Modern System-on-Chip Design on Arm

Modern System-on-Chip Design on Arm

DAVID J. GREAVES

 Education Media

Contents

Preface

Silicon technology has seen relentless advances in the past 50 years, driven by constant innovation and miniaturisation. As a result, more and more functionality has been placed into a single chip. Today, entire systems, including processors, memory, sensors and analogue circuitry, are integrated into one single chip (hence, a system-on-chip or SoC), delivering increased performance despite tight area, power and energy budgets. The aim of this textbook is to expose aspiring and practising SoC designers to the fundamentals and latest developments in SoC design and technologies. The processors within a SoC run a huge body of software. Much of this code is portable over many platforms, but low-level components, such as device drivers, are hardware-dependent and may be CPU-intensive. Power use can be reduced using custom accelerator hardware. Although this book emphasises the hardware design elements, it also addresses *co-design*, in which the hardware and software are designed hand in hand. It is assumed that the reader already understands the basics of processor architecture, computer technology, and software and hardware design.

Is This Book Suitable For You?

We assume that you have some experience with hardware design using an RTL such as Verilog or VHDL, and that you understand assembly language programming and basic principles of operating systems. In other words, you have completed the first two years of a degree in Computer Science or Electronic Engineering.

Many of the principles taught in this book are relevant for all forms of system architect, including those who are designing cloud-scale applications, custom accelerators or IoT devices in general, or those making FPGA designs. But the details of design verification in Chapter 8 are likely to be just of interest to those designing semi-custom silicon using standard cells.

A Git repository of **online additional material** is available at http://bitbucket.org/djg11/modern-soc-design-djg

This contains data used for generating tables and graphs in the book, as well as further source code, lab materials, examples and answers to selected exercises.

The repo contains a SystemC model of the Zynq super FPGA device family, coded in blocking TLM style. It is sufficient to run an Arm A9 Linux kernel using an identical boot image as the real silicon.

Book Structure

This book contains nine chapters, each devoted to a different aspect of SoC design.

Chapter 1 reviews basic computer architecture, defining terms that are used in later chapters. Readers are expected to be largely familiar with most of this material, although the transactional-level modelling (TLM) view of the hardware is likely to be new. A SoC is an assembly of intellectual property (IP) blocks.

Chapter 2 describes many of the standard IP blocks that make up a typical SoC, including processors, memories, input/output devices and interrupts.

Chapter 3 considers the interconnect between the IP blocks, covering the evolution of processor busses and networks-on-chip (NoCs).

Chapter 4 teaches basic principles of system architecture, including dimensioning of busses and queuing theory and arbitration policies. It also discusses debug support.

Chapter 5 presents Electronic System Level (ESL) modelling, where a simulation model for a whole SoC, also known as a virtual platform, is put together. The ESL model is sufficient to test and develop software, as well as to perform architectural exploration, where the throughput, energy use and silicon area of a proposed system implementation can be examined at a high level.

Chapter 6 presents further architectural exploration considerations, including the design of custom accelerators for a specific application. The languages Bluespec and Chisel are described as alternatives to RTL for design entry and the basic principles of high-level synthesis (HLS) are covered.

Chapter 7 is a primer for formal verification of SoCs, comparing the usefulness of formal compared with simulation for bug hunting and right-first-time solutions. A number of useful formal tricks are covered.

Chapter 8 presents semi-custom fabrication flows for making the physical silicon and covers advanced verification and variability mitigation techniques for today's deep sub-micron devices using FinFETs.

Chapter 9 covers what to do when the first SoC samples arrive back from the wafer processing plant, including booting an operating system and checking environmental compatibility (operating temperature and unwanted radio emissions).

Acknowledgements

I am very grateful to Professor Sir Andy Hopper, who was my PhD supervisor, who has been a constant source of inspiration and direction, and who has often been my boss both in industry and at the Computer Laboratory. He introduced me to the field of chip design. I am also very grateful to the late M. G. Scroggie, the principal author of 'Foundations of Wireless', which was a book I read and re-read all through my childhood. I can only hope some people find this current book as valuable as I found his. Certainly I have tried to mix breadth and depth in the same accessible way that he managed. I would like to thank those working in the Computer Laboratory who helped with this book, including David Chisnall, Robert Mullins, Omer Sella and Milos Puzovic. I would also like to thank my wife, Aldyth, for putting up with me for this last year. I've often read such comments in the acknowledgement sections of other books, but now I understand what causes it.

Most importantly, I'd like to thank the many Arm staff who have helped with this book, either by contributing text to large chunks of it, or with additional information and suggestions:

Khaled Benkrid, who made this book possible.

Liz Warman, who kept me on track and assisted me with the process.

Shuojin Hang and Francisca Tan who helped create the scope and reviewed early drafts.

This book would not have been possible without the collaboration of the following Arm engineers who have co-written, reviewed and commented on the book:

- Chapter 2: Processors, Memory and IP Blocks
  Rahul Mathur, Staff Engineer

- Chapter 3: SoC Interconnects
  Anup Gangwar, Distinguished Engineer
  Antony Harris, Senior Principal AMBA Architect

- Chapter 6: Architectural Design Exploration
  Edwin Dankert, Director, Technology Management

- Chapter 7: Formal Methods and Assertion-Based Design
  Daryl Stewart, Distinguished Engineer

- Chapter 8: Fabrication and Production
  Jim Dodrill, Fellow
  Christophe Lopez, Senior Principal Engineer
  Aurelien Merour, Principal Engineer
  Jean-Luc Pelloie, Fellow

Author Biography

Dr. David J. Greaves, PhD CEng. is Senior Lecturer in Computing Science at the University of Cambridge, UK and a Fellow of Corpus Christi College. Born in London, he grew up in a house full of engineering textbooks, circuit diagrams and pieces of telecommunications equipment. His grandfather had built his own television set as soon as television broadcasts started. His father worked at EMI and IBM, developing modems and computer interfaces. With the shift of head office of IBM UK to Portsmouth, the family moved to Romsey in Hampshire.

Plessey Roke Manor was also situated in Romsey, along with IBM's UK research laboratories at Hursley Park. These were, and remain, world-leading research centres in the field of radio communications and computing. The young David J. Greaves was a regular visitor and intern at both sites, and by the age of 17 had designed and built his first computer. The chips had been mostly removed from old circuit boards using a blow lamp. The software, including the disk operating system and a Pascal compiler, had all been written from scratch.

During his A-level studies, Greaves designed a local area network for Commodore PET computers. The design was published in Wireless World magazine and commercially replicated.

As an undergraduate at St John's College Cambridge, he offered consultancy services to various small electronics companies in the field of professional audio, developing MIDI interfaces and low-noise pre-amplifiers. His final-year degree project was a fully digital keyboard instrument that was serialised in Wireless World and copied by many enthusiasts worldwide. A main interest became the design and implementation of compilers, as encouraged by Dr. Martin Richards of St Johns, who had developed the BCPL language, the direct precursor of C.

Greaves designed his first silicon chips during his PhD studies, which were in the field of metropolitan area networks. He designed fibre optic transceivers that sent the first mono-mode signals over the newly installed fibres that criss-crossed Cambridge. In collaboration with Acorn Computer, in 1995 Greaves was the chief network architect for the Cambridge ITV trial, which put ATM switches in the kerbside cabinets belonging to Cambridge Cable Ltd and delivered video on demand to 50 or so homes. It was 20 years later that the last movie rental shop in Cambridge closed.

Also in 1995, he implemented CSYN, one of the first Verilog compilers for synthesising hardware specifically for field programmable gate arrays. This compiler was distributed widely among local companies on the Cambridge Science Park and also used for undergraduate teaching. It was licensed to a multinational to bundle with its own family of FPGAs.

Greaves had visited Arm when it first spun out of Acorn and consisted of six engineers in a barn. At the university, Greaves used a donation of Arm circuit boards for a new practical course in which the students wrote assembly language and Verilog to learn about low-level hardware and software interfacing. These courses still run today and the lecture notes have evolved into this textbook.

Greaves has been on the board or technical advisory board of at least ten start-up companies. He has supervised or examined more than 60 PhD students. He holds at least five international patents in the field of communications and electronics. His company Tenison EDA was, before acquisition, directly providing tools to all major chip makers. His current research interests remain in the field of compilation tools for design automation and scientific acceleration.

List of Figures

List of Tables

Chapter 1

Introduction to
System-on-Chip

1.1 What is a System-on-Chip?

The majority of computers made today follow the System-on-Chip (SoC) approach. A SoC contains the processors, caches, memory and input/output (I/O) devices all on one piece of silicon. This gives the lowest product cost and so is used whenever possible. More complex computers cannot fit onto a single piece of silicon and so multiple chips are used. This is also the preferred approach if the manufacturing process for a single chip is not the best for all of its parts. In a later chapter (Section 6.1), we discuss motivations for using different chips for DRAM and flash memories. However, even when multiple pieces of silicon are used, they are often tightly integrated into a single package using die-stacking or interposers (Section 8.9.1). Packing the computer into the smallest space possible is the primary technique by which computer technology has progressed in the last 60 years. A smaller computer has shorter wires and can operate faster for the same power consumption. The relevant equations are described in Section 4.6.

We start this book with a review of what a computer is and was.

1.1.1 Historical Review

A SoC is a System-on-Chip. In this context, the word **system** originally denoted a computer but today's SoCs have many computers on them. To kick off this chapter, we start by defining some terminology that we will develop and use throughout this book. An **MPSoC** is a SoC containing multiple embedded processors. The four quadrants in Table 1.1 give a traditional view of an old computer system.

Table 1.1 Four quadrants of a computer

Control unit	Execution unit
Primary storage	I/O devices

Each quadrant occupied at least one full-height 19-inch rack in early computers. The execution unit and the control unit are together known as the central processing unit (CPU). When VLSI technology advanced such that a CPU could be put on a single chip, this was called a microprocessor. Famously, Gordon Moore is recognised as the first person to do this, with the invention of the Intel 4004 in 1971.

The **primary storage** contains both programs and data in a von Neumann architecture. This is in contrast to a Harvard architecture that has separate primary memories for programs and data (Section 2.1). Primary storage is also known as **main memory**. Primary storage is directly addressed by the CPU, both for an instruction fetch and for data load and store instructions. With the advent of tape and disk drives as I/O devices, further memory was attached as secondary storage and behaves like any other I/O device. Flash memory is the predominant form of secondary storage today (Section 2.6.8).

An important strand in this book is transactional-level modelling (TLM). Figure 1.1 illustrates a TLM view of a simple computer with no I/O devices. We will describe TLM in detail in Chapter 5. In contrast, Verilog and VHDL are the predominant register transfer languages (RTLs), studied in Section 8.3. We introduce TLM right here at the start and will use TLM examples alongside RTL examples throughout. In Figure 1.1, the microprocessor makes TLM calls on the memory. The processor is an **initiator** and the memory is the **target**. There is only one target in this very simple system, but normally the initiator has a choice of targets on which to invoke transactions. TLM calls are essentially the same as method calls in object-oriented languages such as C++.

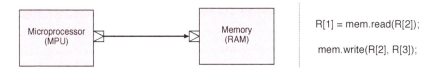

R[1] = mem.read(R[2]);

mem.write(R[2], R[3]);

Figure 1.1 Transactional-level model (TLM) of the simplest computer (left) and code fragments (right)

Personal computers of the 1970s were called microcomputers. Famous models are the Commodore Pet, the Tandy TRS-80 and various Acorn computers, including the BBC Micro, which led to the founding of Arm. These microcomputers can be regarded as the ancestors of today's SoCs. The range of address values that can be put on the address bus is called an **address space**. They used a 16-bit address bus and an 8-bit data bus, so are called A16D8 systems. The microprocessor can make two main TLM calls to access memory space:

```
// Simple A16D8 TLM interface signature
u8_t read_byte(u16_t addr);          // Memory read (load)
void write_byte(u16_t addr, u8_t data);   // Memory write (store)
```

Such microprocessors often also support I/O transactions, again with 8-bit data, but perhaps fewer address bits for the I/O space. Using separate instructions for I/O, such as in and out, was desirable since the A16 primary storage address was a critical resource that was spared by avoiding **memory-mapped I/O**. The I/O calls would be something like:

```
// Simple A16D8 TLM interface signature
u8_t io_read(u8_t io_addr);           // Input instruction
void io_write(u8_t io_addr, u8_t data);   // Output instruction
```

Early microprocessors, such as the original Intel 8080, were A16D8 systems, so could address 64 kbytes of memory. Modern microprocessors commonly have on-chip caches and a memory management unit for translating virtual memory addresses.

As we will see later, TLM modelling of processor operations is at quite a high level, leading to orders of magnitude saving in simulation time compared with modelling each transition of every net that makes up the components and their interconnect. We use the term 'net' throughout this book for a wire between the output of one gate and the input or inputs of others. A net-level description of a SoC is its circuit diagram.

The C++ code fragments on the right in Figure 1.1 would be executed by an instruction set simulator (ISS, Section 5.5) model of the processor when executing load and store instructions using register-indirect addressing. The array *R* models the processor register file.

1.1.2 Simple Microprocessor Net-level Connections

Figure 1.2 shows a basic A16D8 microprocessor with a tri-state bus. A single set of data wires are used, bidirectionally, to alternately send data to and from the processor. At most, only one source can enable its tri-state buffers at a time, otherwise a heavy current will arise in a **bus fight**, during which two sources disagree on the value of data bits. Microcomputers of the 1970s and 1980s used a tri-state bus. This microprocessor uses the net-level connections shown in Table 1.2 for its bus transactions.

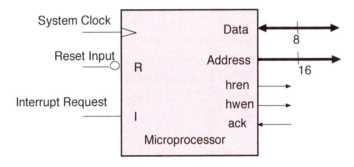

Figure 1.2 Schematic symbol and external connections for a tri-state version of a simple microprocessor

The processor puts its address (and also data for a write) on the busses, asserts `hwen` or `hren` depending on whether it is a write or read and waits for `ack`. For a read, the data present on the data bus when `ack` is asserted is accepted by the processor. This is the essence of the **bus protocol**. We later define the protocol more thoroughly using separate read and write data busses (Section 1.1.4). Having just one bus protocol that is used by all interconnected blocks is a key part in facilitating SoC integration at scale. Large real-world SoCs inevitably use several protocols, but each must be justified by its performance, power use or other capabilities.

Table 1.2 Net-level connections

Connection	Direction	Use
data[7:0]	I/O	Bidirectional data bus
addr[15:0]	Output	Selection of internal address; not all 32 bits are used
hren	Output	Asserted during a data read from the target to the host
hwen	Output	Asserted during a write of data from the host to the target
ack	Input	Asserted when the addressed device has completed its operation

The processor has three control inputs, shown on the left-hand side of Figure 1.2. The **clock input** is a periodic square wave (of a few MHz in the 1970s). The **reset input** causes the program counter to be set to a hardwired value called the reset vector (typically all zeros). An **interrupt input** makes it save the current program counter and load another hardwired vector that is the entry point for an

interrupt service routine (ISR). Typically, the processor hardware will set an interrupt disable bit in the status word at the same time. It is the programmer's responsibility to ensure that the interrupt input is de-asserted before it clears the interrupt disable bit.

Given the definition of a simple microprocessor, we can proceed with the definition of a full microcomputer. Although we expect the readers of this book to be thoroughly familiar with this material in hardware terms, the simultaneous presentation of TLM may be new.

1.1.3 Full Netlist and Memory Map for a Microcomputer

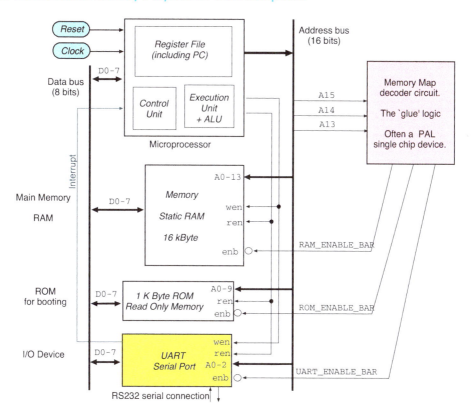

Figure 1.3 A simple A16D8 microcomputer structure. A microprocessor initiates all transactions on a bidirectional/tri-state data bus, which is connected to all other components

Figure 1.3 shows the inter-chip wiring of a basic microcomputer (i.e. a computer based on a microprocessor). The allocation of the 64 kbytes of addressable space to hardware resources is called the **memory map**. Table 1.3 is the memory map generated by the logic of Figure 1.4. The glue logic can be implemented with two invertors and three NAND gates as shown. It is also described in the following RTL:

```
module address_decode(abus, rom_cs, ram_cs, uart_cs);        // Glue logic for address decode
    input [15:14] abus;
    output rom_cs, ram_cs, uart_cs;
    assign rom_cs = !(abus == 2'b00);   // 0x0000
    assign ram_cs = !(abus == 2'b01);   // 0x4000
    assign uart_cs = !(abus == 2'b11); // 0xC000
endmodule
```

Table 1.3 Memory map

Start	End	Resource
0000	03FF	ROM (1 kbytes)
0400	3FFF	Unused images of ROM
4000	7FFF	RAM (16 kbytes)
8000	BFFF	Unused
C000	C007	Registers (8) in the UART
C008	FFFF	Unused images of the UART

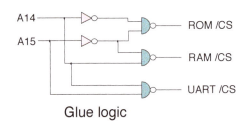

Glue logic

Figure 1.4 Connections to memory

For a thorough equivalent example today, run `cat /proc/iomem` on any Linux machine to see its address map.

In our simple example, the 64-kbyte memory map of the processor has been allocated to the three addressable resources, as shown in the memory map table. The high-order address bits are decoded to create chip enable signals for each of the connected peripherals, which are the RAM (Section 2.6.1), ROM (Section 2.6.2) and universal asynchronous receiver and transmitter (UART, Section 2.7.1). The memory map must be allocated without overlapping the resources. The ROM needs to be mapped so that it encompasses the **reset vector**, which is where the processor starts executing from when it is reset. It is commonly zero, as assumed here. In such a simple computer, the full memory map must be known at the time the code for the ROM is compiled. This requires agreement between the hardware and software engineers. Modern SoCs tend to use programmed memory map discovery techniques so that the software is portable over a variety of hardware devices to accommodate various orderings of pluggable peripherals (Section 3.1.7).

In the early days, the static memory map was written on a blackboard so that all engineers (hardware and software) could see it. For a modern SoC, there can be up to 100 devices in the memory map and a complex device could have several hundred internal registers and fields within such registers. Each register or field will have a protocol update policy (e.g. read/write, read-only etc.) and may or may not change through its own volition. Automatic tooling to manage and document a memory map is vital. Virtualisation and security considerations dictate that some registers have alternative views and access policies. An XML representation called IP-XACT (Section 6.8.2) is one standard that has been adopted for machine-generated memory maps. It allows the glue logic and all the interconnect wiring to be generated automatically.

1.1.4 Separate Read and Write Data Busses

Our example so far used a tri-state bus. These are still commonly used for chip-to-chip interconnects on **printed circuit boards (PCBs)**. However, modern SoCs do not use tri-states on-chip. A lower switched-capacitance solution is achieved using point-to-point wiring, which also avoids wasting the leakage energy in logic gates where the input is floating between logic levels (Section 4.6.2). In this book, for simple reference designs we will initially use a reference bus that we call MSOC1. This uses separate read and write busses instead of a single data bus. Elsewhere, we use real-world busses, like AXI and CHI. For subsequent examples, we will default to using an A32D32 system with separate read and write busses.

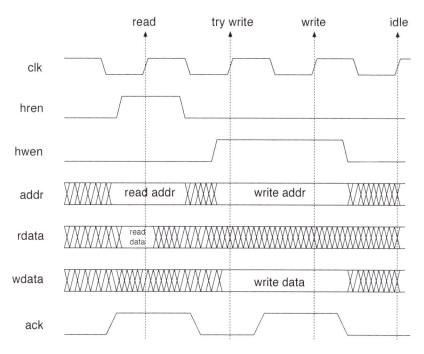

Figure 1.5 MSOC1 reference bus protocol, with read and write examples

Figure 1.5 shows two example cycles for our MSOC1 reference bus. It is a synchronous bus with transactions occurring on the positive clock edge. Each instance of an MSOC1 port in an A32D32 system uses the the net-level connections listed in Table 1.4.

Table 1.4 Net-level connections of an MSOC1 port in an A32D32 system

Connection	Direction	Use
addr[31:0]	Output	Selection of internal address; not all 32 bits are used
hwen	Input	Asserted during a write from the host to the target
hren	Input	Asserted during a read from the target to the host
wdata[31:0]	Input	Data to a target when writing or storing
rdata[31:0]	Output	Data read from a target when reading or loading

The signal directions shown are for a **target**. On an **initiator**, the net directions are reversed. A read transaction occurs on any clock cycle when both hren and ack are asserted. A write occurs on any clock cycle when both `hwen` and `ack` are asserted. The example waveforms show a read followed by a write. The write is extended by a clock cycle since the `ack` signal was not present on the first positive edge when `hwen` was asserted.

The protocol is said to execute a **handshake** with external devices using the `hren`/`hwen` signals, which are the request nets. The `ack` net is an acknowledge. In Chapter 2, we will present the essence of common peripheral blocks using RTL examples. If a device can respond immediately, no `ack` signal is required, as an equivalent can be generated with an OR of the `hren` and `hwen` nets. In practice, contention, cache misses and operations on slow busses delay responses to the processor. Simple processors stall entirely during this period, whereas advanced cores carry on with other work and can process responses received out of order.

In Chapter 2, the examples mostly assume that no acknowledgement signal is required, meaning that every addressed target must respond in one clock cycle with no exceptions. Also we assume that only complete words are stored. The stores are always word aligned, so no lane qualifiers for bytes and half words are needed. A **misaligned access** spans two adjacent word addresses, such as reading or writing a 16-bit word at an odd-byte address.

1.2 Microcontrollers

The term 'microcontroller' briefly denoted an industrial controller based on a microprocessor, as would be used for sequencing and control of a small plant or production line, such as a microbrewery. Microprocessors integrated two of the historical quadrants on one piece of silicon (Table 1.1). As VLSI capabilities grew, the remaining two quadrants – the main memory (primary storage) and the majority of I/O devices – could also be included. This was then called a microcontroller. It has all the system parts on one piece of silicon. It is a SoC.

One of the most famous microcontrollers is the Intel 8051 family, introduced in 1980. Such microcontrollers differed from other microprocessors of the time because they had a rich set of instructions for setting, clearing, toggling and testing individual bits in I/O space. These were useful in that they did not destroy register contents and were faster than the three-instruction sequence (load, operate and store) that would otherwise be needed. Today's SoCs hardly benefit from such instructions since the CPU rate is much faster than normally needed for bit-oriented device control.

Figure 1.6 is a block diagram of a first-generation microcontroller, like the one illustrated in Figure 1.7. The device contains an entire computer, requiring externally only a power supply, an external clock and reset components. All the remaining pins are usable for I/O, such as general-purpose I/O (GPIO, Section 2.7.3). A bus bond-out mode was also supported by some devices so that memory-mapped devices can be connected externally.

Like a microcomputer, program code was stored permanently in the ROM. PROM and EPROM were available in the original devices, as well as masked ROM. Today, a three-stage chain is often used for booting, in which a mask-programmed ROM reads code from a low-performance flash memory into internal RAM. The code thus loaded can be the main application itself, but is often just a bootloader, which itself loads the main operating system (Section 9.1).

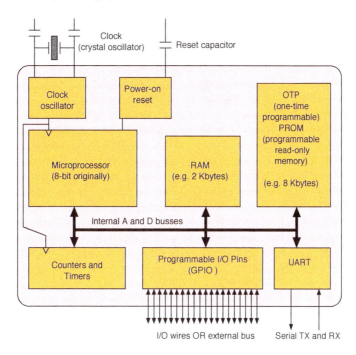

Figure 1.6 Structure of a typical microcontroller, a single-chip microcomputer

Figure 1.7 Hitachi HD614080 microcontroller chip from 1980. Such devices were often in very large, dual in-line (DIL) packages to make a large number of GPIO pins available

A UART was the most advanced peripheral implemented in the early microcontrollers. Also commonly found were pulse-width modulation (PWM) generators and pulse counters (Section 2.7.4). These are still found on today's SoCs, but are being used less and less, with USB and Ethernet taking over in many applications.

Chip-and-pin smart cards contain a microcontroller. Many of these run a cut-down integer-only Java virtual machine (VM). Figure 1.8 shows the contact plate. Clock, reset and power are provided externally and all communication uses a protocol on the bidirectional data pin. Early variants required an external programming supply, on contact C6, but today's devices have an on-chip voltage generator and so there is now a spare pin on the contact plate (Section 8.6.1).

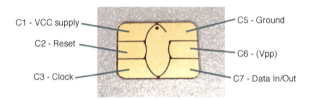

C1 - VCC supply
C2 - Reset
C3 - Clock
C5 - Ground
C6 - (Vpp)
C7 - Data In/Out

Figure 1.8 Contact plate for a smart card. The card reader supplies VCC power, clock and reset. Inputs and outputs are then made via the 1-bit bidirectional data pin

1.3 Later Chapters

Chapter 2, 'Processors, Memory and IP Blocks', is a tour of the many basic building blocks on a SoC. These are known as **intellectual property (IP) blocks**. They may be bespoke or off-the-shelf and include memory, peripherals (I/O devices) and processors.

Chapter 3, 'SoC Interconnect', reviews various approaches to connecting the IP blocks together, taking into account the required throughput and latency requirements to meet the target SoC performance.

Chapter 4, 'System Design Considerations', reviews the basic principles of traffic engineering and design techniques. These are important for guiding the design process and understanding the expected effect of a design change. Debugging and security are also discussed.

Chapter 5, 'Electronic System-Level Modelling', explains the reasons and techniques for building and using a high-level model of a SoC. This is called an **electronic system-level (ESL)** model. It can be used to estimate performance and energy use and to develop the software that will run inside the SoC.

Chapter 6, 'Architectural Design Exploration', considers various approaches to implementing a given function, including using custom processors and hardware accelerators. Advanced hardware design tools are also discussed.

Chapter 7, 'Formal Methods and Assertion-based Design', examines mechanisms for avoiding mistakes in chip design, comparing simulations with a formal proof of correctness.

Chapter 8, 'Fabrication and Production', presents the back-end steps in chip making, during which synthesisable RTL is converted to masks for fabrication. It discusses techniques for squeezing performance out of silicon and ensuring reliable operation despite variations in wafer processing, supply voltage and operating temperature (PVT variations).

Chapter 9, 'Putting Everything Together', rounds up the book. It discusses bootstrapping the code into a new SoC and getting a product ready for consumer use.

1.4 SoC Design Flows

SoC design flow uses a tower of abstractions. Each component is represented at multiple levels with an increasing amount of detail for lower levels. Figure 1.9 illustrates this for an invertor. Components that are generated by synthesis tools, such as for signal buffering or repipelining, do not appear at all in the higher levels.

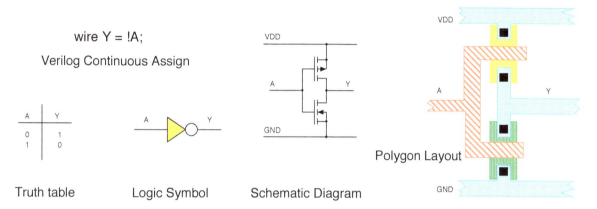

Figure 1.9 An invertor viewed at various levels of abstraction

The design of a SoC requires tens of man years of effort, for even just a variation of a previous SoC. A totally new design requires orders of magnitude greater effort and even then, it makes extensive use of pre-existing blocks, known as **intellectual property (IP)** blocks. As will become clear in the chapter on fabrication, Chapter 8, a new SoC requires half a dozen teams of engineers, each with a different focus, such as hardware, software, packaging, documentation, physical design, verification and testing. Figure 1.10 is an abstract view of the front end of the SoC design flow. This view starts with the functional requirements determined by the marketing department of the company designing the SoC and stops at the level of synthesisable RTL (Section 8.3.8).

1.4.1 Functional Model

A SoC begins with a functional specification. This typically comes from the marketing team at an electronics company in the form of a **product requirements document (PRD)**. The design aims are specified in terms of high-level requirements that cover functionality, throughput, power consumption and cost.

Numerous tools exist for capturing and managing requirements. Examples are IBM Engineering Requirements Management DOORS Next, Orcanos and various tools that support Jenkins, SysML and UML. These support hypertext links between various sub-documents stored in a revision control system and various consistency checks. Ultimately, the design concept and performance needs are transferred from the marketing person's mind, the back of an envelope or a word processor document into machine-readable form.

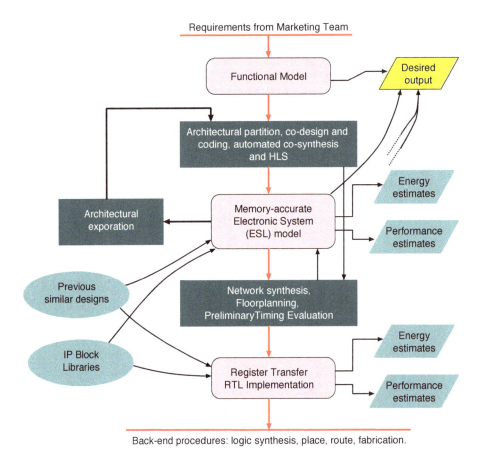

Figure 1.10 Front-end flow in SoC design

Any particular field of application or discipline will adopt its own approach at this level, but in general, creating software to produce the desired output is a useful starting point. For instance, if the SoC is to drive the mechanisms of an inkjet printer, then the desired output is the required signal waveforms for the various stepper motors and ink cartridges. The desired output is shown in yellow on Figure 1.10. The software used to generate the desired output is called a **functional model**. It is the highest level model. Such a program will have little in common with the final product, except that it produces the same desired output. The lower-level models and implementations should generate an identical functional output and are progressively closer to the final product.

Often, we need to design a product with a total silicon area of under $100 \, \text{mm}^2$. This is a good size for a SoC (as discussed in Section 8.11.1). In the past, there were significant obstacles when integrating various forms of electronics on one chip. Difficulties arise, since analogue functions, low-noise amplifiers, optronics and high-density memory have their own optimum wafer recipe for processing the silicon. Progress has made this integration easier. Nonetheless, our example for this chapter, an ADSL broadband modem, is from around 2008, when integration was not as mature.

Figure 1.11 shows the main circuit board of a broadband modem hub made by Belkin. Figure 1.12 is a block diagram at the board level. The main components are a power supply, a Wi-Fi subsystem, a four-port Ethernet switch and an ADSL modem. There is also a USB port, about eight LED indicators and two push switches.

Figure 1.11 Main PCB of an ADSL home modem

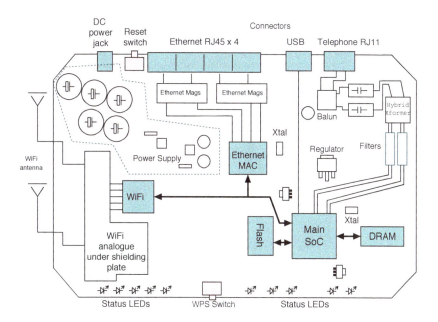

Figure 1.12 Main PCB structure of an ADSL home modem

In a product made today with identical functionality, the Wi-Fi subsystem would have far less PCB area. Much of its functionality would be on the main SoC. Also, either the flash or the DRAM could be on the main SoC, or perhaps die-stacked on top of it. All other aspects of the design would be the same.

1.4.2 Architectural Partition

The collection of algorithms and functional requirements must be implemented using one or more pieces of silicon. Each major piece of silicon contains one or more custom or standard microprocessors. Some of the silicon has a custom design, some of it has a design common to different devices in a product line, some of it has a standard design and some of it has a third-party design. A breakdown of the major categories of integrated circuit is presented in Section 8.4. Chapter 4 explores the design partition problem.

The result of the first-pass architectural design process is a mapping of the design into physical components. Certain electronic requirements, such as high voltage, microwave radio frequencies and optimum memory bit density, are still fulfilled with optimised silicon (or GaAs) processes, but today, almost everything is either a standard part or else can be mapped onto a single SoC. Beyond the fundamental properties of silicon, a design partition must take into account non-technical aspects, such as the stability of the requirements, the design lifetime, ease of reuse and other market forces, such as whether all the required parts will continue to be available during the envisioned production run. It is common for an end customer to require that there is a **second-source supplier** for any part to prevent a shortage from significantly interrupting a production run. This second supplier may either already be making an equivalent part or have signed the required contracts and warranties to ensure it can start production at short notice.

When designing a subsystem, we must choose what to have as hardware, what to have as software and whether custom or standard processors are needed. When designing the complete SoC, we must think about sharing the subsystem load over the processors chosen. Estimates of the instruction fetch and data bandwidth for each processor are needed when deciding how many memories to instantiate and which processors operate out of which memories. The envisioned system data flow between subsystems is another important consideration, affecting how the busses are interconnected and whether a **network-on-chip (NoC)** is justified. For a SoC intended for a single target application, there is greater certainty about the likely data flow compared with a general-purpose chip. Although the transistor count is not a significant design constraint in modern VLSI, hardwired data paths are more efficient than switched structures. Moreover, wiring length and hence, energy are minimised if less area is used. A solution providing a non-blocking full-crossbar interconnection (Section 3.2.3) will generally be over-engineered for all applications.

Energy efficiency is also often a critical consideration. Whether for a battery-powered device or a server farm, low-power design principles are applicable and power control mechanisms affect the design at all levels.

The functional requirements for the broadband modem are, essentially, its hardware and software feature set. There may be requirements relating to its power consumption and throughput, but these are likely to be of low concern because the unit is mains powered and performance is limited by the low-speed interfaces (ADSL and Wi-Fi). There may be a requirement for the wired Ethernet to handle local traffic at a full line rate of 100 Mbps per port full-duplex, but this would more than likely be relaxed for a low-cost residential unit in favour of cost of goods.

The **cost of goods** is the total amount paid by the manufacturer for all the parts that go into a product. It includes the component costs, case costs and cost of the cardboard box, and is always a major concern for a consumer product. Assembly and testing costs are also a consideration. Most digital products are quite easy to test, since they can embody sophisticated self-test mechanisms.

The hardware features are all obvious from the final hardware design. The Wi-Fi has a diversity antenna, which was a strong selling point in 2008, albeit for a considerable increase in cost of goods. Today, all but the most basic designs have multiple antennae to overcome fading arising from reflections and standing waves.

The software features include a firewall and DHCP server, internal web-based management HTML server and so on. We will not cover these in this book. However, one significant feature that the software needs to provide is a degree of flexibility against future changes. Changes could be protocol or security enhancements, or perhaps regional variations to address parts of the world not originally provisioned. A SoC design must anticipate such changes as far as possible by providing sufficient hooks and general-purpose internal interfaces.

Another output available when all of the requirements and proposed algorithms are captured in a high-level software implementation is the total memory and execution cycle budget. The cycle budget might typically be for a serial single-threaded implementation and hence, knowing the target clock frequency for the SoC, the degree of parallelism required in the final implementation can be estimated. Although these figures may vary by perhaps ± 30 per cent from the figure for the final SoC target, insights at this high level can form a basis for feedback to the marketing team regarding the likely final silicon cost and power consumption.

1.4.3 Architectural Partition and Co-design

Given the design requirements, an initial allocation of design features to pieces of silicon and IP blocks within those chips must be made. Normally, we aim to create one SoC and supplement it with as few standard parts as possible to form a board-level product.

There are two principal ways to solve the design partition problem:

1. **Co-design**: Implementing a manual partition between custom hardware and software for various processors.

2. **Co-synthesis**: Automatically creating simple 'device drivers' and inter-block message formats to match the automated partitioning decisions.

The partitioning decisions can, in theory, be automated. This is the **co-synthesis** approach. For well-defined tasks, such as when the whole system functionality is fully described by a single high-level application program, automatic partitioning works. It has been demonstrated in various academic projects and is working today in cloud-based FPGA accelerators (Section 6.4). However, such techniques cannot yet replace human-guided partitioning for typical SoC projects, mainly due to the lack of characterisation of the vast potential design space. There are also problems with hard-to-quantify or intangible advantages of particular design decisions and their mutual interactions.

Industry today uses **co-design**, in which a senior engineer, the **system architect**, makes the partitioning decisions.

In either approach, early and rapid feedback of energy and execution performance is needed. This must be more accurate than the first indications from our initial software functional model. Only a basic or moderate level of accuracy is needed initially, but the polarity of the derivatives is critically important (Section 6.6). A basic level of accuracy is needed for comparing vastly different designs. Accuracy in the polarity of the derivatives indicates whether an incremental change is for the better or the worse. Incremental changes might be, for example, doubling a cache size, doubling the number of cores or doubling the width of a data bus. We compare successive variants of the high-level structure of a system in a process called **architectural exploration** (Section 6.2). If the power and performance partial derivatives have the correct polarity for all major partitioning decisions, then architectural exploration will lead to a good design point.

Typically, an ESL model is used for architectural exploration. We explore ESL modelling in Chapter 5. Another name for such a model is a **virtual platform**. These models can accurately run the software for the embedded cores with zero or very minor modification to the software. Multiple ESL models of target system components are commonly used. These vary in their level of detail and modelling performance. Various whole-system models can then be put together using different levels of modelling for the various subsystems. The level of detail selected for a subsystem depends on what performance metric or behavioural feature is currently of interest.

An important aspect of an ESL model is ease of editing and reconfiguration. The most popular language for ESL models is C++ using the SystemC coding style (Section 5.3). After each edit, static information, such as silicon area and standby power results, are recomputed. Then a test workload is run on the model, and data are collected on dynamic performance and energy use.

1.4.4 IP Blocks

A SoC consists of an assembly of intellectual property (IP) blocks. The same is true for its high-level ESL model. IP blocks are designed to be reusable over a large number of designs. They include CPUs, RAMs and standard I/O devices such as for USB, Ethernet and UART. These will often be provided with a per-use licence by an external supplier, notably Arm or Cadence. The IP blocks in a SoC also include custom blocks that are locally generated specifically for the current application.

An IP block is supplied in various forms in parallel. A machine-readable data sheet has static information, such as silicon area and the power consumption for various activation levels. A high-level model is provided for the ESL. A synthesisable model or cycle-accurate model is provided for net-level simulations, and a hard macro for the layout may be provided for critical high-performance subsystems such as RAMs and CPUs. A test programme and documentation are also provided. Chapter 2 is an in-depth review of IP blocks.

In architectural exploration, different combinations of processors, memory and bus structures are considered in an attempt to find an implementation with good power and load balancing. A loosely timed high-level model is sufficient for computing the performance of an architecture.

In detailed design, we select IP providers for all the functional blocks. Alternatively, previous in-house designs can be used without paying a licence fee, or they can be freshly written.

1.4.5 Synthesis

As shown in the lower half of Figure 1.10, once an architecture has been chosen, implementation can start. Implementation at this level needs to interconnect all the blocks that make up the design. This will involve the final selection of standard parts for the board-level design and generating RTL for custom IP blocks that have so far been modelled only at a high ESL level.

Synthesis is the process of automatically converting a high-level description of something into a lower-level form. A number of synthesis tools are typically used at this stage:

- A **network synthesis** tool is often used to generate memory maps and all the bus structures or NoCs for interconnecting the IP blocks (Section 3.9).

- A **memory synthesiser** tool generates memories with the required number of bits and port structure (Section 8.3.10).

- An **HLS compiler** is sometimes used to generate RTL designs from parts of the high-level model (Section 6.9).

- A **logic synthesiser** is used to convert the RTL to net-level circuits (Section 8.3.8), but much of the simulation is run on the behavioural RTL model. The net-level synthesis is considered to be part of the back-end flow.

In practice, the whole procedure may be iterative, with detailed results from a lower level of implementation sometimes requiring changes at the architectural level, such as the size of scratchpad RAMs.

1.4.6 Simulation

Different types of simulation are used at different levels of representation. Since synthesis steps always expand the level of detail, it is faster to simulate the input level than the output level.

A synthesisable RTL model of the complete SoC can, in principle, be simulated with an RTL simulator (Section 8.3.3). This will be slow. However, it should seldom be necessary, if most of the system can be simulated at a high level with an ESL model. In that case, an RTL implementation is used for only one or two subsystems of interest.

Test bench components need to be coded before simulations can be run. These can be behavioural models that are also suitable for ESL modelling. Sometimes they use data files collected from the real world, such as signals from a telephone line in our broadband modem example.

Logic synthesis converts from behavioural RTL to structural RTL (Section 8.3.8). This results in at least one further order of magnitude increase in detail and hence, simulations of the resulting netlist will run 10× slower. Table 5.2 shows typical simulation speeds.

Apart from the input RTL, the other main input to logic synthesis is the chosen target technology library and directives about what to optimise (area, power or performance). A target technology library is normally a machine-readable semi-custom standard cell library (Section 8.4.1). It has an associated fabrication geometry (e.g. 28 nm) and supply voltage range (e.g. 0.9 to 1.1 V).

1.4.7 Back-end Flow

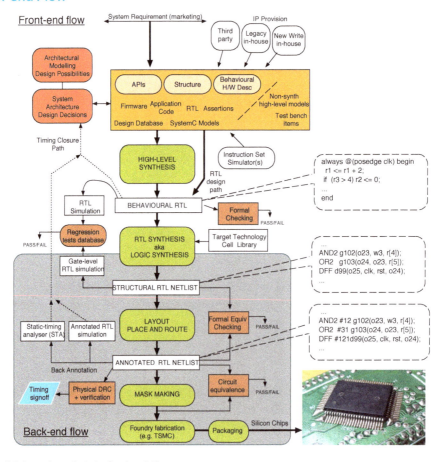

Figure 1.13 Overall design and manufacturing flow for a SoC

Figure 1.13 shows a typical overall design and manufacturing flow from design capture to application-specific integrated circuit (ASIC) fabrication. This might take 6 months and 50 man years. A small FPGA flow (Section 8.5.2), on the other hand, can be executed in just a few days by one person.

Once the design is in synthesisable RTL form, the so-called back-end flows commence. Apart from preliminary logic synthesis, a back-end flow is normally handled by a separate design team. Parts of the back-end flow may be outsourced to other companies. Mask making and foundry services are nearly always outsourced, although certain very large players can do everything in-house (e.g. Intel and Samsung). The back-end steps are discussed in Chapter 8. However, often changes are required at the front end due to discoveries made in the back end. Most notable is timing closure (Section 8.12.16) and testability (Section 8.8.2). Timing closure refers to making sure that each subsystem can clock at its target frequency in all PVT conditions (Section 8.4.4). Modern on-chip bus protocols are designed to tolerate issues arising from meeting timing closure with minimal redesign, albeit with a minor increase in latency and perhaps loss in throughput (Section 4.4.2 and Section 3.1.3).

The output from RTL synthesis is a structural netlist that uses a target technology library. In other words, it is almost the complete circuit diagram of the SoC in terms of individual logic gates. It is not the entire circuit diagram, since components such as CPU cores are typically supplied in hard macro form (Section 8.4.2). Essentially, they look like massive logic gates. The internal circuits for the logic gates in a library are normally available under a library licence, but this may not be possible for hard macros.

The placement step gives a 2-D coordinate to each component. This is often guided by an engineer who makes a high-level floor plan, which divides a SoC into tens of regions. Placement is then automatic within each region and is performed to minimise wiring length. If multiple power voltages and domains are used (Section 4.6.10), placement must normally aim to put blocks with common power supplies close to each other for ease of wiring.

The routing step selects the route taken by each net. Normally digital nets are on the lowest two layers of metal, one being for predominantly vertical runs and the other for predominantly horizontal runs. Interlayer vias are installed if a net needs to change direction. Areas with too many nets may not be routable and a modified placement may be needed. Beyond that goal, minimising the wiring length and the number of layer swaps are secondary goals. The upper layers of metal are used for power distribution. Again, the routing tool will design these layers. A very important net is the clock for each subsystem. The router may use a layer just for clock nets, since this makes it easy to deliver a clock with low skew (Section 4.9.5).

Once routing is complete, an **annotated netlist** may be extracted by another tool. This tool calculates the actual load capacitance on each net. This is important both for power estimation and timing closure, since the performance of a gate degrades as the length of its output net is increased (Section 4.6.4). The RTL can then be back-annotated with actual implementation gate delays to provide a fairly precise power and performance model. Design changes are needed if performance is insufficient. For instance, a gate driving a long net could be changed to a similar gate with increased drive power, but with slightly greater area, so that a row of adjacent gates becomes slightly displaced.

Fabricating masks is commonly the most expensive single step of the design flow (e.g. £1 million), so must be correct first time. As mentioned, fabricating silicon dies is performed in-house by large companies, but most companies use third-party foundries, notably UMC and TSMC. The foundries can also test chips (Section 8.8).

At all stages of the design flow (both front end and back end), a huge library of bespoke tests is run every night and any changes that cause a previously successful test to fail (regressions) are automatically reported to the project manager. Many systems can automatically determine which engineer most likely made the edit that caused the regression and will send them an email to ask them to review it (Section 7.2.3).

1.4.8 Example: A Cell Phone

Figure 1.14 General internal view of a mobile phone (left) and views of both sides of the main circuit board (centre and right). Highlighted in red are the main SoC, which contains several Arm processors, and a multi-chip module containing several memory chips (a proprietary mix of DRAM, SRAM and flash)

A modern mobile phone contains eight or more radio transceivers, including the various cell phone standards, GPS, Wi-Fi, near-field and Bluetooth. Figure 1.14 shows the internals of a typical phone. The main circuit board contains more than 50 pieces of silicon to support the various radio standards. These are on both sides of the main board and are covered with shielding cans, which have been lifted off for the photo. The largest chip package is a **multi-chip module (MCM)** (Section 8.9.1) containing several memory devices. The second largest device is the main SoC.

The **bill of materials (BoM)** for a modern smartphone has the following components:

- main SoC: the application processor with die-stacked or nearby SRAM, flash and DRAM

- display with integrated capacitive touchscreen (instead of an older physical keypad) and miscellaneous push buttons

- haptic vibrator, audio ringers, loudspeaker, earphones and microphones in noise-cancelling pairs or arrays

- multimedia codecs (audiovisual capture and replay in several formats with hardware acceleration, Section 6.4)

- radio interfaces: GSM (three or four bands), Bluetooth, IEEE 802.11, GPS, near-field (contactless ticketing and payments), etc., plus antennas for each (some shared)

- power management: battery charger and regulator, contactless charging through near-field antenna, processor speed governor, die temperature sensor(s), on, off, and flight modes

- infrared IrDA port (older units), magnetic compass, barometer, gravity direction sensor and accelerometer

- front and rear cameras, fingerprint camera, torch and ambient light sensor

- memory card slot and SIM card slot

- physical connectors: USB, power and headset

- case, main battery, secondary battery and PCBs

- Java or Dalvik VM, operating system, bundled applications, security certificates, etc.

1.4.9 SoC Example: Helium 210

A platform chip is a SoC that is used in a number of products although chunks of it might be turned off for a particular application. For example, the USB port might not be available on a portable media player despite being on the core chip. A platform chip is the modern equivalent of a microcontroller. It is a flexible chip that can be programmed for a number of embedded applications. The set of components is the same as for a microcontroller, but each has far more complexity, for example there could be a 32-bit processor instead of an 8-bit one. In addition, rather than putting a microcontroller on a PCB as the heart of the system, the whole system is placed on the same piece of silicon as the platform components. This gives us a SoC.

The example illustrated in Figure 1.15 has two Arm processors and two DSP processors. Each Arm has a local cache and both store their programs and data in the same off-chip DRAM. In the block diagram of this in Figure 1.16 the left-hand Arm is used as an I/O processor and so is connected to a variety of standard peripherals. In a typical application, many of the peripherals are unused and so held in a powered-down mode. The right-hand Arm is the system controller. It can access all the chip's resources over various bus bridges. It can access off-chip devices, such as an LCD display or keyboard via a general-purpose analogue-to-digital local bus.

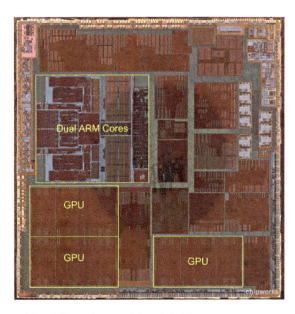

Figure 1.15 An Apple SoC with two Arm and three GPU cores. It was made by arch-rival Samsung

Bus bridges map part of one processor's memory map into that of another so that cycles can be executed in the other's space, albeit with some delay and loss of performance. A FIFO bus bridge contains its own transaction queue of read or write operations awaiting completion.

The twin DSP devices run completely out of on-chip SRAM. Such SRAM may dominate the die area of the chip. If both are fetching instructions from the same port of the same RAM, then they have to execute the same program in lockstep or else have their own local cache to avoid a huge loss of performance due to bus contention.

The rest of the system is normally swept up onto the same piece of silicon and this is denoted with the special function peripheral. This is the sole part of the design that varies from product to product. The same core set of components can be be used for all sorts of different products, such as iPods, digital cameras and ADSL modems, as shown in Figure 1.17.

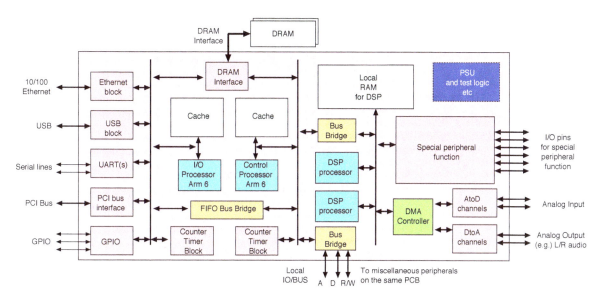

Figure 1.16 A platform chip example: the Virata Helium 210, as used in many ADSL modems

Figure 1.17 Helium chip as part of a home gateway ADSL modem (partially masked by the 802.11 module)

At the architectural design stage of an application-specific SoC, to save the cost of a full crossbar matrix interconnect, devices can be allocated to busses, if we know the expected access and traffic patterns. Commonly there is one main bus master per bus. The bus master is the device that generates the address for the next data movement (read or write operation). The Helium chip illustrates this design pattern.

Busses are connected to bridges, but crossing a bridge has latency and also uses up bandwidth on both busses. Devices should be allocated to busses so that inter-bus traffic is minimised based on a priori knowledge of likely access patterns. Lower-speed busses may go off-chip.

SoC Example: Tablet or Display Panel Device

Another example of a platform chip is illustrated in Figure 1.18. This device was used in a wide variety of consumer devices, ranging from fire alarm control panels to low-end tablets. It integrates two 400-MHz Arm cores and a large number of DMA-capable peripheral controllers using a central bus matrix. For this component, the wide variety of application scenarios implies that traffic flow patterns are not accurately known at design time. This motivates the use of a central switching matrix.

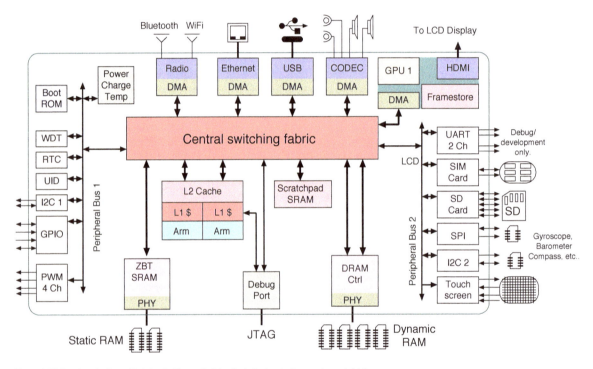

Figure 1.18 Another platform chip intended for use in thin-client display devices, such as a tablet

Both examples demonstrate that DRAM is always an important component that is generally off-chip as a dedicated part. Today, some on-chip DRAM is used, either on the SoC itself or die-stacked (Section 8.9.1).

1.5 SoC Technology

In 1965, Gordon Moore predicted that the number of transistors on a silicon chip would double every two years. Figure 1.19 reproduces one of the many scatter plots of chip sizes against dates that litter the Internet. These demonstrate that his vision was roughly correct. This phenomenon is now well known as Moore's law (Section 8.2).

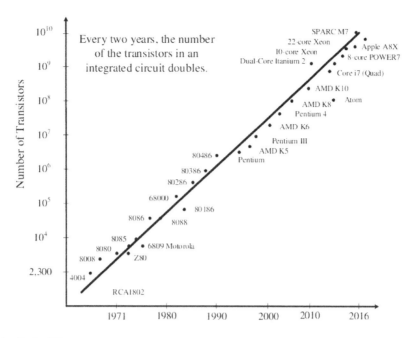

Figure 1.19 Moore's law (Section 8.2)

The most common implementation technique for SoCs is called **semi-custom** and uses a standard cell library (Section 8.4.1). The other main alternative is the **Field Programmable Gate Array (FPGA)**, where, instead of being hard-coded in the manufacturing masks, the user's logic is downloaded into the silicon into programmable logic at power-up time (Section 8.5.2).

Hybrid devices, known as super-FPGAs, are also available. In these the silicon area is partitioned between a large number of everyday IP blocks and general purpose, programmable logic.

For such hardware, we use the terms 'hard' and 'soft' to differentiate between those functions that are determined by the fabrication masks and those that are loaded into the programmable fabric. Before super-FPGAs, it was common to put so-called soft CPU cores in the programmable logic, but this is not an efficient use of silicon or electricity for everyday cores. The super-FPGA always has processors, caches, the DRAM controller and a selection of network interfaces as **hard IP blocks**, since these are always needed.

The high cost of ASIC masks now makes FPGAs suitable for most medium-volume production runs (e.g. sub 10 000 units), which includes most recording studio equipment and passenger-in-the-road detection for high-end cars. The dark silicon trend means we can put all the IP blocks onto one chip, provided we leave them mostly turned off.

1.6 Summary

This chapter has reviewed the basic concepts of digital computers and chip technology. We have introduced some terminology that will be discussed further in the following chapters. A SoC essentially consists of a collection of IP blocks and an associated interconnect. Many of the IP blocks are used in several SoC designs, and they are sourced from IP block vendors. Others are application-specific and embody proprietary IP.

The next chapter will review three classes of IP block: processors, memory and everything else. The chapter after that will discuss how to interconnect IP blocks.

1.6.1 Exercises

1. What is the addressable space of an A32D32 processor in terms of bytes and words?

2. Why is the register space of an I/O device typically mapped so that its base address is a multiple of its length?

3. What are the differences between a PC, a microprocessor, a SoC and a microcontroller? Are they clearly distinct?

4. How would you estimate with a spreadsheet the external DRAM bandwidth needed by a SoC?

5. How could some peripheral devices be made unaddressable by some cores (Section 7.7)?

Chapter 2

Processors, Memory
and IP Blocks

As mentioned in the introduction, a SoC is essentially an assembly of IP blocks. IP blocks may be reusable over a large number of designs. They may include CPUs, RAMs and standard I/O devices such as USB, Ethernet and UART. This chapter will review all of these main forms of IP block in terms of functionality and the external connections they need. We provide illustrative TLM diagrams and RTL code fragments for many of the more simple ones. Bus fabric components are covered in detail in a subsequent chapter (Chapter 3).

2.1 Processor Cores

A SoC typically contains at least one general-purpose CPU. It may be supplied in synthesisable or a hard macro form (Section 8.4.2). In low-performance designs, the unit of instantiation is just a cacheless CPU. The basic system, ignoring I/O, is then as shown in Figure 2.1(a). The CPU just needs to be connected to the main memory. A single cache for both data and instruction is illustrated in Figure 2.1(b), but for mainstream and high-performance systems, the split between the instruction cache (I-cache) and data cache (D-cache) of Figure 2.1(c) is now more common.

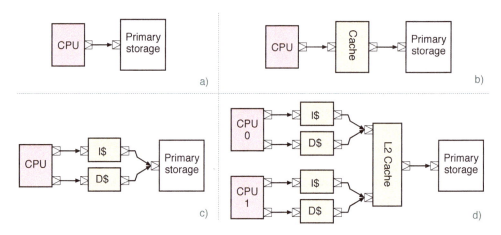

Figure 2.1 TLM connection diagrams for CPU and memory configurations: (a) direct connection, (b) with a cache, (c) with a split cache and (d) two cores with a shared L2 cache. The fan-in to the TLM socket denotes that the bandwidth is shared. In reality, debug and managements ports also need to be connected

With both instructions and data being stored in the same memory and with only one word being transferable at a time over the interface, the architecture of Figure 2.1(a) has an intrinsic structural hazard (Section 6.3). This hazard is called the **von Neumann bottleneck**. It raises no issues for register-to-register operations, but can affect any form of load or store instruction. The advantage of a split cache is called the **Harvard advantage**, which arises from holding programs and data in different memories, as did the early computers constructed at Harvard. The British computers constructed at Manchester and Cambridge used the von Neumann architecture with one memory for both. Two minor disadvantages of the Harvard architecture are: (1) that any form of program loader or self-modifying code needs a back door to be able to write to program memory and (2) that a static partition of memory resources reduces the effective capacity since one will always run out before the other (see statistical multiplexing gain, Section 4.3.3). Further advantages of having separate I- and D-caches are that each can be physically located near where their data will be used, reducing wiring distance and eliminating a multiplexing stage for the address input. The I-cache is next to the instruction decode logic and the D-cache next to the ALU.

The first-level or L1 instruction and data caches are often tightly coupled to the CPU. The composition is known as a **CPU core** or just a **core** for short. Such a core is then the unit of instantiation at the SoC level. This is like Figure 2.1(a) from the system integrator's point of view. The core may also have a memory management unit (MMU; Section 2.2.1) or other memory protection units with any associated translation lookaside buffers (TLBs; Section 2.2.1). A tightly coupled coprocessor, such as a floating point unit (FPU; Section 6.4) or a custom accelerator (Section 6.4), can also be included in the instantiated component. As well as being atomic from the system integrator's point of view, these components are also tightly coupled in the sense that they are mutually optimised for performance. The clock distribution network (Section 4.9.5) is shared, and critical interconnections, such as the byte alignment logic on the data cache read port, may potentially have been optimised using full-custom techniques (Section 8.4). However, for maximum flexibility in SoC design, the coprocessor connections can be wired using the general IP interconnection tooling. This is shown in Figure 2.2. Apart from accelerators, another way to increase processor functionality is by extending the custom instruction set (Section 2.1.3).

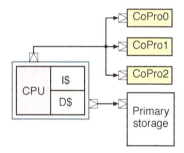

Figure 2.2 TLM diagrams for a CPU core with integrated first-level caches and external coprocessor connections

The level-2 (L2) caches and associated snoop controllers for cache consistency (Section 2.4.1) are likely to be instantiated as separate IP blocks, as shown in Figure 2.1(d). This gives the SoC designer the freedom to experiment with cache structures and bus bandwidths. In these TLM diagrams, where two arrows connect to one TLM port of a component, this is normally taken to denote that the bus bandwidth at that point is shared, but not always (as will be explained in Section 5.4.5). Having a dedicated L2 per core is also a sensible design, as explored in Section 6.6.1.

As well as access to primary storage, a SoC designer needs to implement a number of other connections, including clock, reset, interrupts and a debug port. The debug port provides back door access to the CPU for register inspection, single stepping, triggering and trace logging (Section 4.7).

2.1.1 ISAs

Any processor family is defined by its **programmer's view (PV)** instruction set architecture (ISA). The PV includes the registers and memories that a low-level software programmer needs to know about and which they manipulate with instructions. It does not include any details of the **microarchitecture**, like the registers used for pipelining or present only in some particular hardware implementation of the ISA. The ISA defines both the user-visible registers and the set of available instructions. The two most prevalent ISAs used today are Arm and x86, but both of these have numerous variations. For instance, early Arm architectures supported only 8- and 32-bit data with 16-bit support being added in a later variant. Most recently, the Arm AArch64 architecture with 64-bit addresses was released.

Within each variation of an ISA, multiple implementations usefully co-exist. An ISA can be implemented with different microarchitectures that vary in area, energy and performance. Power consumption tends to be proportional to area, but performance always grows sublinearly. In other words, doubling the processor complexity gives less than a factor of 2 improvement in throughput. **Pollack's rule of thumb**, which is widely quoted, gives the exponent as 0.5. Two cores give twice the performance for twice the power, but, following Pollack, getting twice the performance from a single core requires 4× the power. Hence, if a program can be made to run on multiple cores, then this is better than using fewer but more complex cores.

However, automatic parallelisation of existing programs is difficult. This is often a result of the way they were coded and the programming languages used. Hence, to achieve high performance with legacy code, so-called 'brawny' cores are needed [1]. They have high complexity but are in mainstream use, predominantly using the x86 architecture. Note that the total energy used by the system is divided over the memory system and the cores, which may use roughly equal amounts of energy in some systems. The energy cost of moving data between the memory and core is increasingly significant. The amount of memory traffic for an application is not altered by the processor design (to a first approximation, ignoring prefetches and mispredicts); hence, the core complexity affects less than half the power budget. Indeed, the energy used for memory and communication is becoming increasingly dominant.

These topics are explored further in Section 6.6.2.

High-performance implementations of cores may have powerful but less-frequently used instructions in hardware; the same instructions are emulated on the lower-performance implementations. If such an instruction is missing from the implemented set, an **emulation exception** is raised and tightly coupled machine code or microcode is executed to provide the functionality. Examples are vector-processing instructions.

Early devices relied on complex instruction set computing (**CISC**). Such ISAs had complex and powerful instructions that helped minimise code size but whose execution logic extended the critical path (Section 4.4.2) and hence, reduced the clock frequency. Also, many of these instructions were seldom used. This is not a good design since it penalises the performance of the frequently used instructions. As a result, so-called **reduced instruction set computing** (**RISC**) was introduced, primarily in the early 1980s (although IBM had a RISC project in the 1960s). As well as a streamlined instruction set, RISC aimed to achieve one instruction per clock cycle (IPC). Hence, bus protocols that can transfer a word every clock cycle were needed and a split cache was also deployed to maintain IPC at unity during loads and stores. Famous RISC designs from that period were produced by MIPS, SPARC and Arm, with the first Arm silicon in operation in 1985.

Modern implementations of CISC generally use a conversion phase that expands a CISC instruction to one or more RISC-like instructions. There are three places in which the translation can be performed:

1. In **software** as part of the compiler or in the operating system loader.

2. In hardware, **pre-instruction cache**: An instruction is expanded on cache miss; however, this adds an overhead to branch target identification and checkpointing during exception handling.

3. **Post-instruction cache**: The expansion is handled using **microcode**.

The third option is most commonly used in CISC implementations. An expanded CISC instruction is often called a **uop** or micro-operation, especially in the context of x86 architectures. Simple CISC instructions, such as a register transfer, are converted to a single uop, whereas more complex instructions, such as a block move or a division, are converted to entry points into a microcode ROM, which stores a program with 2 to 20 or so uops. Such cores translate each CISC instruction every time it is used. Assuming an unchanged 95 per cent hit rate in the instruction cache, only 5 per cent of that energy would be needed under option 2 and none at all under option 1. The primary explanation for the world being stuck with these relatively poor designs is market inertia.

2.1.2 Vector Instructions

The energy used by high-performance core implementations is dominated by instruction fetch, decode and scheduling. The actual computation energy in ALUs and register files is typically a small percentage (5–10 per cent). This is the fundamental reason why hardwired accelerators perform so much more efficiently (Section 6.4). It is also a fundamental motivation for **vector-processing** ISA extensions.

A vector instruction is also known as a **SIMD instruction**, since a single instruction operates on multiple data words. Vector instructions implement massively parallel operations on the normal register file, manipulating many registers at once. Alternatively, they operate on additional registers in the PV. (However, register renaming in super-scalar CPUs clouds this distinction (Section 2.2).) The register file can typically be treated as multiple, shorter registers. For instance a swathe of a 32-bit register file might be treated as 4× as many 8-bit registers. By operating on, for example, 16 or 32 registers at once, the fetch-execute overhead is amortised by the same factor. Hence, vector arithmetic of this nature can approach the efficiency of custom accelerators. If a processor has load-multiple and store-multiple instructions, like the Arm family, a multi-register block of data can be transferred to and from the memory system in one instruction.

2.1.3 Custom Instructions

Processors are either placed on a SoC as hard macros (Section 8.4.2) or in synthesisable form. A hard macro is carefully optimised by the IP supplier and cannot be changed by the SoC designer. However, so-called **soft cores** are supplied in RTL form and can be changed in various ways by the SoC designer, although parts of the RTL may be encrypted or obfuscated to protect IP. One change, commonly supported, is for the SoC designer to add one or more **custom instructions** [2]. These share the instruction fetch and decode logic of the standard instructions, but can access new registers, ALUs or custom resources. The mapping for the instruction set opcode typically has various gaps where new operations can be added. The assembler, debugger and other parts of the tool chain can likewise be augmented to exploit new instructions. The benefits of custom instructions are explored alongside custom coprocessors in Section 6.4.1.

2.1.4 The Classic Five-stage Pipeline

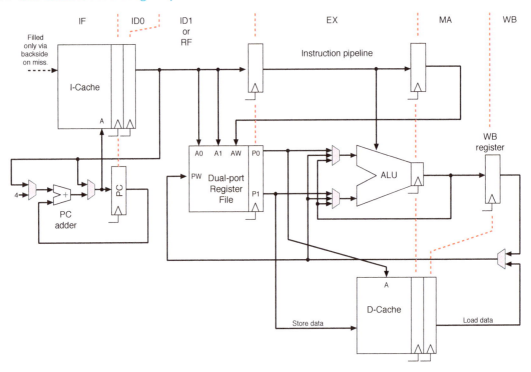

Figure 2.3 Main data paths in a generic five-stage RISC microarchitecture, excluding the back sides of the cache and MMU. Instruction field bit-extracts to control the multiplexes and ALU are not shown

Figure 2.3 is a diagram of a generic microarchitecture for the classic **five-stage pipeline**. It actually shows six stages, since both the ID0 and ID1 stages are used. Getting back to five involves combining the ID0 and ID1 stages, but there are various specific ways of doing this, such as making the main register file combinational for reads or using single-cycle cache access. The five pipeline stages are:

- **Instruction fetch (IF)**: The next instruction is fetched from the I-cache, which behaves like a synchronous SRAM (Section 2.6.4), in that the address must be provided at least one cycle before the instruction comes out. Figure 2.3 shows read operations with a latency of two for both caches.

- **Instruction decode (ID)** or **register fetch (RF)**: Designs vary according to how the instruction decode is precisely pipelined, but there is at least one cycle between the instruction arriving and the register data being input into the ALU.

- **Execute (EX)**: The ALU combines the operands from the register file. The register on the **arithmetic and logic unit (ALU)** result bus makes this a pipeline stage.

- **Memory access (MA)**: Again, since read access to the data cache has a latency of two, the memory access pipeline stage actually takes two cycles. However, in some designs, this is a single-cycle operation.

- **Writeback (WB)**: The writeback stage is just padding to equalise the delay from the output of the ALU for the computed results with the data cache load delay (assuming a two-cycle data cache). The padding ensures that load and arithmetic/logic instructions can be placed back-to-back and that at most one register in the main file needs to be written per clock cycle.

These simple RISC designs have two main types of pipeline hazard. A **control hazard** occurs when a conditional branch predicate is not known at the time it is needed. Hence, there is a good chance that incorrect instructions are fetched and decoded. This is overcome by suppressing the stores and register file updates from such instructions so that they effectively behave as no-ops.

A **data hazard** occurs when the result of a computation or load is not in its intended place in the register file until two cycles later. This is solved for ALU operations with the two **forwarding paths** from the output of the ALU and the output of the writeback register. For loads, it cannot be solved for immediate use and a pipeline bubble is needed (the compiler optimiser should minimise this use pattern as far as possible), but it can be forwarded from two cycles before. The forwarding multiplexors use simple pattern matching across successive stages of the instruction pipeline shown at the top of the figure.

2.2 Super-scalar Processors

A super-scalar processor can execute more than one **instruction per clock cycle (IPC)**. The average is around 2 or 3 with a peak of 6, depending on the nature of the program being run. However, first-generation microprocessors required several clock cycles for each bus cycle. Since the average number of cycles per instruction was at least one, performance was measured in clock cycles per instruction (CPI), which is the reciprocal of the IPC.

Figure 2.4 shows the main features of a super-scalar microarchitecture. Such a processor needs to be able to read multiple instructions from the instruction cache in one clock cycle. The diagram shows

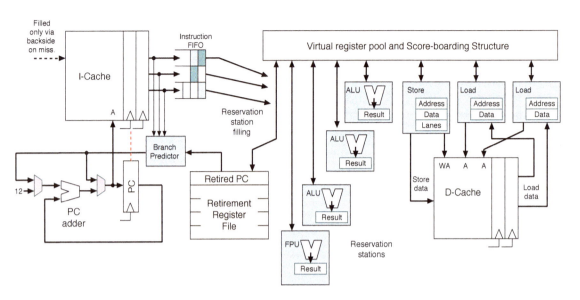

Figure 2.4 Key components of a super-scalar CPU core, excluding the back sides of the cache and MMU

three, but a power of 2 is more common. A branch target is not normally aligned to the instruction width of the I-cache, so realignment is typically needed. Using a FIFO for this can help overcome other sources of pipeline bubble.

The **execution unit** consists of some number of reservation stations. These can be identical in structure, but often are specialised to some degree. The diagram shows four types: load, store, integer ALU and floating-point ALU, but designs vary greatly in detail. Although essential for the instruction cache, it is usual for the data cache to also support super-scalar operation. The diagram shows paths for three transactions on the data cache per clock cycle. This total does not include the back-side cache load/evict operations.

Instructions are placed in empty reservation stations. Complex matching logic triggers a reservation station to execute its saved instruction as soon as its operands are ready. Execution will typically take several clock cycles for a complex instruction, such as a 64-bit multiply or floating-point add. A reservation station is not typically fully pipelined (Section 6.3), so that it is busy until the result is ready. The provisioning mix of reservation stations must match the mix of instructions commonly found in programs. For a design to have a balanced throughput, this mix must be weighted by how long a reservation station is busy per operation. Generally, every fifth instruction is a branch and every third is a load or store. Loads are at least twice as common as stores.

When a result is ready, the reservation station or stations that depend on the new result become ready to run. These will not necessarily be the next instructions in the original program sequence. Hence, we achieve **out-of-order instruction execution**. In general, the execution times for different instructions are neither equal nor predictable. Load and store stations have a variable execution time due to the complex behaviour of caches and DRAM. By executing an instruction as soon as its operands are ready, the hardware dynamically adapts to the behaviour of memory. Certain operations at a reservation station can have a variable latency as well. For example, for a division, the number of cycles depends on the bit position of the most significant 1, because, in a typical mainstream division algorithm, the denominator must be left-shifted until it is greater than or equal to the numerator (which takes forever when dividing by zero!).

Reservation stations operate on virtual registers, not the physical PV registers. A PV register could be updated several times within the window of instructions spread out within the core. This can often be tens of instructions. This is possible only if several virtual registers alias one PV register, which is called **register renaming**. The mapping at any instant is held in complex **scoreboarding logic**. Move operations that merely transfer data between registers can be implemented as just an update to the scoreboard structure, if is clear from the forward instruction window that only one copy needs to be kept.

For an average branch instruction density of about one fifth, four basic blocks are processed simultaneously for an instruction window of 20. This is possible without parallel speculation down multiple flows of control by accurately predicting which way branches will go. The predictions are made by a specialist branch direction cache that monitors the patterns of flow control. If this is accurate to about 0.99 (a typical figure) then, with four branches in a window, the overall misprediction ratio is $1 - 0.99^4 \approx 0.04$. Hence, 4 per cent of instruction executions are wasted and their results must be discarded.

Keeping track of correct execution is handled using the **retirement register file**. This minimally contains the retirement program counter (PC). It contains also either a copy of the PV at that PC value or else a sufficient snapshot of the scoreboarding structure that describes which virtual registers contain equivalent information. The retirement PC denotes the point at which all previous instructions have been successfully executed along the correct control flow. For a branch mispredict or another error, a super-scalar processor discards everything that is in flight and rolls back execution by copying the retirement PC to the fetcher PC. Likewise, PV registers that are needed but not in virtual registers are fetched from the retirement register file.

The multiple ALUs and copies of registers in a super-scalar processor have a correspondingly larger number of control inputs compared with a simple processor that only has one instance, or fewer instances, of each component. Rather than on-the-fly parallelism discovery within a standard instruction stream, the main alternative is to use a **very long instruction word (VLIW)** processor. In these architectures, individual data-path components are explicitly driven in parallel using wide instructions for which the concurrency has been statically optimised, at compile time, by the assembler. Such architectures save energy and silicon area because the interleaving is done off-line. Although it may seem that using fewer but wider instructions could achieve a roughly equivalent instruction encoding efficiency, a naive design will give rise to a low entropy stream due to commonly repeating patterns. Explicitly encoding something that can be readily inferred is bound to be inefficient. As with **high-level synthesis (HLS)** (Section 6.9), a static schedule, generated at compile time, cannot efficiently adapt to out-of-order data returned from today's complex memory systems.

A high-performance microprocessor requires much more from its memory system than the simple read/write byte/word needs of a low-performance core. It will typically have more than one load station and also support vector instructions, both of which require greater data bandwidth from the I-cache. It will also be able to exploit an out-of-order read service discipline. Out-of-order operation also requires sequential consistency interlocks (Section 4.5) to ensure that reads and writes to the same address follow the correct logical ordering. Many of these details are hidden from the SoC designer if the L1 cache is part of the same IP block as the microprocessor. This is a motivation for using the term 'core' to denote the combination of a microprocessor and first-level caches, but other authors use 'core' to denote just a cacheless microprocessor.

2.2.1 Virtual Memory Management Units: MMU and IOMMU

A **memory management unit (MMU)** translates virtual addresses into physical addresses. A simplistic TLM diagram is shown in the top half of Figure 2.5. However, in reality, a decision has to be made about whether each cache operates on virtual or physical addresses. A common configuration is shown in the bottom half of Figure 2.5. Here, the L1 caches operate on virtual addresses whereas the L2 cache operates on physical addresses. The figure also shows the necessary secondary connection to allow the control and configuration registers to be updated by the core. If an L1 cache operates on virtual addresses, the MMU is not part of the performance-critical front-side operations. Using Arm technology, such updates are made via the coprocessor interface, so the MMU of a core appears as a coprocessor.

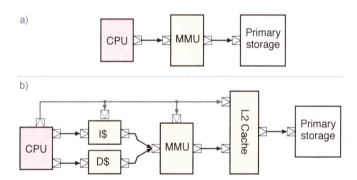

Figure 2.5 TLM connection diagrams for a CPU and memory management unit (MMU): (a) naive view and (b) one possible cache arrangement

An MMU contains a cache of recently translated addresses known as the **translation lookaside buffer (TLB)**. In most processor architectures, misses in this cache are serviced entirely using hardware inside the MMU, which includes a root translation register and table walking logic that uses back-side operations to load the TLB. The alternative, as used by MIPS processors, is for the TLB to be filled with software via a translation fault exception. Having physical addresses in the L2 cache is not always the best design. The cache miss performance penalty, whether pages are to be mapped more than once and how they are shared between cores must also be considered. Such decisions impact only to a small extent the overall SoC design and vary according to the need for a cache-consistent DMA and accelerators (Section 6.4).

Recently, systems have started including an **I/O memory management unit (IOMMU)** for input/output operations. It typically operates in two directions: it controls memory mapping of I/O devices into a processor's address space and it controls what regions of primary storage are addressable by DMA from I/O devices.

Two motivations for an IOMMU are virtualisation and pluggable devices. With the increased use of **hypervisors** (Section 4.9) to enable multiple operating systems to run at once on a computing device, a layer below the operating system is required to virtualise the physical devices, so that, to some extent at least, the device drivers for specialist devices are embodied above the virtualisation layer. With DMA-capable pluggable devices, such as recent versions of Firewire and Thunderbolt, foreign hardware can potentially have unrestricted access to the entire memory contents in the absence of an IOMMU.

Low-power systems may use a **memory protection unit (MPU)** (Section 4.9) instead of an MMU to provide some level of security.

2.3 Multi-core Processing

A **chip multiprocessor (CMP)** has more than one CPU core on one piece of silicon. For a **symmetric multiprocessor (SMP)**, the cores are identical. Although the cores may be identical and see a global flat address space for primary storage, each may have faster access to some local memory than to the local memories of other cores or to centralised memory, which results in **non-uniform memory access (NUMA)**.

Having more than one CPU core is an energy-efficient approach for increasing performance. Another phrasing of Pollack's rule, compared with that in Section 2.1.1, is to say that energy use in a von Neumann CPU grows with the square of its IPC. However, using multiple cores can result in close to linear growth. This contrasts with the increase in energy consumption, which is roughly linearly proportional to the increase in complexity, which in this context refers to the amount of processor logic, i.e. its area. Note that just clocking faster requires at least quadratic energy use (Section 4.6.8).

Computer architectures for parallel programming have converged on cache-consistent shared memories. This is one practical implementation of a so-called parallel random access machine (PRAM; Figure 2.6) [3]. Each processor operates in parallel and has random access to the entire primary store. The memory is partitioned into atomic units (cache lines in contemporary implementations), such that writes of all bits occur together. The interconnect imposes some model of sequential consistency (Section 4.5), which, in the baseline model, is that every change to a word is visible to every other processor the cycle after it is written. A clock or orchestration unit keeps each processor in lockstep, to some granularity. In the baseline model, reads alternate with writes and all cores stop when any core executes a halt instruction. However, in **bulk synchronous processing (BSP)** [4], the granularity is coarser, so that hundreds of instructions may be executed before the processors are synchronised. These architectures are not mainstream, either in terms of implementation or high-level language support. However, some CPU vendors have implemented **hardware transactional memory**, which is similar; the processors can work on multiple cache lines before atomically writing them all out to primary store (raising an exception for any clashes).

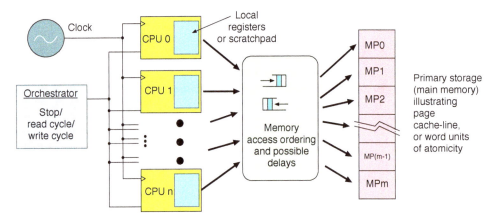

Figure 2.6 A generalised PRAM model of computing. A number of synchronous processors, each with some private local store, make random access and read and write operations on shared memory that has many atomic locations of some size. The interconnect implements some variant of coherence (value and sequential consistency)

There is academic debate over whether cache consistency is really necessary in real-world systems. For a large majority of parallel programs and algorithms, the consistency information can be statically known or easily checked explicitly at runtime. The same is true for operating systems and network interfaces but, perhaps, to a lesser extent. Likewise, for the caches themselves, software-managed scratchpads could instead be used. However, the fundamental advantage of multiple levels of storage technology with different speed-to-density ratios is unquestionable and can be demonstrated analytically (Section 6.6.1). Also, automatic and on-demand loading of data into caches provides parallelism and allows the system to adapt to dynamic program behaviour. These are the principal advantages of hardware-managed caches (except for hard real-time systems). Arguably, the cost of cache consistency for hardware-managed caches (unlike scratchpad memories) is a minimal further overhead. Moreover, it is possible that software-managed scratchpads waste instruction bandwidth by explicitly performing operations that could be inferred.

A **scratchpad memory** is a small region of primary storage that is closely coupled to a CPU core. It is normally implemented in SRAM and may be tens to hundreds of kilobytes in size. Its access time is low (similar to a L1 or L2 data cache) but also predictable, since cache effects are minimised and there is no DRAM delay. Two possible scratchpad configurations are shown in Figure 2.7. Non-determinate cache effects are eliminated if the scratchpad is at the L1 level and small if at the L2 level. Use of memory in scratchpads is managed in software and typically exploited only by hard real-time singleton applications. A singleton application is one that is present at most once on a SoC, such as a global manager for power, security or a specific I/O device.

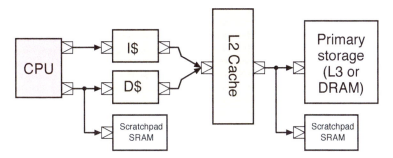

Figure 2.7 Two possible configurations for scratchpad memory

2.3.1 Simultaneous Multithreading

To increase the number of effective processor cores in a CMP, rather than adding further complete cores, **simultaneous multithreading** can be used. This adds further retirement register files to an existing core, which has a much lower area overhead than adding a full core with L1 caches. A thread is defined by the presence of a program counter in each register file, but a full set of all architecturally visible registers is needed. The set of reservation stations is shared over the threads within a simultaneously multithreaded core. There are advantages and disadvantages. Apart from requiring less silicon than a full new core, a new thread benefits from a statistical multiplexing gain (Section 4.3.3) in the utilisation of reservation stations, since there is a higher chance that more of them will be in use at once. A potential disadvantage is that the L1 caches are shared. This potentially leads to greater thrashing (capacity evictions) unless the simultaneously multithreaded cores are running closely coupled parts of the same program.

2.4 Cache Design

In computer architecture, a cache contains key-value pairs. The key is an address and the value is a **cache line** of typically four or eight 32-bit words. The capacity of a cache is the number of key-value pairs it can hold and is typically expressed using the total number of bytes it can store in the value fields. A simple cache has two logical ports: (1) The **front side** gives fast and frequent access to the cache user. It is typically a CPU core or a faster cache. (2) The **back side** uses a wider and slower data bus that connects to wherever the data are served from. The underlying implementation is typically constructed from single-ported SRAM with virtual dual-porting (Figure 4.19). Having levels of caching means that memory components that have different trade-offs between logic speed, storage density and energy use can be combined efficiently (Section 6.6.1). There is always at least an order of magnitude difference in bandwidth, in terms of bits per second, between the front and back sides. A component with the same bandwidth on both sides that merely converts from a narrow bus to a wide bus with a lower clock frequency is called a **gearbox** or **serialiser**.

The bandwidth saving from a cache arises for two reasons:

1. With **temporal locality**, an item recently looked at is likely to be looked at again.

2. With **spatial locality**, items stored in nearby locations are likely to be accessed. A performance gain and saving in complexity are achieved by fetching a cache line that is larger than a single byte or word. The performance increases because adjacent data are prefetched. The complexity is reduced because the data management overhead is amortised.

There are three principal organisation techniques for caches:

1. A **fully associative cache** allows any line to be stored anywhere in the cache. A parallel search of the whole cache is used to determine whether an address is held, which tends to be too energy expensive (except for MMU TLBs, Section 2.2.1).

2. A **directly mapped cache** has just one place where an address can be stored. That location is given by a hash function on the address. The normal hash function, suitable when the cache size is a power of two, is to ignore all higher-order address bits. A directly mapped cache has the advantage that only one place needs to be searched to see whether data are held. Moreover, those data can be returned to the customer in parallel with its validity being checked. The main disadvantage of a directly mapped cache is the high degree of aliasing. Due to the **birthday paradox**, on average, too much of the data that is concurrently needed is mapped on top of itself. This leads to much wasteful thrashing. (The birthday paradox is the popular name for the fact that the probability of 30 people all having different birthdays is surprisingly low).

3. The technique most commonly used is a **set-associative cache**. Each line is stored in a small set of possible places (typically four or eight). When searching, only this small set needs to be checked, which can be done in parallel with a small amount of hardware. However, the effect of the birthday paradox is ameliorated: the chance that more than four lines will concurrently alias to the same set is acceptably low. With eight, it is negligible. However, more ways are sometimes used in larger caches (but this is to prevent the directly mapped bit field from becoming too large, such as bigger than a virtual memory page).

If data are written to a cache but not yet synchronised with the next level of storage in the memory hierarchy, then the cache line with the changes contains **dirty data**. In general, just a few bytes in the whole cache line may be dirty. Freeing up a cache line so that it can be used for entirely different data is known as **eviction**. When dirty data are evicted, the cache must save the modified data out of its back side (to the next-level cache or primary store). This is the **copyback** policy for managing writes, which is also known as a **writeback**. The alternative policy is **write-through**, in which all writes also update subsequent levels as they happen. The disadvantage of a write-through is that bus bandwidth is wasted in the common scenario of multiple, successive updates to the same variable. Moreover, writes can stall the processor because they are slowed down to the rate supported by the next-level cache by backpressure. To reduce the slowdown from backpressure, a **write buffer** is sometimes used. A write buffer holds one or two lines under the fully associative policy. Dirty data are stored in the write buffer and the dirty words are tagged. The buffer performs **write coalescing** of successive writes to the same line. It can reduce back-side bandwidth use since only the dirty words need to be written out to the next level. In this context, the width of a word is the width of the back-side data bus.

A set-associative cache is efficient in terms of hit ratio for the degree of associativity and hence, energy use. A disadvantage is that data can be returned only on the front side after the tag matching is complete. In some designs, an extra memory, called the **way cache**, improves performance by remembering which way was last successful in each directly mapped set and serving its data while the tags are checked. A directly mapped cache can sometimes be improved with a **victim store** that holds one or two additional lines under the fully associative policy. These are filled by lines evicted from the main directly mapped array. This gives a small degree of full associativity.

A **cache hit** occurs when data are found in a cache. A cache needs to have a hit rate of above 80 per cent to be worthwhile; typical hit rates in a data cache are often 95 per cent. They are even higher in instruction caches at around 99 per cent, except for long straight-line code. A miss occurs when the data are not found. There are four reasons for a miss:

1. A **compulsory miss** occurs if the data were never present in the cache. All data read must have an initial reading. This is unavoidable, regardless of cache size.

2. A **capacity miss** arises when the data were present but have been evicted due to the need to reuse the finite capacity.

3. A **conflict miss** arises due to cache mapping strategies. Fully associative caches do not suffer from conflict misses. Instead, they occur because of enforced structures like direct mapping.

4. A **sharing miss** arises from cache-consistency protocols operating between two or more caches. Under the copyback write policy, a cache line may become dirty in one cache and so copies in other caches need to be removed. This is called a **cache line invalidate**. If a local user tries to read the data, a sharing miss occurs.

If a new line needs to be loaded into an associative cache (fully associative or set-associative), the system must decide where to store the new data using a **replacement policy**. The best replacement policy is to evict the data that is not going to be used for the longest amount of time. In general, this cannot be known, but certain characteristics can be dynamically learned with sufficient reliability to be usefully exploited.

A common replacement policy is **random replacement**. No information is used to guide the decision. Silicon testing is very difficult for logic with truly random behaviour, so it is avoided as much as possible (Section 8.8.2). It is better to use a pseudorandom binary sequence (PRBS) generator. In practice, a simple counter is sufficient.

The **least-recently used (LRU)** replacement policy has also been used. In a nominal implementation, counters or timers exist for each cache line to keep track of when it was last used. It is assumed that the line that was used the longest time ago will remain unused the furthest into the future and is, thus, evicted.

The complexity of LRU grows exponentially with the degree of associativity. A naive approach that stores a timer in each associative way would have to compare many timers for each decision, perhaps using a heap for efficiency. A heap is a tree with the most promising candidate at the root. It has a logarithmic update cost. There is a factorial number of relative age orderings over the associative ways, which can be used to create a more compact implementation of LRU. For instance, for a four-way associative cache, there are 4! = 24 orderings, which can be enumerated in a 5-bit field. The update function required when a way is used can be implemented in a compact logic function or a partially populated ROM of 5 × 5 with a further two output bits to specify which way to use at each step. For higher degrees of associativity, the factorial (exponential) complexity becomes infeasible and similar logic functions are used to implement **pseudo-LRU**, which is cheaper but approximate. However, such a noisy solution can have an advantage because certain regular access patterns, such as a linear scan, which would thrash the cache under a perfect LRU, will retain some useful content.

Some designs implement the simple **not recently used algorithm**, which is also called the **clock algorithm** when used in virtual memory paging. The clock algorithm uses a single bit per way, initially clear, which is set when that way is used. Eviction selects a way using round-robin arbitration (Section 4.2.1) from amongst those with clear bits. If setting a bit results in all bits being set in that associative set, they are all cleared at that point. However, a true LRU policy is often useful for caches if an access to the next level of store is expensive, such as for spinning disks or writes to solid-state drives (SSDs).

Another policy variation is known as a **write allocate**, which can evict existing data. A value that is written while its line is not in the cache causes an allocation within the cache. If it is clear the data are not going to be served from the cache, write allocate is a waste of time. Such situations include erasing blocks of memory for security or initialisation or for sending data to other parts of a shared-memory system. Certain bus protocols, such as AXI (Section 3.1.5), enable the writer to indicate whether to write allocate or not, for every write.

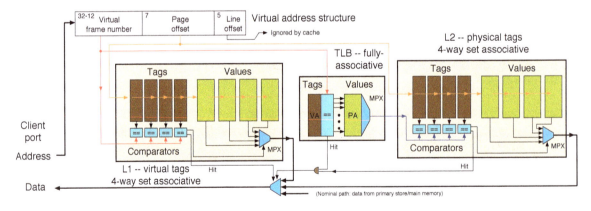

Figure 2.8 Typical arrangement of virtual and physical mapping with L1, TLB and L2. Data are served from L1 or L2, but are unlikely to be served directly from primary storage. Instead, update mechanisms (not shown) are used. Four-way associativity is illustrated, but a higher degree is typically used, to increase both the hit ratio and capacity, since it is generally required that the directly mapped axis is not wider than the virtual memory page size

Figure 2.8 shows a particular arrangement of virtual and physical mapping with L1, L2 and TLB. Numerous other arrangements can be used, but the advantage of having a virtually indexed L1 is that the hits in it, which should be the vast majority of accesses, can be served without lookup delays in the TLB. Additionally, the L2 tag RAMs are accessed in parallel with the TLB lookup, so inputs to the four L2 comparators arrive at roughly the same time.

Implementing a four-way set-associative cache is fairly straightforward. An associative RAM macrocell is not needed. Instead, four sets of XOR gates are synthesised from RTL using the == operator!

```
reg [31:0] data0 [0:32767], data1 [0:32767], data2 [0:32767], data3 [0:32767];
reg [14:0] tag0 [0:32767], tag1 [0:32767], tag2 [0:32767], tag3 [0:32767];

always @(posedge clk) begin
    miss = 0;
    if (tag0[addr[16:2]]==addr[31:17]) dout <= data0[addr[16:2]];
    else if (tag1[addr[16:2]]==addr[31:17]) dout <= data1[addr[16:2]];
    else if (tag2[addr[16:2]]==addr[31:17]) dout <= data2[addr[16:2]];
    else if (tag3[addr[16:2]]==addr[31:17]) dout <= data3[addr[16:2]];
    else miss = 1;
    end
```

2.4.1 Snooping and Other Coherency Protocols

If multiple caches can store the same data, **cache coherency** is used to prevent copies becoming unsynchronised. There are two main aspects to cache coherency:

1. **Data consistency** ensures that all observers see the same data in the same memory location.

2. **Sequential consistency** ensures that observers see the same ordering of updates in different memory locations.

The standard data consistency protocol is MESI, named after the states modified, exclusive, shared and invalid:

▪ An **invalid (I)** cache line is not in use.

▪ An **exclusive (E)** line holds data that are not in any other cache at the same level. The data may be in caches at other levels.

▪ A **shared (S)** line holds data that might also be present in other caches at the same level.

▪ A **modified (M)** line is the same as an exclusive line, but contains modified data. These dirty data must be copied back at eviction.

Each cache line is in one of these states.

System programmers need to be aware of several cache artefacts. Instruction caches are normally not subject to consistency mechanisms, hence giving rise to a Harvard-like architecture. Self-modifying code and loading new code are supported only with specific cache-flush instructions. The programmer must include these instructions. Also, volatile memory areas, such as I/O device status registers, must not be cached, since otherwise any polling-like operations (Section 2.7) will fail. This can be overcome using a combination of **uncacheable regions** specifically denoted in the MMU translation flags or additional attributes in the command field of a bus transaction, such as the AXI uncacheable operation type (Section 3.1.5). Some ISAs contain special cache-bypassing load and store instructions that a systems programmer must use. In general, all programmers really need to be aware of how caches operate if they are to design efficient code and data structures.

Caches cooperating using the MESI protocol need to keep track of what is happening in the other caches. For instance, a read miss will result in a back-side load, but the resulting state will be either exclusive or shared depending on whether the data are already held in another cache. Likewise, a store to a shared cache line needs to convert that cache line to modified but also evict the line from those other caches that had the line in a shared state.

For small-scale systems, the principal communication technique for achieving cache consistency is based around **snooping** of the back-side bus. In early systems, the back-side bus was a physical bus where a common set of conductors connected to multiple caches. Owing to wiring capacitance, using physical busses is no longer a good design point at the physical level (Section 1.1.4), but the term, 'snooping', and its related aspects persist. The important aspects of a logical bus are zero spatial ruse of bandwidth (having at most one active transmitter) and being able to simultaneously broadcast to all connected devices. Structures using **snoop filters** and **directory protocols** are used for larger systems. These are presented presented in Section 3.1.6, after we have discussed cache-coherent interconnect.

Figure 2.9 shows one mapping of snooping cache consistency into reusable IP blocks. The illustrated **snoop control unit (SCU)** has eight target sockets that can connect to up to four cores. A ninth socket is available for connecting cache-consistent accelerators or DMA units. On the back side, it has one or two initiator sockets to the next level of storage. Illustrated are two L2 caches that serve different parts of the physical address space using an address partitioning system inside the SCU. The partition must be set up by the operating system at boot time. Alternatively, with this IP block, the two back-side ports can be connected in parallel to a shared next-level memory system to give twice as much bandwidth but without partitioning. Hard partitioning suffers from a loss of performance due to statistical multiplexing (Section 4.3.3) whereas a parallel connection requires arbitration if both ports address the same primary or next-level region. Note, the TLM model for this SCU is discussed in Section 5.4.2. The setup in Figure 2.9 uses the backchannel inside the TLM sockets on the caches and the snoop controller to initiate invalidate operations on the local data cache of a core (Section 6.7.1).

The MESI protocol can be augmented with a fifth state, owned (O), for shared data that is dirty. The cache is responsible for issuing a copyback before invalidating the line. As long as writes are

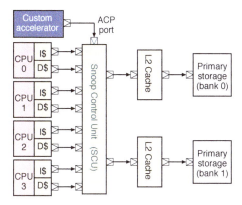

Figure 2.9 An example system using a snoop control IP block from Arm (Cortex A9 family)

communicated between a group of consistent caches, they can exchange dirty data between themselves, thereby avoiding writing out a dirty line to the next level of storage, only to read it in again. Only one cache is permitted to hold the line in the owned state, and others must hold it in the shared state. On the penultimate eviction, a line becomes modified again and the copyback to the next level then occurs as usual on the final eviction from the group. This five-state protocol is called MOESI. Figure 2.10 shows Arm's equivalent to MOESI, as used in the AMBA ACE and CHI coherency protocols. The ACE protocol extends the regular AXI interface with snoop channels to enable communications between peer caches and maintain coherency.

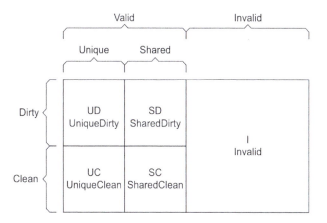

Figure 2.10 MOESI-like state diagram used in the Arm ACE and CHI protocols

If there are several levels of cache, it is sometimes necessary to ensure that a line cannot be evicted from a cache unless it is missing from all (smaller and faster) caches on the front side. In other words, each cached line is also present in all caches on the back side (which are typically larger and slower). A cache level that maintains this policy is called an **inclusive cache**. Although this policy effectively reduces the total number of different lines that can be stored in the cache system as a whole, it helps with the scalability of coherency protocols (Section 3.1.6).

2.5 Interrupts and the Interrupt Controller

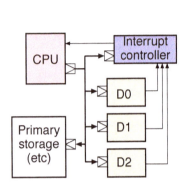

Figure 2.11 Three I/O blocks connected to a CPU, memory and an interrupt controller

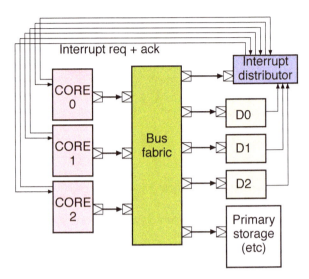

Interrupt req + ack

Figure 2.12 Three I/O blocks with flexible interrupt distribution in a multi-core system

Interrupt priorities and wiring can be hardwired at the SoC level or PCB level, or may be programmable, completely or to some degree. Figure 2.11 shows the typical interrupt structure of a SoC. The single core uses three I/O devices, each of which is a bus target for programmed I/O (PIO) read and write transactions. They can also generate an interrupt for the CPU. An **interrupt controller** can be as simple as a three-input OR gate or it could be programmable, as discussed here.

With only a single interrupt wire to the processor, all interrupt sources share it and the processor must poll each interrupt to find the device that needs attention. An enhancement is to use a **vectored interrupt** that makes the processor branch to a device-specific location. However, there is very little difference in execution cost between having hardware and software handler tables, since an interrupt controller contains a unary-to-binary priority encoder that can be interpreted by interrupt software or hardware. A more important distinction is that interrupts can also be associated with priorities, so that interrupts with a level higher than currently being run will pre-empt.

At the processor core level, a higher-priority interrupt is one that can pre-empt a lower one. Processor cores typically support more than one level of interrupt priority. For instance, the Motorola 68000 had seven. Arm cores typically had only two levels, called IRQ and FIQ, with FIQ being higher. The number of effective levels of priority can be augmented outside the core in the interrupt controller.

Generally, many more devices can raise an interrupt than the number of interrupt priority levels supported by the cores. Hence, a degree of sharing of levels is needed. Those that share a processor priority level can have their own relative priority implemented inside the interrupt controller using a standard priority encoder, as just mentioned. Alternatively, a round-robin arbitration policy can be supported inside the controller. This requires keeping a state for which source was last served (Section 4.2.1).

With only a single core, all interrupts must be routed to that core. The only remaining degree of freedom is then deciding what priority to allocate to each interrupt. As mentioned, this could be a pair of priorities: the core priority and the priority amongst those share a core priority.

With multiple cores, there are many more possibilities. The main new policy decision is whether individual cores should be strongly associated with a given interrupt source or whether to use dynamic allocation of cores to interrupts. Figure 2.12 shows the most generic setup. This is embodied in products such as Arm's generic interrupt controller (GIC). Interrupts can be routed statically to a core or dynamically dispatched based on a core being available that is not already interrupted or that is running a lower-priority interrupt. These policies are controlled by the **boot-up core**, which sets the values in tens of configuration registers (Section 9.1) [5].

Two nets, an interrupt request and an acknowledge run bidirectionally between the core and the controller. Although the core may not implement interrupt priorities, the controller can implement pre-emption by having the core re-enable interrupts as soon as it has acknowledged an interrupt from the controller and then relying on the controller to interrupt the core again only if there is higher-priority work.

2.5.1 Interrupt Structure Within a Device

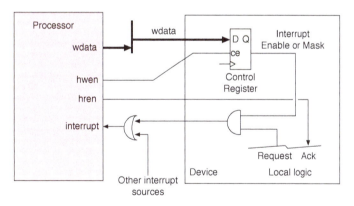

Figure 2.13 Interrupt generation: general structure within a device and at system level

When discussing I/O devices, the term **host** refers to the CPU or code that is looking after the device. When a device is newly reset, it has not been configured. It should not generate interrupts until after it has been set up by its device driver code running on the host. Moreover, interrupts need to be turned off during operation if the device goes idle (especially transmit-ready interrupts, Section 2.7.1). Although on/off control is possible inside the CPU and inside most interrupt controllers, a device typically has a master interrupt enable control register bit that can be set and cleared by PIO by the controlling processor. A PIO register that holds on/off control for an interrupt is called an **interrupt**

mask. As well as this master flag, a device commonly has further interrupt masks for specific local causes of interrupts. Its output is just ANDed with the local interrupt source. This is shown in Figure 2.13. This is illustrated for the UART device driver, which turns off transmit interrupts when there is nothing to send (Section 2.7.1).

PIO uses the write-enable (`hwen`) signal to protect the transfer of data from the main data bus into the control register. A `hren` signal is used for reading back a stored value.

The widely used pattern of interrupt programming is demonstrated for the UART device driver code in Section 2.7.1:

- The receiving side keeps the interrupt always enabled. The device then interrupts when received data are ready.

- The sending side enables the interrupt only when the driver's software output queue is not empty. The device then interrupts when the hardware output queue is ready, but not if there is nothing to send.

These two general patterns arise with all I/O devices. Moreover, if DMA is used (Section 2.7.5), the same principle still applies, but the memory pools used for DMA now logically belong to the device and interrupts occur when these pools need a service from the host.

2.6 Memory Technology

More than half the silicon area of nearly every SoC consists of memory, mainly SRAM (Table 2.1). Memory is always a bus target and, with its details abstracted, can be thought of as quite simple. However, a memory subsystem may embody error detection and correction, in which case it usefully needs to have a fault indication output for uncorrectable errors. It may also have a built-in self-test (BIST) (Section 4.7.6), in which case it will have test modes and control inputs. Certain error-correcting memory requires that scrub commands are executed periodically (Section 4.7.6). DRAM needs to be refreshed and ideally put into a low power state if about to become idle. Flash needs wear levelling and bulk erase control, so memory can have a significant amount of complexity.

Table 2.1 Principal characteristics of memory technologies currently used for booting, caches, primary storage and secondary storage

Memory	Volatile	Main applications	Implementation
ROM	No	Booting, coefficients	Content set by a tapeout mask
SRAM	Yes	Caches, scratchpads, FIFO buffers	One bistable (invertor pair) per bit
DRAM	Yes	Primary storage	Capacitor charge storage
EA-ROM	No	Secondary storage	Floating-gate FET charge storage
Memristive	No	Next generation	Electrically induced resistance changes

Figure 2.14 illustrates the relative dominance of memory arrays in area terms. For a high performance processor [6], the L1 and L2 cache memory arrays were placed on a separate piece of silicon from all of

the other logic. Both dies were 10 × 10 mm using 7 nm FinFET transistors, and the two dies were stacked (Section 8.9.1). The instruction and data L1 caches are each 64 KB, set associative. The L2 cache size is 1 MB using two banks. The two dies were designed in close conjunction, as required for inter-chip bonding using the third dimension, and to avoid vertically aligned hot spots. The memory array area has dominated the overall chip size, since that die is fully filled, whereas the coloured logic layer can be seen to not need all of its die. Hence more than 50% of the silicon area is memory.

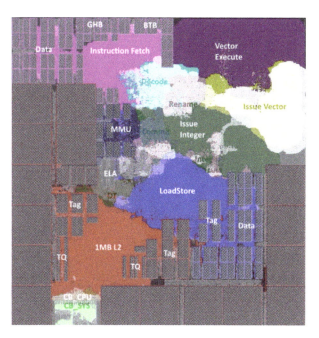

Figure 2.14 Floorplan visualisation of a 3D implementation of the Arm Neoverse N1 design using two chips, vertically stacked. The cache memories are placed on the lower piece of silicon, shown in monochrome, whereas the logic for the ALUs, register files and everything else is shown in colour on top. The 1MB L2 label is the L2 logic and not L2 memory arrays

2.6.1 Logical and Physical Layouts

Most typical applications of ROM and RAM require both the number of address bits and the number of data bits to be in the tens. The widest data words typically encountered might be $4 \times 8 \times 9 = 288$, corresponding to four 64-bit words with error correction (Section 4.7.6). However, the number of bits stored is exponential in the number of address bits and linear in the number of data bits. So even with a wide word, this leads to a very long and skinny logical arrangement. For instance, a 16k-word RAM with 16 address bits and 256 data bits is said to have an arrangement of $65\,536 \times 256$. Designing a memory macro of this shape will be impractical, since its performance would be very poor due to the high capacitance of the long nets. A low aspect ratio (square-like) array of bit cells is desirable for a balanced **floor plan** (Section 8.6) and leads to lower power operation (Section 4.6).

The total number of bits can factorised in a close-to-square way using Napier's rule:

$$2^{16} \times 2^8 = 2^{24} = 2^{12} \times 2^{12}$$

We would, therefore, use a square array with 4096 bits on a side, or perhaps 2048 rows of 8192 columns, or vice versa, depending on the details of the target technology, which may marginally prefer rows to columns. For arrays that require a number of rows or columns beyond what can be supported with appropriate noise margins, then multiple smaller arrays are used. For example, multiple arrays are illustrated in the DRAM micrograph of Figure 2.21.

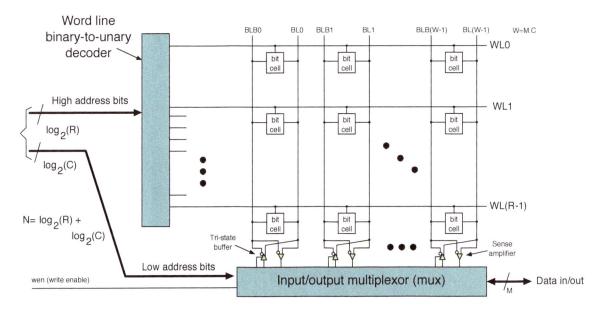

Figure 2.15 Low-aspect-ratio RAM array showing the shared peripheral circuitry, which includes the word-line decoder, sense amplifiers, tri-state buffers and I/O multiplexor. Externally it offers 2^N words of M bits where $N = \log_2(R) + \log_2(C)$. Internally it uses R rows each with $(M \times C)$-bit cells

For a single-array design, the general setup is illustrated in Figure 2.15. The N address bits are presented externally in binary format and address 2^N locations of M bits. $N - \log_2(C)$ bits of the address field are fed to the binary-to-unary row decoder, which raises one active row line. This horizontal net is also called a word-line net as, on assertion, it selects the appropriate bit array word, which is one row. The values stored in all cells of the word are simultaneously read out to the vertical nets, which are called bit lines. The remaining address bits are used to select which M-bit word to update or to deliver externally. The write-enable input controls the operation on the word. For a read, the appropriate bits are delivered on the data in/out nets, whereas for a write, the data received on these nets are forwarded by M enabled tri-state buffers to the bit cell (Figure 2.17).

To reduce noise and to facilitate writing in RAM, the bit lines are present in true and negated form, so there are twice as many of them as bit cells in the row. ROM often uses a single bit line per bit.

Memory access timing is composed of the address decoder delay, the word-line delay and the bit-line delay. With technology scaling, word-line and bit-line parasitic resistance has increased manifold and now these components dominate the memory access time.

Non-volatile memory retains its value when the power is removed. This is essential for secondary storage. Classically, the main forms of secondary storage have been tapes and disks. For booting, it is critical to have a non-volatile store in the boot ROM (Section 9.1). Non-volatile stores were used as primary storage in ferrite core memories of the 1960s, and there has been some resurgence with the use of flash and Optane (©Intel), but most current non-volatile technologies cannot replace SRAM or DRAM for primary data storage due to limitations in access times and write endurance.

2.6.2 Mask-programmed ROM

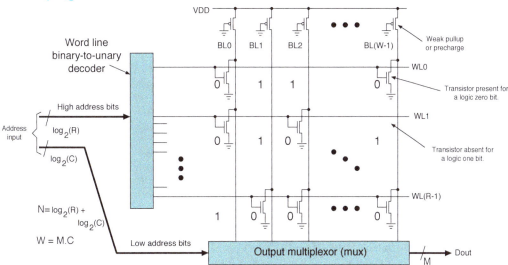

Figure 2.16 Mask-programmed NMOS ROM structure with a capacity of 2^N locations, each holding an M-bit word

Read-only memory (ROM) is non-volatile and has restrictions on how it can be written. The most simple bit cell of all memory types is found in mask-programmed ROM, as illustrated in Figure 2.16. A zero is represented by the presence of a transistor in the bit-cell array and a one by the absence of a transistor. The contents (stored data) must be known at tapeout (Section 8.7.7), which is when the photolithographic masks are made for production. They cannot be changed post-fabrication. In a SoC design, such ROM is used for bootstrap code, secret keys (Section 9.1.1) and coefficient tables in certain accelerators.

An NMOS structure is shown in the figure. It uses a weak pull-up transistor for each bit line. An alternative is **dynamic logic**, which is also commonly used. Dynamic logic uses the two phases of a clock. The bit lines are precharged, usually to VDD on one phase, and then allowed to float. Using the high address bits, the row address is decoded and an entire word is selected by the assertion of the corresponding word line on the other phase of the clock. Depending upon the value stored in each cell, bit lines are either pulled low or not as the charge on the line discharges through the bit cell. The externally required bit or word of *M* bits is selected for output using the remaining (low) bits of the address field.

2.6.3 Static Random Access Memory

The size and number of ports of static RAM (SRAM) vary. Single-ported SRAM is the most important and most simple resource. It can be connected to a bus as an addressable scratchpad target. It is also used inside caches for tags and data.

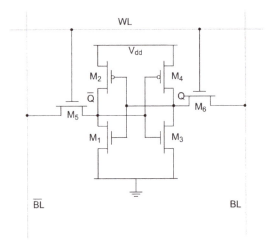

Figure 2.17 Transistor-level view of a standard six-transistor (6T) SRAM cell. M1, M2, M3 and M4 are used for storage. M5 and M6 are used to access the cell for read and write operations

An SRAM cell is shown in Figure 2.17. Data are stored in a pair of cross-coupled invertors (M1 to M4) that form a bistable. Two access transistors (M5 and M6) are used for read and write operations on the cell. The transfer function of the cross-coupled invertors has three equilibrium points, two of which are stable (Section 3.7.2), giving a standard bistable.

A simple bistable consumes a few per cent of the area of a full edge-triggered flip-flop. The word 'static' in SRAM denotes that data are retained in the memory for as long as its powered on (in contrast to DRAM, Section 2.6.6). The 'random access' in SRAM denotes that the ordering in which data are stored does not affect the access time. The 'RAM' in DRAM means the same thing, but, as we explain, access times vary with DRAM depending on what was last accessed. Shift registers, FIFO buffers and, historically, drum drives are examples of non-random access memory. If the memory system is complex, the different RAM devices will be at different distances from the point of access, resulting in an architecture with **non-uniform memory access (NUMA)**.

The read operation for SRAM is the same as described for ROM. The only caveat is that the capacitance of the bit lines must be sufficiently small to avoid upsetting the tiny RAM cell when connected to the bit line. This is the **read-disturb problem**. It is preferable to precharge all bit lines to a minimally disruptive voltage in advance of asserting the row line. Certainly, they should be precharged to the same voltage to avoid a bias that will tend to flip the RAM cell content. SRAM and DRAM both require a **precharge time** between operations. Although this does not affect the read latency, it does extend the total read cycle time.

For the bit cells that are to be updated by a write operation, BL and $\overline{\text{BL}}$ are driven to VDD and GND, respectively, or vice versa, depending upon the data to be written. Again, the row address is decoded, and an entire word is selected by asserting the corresponding WL. If the data to be written are different from what is already stored in the cell, the BL and $\overline{\text{BL}}$ pair overpower the feedback of the cross-coupled invertor to flip the cell to its new value.

Due to RAM fabrication overheads, RAM below a few hundred bits should typically be implemented as **register files** made of flip-flops. However, larger RAM has better density and power consumption than arrays of flip-flops.

SRAM Noise Margins

The **noise margin** for a net is the voltage offset it can sustain before correct operation of the circuit is compromised. The **DC noise margin** is the offset before a zero is interpreted as a one or vice versa. The **AC noise margin** is the offset before the circuit moves from a gain less than unity to greater than unity. If a circuit is operating above its AC noise margin, random noise is amplified instead of being attenuated and the fundamental digitalness of the system is lost. The noise voltage offsets can equivalently be in the supply rails or the signal nets.

For a manufacturing process node (Section 8.2.1), the wiring capacitance for a given length is predetermined. The only freedom the RAM designer has is setting the size of the transistors. These considerations determine the maximum column length possible. An SRAM cell has a ratioed logic design: the transistors must be sized carefully for correct operation. It is also very important to consider the spatial variation, as typically a memory array has millions of cells and each bit cell must work correctly. The variations become larger with process and voltage scaling (Section 8.4.4). This degrades the SRAM noise margins, which is the key challenge in SRAM design for advanced semiconductor process nodes.

2.6.4 Synchronous Static RAM

Although RAM bit cells do not require a clock, it is common to wrap up the main bit array within a synchronous wrapper, resulting in **synchronous static RAM (SSRAM)**, as shown in Figure 2.18. SSRAM has at least one clock cycle of read latency, which arises by putting a broadside register on the data output. A second cycle of latency arises if there is an input register as well in the binary-to-unary row decoder. Such memory may be denoted as SSRAM2. The design must be aware of the read pipeline delay. This was illustrated on the front side of the two caches in the five-stage RISC in Figure 2.3. For writes, there is no pipeline effect, as the write-enable, write-data and write-address are all presented in the same clock cycle.

The RAM illustrated has a read latency of one clock cycle. Note than when a write occurs, the old value at the addressed location is still read out, which is commonly a useful feature. The en input signal is not strictly needed since the RAM could deliver read data on all cycles. However, not having it would waste power.

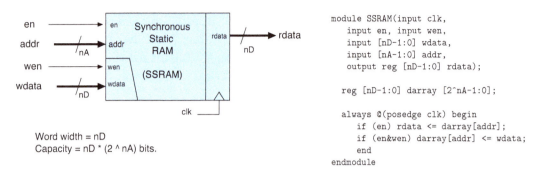

```
module SSRAM(input clk,
    input en, input wen,
    input [nD-1:0] wdata,
    input [nA-1:0] addr,
    output reg [nD-1:0] rdata);

    reg [nD-1:0] darray [2^nA-1:0];

    always @(posedge clk) begin
        if (en) rdata <= darray[addr];
        if (en&wen) darray[addr] <= wdata;
    end
endmodule
```

Word width = nD
Capacity = nD * (2 ^ nA) bits.

Figure 2.18 SSRAM with a single port, showing the logic symbol (left) and internal RTL model (right)

2.6.5 Dual-ported Static RAM

Many memories need to be accessed from many different places within the SoC. This is possible using multiplexers in the SoC interconnect (Chapter 3), but having two physical sets of wiring to the bit cells is also quite often used for SRAM. A bit cell for SRAM with two complete sets of row and column logic is shown in Figure 2.19. One version of such a dual-ported SRAM contains eight transistors instead of the usual six. The corresponding logic symbol is shown in Figure 2.20. This shows a single clock input, but having two clock inputs, one per port, is also common and useful for sharing data between clock domains.

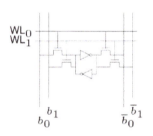

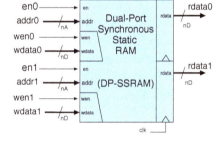

Figure 2.19 8T SRAM cell with true dual-porting

Figure 2.20 Dual-ported SSRAM logic symbol

An 8T dual-ported SRAM cell is not as dense as a 6T SRAM. Furthermore, the internal node of the cell has greater capacitive loading due to its connections to multiple access transistors, which leads to greater latency and power use. Another design implication is that such a memory needs collision circuitry to avoid multiple writes of different data to the same cell. A collision detector will tacitly give priority to one port, but in principle, the output from a collision detector could be made available for system-level use.

2.6.6 Dynamic RAM

The word 'dynamic' in **dynamic RAM (DRAM)** denotes that it uses charge as the mechanism of storage. Charge is used in both DRAM and flash memory, but in DRAM there is leakage and this charge needs to be refreshed at a few hundred hertz or else the DRAM cell will lose its content. Figure 2.21 shows a micrograph of a DRAM chip. Externally, this device is accessed with row and column addresses of ten

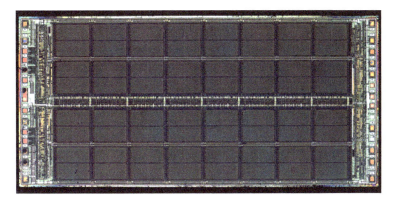

Figure 2.21 Micrograph of a simple DRAM chip circa 1994. This is a Micron Technology MT4C1024 device with organisation 1024x1024x1 (source: ZeptoBars 2012. Reproduced under the terms of the Creative Commons Attribution Licence, CC BY 3.0 <https://creativecommons.org/licenses/by/3.0>)

bits each, so logically it is organised as a single array of 1024 columns of 1024 bits. But the micrograph shows the physical layout uses sixteen sub-arrays. The physical layout is selected for optimum noise margin reasons (Section 2.6.3). Also visible are the 24 orange-looking bond pads, 12 on each side.

Figure 2.22-left shows the external connections where the 24 bond pads are connected to 20 external pins. The difference arises since several bond pads may be connected in parallel to the V_{SS} and V_{DD} supply pins for reduced inductance and resistance.

As shown on the right of Figure 2.22 each bit cell consists of a capacitor, which stores the state of one bit, and an access transistor. For maximum density, these are normally vertically organised with the transistor on top of the capacitor. The capacitor may actually be a reverse-biased diode with a large

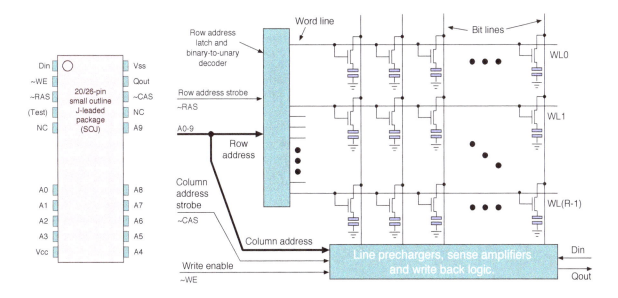

Figure 2.22 Left: pinout for a typical asynchronous DRAM, such as the MT4C1024 pictured above, that is controlled by the RAS and CAS signals instead of a having a clock input. Right: basic internal structure schematic. This device only has a single bank so there are no bank address inputs

junction area or it may be a stacked arrangement with interleaved conducting fingers. The capacitor can be in either a charged or discharged state, which denotes a logical 1 or 0, respectively.

DRAM is slower but much more compact than a six-transistor SRAM cell. DRAM is principally used as the primary storage (main memory) of SoC systems. Manufacturing capacitive structures in silicon that are compact yet highly capacitive is difficult and needs a specialised process. However, this process is not good for most other forms of logic and this is one reason why DRAM is normally on a separate piece of silicon, die-stacked or nearby on the printed-circuit board (PCB). Another reason is the area versus yield trade-off (Section 8.11.1). Moreover, DRAM is a commodity device rather than application-specific (Figure 8.31).

DRAM: Activate, Read and Write

The DRAM read cycle is based on the **row-activate operation**, which is the lowest-level DRAM operation, with all other significant operations being built on top. In a row-activate operation, the row address is decoded from binary to unary and the corresponding word line then becomes asserted. The bit lines must first have been precharged, usually to V_{DD}, and then allowed to float. The bit-line capacitance will generally be larger than that of a bit cell capacitor, but as the word line is asserted, the bit line shares charge with the cell capacitor and the bit line will change in voltage by a sufficient amount to be reliably detected. If a row has its row line asserted, the row is said to be open and that row is called the open page.

Unlike SRAM, a row-activate operation is destructive: the charge redistribution causes a large change in the original value of the charge stored on the capacitor so that a follow-on read will fail. Hence, any read must be followed by a writeback when the row is closed (deactivated). To perform the writeback, the bit line is driven to the value of the data to be written. This value is then transferred onto the capacitor of the cell through the access transistor before the word line is de-asserted.

As with SRAM, the values detected on bit lines of interest are selected by the remaining address bits (called the column address) and read out from the chip. It is common for external logic to successively supply multiple column addresses from the active row. The system-level hardware and software are optimised to make use of the random access available within a row once it is activated.

A refresh operation is a row activation without any column address being supplied. The row closure writes the data back, ameliorating the effect of leakage. Every row must have been activated and closed, within a prescribed period of a few milliseconds. A counter is provided on the DRAM chip that selects which row will next be refreshed. If there are 1024 rows in the bit cell array, then a refresh operation is needed every few microseconds on average. This presents a low overhead considering that hundreds of activations per microsecond are typically supported (see the timing figures in the next section). Often the refresh can be entirely hidden with a line in one bit-cell array being refreshed while another bit-cell array is being used for a read or write.

A DRAM write operation is a further variation of the row-activate operation. The values written back are different from those read out in the places where write operations have been performed.

DRAM: Banks, Ranks and Channels

Table 2.2 shows the data organisation in a typical DRAM channel that uses four **dual in-line memory modules (DIMMs)** each with 16 DRAM chips. The chips are shown in Figure 2.24. The address is provided via 3 bank bits and 14 address bits. Only 12 of those are used when the row address is being provided. (Note, for clarity, Figure 2.24 shows only two bank bits.) A **DRAM channel** is the set of nets between a DRAM controller. It raises a structural hazard (Section 6.3) in terms of simultaneous access to each rank. A rank is a set of DRAM chips with their data, address and enable signals in common. This is also true for a DIMM, but a rank enables a physical DIMM to host some number (two or four) of logical DIMMs on the same PCB.

Table 2.2 DRAM address terminology and hierarchy with typical sizes

Quantity	Aggregate capacity	Description
1 channel	16 GB	A physical bus: 64 data bits, 3 bank bits and 14 address bits
4 DIMMs	16 GB	Multiple DIMMs are connected on the PCB to one channel
1 rank	4 GB	A number of logical DIMMs within a physical DIMM
16 chips	$16 \times 0.5 = 4$ GB	This DIMM uses 16 4-bit chips making a 64-bit word
Lanes/chip	4 bit lanes = 1 GB	Each chip serves a word 4 bits wide
8 banks	$2^{14+12+8} = 0.5$ Gbit	Each bank has its own bit-cell arrays (simultaneously open)
2^{12} rows	64 Mbit	A page or row is one row of bit cells in an array
(Burst)	8 words = 64 bytes	The unit of transfer over the channel
2^{14} columns	16 kbit	The data read/write line to a bit cell

*Figure 2.23 4-Gbyte DRAM dual in-line memory module (DIMM) for a laptop computer. Eight chips are mounted on a small PCB, four on each side. A label on the back says '1600 11-11-11'. More detailed information, including the supply voltage, is stored electronically in a small **serial presence detect (SPD)** ROM in the centre of the DIMM*

A modern DRAM chip contains multiple bit-cell arrays, not only to provide multi-bit words and guarantee noise margins, but also to offer **DRAM banks**. Banks are very useful. If pages are in different banks, a DRAM chip can have multiple pages open at once. To ensure performance, a good closure policy must be implemented in the DRAM controller. It can be premature to close a page immediately after a read or write operation because the next read or write may be to the same page and the page will have to be reopened. However, if the next operation for a bank is on a different page, leaving the bank open on the last page will delay access since the open page will have to be closed before the required page can be opened. Moreover, a writeback needs to be made and the bit lines need to be precharged between any close and the next open on a bank. Getting the controller to delay a write does not affect system performance and can even increase it due to write coalescing. However, the customer of a delayed read will be held up by the increased access time latency. Hence, although DRAM is called random access memory, it has very non-uniform access times depending on what state a requested page is in.

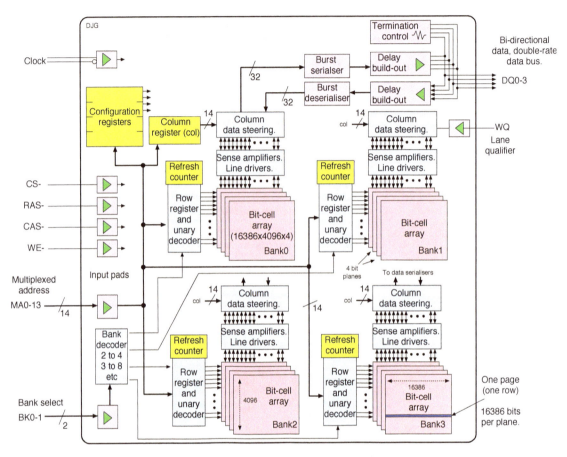

Figure 2.24 Internal block diagram of a 4-bit-wide DRAM device. There are four banks, although eight are normal. (The data strobe (DS) signal is omitted for clarity)

DRAMs for use in PCs are mounted on single-in-line memory modules (SIMMs) or DIMMs. However, for embedded applications, they are typically just soldered onto the main PCB. Normally, one DRAM chip (or pair of chips to make $D = 32$) is shared over many subsystems in, say, a mobile phone. SoC DRAM compatibility might be a generation behind workstation DRAM. For example, a SoC may use DDR3 instead of DDR4. Also, the most recent SoCs embed some DRAM on the main die or flip-chip/die-stack the DRAM directly on top of the SoC die in the same package as a **multi-chip module (MCM)** (Section 8.9.1). Table 2.3 gives the pin connections for a typical DIMM.

DRAM Performance

The design and provisioning of a DRAM subsystem is one of the most critical aspects of a SoC. More than one DRAM channel is used in high-performance desktop workstations and supercomputers, but

Table 2.3 Typical DIMM connections

Clock±	Clock (400 MHz)
RAS−	Row address strobe
CAS−	Column address strobe
WE−	Write enable
DQ[63:0]	Data in/out
Reset	Power-on reset
WQ[7:0]	Write-lane qualifiers

DS[7:0]	Data strobes
DM[7:0]	Data masks
CS−	Chip select
MAddr[15:0]	Address input
BK[2:0]	Bank select
spd[3:0]	Serial presence detect

for everyday laptops, cellphones and embedded systems, a single DRAM channel is used. Also, a single rank is used, whether in DIMM form or on the PCB or MCM. The mid-range laptop DRAM in Figure 2.23 was specified as 1600 11-11-11. This denotes the effective clock frequency in MHz and the number of clock cycles for row addressing, column addressing and precharge. This is a **double data rate (DDR) DRAM** so the physical clock net runs at half the quoted clock frequency and is, therefore, 800 MHz, since both clock edges are used to transfer data.

The maximum throughput of a DRAM is often quoted in MT/s or million transfers per second. For a low-performance memory system, the data bus width and clock frequency are the main performance parameters. The bottom end is 16 bits at around 200 MHz. Using both edges of the clock, we can achieve 400 MT/s but due to the narrow bus, this is only 0.8 gigabytes per second (GB/s). This is suitable for an inexpensive smartphone. For high-performance memory systems, a 2.166-GHz clock might be used, giving 4.3 GT/s on a 64-bit bus, making 34 GB/s. This is suitable for a server cloud blade. For further performance, several such channels are connected to one CMP (Section 2.3).

The maximum transfer rate of a data bus cannot be sustained except when reading all the data from a row before activating the next row. The provision of the column address within the row is overlapped with the actual data access, but if there are 11 clock cycles for the column address operation, the data burst size needs to be sufficiently large to exploit the overlap. Reading an entire row is infrequent, since a row stores more than a cache line. The maximum throughput is degraded by the need to close rows and open other rows.

With higher clock rates, the row and column clock counts also tend to increase, so become comparatively longer while staying similar in real terms. A high-performance DRAM may be specified as 19-21-21. In the worst case, if this DRAM is currently open on the wrong row, 61 clock cycles are then needed to change to the new location. Roughly the same number of clock cycles again will be used in pipeline stages through the various memory hierarchy levels of the controller.

There is a further description of DRAM configuration and controllers in Section 4.5.0.

2.6.7 Electrically Alterable ROMs

An **electrically alterable ROM (EA-ROM)** is non-volatile, but its contents can be changed by applying electric fields or currents. One of the earliest forms used metallic **fusible links** that can be melted with a heavy current. These still have limited use during post-fabrication testing for speed binning

(Section 8.8.4) and redundancy zapping (Section 8.8.4). Most forms today use charge stored on a floating gate.

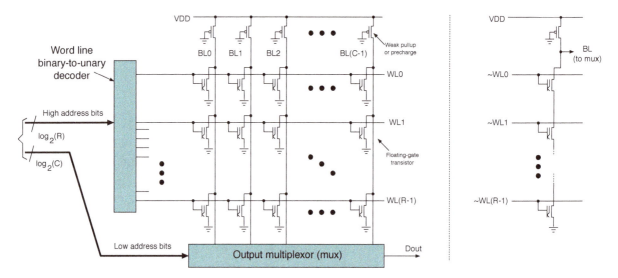

Figure 2.25 NOR ROM block diagram (left) with capacity $2^{(R+C)}$ bits and alternative NAND ROM array detail (right). For a ROM more than 1 bit wide, the Dout connection is a bus of width M and the low address bus width is reduced by $\log_2(M)$ bits

Figure 2.25 shows the two basic configurations of ROM arrays. Only the transistors in one polarity of the bit cell programming are present. Both forms use a weak NMOS pull-up on the bit lines, which acts like a resistor, but a dynamic precharge to V_{DD} can also serve and trade off static and dynamic power (Section 4.6.1).

A NOR ROM resembles a NOR logic gate since the NMOS transistors are connected in parallel to the output bit line. A logic zero is produced if a word line is asserted (taken high) and a transistor is actively preset to pull down the bit line. The absence of a transistor means the bit line will remain undisturbed at 1.

NAND ROM operation uses negated word lines, which are normally high. The row binary-to-unary decoder makes one of them low. Since, initially all word lines are high, the default output value of bit lines is 0. The presence of an active NMOS transistor in the bit cell turns off the NMOS stack, enabling the bit line to go high. If there is no cell transistor, the top and bottom of the cell are effectively joined by a wire, although this is a permanently on transistor in a NAND EA-ROM.

NOR ROMs are fast, as the pull-down stack has only a single NMOS compared to the series of NMOS devices in a NAND ROM. On the other hand, a NAND cell is more compact as it does not require a ground wire or the associated contacts for connecting to the bit line and ground. The whole stack of transistor channels can be made as a single, contiguous channel polygon in the fabrication masks.

2.6.8 Floating-gate EA-ROMs and Flash

Most EA-ROM technology uses a **floating-gate transistor**, which is like a regular MOS transistor except that it has an extra layer in its gate structure. Instead of one polysilicon gate, it has two polysilicon gates, one on top of the other. This is shown as part of Figure 2.27. The upper gate connects to the word line or ground, while the lower is completely floating, since it is surrounded by gate oxide on all sides. In electronics, a **floating conductor** is disconnected from anything that alters its electrical potential. The key idea is that the threshold of a floating-gate transistor is altered by the static charge stored on the floating gate. By adjusting this charge, the transistor can be changed from being always on, always off or behaving normally. Moreover, by applying a high voltage at the connected gate, charge is moved onto the floating gate through **hot carrier injection** (Section 8.12.15) or **electron tunnelling**. The trapped charge on the floating gate can be retained for decades, thereby making the bit cells non-volatile.

Two directions of charge movement are needed to change the value stored in a floating-gate transistor, depending on its current state. Different mechanisms are used for the two directions of transfer, with one direction generally taking orders of magnitude longer than the other. The fast direction is commonly not any slower than a read operation.

The first generation of floating-gate devices were for **erasable programmable read-only memory (EPROM)**. The erase procedure for these devices required them to be placed inside a sealed box with a high-intensity ultraviolet light source. As shown in Figure 2.26, the chip package had a glass window in the top to let the light in. Such a package was expensive. For production runs where reprogramming was never expected, the same chip was also available in opaque plastic packages. The first EPROM chips used by the author required three supply rails for normal operation (+5, −5 and +12 V) and a fourth supply (+27 V) during programming. Today's devices generate all the required voltages on-chip from a single external supply of 3.3 V.

Figure 2.26 EPROM device from the 1980s. The silicon die is visible through the top window

In contrast to the single-transistor bit cell shown in Figure 2.25, Figure 2.27 shows a two-transistor bit cell. The design is tolerant to large margins in the lower transistor since it just has to be always on or always off. Single-transistor designs are widely used; the word line is connected to the floating-gate transistor's non-floating gate. A one-transistor cell requires more careful erasing since the floating charge must be brought back into the range where the transistor operates normally. NOR and NAND structures, as illustrated for the EA-ROM in Figure 2.25, are commonly used with floating-gate ROMs.

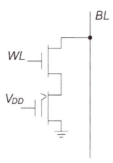

Figure 2.27 Schematic of a possible bit cell for EPROM and EEPROM. There is a kink on the top of the extra gate of this floating-gate transistor to denote that tunnelling is possible

A major step forward was **electrically erasable programmable read-only memory (EEPROM)**. In such devices, bits can be programmed in not just one, but both directions, by electron tunnelling and/or carrier injection. The predominant EA-ROM used today is **flash memory**. Programming is performed on a per-bit basis and is fast, but erasing is done on a large block basis, with the silicon die typically having eight erase regions. Erasing a region takes milliseconds. These devices use internal timers and measurement mechanisms to apply just the right amount of reverse charge. Erasing does not eliminate all the stored charge, so eventually such memory will fail. It is guaranteed for some finite number of erase cycles per block, such as one million.

Solid-state drives (SSD)s with EEPROM are replacing spinning magnetic disks. Flash USB memory sticks use the same technology. Although these devices give the impression that writing either polarity of data is equally easy, internally they include additional, unadvertised storage, some of which is kept erased and dynamically mapped into the memory map as appropriate. They also maintain counters for **wear levelling** to ensure that, whatever the application's use patterns, there is a balanced pattern of erase operations over the physical erase regions.

2.6.9 Emerging Memory Technologies

Today's memory technologies are having trouble keeping up with ever-increasing demands on density, access time and energy use. Although performance continues to rise by using ever smaller geometries, noise margins are being eroded. SRAM faces challenges from increased process variation and the degradation of noise margins. Shrinking a DRAM capacitor means that the stored charge is more susceptible to noise and disturbance from nearby rows and columns. A lower capacitor charge also means less charge is shared and the voltage swing is reduced, which is a problem for reliable sensing. Also, the contact resistance between the cell capacitor and the access transistor is higher. The resistivity of a smaller cell transistor impacts DRAM speed. Moreover, flash is reaching the fundamental limits for device size. Thus, accidentally losing even a few electrons from a floating gate can result in data retention issues. Besides, write endurance has become worse as the electric field stress during programming is higher for smaller geometries.

The second major problem is standby power. An SRAM cell is a four-transistor bistable that consumes static leakage power. These cells must always be powered on to retain their state, even if they are idle. One mitigation is to drop the supply voltage if the bit array has not been accessed recently. This retains data but the cell is no longer powerful enough to be read reliably. If the cell transistor in DRAM is made smaller, its leakage grows. Combined with the smaller cell capacitance due to shrinking, the reliable retention time is reduced. As a result, refreshes must be performed more frequently and energy use due to refreshing contributes more to the system power budget.

There is commercial interest in new memory technologies that sit between DRAM and SRAM in terms of density and access time. Three-dimensional, non-volatile memory is one possibility. Intel and Micron released one form of this, branded Optane. It uses **memristive** technology, in which arrays of resistors made from special compounds are measured with a small electrical current and modified with a higher current. Such memories are non-volatile and have zero standby power. The number of write cycles and the speed of writing are both significantly improved with respect to floating-gate EA-ROM. Motherboards with slots for such memories became available, but many of the products were cancelled in early 2021 [7]. Moreover, the long-established distinction between primary and secondary storage is being challenged by such technologies, so fully exploiting them will be highly disruptive.

2.6.10 Processor Speed versus Memory Speed

The speed of processors has doubled every two years, whether by increasing the clock frequency or by using a multi-core design. Memory density has likewise roughly doubled every two years. Both trends have lead to increasingly powerful and affordable computers. However, the memory access latency decreases at only half this rate.

This ever-expanding gap between main memory and CPU performance is known as the **memory wall**, as it is a barrier to further progress. Figure 2.28 illustrates the memory wall issue. It plots the increase in single-threaded performance as cache sizes are increased above a baseline value. Each data point represents the average performance of SPEC-Integer-2006, a well established benchmarking suite [8]. Increasing the number of cores does not benefit workloads with few options for parallelism (Section 4.2), so increasing the size and complexity of caches are the main solutions. This essentially brings the computation closer to the data that are being operated on, which is a basic form of **near-data processing** [9].

Babbage's two main computer architectures differed in that the ALU associated with each storage location in his Difference Engine was replaced with a centralised resource in his Analytical Engine. The motivation was cost. Today, it would be inexpensive to distribute tens of thousands of ALUs throughout a memory device, so a return towards Babbage's original design is potentially feasible. However, this results in a radically new computing architecture. DRAM and high-performance logic would have to be mixed by the same silicon process, which raises new fabrication challenges (Section 6.1). It is possible such approaches will gain commercial traction within a decade, but such ideas are currently just academic.

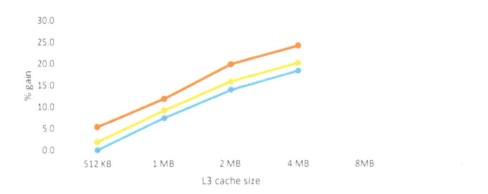

Figure 2.28 Typical increase in benchmark performance in response to L3 cache size enlargement for L2=64 KB (blue), L2=128 KB (yellow) and L2=256 KB (red)

2.7 SoC I/O Blocks

In this section, we review some common I/O standards and associated IP blocks used for I/O in many SoCs. Another term for an I/O device is a **peripheral device**. I/O is always performed in one of three ways:

1. Under **polled I/O**, a processor periodically inspects the status register of an I/O device to see whether any data have arrived or whether it is ready to send new data. Polling wastes processor cycles and is normally avoided. It is used only in very simple bootloaders and error handlers when the main operating system is not running.

2. Under **interrupt-driven I/O**, a device raises an interrupt request signal when it requires service. The processor then saves what it was doing and inspects the status registers, as with polling. However, the periodic overhead is avoided.

3. Under **direct memory access (DMA) I/O**, the device itself initiates transactions on the bus and can load and store its data to primary storage. Interrupts are raised only when a new memory region needs oto be provided or serviced by the processor. For further details, see Section 2.7.5.

The first two of these are known as **programmed I/O (PIO)**, since the processor moves the data.

A complex SoC may have many hundreds of device registers. Processors with a narrow address bus, such as the A16 microprocessors mentioned in Section 1.1.1, generally provide `write` and `read` instructions for transferring data to and from I/O devices. These access a different address space from primary storage. It is called the I/O space. This avoids using up primary address space with I/O device registers. A32 processors have such a large primary space (4 Gbyte) that the overhead of hundreds of device registers is insignificant. So, such processors, like the Arm architecture, do not have I/O instructions. Instead, they access devices with memory `store` and `load` instructions. This is called **memory-mapped I/O**.

2.7.1 Universal Asynchronous Receiver-Transmitter (UART)

A **universal asynchronous receiver-transmitter (UART)** is the IP block associated with the RS-232 serial port. UARTs were widely used in the 20th century for character I/O devices (telepritners, printers and dumb terminals). They are still commonly used in practical SoC designs since they are some of the most simple and easy devices to get working. The first test that nearly any newly developed SoC runs is to print 'Hello, world' from its UART. UARTs are also found in virtualised form entirely inside a SoC. For instance, it might be used instead of a bus connection to a ZigBee IP block.

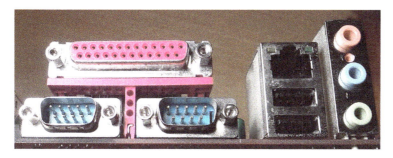

Figure 2.29 Typical I/O ports. Shown are two serial ports, one parallel port, one Ethernet port, two USB ports and three audio ports

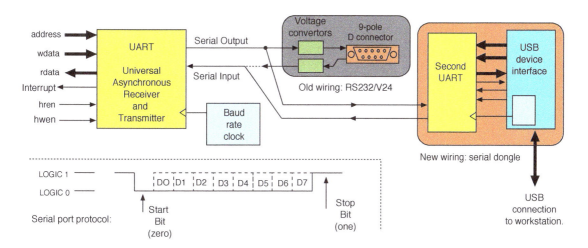

Figure 2.30 Two typical configurations for a serial port using a UART. Inset: Serial port timing diagram. The old wiring to a D9 connector for an RS-232 port is today often replaced with a very short connection to a second UART inside a USB dongle for connecting to a laptop

A serial port uses two independent simplex channels, one for output and one for input, to make a full duplex channel. A nine-pin D-connector is used for the serial ports in Figure 2.29, but only one wire is needed in each direction, as shown in Figure 2.30. The two data directions plus a ground pin mean that only three out of the nine pins are actually used. The additional connections are sometimes used to indicate device ready status and to implement **Xon/Xoff flow control** (Section 3.4.4). Data are sent serially at a pre-agreed baud rate. The **baud rate** is the maximum number of transitions per second on one of the signals. The effective data rate is less than the baud rate due to the overhead of the start and stop bits. The baud rate and number of bits per word must be pre-agreed at each end, such as 19 200 bps and 8 bits. The device internally contains status and control registers and transmit and receive data FIFO buffers. In essence, any byte stored in the transmit FIFO buffer is converted to serial form and sent. Received data are converted back to parallel form and stored in the receive FIFO buffer. Interrupts are generated when the transmit FIFO buffer is empty or the receive FIFO buffer is not empty.

Interrupt-driven UART Device Driver

A **device driver** is a piece of software that connects an I/O device to the operating system. Although devices vary greatly in structure and detail, a homogeneous interface is needed for the operating system. At the lowest level, Linux and Unix have only two device types: character and block. Higher-level classifications split devices into classes such as printers, storage devices, network interfaces, cameras, keyboards and so on, but these classifications are for ease of management and do not effect the device driver interface. A UART is a character device, since it nominally presents one byte at a time. Ethernet and disks are block devices, since the unit of data transfer is an array of bytes. The characters from a character device are normally aggregated to some extent to amortise handling overheads. For instance, a `write` system call may transfer a buffer of characters to a UART, but no semantic boundary is introduced.

The device driver code starts with a definition of the registers accessible by PIO. Device drivers are normally written in C. Here is C preprocessor code to define the I/O locations in use by a simple UART device:

```
// Macro definitions for C preprocessor enable a C program to access a hardware
// UART using PIO or interrupts.

#define IO_BASE 0xFFFC1000 // or whatever

#define U_SEND    0x10
#define U_RECEIVE 0x14
#define U_CONTROL 0x18
#define U_STATUS  0x1C

#define  UART_SEND()  \
   (*((volatile char *)(IO_BASE+U_SEND)))
#define  UART_RECEIVE()  \
   (*((volatile char *)(IO_BASE+U_RECEIVE)))
#define  UART_CONTROL()  \
   (*((volatile char *)(IO_BASE+U_CONTROL)))
#define  UART_STATUS()  \
   (*((volatile char *)(IO_BASE+U_STATUS)))

#define UART_STATUS_RX_EMPTY (0x80)
#define UART_STATUS_TX_EMPTY (0x40)

#define UART_CONTROL_RX_INT_ENABLE (0x20)
#define UART_CONTROL_TX_INT_ENABLE (0x10)
```

The following code implements a polled receiver. It spins until the empty flag in the status register goes away. Reading the data register makes the status register go empty again. The actual hardware device may have a receive FIFO buffer, so instead of going empty, the next character from the FIFO buffer would become available straight away:

```
char uart_polled_read()
{
    while (UART_STATUS() &
        UART_STATUS_RX_EMPTY) continue;
    return UART_RECEIVE();
}
```

The output function is exactly the same in principle, except it spins while the device is still busy with any data previously written:

```
uart_polled_write(char d)
{
    while (!(UART_STATUS()&
        UART_STATUS_TX_EMPTY)) continue;
    UART_SEND() = d;
}
```

Here is an interrupt-driven UART device driver:

```
char rx_buffer[256];
volatile int rx_inptr, rx_outptr;

void uart_reset()
{ rx_inptr = 0;    tx_inptr = 0;
  rx_output = 0;   tx_outptr = 0;
  UART_CONTROL() |= UART_CONTROL_RX_INT_ENABLE;
}
// Here we call wait() instead of `continue' in case the scheduler has something else to run
char uart_read() // called by application
{ while (rx_inptr==rx_outptr) wait(); // Spin
  char r = buffer[rx_outptr];
  rx_outptr = (rx_outptr + 1)&255;
  return r;
}

char uart_rx_isr()  // interrupt service routine
{ while (1)
    {
      if (UART_STATUS()&UART_STATUS_RX_EMPTY) return;
      rx_buffer[rx_inptr] = UART_RECEIVE();
      rx_inptr = (rx_inptr + 1)&255;
    }
}

uart_write(char c)  // called by the application
{ while (tx_inptr==tx_outptr) wait(); // Block if full
  buffer[tx_inptr] = c;
```

```
    tx_inptr = (tx_inptr + 1)&255;
    UART_CONTROL() |= UART_CONTROL_TX_INT_ENABLE;
}

char uart_tx_isr()    // interrupt service routine
{ while (tx_inptr != tx_outptr)
    {
      if (!(UART_STATUS()&UART_STATUS_TX_EMPTY)) return;
      UART_SEND() = tx_buffer[tx_outptr];
      tx_outptr = (tx_outptr + 1)&255;
    }
  UART_CONTROL() &= 255-UART_CONTROL_TX_INT_ENABLE;
}
```

This code fragment illustrates the complete set of five software routines needed to manage a pair of circular buffers for input and output to a UART using interrupts. If a UART has a single interrupt output for both send and receive events, then two of the five routines are combined with a software dispatch between their bodies. Not shown is that the **interrupt service routine (ISR)** must be prefixed and postfixed with code that saves and restores the processor state (this is normally written in assembler and provided by the operating system).

2.7.2 Parallel Ports Using General-purpose I/O

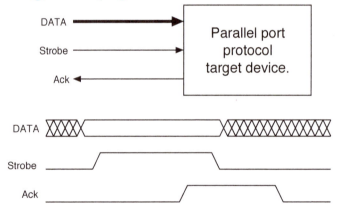

Figure 2.31 Timing diagram for an asynchronous four-phase handshake

The second connector in Figure 2.29 is a parallel port. Although parallel ports are hardly used these days, they provide a useful example for explaining **general-purpose I/O (GPIO)** blocks. They also demonstrates a class of very important asynchronous protocols. A parallel port is simplex: it carries data in one direction only. It is asynchronous and its protocol is suitable for clock-domain crossing within a SoC (Section 3.7.3). It follows the initiator/target paradigm with data being transferred from the initiator to the target. The parallel port protocol defined originally by Centronics uses a total of three handshake wires, but this is not necessary. Here we present the standard **four-phase handshake** protocol, which uses a single control wire in each direction. The protocol is illustrated in Figure 2.31. The initiator first puts a word on the data bus, then raises the strobe signal. When the target notices the `strobe` and is ready to accept the data, it raises its `ack` signal. The initiator then de-asserts the `strobe`, ready for the next cycle. This makes a total of four phases. Note that the various wires from the initiator to the target may vary slightly in length and stray capacitance. Therefore, the initiator must pause for a **de-skewing delay** between setting the data on the data bus for longer than the likely difference in any signal propagation time in the wires. This guarantees that the data are valid at the target when the target sees the `strobe`.

A variation of the four-phase handshake is the **two-phase handshake protocol**. The third and fourth phases are not used. The initiator places the data on the data bus, waits for the de-skewing delay, and then toggles the `strobe` wire. It then waits for the target to toggle the `ack` wire. A toggle is a change of state: one to zero or zero to one.

2.7.3 General-purpose Input/Output Pins

A parallel port can be implemented using a GPIO block, which has a number of GPIO pins. Such pins can be for an input or an output that can be sensed, set or cleared under software control. GPIO pins are commonly used for connecting to simple LED indicators and push switches. Commonly, they can also generate interrupts. As noted above (2.7.1), a UART device requires two I/O pins, one for input and one for output. These are for special-purpose I/O. A SoC may have two or four UART devices, but not all of them are used in every design. The special-purpose I/O pins for unused I/O blocks can normally be put into GPIO mode and used for GPIO. We will illustrate the details.

Figure 2.32 shows the general structure of a GPIO block schematically and in RTL. The block connects to our MSOC1 bus from Chapter 1. All the internal registers are accessible from the host using PIO. Each pin may be for either input or output as controlled by the corresponding bit in the data direction register. When an output, the special function register enables it to be controlled from either the GPIO block or a special function block, such as the UART, which is not shown. When a pin is GPIO output, the data bit is whatever was stored in the data register by PIO. Interrupt polarity and masks are available on a per-pin basis for received events. A master interrupt enable mask is also provided.

Other features typically found, but not illustrated, include a programmable pull-up or pull-down resistor and slew rate control. The voltage gradient when changing from zero to one or back again is called the **slew rate**. Many applications do not require a high transition rate, such as an LED. Low slew rates, such as under 10 V per microsecond, minimise **radio-frequency interference (RFI)** (Section 9.2) and save energy too.

Using GPIO for a Parallel Port

The four-phase protocol can simply be implemented using polling and GPIO. Such code has often been used to connect to Centronics-style printers. The data-direction register is initialised with nine output bits for the strobe and data and one input bit for the `ack` signal. The code then proceeds as described in Section 5.4.8.

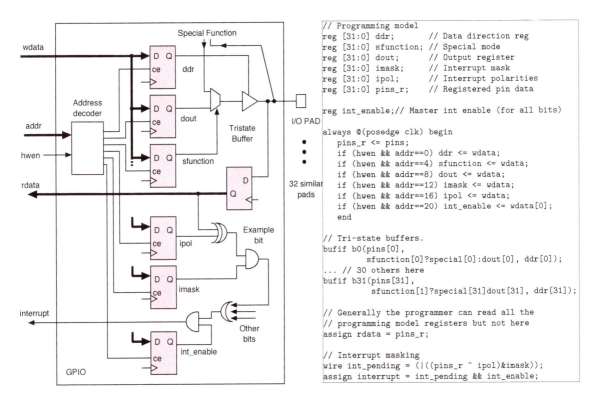

```
// Programming model
reg [31:0] ddr;        // Data direction reg
reg [31:0] sfunction;  // Special mode
reg [31:0] dout;       // Output register
reg [31:0] imask;      // Interrupt mask
reg [31:0] ipol;       // Interrupt polarities
reg [31:0] pins_r;     // Registered pin data

reg int_enable;// Master int enable (for all bits)

always @(posedge clk) begin
    pins_r <= pins;
    if (hwen && addr==0) ddr <= wdata;
    if (hwen && addr==4) sfunction <= wdata;
    if (hwen && addr==8) dout <= wdata;
    if (hwen && addr==12) imask <= wdata;
    if (hwen && addr==16) ipol <= wdata;
    if (hwen && addr==20) int_enable <= wdata[0];
    end

// Tri-state buffers.
bufif b0(pins[0],
        sfunction[0]?special[0]:dout[0], ddr[0]);
... // 30 others here
bufif b31(pins[31],
        sfunction[1]?special[31]dout[31], ddr[31]);

// Generally the programmer can read all the
// programming model registers but not here
assign rdata = pins_r;

// Interrupt masking
wire int_pending = (|((pins_r ^ ipol)&imask));
assign interrupt = int_pending && int_enable;
```

Figure 2.32 Schematic and RTL implementation of 32 GPIO bits connected to an MSOC1 bus

2.7.4 Counter/Timer Blocks

Various counter/timer blocks are found in SoCs. Such a block can contain several independent timers and counters, which are known as channels. A versatile channel can operate in several different modes. Four to eight, versatile, configurable counter/timer channels are generally provided in one IP block. The timer mode counts clock cycles and can generate periodic events, such as interrupts. The counter mode counts events on an external input or measures clock pulses seen while the external input is at a particular logic level. Timers are used as the basis of operating system timeouts and the periodic context switch in an operating system, such as 10 or 100 ms. Counters, for example, are used with certain types of shaft encoder applications such as a car rev counter. One of the channels is often dedicated as the system **watchdog timer (WDT)**, which performs a hard reboot if it is not serviced within some time by the CPU (e.g. 500 ms).

A channel may operate in a third mode, acting as a **pulse-width modulation (PWM)** generator. Channels in this mode produce a square wave of adjustable frequency and adjustable duty cycle. PWM controllers are often used to control heaters, the brightness of LEDs or the colour of a multi-colour LED. The frequency is relatively unimportant, but the duty cycle alters the brightness or colour.

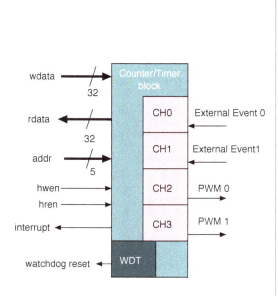

```
// RTL for one channel of a typical timer

// Programmers' model state
reg int_enable, int_pending;

reg [31:0] prescaler;
reg [31:0] reload;

// Programmer-invisible internal state
reg ovf;
reg [31:0] counter, prescale;

// Host write operations
always @(posedge clk) begin
    if (hwen && addr==0) int_enable <= wdata[0];
    if (hwen && addr==4) prescaler <= wdata;
    if (hwen && addr==8) reload <= wdata;
    // Write to addr==12 to clear the interrupt
    end
wire irq_clr = hwen && addr == 12;

// Host read operations
assign rdata =
    (addr==0) ? {int_pending, int_enable}:
    (addr==4) ? prescaler:
    (addr==8) ? reload: 0;

// A timer counts system clock cycles
// A counter counts transitions from an external input
always @(posedge clk) begin
    ovf <= (prescale == prescaler);
    prescale <= (ovf) ? 0: prescale+1;
    if (ovf) counter <= counter -1;
    if (counter == 0) begin
        int_pending <= 1;
        counter <= reload;
        end
    if (irq_clr) int_pending <= 0;
    end

// Interrupt generation
assign interrupt = int_pending && int_enable;
```

Figure 2.33 Schematic symbol for a counter/timer block and internal RTL for one timer function

All forms of channel are essentially a counter that counts internal clock pulses or external events. A channel can either interrupt the processor on a certain count value or toggle its output wire. An automatic reload register accommodates poor interrupt latency, so that the processor does not need to reload the counter quickly before the next event. In PWM, the output line is driven by a comparator that checks whether the counter is above a parameter register written by PIO.

The timer mode channel illustrated in the RTL of Figure 2.33 counts a prescaled system clock. All registers are configured as bus addressable read/write resources for PIO. The SoC system clock can be 100–600 MHz, so the prescaler is a simple divider that brings it down to a more useful frequency. Instead of the prescaler, a counter counts cycles of an external input, as shown on the schematic symbol. In this example, the interrupt is cleared by host PIO when it accesses a location that does not provide any data at offset 12.

2.7.5 DMA Controllers

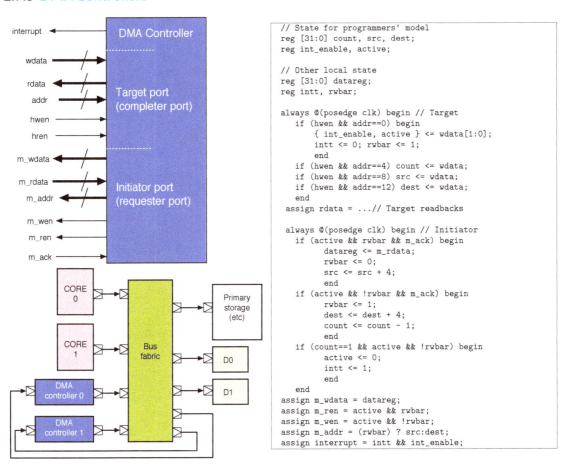

```
// State for programmers' model
reg [31:0] count, src, dest;
reg int_enable, active;

// Other local state
reg [31:0] datareg;
reg intt, rwbar;

always @(posedge clk) begin // Target
    if (hwen && addr==0) begin
        { int_enable, active } <= wdata[1:0];
        intt <= 0; rwbar <= 1;
        end
    if (hwen && addr==4) count <= wdata;
    if (hwen && addr==8) src <= wdata;
    if (hwen && addr==12) dest <= wdata;
    end
assign rdata = ...// Target readbacks

always @(posedge clk) begin // Initiator
    if (active && rwbar && m_ack) begin
        datareg <= m_rdata;
        rwbar <= 0;
        src <= src + 4;
        end
    if (active && !rwbar && m_ack) begin
        rwbar <= 1;
        dest <= dest + 4;
        count <= count - 1;
        end
    if (count==1 && active && !rwbar) begin
        active <= 0;
        intt <= 1;
        end
    end
assign m_wdata = datareg;
assign m_ren = active && rwbar;
assign m_wen = active && !rwbar;
assign m_addr = (rwbar) ? src:dest;
assign interrupt = intt && int_enable;
```

Figure 2.34 A simple DMA controller: schematic symbol, example TLM wiring and RTL for one channel

A DMA controller makes direct memory access transfers. DMA controllers are either stand-alone, as illustrated in Figure 2.34, or built in to other I/O devices, such as a streaming media device (Section 2.7.6). They move blocks of data from one part of the system to another. A DMA controller needs to be both a bus target (so that it can be programmed by the host CPU) and also a bus initiator (so that it can manipulate primary storage). The schematic symbol shows that it has two complete sets of bus connections. Note the reversal in the direction of all nets on the initiator port. The TLM diagram in the figure shows the bus connections required for a small system with two CPUs and two DMA controllers. These four devices are initiators for bus transactions.

Our simple DMA controller has one channel, which can perform only one operation. Real-world DMA controllers tend to have multiple channels, which is semantically the same as having multiple single-channel DMA controllers, give or take a master control register for interrupts etc. The illustrated RTL for the controller can just make block copies. It uses source and destination pointer registers, which must be set up by the host CPU. Likewise, the block length is set in a third register.

Finally, a status/control register controls interrupts and kicks off the procedure. Real-world DMA controllers are often more complex. For instance, they can load the block move parameter registers from meta-blocks set up in memory by the host CPU and can follow linked lists of such meta-blocks.

The RTL code for the controller is relatively straightforward. Much of it is dedicated to providing the target-side PIO access to each register. The active RTL code that embodies the function of the DMA controller is contained in the two blocks qualified with the `active` net in their conjunct. A concrete TLM model of this same DMA controller is given in Section 5.5.2 and can be downloaded from the supporting material.

The figure shows two simple target I/O devices, D0 and D1. Quite often these may have data registers such that a packet or block is formed using successive words written or read to a single data-register location. In these cases, the DMA controller needs a mode in which either the destination or source pointer is not adjusted inside the loop, depending on whether it is sending or receiving, respectively. For instance, to play audio out of a sound card, the destination address could be set to the PIO address of the output register for audio samples and set not to increment. The block size would need to be smaller than the device's staging FIFO buffer (Section 2.7.6).

Another processor core can be used instead of a DMA controller. If the processor 'runs out of' (i.e. fetches its instructions from) a small local instruction RAM or cache, then the code reads will not impact the main memory bus bandwidth. The silicon area of a very basic processor is not necessarily much larger than that of a DMA controller.

2.7.6 Network and Streaming Media Devices

Network devices, such as Ethernet, USB, Firewire and IEEE 802.11, are similar to streaming media devices, such as audio, and modem devices. All such devices commonly have embedded DMA controllers. Only low-throughput devices, such as a UART, are likely not to use DMA.

Figure 2.35 shows a schematic symbol of a network or streaming media device. It is the same as the DMA controller in Figure 2.34 except for additional device-specific functionality and wiring. In particular, there is a physical-layer interface to the external medium. The physical medium is generally glass fibre, copper or wireless. Wireless interfaces are illustrated in more detail in Figure 6.1. Each type of media requires specialised circuitry to drive it. This is called the PHY or **analogue front end (AFE)**. Sometimes this circuitry can be fully embedded on the main SoC chip (which is very common for USB) and other times it cannot, due to voltage swings, the operating frequency or noise levels (Section 8.4). Copper cables, such as used for the Ethernet CAT5 RJ45 shown on the right-hand side of Figure 2.29, require electrical isolation and miniature transformers. Further transformers, known as baluns (balanced-to-unbalanced transformers) and further inductors can suppress **radio-frequency interference (RFI)**. This entire block is known as the **PHY magnetics** and is often integrated inside the RJ45 connector.

A network interface IP block is known as a **network interface card (NIC)**. However, for SoC use, a better acronym would be **network interface controller** since it is integrated on the chip instead of

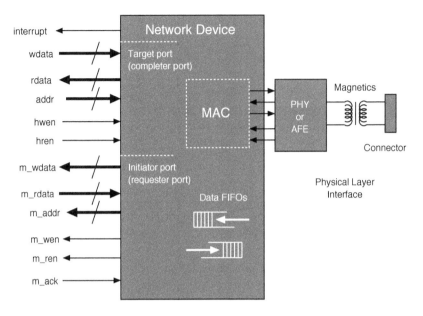

Figure 2.35 Net-level schematic symbol for a DMA-capable network interface IP block

being a pluggable card. A NIC contains a block known as the **media access controller (MAC)**, which handles the framing preambles, postambles and CRCs. It also decides when to transmit, using a protocol such as **carrier-sense multiple access with collision detection (CSMA-CD)** for Ethernet.

For streaming media with hard real-time characteristics, such as audio, video and modem devices, small staging FIFO buffers are needed in the device because the initiator port may experience latency when it is serviced by the bus fabric. The embedded DMA controller then initiates the next burst in its transfer when the local FIFO buffer reaches a trigger depth. Using DMA offloads work from the main processor, but, equally importantly, using DMA requires less data-staging RAM or FIFO buffering in a device. For the majority of SoC designs, RAM is the dominant cost in terms of SoC area. If the staging FIFO buffer is too small, then overruns or under-runs can occur. An **overrun** occurs when too much data are received and the memory system is not responsive enough for the data to be saved before the staging FIFO buffer overflows. The data must be deleted, causing knock-on effects (such as audio artefacts or packet retransmissions). Likewise, an **under-run** occurs when the sending FIFO buffer becomes empty because the memory system has not been fast enough in servicing it. This can also cause glitches in hard real-time media, such as audio, but may be less of a problem with packet-based network interfaces that allow gaps between packets.

A DMA controller in a network or streaming media device can often follow elaborate data structures set up by the host CPU, such as linking and delinking buffer pointers from a central pool. Due to the virtualisation requirements for a NIC in cloud computing, for server-grade NICs, the DMA system may be able to demultiplex packets based on VLAN number and store them in different buffers.

2.7.7 Video Controllers and Frame Stores

A bit-mapped frame store or video controller presents each word in its memory as a different pixel on a screen. For monochrome, the words can be 1 bit wide, denoting black or white. The designs of video interfaces have evolved along with the history of television. Today's flat panel displays use essentially the same signal set and protocols as an analogue video monitor from 1950. A frame store reads out the contents of its frame buffer over and over again at the **frame refresh rate**, which is commonly 60 Hz.

A 3-bit RGB word can render the eight basic saturated colours: black, white, magenta, cyan, red etc. To show other colours, a video **digital-to-analogue convertor (DAC)** is used to drive the red, green and blue primary colour signals. In modern DVI and HDMI ports, the DAC is at the display end of the monitor cable, which is then digital. A DAC is typically integrated into the driver ICs that directly connect to the transparent conductors within the panel.

In our simple reference implementation of Figure 2.36, the memory is implemented in a Verilog array, which has two address ports. Another approach is to have a single address port and for the RAM to be simply 'stolen' from the output device when the host makes a write to it. This causes noticeable display artefacts if writes are frequent. Real-world implementations use pseudo-dual-porting (Figure 4.19). This frame store has a fixed resolution and frame rate, but real ones have programmable values read from registers set up by the host CPU under PIO instead of the fixed numbers 230 and 110. This frame store is an output-only device that never becomes busy or ready, so it generates no interrupts. The device driver needs to know the mapping of RAM addresses to screen pixels and has zeroed the locations read out during horizontal and vertical synchronisation. Real implementations do not waste memory in this way and pause the supply of video data during the blanking intervals. A secondary link is included in contemporary video cables so that the display size can be read from an electronic data sheet stored in serial ROM inside the display. This is called a **display data channel (DDC)**.

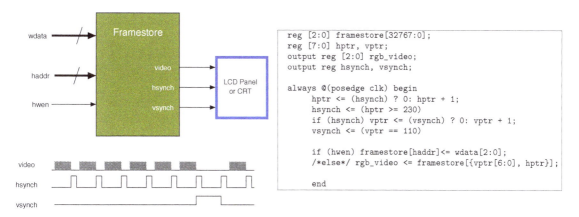

```
reg [2:0] framestore[32767:0];
reg [7:0] hptr, vptr;
output reg [2:0] rgb_video;
output reg hsynch, vsynch;

always @(posedge clk) begin
    hptr <= (hsynch) ? 0: hptr + 1;
    hsynch <= (hptr >= 230)
    if (hsynch) vptr <= (vsynch) ? 0: vptr + 1;
    vsynch <= (vptr == 110)

    if (hwen) framestore[haddr]<= wdata[2:0];
    /*else*/ rgb_video <= framestore[{vptr[6:0], hptr}];

    end
```

Figure 2.36 Structure of a simple frame store, RTL implementation and generated timing waveforms

The frame store in this example has its own local RAM. This reduces RAM bandwidth costs on the main RAM but uses more silicon area, a delicate trade-off. Video adaptors in PCs have their own local RAM or DRAM and also a local **graphical processing unit (GPU)** that performs polygon shading and so on.

2.7.8 Doorbell and Mailbox Blocks

An **inter-core interrupt (ICI)** facility is needed for basic synchronisation between separate cores within a SoC, for instance, if one CPU has placed a message in a shared memory region for another to read. The ISA for a processor may have a specialist ICI instruction, but this instruction may not work between different types of processor. An external IP block is then needed. The ICI function could be included in the interrupt distributor, which allows any device interrupt to be routed to any core with any priority (Section 2.5). Alternatively, a bespoke doorbell and mailbox block can be used.

Such a device offers multiple target interfaces, one per client bus. Figure 2.37 shows a dual-port device, but *n*-way can be deployed as required. The basic operational sequence is for one core to write a register in the interrupt that asserts an interrupt net connected to another core. The ISR of the interrupted core reads or writes another register in the interrupter to clear the interrupt.

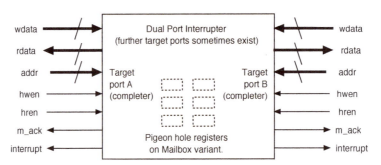

Figure 2.37 Doorbell and mailbox block

The mailbox variant supports message passing using a small internal FIFO buffer or scratchpad RAM inside the device. The interrupt is then generated after the message has been entered into the internal storage. Likewise, it is cleared as the receiver reads out the message.

2.7.9 Performance Management Units

A **performance management unit (PMU)** contains counters that can be programmed to count architectural features, such as instruction fetches and cache misses. A typical PMU has a small set of event counters, usually at least 10× fewer than the number of possible event sources. Hence, a programmable event routing matrix is needed to map events to counters. Moreover, the event counters may be limited in range, such as to 32 bits. To reduce any overflows at the expense of precision, the prescalers can be programmed so that the readable counter is incremented only after, say, 1024 real events have occurred. Even so, the counters may still overflow and it is not uncommon to use an operating system daemon, such as `oprofile` in Linux, to convey the hardware counts to software mirrors at a rate of 10 to 100 Hz.

For a core, events typically include page table misses, branch mispredicts, instructions retired, cycles out of halt mode or at various privilege levels, loads, stores, stalls and interrupts. For a cache, the number of hits, the number of sharing evictions and each type of miss may be recorded, although compulsory and capacity misses cannot be distinguished by the hardware.

2.8 Summary

A simple processor consists of a register file, an **arithmetic and logic unit (ALU)** and a control unit. The register file and ALU collectively form the **execution unit**. A SoC typically contains multiple processors, perhaps of different specialised types. A processor, together with any dedicated cache and coprocessors is known as a **core**. At reset, one of the cores, the **boot-up core**, starts execution, which initiates the start-up of the other cores (Section 9.1).

Memory systems are complex, especially if there are multiple initiators of bus transactions, such as multiple processor cores and DMA engines that all need to move data around. The designer needs to select which initiators can access which memory resources and whether cache consistency is worthwhile. The whole of the memory system, including its caches, is normally placed on the main SoC, except for the DRAM. DRAM may be placed in the same chip package as an MCM (Section 8.9.1).

As well as the memory system, numerous I/O peripherals and other IP blocks are placed on the SoC. Some are general purpose (such as USB) and others application-specific, such as a printer mechanism controller. Arranging a DRAM and designing its controller are very important. These are discussed later in Section 4.5, after we have discussed interconnects in the next chapter.

2.8.1 Exercises

Note: The exercises in this chapter are somewhat different from those in other chapters, since they assume a broad basic knowledge of processor architecture and assembly language programming. They may require materials not presented here.

1. Give examples of assembly language programs for a simple in-order processor that could suffer from each of the following problems and describe hardware or software mitigations: (i) a control hazard, (ii) a hazard arising from the ALU being pipelined and (iii) a load hazard, even though the data are in the cache.

2. If the front side of a cache has the same throughput as the back side, since it has half the word width and twice the clock frequency, for what sort of data access pattern will the cache provide low performance?

3. If a super-scalar processor shares FPUs between several hyper-threads, when would this enhance system energy use and throughput and when will it hinder them?

4. Why has serial communication been increasingly used, compared with parallel communication? Compare the parallel ATAPI bus with the serial SATA connection in your answer.

5. Assume a processor has one level of caching and one TLB. Explain, in as much detail as possible, the arrangement of data in the cache and TLB for both a virtually mapped and a physically mapped cache. If a physical page is in more than one virtual address, what precautions could ensure consistency in the presence of aliases? Assume the data cache is set associative and the TLB is fully associative.

6. What are the advantages and disadvantages of dynamically mapping a device interrupt to a processor core? What should be used as the inputs to the mapping function?

7. If a new variant of a microcontroller uses a single non-volatile memory technology to replace both the static RAM and mask-programmed ROM, what are the possible advantages and disadvantages? Is this even possible?

8. Some PC motherboards now have slots for high-performance non-volatile memory cards. How can these be used for primary or secondary storage? Should computers continue to distinguish between these forms in their architecture?

9. Briefly describe the code and wiring needed for a seven-segment display to count the number of presses on an external push button accurately. Note that mechanical buttons suffer from **contact bounce**. Use polling for your first implementation. How would you adapt this to use a counter/timer block and interrupts? What are the advantages of the button and the display?

10. A SoC is required to have frame stores for video input and output. Could these follow essentially the same design with minor differences? Would it be sensible to support a number of dual-purpose frame stores that can operate as either an input or output?

References

[1] Urs Hölzle. Brawny cores still beat wimpy cores, most of the time. Technical report, Google, 2010.

[2] Lauranne Choquin. Arm custom instructions: Enabling innovation and greater flexibility on Arm. https://armkeil.blob.core.windows.net/developer/Files/pdf/white-paper/arm-custom-instructions-wp.pdf, 2020.

[3] Joseph F. JaJa. PRAM (parallel random access machines). In David Padua, editor, *Encyclopedia of Parallel Computing*, pages 1608–1615. Springer US, Boston, MA, 2011. ISBN 978-0-387-09766-4. doi: 10.1007/978-0-387-09766-4_23. URL https://doi.org/10.1007/978-0-387-09766-4_23.

[4] Leslie G. Valiant. A bridging model for parallel computation. *Commun. ACM*, 33(8):103–111, August 1990. ISSN 0001-0782. doi: 10.1145/79173.79181. URL https://doi.org/10.1145/79173.79181.

[5] Arm Ltd. The Arm CoreLink generic interrupt controllers. https://developer.arm.com/ip-products/system-ip/system-controllers/interrupt-controllers, 2021.

[6] R. Mathur, C. Chao, R. Liu, N. Tadepalli, P. Chandupatla, S. Hung, X. Xu, S. Sinha, and J. Kulkarni. Thermal analysis of a 3D stacked high-performance commercial microprocessor using face-to-face wafer bonding technology. In *IEEE 70th Electronic Components and Technology Conference (ECTC)*, pages 541–547, 2020.

[7] Brad Chacos. "Intel quietly kills its face-melting Optane desktop SSDs," [Online]. Available: https://www.pcworld.com/article/3604093/intel-quietly-kills-its-face-melting-optane-desktop-ssds.html, January 2021.

[8] Standard Performance Evaluation Corporation. Spec CPU 2006. https://www.spec.org/cpu2006/, 2006.

[9] M. Gao, G. Ayers, and C. Kozyrakis. Practical near-data processing for in-memory analytics frameworks. In *International Conference on Parallel Architecture and Compilation (PACT)*, pages 113–124, 2015. doi: 10.1109/PACT.2015.22.

Chapter 3

SoC Interconnect

3.1 Interconnect Requirements

As discussed in the previous chapter, a SoC contains a large number of reusable IP (intellectual property) blocks. These need to be wired together by a SoC interconnect, which is the subject of this chapter. An interconnect primarily carries **transactions** that are started by a **transaction initiator** (also known as the **requester** or **manager**) and served by a **target** (also known as the **completer** or **subordinate**). The interconnect conveys the command from an initiating IP block to a target block and a response back again.

The traditional way to connect such blocks is to use a so-called bus, but, as we explain here, the term has evolved in meaning and is now pretty much a misnomer. In all but the most basic SoC designs, more than one initiator needs to be supported. As well as CPUs, **direct memory access (DMA)** controllers and other devices that perform DMA are initiators. Contention (competition) for resources can arise. Arbitration is required to manage how they are shared. There are two main forms of contention – fabric and target – as discussed in Section 4.2.1. So, an important aspect of designing an interconnect is providing sufficient bandwidth and implementing management techniques that allocate what is available.

In modern SoC flows, we expect all of the interconnect details to be designed by one or more **system interconnect generator** tools, which also generate documentation, device driver header files and test software (Section 6.8.2). An interconnect generator will ideally use the same architectural design files as used in the high-level ESL models used in the virtual platform (Chapter 5).

The transaction types typically provided by an interconnect can be classified as follows:

1. **Single-word reads and single-word writes** are the smallest individual operations or transactions. Data are moved from the initiator to the target for a write or store operation and in the other direction for a read or load operation. The initiator is typically a processor (or the back side of a cache) and the target is typically a memory or peripheral device. Word writes are often accompanied with **lane** flags so that only certain bytes within the word are updated. The flags are used when storing bytes and half words and for unaligned writes that straddle word boundaries.

2. **Uncached** reads and writes are also commonly required for I/O devices (when an MMU is not being used to define what is cacheable). For instance, the AMBA AXI protocol supports 12 different read and write semantics for the detailed interactions with caches, just for read and write data (e.g. write-through, write-allocate, write-back, etc.) [1].

3. Since individual reads and writes have too much overhead when more data needs to be moved, most forms of interconnect support **block** or **burst transfers**, in which larger quantities of data (128 bytes to 4 kB) are moved as a single transaction.

4. Broadcast and **multicast** transactions allow the same data word to be written to more than one destination at a time. A similar transaction type is **pseudo DMA**, in which data are moved between two target devices, one reading and the other writing, while the initiating CPU core ignores the

data on the bus. Real DMA can follow the same pattern (Section 2.7.5), the difference being that the initiator is a dedicated controller instead of a CPU core that is executing a dummy read transaction.

5. **Atomic operations** are needed in all multiprocessor systems. The conventional operations are **test-and-set** and **compare-and-swap**. These require two successive operations on an addressed location without pre-emption. This does not scale well to multi-initiator systems, so **load-linked** and **store-conditional** single-word operations are, typically, more common today (Section 3.1.7).

6. If the order of delivery of the data is critical (which is the normal case), the interconnect must observe **sequential consistency primitives** or **memory fences** (Section 4.5). For instance, the arguments to a device command must arrive at an I/O device before the go command is received. An interconnect that supports transaction buffering can allow transactions to arrive out of order, unless sequential consistency is managed implicitly or through explicit fence operations.

7. Cache consistency or **data coherency** messages are also conveyed between components that perform caching to ensure that out-of-date data are not erroneously served for a read (e.g. the AMBA ACE protocol).

8. It is common for an interconnect to carry **read-ahead** or **warm-up traffic**. These are read cycles whose results might not be needed but allow data to be loaded speculatively so that the data are available with lower latency if needed.

9. There will frequently be a completely separate interconnect network for **debug transactions** (Section 4.7). One advantage of a separate network is its unobtrusiveness, since certain bugs are hard to track down if the bug's behaviour changes when debug instrumentation is enabled. Also, there may be a considerable amount of data moving over the debug network if intensive logging of the main network traffic is enabled. The dark silicon argument (Section 8.2) enables the provision of extensive, yet seldom-used, additional infrastructure at costs lower than might be expected.

10. Configuration operations, such as **presence probing** and other miscellaneous operations, must also be conveyed in some systems. For instance, several instances of an identical IP block need to be given different base addresses. Alternatively, the operating system would need to determine which IP blocks are present on the platform it is running on. When the base address is not hardwired at SoC tapeout (Section 8.7.7), there must be transactions to configure the base address before normal programmed I/O can proceed. These can also make device drivers more generic (Section 3.1.7).

11. Secure systems, such as those using hardware capabilities or which otherwise track ownership of the data using hardware (Section 3.1.4), need to convey **tagged data**. Tags are also used for associating transactions with their responses in some bus protocols that we will cover. These tags are generated by the hardware and not visible to the programmer.

Interrupts must also be conveyed from devices to processors (Section 2.5). Interrupt wiring was traditionally part of the 'bus' standard when child boards were plugged into a motherboard bus. However, for SoC design within the ASIC, interrupts are typically conveyed by separate wiring that is not related to the nets carrying transaction data. The same goes for power management signals that ensure that a peripheral is suitably able to handle a request (Section 3.7.5). The system integration tool must instantiate these nets as it configures the interconnect.

A read transaction clearly requires a response that contains the data. A write transaction does not strictly require a response. The initiator may proceed optimistically, assuming success. This is known as **write posting**. However, it is normal practice for all transactions to receive an acknowledgement containing a **response code**. Since an interconnect is designed to be reliable, the standard assumption for simple microcontroller systems is that there are no errors in the hardware. Hence, transactions always complete successfully and no fault handlers are required (except for a watchdog timer (Section 2.7.4)). However, a number of possible errors can arise in modern SoC designs and these need to be handled appropriately, which could be a retry in hardware or an exception interrupt being raised for software handlers to deal with.

Sources of bad response codes include:

▪ The addressed target may be **powered down, disconnected** or otherwise **not ready** for the operation.

▪ **Unused address**: No device is mapped at the target address.

▪ **Address translate error**: The address translation unit (or I/O MMU) does not contain an entry for the initiator-supplied address.

▪ **Parity, CRC or ECC failure**: A data integrity error was encountered in the interconnect circuits or else a checked memory target was addressed and the memory parity or CRC check failed (Section 4.7.6).

▪ **Store-conditional fail**: The atomic operation was pre-empted (Section 3.1.7).

▪ A **dirty data** failure arises in some cache consistency protocols (Section 2.4.1).

▪ A **single-event upset** arises from a burst of radiation or an alpha particle hitting the silicon (Section 8.2.1). This may be detected or corrected using parity or ECC mechanisms, or it may be an undetected error at the interconnect level.

An **interconnect standard** defines a set of nets and a net-level **protocol** that together support the various transactions. An example is the nets and protocol of MSOC1 in Figure 1.5. According to the context, we normally use the short word 'bus' interchangeably for 'interconnect standard' and elsewhere for all of the components that make up the interconnect of a particular SoC. Preferably, the various IP blocks must all be designed according to the interconnect standard. They may have more than one port, but each port follows the standard. SoC assembly is easiest if all IP blocks use the same interconnect standard. Modern interconnect standards, such as AXI, have defined functional profiles in which a subset of the full functionality is present within a profile. Having predefined functional profiles makes it easy also to provide a set of protocol adaptors that map between the profiles.

3.1.1 Protocol Adaptors

For each parameterisable bus standard, an exponentially large number of **protocol adaptors** and bus bridges is required. There is a small number of basic operations, such as FIFO buffering, policing, width converting, domain crossing, multiplexing and demultiplexing. Some set of these functions needs to be deployed in a protocol adaptor. The number of ports, the direction of the ports, port widths, protocol profile (e.g. the Lite variant) also vary. Enumerating all possibilities as library components is not practical. Hence, a tool that generates efficient RTL implementations is generally required.

Given the required functionality, further variation arises from the order of composition of the basic operations. For example, a simplex demultiplexer that also converts the bus width and embodies a short FIFO buffer can be constructed in many ways. Four of the six basic permutations are shown in Figure 3.1. Although these vary in terms of head-of-line blocking behaviour (Section 4.3.2), they otherwise behave almost identically provided the re-arbitration points are appropriately constrained to avoid misinterleaving of transaction beats for a burst transaction (e.g. AXI has the LAST signal for this purpose but AXI-Lite handles only single-beat transfers).

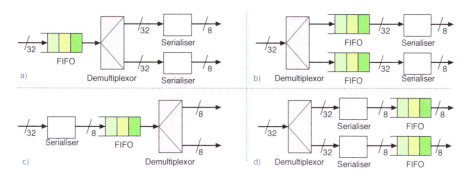

Figure 3.1 Four of six permutations that implement a simplex protocol adaptor. Each has the same signature of one input and two output ports of 32 and 8 bits, respectively. More typically, duplex implementations are required

Design Considerations and Physical Constraints

The aim of an interconnect design is to be as unobtrusive as possible, both at design time and in use. Broadly speaking, these are the most fundamental parameters for an interconnect:

- The baseline **connectivity matrix** records which initiators need to communicate with which targets.

- The **throughput** is the amount of data it can move per unit time, normally measured in MB/s (megabytes per second). For instance, in 2005, a bus that was 128 bits wide and had a clock frequency of 200 MHz could convey a peak of 3200 MB/s, or roughly 3 GB/s. A typical application processor today may use a 1 GHz clock for cross-bar interconnect and up to 2 GHz for mesh or ring interconnect. Hence throughputs five or ten times greater are typical.

- The **latency** is the time a transaction takes to complete. For many applications, a transaction cannot be initiated until the previous transaction has returned its result, such as when following a linked-list structure. Hence, latency is very important.

- A quantified version of the connectivity matrix records the expected traffic pattern in terms of peak and average bandwidth needs between each end point. Ideally, an interconnect is planned and dimensioned using this information. Both the throughput and the latency will tend to degrade if the actual traffic patterns vary significantly from the expected use pattern, unless the interconnect supports a high degree of **connectedness** such that all possible patterns of use are equally well served. However, this can lead to over-engineering.

- The **energy consumption** of an interconnect is also very important in modern SoCs. Energy use is proportional to the distance that data moves across the chip (Section 4.6), which may depend on the amount of deviation from the planned traffic flow.

- Support for **real-time traffic** with a guaranteed **quality of service (QoS)**, is commonly needed. The QoS can be quantified, as discussed in Section 4.3, and recorded in the connectivity matrix. QoS mechanisms within an interconnect ensure that tasks can be completed by relevant deadlines while avoiding **starvation** for lower-priority traffic.

- All types of interconnect tend to contain loops. They could be in the forward and reverse handshaking logic on a simple path, or composed of multiple switched segments in a mesh. Such loops are liable to become deadlocked. A deadlock is a ring of components each waiting on the next. The need to avoid deadlocks restricts the interconnect design space and must always be taken into account (Section 3.4.3).

Physical Constraints

Today, it is not sensible to send data at a high rate from one side of a chip to the other using just wiring. Buffering and re-timing are needed. The normal approach today for a single clock domain (CD) is to add a pipeline stage (Section 4.4.2) to all nets of the bus. The protocol must tolerate this. A pipeline stage may also be needed in the reverse flow direction.

Crossing CDs requires domain-crossing logic. If the clocks originate from the same master source, they are synchronous (**harmonically locked**) and domain crossing can be relatively simple and efficient. If the clocks are asynchronous, then the logic must be carefully designed to avoid signal sampling issues, such as metastability (Section 3.7.1). Transmitting data consumes energy and incurs a delay. In the absence of electrical resistance, the speed of propagation of an electrical signal c

depends on the dielectric constants of the materials. The speed is also the product of the wavelength and frequency:

$$c = \frac{1}{\sqrt{\epsilon_0 \mu_0 \epsilon_r \mu_r}} = \lambda f$$

The propagation constant relevant for silicon chips is the relative permittivity since there are no magnetic effects from any of the materials in use. For silicon dioxide, $\epsilon_r = 3.9$, which means signals are limited to $1/\sqrt{3.9}$, which is about half the speed of light in a vacuum. The capacitance per unit length of a conductor that is spaced a diameter away from the next one is approximately 83 pF/m. The inductance of conductors that are much longer than their diameter (e.g. 500 times longer) is about 1.4 µH/m. To achieve a propagation speed that is half the speed of light, which is 150 m/µs, means that for a clock frequency of 2 GHz, the wavelength must be 7.5 cm. The clock will be 180° out of phase (i.e. inverted) within 3.75 cm, even in the absence of resistance. However, the principal idea of digital logic modelling (Section 4.6.4) is that all parts of a net are at the same voltage. This is approximately true for up to 1/10th of a wavelength, so the speed of light limits the length of a conductor to 75 mm, which is less than the diagonal of many SoCs.

L and C are independent of manufacturing geometry and their ratio remains constant with technology scaling. Resistance is a different matter. Aluminium nets have a conductivity of about $2.7 \times 10^{-8}\ \Omega$ m. Their resistance per unit length increases as they are made thinner. The wiring pitch for the finest nets is typically about 5λ and their thickness and height are both about 2.5λ, where λ is now not the wavelength, but a measure of the the fabrication geometry (Section 8.2). Because both height and width have been made finer and finer over recent decades, there has been a near quadratic growth in resistance (the height has not been reduced as much as the width). This increase in electrical resistance creates an RC propagation delay that now reduces propagation speeds well beyond the LC transmission line (speed-of-light) delay.

Figure 3.2 plots the RC delay against net length for fine-pitched nets made in 45 nm and 16 nm processes. These are computed using the simple Elmore delay model (Section 4.9.5) that ignores inductance. Also shown is the transmission line delay for a lossless LC line, which should be included when significant. System design rules based on these figures dictate how frequently a signal needs regenerating as it traverses a chip. Clearly, several D-types are needed if it passes from one corner of even a small 8 mm SoC to the opposite corner. For any geometry, the design rule used for timing closure (Section 8.12.16) must be conservative. The plot shows a simple linear bound of 1600 nm/µs, as used in a recent 16 nm tapeout. Since any net that is required to be faster than this conservative bound violates the rule, it must be redesigned. The delay, as given by the Elmore curve, will exceed the delay anticipated by the simple linear rule for long-distance nets, but such nets are either not allowed by other design rules or else routed on higher metal layers with perhaps twice the width and thickness, and hence, 4× less delay.

The signal restoration and amplification considerations are the same whether a signal is conveyed across the chip using combinational or synchronous buffers. Digital **signal restoration** is the process of removing noise and ensuring the voltage falls properly within the logic margins that define a zero or one. As explained in Section 2.6.3, the **logic margin** is how far the signal is below the maximum

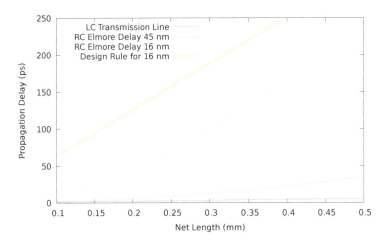

Figure 3.2 Comparison of speed-of-light (LC) and RC-based Elmore delay models for propagation along a net. Also shown is a real-world design rule for 16-nm geometry

specified logic zero voltage or how far above the minimum logic one voltage it is. A plot of output voltage against input voltage for a logic gate is called its **voltage transfer characteristic**. All logic gates have an amplification factor (gain) of well less than unity within the logic zero and logic one input regions, with a high gain region in between (Figure 3.33). If this were not the case, digital logic would lose its fundamental property of keeping the zeros and ones properly distinct. The circuit noise will become amplified if the signal is in a region with an absolute gain greater than unity.

Two extreme approaches to sending a signal a long way over a chip are:

1. Use many low-power buffers spaced evenly along the signal path.

2. Use one powerful buffer at the start of a single piece of metal track.

Neither of these is good. A large buffer will have wide transistors and a large input capacitance. Moreover, invertors are far more efficient than buffers in CMOS, so having two invertors with a section of wire between them is better than a buffer. Generally, spacing out four invertors can be a good design for a long net. If these have different drive strengths (Section 8.4.1), the lowest power invertor is placed at the start of the chain. If the net has to fan out to multiple destinations, the best structure can be manually determined using **logical effort analysis** [2], or simply left to a logic synthesiser tool (Section 8.3.8).

Another physical constraint for an interconnect is its wiring density. Wiring congestion is an issue for crossbar interconnects (Section 3.2.3) or narrow routing channels (Section 8.3.12). However, the wiring problem has been reduced to a large extent with newer interconnect technologies, such as a **network-on-chip (NoC)**, unless the channels are very narrow. The wiring density on the lowest levels of metallisation is similar to the transistor size, but it becomes coarser at the higher levels. The highest levels are always reserved for power distribution, since this requires the lowest fidelity. Any modern technology can support thousands of nets per millimetre per layer. Hence, busses 128 bits wide or wider, which would cause layout difficulties for PCB design, are not a serious concern for VLSI, although the area penalty of turning 90° at a corner is not trivial. As mentioned, very thin nets have a high resistance, which can be a consideration for exceptionally dense wiring owing to the increase in the RC signal delay.

The ability to use wide busses and the need to use delay-tolerant protocols have led the industry towards bus protocols that are optimised for large transactions. For a given data rate, a wider data bus means a lower transaction frequency. Architectural design approaches reflect this. For instance, the traffic at the back side of a cache has a pattern much more like this than the front-side traffic.

3.1.2 On-chip Protocol Classes

On-chip interconnects can be broadly classed as **circuit switched** or **packet switched**. A basic **circuit-switched** configuration makes an electronic connection between a number of wiring segments to form an initiator-to-target connection that lasts for the duration of a transaction. Our MSOC1 protocol is an example (Section 1.1.4). Most modern forms of interconnect decouple the initiation and response phases of a transaction but retain the circuit-switching concept for each half, certainly for short distances. The wiring segments are joined by multiplexer structures. The presence of D-type re-timing (pipeline stages) at the joints does not alter the classification because, to a first approximation, all of the bus resources used for the transaction (or transaction phase) are tied up for the duration and cannot be concurrently used by other transactions.

On the other hand, in a **packet-switched** configuration, each interconnect resource is tied up only while it is forwarding part of the transaction to the next interconnect resource. A transaction typically has a longer duration than the involvement of any interconnect component in handling that transaction. This forms the basis for one type of NoC that we discuss in Section 3.4.

3.1.3 Simple Bus Structures

Leaving aside bridged bus and NoC structures, the following taxonomy is useful for discussing protocols for simple bus structures. These simple structures also form the baseline for discussing individual links in a NoC mesh.

1. **Reciprocally degrading busses**: The throughput is inversely proportional to the target latency in terms of clock cycles, such as the four-phase handshake (described next) and AHB (described below).

2. **Split-port busses**: These have separate request and acknowledge channels that carry different **transaction phases** with independent timing. (Note: A different use of the word 'split' describes a burst transaction that is temporarily paused while a higher-priority operation takes place.)

3. **Delay-tolerant busses**, such as AXI4-Lite (Section 3.1.5) and BVCI (described below): New commands may be issued while awaiting responses from earlier commands.

4. **Reorder-tolerant busses**: Responses can be returned in a different order from the transaction commands. This is highly beneficial for DRAM access and is needed for advanced NoC architectures (Section 3.1.4). Examples include full AXI (Section 3.1.5).

A simple bus provides data movement, addressing and flow control. A **simplex** connection sends data in one direction only. A **half-duplex** connection sends data in both directions, but only in one direction at a time. Another name for half-duplex is **time-division duplex**. A **full-duplex** connection can send data in both directions at the same time. A **streaming** connection does not include any addressing capabilities. It is often simplex. A pair of streaming connections, one in each direction, can be used to form a duplex streaming connection. For instance, the AXI4-Stream port is essentially the same as one direction of a standard AXI port but without the address bus. It is like the standard synchronous interface (see below). The AXI bus is described in Section 3.1.5.

For lossless reliable behaviour, a bus must also provide **flow control**, so that, on average, the rate at which data or transactions are generated at the initiators exactly meets the rate at which they are processed at the targets. If a destination (target) is slow, or not ready, it applies **backpressure** on the source (initiator), so that new transactions or data are not generated until it is ready. If the source cannot generate its next transaction because that transaction depends on the response to the current transaction, we have a **data hazard** (Section 6.3). This is a common situation. The overall system **throughput**, in terms of transactions per second, then depends on the round-trip **latency**, which is the time between issuing a transaction and receiving the response.

Four-phase Handshake

Bus protocols vary in the **maximum number of outstanding transactions** they support. This is a key metric that affects how throughput degrades as latency is increased. The simplest protocols allow only one outstanding transaction.

A four-phase handshake (Figure 3.3) provides flow control for a parallel data channel of any number of bits. It supports a simplex, in-order, lossless, infinite sequence of word writes. It was used on parallel printer ports from the 1950s until replaced with USB. It has at most one transaction in flight, so its throughput is inversely proportional to the round-trip latency. It is normally implemented without a clock net and so is asynchronous. We cite it here as an important historic example. It also serves as the basis for an asynchronous CD-crossing bridge (Section 3.7.3). The two-phase variant transfers data on both edges of the strobe signal.

MSOC1 and AHB Protocols

As established in Section 3.1.1, nets can no longer pass a significant distance over a chip without buffering. Registering (passing through a D-type pipeline stage) is the best form of buffering within a CD, since it enables a higher clock frequency (Section 4.4.2). Hence, we must use protocols that are tolerant to being registered on modern SoCs. Within a clock domain, it is always appropriate to use

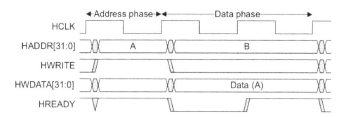

Figure 3.3 Timing diagram for AHB bus write cycle with one wait state

synchronous bus protocols. However, older synchronous bus protocols either intrinsically cannot tolerate additional pipeline stages as their definition requires a response within some predefined number of clock cycles (normally 1 or 2) or if they can tolerate it, tend also to suffer from the reciprocal degrading problem. Our MSOC1 reference protocol (Figure 1.5) suffers in this way.

A real-world example is the AHB bus. This protocol was defined in the 1990s. Figure 3.3 shows the principal nets used for a data write. The clock is shared by all participants. The address, write guard and data are generated by the initiator and the HREADY signal is the handshake response from the target. The figure shows that one wait state arising from the addressed target (or some intermediate fabric part) is not ready for the write data. Hence, HREADY is de-asserted until progress can resume.

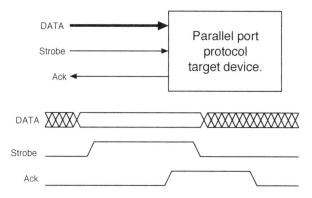

Figure 3.4 Timing diagram for an asynchronous four-phase handshake

In a basic AHB implementation, only one transaction may be outstanding at one time and the bus nets are idle in wait states. This is wasteful. However, unlike our simple MSOC1, AHB supports burst transactions, in which multiple data words can be sent or received without re-arbitration. A full AHB implementation that supported interruptible transactions with long bursts and retry mechanisms was developed. Its retry mechanism enabled a target to reject a transaction with a request for it to be started again. The mechanisms for bursts and interruptible transactions were similar in how they extended the baseline protocol and its implementation. Overall, the complexities arising from supporting a complex set of behaviours became undesirable and unnecessary as SoC and VLSI technology advanced. The preferable way to attain high performance is always to use split port transactions and, optionally, to use simpler MSOC1-like protocols for lower-performance I/O subsystems where appropriate. A real-world simple bus example is the **AMBA peripheral bus (APB)** standard defined by Arm. Overall, reciprocally degrading protocols are not suitable for modern SoCs in which net pipelining and registering are needed to traverse any distance over the chip.

The Standard Synchronous Handshake

The four-phase handshake, as described above, is suitable for asynchronous interfaces. On the other hand, a very common paradigm for synchronous flow control of a simplex bus is to have a handshake net in each direction with bus data being qualified as valid on **any positive clock edge where both handshake nets are asserted**. This protocol is called the **standard synchronous handshake**. A simplex bus is unidirectional: all data lines go in the same direction. The handshake nets are typically called 'valid' and 'ready', with valid being in the direction from the initiator to the target and ready in the opposite direction. For simplex interfaces, the data source is nominally denoted the initiator. This paradigm forms the essence of the LocalLink protocol from Xilinx and is used in many other synchronous protocols, such as for each **channel** of the AXI protocol (Section 3.1.5). Timing diagrams are shown in Figure 3.5. The interface nets for an 8-bit transmit-side LocalLink port are:

```
input  clk;
output [7:0] data;  // The data word - here just a byte but any size is possible
output src_rdy_n;   // This is the `valid' signal
input  dst_rdy_n;   // The reverse-direction `ready' signal
output sof_n;       // Start of frame
output eof_n;       // End of frame
```

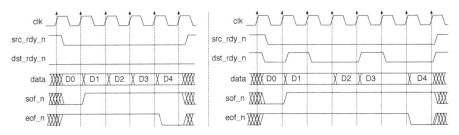

Figure 3.5 Timing diagrams for the synchronous LocalLink protocol. Left: Back-to-back transfer of words because the destination is always ready. Right: Pauses to match the acceptance rate of the destination. Note that all control signals are active low (denoted with the _n RTL suffix) in LocalLink

As well as word-level handshake signals, LocalLink defines start-of-frame and end-of-frame signals. These provide a packet delineation layer that is 'above' the word-level protocol in that the framing nets are qualified by the conjunction of ready and valid, alongside the data nets. Having both start and end frame delimiters is technically redundant, as discussed in Section 7.5, but can simplify arbitration circuits, for instance, in a multiplexor that should not switch between sources mid-frame. An ESL model for LocalLink is presented in Section 5.4.9.

A feature of the standard synchronous handshake is that both sides can freely assert and de-assert their handshake net at will. Sometimes, in an implementation, one side will wait for the other side to assert its handshake net. Such waiting should be avoided where possible since it adds to the delay. It is very bad if both sides wait in this way, either synchronously or combinationally, since we have an instant deadlock. Any instance of this communication paradigm must eliminate potential deadlock scenarios by specifying permitted and illegal dependencies.

Note, adding a pipeline stage to the standard synchronous handshake is not a matter of just putting a broadside register across all of the nets: the handshake nets travel in both directions, so re-timing one or both will disrupt their points of conjunction. As described in Section 3.4.4, this is one reason to use **credit-based flow control** instead.

Multiple Outstanding Transaction Protocols

To overcome the round-trip latency arising from the pipeline stages, protocols that can keep multiple transactions in flight are needed. These generally use multiphase transactions in which the request and response phases are conveyed over different channels that together form a bus port. A **multiphase transaction** (aka **split transaction**) has a temporal separation between the issuing of the command and the receipt of the result. Multiple outstanding transactions are then possible and arise if further commands are issued before the results are received. Likewise, interconnect components are free to operate in a streaming pipelined mode, as they can handle the next transaction before the current transaction is complete.

This shift in bus protocol design went hand-in-hand with a related shift in how bus arbitration was performed (Section 4.2.1). The principal interconnect definition now relates to the port on the IP block. Bus arbitration signals are no longer defined as part of the port and the system integrator is given complete freedom over the actual bus topology. Hence, an IP block can be connected to a NoC or a simple bus without (substantially) changing its interface.

If multiple outstanding transactions are supported, the option arises for responses to be received out of order. We consider this in Section 3.1.4, but first, we look at the BVCI protocol, which does not support out-of-order responses. The BVCI protocol, defined as part of the **Open Core Connect (OCP)** standard [3], was a popular alternative to the AHB protocol because it supports multiple outstanding transactions and does not tie up interconnect resources for the duration of a transaction.

BVCI has separate command and response channels and each channel uses an instance of the standard synchronous handshake. As well as being amenable to larger delays over the interconnect, a multiphase protocol can tolerate varying delays, as arise when crossing CDs (Section 3.7.3). Older-style single-channel protocols, in which the targets had to respond within a prescribed number of clock cycles, cannot be used in these situations.

The standard synchronous handshake in each channel guards all of the other nets in that channel. Data are transferred on any positive edge of the clock where both are asserted. If a block is both an initiator and a target, such as the DMA controller example from Section 2.7.5, then there are two complete instances of the port in an IP block. However, BVCI requests and responses must be preserved in their respective order at any given port, whether that is an initiator or a target.

For BVCI core nets (Figure 3.6):

▪ All IP blocks can support this interface.

▪ There are separate request and response channels.

▪ Data are valid if there is an overlap of `req` and `ack`.

▪ The temporal decoupling of directions allows pipeline delays for crossing switch fabrics or crossing CDs.

▪ Sideband signals, such as interrupts, errors and resets, vary per block.

▪ Two complete instances of the port are needed if the block is both an initiator and a target.

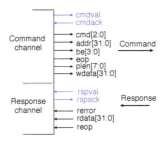

Figure 3.6 BVCI core nets. Arrows indicate signal directions on the initiator. All of these are reversed for the target

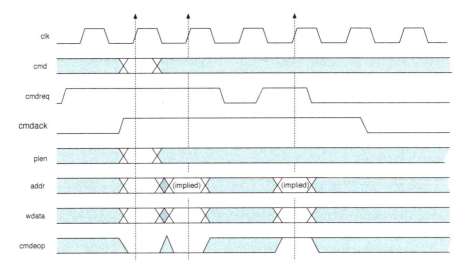

Figure 3.7 BVCI protocol: Command phase timing diagram

BVCI supports burst transactions, in which multiple consecutive reads or writes are performed as a single transaction with subsequent addresses being treated as offsets from the first address. Figure

3.7 shows a write transaction where three words are stored. The implied addresses may wrap modulo some pre-agreed basis, such as the cache line size. This allows a complete cache line to be retrieved, but with the first-needed offset being served first. Because the standard synchronous handshake allows back-to-back transactions without wasting clock cycles, there is no protocol-level performance advantage to supporting a burst facility with this bus structure. However, target devices, especially DRAM subsystems (Section 4.5), are highly optimised for burst operations. Hence, a burst must be maintained as an ordered sequence over the interconnect.

Figure 3.8 shows a response to a read request that was also for three words.

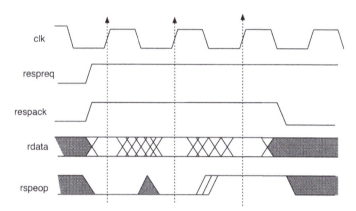

Figure 3.8 BVCI protocol: Response phase timing diagram. Operations are qualified with the conjunction of req and ack. Response and acknowledge cycles maintain their respective ordering. Bursts are common. Successive addressing may be implied

3.1.4 Ordered and Unordered Interconnects

Some initiators, particularly out-of-order CPU cores (Section 2.2) and massively parallel accelerators (Section 6.4), issue multiple outstanding reads and can do useful work as soon as any of these are serviced. Some targets, particularly DRAM, can perform better by servicing requests out of order. Some bus fabrics, especially those with multiple paths, can perform better if they are not constrained to deliver messages in order. Thus, it is clear that an interconnect that supports an out-of-order service is useful. However, there are many occasions when ordering must be controlled so that **sequential consistency** is preserved (Section 4.5).

Importantly, if we multiplex a pair of in-order busses onto a common bus, yet tag all of the traffic from each bus on the common bus according to its in-order initiator, we have a tagged out-of-order bus. This is illustrated in Figure 3.9. A **transaction tag** is a positive integer that associates either a command with a response or a group of consecutive commands with a group of consecutive responses in the same order. The semantics are that for any given tag, the requests and replies must be kept in order. The devices on the left may be separate initiator blocks, like processors and DMA controllers, they may be different load/store stations (Section 2.2) on a common IP block or, in theory, they may be any mix. For the targets on the right, there is no difference between demultiplexing to separate in-order targets and using a single target that understands tags.

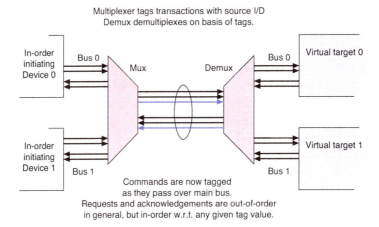

Figure 3.9 Out-of-order bus formed from a pair of in-order busses with added tags (blue)

The tag size must be large enough to distinguish between different initiators that are multiplexed together and also to support the maximum number of differently numbered outstanding transactions generated by an initiator. For an interconnect that maintains order within a tag value, any number of transactions with a given number can be safely outstanding. The simplest management technique is for each individual source to generate tags with a width sufficient to enumerate its number of load/store stations and for the command tag width to be extended at each multiplexing point by concatenating the source port number with the source's tag. This is illustrated in Figure 3.10. In demultiplexing stages, the tag width may be unchanged, with an end point preserving the widest form of the tag to send back to the originator. The reverse approach provides simple demultiplexing of responses back to the appropriate source. A tag will then never get reused while it is in use because each originating load/store station has a unique encoding and such a station will not issue a new command while it has a request outstanding.

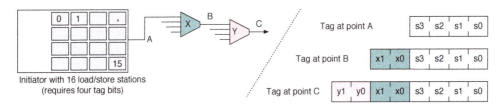

Figure 3.10 Augmenting the tag width through successive multiplexing stages

The tag mechanism just described is sufficient to correlate results to replies over an out-of-order bus. However, to preserve sequential consistency (Section 4.5) between, say, separate load/store stations on a CPU, which would have their own IDs, a **memory fence** mechanism is also needed. With so-called **weak memory ordering models**, the physical memory operates deterministically, but the interconnect or memory controller allows messages to overtake each other. Fences, also known as **barriers**, preserve RaW and WaW orderings: no transaction is allowed to overtake others in a way that would make it jump over a fence in the time domain. A programmer must insert fences in their software to sequence requests correctly to different addresses, as illustrated in Figure 4.17. In a variant of the OCP/BVCI bus, tag numbers were used in a different way from AXI: a fence was implied when an initiator increased a tag number.

3.1.5 AMBA AXI Interconnect

The first **Advanced eXtensible Interface (AXI)** standard was defined by Arm in 2003. This marked a move away from a conventional bus by defining the interface to a compatible IP block. It uses multiphase transactions and hence, enables an arbitrary number of clock cycles to be consumed as traffic moves across the interconnect. The standard also has many other freedoms. For example, the data bus width can change inside the interconnect (using a resizer Section 3.6) and the clock frequency can vary, for either a harmonic or an asynchronous clock (Section 3.7.1).

As shown in Figure 3.11, one AXI port has five separate channels. Each channel has its own standard synchronous handshaking using a contra-directional READY/VALID pair with all the other nets running in the VALID direction and qualified by the conjunction of ready and valid on a clock edge.

BVCI has two independent channels, which is the minimum required for multiple in-flight transactions. The number is increased in AXI by first completely separating the read and write transactions into independent channel groups and second, by splitting the write group further using separate address and data channels. Using separate channels for reads and writes not only increases the bandwidth owing to the spatial reuse principle (Section 3.2), it also tends to reduce the complexity of the implementation of the logic overall, but at the expense of wiring area. The interface is simple because the data are moving in only one direction in each of the channels. No additional energy is needed by the additional wiring area (principally two address busses instead of one), indeed the number of transitions on the split address busses can typically be lower than on a shared bus owing to the spatial locality of access.

The complete decoupling of the read and write aspects immediately raises the prospect of uncontrolled RaW and WaR hazards and related sequential consistency problems (Section 4.5). These hazards arise if the most recent data are not read back after a write has nominally occurred. The AXI protocol lays down no ordering requirements between read and write transactions over the separate channels. Same-address RaW/WaW hazards are generally handled in hardware, either by detecting and stalling a request that is to the same address as an outstanding write or by serving it from the write queue.

To maintain sequential consistency, fences have been deprecated within the AXI specification because fences are more efficiently handled within the initiator. Supporting fences within the interconnect requires a significant amount of state storage and goes against modern interconnect design techniques in which components are designed to be simple so that they are easy to verify and can run at a high frequency. Hence, for AXI systems, an initiator must wait for all outstanding responses to come back before issuing a transaction on any of its load/store ports, which needs to be after a fence.

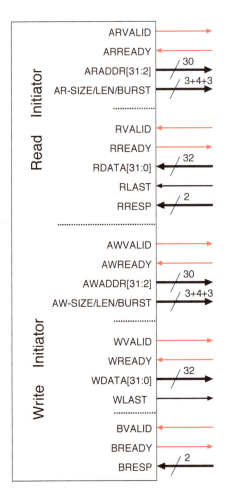

Figure 3.11 The baseline port structure for an A32D32 AXI standard initiator showing the five temporally floating channels, two for reads and three for writes. Parity bits may be present on any of the busses. Writing an address and writing data operate close to lockstep for single-word writes, but are split to support multi-word bursts. Signal directions are reversed for a target

The AMBA AXI and ACE specification includes major revisions (3, 4 and 5) and interface variants, e.g. AXI4-Lite and ACE5-Lite, as summarised in Table 3.1. Each row in the table defines multiple possible forms due to further parametrisation being used to define the address, data, tag and other bit widths. AXI can be used with a tag width (Section 3.1.4) of any size. A size of zero bits is allowed, which gives an untagged port. The AXI3 and AXI4 protocols are very similar. Both support burst transfers. However, for both reads and writes, a burst transaction sends only one address to accompany multiple data words, with the addresses incrementing according to one of several predefined patterns. AXI4 extended the maximum number of **data beats** in a burst transaction from 16 to 256. A beat is a clock cycle during which a data word is transferred. It also added a QoS dimension (Section 4.3) and a richer set of commands and protection levels. The Lite variant of AXI4 is cut down, as it has no tags or byte lanes and a burst size always of one beat. AXI5-Lite bridges the gap between AXI5 and AXI4-Lite by permitting response reordering but with single-beat transactions.

Table 3.1 Major predefined AMBA AXI bus standards and profiles. Within each profile, there can be variations in address, data, tag and other bus widths per instance

Profile	Channels	Other nets	Description
AXI3	AR+R, AW+W+B	Tag ID, WLanes	Bursts 1–16 beats
AXI4	AR+R, AW+W+B	Tag ID, WLanes, QoS	Bursts 1–256 beats
AXI4-Lite	AR+R, AW+W+B		No burst transfers. No byte lanes
AXI4-Stream	W		Simplex. No addressing. Unrestricted length
AXI ACE	All of AXI4	AC+CR+CD	Cache coherency extensions
ACE5-Lite	All of AXI4	AC+CR+CD	Single beat. Out-of-order responses

AXI Coherency Extensions (ACE)

The **AXI Coherency Extensions (ACE)** protocol extends AXI with three further channels to support cache consistency. It defines the messages required on these channels to keep multiple caches consistent with each other, using MESI-like protocols (Section 2.4.1). The new channels are:

1. **AC**: The snoop address channel is an input to a cached master that provides the address and associated control information for snoop transactions. This supports operations such as reading, cleaning or invalidating lines. If the snoop hits a line in the cache, the line may have to change state. The type of snoop transaction informs the cache which states it is permitted to change to.

2. **CR**: The snoop response channel is an output channel from a cached master that provides a response to a snoop transaction. Every snoop transaction has a single response associated with it. The snoop response indicates whether an associated data transfer is expected on the CD channel.

3. **CD**: The snoop data channel is an optional output channel that passes snoop data out from a master. Typically, this occurs for a read or clean snoop transaction when the master being snooped has a copy of the data available to return.

With ACE, the AXI bus has evolved into a total of eight channels. As will be discussed in Section 3.4, this is a bit cumbersome for a NoC. A protocol like AMBA CHI (Section 3.4.5) is more appropriate, since a single 'link' carries all the relevant information between one interconnected component and the next. Having many channels is not necessarily bad (especially in low-leakage technology Section 4.6.3): many channels means more nets, which means more bandwidth. Provided these nets see reasonable utilisation, bridge or hub-based AXI remains a sensible interconnect system for medium-complexity systems.

3.1.6 Directory-based Coherence

The snooping approach to cache consistency was presented in Section 2.4.1. For a single level of caching, snooping suffers from a quadratic growth in energy as the number of initiators (cores) is increased because on each cache miss, all the other caches must be checked to see if they contain the line in question. Moreover, the traffic load on a broadcast snoop bus grows linearly and will eventually saturate. One solution is to use multi-level caches and another is to use a directory-based system.

Having multiple levels of cache, either with successively higher density or lower performance, is good in terms of energy use, as is well known and demonstrated in Section 6.6.1. In addition, it also helps with saturation of the snoop bus. Having caches arranged in an **inclusive cache tree** is also good. The root of the tree is the main memory. It is accessed by some subsystems, each with a local cache and with snooping used between these caches. However, the structure repeats inside each subsystem with the snooping being localised to each subsystem. Nesting this structure generates the tree. Every cache is inclusive, so that if a line is present, it is also present in every other cache on the path to the root. Suppose that all the caches have a good hit rate of 95 per cent and a front-to-back clock ratio of 2 to 1 and that the bus width increases with line size. In this case, they will have a transaction rate of 10 to 1 between their front and back sides. Thus, having 4 or 8 subsystems in a snoop group is quite feasible.

Although cache trees scale quite well in terms of coherency and main data bandwidth, their latency increases with the tree depth. The rapid exchange of cache lines between initiators that are a long way apart in the tree is slow. This use case can occur, dependant on operating system policy and software structure. The number of feasible RAM densities and clock frequencies in a silicon process is typically at most three, so having more than three levels of caching to span the gap is not necessary. However, the memory capacity and bandwidth must be continually increased due to the ITRS roadmap and market pressure. With the end of Dennard scaling (Section 8.2), the processor clock frequency is no longer the driving force, so that the number of cores on a SoC has had to increase. Having more cores motivates a wider cache tree. However, using only three or four levels of cache tree requires a wider fanning out at each level, which is not possible since a bus wider than a cache line does not help, and hence, system growth is limited.

Snooping-based coherency can be extended with a **snoop filter** [4]. A snoop filter block reduces the amount of snoop traffic by not forwarding consistency messages that are clearly redundant. The filter can operate in an approximate manner, provided that it does not remove essential messages. Various forms of approximation are possible, including those based on memory addresses or replicated data structures that are not necessarily up-to-date. In general, different cores can have widely disjoint memory footprints, which can be distinguished adequately just by looking at a few bits of the physical address. Combining several different bit fields or hashes from the physical address gives the **Bloom filter** an advantage [5]. Like a set-associative filter, a Bloom filter overcomes the birthday paradox (Section 2.4) by using a number of parallel hash functions, so that the chances of an entry aliasing with another under all the functions is reasonably low.

The main alternative approach is to use multiple independent caches under **directory-based coherence**. The memory map is hashed to some directory servers using bit-field masking. The MOESI status and relevant cache list for a cache line are stored in its directory server. This approach is ideal for NoC-based multiprocessor systems. Cache misses are served by sending an inquiry to the appropriate directory. For a simple read, the server can send its reply to the relevant cache, which can then forward on the data to the reader, minimising latency. Every situation requires a bespoke set of messages to be exchanged, but these are relatively straightforward to implement. The internal data structure of a directory needs to be designed carefully to handle cases where a large number of caches hold the same line. Solutions to this problem were presented in the seminal paper 'An economical solution to the cache coherence problem' [6].

One option is to make an approximate directory. For example, instead of keeping a list of all the caches that hold a line, the directory records one cache, which has the line, and a flag, which indicates whether the line is also in another cache somewhere. If the flag is set, then all caches would need to be snooped. This can be an efficient implementation in a common use case where most lines reside in only one processor's cache at a time. However, directories rely on caches indicating when they allocate and evict lines, whereas with snooping, a clean line can be silently evicted. So, directories suffer from an overhead in signalling these events.

With the move from defining complete bus standards to just standardising the interconnect port on an IP block, a wide variety of innovative hybrids of snooping and directory-based approaches can be implemented without upsetting other aspects of the system design. Open-standard protocols, like ACE and CHI, enable innovations to be made in cache structures and offer a better degree of future-proofing.

3.1.7 Further Bus Operations

The list of bus operations in Section 3.1 included much more than just simple single-word and burst read and write transactions. Today, the vocabulary of operations has expanded, with an opcode space of 32 possible commands becoming commonplace.

Load-linked and Store-conditional Instructions

Older generation atomic instructions, such as test-and-set or compare-and-swap, involve both a read and a write operation. If implemented as separate bus transactions, to avoid pre-emption, the relevant memory system had to be locked for the duration. This restricted the concurrency and could leave a memory bank permanently locked under certain transient failures.

A new approach to providing exclusion between load and store instructions to the same word is provided by the **load-linked** (LL) and **store-conditional** (SC) instruction pair. These can be equivalently implemented in the cache system, the TLB or the memory system. The semantics for a memory-based implementation are that an initiator (CPU core) performs an LL on a memory address. As with a normal load, this retrieves the memory contents at that location, but as a side effect, it also stores the initiator identifier (core number) and the address, rounded to some number of bytes, in some hidden register pair associated with the memory region or bank concerned. The same core then performs an SC to the same address, perhaps attempting to acquire a mutex by placing a one where a zero was found (the test-and-set operation). However, hardware matching makes sure the SC succeeds only if the initiator's identifier and the same address remain held in the hidden pair. When SC fails, no write is made and the initiator is given an appropriate return code. In the Arm architecture, the success or fail return code is loaded into an extra register specified as an operand to the `strex` instruction.

If any other initiator attempts any memory access on the same address, the first core's ID is removed and replaced with a null value. Similarly, if any other initiator attempts an LL instruction on the region of addresses that shares the hidden register pair, the first core's ID is overwritten by the new core's ID. Either way, the LL/SC sequence fails for the first core. This is called **optimistic concurrency control**. It requires clients to retry on failure. Another possible problem is periods of livelock, during which two or more clients compete for the same mutex, each causing another to fail and retry. In a well-engineered system, failure should be rare and cause minimal overhead.

Rather than being implemented in the memory as described, the LL/SC mechanisms can be efficiently implemented in the data cache or address TLB where present (but not in microcontrollers for instance). A data cache implementation of LL loads a cache line as usual, but the line is placed in the MOESI 'exclusive' state (Section 2.4.1). The core ID may be intrinsic to the physical cache slot or may already be held for a shared L2 cache as part of the exclusive tagging. Likewise, the effective address is in the cache tag, save for the last few bits, which will alias. Existing coherency mechanisms, such as snoop requests, can then be used to erase the exclusive state should another core attempt to access the same memory location. Using C structs with padding, or whatever, the programmer should pad out mutex and semaphore variables so that they do not alias by sharing a cache line. Sharing would lead to unnecessary SC failures.

Atomic Interconnect Effects

LL/SC is one option for atomic operations. Concurrency control is tricky because an operation is performed at the initiator but needs to have the semantics of an atomic operation at the target. The obvious alternative is to implement the atomic operation close to the actual storage. This is called **near-data processing (NDP)**, and often has the advantage that a computation can be performed with less data movement, which is the greatest energy user in modern VLSI.

Many atomic operations have **hazard-free and commutable effects**. By 'effects', we mean side effects: i.e. imperative mutations of the surrounding state. By 'hazard-free' and 'commutable', we mean that the order of application is unimportant. For an effect to be commutable, the operator does not need to be commutative since there is no loss of control of operand order. Instead, the operator needs to be associative and cumulative. Standard **far atomic operations** include XOR, MAX, MIN, ADD, BIT-CLR and BIT-SET. Each of these mutates a location held in memory using an immediate operand. Increment, decrement and subtract can all be implemented via the generic ADD command. There can be both signed and unsigned variants of MAX and MIN. The final result from most sequences of these commands is the same, regardless of the order in which the sequence is applied. However, for instance, BIT-SET and ADD cannot be permuted in a sequence, so effects reside in classes within which their order is unimportant. Moreover, test-and-set (or compare-and-swap) operations, despite being atomic, are **not** commutable: they not only cause side effects, but they also return a result that alters the caller's behaviour.

A simple yet useful atomic operation is a multi-word read or write. If write data uses a separate channel from the write command and address, as is the case with AXI and CHI, a **store zero** or multi-word memory clear operation can be usefully implemented. This does not need an operation on the write data channel.

Erasure Data Channels and Poison

Within a SoC, data can be corrupted by a variety of effects, such as nearby electric sparks or atomic radiation, which can cause a **single-event upset (SEU)** (Section 8.2.1). This is typically detected when a parity or an **error-correcting code (ECC)** check fails to tally properly. An **automatic repeat request (ARQ)** is typically used when errors are detected by an on-chip interconnect. This results in the initiator reattempting the transaction. For large burst transfers or streaming channels, either the latency overhead from a retry is intolerable or retries are infeasible. Forward error correction and error concealment are then the only possible options. ARQ is also occasionally known as **backward error correction**.

With **forward error correction (FEC)**, check digits are added to the data such that if a small amount of data is corrupt, any errors can be found and corrected from the redundant information. One of the most common FEC techniques is **Reed–Solomon coding**. The additional check digits are very easy to generate in hardware using shift registers and XOR gates. Checking and correcting are also relatively easy for an erasure channel. In an **erasure channel**, the location of corrupt data are marked. These parts of the data are treated simply as being missing, instead of being corrupt. One technique for marking erased data uses **poison bits**. For instance, in the AXI standard, for each 64 bits of a data bus, an additional poison bit may be conveyed to mark a data erasure. Clearly, it is better to check the data near the final receiver than to check it close to the source and then convey the poison flags a long distance, as the poison flags may become corrupt.

If data have errors to the point where these cannot be corrected or if no FEC check information is present, **error concealment** is used instead. This is widely used for audio and video data. Concealment techniques typically repeat the last accurately conveyed data or fall back to a lower-resolution copy that was also conveyed in case of error. However, concealment is application-specific and should not be embodied in general-purpose hardware.

Persistent Operations

When a **non-volatile store** is used for secondary storage, such as SSD (Section 2.6.1 and Section 2.6.8), memory transfers are made by a specific device driver as part of the operating system's file system. However, increasingly, especially in smartphones and embedded systems, non-volatile memory is used as the primary store and operated on, via the cache hierarchy, by the everyday instruction fetch and load/store operations. Each memory location has a point in the hierarchy at which data can be relied upon to be persistent when power is removed. This is known as the **point of persistence (PoP)**. A write instruction that is supposed to update a persistent store will often be buffered (Section 2.4). This improves performance in general and also reduces write wear on memories that have a limited write lifetime (Section 2.6.8). A **persistent write** transaction is a write that flushes itself to the PoP. It is similar to the `sync` system call in an operating system, which results in software writing out the buffer cache to disk. In contrast, a persistent write transaction operates on the primary store and the implementation is in hardware: write buffers and dirty cache lines are propagated to their persistent store.

Cache Maintenance Operations

Normally, the caches present in a memory system are designed to offer transparent performance gains without programmers or the software being aware. An interconnect carries various forms of **cache maintenance operation (CMO)**. These are mostly generated automatically by hardware, such as an eviction message between caches when a line needs to be moved to the exclusive state. However, others are generated explicitly by software. For instance, instruction cache coherence is not generally implemented in hardware, so with self-modifying code, such as when a dynamically linked library is loaded by the operating system loader, an instruction cache flush CMO must be issued.

A remote cache write or **cache stash** enables an initiator to update the local cache of another component [7]. This is essentially a store instruction, issued by one core, that behaves as though it was issued by another. In simple terms, it does not matter which core issues a store, given that it is issued at least somewhere, since ultimately the target address will be updated accordingly. However, due to write buffering, as discussed above, a store is often not written out to its ultimate destination, especially if another store writes fresher data before the writeback occurs. In many inter-core communication patterns, the cache would behave much better if the core that is to receive a message had stored it in the first place. This is what a remote cache write enables. The data that the receiver wants to examine is already in its cache. The receiver remains free to overwrite it or ignore it, or anything in between. Often, no main memory traffic is needed to support the complete transaction.

Alternatively Translated Operations

A simple SoC may have virtual address spaces for each core and one homogeneous physical address space for everything else. In more complex designs, the MMU(s) may be within the interconnect and multiple address spaces may share the same physical bus segment, especially in a NoC. A common requirement is for a core to issue a load or store instruction that is not translated or which is translated with a mapping that is not the current mapping of that core. A common example is a user-space linked list in an operating system kernel or a smart DMA engine. Hence, an interconnect must support various alternatively translated transactions.

It is common for a system to employ distributed MMUs using a common set of translations. This enables a task to run seamlessly on any one of a set of processors. MMUs cache translations in their local TLBs, fetching a translation from memory only if it is not present in their TLB. If a change to a page table must be applied to all MMUs, then these TLB entries must be invalidated.

Peripheral Probe Operations

The job of allocating programmed-I/O (PIO) base addresses (Section 1.1.3) for each peripheral is not very difficult to automate for a single SoC. However, for a family of similar products, which may have evolved over decades, and for multiple release of the operating system, static management of the memory map is cumbersome. For the cost of very little logic, it is possible to support dynamic device discovery so that a software build can find the I/O devices present on the platform it hits. A variety of techniques is possible, including putting a device data sheet in a ROM at a well-known location. However, this cannot easily cope with pluggable upgrades. If a peripheral's internal register space starts with a few read-only locations, these can easily contain the model and version number of that IP block. They might even contain a URL for downloading the device driver. This solves the peripheral identification problem. However, a boot-time prober or **hardware abstraction layer (HAL)** needs a lightweight presence-detect read operation so that it can attempt to read the identifying information from likely places. Instead of a bus-error interrupt being raised in response to reading from an undecoded address space, a probe read instruction will return a well-known value, such as 0xDEADBEEF.

NoC Maintenance Operations

Most NoC designs require a certain level of management by a control processor. Although PIO to dedicated register files is always the preferred interface for low-level management and configuration, some configuration may be required before everyday PIO can operate. Operations may be needed to establish routing maps (Section 3.4.1) and flow control credit may need to be distributed manually (Section 3.4.4). Null transactions that have no response and null responses that have no command are also commonly needed. These can be used to return one spare credit to a destination node.

3.2 Basic Interconnect Topologies

In an ideal SoC design flow, the topology of the interconnect should be one of the last high-level design decisions. The design should be automated or semi-automated from a traffic flow matrix collected from high-level models. Once the topology is chosen, a system interconnect generator can create all of the RTL, which contains all the component IP blocks and fabric IP blocks (such as bus adaptors and bus bridges) (Section 6.8.2). In this section, we review basic topologies that use arbitrated busses and bus bridges. NoC topologies will be considered in Section 3.5.

The bus in early microcomputers (Section 1.1.3) was a true bus in the sense that data could get on and off at multiple places. SoCs do not use tri-states, but, as mentioned earlier, we still use the term 'bus' to describe the point-to-point connections used today between IP blocks. Our MSOC1 protocol (Figure 1.5) is more practical because there are separate read and write data busses.

One feature that largely remains from the older definition is a lack of spatial reuse. **Spatial reuse** occurs when different busses are simultaneously active with different transactions. For instance, a traditional 32-bit data bus with a clock frequency of 100 MHz can convey 400 MB/s. Owing to the original tri-state nature, such a bus is half-duplex, meaning that reading and writing cannot happen simultaneously. The total read and write bandwidth is limited to 400 MB/s. Today's SoC busses are largely full-duplex, with separate nets carrying the read and write data, so the throughput would approach 800 MB/s if there were an even mix of loads and stores. (In reality, the store rate might typically be 25 per cent or less of all transactions.) In all cases, as more devices are attached to a bus, sharing reduces the average amount of bandwidth available per device. This is in contrast to the switched networks we present later (Section 3.2.3), which enable genuine spatial reuse of the data bus segments. With NoCs (Section 3.5), the available bandwidth increases since more of the interconnect is deployed.

In contrast to a traditional PCB-level bus, interrupt signals do not need to be considered alongside bus topologies. In a small to medium-sized SoC, they can just be dedicated wires running from device to device. However, like other parts of a bus configuration, they need representation in higher-level descriptive files. Moreover, the allocation and naming of interrupts need to be managed in the same way as the data resources in a memory space.

As systems become larger with more processors, the sheer number of interrupt lines becomes difficult to route across a large SoC. Also, off-chip processors may require interrupts to be communicated between chips, although signal pins are at a premium. For these applications, **message-signalled interrupts (MSI)** can be used. In MSI, interrupts are communicated using packets similar to data. In a general NoC implementation, they might use the same interconnect as other traffic, but care must be taken to meet the system's latency requirements for an interrupt.

We will, first, review the area, energy, throughput and latency for various simple interconnect topologies.

3.2.1 Simple Bus with One Initiator

The most simple interconnect topology uses just one bus. Figure 3.12 shows such a bus with one initiator and three targets. The initiator does not need to arbitrate for the bus since it has no competitors. Bus operations are just reads or writes of single 32-bit words. Unbuffered wiring can potentially serve for the write and address busses/channels, whereas multiplexers are needed for read data and other response codes. Following the physical constraints outlined in Section 3.1.1, buffering is needed in all directions for busses that go a long way over the chip. The network generator tool must instantiate multiplexers for the response data paths. As explained in Section 1.1.4, tri-states are not used on a SoC: the multiplexers are fully active or, in some localised cases, may use pass transistors (Section 8.5.1). In a practical setting, the bus capacity might be 32 bits × 200 MHz = 6.4 Gb/s. This figure can be thought of as unity (i.e. one word per clock tick) in comparison with other configurations that we will consider.

3.2.2 Shared Bus with Multiple Initiators

A single bus may have multiple initiators, so additional multiplexors route commands, addresses and write data from the currently active initiator to drive the shared parts of the bus, as shown in Figure 3.13. With multiple initiators, the bus may be busy when a new initiator wants to use it. This requires arbitration between contending initiators, as discussed in Section 4.2.1. The maximum bus throughput of unity is now shared amongst the potential initiators. If a device is both an initiator and a target, such as device 2 in the figure, it has two complete sets of connections to the network.

When granted access to the bus, an initiator may perform multiple transactions before releasing it. One motivation for this is to support atomic actions, as discussed in Section 3.1.7. The bus may or may not support burst transactions or the burst size supported may be insufficient for the amount of data that needs to be moved. As explained in Section 4.3.1, the real-time performance of the system can fall if the bus is not shared sufficiently finely. A system-wide maximum **bus holding time** may be specified to mitigate this.

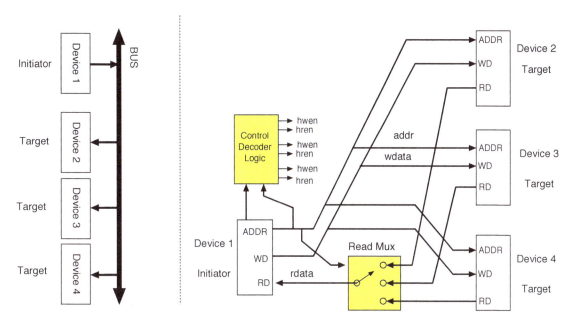

Figure 3.12 A basic SoC bus structure for the MSOC1 protocol. One initiator addresses three targets (high-level view and detailed wiring)

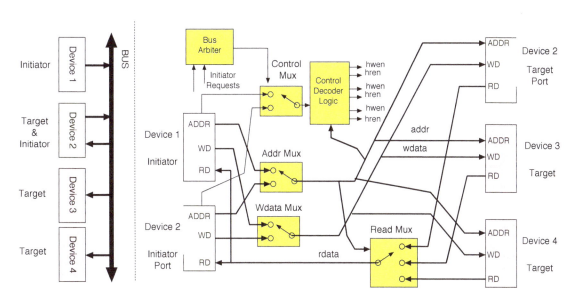

Figure 3.13 Example where one of the targets is also an initiator (e.g. a DMA controller)

3.2.3 Bridged Bus Structures

Two busses can be joined by a **bus bridge**, which potentially allows them to operate independently if traffic is not crossing. Essentially, bus operations received on one side of a bus bridge are reinitiated on the other side. The bridge need not be symmetric: CDs, clock speeds, protocols and data widths can differ on each side. However, in some circumstances, especially when bridging down to a slower bus, there may be no initiator on one side, so that that side never actually operates independently and a unidirectional bridge is all that is needed. In a **multi-socket system**, bridges may interconnect busses on different pieces of silicon.

Two busses potentially means twice the throughput (spatial reuse principle). However, when an initiator on one bus requires access to a target on the other bus, the bridge will convey the transaction. This transaction consumes bandwidth on both busses.

Figure 3.14 shows a system with three main busses and one lower-speed bus, all joined by bridges. To make full use of the additional capacity from the multiple busses, there must be at least one main initiator for each bus that uses it most of the time. Hence, knowledge of the expected traffic flow is needed at design time. However, a low-speed bus might not have its own initiators, as it is just a subordinate bus to the other busses. The slow bus may also use a lower-performance lower-complexity protocol, such as the APB standard. The maximum throughput in such systems is the sum of that of all the busses that have their own initiators. However, the throughput realised will be lower if the bridges are used a lot, since a bridged cycle consumes bandwidth on both sides.

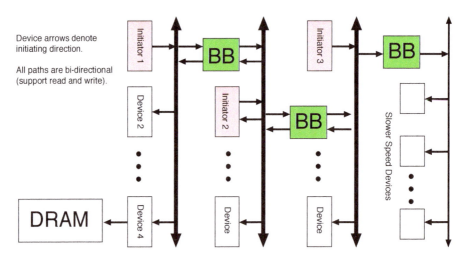

Figure 3.14 A system design using three bridged busses. Each main bus has its own primary initiator (pink), which is typically a CPU, but the bus bridges (green) also initiate transactions

There is a wide potential design space for a bus bridge, but the external connections, shown in Figure 3.15, remain the same. A bus bridge may make address space translations using simple arithmetic. Alternatively, logical functions may be applied to the address bus values. The SoC as a whole might be defined with a unified global address space, but with non-uniform (i.e. different) access times between various pairs of initiators and targets. This gives a **non-uniform memory access (NUMA)** architecture (Section 2.3). For debugging and testing, it is generally helpful to maintain a flat address space and to implement paths that are not likely to be used in normal operation, even if there is a separate debug bus (Section 4.7). However, for A32 systems (with an address bus width of 32 bits), the address space may not be large enough to hold a flat address space. For secure systems, a flat address space increases the attack space. A bus bridge might implement write posting using an internal FIFO buffer. However, generally it must block when reading. As mentioned earlier,

write posting is where the initiator does not wait for a successful response indication from a write transaction. This reduces the amount of time that multiple busses are occupied in old busses. Split busses, with separate command and response ports, do not suffer from this. For cache-coherent buses, the bus bridge may carry coherency traffic or else consistency resolution may be left to the system programmer.

A bus bridge with different bus parametrisations or bus standards on each side acts as a **bus resizer** or **protocol converter**. A bridge with more than two target ports may be called a **hub**, but this term is also used loosely for a demultiplexer with just one target port. By using multiphase protocols, a demultiplexer for commands acts as a multiplexor for responses.

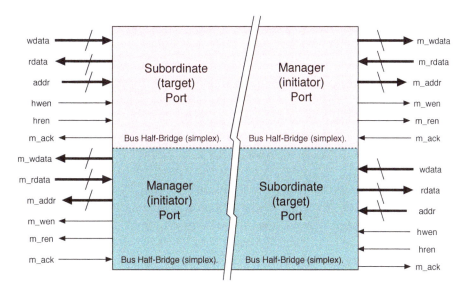

Figure 3.15 Bidirectional bus bridge for the MSOC1 protocol. It has a pair of back-to-back simplex bridges. It could be a single IP block on a single chip, or the two halves could be on different chips with a SERDES (Section 3.8) serial link between them

Figure 2.12 shows an abstract centralised hub labelled the **bus fabric**. This could represent a multi-port bus bridge or a NoC. A **crossbar** switching element enables any input to be connected to any output and for every input to be connected to an output at once, provided at most one input is connected to any output. Figure 3.16 illustrates various circuit structures that achieve crossbar switching. The number of inputs and the number outputs, $N = 4$. The left-hand panel shows a **time-division multiplexed (TDM)** bus that must have a bandwidth of N times the input bandwidth by using a faster clock. Instead of increasing the clock rate, the bit width can be increased by a factor of N. This gives the central and right circuits, which are two ways of depicting the same circuit. In the centre diagram, N^2 **basic crossbar elements** are used. A basic crossbar element can either be in the bar state (shown pink), in which signals are routed from top to bottom and left to right, or be in the cross state (shown green), in which a horizontal signal is redirected to the vertical nets. In the right-hand panel, a broadcaster at each input sends a copy to each output and a multiplexer selects one of the arriving inputs. The broadcasters may be just passive wiring if noise margins can be satisfied (Section 2.6.3).

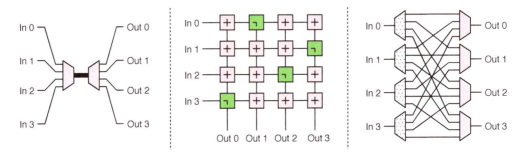

Figure 3.16 Crossbar 4 × 4 connectivity implemented in three different ways: with a high-capacity TDM bus (left), crossbar elements (centre) and multiplexors (right)

A crossbar does not suffer from **fabric contention** (defined in Section 4.2.1), but the limit of one input connected to each output inevitably leads to output port contention. Analytically, the saturated throughput per port for balanced random traffic is $1/e$, but real SoC traffic patterns are never balanced. We return to network dimensioning in Section 3.9 and Chapter 6.

The standard analysis for output port contention is given by

$$\text{Maximum throughput} = 1 - \left(\frac{N-1}{N}\right)^N$$

This is simply a binomial distribution applied to the probability that, for an output port, no input queue has a packet at its head destined for it, given that all inputs have something at the head of their line. Counter-intuitively, this gets progressively worse for larger crossbars. For one input, the throughput evaluates to unity, which is not surprising. For two inputs, it is 0.75, which is obvious, since half the time the two inputs will select the same output and the other output will be idle. For three inputs, it is 0.740 and for arbitrarily large switches, the limit is $1/e \approx 0.632$.

3.3 Simple Packet-Switched Interconnect

As mentioned, protocols such as AXI are classed as **circuit-switched**. However, if we have different channels for requests and responses and the messages are shorter than the time-of-flight along the channel, the distinction between a circuit-switched bus and a **packet-switched** NoC becomes blurred.

Figure 3.17 shows the essential structure of a demultiplexer for a multiphase bus protocol along with the remultiplexer necessarily required to route responses back to the appropriate initiator. It shows a radix-2 component, but typically there will be several inputs, say N. Moreover, there may be M such demultiplexers in an $N \times M$ bus fabric hub (multi-way bus bridge).

There are two main approaches for controlling the remultiplexor. In the tagged-bus approach (Section 3.1.4), the tag width can be expanded (or introduced if not already present), so that the transaction carries the reverse routing information with it. This is stripped off when used. Hence, this is a form of **source routing** (Section 3.4.1), which is perversely introduced by the target of the transaction and which has disappeared by the time the response gets back to the transaction source.

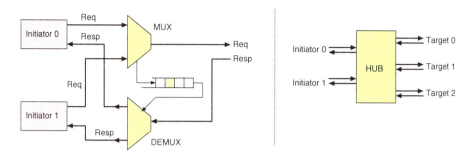

Figure 3.17 Multiphase (split transaction) bus demultiplexor and remultiplexor for responses (left). Three of these structures could be used to implement the 2 × 3 bus fabric hub (right)

The other way, as shown, is to rely on the order of requests and responses being preserved and to store the routing information in a local FIFO buffer. The depth of the FIFO buffer must be sufficient for the number of outstanding transactions expected downstream of this point, but when the requested channel is full, backpressure can be used to hold off further load.

3.3.1 Multi-access SoC and Inter-chip Interconnect

Multi-access techniques, as used in first-generation **local-area networks (LANs)**, use only source queuing. The lack of queues in the switching elements reduces hardware costs. Such structures are sometimes used in SoCs or between SoCs for a high-performance interconnect. The two main topologies are the ring and the folded bus. Ring media access protocols include **register insertion**, **slotted ring** and **token ring**. The links of the network are a shared resource. These different protocols moderate access to the resource, by making traffic wait at the initiator until it can be served. Hence, no further logic is required to implement flow control for the interconnect. Messages are packetised with a header that contains the destination address. Receivers see all traffic and selectively filter it based on the address. Broadcast and multicast are also trivial to implement due to the underlying broadcast nature of the medium.

The multi-access technique can level the delivered load, by limiting the maximum delivery rate at a destination. Beyond that, fine resolution throttling of the bandwidth for a destination is possible using a **virtual channel (VC)** overlay on the slot structure. For instance, a dynamic yet predictable mapping of slots to VCs can be used as presented in Section 4.6.6 of [8]. Each receiver is permanently allocated a particular VC and arrivals at the receiver are limited by the capacity of that VC, which was established during the design of the mapping function.

Since each receiver is allocated a VC number, it needs to look only in slots that have that channel. The mapping establishes the density of slots and hence, the maximum delivery rate to a receiver. Transmitters must use the correct channel number for the addressed receiver. The mapping can be as simple as alternately labelling slots odd and even, to provide two channels and get a 50 per cent throttling of bandwidth. Alternatively, the mapping can be a carefully constructed many-to-one hash function, based on labelling slots using a **pseudorandom binary sequence (PRBS)** (Section 3.8).

Such multi-access techniques are ideal for applications where the destination has a guaranteed throughput. However, if lossless operation is to be preserved, additional end-to-end flow control is required if the response times of the receiver can vary. The network can carry a response indicating whether a message was properly received, but traffic to a busy destination needs to be retried again by the originator as there is no intermediate storage in the network. This means delivery latencies are multiples of the round-trip time. This also requires considering the ordering if multiple transactions are in progress.

A slotted ring has its sequential delay (the number of clock cycles to traverse it) formatted into a fixed number of slots. Each may be full or empty. A transmitter waits for an empty slot and fills it. The receiver may free up the slot or use it for a response to the transmitter. The **pass-on-free rule**, if used, requires the transmitter to empty the slot and pass it on to the next potential transmitter, making sharing fair. If the transmitter directly reuses the slot or the receiver reissues the response, other access control protocols are needed [9]. The Knights' Corner processor from Intel, and many succeeding designs, notably used a pair of counterrotating slotted rings for cache consistency.

A register-insertion ring places its message in a shift register that it inserts into the ring to send the message. When the message has rotated all the way around, it can be removed. A token ring passes a specific non-data word around the ring. A transmitter that needs to send, holds the token and sends its message instead, putting the token at the end of the message.

Ring networks are suited well to simple broadside pipeline register stages, as ring links do not require low-level flow control due to the media access protocol. If it is known that it is rare for a destination to be busy, instead of making the transmitter send again, a simple alternative is to stall the whole ring for one or more clock cycles. Sadly, this can lead to a deadlock if the reason for the destination being busy is not going to go away while the whole ring is stalled. A better multi-access network in this respect is a **folded bus**.

3.3.2 Multi-access Folded Bus

Figure 3.18 shows two topologies for a folded-bus multi-access network. The basic behaviour is very similar to that of the ring topology. The multi-access shared medium has a transmit region that feeds into a receive region at the fold, with any amount of simple broadside registering being allowable in each branch, except for the tree-form transmit region, which requires a backwards handshake net. The switching elements forward traffic from either input that is not idle. In the linear form, the elements typically give priority to existing traffic over new traffic from the local end point. In the tree form, the elements may use round-robin arbitration. A higher priority will then be given to any transmitting station that is closer to the root if an unbalanced tree is used.

Without hop-by-hop flow control along the transmitting half of the linear form, sources furthest from the fold would effectively have priority, since they see less competition for bandwidth. Switching elements are, by design, not allowed to buffer traffic and cannot stop it from arriving. The tree form, however, typically uses backpressure, but the paths are logarithmic only in length and this path can

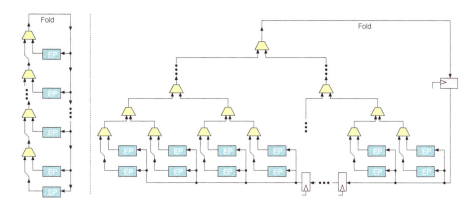

Figure 3.18 Two folded busses that have similar component counts. For each, the number of switching elements grows linearly with the number of end points (EP). The linear form (left) is suitable for multi-chip use, but the tree form (right) has lower latency. The receive half of the tree form often has a tree structure running exactly parallel to the transmit half, but here it is shown flattened to almost a bus

tolerate some delay through synchronous logic, without the network losing performance overall. This approach was used in the reliable Hubnet LAN [10]. It avoids excessive combinational path build-up. Alternatively, fully registered FIFO stages can be added to break the paths (Section 6.3.4). For the linear form, media access control, if needed, is typically achieved using request tokens piggybacked on the forward traffic to establish a path for higher stations to instruct lower stations to defer sending. This was the basis for the Dual-Queue/Dual-Bus LAN standard [11].

A folded bus has twice as much wiring as a simple ring, but the presence of the break enables any part of the transmit half of the bus to be stalled without interrupting the delivery of traffic to the receiving side. This eliminates a major form of deadlock, as discussed in Section 6.6.3.

3.4 Network-on-Chip

A **network-on-chip (NoC)** consists of end points, switching elements, domain-crossing elements and bus resizers. These are interconnected by nets known as NoC links. The main forms are listed in Section 3.6. If **cache coherence** and **virtual memory (VM)** are required, quite a large set of different types of data have to be conveyed. As well as both logical and physical addressed data transactions, cache coherency traffic and additional transactions are needed just to set up and manage the NoC. Circuit-switched architectures use spatial isolation with separate busses for each of these traffic types, whereas NoC designs multiplex all forms of data onto a few channel types. This means caches and VM translation units (Section 2.2.1) can be freely connected to the NoC along with traditional IP blocks, such as CPU cores and memory.

Above a certain minimum size, NoCs lead to scaling gains over circuit-switched busses. The principal advantage of packetised communication is better utilisation of the physical channels while still providing data isolation and QoS guarantees. VCs (Section 3.4.2) are commonly used, leading to even better utilisation of the physical nets and an ability to handle disparate traffic requirements without deadlock.

In a complex SoC, quite often parts of the SoC will have their own local interconnect. Such a local interconnect follows traditional design patterns and is not part of the NoC architecture. Protocol adaptors are needed to map circuit-switched busses, such as AXI, on and off the NoC. This is a strict requirement if IP blocks have AXI ports, but increasingly, IP blocks have native NoC ports that conform to a standard such as AMBA CHI (Section 3.4.5).

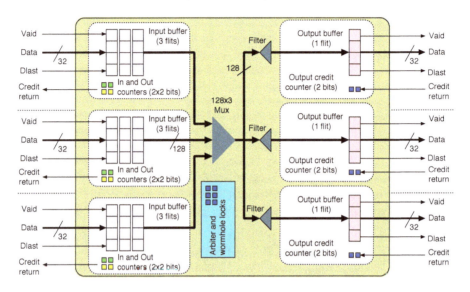

Figure 3.19 A radix-3 switching element for a NoC using a broadcast bus at 4× the link bandwidth and credit-based flow control

Based on a broadcast bus implemented as a crossbar (left-hand structure in Figure 3.16), Figure 3.19 shows a simple switching element for a baseline NoC. The element is 3 × 3 and uses 128-bit flits on 32-bit busses. A **flit** is a unit of flow control, where the 128 bits would be conveyed in 4 back-to-back words on the 32-bit bus. (All the terms in this illustrative summary are defined elsewhere in this section.) The element has an input buffer with three flits' worth of input storage per port. Each output port has 2-bit credit counters to hold the credit available (0–3) in the successive inputs. No VCs are used in this simple example, but per VC output credit would be needed if VCs are used. The input queues are organised as ring buffers with 2-bit in and out pointers. Wormhole routing is used (Section 3.4.1), so that routing is locked until the last word of a flit is indicated with the Dlast signal. The routing locks and arbitration logic are in the central block. Switching is performed with a 128-bit bus that has four times the bandwidth of each input port, which might look as though it is more than enough for full throughput. The bus width is sufficient for a whole flit to be transferred atomically. However, the throughput will be degraded (under theoretical random traffic) by output port contention to $0.704 \times 4/3 = 0.938$ of the full load, assuming an infinite output queue size. A finite output buffer can reduce this slightly, but this is negligible compared with the intrinsic inaccuracy of the random traffic destination assumption. (The illustrated output buffer has one word pending and one word currently being serialised, so its capacity is one or two depending on how you count it.)

Figure 3.20 illustrates a 2-D unidirectional torus topology fabricated with radix-3 elements. This is intrinsically deadlock free, since traffic can turn in only one direction (anticlockwise at bottom left).

The input buffers that are directly connected to end points will likely be simplified in reality, with the queue structures shared between the element and the end point.

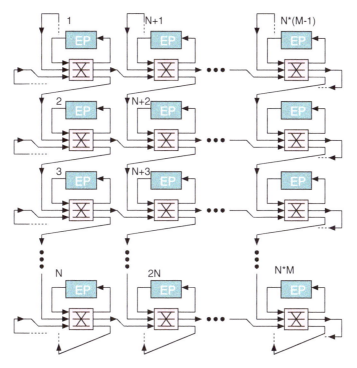

Figure 3.20 Example of a NoC fabric using radix-3 switching in a unidirectional torus mesh

The aim of a NoC design is low latency. If the parallelism available in an application is limited, which is often the case, the application performance degrades reciprocally as latency is increased. However, pipeline stages are required to close timing for the longer links within the design (Section 8.12.16). Hence, the links of a NoC must be designed to attain efficient re-timing stages. As explained in Section 3.4.4, this leads to a preference for **credit-based flow control** instead of the standard synchronous interface used in AXI. Different parts of a NoC have different traffic densities, and the width of the most appropriate data bus may vary accordingly. Hence, resizers, which either increase or decrease the width of a physical bus (aka channel), are needed at various points, perhaps associated with CD and power domain (PD) crossing. There are a large number of feasible designs and arrangements of the building blocks. These need to be connected and configured appropriately to give a solution with the desired **power, performance and area (PPA)** (Section 5.6). NoC design optimisation is discussed in Section 3.5 and Section 6.2.

3.4.1 NoC Routing and Switching

Conventional busses essentially route traffic based on an address. There is notionally one **address space** associated with a bus (Section 1.1.1). The same address will denote the same device or location, regardless of which bus master issues the request to that bus. However, the same address issued to different busses may well have different meanings. At a higher level of system design, such reuse of the address space may increase the complexity of management and cause potential confusion during debugging. The advice for A64 systems is to avoid such reuse, unless it is really needed for efficiency.

For a NoC, it may be unavoidable to have multiple active address spaces. Moreover, not all transactions or transaction phases carry a conventional address. Address spaces can be virtual or physical, and there can be considerable overlap in the addresses used in different address spaces. Hence, for NoC routing, every destination on the NoC has its own network identifier (NoC ID). The initiator of a transaction must have a way to select the target NoC ID. This can be hardwired or held in a local map implemented as a few PIO registers or a small RAM.

Routing is the process of deciding the path across the NoC that a transaction will take. Switching is the process of physically conveying the transaction and its response over the NoC. Routing may be performed in one of four main ways:

1. With **static destination routing**, the transaction carries its destination NoC ID. Each switching element can apply a simple function, such as bit-field extraction, on the destination address, which specifies which output link to use.

2. With **dynamic destination routing**, the transaction again carries its destination NoC ID, but switching elements have greater freedom over route selection. For instance, a message going north-east can sensibly be forwarded north or east at the next step. The choice is typically determined by which output port is currently idle or is based on a maximal matching of input to output ports for the next time slot.

3. With **source routing**, the route is explicitly put in the transaction by the source as a list of intermediate nodes or output port numbers for an element. Each switching element then removes an item from the node list and follows that item.

4. With **virtual-circuit routing**, a route is set up and stored in the switching elements. The transaction carries a virtual circuit number or locally scoped **routing tag**, which is looked up at each switching element and used to select the next step of the path. Although virtual-circuit routing is not commonly used for on-chip networks, it is mentioned here to emphasise that it is not the same as a VC, which is defined shortly.

If there is only one path between the source and the destination, the routing decision is moot. In dynamic routing, there can be an ordering issue for legacy protocols in which order must be preserved. Super-scalar architectures, however, exploit the additional performance available by ignoring order and deploy specific mechanisms, such as memory fences, where necessary.

In reality, many current NoC designs are comparatively simple. They use only one address space and use static routing based on bit-field extraction of the target address. This results in minimal hardware complexity and is optimised well during logic synthesis (Section 8.3.8). Response routing is based on similar direct decodes of the source NoC ID that was placed in the command by the initiating bridge.

Although very wide busses are relatively common in modern VLSI, certain transactions require multi-word transfers over a bus. These could be large payload reads and writes or any transaction that crosses a narrow bus (e.g. of 32 bits or less). As a result, a phase of a transaction (request, response, snoop, etc.) can quite often take multiple clock cycles to be delivered. A large transaction will always be split up into multiple flow-control units known as **flits**. These are the atomic units of exchange between switching elements. However, even one flit can contain more bits than the bus width. By definition, a flit is delivered without pre-emption by another (on the same VC). A multi-word flit is typically forwarded between switching elements using **cut-through** or **wormhole routing**. Figure 3.21 (left) illustrates cut-through operation. Cut-through means that the head of a flit has already left the element on the egress port before the tail has fully arrived. Alternatively, the elements can be **store-and-forward** elements, meaning that the entire flit is received into an internal buffer before its head emerges from the element. This results in a **packet-switched** network like the Internet. Store-and-forwarding increases latency and buffer requirements, but suffers less from deadlocks. A NoC design generally does not use store-and-forward elements but instead solves the deadlock problem. Both types of routing experience a structural hazard in that two flits cannot share the same link (without VCs) at once. Figure 3.21 (right) illustrates that link contention can lead to a deadlock, as will be discussed shortly.

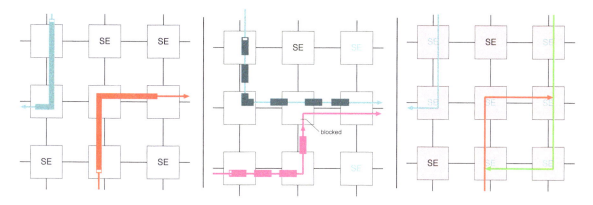

Figure 3.21 Illustration of cut-through routing on a 2-D mesh NoC (left), wormhole operation (centre) and potentially deadlocking routes (right). The thin black lines are the NoC links, which are bidirectional. The thick coloured lines are the routes chosen for a packet. The white marks indicates the end of a packet

Cut-through cannot apply for flits that are just one bus word in length, and a registered switching element will intrinsically use store-and-forwarding. For longer flits, the routing information needs to be at the start. With **wormhole routing**, as shown in Figure 3.21 (centre), the switching element loads an active path register when the head of the flit is encountered. The value persists while the remainder of the flit is forwarded. The path register is cleared at the end of the flit (shown with a white marker). Hence, the routing is not pre-empted and the flit is never split. It is not necessary for the unit of flow control to be the unit of wormhole routing. Another common design point is for the wormhole to last for the duration of a phase of a transaction.

3.4.2 Virtual Channels

A **virtual channel (VC)** is a **time-division multiplexed (TDM)** slice of a physical channel or link. The physical link might carry two to ten VCs. These normally share a resource using round-robin arbitration (Section 4.2.1) rather than statically allocating slots, which would be too wasteful. To allow demultiplexing, the word width can be extended with the VC number that is active. For a multi-word flit, an additional field is added.

VCs, when used judiciously, help in improving performance and optimising wire utilisation. Different VCs can be used to provide fine-grained sharing of the fabric (sub-transaction level). They commonly support a differential QoS and can help to prevent deadlocks. VCs preserve isolation, both between separate classes of traffic and between requests and responses. The isolation of requests from responses also helps to avoid deadlocks, as explained in Section 3.4.3. However, the use of VCs, in general, leads to an increased number of buffers, which, in turn, increases the silicon area and power consumption. An inefficient VC assignment can lead to NoCs that are at least an order of magnitude inferior in terms of PPA. Hence, an optimal allocation of VCs is crucial in NoC design and an important part of NoC synthesis.

A crucial step when designing an interconnect is to assign VCs to traffic classes so that its PPA meets the design objectives while also avoiding deadlocks. The VC assignment problem for a NoC is tightly coupled with topology generation and routing. However, combining VC assignment with topology generation further complicates an already complex problem, and it is difficult to solve both effectively. Traditional methods for VC mapping usually involve a greedy algorithm or use a different VC for each QoS level. These methods are inefficient. If we have to use a constructive design approach, which cannot iterate (Section 6.2), it is better to perform VC assignment after topology generation [12, 13]. However, generating a topology without partitioning the traffic into VC classes usually results in a NoC that has a suboptimal PPA, as both the silicon area and net count will be higher. The co-dependent nature of these two NP-hard problems poses a major challenge in creating efficient solutions for both of them, so, as with most aspects of *design space exploration*, an iterative optimisation technique is applied (Section 6.2).

3.4.3 NoC Deadlocks

An interconnect can experience various forms of deadlock. A deadlock arises when a path with a circular dependency is activated such that each participant is waiting for the next to do something. Figure 3.22 shows one typical pattern that can arise with wormhole and cut-through routing. This is a **fabric deadlock** since two (or more) messages, both present in the NoC switching fabric, are stopping each other from being delivered. The figure shows radix-3 switching elements in a 2-D grid. The bidirectional links between each pair of elements either do not use VCs or else both the red and green transactions are using the same channel. Hence, there is structural contention (Section 6.3), as at most one transaction phase can be active on each direction of a link. The red and the green transactions are deadlocked: each is blocked by the other at the parts shown as dashed lines. Red is waiting for green at element B0 and green is waiting for red at element A1. The example is small and

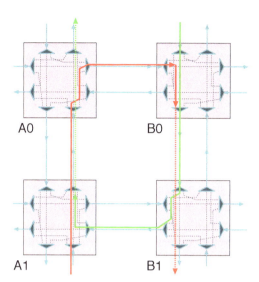

Figure 3.22 Four elements in a 2-D mesh. Two transactions, red and green, are in a fabric deadlock, since unconstrained cut-through switching with wormhole routing has allowed each to block the other. The dashed parts cannot complete

both transactions are taking unusually circuitous routes, but it demonstrates how the problem can arise with unconstrained routing.

The main mechanism for aviding deadlocks in current interconnect designs is **restricted-turn routing** [14]. Figure 3.23 (left) shows the eight named turns possible in a 2-D mesh. Four are clockwise turns and four are anticlockwise turns. A clockwise cyclic dependency cannot form unless all four clockwise turns are used. Similarly, an anticlockwise cycle requires all four anticlockwise turns. A simple blanket prohibition on certain patterns of turns is typically used. There are many possible policies that vary in complexity and suitability for different numbers of dimensions. Examples are:

- **Dimension-ordered routing**: The various dimensions of movement are made in an overall order. For instance, in 2-D, traffic should always move as far as it needs in the Y (north/south) direction before moving any distance in the X (east/west) direction. Figure 3.23 (centre) shows the four turn directions then allowed. This is known as **Manhattan routing**. The turn direction can also be restricted in torus-like topologies, such as making negative movements first.

- **2-D spanning-tree routing**: A spanning tree is imposed over the mesh. Only links that are part of the tree are used. This is very wasteful (albeit widely used for LANs), but is potentially useful due to redundancy, as the tree can be recomputed after a failure. A variation is **up–down routing**, in which a rooted spanning tree is imposed over the mesh. Traffic must always move first along up links (towards the root) and then only along down links.

- **2-D three-turn routing**: In each of the clockwise and anticlockwise turn sets, one possible turn is prohibited. This allows a dynamic choice from a richer set of paths compared with the static routing of dimension-ordered routing.

- **General prohibition**: Given a regular topology with any number of dimensions or an arbitrary topology, the allowable set of turns at any given element is judiciously chosen using static analysis such that full connectivity is retained. Thus, certain turns are removed from each element. In the absence of VCs, this does not involve storing additional information at an element. On the contrary, it involves removing the multiplexor inputs and nets that would have provided that turn. An advanced approach would take the traffic matrix (Section 3.5.1) into account and implement different restrictions for different VCs.

A deadlock can also arise at higher levels. All deadlock-avoidance strategies are based on understanding the dependencies between various actions. The most direct way to avoid a higher-level deadlock is to use physically separate interconnect resources for conveying traffic that might interfere. VCs provide logical separation instead, which is also sufficient. The interconnect is then logically composed of a number of independent subnetworks. The individual subnetworks need to be deadlock free, to avoid a fabric deadlock, but, as just described, this can be determined by a static analysis of each in isolation and without knowledge of how the traffic on different VCs is correlated.

The next higher source of deadlocks is due to **phase dependency**. Multiphase transactions have separate command and response phases in which the response phase is triggered by a command. AXI (Section 3.1.5) is predominantly a request–response protocol wherein there is an implicit dependency between the request receipt at the egress port and the triggered response from the same port. With AXI on wide NoC links, either the command or the response can be multi-word. The command is multi-word for burst writes and the response is multi-word for burst reads. However, it is never multi-word for both. Moreover, the response is generated only after full receipt of the command. An interphase deadlock on uncached AXI is, therefore, unlikely. A protocol that supports long burst reads with explicit instead of implied addresses would have overlapping command and response phases and could potentially allow phase-dependent deadlocks.

Figure 3.23 (right) shows how phase dependency can become manifest as an illegal turn, despite strict north–south first routing being used. We show two transactions between four peers. Both the request and response phases are quite long, giving significant opportunity for interference. The red path shows initiator I1 at s00 making a two-phase transaction on target T1 in the opposite corner. The response is shown in green. However, before the response arrives, a second initiator, I2, starts to use the required link between s22 and s21. Its traffic is shown in blue. The link is now tied up since wormhole routing is being used and the requests and responses are not on separate VCs. Moreover, this second transaction also becomes blocked since target T2 needs to use the link from s01 to s02 for its response, but that link will not become free until initiator I1 has sent the end of the first transaction. Inevitably, limited buffering is available in the switching elements and targets, so a deadlock arises as soon as every resource along the contending paths is occupied.

The essence of the problem is that the targets have effectively implemented a bottom right anticlockwise (BRA) turn, thus defeating the north–south first policy, which does not allow BRA. Many application programs avoid deadlocks by chance, due to their traffic routing patterns or short

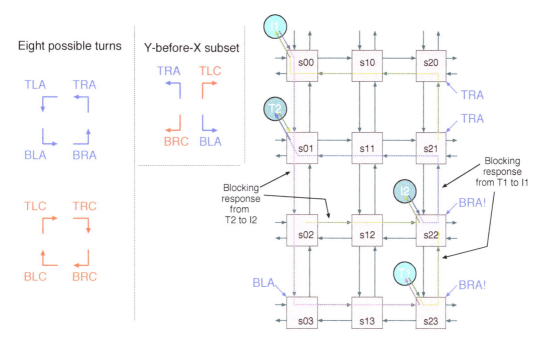

Eight possible turns

TLA   TRA

BLA   BRA

TLC   TRC

BLC   BRC

Y-before-X subset

TRA   TLC

BRC   BLA

TRA

TRA

Blocking
response
from T1 to I1

BRA!

BRA!

BLA

Blocking
response
from
T2 to I2

Figure 3.23 The eight possible 2-D turns (left), the allowable 2-D turns with Y-before-X (north–south first) routing (centre) and an example set of turns used by two transactions that obey the north–south first global policy but still manage to deadlock owing to interference between requests and responses. The turns that violate the global policy are marked with an exclamation mark. BLA: bottom left anticlockwise; BRA: bottom right anticlockwise; TRA: top right anticlockwise; TLA: top left anticlockwise; BLC: bottom left clockwise; BRC: bottom right clockwise; TRC: top right clockwise; TLC: top left clockwise

transaction lengths, but a small edit to their code, or just running alongside another incompatible application, could lead to a deadlock.

As well as between the phases of a transaction, dependencies can arise when complete transactions need to be cascaded, such as when the front and back sides of a data cache or TLB (Section 2.2.1) share the same fabric. Cache miss operations typically require a fresh transaction to be issued and need to complete before the triggering transaction completes. To remove this next higher level of potential deadlock, we use a behavioural traffic specification, such as the one in Figure 3.24. This shows a dependency between two ports, since the receipt of the read phase of a transaction at port u_S0 triggers a new read transaction at u_M0. It is important to note that one transaction triggering another transaction is not the same as a transaction needing a further transaction to complete before it can complete itself. The former is common and does not lead to a deadlock of the first transaction since it has completed. The latter must be captured as an explicit inter-transaction phase dependency and considered during deadlock avoidance.

Fully factoring all the higher-level phase and cascade transaction constraints into a scheme like turn restriction can become fragile or infeasible. The resulting design can be highly sensitive to an undocumented dependency. The approach often preferred is to use different VCs for the different phases of transactions. Given that many transactions are fairly simple client–server operations, the universal use of a large number of VCs could seem extravagant. However, the set of potentially active VCs on a hardware link is easy to collate statically given the routing basis. Hence, post-processing to

```
1  Profiles:
2      t0: { src: u_M0, type: readRequest, avg: 10, peak: 100, req_beats: 1,
3             resp_beats: 4, qos: 0, lc: false, dst: u_S0 }
4      t1: { src: u_M0, type: writeRequest, avg: 10, peak: 94.3, req_beats: 4,
5             resp_beats: 1, qos: 0, lc: false, dst: u_S0 }
6  Dependencies:
7      # Receipt of readRequest at u_S0, triggers a transaction at u_M0
8      d0: { from: u_S0.readRequest, to: u_M0.readRequest }
9
```

Figure 3.24 Sample behavioural traffic specification containing a load profile and a transaction phase dependency

remove support for unused VC code points on a link can be applied as a design optimisation step. Of course, VCs also provide QoS isolation.

No amount of interconnect engineering can stop a programmer writing software that deadlocks. Hardware support for this highest level of deadlock typically amounts to a bus timeout on a transaction, implemented at the initiator. More heavy-handed is the watchdog timer (Section 2.7.4)!

3.4.4 Credit-based Flow Control

Flow control is the process of matching sending and receiving rates between components (Section 3.1.3). As mentioned, for a NoC, the unit of flow control is called a **flit**. This term is loosely used for other units of transfer over a NoC, such as a unit that is routed homogeneously or a unit that is not pre-empted by any other.

Also, as pointed out in Section 3.1.3, the standard synchronous interface cannot be re-pipelined with just the addition of a broadside register since the forward and reverse handshake nets will be offset in opposite directions in the time domain. Instead, a FIFO structure must be used, which is more complex than a simple broadside register owing to the presence of handshake logic. Moreover, various FIFO designs exist, which either introduce bubbles, waste capacity or introduce undesirable combinational chains of handshake logic. A FIFO bubble is a clock cycle where data could potentially move in or out of the FIFO, but is not allowed to owing to the desire to avoid combinational paths through the control circuitry (Section 6.3.4). For instance, if new data were enabled to enter a long FIFO chain structure as soon as a word was read out at the far end, there would have to be a combinational reverse path from the output handshake back to the input ready signal.

Long combinational paths reduce the achievable clock frequency (Section 4.4.2). Thus, the hardware complexity can become troublesome and it is difficult to select a good balance between FIFO complexity, the potential for bubbles and combinational path delays in the handshake logic.

Instead, many NoC designs use **credit-based flow control**. In this type of control, the source keeps track of how much receive buffer space is available at the destination. A source cannot send a flit unless it has at least one credit. When links are activated, each receiver must provide at least one credit to each sender that might send to it. A receiver must guarantee that it can accept all the flits for which it has issued credits.

Credit-based flow control can be operated hop by hop (link-level) only, but also end to end for a source/destination pair. If multiple senders share one receiver, the receiver may dynamically reallocate the available credits according to priority or observed recent behaviour, but each sender must be granted at least one credit or else a separate request-for-credit mechanism must exist. Under end-to-end flow control, a sender that sends to multiple destinations will maintain separate credit accounts for each destination, whether the traffic shares a common egress VC or not.

A basic hop-by-hop setup is illustrated in Figure 3.25. An up/down counter at the sending end of a link (the source) is initially loaded with a count value, known as the credit. This is equal to the capacity of the sink to receive data without overruns. The sink must have an effective FIFO buffer or equivalent of that capacity. Data forwarded between the components is simply qualified by a valid net, but the source may send only when it has credit greater than zero. The source decrements its credit count for each word sent. A credit-return mechanism notifies the sender when it may increment its counter. This can be a single net in the return direction, as shown, or a **piggyback** field in traffic that is returning in the other direction. However, relying on traffic in the other direction can cause cyclic dependencies and hence, a fabric deadlock, so such mechanisms must be designed with great care. An explicit backward flit can also be used to establish the initial credit or retract it.

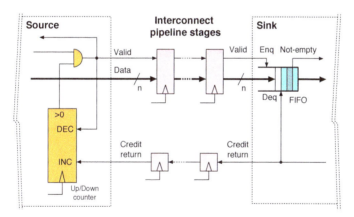

Figure 3.25 One possible structure using link-level credit-based flow control, showing tolerance to pipeline stages in the interconnect nets. The forward and return paths need not be matched in delay terms

In the above description, the unit of flow control, the flit, was a word, equal in width to the data bus. If a flit has more than one word, it retains that fixed size and a fixed-size packet containing the several words are sent per credit.

A crude form of flow control that also avoids combinational paths is called **Xon/Xoff flow control**. A binary value is conveyed over the return path, which turns the source on or off. This technique is also commonly used on RS-232 serial ports (Section 2.7.1). Both on-SoC and for the serial port, the reverse path can be either a physical wire or a token sent via piggyback in the reverse direction traffic (if duplex). Compared with credit-based control, Xon/Xoff requires receiver buffering proportional to the round-trip delay. Since it is coarse-grained, it can also increase the burstiness of the data. Nonetheless, it is used in some NoC designs.

3.4.5 AMBA 5 CHI

The AXI family of protocols is not ideal for a NoC. AXI has a different structure for reading and writing whereas a homogeneous NoC fabric is symmetric. Thus, the same data nets should equally well be able to carry write data from an initiator on the left of the chip as read data to an initiator on the right of the chip. Arm designed the **AMBA Coherent Hub Interface (CHI)** protocol for NoC applications, although it can also be used for an over-engineered point-to-point connection. CHI uses credit-based flow control.

Compared with AXI, CHI was a fresh start at a bus definition. It provides greater support for NoC systems. It has a four-layer protocol stack, as shown in Figure 3.26. The top layer, called the protocol layer, generates and processes transactions at end points and implements end-to-end flow control. The network or routing layer packetises protocol messages into flits and manages routing over the NoC. The second-bottom layer is the link layer. It provides hop-by-hop flow control between connected components (end points or switching elements). The bottom layer is the physical layer, which controls the nets between components. Commonly the flit size in bits is some multiple, N, of the physical bus width. Each flit must then be transferred as N separate words over the bus. These are called **phits**.

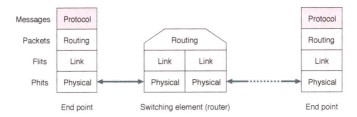

Figure 3.26 Two end points interconnected via some number of switching elements. The AMBA 5 CHI protocol layers are shown

In CHI, each NoC component that is connected to a neighbour has a so-called link in each direction. The links are simplex and consist of CHI channels. All channels can operate at once, so overall we have a full-duplex bidirectional port. Credit accounts operate for each individual channel, so that a transmitting channel cannot send a flit unless it has a credit. A single link carries all forms of transaction, whether reads, writes or any other type listed in Section 3.1.

The left-hand panel of Figure 3.27 shows a minimal CHI implementation, connecting a requester (initiator) to a completer (target). Transactions are issued on the request channel (TX–REQ). If an issued transaction has associated data, such as the data for a write transaction, those data are conveyed over the TX–DAT channel. Responses to transactions are received on the response (RX–RSP) channel. If the responses have data, such as a read, the data are conveyed over the RX–DAT channel. These four channels are sufficient for a simple initiator or target that does not participate in cache coherency.

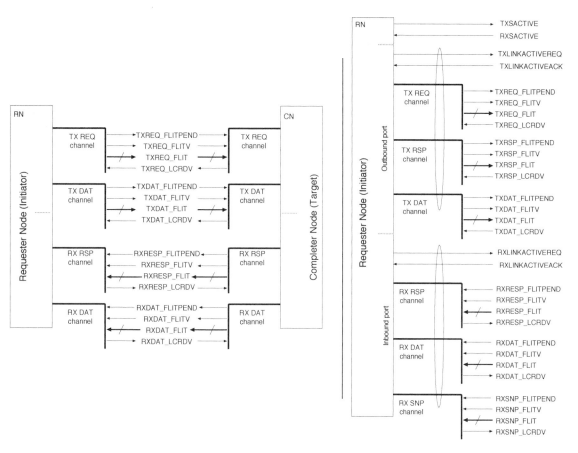

Figure 3.27 A minimal application of the AMBA 5 CHI specification between a requester and a completer (left) and full net-level details of the six channels found on a more-typical request node (RN) (right)

The right-hand panel of Figure 3.27 shows the full port found on a typical CHI requester node (RN). The top two nets form part of a start/stop protocol that is exercised as a port joins or leaves the NoC. When a credit-controlled channel is being activated or deactivated, care must be taken with the credit tokens. Each channel of the port has a further pair of nets to implement the start/stop protocol. On activation, the transmitter must be granted some credit. On deactivation of a transmitter, credit might be lost and a buffer space in the receiver might become permanently wasted. An explicit deactivate phase in the link management protocol avoids this problem. During deactivation, a transmitter sends NOP flits until it has run out of credit. The receiver should not issue credit returns during that phase. The figure shows six channels. The transmit (TX) group has request (TX-REQ), response (TX-RSP) and data (TX-DAT) channels. All three channels transmit data. The receive (RX) side, likewise, contains three receiving channels, called response (RX-RSP), data (RX-DAT) and snoop (RX-SNP).

Each direction of a link has more than one channel for three principal reasons:

1. **Deadlock avoidance**: Application-level transaction dependencies are complex and varying. They can be statically enumerated for simple IP blocks, such as a PIO register file. Thus, it is theoretically

possible to undertake a whole-system deadlock analysis, but this is generally infeasible for anything other than small systems with simple components. Moreover, the analysis may have to include the behaviour of the application code, which is highly undesirable. It is much better if the hardware works as expected for any application code. Hence, as explained in Section 3.4.3, it is better to keep transaction phase responses separate from the request phases, so that static deadlock avoidance mechanisms can be deployed for each separately, without having to worry about how they interact with each other. The multiple physical channels in CHI are not sufficient to avoid all deadlock scenarios, so they must be augmented with a moderate degree of phase separation using VCs.

2. **Loose coupling**: The data phase for a burst read or write transaction is much longer than the request or response phase of a typical transaction. Some transactions are data-less (e.g. a reset command). Loose coupling between phases maximises the available parallelism (this is the same reason that write data and write addresses have separate channels in AXI).

3. **Spatial reuse**: Having more channels increases the throughput for a prescribed maximum word width. The sizes of the data busses for each channel can be precisely tuned to the widest word they need to carry.

Looking at the net level, FLIT is the main data-carrying bus of a channel. For the data channels, its fundamental width is 128, 256 or 512 bits, augmented with about 50 further protocol bits plus any additional parity and poison bits. For the other channels, the FLIT bus tends to be in the ballpark of 100 bits wide. This will depend on the NoC topology and will be higher for larger NoCs with larger node indexes. Implementations may also add further **AXI user** sideband bits as required.

Going in the same direction as a FLIT are the FLITPEND and FLITV nets. Each channel also has a LCRDV net that sends signals in the reverse direction. FLITV is the forward data qualifier net. It holds true in any clock cycle when FLIT has a valid word. The FLITPEND signal is asserted one clock cycle in advance of FLITV. It wakes up the clock gating (Section 4.6.9) at the receiving end of the link. LCRDV is the credit-return net. It operates as illustrated in Figure 3.25, by returning a credit token to the sending end on each clock edge where the link credit is asserted.

3.5 Advanced Interconnect Topologies

Designing an interconnect involves choosing a topology and then deploying the various interconnect canvas components and configuring them by choosing bus widths. An important first decision is whether to use a NoC, a centralised hub or one or more bridged busses. Often a combination of all approaches will be used. The design will be greatly influenced by the floor plan of the chip (Section 8.6) and the needs of the PD and CD.

Over the past decade, on-chip communication networks have seen rapid changes. These have been mostly driven by a desire to customise on-chip interconnects to enhance PPA (Section 5.6). However, optimising the PPA has become more complicated due to the many changes in communication requirements across generations of chips along with pressure on **time-to-market (TTM)**. While bus-based and centralised fabric designs have been the traditional approaches for on-chip communications, due to the demands for scalable solutions with tight PPA and quick TTM, designing such systems has become complicated. The problem is further compounded by the unavailability of tools and the use of back-of-an-envelope and heuristic solutions, which lead to poor PPA and over-engineering.

Whether designing a custom bridged-bus structure or a NoC, the same traffic engineering models and synthesis procedures broadly apply. A combination of manual and automatic tooling is possible at all levels, from choosing the overall topology to setting minor configuration options for each interconnect component. Manual design typically uses an IP-XACT based GUI editor (Section 6.8.2). The Socrates tool from Arm is an example. One procedure for automatically generating the topology is presented in Section 3.9. However, in modern SoC flows, whatever the mixture of automatic and manual design, we expect the output from each automated tooling level to be amendable in a graphical editor. Regardless of how the high-level design was created, we certainly expect all the interconnect details to be designed by a **system interconnect generator** that also generates documentation and device driver header files and automatically configures the test procedures (Section 8.8.1).

3.5.1 Traffic Flow Matrix

Standard NoC topologies based on geometric shapes, such as a ring or torus, are briefly reviewed at the end of this section, but with today's tools, the only reason for using a standard shape is a lack of prior knowledge of the expected traffic flow matrix. This use case still arises for certain general-purpose chips, such as accelerators for scientific computing (Section 6.4).

A **traffic flow matrix** contains the actual bandwidth and burstiness of traffic between each initiator and target IP block. It will not generally be symmetric since, for instance, a typical memory location is read three times more often than it is written. Moreover, some cores will not interact with some peripherals. If traffic flows share a common resource, the burstiness is used to compute the **effective bandwidth** (Section 4.3.3). Policers (Section 4.3.4) can be installed as canvas components if the link bandwidth that would have to provisioned to otherwise avoid starvation and under-runs would be very high. For any interconnect design, the performance is highly dependent on the characteristics of the offered traffic load. Although important as the basis for design, a traffic flow matrix is not sufficient for simulating or verifying a design. Instead, synthetic traffic generators and real applications can be used to create an actual workload. The traffic generated can be measured and combined to form or refine the traffic flow matrix. If a design is to handle all loads envisaged, the maximum throughput and burstiness for these loads should be used at each point where traffic flows meet and contend.

Although adding pipeline stages enables higher clock frequencies and hence, a higher interconnect throughput, pipeline stages also add to the latency. It is important to include a synthetic workload to model closed-queue systems (Section 4.3), in which a task is performed by a fixed number of threads or a fixed super-scalar factor (Section 2.2) and the offered load decreases as the round-trip latency increases. This is because each closed-system worker will not create a new interconnect transaction before its previous transaction is complete. Without this, it is easy to think that a high throughput design that also has high latency (e.g. because traffic is using otherwise free, circuitous paths) will perform well.

Traffic models that can comprehensively capture all possible traffic behaviour in on-chip networks across any design are critical for rapid development and for meeting TTM requirements. However, there are several challenges in designing traffic models and generating network traces for the detailed analysis of NoC performance that is need to achieve an optimal design.

The synthetic traffic models typically used for NoC modelling generate uniform random flows, bit-reversal flows, transpose flows and so on. These are abstractions of communication mechanisms across a broad class of applications. They exercise the interconnect using regular, predetermined and predictable patterns. Although they tend to be simplistic, they are valuable for stress-testing a network.

Table 3.2 Some (simplified) synthetic traffic generation vectors and their descriptions

No.	Name	Description
1.	Rate: open loop Flows: all to all Length: 8 Spacing: Regular	Average rate injection from all ingress ports to all egress ports of 8 byte payloads, with no burstiness
2.	Rate: open loop Flows: all to one Length: 8 Spacing: Regular	Average rate injection from all ingress ports to one egress port, with no burstiness.
3.	Rate: saturated Flows: all to all Length: 8 Spacing: Regular	Injection at peak capacity from all ingress ports to all egress ports, with no burstiness.
4.	Rate: open loop Flows: all to all Length: 8 Spacing: Random	Average injection rate with random delays between injections, from all ingress ports to all egress ports.
5.	Rate: open loop Flows: all to all Length: Variable Spacing: Regular	Average injection rate from all ingress ports to all egress ports, with variable length packets.
6.	Rate: closed loop Flows: all to all Length: 32 Spacing: Regular	Ingress port only generates a new message after previous response. All packets are long (32 bytes).

Example synthetic scenario vectors and their descriptions are presented in Table 3.2. These embody key spatio-temporal characteristics using four independent control parameters: injection rate, flow matrix, payload size distribution and ingress burstiness. These parameters may be set to generate a wide range of traffic profiles. A **saturated source** is one that generates a new transaction as soon as enabled by the handshake mechanisms. A closed-loop source has some maximum number of transactions outstanding and when this is reached, it waits for a previous transaction to complete before generating any further work. An open-loop source generates traffic at a prescribed average rate, λ, as described in Section 4.3.

A generation framework can simultaneously apply any number of vectors. Its parameters are dependent on minimal and abstract input information about the system-level design, available even in the early phases of network design. The input mainly comprises network end points and the communications between end points. It is agnostic to system design and its interconnect topology.

On the other hand, there are few realistic traffic traces for any chip architecture, especially with the rapid pace of chip development. Most standard application benchmarks are suitable only for large-scale homogeneous architectures. These include realistic traffic benchmarks like SPLASH-2 [15], Parsec [16] and MediaBench [17], which can simulate traces from actual applications. Processing systems meeting diverse application requirements are being developed. These have highly application-specific architectures and organisations. The associated NoC infrastructures, traffic characteristics and volumes are significantly affected by the design goals. However, to record the matrix, these applications can be run on instrumented ESL virtual models of the SoC (Chapter 5).

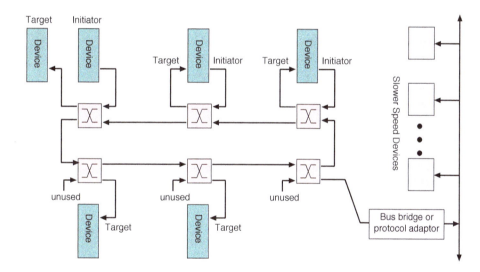

Figure 3.28 A ring network. This is a low-complexity NoC structure

Network-on-chip: Simple Ring
Figure 3.28 shows a unidirectional **ring topology**. The closed loop has two-by-two switching elements. Each switching element is registered; hence, the ring network can easily span the chip. It can go off-chip as well, provided it comes back on again. A higher-radix switching element allows more devices to be connected at a station. A 'station' is the traditional name for an access node on a ring. Alternatively, several stations can be placed together. A protocol-converting bridge is needed to adapt to a conventional bus.

Ring switching elements give priority to traffic already on the ring. They use **cut-through** switching to minimise latency (Section 3.4.1). A ring has local arbitration in each element. Global policies are required to avoid deadlocks and starvation or else tokens and slot-full markers can be carried on the ring, like the first generation of local-area networks (LANs). Like those LANs, a ring will typically use **source buffering** and **backpressure**: a source is held up until there is sufficient network capacity to send a message. Hence, there is not always a requirement for queuing in an element. However, there are significantly different consequences between holding up a request and holding up the acknowledgement parts of a split transaction. Holding up a requesting channel with backpressure reduces the applied load and overall throughput. This is a good aspect. However, holding up a response can lead to a deadlock (Section 3.4.3); hence, it is generally necessary to consider the static priority of responses over requests.

For a simple unidirectional ring, traffic will travel halfway round the ring on average, so the throughput compared with a simple bus is 2×. Counter-rotating rings are sometimes used. Each link is bidirectional and two separate rings operate at once, one in each direction. Traffic is then sent in the ring direction with the shortest number of stations to the destination. Traffic will now travel one quarter of the way round the ring, so the bandwidth multiple is 4×.

A two-level hierarchy of bridged rings is sometimes a sweet spot for SoC design. For example, the Cell Broadband Engine uses dual rings [18]. At moderate size, using a fat ring (wide bus links) is better than a thin crossbar design for the same throughput in terms of power consumption and area use, as shown in Section 6.6.3.

Network-on-chip: Torus Topology

A rectangular mesh network that wraps at the top to the bottom and at the right edge to the left edge has, mathematically speaking, a **torus topology**. A unidirectional torus is illustrated in Figure 3.20. It can be constructed in the same way as a ring. Indeed, a ring is a degenerate torus with one dimension set to unity. The switching elements in a bidirectional torus need to be radix 5, with connections for the local traffic and mesh connections north, south, east and west.

Network-on-chip: Hypercube Topologies

Another interconnection topology used, especially in a supercomputer interconnect, is an n-dimensional cube, also known as a hypercube. A 2-D square when logically extended to 3-D becomes a cube. As shown in Figure 3.29, a cube projected to 4-D becomes a tesseract. The nodes in a square have two edges; those in a cube have three edges and those in a tesseract have four edges. Such **hypercube** structures provide defined relationships between the number of nodes and the average number of hops to get to a random other node. The diameter grows with a low exponent (such as a square root) in the number of dimensions, while the number of nodes grows exponentially, such as squaring with the hypercube. A hypercube has the smallest diameter for the number of nodes.

High-dimensionality hypercubes are not too hard to wire up at the supercomputer rack scale due to the freedom of the 3-D world. However, a silicon chip is essentially 2-D with a little bit of extension into the third dimension from multiple wiring layers. Hence, pragmatic regular on-chip topologies tend to use a torus structure with a low density of **long links** that span multiple mesh hops in one step. These tend to approximate a hypercube of dimensionality 2.25.

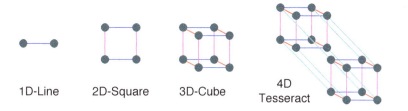

Figure 3.29 Regular cubic structures with 1, 2, 3 or 4 dimensions. 5-D and above are hard to draw

Network-on-chip: Classic Switching Structures

Classic network switching theory was developed for telephone networks, but exactly the same approaches can be used on-chip. Using a complete crossbar network to connect n inputs to n outputs has area cost n^2 and is prohibitive above moderate values of n. There are a number of well-known switch wiring schemes, with names such as Benes, Banyan, Clos, delta, express mesh and butterfly. These vary in terms of the complexity and fabric contention factor (also known as blocking factor) (Section 4.2.1). Each network pattern consists of approximately $n \log(n)/k$ switching elements, where there are n inputs, the same number of outputs, and each switching element is a crossbar of radix $k \times k$. The butterfly pattern, also known as a **shuffle network**, is illustrated in Figure 3.30 (and also Figure 6.50 for the fast Fourier transform).

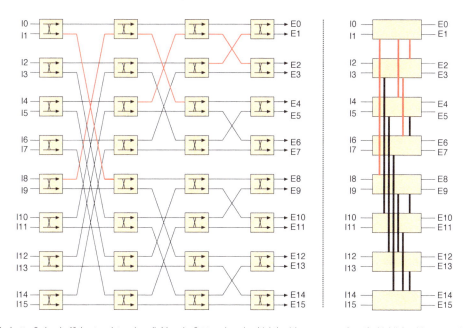

Figure 3.30 The butterfly (or shuffle) network topology (left) and a flattened version (right), with some example paths highlighted for comparison. The vertical links in the flattened form are bidirectional

Figure 3.31 illustrates the delta wiring pattern. The figure shows 12 switching elements, each of which would contain two 2-input multiplexers; hence, the total cost is 24 multiplexers. A crossbar would require 7 equivalent multiplexers for each output, making a total of 56. (You could argue that higher-radix multiplexers should be used for a crossbar, but multiplexer fan-in is bounded in any technology and eventually the full crossbar becomes infeasible.) Hence, the delta pattern provides full complexity at the cost of some fabric contention. For instance, the links highlighted in blue make it clear that there is only one path by which initiators 1 and 6 can reach targets 6 and 7; hence, both routes cannot be active at once. A switch controller is aware of these constraints and can take them into account as a side condition when creating a schedule (succession of I/O matchings) that overcomes the main problem of output port contention (Section 4.2.1), which arises even for a full crossbar. The delta and butterfly have the minimum number of elements for full connectivity, whereas richer patterns, such as Clos, folded Clos and Benes (not illustrated), have at least one additional layer of switching elements to provide routing diversity [19]. This reduces fabric contention.

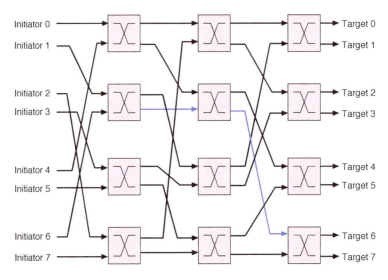

Figure 3.31 Example of an 8 × 8 switching fabric that uses radix-2 elements and the delta wiring pattern. Interchanging the initiators and targets is equally valid

In real-world use, elements with a radix greater than two are typically used. The sub-quadratic growth yields greater return for larger n. These regular structures provide as many inputs as outputs, but a NoC typically does not need as many initiators as targets, so a symmetric switch system can be over-provisioned for small networks, but they scale up well [20]. The overall interconnect may use a hierarchy, with local crossbars interconnecting low-latency clusters. Arm has the **Coherent Mesh Network (CMN)** product family [21]. A typical use would interconnect eight local clusters, each with eight Arm-8 cores. Multiple clusters can be interconnected using CXIX and CCX links (Section 3.8.2) with memory coherency spanning the whole system.

The physical layout of a switching network does not have to match its logical topology. Clearly this is impossible for more than three dimensions. For a torus, a 2-D layout is relatively easy, but the flyback wiring arising from a straightforward 2-D mesh projection, as was shown in Figure 3.20, is undesirable. The solution is to apply an interleaved logical to physical mapping, such as 1, 7, 2, 6, 3, 5 or 4. Coalescing several switching elements into one higher-order element can also be a good idea. Figure 3.30 shows a butterfly network (left) that is implemented (right) from large blocks that combine a complete row of elements. This is called a **flattened butterfly topology** [22]. That paper, although quite old now, contains a good introduction to switching network design.

3.6 Interconnect Building Blocks

SoC interconnect uses various building blocks, such as switching elements, width resizers, FIFO buffers, policers, protocol bridges, power and clock domain converters (PCDCs), pipeline elements and so on. These are collectively called **canvas components**. Many of them are generated by synthesis tools that macro-generate specific instances from stored templates or synthesise them from protocol specifications [23]. Each canvas component has some ports that accord to a parametrised instance of the relevant bus or port standard. Design rules prescribe what sort of inter-port wiring is allowed. For any given bus standard, a modular *kit-of-parts* approach is normally taken, so that virtually any component can be connected directly to any other, subject to design rules and appropriate reparametrisation. The two common patterns are one-to-one (e.g. initiator to target) and single-source multiple-destination broadcast.

Specifically for a NoC, the main interconnect components are as follows:

1. **Switching element**: A typical NoC switching element (aka router) is a crossbar. Hence, it has no internal fabric blocking but suffers from output port contention. It has a strictly limited amount of flit buffer and hence, buffer allocation schemes must also be carefully implemented. A switching element arbitrates at two levels: packet and link. At the packet level, which is the upper level, an incoming packet must be routed to a pair composed of an output port and a VC number. Using wormhole routing, once a VC is locked after arbitrating, it stays locked until the end of the packet. The lower level is the link level. In a per-output VC multiplexer, this level chooses which VC will send next. The two levels interact and decisions must be based on the available credit, priority and possibly other QoS and traffic shaping factors. At the higher level, higher priority traffic should be given an expedited service, i.e. served first (Section 4.3.2). However, the lower level of arbitration can often be implemented as simple round-robin arbitration over the available VCs that are ready to send because the granularity of sharing is much finer, which largely overcomes head-of-line blocking.

2. **Protocol bridge**: These convert one protocol to another. For a NoC, the outside world protocol is typically circuit-switched (e.g. AXI) or some other protocol. It will tend to have a different behaviour and flow control paradigm compared with the internal NoC protocol, which is packetised. A specific protocol bridge adapts between the NoC and external protocols. For a protocol with more than one channel in a given direction, like AXI, these may map to the same VC (e.g. write data sharing with write address). Like a switching element, a protocol bridge may make scheduling decisions, but the search space is much smaller or zero, owing to the lack of output port contention.

   The processing of credits is also different. In some implementations, credit is available for consumption in the same cycle in which it arrives. Others avoid combinational timing paths by delaying credit use or by returning it within a clock cycle.

3. **Resizer**: These convert between links with differing bus widths. One design approach is that a flit is always one word on the parallel bus, whatever width is locally in use. Hence, a flit will contain a different number of bits on different-sized busses. Moreover, the resizer must also do a currency conversion for credit-based flow control. A similar situation arises when moving to a different clock frequency with the same word width. Alternatively, a flit can contain a fixed number of bits across the SoC and occupy multiple consecutive words on all but the widest busses. Also, the flit sizes in different channels, such as request and response, are independent.

In certain designs, the resizing logic is within a switching element. The resizing operation can potentially be placed on either the input or the output port of the element. As discussed in Section 4.3.2, an **input-buffered switch** has intrinsically lower performance than other designs, but this can be mitigated by using a higher bandwidth through the multiplexers that perform the actual switching. The best site for a resizer that transitions to a faster link rate is on the input to the element. This again accelerates the transfer rate through the switch, potentially freeing up the output VC for arbitration earlier. However, such a design may limit the maximum clock frequency at which the element can operate in a real design. Hence, an alternative design of having separate resizing logic is also used.

4. **Pipeline elements**: These are inserted in a credit-based NoC to ensure timing closure on long paths. These are often **uncredited buffer stages**, which operate at the same clock on both sides and act as store-and-forward elements in each cycle. There are three design approaches:

   ▪ **Unbudgeted simple pipeline stage**: A broadside register across all forward nets is shown in Figure 3.25. Independently, the reverse path may or may not be pipelined. The correctness is unaltered by either of these steps, which was a primary advantage of the credit-based approach. Although this stage ensures timing closure, the round-trip latency is extended by one or two clock cycles: one for data and one for the credit return. The higher latency will degrade the throughput if there is insufficient credit available. If the total issued credit is C and the number of clock cycles in the round-trip loop is R_{TT}, then the maximum average throughput of single-word flits on the link is C/R_{TT}. Unbudgeted pipeline stages do not necessarily degrade link performance, however. Typical traffic is bursty. The peak rate is unaffected by credit-based flow control and the mean can often be considerably less than the peak. Moreover, for multi-word flits, the parameter R_{TT} needs to be divided by the flit length, so that a single pipeline stage has proportionally less effect.

   ▪ **Budgeted simple pipeline stage**: The performance degradation compared to the sustained average rate from an unbudgeted pipeline stage can be alleviated by supplying additional credit. However, the initial credit cannot be simply increased without penalty: it must be matched with an additional flit buffer at the receiver. This replication of the additional logic is not a severe consideration in practice: the distance that the data moves is almost unaltered and hence, energy use hardly increases.

- **Fully credited stage**: A FIFO stage that lends its capacity to the surrounding credit loop is shown in Figure 3.32. The output side behaves like any credit-controlled source, with its associated up/down counter to hold its credit. As always, the stage can send data only when it has credit. However, the stage passes this credit back to earlier flow points and issues credit for its own capacity. This example has a capacity of unity, so its initial credit of one is held in a single synchronous S/R stage that is set during a system reset. The credit is passed backwards after a reset. If there is an optional D-type in the credit-return path, this FIFO stage is fully registered.

Although a fully credited stage is the most complex, it solves all the problems. Moreover, the complexity it adds can largely be removed from the final receiver. In effect, the logic at the receiver is spread out over the forward path. The buffering is distributed across a wider physical region, which makes it more tractable for the P&R tool to meet the timing. The number of stages to include will be finalised during design optimisation and revisited after the negative slack analysis (Section 4.9.6). The spreading of the stages can be controlled during placement with the same algorithms used for D-type migration (Section 4.4.2). These use force-directed techniques where the number of stages is the quanta of force. The switching-element port assignment can also be remapped under the same framework to minimise wire crossing. A two-place fully credited FIFO buffer has lower complexity than two one-place FIFO buffers due to the shared credit counter, but this might mean the difference between $2 \times 3 = 6$ and $1 \times 4 = 4$ flip-flops, which, even considering supporting gates, is hardly significant.

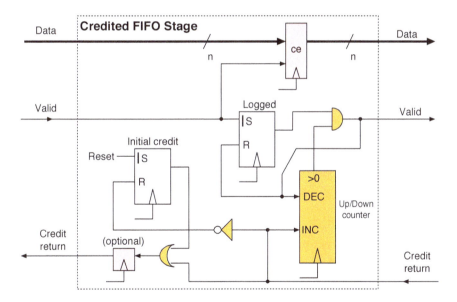

Figure 3.32 A one-place pipelined FIFO stage using credit-based flow control. A multi-place FIFO stage would replace the synchronous S/R flops used for the initial credit and backlogged state with counters, which result in better density than cascading one-place stages. (The vertical line on the S input denotes that setting has priority over resetting when both are asserted)

3.7 Long-distance Interconnects

A long-distance interconnect spans multiple CDs and PDs and can span between chips using gigabit links. A long-distance interconnect that supports remote initiators or other forms of DMA is often required to be cache consistent.

3.7.1 Domain Crossing

A **power domain (PD)** is a region of logic that is adjusted in supply voltage or power gated together. A **clock domain (CD)** is a region of synchronous logic with exactly one clock. A domain boundary arises where either of these changes. Sometimes they both change on the same boundary. The SoC floor plan (Section 8.6) defines which component instances are in which domain. Nets cannot simply pass between domains without care. PDs are either explicitly managed by the SoC user or managed automatically in hardware (Section 3.7.5). On the other hand, CD crossing, which we discuss first, is always expected to be automatic between any powered-up regions.

Multiple CDs are used for two main reasons:

1. **Power and performance folding**: Above a certain frequency, high-frequency logic requires more power than lower-frequency logic. Hence, a good design often has a larger amount of lower-speed logic than needed for a compact alternative that is clocked faster. This is part of the folding in time versus folding in space argument presented in Section 4.4.2. A good example is the L1 and L2 cache system of a processor; the trade-off is analysed in Section 6.6.1. Hence, it is energy efficient to operate parts of a circuit with a lower-frequency clock than is needed elsewhere. Another example is the DRAM subsystem. DRAM chips are available at standard clock frequencies that may not be appropriate for the main SoC. Alternatively, the desired DRAMs may not be available during the factory production window and substitution with a DRAM with a slightly different frequency is forced, but this needs to be done without changing the frequencies for the rest of the design.

2. **Physically separate clocks**: Systems must continue to operate when networking cables, such as Ethernet, are disconnected. Thus, each such system has its own clock generator. Data are normally driven down a networking cable (or fibre or radio link) using the local clock of the transmitter. Hence, it will not be accurately synchronised with the local clock at the receiving end. Quartz crystal oscillators are generally used as local clocks (Section 4.9.4). Two crystals each nominally of 10 MHz will actually be different by tens of hertz and the error will drift with temperature, supply voltage and crystal age.[1] As explained in Section 3.8, a transmitter's clock is recovered at the receiving end using some amount of digital logic. Hence, there are two CDs in the receiver and the received data must be re-timed against the local transmit clock.

---

1. Atomic clocks are far better, of course. Their accuracy is higher than one part in 10^{12}, but they are still not accurate enough to avoid rapid metastable failure. Moreover, it is infeasible to incorporate an atomic clock in everyday equipment.

The second situation is genuinely asynchronous, whereas the first is often handled using harmonic clocks, as explained shortly (Section 3.7.4).

3.7.2 Metastability Theory

An input from an asynchronous CD is bound to violate the registers in the receiving CD from time to time. This cannot be avoided, but it must be mitigated. As will be illustrated in the flip-flop timing parameter Figure 4.12, a transparent latch or D-type must not be clocked when its input is changing.

A system that is balanced so that it will not move under its own volition, but which will locomote (move under its own power) when slightly disturbed, is said to be **metastable**. A pencil exactly balancing on a razor's edge is a typical example, as illustrated in Figure 3.33 (left). We expect it to flop to one side or the other, but how long this will take depends on how finely balanced it was initially. A bistable device is essentially two invertors connected in a ring. It has two stable states, but there is also a metastable state. The three states are where the transfer function (the heavy line in Figure 3.33 centre) intersects the $y = x$ line (blue line). The metastable state is the middle one.

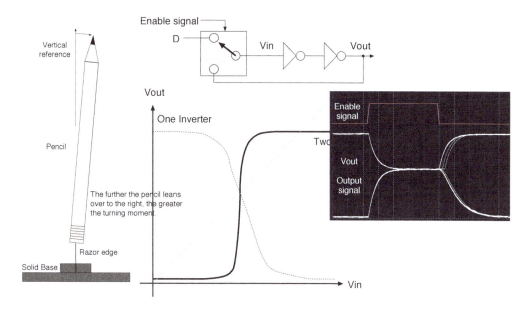

Figure 3.33 Metastability illustrated by a pencil balancing on a razor's edge (left). The essential structure of a transparent bistable (latch) and a transfer function (centre). The gate signal and measured responses from a transparent latch with an input wired to a voltage source close to the metastable point (right)

If the metastable behaviour takes more than a clock cycle to resolve in a receiving flop, further flops connected to its output have the potential, in theory, to become metastable too. The principal mitigating technique is to use a high-gain flip-flop to receive asynchronous signals but not to look at their output until one whole clock cycle later. With a fast transition band (high gain) in the transfer function, the probability that the next flop will be violated can be reduced to make it unlikely in the lifetime of the universe. This is sufficiently reliable.

The oscillogram on the right of Figure 3.33 shows metastable waveforms at the output of a transparent latch whose input is approximately at the metastable voltage. If a D-type is violated by clocking while the input is changing, it can likewise be set close to its metastable state. It will then drift off to one level or the other, but, sometimes, it will take a fair fraction of a clock period to settle. The settling times are given by an exponential distribution and could, in theory, last many clock cycles.

A related problem is that a parallel bus that crosses between CDs will have a skew. It cannot be guaranteed that all receiving flops will make the same decision about whether it has changed since the last receiver clock edge.

3.7.3 CD-crossing Bridge

Therefore, a domain-crossing bridge is needed between CDs. This is often called a **CD-crossing bridge (CBRI)**. The generic name for either a power or clock bridge is a **PCDC bridge**. The basic domain-crossing technique is the same whether implemented as part of an asynchronous FIFO buffer, a bus bridge or inside an IP block (e.g. network receive front end to network core logic). Figure 3.34 illustrates the key design aspects for crossing in one direction, but generally these details will be wrapped up into a carefully designed library block, like the domain-crossing FIFO buffer described elsewhere (Section 6.3.4 and Figure 6.7). Data signals can also suffer from metastability, but the multiplexer ensures that these metastable values never propagate into the main logic of the receiving domain.

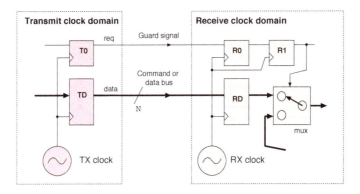

Figure 3.34 Generic structure of a simplex CBRI. Parallel data are reliably sent between CDs

Figure 3.34 demonstrates the following CBRI design principles:

- Use a one-bit request signal whose transition is a guard or qualifier signal for all the data signals going in that direction.

- Make sure all the data signals (from TD to TR) are changed one cycle in advance of the guard.

- Pass the guard signal through two registers (R0 and R1) before using it (metastability avoidance).

- Use an expanded width data bus (large N) because crossing operations cannot occur every cycle.

Here is the receiver-side RTL:

```
input clk;  // Receiving domain clock

input [31..0] data;
input req;
output reg ack;

reg [31:0] RB;
reg R0, R1;
always @(posedge clk) begin
    R0 <= req;
    R1 <= R0;
    ack <= R1;
    if (R1 && !ack) RB <= data;
    // ack typically not sent back to sender
```

An asynchronous signal should be registered in exactly one flip-flop and its output should be further registered before being fanned out or otherwise used.

A simplex CD-crossing bridge carries information in only one direction. Carrying data in both directions is commonly required, so a duplex CBRI is formed by a pair of contra-directional simplex clock bridges. Because the saturated symbol rates are not equal on each side, we need a protocol with insertable and deletable padding states. These are known as **justification symbols**, and they have no semantic meaning. For a processor interconnect, this typically means that the protocol must have elidable idle states between or within transactions. The elidable symbols in Figure 3.34 are nominally conveyed in every clock cycle in either domain where the request net does not transition from zero to one. For the standard synchronous protocol, the justification symbols are simply the clock cycles where either ready or valid is deasserted.

3.7.4 Harmonic Clocks

When crossing truly asynchronous CDs, 100 per cent utilisation is impossible. The simple four-phase handshake outlined in the RTL above limits utilisation to 25 per cent at best. A two-phase protocol, where data are transferred each time the guard net is toggled, restores this to closer to 50 per cent. Other protocols can get arbitrarily close to saturating one side or the other, provided the maximum tolerance in the nominal clock rates is known. However, since the clock frequencies are different, 100 per cent of one side is either less than 100 per cent of the other or else overloaded. Hence, some overhead in justification symbols is always required. Their minimal density can be computed from the maximum clock tolerances. Latency remains an issue due to the need for additional register delays to overcome metastability. With a 1:1 clock ratio, in many real designs the domain-crossing latency can be as high as 3 or 4 cycles in one direction. Lower-latency domain crossing, down to one cycle, can be achieved using **harmonically locked clocks**. These are also known as **ratioed clocks**.

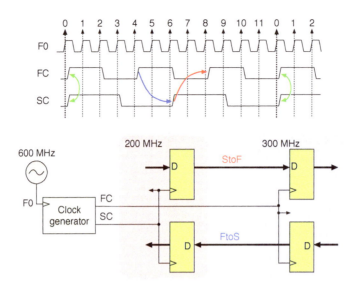

Figure 3.35 Timing diagram (top) and a basic structure for two systems that use harmonically locked clocks (bottom). Relative edge timings that require tight phase control are highlighted

Figure 3.35 shows the timing pattern and hardware arrangement for two CDs that have **harmonically locked clocks**. In this example, these have a prescribed ratio of exactly 3:2 with no relative error. Hence, there is no relative phase progression and the timing pattern is fixed. Other natural number ratios are commonly used, each with its own repeating pattern of relative phases. A ratio of 3:2 can also be quoted as 1.5 to 1. For instance, an Arm 9 **snoop-control unit (SCU)** specifies ratios such as 1, 1.5 and 2.5 to 1 as the clock ratio between the L1 and L2 caches.

The clocks for each domain are locked to a master source. Our diagram shows an oscillator at the lowest-common-multiple frequency, but alternatives based on phase-locked loops (Section 4.9.5) are commonly used to avoid the need for excessively high master clocks. Even though there may be a frequency error in the primary reference clock, a common reference results in zero *relative* frequency error in the derived clocks: the ratio is exact.

As well as having an accurate frequency, the generator outputs need to be tightly controlled in terms of relative phase for simple domain crossing. Data can be transferred on every active edge of the lower-speed clock. The blue and red arrows show pattern offsets at which data can easily be transferred in the fast-to-slow and slow-to-fast directions, respectively. The green arrow shows a pattern offset where data are being transferred in both directions at once, but this requires very tight phase margins to be maintained, akin to the level of clock skew tolerable in a single domain to avoid shoot-through (Section 4.6.9).

An alternative to having tight phase margins in the generator and distributor is for the crossing logic to select dynamically the best phase of its clock edge to use for the transfer. This is a long-term decision made at boot time or when clock frequencies are adjusted. Changing the clock edge can alter the effective number of pipeline stages in the path, so protocols that are amenable to this, like AXI and CHI, must be used, and the change of edge made only when the bus is idle.

Although significant design care is needed, with harmonically locked domains, the risks of metastability are eliminated and domain crossing can be achieved with a lower latency because there is no need to separate the guard and the qualified signals into different clock cycles.

3.7.5 PD Crossing

As well as crossing CDs, an interconnect encounters PDs, where, at any instant, some parts of the SoC can physically be turned off (Section 4.6.10) or be in a sleep state. Data cannot be forwarded through powered-down regions, so an interconnect structure must be aware of PD control policies. There are two styles of operation:

1. The powered-down structure is brought up before transactions are issued.

2. The transactions are issued and this brings up the powered-down structures.

The former is typically managed by a software programmer who is aware of the requirements. In case a mistake is made, the hardware should be structured to make the bus transaction abort. The power isolation barrier will return a failed transaction code, which will raise an interrupt on the issuing core. The latter can be handled by Arm's P-channel protocol, or the power disconnect protocol that accompanies BVCI as part of the OCP family.

The P-channel and Q-channel protocols from Arm [24] use an asynchronous four-phase handshake (Section 3.1.3) to request a subsystem to change its power mode. Figure 3.36 shows the nets for the P-channel variant. The PACTIVE output bus from a device reflects its current power mode. Typically, only a few modes are supported, such as off, sleep and active, so only a few bits are needed. A request to transfer to a new power mode starts with the power controller encoding the requested mode on the PSTATE nets and asserting PREQ, as the first two steps in a four-phase handshake. The device then responds with an active state on either of PACCEPT or PDENY. This response is held until the controller removes the request. Because only one handshake net transitions at a time, independent of any clock, the P interface can be implemented safely between CDs.

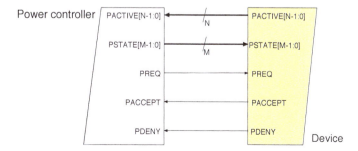

Figure 3.36 Net-level view of the AMBA P-channel interface for device power control

For an automatic power-up when a transaction is approaching, the P-channel can be driven in hardware. The device will be brought to a sufficient state to handle the bus transaction. For instance, a PIO write to a configuration register does not require the whole device to be awake. There could be orders of magnitude difference in power use for a subsystem, such as a Gigabit Ethernet interface. A power wake-up increases transaction latency. If both PD and CD crossing are needed and the target is asleep, an overhead of tens of clock cycles will be required.

The **AMBA Q-channel protocol** is a simpler variant that can only ask a device to go quiescent. The `QACTIVE` output is high if it is running or may have more work to do. When low, the device may be prepared to go to sleep (power down) if requested. In this interface, several of the nets are active low. These polarities are chosen so that, in the quiescent state, all nets are logic zero. This facilitates simple default isolation rules.

3.8 Serialiser and Deserialiser: SERDES

Figure 3.37 shows the main components of a **serialiser/deserialiser (SERDES)**. At the transmitter, parallel data are converted to bit-serial form for inter-chip communication. They are converted back to parallel form at the receiver. This kind of structure is used for the **serial AT attachment (SATA)** interface to disks, each channel of PCIe, Gigabit Ethernet and as the basis of many other links. A very small amount of logic needs to operate at the serial data rate. Careful design, using balanced delay lines and structures like a Johnson counter (Section 4.4.2), enables standard CMOS processes to achieve a serial clock frequency of 10 or 20 times the rate used for general logic.

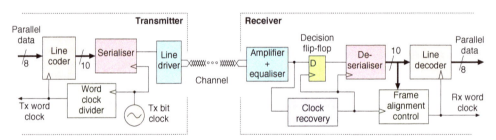

Figure 3.37 Main components of an 8b10b, block-coded SERDES (serialiser/deserialiser) transceiver (transmitter/receiver) operating over a twisted-pair channel

The figure shows the details for 8b10b **block coding**, where eight user data bits are transmitted serially as 10 bits on the channel using a clock frequency 10 times higher. Block coding is an example *line code*. There are numerous line codes, each suitable for different types of media. For instance, on a DVD, the optical channel can carry consecutive groups of ones and zeros with high accuracy, but the minimum run length of either digit must be above a minimum number, such as 3, or else the mark will not be made on the media. For most binary channels, the line code must be **balanced**, meaning that the average number of zeros and ones should be the same. This means it can be AC coupled and passed through transformers. Often binary channels need to use **polarity-insensitive coding**, especially over twisted pairs, where the two wires might be interchanged. This can be accomplished using **non-return-to-zero invert-on-ones (NRZI)** coding where a one is transmitted as a change in the channel polarity and zero as a no-change. Transformers (not shown in the figure) provide **galvanic isolation**. This prevents ground loops being created between equipment and is recommended for inter-building data wiring. Fibre optic transceivers can be used instead, without any design changes to the SERDES logic. These also provide electrical isolation since fibre does not conduct.

Most short-distance digital links use **low-voltage differential signalling (LVDS)**. The advantage of differential transmission is **common-mode rejection**. The signal is represented by the difference in voltage between the two conductors and this is unaffected by any noise voltage or ground potential mismatch that is suffered equally by both wires. The differential pair is terminated at the receiving end with a resistor equal to the **characteristic impedance** of the pair, which prevents reflections and standing waves. LVDS is a baseband digital signal. Higher-frequency elements of the square waves that make up a digital signal are severely attenuated, mainly due to the **skin effect** in electrical conductors, since higher frequencies are carried only on the outside of the conductor and hence, experience higher electrical resistance than lower frequencies, which can use all of it. At the receiver, equalisation is required. **Equalisation** is the process of amplifying different frequencies by different amounts to restore the original pulse shape.

After equalisation, the signal is converted to digital form by the decision flip-flop. This is a high-quality component that internally has high gain and fast transistors. The clock-recovery unit must ensure that the new clock has a suitable phase for tidy clocking by the decision flip-flop. It must be clocked at the precise phase where the signal-to-noise ratio is best. This is known as the **optimum eye opening**. A poor phase will lead to bit errors along the link and can cause metastable violations (Section 3.7.2).

The receiver regenerates the transmitter's clock using a **clock-recovery unit**. The transmit clock can be recovered from the transitions in the equalised signal provided they are sufficiently common for the recovery unit not to have drifted so far as to miss the correct bit cell delineation. Using NRZI encoding, this relates to not having long runs of zeros in the unencoded data, since a one is communicated as a transition.

Sufficient transition density is ensured using a **scrambler**, **block coding** or **bit stuffing**. With the illustrated 8b10b block code, only 256 of the possible 1024 ten-bit patterns are used. These are selected to chose a **codebook** of only those that have a high density of ones. It is also possible to maintain the short-term DC balance by monitoring the history and selecting from alternatives that decode to the same value but which have an odd or even number of ones, according to which direction of balancing is required. On the other hand, a scrambler exclusive-ORs the data with a hash of the data generated by a **pseudorandom binary sequence (PRBS)** generator, which ensures DC balance and the transition density probabilistically. A PRBS generator is a shift register and XOR arrangement that generates a random-looking stream of bits based on irreducible polynomial theory [25]. This has the advantage that the 25 per cent overhead of 8b10b block coding is not encountered, but the disadvantage that a bit pattern that encounters a communication error due to the way it hashes will deterministically fail on a retry. Bit stuffing detects a long run of consecutive bits and then inserts a transition and a further bit to indicate whether the transition arose from genuine data or stuffing. This is efficient, but has the disadvantage that the data rate varies slightly according to the data sent.

Hence, block coding is most commonly used in SoC applications. Old-fashioned **Manchester coding** is a 1b2b code.

When the receiver deserialises 8b10b data, ten different phase offsets are possible. Only one is correct. The receiver needs to acquire the correct **frame alignment** at start-up, but should not thereafter lose synchronisation. A variety of techniques can be used. If not correctly synchronised, the patterns received will lie outside the codebook and can be flagged as coding violations. The receiver can keep adjusting its phase until there are no or a very small number of violations. More commonly, an idle symbol is also defined, using an extra entry in the codebook. This allows data qualified with a clock-enable to be conveyed. When there is no word to send, the idle character is sent. The idle character can be chosen so that it has a unique signature under all cyclic bit rotations and hence, also serves as a **frame-alignment word (FAW)** to indicate the correct receiver phase [26]. The receiving circuit will typically generate a 'link active' status output once it has correctly locked at the bit and word level. It can also report the link quality based on the rate of codebook violations.

3.8.1 PCIe and SATA

The switch away from parallel busses for board-level interconnects is best exemplified by the **peripheral component interconnect express (PCIe)** family of bus standards. These use a **bonded serial interconnect**, in which a number of so-called serial **lanes** run in parallel. Although the skew across lanes can be multiple bit times, this has no effect when the data are converted back to parallel form at the deserialiser, since the worst skew is less than one word time. Although totally different in hardware structure from the parallel bus implementations of PCI, PCIe was made to appear exactly the same to device configuration and driver software.

PCIe slots are commonly available with different configurations, denoted as $\times 1$, $\times 4$, $\times 8$, $\times 16$ and $\times 32$, where the natural number denotes the number of lanes. Each lane has a pair of simplex channels in each direction. Different generations of PCIe have successively increased the throughput per lane. The first generation used LVDS at a **baud rate** (Section 2.7.1) of 2.5 GHz and 8b10b coding, giving a throughput of 250 MB/s per lane. Subsequent generations moved to 128b130b, with a lower coding overhead. The most recent generations use multi-level signalling, giving multiple bits per baud. Combined with an increase in baud rate, lane data rates have increased by a factor of 16 for the fifth generation, with further increases envisioned.

3.8.2 CCIX, CXL and NVLink

PCIe has no cache coherence protocol, so explicit cache evict and clear operations must be implemented by device drivers. The physical layer for PCIe has recently served as the basis for various cache-coherent accelerator connections (Section 6.4). A different transaction-level protocol is carried over the same serial technology. Two examples from competing trade consortia are **Compute Express Link (CXL)** and **cache-coherent interconnect for accelerators (CCIX)**. Both effectively implement a distributed MOESI protocol (Section 2.4.1). Currently CXL only supports unidirectional coherency, whereas CCIX supports bi-directional, symmetrical coherency. Compared with a NoC interconnect, which can use wide busses, these accelerator interconnects inevitably have much higher latency. This arises from the longer distances travelled and deserialisation delays of at least one word. However, every trick possible is used to minimise latency, such as using harmonic clocks (Section 3.7.4) instead of operating asynchronously.

The *NVLink* board-level mesh network from Nvidia also has SERDES channels using 128b130b. This was developed for GPU interconnections. There are opposing market forces, since system integrators want as few board-level interconnect standards as possible whereas technology providers want to enforce lock-ins to their own particular variant.

3.9 Automatic Topology Synthesis

The goal of topology generation is to deploy switching elements, bus resizers and various other canvas elements to meet the PPA targets. Several well-known algorithms in graph theory aid in topology generation. However, none of these is directly applicable. The topology generation problem consists of multiple NP-hard (Section 6.2) sub-problems. These must be solved in turn and then, as with all aspects of architectural exploration, the procedure is iterated. The same principles apply to designing and dimensioning the debug network in Section 4.7.

Here we present one topology generation procedure. The approach is to start by creating a Steiner tree and then successively refining the solution to meet the PPA objectives. From graph theory, a **minimum Steiner tree** [27] is a tree that connects a set of terminals using the lowest number of connecting nodes. For a NoC, a node is a switching element. A Steiner tree is intrinsically singly connected, meaning that there is exactly one route from each point to every other point.

A Steiner tree is generated on a canvas that is overlaid on the user-supplied floor plan (Section 8.6). The NoC provides connectivity between protocol bridges and other directly connected end points whose position the user has also provided. The canvas defines the locations of switching elements (routers). For a mesh NoC, the canvas is a rectangular grid. The end points are connected to all adjacent routers and the Steiner tree is then computed on the mesh. Note that there are still unused links in the underlying grid. We then compute the shortest paths on the Steiner tree and make an allocation of flows to VCs. The VC allocation must provide full connectivity but not involve edges prohibited by deadlock considerations, such as via the turn-restriction algorithms presented in Section 3.4.3. At the end of route generation, the NoC is functional but not optimised. It is also the tightest topology, since a Steiner tree was used.

3.9.1 Domain Assignment

Once a candidate NoC topology has been generated, the connectivity, routes and VC assignment are all known. The CD and PD for each switching element must then be determined. Domain-crossing bridges (Section 3.7.1) will later be inserted at every boundary.

The domains for each switching element can, in principle, be set independently. A domain-assignment algorithm starts from the end points and computes the most favourable domain at each of the switching elements based on availability, certain metrics and the route. Once the most favourable domain at each element has been computed, a second pass is made over the information to make a final allocation based on minimising the total number of domain-crossing bridges needed. The domains for the remaining NoC components, which have exactly one input, such as policers, pipeline stages and resizers, can default to that of the canvas component that drives them.

3.9.2 FIFO Buffer Sizing

Buffering can be placed in the source, switching elements or the destinations. Using the standard synchronous handshake for flow control (Section 3.1.3), augmented with static deadlock avoidance at the routing level, an interconnect will operate correctly without packet loss and without any queuing at switching elements. It relies on source buffering (Section 3.5.1). Credit-based flow control, on the other hand, must have some overt buffering since credit is issued proportional to buffer space, but again this could be just one flit space per destination. However, this would lead to poor link utilisation. Buffering must be provided in proportion to the delays in the flow control loop and the peak and average bandwidth needs of each flow. Moreover, relying on source buffering causes unnecessary head-of-line blocking (Section 4.3.2) and if there is only a small amount of source buffering, devices will stall unnecessarily.

With credit-based flow control, the average sustainable bandwidth on a link is given by the ratio of credit available to the round-trip time R_{TT}, as described in Section 3.6. The peak rate is the rate of the lowest throughput link on the path, which will be close to that link's raw throughput when all traffic is bursty. If a source generates highly bursty data, a source buffer may sensibly be added, but it should be kept small with buffering preferably provided at the destination. The buffering in the switching elements should also be kept small and rely on flow control instead to ensure congestion-free operation.

The **traffic flow matrix**, from Section 3.5.1, gives the expected bandwidth and burstiness of traffic flowing from each point to every other point. As discussed in Section 4.3.3, it is then possible to compute the **effective bandwidth** needed on each link of the NoC. Alternatively, since the aim here is to generate a starting design for subsequent optimisation, various alternatives can be created, based on peak, effective or mean traffic. Each design can be a seed point for **design space exploration (DSE)** and NoC optimisation (Section 6.2.5). At this point, the round-trip time in clock cycles R_{TT} is known, the clock frequency f_{TX} is known from the domain assignment and the throughput required g has been estimated according to one of the models. For each design point, the destination buffer depth (or total amount of credit if there are multiple budgeted stages in the loop) can be directly computed. To meet the throughput, the depth needed is $\lceil R_{TT} \times g/f_{TX} \rceil$. To serve bursty peaks for the greater-than-mean allocation design points, the available credit needs also to be at least the burst size.

3.9.3 Link Sizing

The final step is to select the width of each link, rounding up to a preferred word size. The link width in bits is easy to compute based on the peak or average throughput, summed over all VCs that share the link. Note that in dynamic TDM, such as round-robin arbitration over active VCs, the effective bandwidth needed on a link is lower than the sum of the individual effective bandwidths of the VCs due to a further statistical multiplexing gain. Moreover, bus width provisioning should use a clustering approach to avoid deploying too many resizers.

The resulting design will nearly always miss the PPA objectives, since it has only taken performance into account. The tightest tree in terms of number of elements in the design is inherently suboptimal when dynamic performance is considered due to the arbitration overhead, head-of-line losses (Section 4.3.2), priority crosstalk and queuing delay. Thus, this is a multiple-objective combinational optimisation problem. The design will then be subject to a sequence of automatic and manual refinements to explore performance improvements. This is discussed in the design space exploration section (Section 6.2.5).

3.10 Summary

This chapter has traced the story of SoC interconnects from the early days of a single bus to today's highly-complex NoCs. Apart from the desire for ever-increasing bandwidth, the main motivations for change have been the increasing number of initiators and the increasing difficulty of sending a signal all the way across the silicon die.

The fundamental requirement of an interconnect is to provide connectivity between initiating components (processors, I/O, etc.) and target components (memory, peripherals, etc.). Not every initiator requires access to every target and the optimal solution may be an irregular interconnect, with asymmetric connectivity. Performance requirements will typically be known in advance. For example:

1. A graphics processor might need a guaranteed memory bandwidth to reach its frame rate target for a given screen resolution and scene complexity.

2. A CPU might have a hard deadline within which to service an interrupt. In this case, the interconnect latency (time taken for a transaction to be serviced) could be critical in meeting its requirements.

The main factors that influence interconnect performance are topology, clock frequency, bus width, bridge crossing, physical distance and congestion. Furthermore, these are all interlinked, so finding a near-optimal solution for a set of requirements can be very difficult and time-consuming.

An application-specific SoC may use bridged busses or a custom NoC architecture whereas a general-purpose SoC that embodies heterogeneous compute cores and accelerators will tend to use a regular mesh NoC. Going forward, such a NoC is increasingly likely to be cache coherent, with L2 and

L3 caches connected to the network instead of directly connected to the cores they serve. The mesh may have some number of longer links that are effectively in the third dimension. There is a much greater exploitation of the physical third dimension for multi-chip tiles and stacks. For longer distances, parallel interconnects have been replaced with bonded serial channels, but DRAM currently remains parallel and instead uses line termination and a buildout that is calibrated at boot time.

An interconnect, as a whole, needs to convey a variety of different operations. As well as memory reads and writes, which are usually done in bursts, there are programmed I/O operations on peripherals, which need to be non-cacheable. Again these are reads or writes, but they usually transfer one word at a time when initiated by a processor, otherwise DMA is used. Both occasionally require atomic operations. A variety of broadcast messages also needs to be conveyed, especially for cache and TLB maintenance. Communications are also required for debug (Section 4.7) and interrupt traffic. These can use separate wiring or else be multiplexed over the main data plane.

An interconnect is normally synthesised automatically from specifications of the end points and their traffic matrix. SoCs can have circuit-switched or packet-switched structures and these may be coherent or incoherent. Synthesis tools include the CMN-600 Coherent Mesh Network Generator from Arm [21], and a companion tool for a non-coherent interconnect [28]. These are typically invoked from a GUI-based system integrator tool, as will be discussed in Section 6.8.2.

3.10.1 Exercises

1. What is the principal reason that protocols that fully complete one transaction before commencing another have gone out of fashion? Estimate the throughput of a primitive MSOC1-like bus protocol implemented with modern technology.

2. What affects interconnect energy consumption as the number of channels that make up a port is increased from two (for BVCI) to five (for AXI)?

3. Why is a mix of coherent and non-coherent interconnects always found on a SoC? Why are some peripheral devices connected to a special-purpose bus?

4. Sketch circuit diagrams for a registered pipeline stage inserted into an AXI channel and a CHI channel. What design decisions arise in each case and what effect do they have on performance and energy use?

5. Sketch the circuit for a bus width converter for an AXI channel if the same clock frequency is used on each side. What are the differences from credit-based flow control? When credit-based flow control traverses a bus width changer, what is the most sensible meaning for a credit token?

6. A NoC uses static TDM to separate VCs on a link with the schedule fixed at tapeout. Should the receiving link have a shared buffer pool or a pool that is statically partitioned for use by different VCs?

7. Another NoC uses dynamic TDM. Additional nets convey a VC number that identifies the data on the remainder of the data nets. Discuss the likely performance and energy differences compared with static TDM. (You should be able to improve your answer after reading the next chapter!)

8. For what types of application does NoC latency affect system throughput?

9. What are the advantages of having fully automatic hardware support for memory coherency compared with leaving it up to the programmer to insert special instructions?

10. A C programmer writes `pthread_mutex_t locks[32]`. A friend says this will have very poor cache performance. Why might the friend say this? Are they correct?

References

[1] Arm Ltd. AMBA AXI and ACE protocol specification, version H. https://developer.arm.com/documentation/ihi0022/h, 2020.

[2] I. Sutherland, R. F. Sproull, and D. Harris. *Logical Effort: Designing Fast CMOS Circuits*. Morgan Kaufmann, 1999. ISBN 9781558605572.

[3] OCP-IP Association. Open Core Protocol Specification Release 1.0. http://www.ocpip.org, 2001.

[4] V. Salapura, M. Blumrich, and A. Gara. Design and implementation of the Blue Gene/P snoop filter. In *2008 IEEE 14th International Symposium on High Performance Computer Architecture*, pages 5–14, 2008. doi: 10.1109/HPCA.2008.4658623.

[5] Burton H. Bloom. Space/time trade-offs in hash coding with allowable errors. *Commun. ACM*, 13(7): 422–426, July 1970. ISSN 0001-0782. doi: 10.1145/362686.362692. URL https://doi.org/10.1145/362686.362692.

[6] James Archibald and Jean Loup Baer. An economical solution to the cache coherence problem. *SIGARCH Comput. Archit. News*, 12(3):355–362, January 1984. ISSN 0163-5964. doi: 10.1145/773453.808205. URL https://doi.org/10.1145/773453.808205.

[7] Meredydd Luff. Communication for programmability and performance on multi-core processors. Technical Report UCAM-CL-TR-831, University of Cambridge, Computer Laboratory, April 2013. URL https://www.cl.cam.ac.uk/techreports/UCAM-CL-TR-831.pdf.

[8] David J. Greaves. *Multi-Access Metropolitan Area Networks*. PhD dissertation, University of Cambridge Computer Laboratory, 1992. URL https://www.cl.cam.ac.uk/users/djg11/pubs/david-j-greaves-phd-dissertation-dec-1992.pdf.

[9] David J. Greaves. The double-slot slotted ring protocol (DSR). In *SBT/IEEE International Symposium on Telecommunications*, pages 238–242, 1990. doi: 10.1109/ITS.1990.175605.

[10] E. Lee and P. Boulton. The Principles and Performance of Hubnet: A 50 Mbit/s Glass Fiber Local Area Network. *IEEE Journal on Selected Areas in Communications*, 1(5):711–720, 1983. doi: 10.1109/JSAC. 1983.1145990.

[11] *IEEE Standards for Local and Metropolitan Area Networks: Supplement to Distributed Queue Dual Bus (DQDB) Access Method and Physical Layer Specifications. Connection-Oriented Service on a Distributed Queue Dual Bus (DQDB) Subnetwork of a Metropolitan Area Network (MAN).* IEEE, 1995. Std 802.6j-1995.

[12] A. B. Kahng, B. Lin, K. Samadi, and R. S. Ramanujam. Trace-driven optimization of networks-on-chip configurations. In *Design Automation Conference*, pages 437–442, 2010. doi: 10.1145/1837274.1837384.

[13] G. N. Khan and A. Tino. Synthesis of NoC interconnects for custom MPSoC architectures. In *2012 IEEE/ACM Sixth International Symposium on Networks-on-Chip*, pages 75–82, 2012. doi: 10.1109/NOCS.2012.16.

[14] David Starobinski, Mark Karpovsky, and Lev Zakrevski. Application of network calculus to general topologies using turn-prohibition. *IEEE/ACM Transactions on Networking*, 11:411–421, 2002.

[15] Steven Cameron Woo, Moriyoshi Ohara, Evan Torrie, Jaswinder Pal Singh, and Anoop Gupta. The splash-2 programs: Characterization and methodological considerations. *SIGARCH Comput. Archit. News*, 23(2): 24–36, May 1995. ISSN 0163-5964. doi: 10.1145/225830.223990. URL https://doi.org/10. 1145/225830.223990.

[16] C. Bienia, S. Kumar, J. Singh, and K. Li. The PARSEC benchmark suite: Characterization and architectural implications. In *2008 International Conference on Parallel Architectures and Compilation Techniques (PACT)*, pages 72–81, Los Alamitos, CA, USA, October 2008. IEEE Computer Society. URL https://doi.org/ 10.1145/1454115.1454128.

[17] M. Potkonjak, C. Lee, and W. Mangione-Smith. Mediabench: a tool for evaluating and synthesizing multimedia and communications systems. In *2012 45th Annual IEEE/ACM International Symposium on Microarchitecture*, page 330, Los Alamitos, CA, USA, December 1997. IEEE Computer Society. doi: 10.1109/MICRO.1997.645830. URL https://doi.ieeecomputersociety.org/10.1109/MICRO.1997.645830.

[18] Michael Kistler, Michael Perrone, and Fabrizio Petrini. Cell multiprocessor communication network: Built for speed. *IEEE Micro*, 26:10–23, 2006. doi: 10.1109/MM.2006.49.

[19] C. Clos. A study of non-blocking switching networks. *The Bell System Technical Journal*, 32(2):406–424, 1953.

[20] A. Banerjee, R. Mullins, and S. Moore. A power and energy exploration of network-on-chip architectures. In *First International Symposium on Networks-on-Chip (NOCS'07)*, pages 163–172, 2007. doi: 10.1109/ NOCS.2007.6.

[21] Arm Ltd. Corelink CMN-600 coherent mesh network. https://developer.arm.com/ip-products/ system-ip/corelink-interconnect/corelink-coherent-mesh-network-family/corelink-cmn-600, 2020.

[22] John Kim, William J. Dally, and Dennis Abts. Flattened butterfly: A cost-efficient topology for high-radix networks. In *Proceedings of the 34th Annual International Symposium on Computer Architecture*, ISCA '07, pages 126–137, New York, NY, USA, 2007. Association for Computing Machinery. ISBN 9781595937063. doi: 10.1145/1250662.1250679. URL https://doi.org/10.1145/1250662.1250679.

[23] David J. Greaves and M. J. Nam. Synthesis of glue logic, transactors, multiplexors and serialisors from protocol specifications. *IET Conference Proceedings*, pages 171–177(6), January 2010. URL https:// digital-library.theiet.org/content/conferences/10.1049/ic.2010.0148.

[24] Arm Ltd. *AMBA Low Power Interface Specification Q-Channel and P-Channel Interfaces*. Arm Ltd., 2016.

[25] W. W. Peterson. *Error Correcting Codes*. M.I.T. Press, Cambridge, Mass, 1961. ISBN 9780262160063.

[26] David J. Greaves and S. Montgomery-Smith. Unforgeable marker sequences. https://www.researchgate. net/publication/242390959_Unforgeable_Marker_Sequences, 01 1990.

[27] M. Garey and David Johnson. The rectilinear Steiner tree problem is NP-complete. *SIAM Journal of Applied Mathematics*, 32:826–834, 1977. doi: 10.1137/0132071.

[28] Arm Ltd. Arm CoreLink NI-700 Network-on-Chip Interconnect, Technical Reference Manual. https://developer.arm.com/documentation/101566/0100/Introduction/About-the-CoreLink-NI-700-Network-on-Chip-Interconnect, 2020.

Chapter 4

System Design
Considerations

Good SoC design involves simultaneously optimising a number of performance targets. Some targets are hard to quantify, such as how flexible the chosen solution will turn out to be for future applications that are currently unforeseen. Others have quantitative metrics whose values can generally be predicted by analysis or from high-level **electronic system-level (ESL)** models of the solution and accurately predicted by a low-level simulation where necessary. To avoid bottlenecks, SoC design should instantiate a balanced set of resources. In this chapter, we present some theory and some practical techniques behind these metrics. We discuss several principles of system design that are widely applicable outside the sphere of SoCs, such as parallel processing theory, traffic theory and queuing theory. We look at where the electrical energy goes and how to design secure and debuggable chips.

4.1 Design Objectives and Metrics

The main design objectives for a SoC are as follow:

1. **Performance**: Traditionally, the most important parameter for computing systems is their processing throughput, measured as **million instructions per second (MIPS)** or **floating point instructions per second (FLOPS)**. Although this remains a key metric, it cannot be reduced to a single figure in a complex modern design, especially one that contains heterogeneous processors and accelerators. For embedded and mobile applications, video processing rates are often more important than main processor performance. Video compression is especially challenging and the design objective will be expressed using metrics such as frame rate and resolution.

2. **Memory bandwidth**: Directly related to processor performance is main memory bandwidth. Generally, there is one DRAM channel and all the on-chip processors use it to a greater or lesser extent. The data width and clock rate for the memory channel between DRAM and the SoC are critical design decisions, both for performance and energy use. It is common to support more than one point in this design space, with the final choices being based on the PCB or MCM assembly time for data width and the boot time for the clock rate.

3. **Energy use** or **battery life**: Energy efficiency is, today, also often a critical consideration. Whether for battery-operated devices or a server farm, low-power design principles are applicable. The power control mechanisms selected affect the design at all levels. Electricity and cooling are major costs for cloud servers and data centres, comparable to the depreciation costs of the hardware. For portable equipment, battery life remains a design consideration despite significant advances in battery power density in the last decade. A mobile phone should offer at least one day's operation between charges, whereas a ceiling-mounted smoke and intruder sensor may target a 10-year battery life.

4. **Power modes**: A SoC as a whole will support various **sleep modes** or **standby modes** (Section 4.6.10) and various regions of the SoC can be **power gated** to be on or off at any one time (Section 4.6.10). When powered on, various clock rates and power supply voltages may be dynamically selected by **dynamic voltage and frequency scaling (DVFS)** (Section 4.6.8).

5. **Production costs**: The production cost for most SoCs with a particular geometry (technology node) is a simple function of the silicon area. Cutting-edge silicon production, in which the geometry is less than 10 μm, is much more expensive than older lines producing 45 μm. The production lines for the larger geometry are mature and ultra reliable, whereas the newer ones can have significant yield problems. For a geometry, the yield is inversely proportional to area (S8.11.1). Expenses related to each chip are called **recurring costs**. Apart from silicon wafer processing, they also include testing and packaging overheads (Section 8.8.3).

6. **Design costs**: The one-off costs in designing a SoC are called **non-recurring expenses (NRE)**. As discussed in Section 8.11, these include engineering time, computer time and mask-making costs. Engineering time includes the creative aspects of hardware and software design and the extensive effort required for design verification and test program generation. Pricing structures for IP block licences depend on the supplier, but typically include both recurring and non-recurring components.

7. **Security**: Increasingly, SoCs need to be secure. It is better if the design IP and embedded software are relatively secure against reverse engineering. Also, boot-time and runtime security mechanisms are increasingly important. Secret keys for various **public-key infrastructure (PKI)** resources need to be held securely for secure booting (Section 9.1.1), digital rights management of copyrighted media and secure applications, such as online purchases or unlocking doors. The security architecture for a SoC may include multiple **roots of trust**, in which information isolation follows a partial order different from the simple total ordering imposed by a traditional supervisor mode privilege flag. For instance, the telephony API on a phone may need to be insulated from user applications before the network provider approves the platform. Moreover, the user's files should be protected from rogue network providers.

8. **Observability**: A device must be testable and debuggable, which conflicts with its security. Test modes and a trace and monitor infrastructure must be deployed to capture behaviour so that bugs, especially software bugs, can be found.

9. **Flexibility**: Due to the high NRE of a SoC design, it is normal to address a family of related applications with one SoC. For instance, one design could be used for a printer, a scanner and a printer/scanner. Certain parts of the SoC may then never be used in the lifetime of the more specialised products. The same goes for the broadband modem example in Figure 1.11, in which the main SoC might have two USB ports but zero, one or two might be wired out on the PCB, depending on the product. If a SoC is intended for a single target application, there is greater certainty about the likely data flow between internal IP blocks compared with a general-purpose chip. Although transistor count does not present a significant design constraint in modern VLSI, hardwired data paths are more efficient than switched structures: wiring length and hence, energy are lower if less area is used. A solution providing a non-blocking full crossbar interconnection will generally be over-engineered.

10. **Safety and reliability**: Functional safety levels need to be higher in some application areas than others. To achieve high reliability, memory can have error correction (Section 4.7.6) and busses can have parity bits. Processors can be duplicated and work in lockstep for error detection, or triplicated, giving **triple modular redundancy (TMR)**, which seeks a majority vote in most cases of disagreement.

The three major metrics of power, performance and area are often considered together using the acronym *PPA*.

4.2 Parallel Speedup Theory

In an ideal world, if work can be divided *n* ways and performed in parallel, then an *n*-times speedup should be achieved. Alternatively, for zero speedup, running a workload in parallel on multiple slower processors gives a considerable energy saving compared to a faster serial execution, with benefits arising from both the CMOS speed law (Section 4.6.6) and Pollack's rule of thumb (Section 2.1.1). Hence, parallel processing is preferred, provided the workload can adequately expressed as parallel tasks. In this section we present basic parallel processing theory.

Figure 4.1 illustrates a task consisting of 35 units of work using parallel processing arranged over four processors. Like many tasks, the work that can be done in parallel depends on a common core of work that cannot easily be done in parallel. This is the initial, serial and start-up phase of four work units. A further two serial units are shown at the end, typically to aggregate the final result. A dependency arises when the input to a unit is computed by a previous unit. In general, the dependency graph can have any structure, but one path (or several equal paths) between the start and finish will have the maximal length. In our figure, this is $4 + 8 + 2 = 14$, which is known as T_∞. This is the fastest possible execution time given sufficient parallel processors. Using four processors, the actual execution time is the same: $T_4 = T_\infty = 14$. Using three processors with a good interleaving of work that reflects the dependencies allows the 5 units from the lower strand to be run as $2 + 2 + 1$, which extends the central region from 8 to 10 units, extending the execution time from 14 to 16 units. Finally, by using one processor to run everything, the job would take $T_1 = 35$ units. It does not matter which server runs the serial part of the problem, as no context-switching work between processors can help. The speedup achieved is $35/14 = 2.5$. The **available parallelism** of the task is $T_1/T_\infty = 2.5$. Since we achieved this with four processors, adding a further processor would not help.

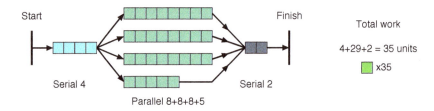

Figure 4.1 Example of parallel speedup. 35 units of work run across four servers, showing dependency arcs typical in the **map-reduce** design pattern. Arcs implicitly exist between all adjacent work unit boxes

It is worthwhile memorising the structure and behaviour of two formulae that are rather grandly called laws. These formulae give fundamental insight into any system design, such as a SoC, where parts of a task are to be accelerated with parallel or custom processing elements:

▪ **Amdahl's law**, which assumes that the problem size remains constant as the system grows

▪ **Gustafson's law**, which proposes that the problem size should scale while being bound by a fixed amount of time.

Amdahl's law gives the speedup of a job due to accelerating some fraction of it. The Amdahl speedup arising from parallel processing is given by $S + (1 - S)n$, where S is the fraction of the job that cannot be accelerated by parallel processing and n is the number of processors. For our example, $n = 4$ and $S = 6/35$, so Amdahl's formula gives 3.5. This is an upper bound for the speedup. The real speedup was lower due to dependencies within the parallel part of the task, which was not uniformly parallel.

An **embarrassingly parallel** problem is one where there is zero dependency between work units that can be done in parallel. An example is computing pixels in the Mandelbrot set or the inverse DFT computation when decompressing a JPEG. Each pixel or pixel tile can be processed fully independently. Such problems should get close to a linear speedup with parallel processing, whereas typical examples, like that of Figure 4.1, have a sublinear speedup.

In general, as a system grows in computational power, the problems run on the system increase in size. Gustafson's law gives the effective speedup as parallelism is added when the workload is increased so that the overall time taken is unchanged:

$$speedup(n) = n + (1 - n)S$$

This law tends to describe real-world situations where users have a preferred maximum processing time and want the best quality result for the number of available processors.

4.2.1 Contention and Arbitration

To create a balanced system, it is also critical to understand queuing and contention. When multiple clients wish to share a resource, we have **contention** and an **arbiter** is required. Typical shared resources are busses, memory and multipliers. At such a multiplexing point, an arbiter decides which requester should be serviced next. In SoC design, we encounter two forms of contention:

▪ **Target contention** occurs when multiple initiators desire access to the same target. As mentioned in Section 4.5, managing target contention for memory systems that share data between parallel processing elements is one of the most critical design decisions.

▪ **Fabric contention** occurs when initiators are accessing different targets but their flows of access traffic interfere in the interconnect. Using additional or wider interconnect paths reduces fabric contention, but over-engineering the interconnect wastes energy and requires more area, which ultimately costs even more energy (Section 4.6.2).

Contention must be managed by a combination of queuing and flow control. Unlike a packet-switched network, such as the Internet, a SoC interconnect is normally designed to be lossless; hence, traffic cannot simply be discarded at an overflowing queue. Another difference is that there is a relatively low latency reverse path in terms of handshake nets or credit-return mechanisms, which means that it is easier to provide lossless operation, but at the risk of a fabric deadlock (Section 3.4.3). The two main forms of flow control used for SoCs are:

- Link-by-link handshakes, which cumulatively apply backpressure on an initiator or traffic source to prevent it from introducing new work into a congested system.

- Transport protocols, typically based on credit-based flow control (CBFC), which is discussed in Section 3.4.4.

The way a multiplex arbiter chooses which source to service next is called the **arbiter service discipline**: Complex arbitration schemes can be created from three basic disciplines:

1. **Static priority**: Each source has a permanently allocated priority and the requesting source with the highest priority is selected. The priority could be the port number. This is stateless.

2. **First come, first served**: This is a FIFO queuing discipline, in which work is maintained in its arrival order.

3. **Round robin**: The sources are placed at points around a virtual circle and, always moving in the same direction around the circle, service is granted to the next requester after the last-served requester. A last-served state variable must be maintained inside the arbiter.

A complex discipline might be to have sources classified into several levels of priority and for round robin to be used within a priority level. All disciplines can be considered a variant of priority service if priorities are dynamically calculated based on various factors. For instance, the **earliest-deadline-first** discipline uses hard real-time timing requirements as the basis for priority. Another major policy type is **pre-emptive**, in which a granted resource is de-assigned while the request is still asserted. Complex disciplines involve dynamic priorities based on use history to avoid starvation. Alternatively, they implement a maximal matching between a number of requesters and a number of resources.

Arbiter Circuits

Arbiters can be implemented in software or as physical circuits. The circuits may be synchronous or asynchronous. Figure 4.2 is a schematic of an example three-input arbiter with the RTL implementation. It has three request inputs and three grant outputs. Figure 6.31 shows Chisel HDL, which parametrically generates circuit arbiters with any number of inputs.

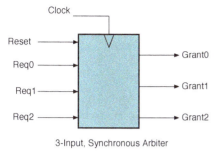

3-Input, Synchronous Arbiter

```
module arbiter(input clk,
               input reset,
               input [2:0] reqs,
               output reg [2:0] grants);

  always @(posedge clk) if (reset) grants <= 0;
      else begin
          grants[0] <= reqs[0]; // Highest static priority
          grants[1] <= reqs[1] && !(reqs[0]);
          grants[2] <= reqs[2] && !(reqs[0] || reqs[1]);
      end
```

Figure 4.2 A schematic of a typical arbiter (left) and the RTL implementation (right) for a three-port synchronous example using static priority with pre-emption. See also Figure 6.31

4.3 FIFO Queuing Theory and QoS

A SoC consists of many interacting subsystems. Work items generated by one subsystem are often queued while waiting to be served by another. These queues could be in-memory structures managed by software or hardware FIFO buffers in the NoC interconnect with protocol adaptors. Queuing analysis provides high-level insights into how a system will behave in terms of throughput and latency. Such an analysis is essential when working out how much waiting area to provide (FIFO depth) and can influence the overall system design. In this section, we present the basic analytical models of open queuing theory as applied to simple components. These give insights in their own right and will also be used further when making abstractions for ESL models in Chapter 5.

Classical queuing theory applies where there is a FIFO queue between any two IP blocks in a SoC. Each task or work item entering a queue is called a **customer** and each IP block that removes an item from a queue is called a **server**. A queuing system may be **open** or **closed**. In a **closed queuing system**, there is a finite number of customers, which continuously circulate between IP blocks. In the SoC context, these can be analogous to threads running on in-order application processors that block waiting for a read response before they can proceed.

The **quality of service (QoS)** that a customer receives depends on how many other customers are contending for a resource and the relative arbitration policies. QoS can be analysed in terms of deadlines and fairness under normal and overloaded operating conditions. Using a static priority will result in **starvation** of lower-priority classes during periods of heavy higher-priority traffic.

If traffic flows pass through a number of shared resources, providing fairness is generally incompatible with maximising system throughput. Various **water-filling algorithms** reconcile fairness with throughput. A typical algorithm starts by nominally allocating zero resource to each flow and gradually increasing the actual allocation to each flow in proportion to its target allocation. When resources start to saturate, no further allocation is made to the flows that have become restricted. This maximises the utilisation at pinch points while accurately tracking the desired relative weighting between flows and allocating as much as possible.

A complete system with a closed queuing model is normally too complex for an analysis with queuing theory to be worthwhile. However, an ESL model may give sufficient insight. With super-scalar processors or write posting (Section 3.2.3), the number of customers for the fabric and the targets are dynamic, so closed queuing theory cannot be applied.

An open queue model is typically used to understand the behaviour of an individual queue in a subsystem containing several queues and servers. In an **open queuing system**, customers randomly enter the system and subsequently leave the system once they are processed. The random entries are modelled using a standard customer generator with prescribed characteristics, such as the mean generation rate and the variance and distribution of inter-arrival times. By varying the mean generation rate, denoted λ, it is possible to explore the local behaviour of a subsystem and gain insights into appropriate memory sizes and bus widths. However, we must be aware that finite-customer effects may make the modelling incorrect. For instance, any queue that has a capacity greater than the closed number of customers cannot overflow in reality. However, there would be a finite probability of it overflowing under an open model with random arrivals.

4.3.1 Classical Single-server and Open Queue Models

Figure 4.3 presents the most basic queue configuration. The average **arrival rate** of customers per second is λ. The average **service time** for a customer at the server is $1/\mu$ s, meaning that the maximum sustainable service rate is μ jobs per second. The server **utilisation** is

$$\rho = \frac{\text{Mean arrival rate}}{1/\text{Mean service time}} = \frac{\lambda}{\mu}$$

The utilisation is always less than unity in a stable system. If the long-term average arrival rate is greater than the mean service rate, the server will become overloaded and the queue will overflow.

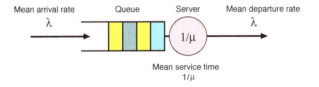

Figure 4.3 General structure of a queue/server pair with mean customer rate λ and mean service rate μ

A FIFO queue is typically used to match the arrival process to the server. An implementation of a queue always has a bounded capacity N_{max}, and so being able to estimate the average number of customers waiting in the queue is critically important for queue dimensioning during system design. The average time waiting in the queue W and the average length of the queue (number of customers in it) N are fundamentally connected by *Little's law*: $N = \lambda W$. Moreover, the overall time a customer is delayed at this point in the system D is the sum of its queuing time W and its mean service time $1/\mu$, so that $D = W + 1/\mu$.

A FIFO queue with N servers is often denoted using Kendall's notation $A/S/N$. A and S indicate the arrival and service delay distributions. The most two common distributions (also known as disciplines in this context) are Markovian (denoted as *M*) and deterministic (denoted as *D*). The behaviour of a **stochastic system** can be modelled with a random number generator. The most important stochastic source is a Markovian generator, whose emissions have random, exponentially distributed spacing. The most quoted example is the spacing between Geiger counter clicks in radioactive decay. When *D* is quoted, it generally means constant and fixed and not merely deterministic. Three basic queueing configurations are illustrated in Figure 4.4. These are:

1. *M/M/1*: Markovian arrivals, Markovian service times, one server.

2. *M/D/1*: Uniform arrivals, uniform service times, one server. This has half the queuing time of *M/M/1*.

3. *D/D/1*: Uniform arrivals, uniform service times, one server. This has a very flat delay until it jumps to infinity when overloaded.

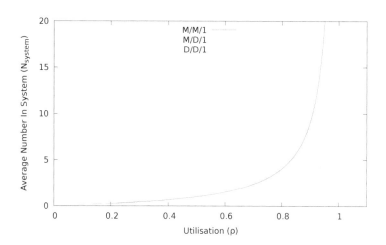

Figure 4.4 Plots of the average number of customers in a system versus the utilisation ρ for three common arrival/service disciplines

Table 4.1 Formulae for N_{system} and N_Q where $N_{system} = N_Q + N_{server}$

Discipline	N_{system}	N_Q
M/M/1	$\dfrac{\rho}{1-\rho}$	$\dfrac{\rho^2}{1-\rho}$
M/D/1	$\dfrac{\rho^2}{2(1-\rho)} + \rho$	$\dfrac{\rho^2}{2(1-\rho)}$
D/D/1	$N_Q + \rho$	$\approx \dfrac{1}{(1-\rho)^\infty}$

The formulae in Table 4.1 show the general trend that the delay goes up according to $1/(1-\rho)$. Markovian systems have higher average delays than deterministic systems. The latter saturate much more abruptly. When connecting two existing components together, we have no control over their traffic patterns, but as we aggregate sources and servers, the patterns become more Markovian as a consequence of the **central-limit theorem** and we benefit from the gain due to statistical multiplexing (Section 4.3.3).

The Markovian approximation is often not a good approximation of reality, but it still gives highly useful insights and has a number of beneficial properties:

1. **Multiplexes of Markovian sources are Markovian**: If two or more Markovian sources are multiplexed, the resultant stream is Markovian with mean arrival rate the sum of the means.

2. **Multiplexes of anything become Markovian**: Due to the central-limit theorem, if uncorrelated arrivals are combined from any distribution, the composite arrival process is Markovian.

3. **Poisson arrivals**: The number of customers arriving in any fixed measurement interval is given by a Poisson distribution.

4. **Demultiplexes are Markovian**: Splitting a Markovian stream with any weighting or time-invariant policy produces Markovian child streams.

5. **Memory-less property**: The probability of an arrival in the next time unit is unaffected by how long it has been since the last arrival.

6. **Markovian arrivals see time averages**: The PASTA theorem is that Poisson arrivals see time averages. If a Markovian source generates a customer, the expected state of the system it enters is the average state.

The memory-less property results in the **paradox of mean residual life**. The residual life of a process is how long it is expected to run into the future. For example, if omnibuses pass a bus stop with a uniform distribution of once per hour, then the average wait for a person randomly arriving at a bus stop is half an hour. However, if the busses arrive with a Markovian distribution with a mean rate $\lambda = 1$ per hour, then the average wait is 1 hour!

The **coefficient of variation** for a component in a queueing system is the ratio of the standard deviation to the mean for its discipline. This is zero for a deterministic component and unity for a Markovian (random) discipline. If we use G to denote a generalised discipline for which we know the two mean service rates and the coefficients of variation c_a, then the **Kingman** $G/G/1$ approximation gives the average queuing delay and number in the queue as:

$$D_Q \approx \frac{\rho}{2(1-\rho)}(c_\lambda^2 + c_\mu^2)\frac{1}{\mu} \qquad\qquad N_Q = D_Q \lambda \approx \frac{\rho^2}{2(1-\rho)}(c_\lambda^2 + c_\mu^2)$$

For the equivalent totals for a queue-plus-server subsystem, the time and number in the server need to be added to the queue figures, respectively, $1/\mu$ and ρ.

There are numerous extensions to the basic Kendall form for describing a queue. Often arrivals or a service are batched for some number of customers arriving or being served together. These are known as **bulk arrival processes** and **batch servers**. Equations are widely available for the average queue length and loss probability for a given queue capacity and the 99th percentile of queue time. The **99 percentile delay** is important for real-time media, such as audio, since the playout buffer must be dimensioned according to the tail of the delay distribution to avoid frequent under-runs.

4.3.2 Expedited Service Queuing

For systems that support traffic with different static priorities, it is usual to give an **expedited service** to the higher priorities. This simply means serving them first. If the system is well designed, the expedited traffic should experience very little **priority crosstalk**, which occurs when one flow alters the service given to another. With strict priority, a flow should experience interference only from higher priorities. Figure 4.5 shows a typical setup that uses two queues for two priorities. For example, if work is being conveyed on an AXI4 streaming bus (Section 3.1.5), the priority can be indicated in the `AxQOS` field. A work item arriving at a higher-priority queue will not experience any queuing delay from lower-priority traffic. The crosstalk it will experience is just the mean residual life of a single customer's service on the server. Hence, provided individual service operations are short, the higher-priority traffic will hardly see the lower-priority traffic. For this reason, longer operations are often fragmented into smaller tasks with correspondingly shorter service times, so that they can be effectively pre-empted. A good example of this is the use of **flow-control elements (flits)** in NoCs (Section 3.4.4). Using two separate queues avoids priority crosstalk of a specific form known as **head-of-line (HoL) blocking**, which occurs when higher-priority work is behind lower-priory work in a queue and cannot be served straight away, due to the first come, first served dequeuing discipline of a FIFO buffer.

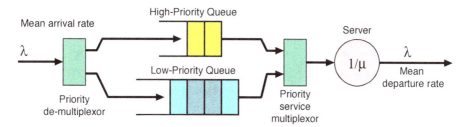

Figure 4.5 Separate queueing for high-priority and low-priority traffic gives an expedited service

If queues are implemented as part of a switching element that routes traffic from some number of sources to various destinations, the queues (known as buffers) can physically be at the output or input links. Figure 4.6 illustrates both types of queuing, though it is not necessary to have queuing at both the input and the output. In an **input-buffered switch** (with queues only at the input ports), the data rate in and out of the input queue is the same as the link rate, assuming that all links to and from the switch are the same. On the other hand, for an **output-buffered switch** (with queues only at the output ports), the data rate into the output queue can be, in the worst case, the sum of all the input port rates. This creates a considerable design challenge for a switch with a large number of inputs.

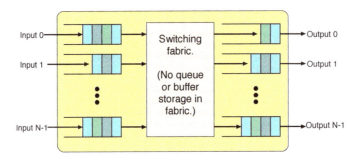

Figure 4.6 Generic switch that includes both input and output buffering on the input and output ports, respectively, of a buffer-less switch fabric. Flow control operates between the switch fabric and the buffers in the switch

Output buffering is the ideal design, since input-buffered switches have lower throughput owing to HoL blocking in the input queues, which can leave the output ports idle while traffic is served in arrival order from each input queue. Typical designs use additional levels of storage, virtual queues at the input per output port or intermediate levels of store. A simpler approach is to use both input and output buffers such that the transfer rate between the input and output buffers is 1.5 or 2 times the link rate. If the switch ports use link-level flow control, one further design point is to rely entirely on **source buffering** and have no buffers in the switch. This is how first-generation multi-access LANs operated, such as rings and shared-bus Ethernet designs.

4.3.3 Statistical Multiplexing Gain

In terms of processing delay, a powerful, monolithic server with a single queue always performs better than a number of queues that feed individual smaller servers if the smaller server capacities sum to the same total as the monolithic server. This is due to **statistical multiplexing gain**. On the other hand, a collection of smaller servers may require less energy in total (Section 2.1.1).

If a channel with a given bandwidth carries a number of traffic flows, the effective bandwidth of an individual flow is the share of the channel bandwidth that is consumed by carrying it. The effective bandwidth can also be defined as the amount of bandwidth that needs to be allocated for a flow to be conveyed without experiencing excessive loss or delay. For uniform flows, the effective bandwidth is just the mean rate. If the sum of the mean rates equals the channel capacity, no further traffic can be conveyed, which is not surprising. However, for bursty traffic, in the absence of flow control or backpressure, the effective bandwidth of a flow is greater than its mean and is closer to its peak rate. Except for constant-rate multimedia streams, computer-generated traffic is always bursty.

Figure 4.7(a) shows a concentrator that simply combines 10 flows. Each flow has an average rate of 100 kbps, so the combined flow has an average rate of 1 Mbps. However, each flow has a peak rate of 100 Mbps. The peak-to-mean ratio, known as the **burstiness**, is 1000. If the combined channel was dimensioned to support all sources bursting at once, it would need to support 1 Gbps. However this is unnecessary. The probability of all flows bursting at once is 1 in $10^{3\times10}$. This situation would last for one average burst time. Assuming this is 1 ms, the all-bursting situation would be expected every 10^{27} seconds, which is 10^{19} years. This can be ignored, since the lifetime of the universe is only 10^{10} years.

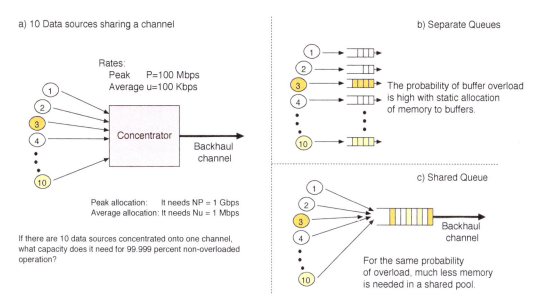

Figure 4.7 *Two scenarios that demonstrate statistical multiplexing gain for N = 10 sources. Sharing the channel bandwidth (a) raises the question of whether reservations are made on a peak or average basis. If N is small, we should use peak allocation, but for large N, we can use average allocation. The law of large numbers states that N needs only to be about 50 for an average allocation to be acceptable. Buffer pools can be partitioned (b) or shared (c)*

To ensure the channel is overloaded at a more realistic rate of once per year, the headroom above the mean is roughly

$$0.001^{headroom} = \frac{1\,ms}{1\,year} = 3.2 \times 10^{-10} \quad \Rightarrow \quad headroom = 3.2$$

Hence, a channel of 3.2 times the mean aggregate rate is sufficient to handle peak demands. This is 3.2 Mbps, and the effective bandwidth of each of the 10 participants is 0.32 Mbps.

Note these overloads are likely to cause a critical fault only in a **hard real-time system** that has no mitigation mechanism. In most other systems, there are recovery techniques at many layers of the system structure, ranging from FIFO queuing and link-level flow control to a human reboot. An example hard real-time application is the output stage of a television system that is broadcasting a live stream. This offers no opportunity for error recovery, but a tiny glitch once per year is a reasonable design margin.

If two or more sources of traffic are known to be highly correlated, statistical multiplexing cannot be used. Such sources should be considered as a single source with aggregated peak and mean statistics. The effective bandwidth will then correctly apply to some number of aggregated sources sharing a resource, provided they are truly independent.

Figures 4.7(b) and (c) illustrate another benefit of multiplexing. Given a resource, such as packet buffers, it is obvious that a shared pool behaves better than a pre-partitioned pool in terms of effective utilisation. A pre-partitioned pool will run out of resource at some point although there is free resource in other partitions. Combined with flow control, this can be a useful aspect of a load-balancing or anti-hogging feature, but on its own, it offers no benefit and should be avoided to allow more effective use of the resources.

As mentioned, a monolithic server performs better than a number of smaller servers that together have the same total capacity. Consider the $M/M/1$ system with a monolithic server loaded to utilisation ρ. The average service time is $W = W_{\text{queue}} + W_{\text{server}} = \rho/(1-\rho)/\mu$. If instead there were 10 smaller servers, each with service rate $\mu/10$, the system capacity is unchanged. Consider the best case where the servers are evenly balanced; each will have the same utilisation as the monolithic server. If customers are not allowed to jump queues between servers, the same formula for W applies with the same value of ρ, but because μ is 10 times smaller, customers experience a 10 times longer service time, $10W$. In a better design where customers are allowed to jump between queues, the monolithic server is hardly better under heavy loads, but for light loads, the average service times are significantly shorter. This is because the queuing delay is greater than the server time for heavy loads and less than the server time for light loads.

These basic aspects of multi-server behaviour are important when considering what mixture of processor cores to use in a SoC design. Equations from queuing theory are helpful when creating a high-level ESL model of a SoC. One modelling technique is to replace queue details with immediate service and simply add on a timing correction computed from the W_{queue} formula (Section 5.2.1).

4.3.4 QoS Policing

A **leaky bucket policer** is the standard mechanism for regulating peak and average rates of flow of packets or flits over an interface.

Figure 4.8 shows QoS policing applied to a queue. The queue can be regulated on either the input or output with output being preferable for a queue that is not shared with other traffic classes. The arrival gate either receives a packet and puts it in the queue or discards it by throwing it on the ground (togging), generating a **togged packet**. In a networking context, if a packet arrives at a full queue, at least one packet has to be togged, and with a simple FIFO queue, it would be the most recently arrived. In a SoC context, with backpressure being possible through the handshaking system, stopping a packet from arriving is also commonly used. The output gate policer will cause packets to accumulate in the queue when the arrival rate is faster than allowed.

Each policer has a number of rate-limiting channels. Using two channels to police a flow is common, and the two channels, respectively, police the peak and mean rates. Each channel has one state variable (a value that changes over time), the **credit**, which must be greater than zero for the channel to authorise an operation. Each channel also has two parameters that are set up by the controlling host. If there is no traffic, credit accumulates while it is less than the `burst_tolerance`. It builds up at the rate set by `credit_rate`. The pseudocode in Figure 4.9 outlines an implementation of one channel, although hardware implementations are commonly found, such as in the QoS-301 IP block from ARM. If the `burst_tolerance` is set to unity, the regulator controls the minimum inter-packet spacing, which is the peak rate. The credit can be Boolean for this case and the implementation can be

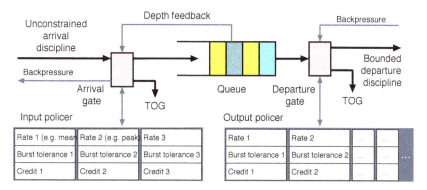

Figure 4.8 A policed queue showing both input and output regulators, although commonly only one site would be policed. Each policer has a number of rate channels (e.g. three are shown for the input site)

```
int burst_tolerance, credit_rate; // Set up by PIO
int credit;                       // State variable
void reset() // Complete setup
{ credit = 0;
  register_timer_callback(crediter, credit_rate);
}
void crediter() // Called at 1/credit_rate intervals
{ if (credit < burst_tolerance) credit += 1;
}
bool police() // Check operation currently allowed
{ if (credit==0) return false;
  credit -= 1;
  return true;
}
```

Figure 4.9 Essence of a software implementation for one channel of a generic traffic policer or regulator

hardwired to allow one of the channels to support this common, degenerate setting. The product of burst_tolerance and credit_rate determines an averaging interval over which the mean credit_rate cannot be exceeded. The illustrated police() operation returns true if an operation is allowed at the current instant. As shown, it also decrements the available credit if the operation is allowed, although a multichannel implementation must check that all channels allow the operation before decrementing the credit for each of them.

Additional policing channels are sometimes used. Implemented in hardware, they consume energy and area but do not give rise to a performance penalty. Beyond the peak and mean rates, a third channel can be used to set a longer-term average limit, or channels may be flexibly assigned to different policing points using a configuration matrix. For instance, separate channels may be used for the peak read and peak write rates, with a shared average-rate channel. Another form of policing channel is independent of time and just counts events. A channel to control the **maximum number of outstanding transactions** has its credit debited when an operation starts and re-credited when the response is received. Starting a new transaction is blocked while the credit is zero.

4.4 Design Trade-offs

Any design process involves a myriad of design decisions at small and large scales. The left plot in Figure 4.10 has two principal design axes: parallelism and clock frequency. System throughput is increased by advancing in either direction, when possible. Ideally, their product defines contours of constant execution design for a task. Higher parallelism leads to a greater throughput at the cost of more silicon area. The power supply voltage and energy use, which are related to clock speed, are affected, as discussed in Section 4.6.1. However, higher clock frequencies require a superlinear increase in energy. Likewise, a higher throughput per processor core requires a superlinear growth in area, as given by Pollack's rule (Section 2.1.1). However, depending on the nature of the workload, the available parallelism may be restricted, so the ability to use a greater area at a lower clock frequency can be limited. A third dimension is the efficiency of hardware: bespoke hardware structures, such as mask-programmed (or FPGA) accelerators (Section 6.4) are far more energy efficient than programmable structures such as processor cores and should be deployed if Amdahl's rule indicates that there is a performance benefit.

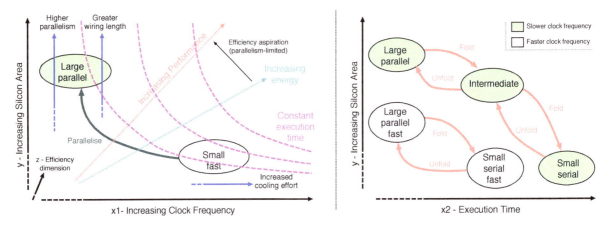

Figure 4.10 Abstract views of the principal axes that span the SoC design space for a task. Parallelism can be traded for clock frequency (left), which shows two design points. At a given clock frequency, the silicon area (and parallelism) can be traded for execution time using a time/space fold/unfold (right)

The right-hand plot illustrates the trade-off between silicon use and throughput. The fold/unfold transformation (Section 4.4.2) for a task is an automatic or manual alteration to the number of processors used. Alternatively, it can alter the structure of an individual subsystem to change the degree of parallelism without changing the clock frequency. Clearly, the clock frequency can also be adjusted, so two clock frequencies are illustrated. (There are intermediate design points at all clock frequencies, but these are not shown for clarity.)

Many of the trade-offs can be summarised with basic analytic models that demonstrate interesting interactions between high-level design decisions. Andre DeHon presented several of these in interesting publications [1].

4.4.1 Thermal Design

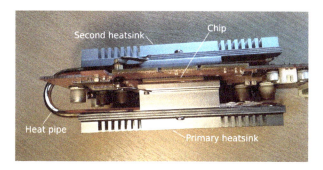

Figure 4.11 Thermal management of a high-power chip. The primary heat sink makes thermal contact with the chip. A heat pipe is connected to a second heat sink. There is no other connection to the second heat sink

The largest challenge for today's SoCs is effective heat dissipation. Thermal circuits work largely like electrical circuits: they have resistance and capacitance (but there is no thermal equivalent of inductance). Charge corresponds to heat, voltage corresponds to temperature and capacitance corresponds to heat capacity. The temperature of a lumped-element node is the integral of the running difference of net heat flow in or out of it divided by its thermal capacity C. Figure 4.12 shows a simple thermal dissipation model with one node. Heat is generated by the source on the left at a rate P J/s (i.e. P watts) when it is active. Heat is delivered to the sink on the right-hand side. The sink models ambient air at temperature T_0. We assume there is no heating of the ambient environment, so T_0 remains constant. In the diagram, the thermal node is simply 'connected' to the ambient air by a thermal path of just one link, although a more detailed model of the various structures involved is usually used. The thermal equivalent of Ohm's law is **Newton's law of cooling**, which states that the rate of flow of heat w through a thermal path is the difference in temperatures $T_1 - T_0$ divided by the thermal resistance of the path. Hence, when cooling, the system is governed by the equation

$$w = \frac{1}{R_{\text{thermal}}}(T_1 - T_0) = -C_{\text{thermal}}\frac{dT_1}{dt}$$

where w is the rate of heat flow between the components (in J/s), which are connected by a material of thermal resistance R_{thermal}. Recall that 1 J/s = 1 watt. When the power is off, the thermal node cools exponentially to ambient temperature. The heat capacity of the thermal node is C_{thermal}. This depends on its mass and material and has units of J/K.

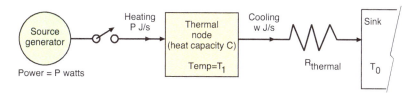

Figure 4.12 Generic thermal circuit, showing on/off heat source, thermal node and thermal resistance between the node and its heat sink

Silicon chips designed to dissipate more than a watt are mounted on a heat spreader plate that consists of about 10 grams of copper. The thermal conductivity of copper is exceptionally good at

401 W/m per degree, so if the spreader plate has a thickness of 2 mm and an area of $1\,cm^2$, the thermal conductivity to the back of the chip is $401 \times 10^{-4}/0.002 \approx 20\,W/K$. So, it will convey 10 W for a small temperature drop of half a degree. Two other components of the thermal path need to be considered: the silicon wafer itself and the air around the heat spreader.

The thermal conductivity of silicon is about 130 W/m per degree. The electronics on the top of the silicon chip are a wafer thickness away from the spreader plate on the back of the chip, which is about 1/3 mm. Uniform electronic heating of 10 W will cause the top of a $1\,cm^2$ chip to be 0.25°C hotter than its backplate, but if most of the heat is dissipated in just 10 per cent of the silicon, as may be the case for a typical SoC, the temperature difference rises to 2.5°C. The temperature at the top affects the behaviour of transistors and is known as the **junction temperature**, denoted T_J. For everyday commercial chips, design margins normally allow a maximum T_J of about 100°C. Given the thermal path to the outside of the chip, this allows an upper ambient temperature of 70°C to be specified. Medical, military and aerospace applications may require chips to operate correctly for a much wider ambient range, for example, as large as -40 to $+125°C$.

Packaged chips are cooled using free air, forced air, heat pipes or pumped liquids. Depending on the size of the heat sink, a free-air cooling arrangement will dissipate up to 1 W per degree rise above ambient. With fan-forced air, twice as much heat can be extracted. With water or glycol cooling, massive amounts of heat can be extracted, resulting in effective thermal resistances of more than 100 W/K. For handheld devices using free-air dissipation, the rise in case temperature must be less than about 6–8°C before it becomes uncomfortable to hold, limiting power use to roughly the same number of watts.

One gram of copper has a heat capacity of 2.6 K/J, so a 20-gram heat plate will rise by 0.13°C for each joule stored. If it absorbs 10 W for 10 seconds, it would rise by 13°C in the absence of a heat dissipation path.

Like its electrical equivalent, the **thermal time constant** of a system is the time for its temperature to decay to $1/e \approx 0.368$ from ambient and is given by the product of the heat capacity and the thermal resistance. For our example, this is

$$\text{Thermal time constant} = \frac{\text{Thermal capacity}}{\text{Thermal conductance}} = \frac{52\,J/K}{20\,W/K} \approx 2.6\,\text{seconds}$$

Hence, techniques such as **computational sprinting** (Section 4.6.10) can use a peak power much greater than the average power use, provided there are gaps every few seconds to allow the chip to cool down after each burst.

It is common for an **embedded temperature monitor** to be incorporated somewhere on a chip. The diode V/I curve given by the Shockley equation depends strongly on the temperature term. This enables T_J to be cheaply and accurately measured given suitable analogue support circuits. Operating system governors can typically sense a reading via an ADC channel. The channel can be hardwired into the DVFS controllers (Section 4.6.8) as a **thermal throttle** (Section 4.6.10) or an overload protection mechanism.

Heat is also extracted from a SoC via its wired connections, which are made of aluminium. Although aluminium has twice the thermal resistance of copper for the same geometry, the power wires and signal nets connect directly to the top of the chip and some have fully metallic connections to the heat-generating transistors. Hence, they provide an additional heat extraction route that should be considered in detailed modelling.

4.4.2 Folding, Re-timing and Recoding

As was summarised in Figure 4.10, a principal design trade-off is between high performance and low power. The **time/space fold** and **unfold** operations trade execution time for silicon area. A function can be computed with fewer clocks by 'unfolding' it in the time domain, typically by **loop unwinding** and predication. The following pair of RTL-like code fragments illustrate the transform. The left-hand fragment denotes a runtime loop that uses a single adder and multiplier whereas the right-hand fragment shows the unwound loop that uses three times more hardware. The predication step is the insertion of the `if` statements.

```
LOOPED (time) option:               | UNWOUND (space) option:
                                    |
for (i=0; i < 3 and i < limit; i++) |  if (0 < limit) sum += data[0] * coef[j];
   sum += data[i] * coef[i+j];      |  if (1 < limit) sum += data[1] * coef[1+j];
                                    |  if (2 < limit) sum += data[2] * coef[2+j];
```

Successive loop iterations interact using the '+=' operation. Addition is an associative operator. In this context, it is said to perform an **associative reduction** from a vector to a scalar (Section 6.9.1). If the only interactions between loop iterations are outputs via such an operator, the loop iterations can be executed in parallel. On the other hand, if one iteration stores a variable that affects the next iteration or determines the loop exit condition, then the unwinding possibilities are reduced. Given that multiplication tends to be a pipelined operator at the hardware level for any significant word size, the above example is an oversimplification in terms of input to a low-level RTL logic synthesiser (Section 8.3). High-level synthesis tools (Section 6.9), however, can operate from this style of coding, deploying pipelined implementations of the arithmetic operators. High-level tools generate ancillary logic that is needed to sequence the operands correctly to the multiplier instances. Some such tools will also automate the decision about whether to unwind the loop whereas others will perform loop unwinding based on user annotations called **pragmas**.

Critical Path Timing Delay and Pipelining

Meeting the **timing closure** is the process of manipulating a design to meet its target clock rate (as set by a marketing department, for instance) (Section 8.12.16). A design can be **re-timed** with and without changing the state encoding of the existing state flip-flops. Re-timing is the process of modifying the sequential behaviour of a circuit (i.e. its next-state function) so that it meets timing constraints. Adding a pipeline stage increases the number of states without **recoding** an existing state. Inserting a pipeline stage is the **go-to** manipulation.

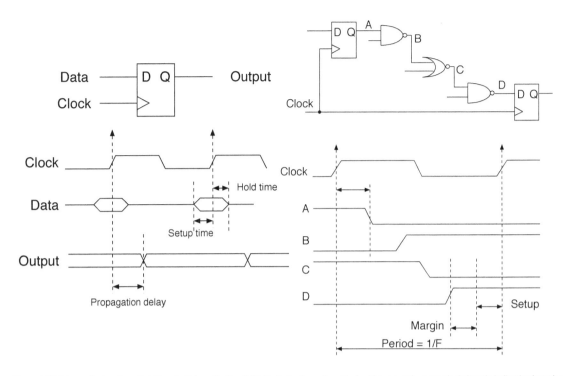

Figure 4.13 Primary timing characteristics of a D-type flip-flop (left). Typical nature of a critical path in a synchronous clock domain indicating how the maximum clock frequency (F) is calculated (right)

The maximum clock frequency of a synchronous clock domain is set by its **critical path**. Figure 4.13 shows the general nature of a critical path. The output of one flip-flop in a clock domain feeds through a chain of combinational gates and arrives at the D-input of the same or another flip-flop in the domain. One of the paths of this nature must be the slowest. Several, very similar paths may compete to be the slowest depending on the PVT variation (Section 8.4.4), but one will be dominant at any instant. The slowest path of combinational logic must have settled before the setup time of its destination flip-flop starts. As shown, the maximum clock frequency is the reciprocal of the path length. If a higher frequency clock is set, the subsystem is said to be **over-clocked** and will be unreliable. Depending on the engineering margins, it may fail and crash in certain PVT corners. The hold time requirement is an ancillary timing specification that is important if the output of one flop is directly connected to the input of another, such as in a shift register. The D-input must be held for at least the **hold time** after the clock edge. The **clock-to-Q propagation delay** must be greater than the hold time for such shift register structures to be valid.

As noted, pipelining is commonly used to boost system performance. Introducing a pipeline stage increases latency but also shortens the critical path and hence, raises the maximum clock frequency (Figure 4.14). Fortunately, many applications are tolerant to the processing delay of a logic subsystem. Consider a decoder for a fibre optic signal. The fibre might be many kilometres long and a few additional clock cycles in the decoder would increase the processing delay by an amount equivalent to a few coding symbol wavelengths, e.g. 20 cm per pipeline stage for a 1 Gbaud modulation rate.

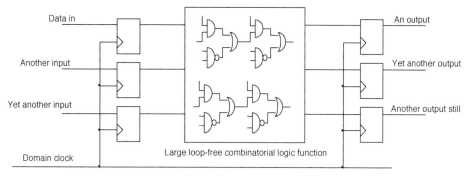

Figure 4.14 A circuit before (top) and after (bottom) insertion of an additional pipeline stage

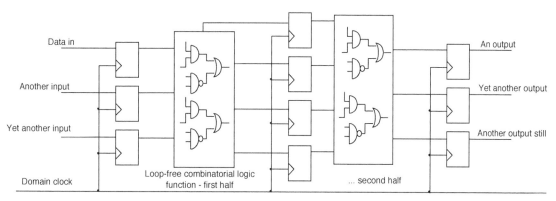

Pipelining introduces a new state but does not require existing state flip-flops to change meaning. On the other hand, **flip-flop migration**, as illustrated in Figure 4.15, does alter the encoding of existing states. Migration may be manually turned on or off during logic synthesis by typical RTL compiler tools. Migration exchanges the delay in one path for a delay in another to balance delay paths. A well-chosen sequence of such transformations can lead to a shorter critical path overall.

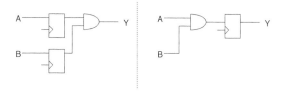

Figure 4.15 Flip-flop migration. Two circuits that behave identically but which have different state encodings

Although migration is very useful and is automated in logic synthesisers, it cannot always be applied. For instance, in the following RTL example, the first migration is a local transformation that has no global consequences:

```
Before:                Migration 1:                 Migration 2 (non causal):
  a <= b + c;            b1 <= b; c1 <= c;            q1 <= (dd) ? (b+c): 0;
  q <= (d) ? a:0;        q <= (d) ? b1+c1:0;          q  <= q1;
```

The second migration, which attempts to perform the multiplexing one cycle earlier, will require an earlier version of d, here termed dd, which might not be available (e.g. if it were an external input and we need knowledge of the future). An earlier version of a given input can sometimes be obtained by delaying all the inputs, but this cannot be done for applications where the system response time (in-to-out delay) is critical (such as generating the not-ready handshake signal in older bus protocols). Further problems that prevent migration from being used are:

- Circuits containing loops (proper synchronous loops) cannot be pushed further than the loop circumference, which can be quite short. An example is the control hazard in the RISC pipeline conditional branch, which is short (Section 2.1.4).

- External interfaces that do not use transactional handshakes (i.e. those without flow control) cannot tolerate automatic re-timing since information about when data are valid is not explicit. A related problem is that in standard RTLs, even when the interface is transactional, the logic synthesiser does not understand the protocol. This has been solved in higher-level design expression languages, such as Chisel (Section 6.8.3) and Bluespec (Section 6.8.5).

- Many structures, including RAM and ALUs, have a pipeline delay (or several), so the hazard on their input port needs resolving in a different clock cycle from hazards involving their result values. Again, this information is not manifest in RTL descriptions and so the transformation cannot be automated during logic synthesis.

However, re-timing can overcome structural hazards (e.g. the writeback cycle in a RISC pipeline, Section 2.1.4).

Recoding without changing the number of flip-flops can also be helpful. Logic synthesiser tools can convert from binary to Gray or one-hot coding. **Gray coding** is a binary number ordering such that two successive values differ in only one bit. For instance, a 3-bit Gray code goes 000, 001, 011, 010, 110, 111, 101 and 100. Although originally designed for mechanical systems, such as shaft encoders, Gray-coded digital logic is intrinsically safe for clock domain crossing (Section 3.7.3). Automatic recoding to Gray values causes a long bus to take consume less dynamic power (Section 4.6.2) than if driven by a binary counter since it has fewer transitions. Another recoding is to unary or **one-hot coding**. These are the same thing. They use 2^n bits to encode an n-bit binary number with just one bit being asserted for a given count value. The next-state logic for a one-hot coded counter is exceptionally simple, leading to very short critical paths. Also, no binary-to-unary output decoder is required in applications that need to command different operations on different count values.

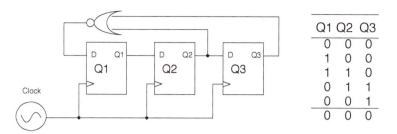

Q1	Q2	Q3
0	0	0
1	0	0
1	1	0
0	1	1
0	0	1
0	0	0

Figure 4.16 Schematic and count sequence for a divide-by-five counter using Johnson encoding

Figure 4.16 shows a **Johnson counter** that divides by five using three flip-flops. A Johnson counter uses a hybrid of one-hot and Gray coding with a maximum of $2n$ states out of an n-bit word being used. It is based around a shift register and has minimal next-state logic. Hence, this design is always used when the fastest possible counter is required, e.g. in GaAs logic for microwave radio-frequency synthesisers.

Automatic recoding from binary to one of these other forms is often performed by a logic synthesiser (Section 8.3.8). Large finite-state machines (FSMs) are commonly recoded so that the output function is easy to generate. This is critical for good performance with complex sequencers, as used, for instance, in HLS. In a flip-flop-rich technology, such as an FPGA, there is zero effective area overhead using such encodings, just a speed and energy benefit. A trivial recoding used for some target cell libraries is to invert logic polarity in a flip-flop. This enables a reset to act as a preset and flips the starting value held in the flop. Despite its benefits, automated recoding has the disadvantage that it makes low-level debugging more complex.

4.5 Design Trade-offs in Memory Systems

Memory systems frequently need to be multi-port, meaning that a given storage location is accessible to some number of transaction initiators. The underlying hardware implementation of a simple SRAM can be single or dual ported (Section 2.6.5), but often a greater number of effective ports are required. Also dual-ported RAM has an area overhead, which means it is commonly not a good solution. Whether cached or not, a memory system will typically consist of an aggregation of individual RAMs. In this section, we discuss aggregation techniques for homogeneous RAMs. The case for using heterogeneous RAMs that vary in terms of clock speed and capacity for hierarchic memory systems is made in Section 6.6.1.

Sequential Consistency

An important design decision is what level of sequential consistency to provide. If some reads and writes to nominal memory are actually served from intermediate caches, write buffers or other forwarding paths in the interconnect, it is possible for the relative order of writes to different locations to appear differently from different points of view. This is the **sequential consistency problem**. A typical programming paradigm is for one initiator to write data to a buffer in shared memory and then to update a flag, pointer or counter to reflect that the buffer is ready to be inspected by other initiators. Figure 4.17 illustrates the essence of this situation. Here, the flag is the first word of a shared memory buffer being non-zero.

```
        Thread 1 - Requestor          |          Thread 2 - Server
                                      |
        ...                           |    while(true)
        buffer[1] = operand1;         |    {
        buffer[2] = operand2;         |      if (!buffer[0]) { yield(); continue; }
        write_fence();                |      read_fence();
        buffer[0] = COMMAND;          |      handle(buffer);
        ...                           |      buffer[0] = 0;
                                      |    }
```

Figure 4.17 Two code fragments using message-passing in shared memory with explicit memory fences. The yield() call could be to the suspend primitive of the operating system scheduler. Alternatively, if running on **bare metal**, it is a dedicated instruction (called YIELD in the Arm ISA) that interacts with hardware hyper-threading if present

However, in a memory system that does not observe sequential consistency, an observer might see erroneous data if it reads the buffer contents after seeing a change to the first word although the writes to the remainder of the buffer are not yet visible. An equivalent problem arises if reads are serviced out of order. Three primary system-level models that address sequential consistency are:

1. Ensure that all shared memory components observe strict sequential consistency.

2. Use a weaker model, known as **processor consistency**, in which all readers see items in a buffer in the same order as they were written by a single initiator but see an arbitrary view of how writes from different initiators are interleaved.

3. Use **relaxed consistency**, for which the programmer must insert explicit fence instructions.

A **memory fence instruction**, also sometimes called a barrier, is inserted by a programmer to constrain the order of memory operations. The three main forms are read fences, write fences and everything fences, which are the same as a read fence followed directly by a write fence or vice versa. A write fence ensures that for any data written before the fence, the data are committed to a store before any data from subsequent writes. Likewise, a read fence ensures that for all reads issued before the fence, the reads have completed before any subsequent read. Hence, as shown in the above example, a write fence should be issued between writing the last word of data to the buffer and writing the flag that acts as the transaction commit. Equivalently, a read fence can be issued between checking the flag and reading the data from the buffer. Real-world busses, as discussed in Chapter 3, support a broader class of bus transactions, beyond just reads and writes. Hence, the operand to a generic fence instruction is a square matrix of Boolean flags indicating which classes must complete before which others.

Memory Bank Arrangements

A single-ported SRAM array presents a structural hazard in that the single address bus can select only one location at a time (Section 6.3). For a given clock frequency, the data transfer rate per bit of a read or write port is fixed at that clock rate. Two basic approaches are used to increase memory bandwidth: **multiple banks** and **wide words**. Smaller SRAM arrays imply simpler and faster decoding and shorter word-line and bit-line lengths. This reduces access times and increases power efficiency at the expense of some loss in area efficiency due to peripheral logic. In a multiple bank, different locations can be accessed simultaneously, whereas just one location at a time can be accessed for memories with wider words. With banking, concurrent accesses ideally hit different banks, therefore providing parallelism.

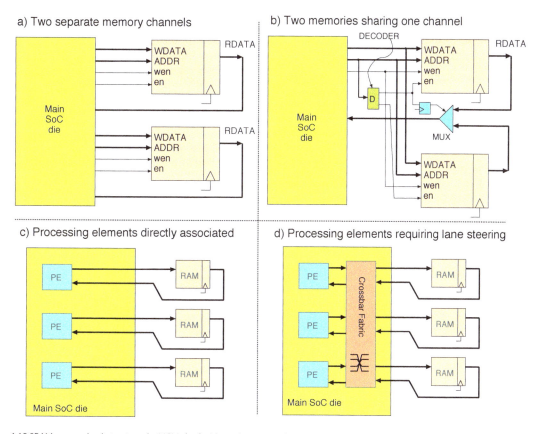

Figure 4.18 SRAM memory bank structures for MCMs (top) with two interconnection patterns inside the SoC (bottom)

Figure 4.18 illustrates typical memory banking arrangements for multi-chip modules (MCMs) (Section 8.9.1). The SRAM memory is die-stacked on the main SoC, but equivalent considerations apply to DRAM and on-chip and PCB-level design. Configuration (a) is simple. Each RAM instance has its own dedicated wiring to the main SoC. This is ideal for use case (c), since each memory channel needs to be accessed by only one core or other processing element. Configuration (b) has two memory devices connected to one channel. This reduces the pin and net count but can consume more dynamic energy than dedicated wiring under low to medium loads due to the greater switched charge (Section 4.6.1). Also the single-channel structural hazard limits bandwidth to a factor of $1\times$.

Figure 4.18(d) also uses external channels but has an on-SoC switch so that unrestricted access is allowed under an address interleave scheme. Given a uniform, random addressing pattern, the probability that two locations of interest are in the same bank is inversely proportional to the number of banks. Hence, more banks are better. With multiple RAMs, the data can be arranged randomly or systematically among them. To achieve a 'random' data placement, some set of the address bus bits are normally used to select the different banks. Indeed, if multiple chips are used in a single bank, this arrangement is inevitably deployed. The question is, which bits to use. Using the low bits for a bank select creates a fine-grained interleave, but tends to destroy spatial locality in the access pattern. The best bit field to use also depends on whether the memory elements are truly random access. SRAM is truly random access, whereas DRAM will have different access times depending on which rows are open. However, even SRAM expends greater energy when switching between bit-cell words compared with selecting different bit lanes from the addressed word.

If data access patterns are known in advance, which is typically the case for HLS, then data access can be maximised or even ensured by careful bank mapping. Interconnection complexity is also reduced if it is manifest that certain data paths of a full crossbar will never be used. In the best cases (easiest applications), no lane-steering or interconnect switch is needed and each processing element acts on just one part of the wide data bus. This is basically the GPU architecture.

An architectural technique that offers pseudo-multi-porting is shown in Figure 4.19. Here, two memory banks store the same data. It can be generalised to any number of so-called **mirror copies**. Disjoint loads can happen in parallel, but the stores update all copies simultaneously. This increases the read but not the write bandwidth. However, since most data are read more often than written, it works. The advantage of this scheme is that fewer physical ports are needed for each memory bank. On the other hand, the obvious disadvantage is the area and power overhead of requiring multiple memory banks, since the number of memory banks is proportional to the number of read ports required.

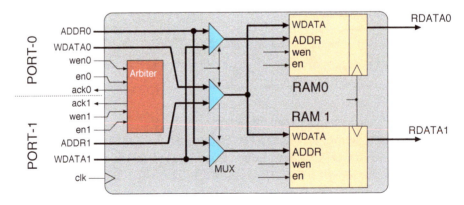

Figure 4.19 Pseudo-dual porting of RAM (using write mirroring)

One disadvantage is that arbitration is required, which in turn means that an acknowledgement reverse handshake is required, as illustrated. This introduces a level of timing crosstalk between the ports, which does not arise with actual dual porting and which may be a problem for hard real-time systems. An alternative approach uses static time-division multiplexing or several successive memory accesses in a single cycle. However, these approaches are possible only if cache access is much faster than the clock cycle. This is usually not the case, and hence, this method is not scalable to multiple ports. Real dual porting is sometimes more suitable for clock-domain crossing, especially if high-level protocols avoid read/write clashes on a common location such that no low-level mechanisms are needed to provide a specific resolution semantic.

Design Trade-offs in a DRAM Controller

As described in Section 2.6.6, addresses are sent over a DRAM channel in two halves: row then column. DRAM is slow to access and certainly does not provide random access compared with on-chip RAM. A modern PC might take 100 to 300 CPU clock cycles to access a random location of DRAM since the CPU may clock considerably faster than the DRAM. However, the ratio is often not as severe in embedded systems that use slower system clocks. Nonetheless, it is nearly always helpful to put at least one level of DRAM caching on a SoC. This can be associated with CPU cores or part of the memory controller or both may be used.

A **DRAM/dynamic memory controller (DMC)** sequences the operations on a DRAM channel. The DMC controller may have embedded error detection or correction logic using additional bit lanes in the DRAM. Caches will access the DRAM in localised bursts, saving or filling a cache line, and hence, cache lines are always arranged to lie within a DRAM row. The controller will keep multiple DRAM pages open at once to exploit spatio-temporal access locality. The high random-access latency and writeback overhead of DRAM requires a bank-closing policy in which mainstream controllers look ahead in a pool of pending requests to assist in deciding when to close a row. Closing a row is also known as closing a page or deactivation. It is normal to prioritise reads over writes, but for data consistency, overtaking must be avoided. Alternatively, reads can be served from the write queue. However, a new request in a previously open line could arrive just after the controller closes it. An **open-page policy** does not write back after the last apparent operation on a row has been processed. It keeps the bank open in case another operation on that row shortly arrives, up to a timeout duration. A **closed-page policy** writes back when there is no work to do. This allows precharging of the bit lines and reduces the latency of the next operation to use that bank. It is best if clients can tolerate responses out of order and hence, the interconnect must support tagged transactions (Section 3.1.4). In reality, DRAM banks are often partitioned into **bank groups**. Within a bank group, power supply and noise issues dictate additional timing constraints on successive operations, which is a further dimension to be considered in access scheduling.

DRAM energy use is discussed in the chapter on ESL, Chapter 5. A major use of energy is for the static power in the high-speed PCB driving and receiving pads. These pads are collectively called the **DRAM physical interface (PHY)**. Each row activation, deactivation, data transfer or refresh consumes a quanta of dynamic energy.

Figure 4.20 shows the structure and board-level nets for a 32-bit DRAM channel. Four separate column address select (CAS) nets are used so that writes to individual byte lanes are possible. For large DRAM arrays, there will also be multiple row address select (RAS) lines that serve as the rank

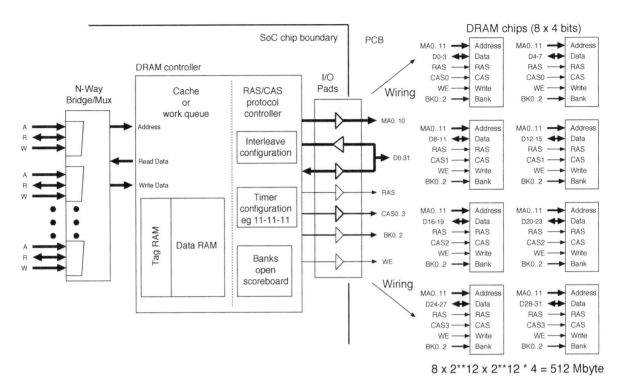

Figure 4.20 Typical structure of a 32-bit DRAM controller connected to DRAM devices. The on-SoC controller manages a DRAM channel with one rank made of eight individual DRAM chips. Each chip has eight banks with four bit planes. Each bit plane has $2^{12} \times 2^{12}$ bits. A DRAM is typically made available to various on-SoC subsystems using a multi-way bus multiplexor

address decode. These help to save power by not sending a RAS to devices that will not be given a following CAS. The controller essentially has two halves. The left half keeps track of outstanding work and caches recent results. The right half keeps track of which rows are open in each bank using a scoreboard and generates carefully timed control-signal waveforms. A modern DRAM controller has an elaborate boot-up procedure that involves:

- if present, reading data from an on-DIMM **serial presence detect (SPD)** ROM that contains the electronic data sheet for the device

- setting the supply voltage and data clock frequency

- calibrating clock and data lines by configuring programmable delay lines and termination impedances

- setting up many internal registers inside the DRAM devices that control the burst addressing and mode wrapping policy

- implementing specific RAS-to-CAS latencies and many other timing details including writeback (precharge) times

- setting up hardware timers to meet the refresh rate targets.

Given the complexity of the task, a controller may have a tiny CPU to interrogate SPD device data and gets the DRAM operating before the main SoC bootloader starts.

In the worst case, the DRAM refresh overhead has a 1 or 2 per cent impact on bus throughput. For example, if 1024 refresh cycles are needed over a 4 ms interval, then a refresh operation is needed on average every 4 μs. This might take 100 clock cycles or so. However, as long as each row is refreshed at some point in a 2 ms slotted time window, the specification is met. Most refresh operations can be slotted in when no other commands need to be issued.

Given the multi-level address structure of a DRAM, which has fields `row`, `column`, `bank`, `rank` and `channel`, another design consideration is how a physical address is mapped to the various physical bits making up these fields. This alters how the memory layout affects performance. Most DRAM controllers are programmable in terms of this physical address interleave. A baseline example, shown in Figure 4.21(a), starting with the most significant bit in the physical address space, uses the order: `row`, `bank`, `column`, `burst offset` and `byte lane`. The fields `channel` and `rank`, if present, are the most significant. The field `byte lane` is always at the bottom, as defined for a byte-addressed memory space. For the spatial locality, `burst offset` must come next and `column` must be lower than `row`. However, having `bank` lower than `column` allows interleaving of accesses to open pages, which is sensible when the system workload has a large amount of activity localised to one large area. In arrangement (b), `bank` has been moved as low as it can go without disrupting cache lines and burst transfers. On the other hand, having `bank` higher can make sense if the system has various concurrent active hot spots, such as is typical with heap, stack, code and static segments.

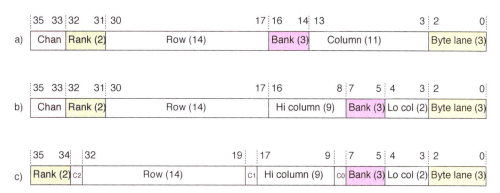

Figure 4.21 Three possible arrangements of DRAM address fields within a physical address. In the centre arrangement (b), the bank field is lower than its naive position in the top arrangement (a). This improves load balancing over banks, but the field is not moved so low that a cache line or burst transfer is split over banks. The rank and channel fields can also be moved lower. Arrangement (c) shows a channel field that has been split and dispersed

If `rank` and `channel` are also present, there are more options! Due to spatial locality in access patterns, address bit behaviour becomes increasingly correlated as the bit number increases. Arrangement (c) shows one way of spreading out some of the `channel` bits. There is a further discussion in Section 6.9.1. Using virtual memory (VM) and its page management policy, the operating system can freely redistribute the top bits. For the lower address bits that form the offset within a VM page, it is possible to use a hardware XOR-based function to whiten the row access patterns.

4.6 SoC Energy Minimisation

A mobile phone battery typically has a capacity of around 10 W h (watt-hours), which is 36 kJ. Energy in an electronic device gets used in several different ways. For a mobile phone, we might see the following budget:

- screen backlight: 1 to 2 W

- RF transmissions via the various transmit antennae: up to 4 W

- sound and vibrations through the speaker and little shaker motor: 200 mW

- heat wasted in the electronics: up to 5 W.

Battery life is very important for portable devices. In data centres, electricity is used both for power and heat extraction, and generally, the electricity bill is the biggest operating cost. Saving energy in computing is always a good idea. In this section, we will examine how digital logic uses energy and how it can be saved.

4.6.1 Power, Resistance and Capacitance

Figure 4.22(a) shows a battery pack for a mobile phone. Strictly, this is not a battery since it has only one cell, though it contains other components as well. If the external terminals are accidentally shorted, a fuse prevents excessive heat or fire. A small-valued series resistor acts as a current shunt for measuring the charge and discharge currents. The voltage across this resistor is measured with an amplifier in the associated battery monitor electronics. The amount of energy remaining in the battery is computed by measuring the terminal voltage and integrating the charge and discharge currents over time. Extra electricity applied to a fully charged cell just creates heat. This condition is detected by the thermistor, whose resistance varies with the temperature of the battery. Being fully charged serves as a boundary condition, which eliminates the arbitrary constant arising from integration over an indefinite period. A complete history of charge and discharge operations may also be stored to assess battery ageing and to trim the charge state estimator function that is based on the terminal voltage. The external **battery state indication (BSI)** connections enable the charge status to be read remotely by the portable device. A battery also typically contains a data sheet in internal ROM that identifies the battery model and its characteristics.

When electricity is consumed, the power law, $P = VI$, states that the power in watts is equal to the supply voltage (volts) multiplied by the supply current (amps). Power is defined as the rate of energy use and 1 W is 1 J/s. Also, 1 J of energy is 1 C of charge dropping 1 V in potential. For the battery illustrated, the terminal voltage is 3.7 V and the capacity is quoted as 1650 mA h, which is equivalent

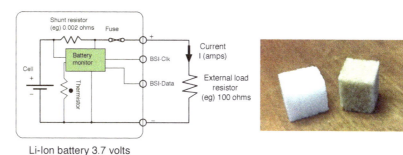

Li-Ion battery 3.7 volts

Figure 4.22 (a) Lithium-ion battery for a mobile phone (3.7 V, 1650 mA h, 6 W h or 22 kJ), external view. (b) Typical internal structure. (c) Two sugar cubes

to $3.7 \times 3600 \times 1.65 = 22$ kJ of energy. For comparison, two standard 4-gram sugar cubes have 32 kcal of energy, which is about 134 kJ (Figure 4.22(c)).

If a load resistor of 100 Ω is applied, as shown, **Ohm's law** gives the external current as $I = V/R = 3.7/100$, which is 37 mA. The power being used is $37 \times 3.7 = 140$ mW or 140 mJ/s and the battery life is $22 \times 10^3/(0.14 \times 3600) = 45$ hours, which is nearly 2 days.

Power can also be expressed as $P = Ef$, where E is the amount of energy used in an event and f is the frequency of that event. For synchronous digital electronics using CMOS, the event of interest is the active clock edge. In transaction-level modelling (Chapter 5), we assign energy use to each transaction. Our power estimate is then the sum of all the transaction energies divided by the runtime, which is also the energy of each transaction multiplied by the average frequency at which it takes place.

4.6.2 Dynamic Energy and Dynamic Power

Power use in digital electronics can be partitioned into **static power use** and **dynamic power use**. Dynamic power is defined to be the electricity usage rate that arises in proportion to how often a net changes state. The static power is the remainder: it is unaffected by net-level activity. In modern CMOS devices, dynamic power tends to exceed static power by a factor of 3 or 4, but the ratio can sometimes be much higher by several orders of magnitude. The high-ratio scenario used to be the only design point for mainstream CMOS technology, but today that design point is used only in specialised low-leakage, low-frequency CMOS technologies that are targeted at long-lifetime, battery-powered applications.

Figure 4.23 is an electrical equivalent circuit for modelling the dynamic power of a CMOS SoC. A switch is used to alternately charge and discharge a capacitor through a resistor. On both the charge and discharge halves of the cycle, the resistor dissipates energy as heat. The resistance R partly determines the time constant $\tau = CR$. If the time constant is sufficiently shorter than the switching cycle, $\tau \ll 1/f$, the capacitor will become fully charged and discharged in each cycle. The energy dissipated on discharge is the energy in the capacitor, which is $E = CV^2/2$. By symmetry, the energy dissipated in the resistor during the charge phase is the same amount, so the total energy use per cycle is CV^2. The power used is $P = fE = fCV^2$. In a real SoC, not all of the nets change state every clock

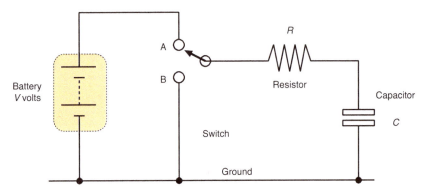

Figure 4.23 Lumped-element electrical equivalent modelling of dynamic power use of a CMOS SoC. The energy drawn from the battery each clock cycle is essentially 'wasted' as heat in the distributed resistance of the active parts of the SoC

cycle: some parts of the chip may be in power-down mode and other parts may be switched on but not doing anything. So, in this electrical equivalent circuit, the switch models the system clock and the capacitor models the average amount of capacitance that is discharged each clock cycle. The general rule is that **energy use is proportional to clock frequency and quadratically proportional to supply voltage**. This second effect is the primary motivation for moving digital systems from the 5-V supplies used between 1950 and 2000 to the lower voltages (e.g. 1.1 V) used today. Also, note, somewhat counter-intuitively, that the energy used does not depend on the value of the resistance. In reality, the resistor is the effective sum of resistive effects in the wiring and the transistors. Both forms of resistor are illustrated in Figure 4.24.

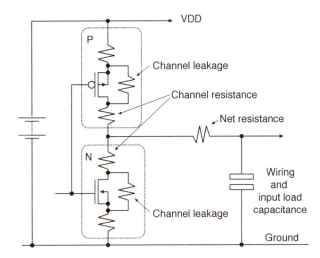

Figure 4.24 A generic CMOS invertor structure shown with explicit parasitic resistances and lumped-equivalent output loading. This illustrates the primary electric paths in CMOS logic

Second and less-significant contributors to dynamic power use are **short-circuit currents**. These are also known as **crowbar currents** (named after the so-called crowbar power protection mechanism that permanently shorts the power rails with a heavy-duty thyristor under error conditions). A short-circuit path is visible in Figure 4.24. The short-circuit current flows directly from the supply to ground at any time that both the P and N transistors are simultaneously conducting. In CMOS, this theoretically never happens: one or the other transistor is off at any instant. In reality, the transistors are not digital switches that are either on or off; they are analogue amplifiers that gradually transition between strongly conducting and very weakly conducting. When the input voltage is between logic levels, both transistors are partially conducting and the so-called short-circuit current flows. Every time the input net transitions, it passes through an intermediate voltage. This can be especially bad with tri-state busses, which, in a basic design, are floating when not being used and can float to an intermediate voltage causing significant short-circuit currents. Tri-state busses are normally totally avoided in modern SoC designs. If they are used, the floating state must be avoided using a **bus holder** on each net (also known as a **bus keeper**). A typical bus holder structure is shown in Figure 4.25. A reset-set (RS) latch is connected to each tri-state data line. An RS latch has a very weak output drive, due to its implementation, which uses small transistors, and so is simply overridden when one of the primary drivers controls the bus line. Of course, there is still a small short-circuit current each time the bus holder's weak drive is overcome, but, if the transistors are optimised for speed, this is much lower than the short-circuit current possible in one of the sensing buffers.

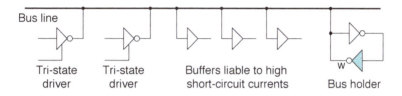

Figure 4.25 A tri-state data line showing driving gates, sensing buffers and a bus holder (or keeper). The bus holder has a weak output driver, denoted 'W', which acts like a series resistor to reduce the output current during transient bus fights (Section 1.1.2)

Clearly, the dynamic power used by a net depends on its **activity factors**, such as the probability of being at logic one and its **toggle rate**. For a synchronous system, the toggle rate is the fraction of clock cycles on which it changes value. The maximum toggle rate for a flip-flop output is 100 per cent, but a flip-flop that changes to a new, uniform random value every clock cycle has a toggle rate of 50 per cent. The clock net itself has a toggle rate of 200 per cent and figures above 100 per cent are also possible for double-data rate busses, as used for DDR DRAM. Simulators can measure activity factors and report them in a **switching activity interchange format (SAIF)** file (Section 5.6.1), which can be imported into a power modelling tool.

4.6.3 Static Power Use

Figure 4.24 also shows the two leakage paths, indicated by the channel leakage parasitic resistors. A transistor that is supposedly off still conducts to some extent. The current it carries is called **static leakage current**. P and N transistors typically have the same off-resistance, so the same static current passes regardless of the dynamic state or amount of dynamic activity in the circuit. The first generations of CMOS technology had exceptionally low leakage currents; thus, static power consumption could be neglected during design. They used relatively large transistors and supply voltages in the 5–15 V range. However, as noted earlier, the V^2 term for dynamic energy has motivated significant reductions in supply voltage. Lower voltages mean that an off transistor is less off than it was with higher voltages (see Eq (4.1) in Section 4.6.6) and hence, has higher leakage. With modern technology, a trade-off exists in the choice of dopant levels and other aspects of transistor geometry. These affect the **threshold voltage** V_T for transistor switching. This is the smallest gate voltage at which (additional) current starts to flow in a straightforward, enhancement-mode field-effect transistor (FET) (beyond the leakage current). In the simple switch view of a FET, when the gate voltage is above this level (for an N-type transistor), the device is on and when below, it is off. The logic swing must comfortably exceed the threshold voltage. With lower supply voltages, lower threshold transistors must be used. However, a low threshold means the transistors are less turned off when they are supposed to be off; hence, there is higher leakage. A higher threshold means the input must swing further up before the transistor turns on, which is poor switching performance and hence, there are longer logic delays. Equivalent arguments apply to the on-resistance; a lower on-resistance overcomes the load capacitance more easily, resulting in faster logic, but larger or faster transistors leak more.

A large number of techniques have been used to tackle the leakage versus performance trade-off. A simple approach is to use a single design point over the whole SoC and aim for static power to be about half as much as dynamic power. This is becoming less attractive, since it rapidly encounters **dark silicon** constraints (Section 8.2). A mainstream approach is to use two different transistor designs. Low-threshold, leaky transistors are used on the critical paths (Section 4.4.2). These switch fastest. Slower transistors with less leakage are used elsewhere. This is a static approach; these transistors are manufactured with different geometries and dopant levels. Other techniques are dynamic, such as **partial power gating** (Section 4.6.10) and **dynamic body bias** (Section 4.6.10).

4.6.4 Wiring and Capacitance Modelling

Capacitance[1] is caused by two conductors being close to each other. Capacitance is increased beyond what would occur in a vacuum due to the relative permittivity of the surrounding material ϵ_r. The wiring capacitance for a pair of conductors with radius a and separation d is given by

$$C = \frac{\pi \epsilon_0 \epsilon_r}{\cosh^{-1}(d/2a)}$$

in farads per metre (F/m). For VLSI nets for which the spacing is the same as their width (i.e. $d \approx a$), the denominator is unity. If the insulator is silicon dioxide ($\epsilon_r \approx 4$), as used in VLSI, the capacitance is roughly 100 pF/m. At sub-centimetre chip dimensions, expressing this in units of 0.1 pF/mm or 0.1 fF/µm per net is more useful. If capacitance arises unintentionally, we refer to it, interchangeably, as stray or parasitic capacitance. Capacitance negatively contributes to both energy use and delay performance. Detailed analogue simulations that include capacitance and the transfer characteristics of a transistor are used to study circuit performance. An example using SPICE is presented in Section 4.6.7. However, this level of modelling is slow to run and unnecessary. The basic behaviour of digital logic can be adequately understood by lumping all the capacitive effects and then all the delay effects. These lumped figures are then used in simple formulae that also contain detailed **derating**

---

1. Strictly speaking, we are referring to mutual capacitance.

factors that have been carefully analysed for the nine PVT corners. The PVT corners relate to a cuboid space defined by variations in wafer processing, supply voltage and operating temperature (Section 8.4.4). This space has eight corners and the ninth point (or corner) is the nominal operating point in the centre of the cube.

Both the power consumption and effective delay of a gate driving a net depend mainly on the length of the net being driven.

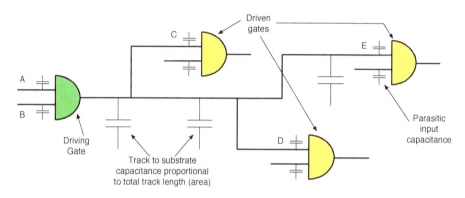

Figure 4.26 Logic net with a single source and three loads, showing tracking and input load capacitances

In CMOS VLSI, the main sources of capacitance are between the gate and channel of a FET and between a net and other nets in the wiring. Figure 4.26 shows a typical net that connects a source gate to three load gates. To change the voltage on the net, the source must overcome the net's stray capacitance and the input load capacitance. The **fanout** of a gate is the number of devices that its output feeds. (The fanout is three in the figure.) The gate will normally come from a **standard cell library** (Section 8.4.1). The net's stray capacitance is the track-to-substrate capacitance, which is a library constant times the track area. For constant-width nets, the area is proportional to length. Precise track lengths are known only after placing and routing. As shown in Figure 1.13, this information can be fed back into a high-level model in a **back-annotated post-layout simulation** (Section 8.7.4). Before synthesis or before layout, tools can predict net lengths from Rent's rule and RTL-level heuristics (Section 5.6.6). The load-dependent part is the sum of the input loads of all the devices being fed. These do not depend on the layout and so can be determined earlier in the back-end design flow.

In digital modelling of non-clock nets, the following principal simplifying assumption is commonly used: **All parts of the logic net change potential at exactly the same time.** The loading effects are then all absorbed into the delay model of the driving gate. This model is accurate when the output resistance of a gate is significantly higher than the net track resistance. For example, the points C, D and E in Figure 4.26 all change from 1 to 0 at the same time. Due to the AND functionality, the switching instant is a fixed pre-computed delay after either A or B goes from 1 to 0. The driving fixed device delay is computed with a lumping formula:

$$\text{Device delay} = (\text{Intrinsic delay}) + (\text{Output load} \times \text{Derating factor})$$

The output load is the sum of the wiring and gate input capacitances. The derating factor models the output strength of the driving gate and is taken from the gate's data sheet. The formula model estimates the delay from the input to a gate, through the internal electronics of a gate, through its output structure and down the conductor to the input of the successor gates. It effectively has three terms that are summed:

1. The internal delay of the gate, termed the intrinsic delay.

2. The reduction in speed of the output stage, due to the fanout/loading, termed the **derating delay**.

3. The propagation delay down the conductor.

For clock nets, which must be specially designed with low skew and known delays, more detailed techniques are used (Section 4.9.5).

The on-chip net delay depends on the distributed capacitance, inductance and resistance of the conductor material and the permittivity of the adjacent insulators. A detailed computation, using the Elmore model for nets that feed more than one destination, was presented in Section 3.1.1. For circuit board traces, the resistance can be neglected and the delay is just the **speed of light** in the circuit board material. Most PCBs are made from **FR-4 fibreglass**, which has a relative permittivity of $\epsilon_r \approx 4.7$, so the propagation speed is about $1/\sqrt{4.7} = 0.46c$, which is 138 m/µs. On the other hand, for the shorter nets found on a chip, the propagation delay is not a free-standing term in the above formula and its effects are bundled into the output derating, since a net that is longer has a larger capacitance.

To attain the maximum performance from logic, simple models of gate delay may have over conservative design margins. Today, the delay can be characterised additionally by the **slew rate** of the arriving signal, as described in Section 8.4.6. Moreover, the resistance of very thin nets, which are sometimes used in highly dense wiring, contributes to the effective delay. Moreover, if such a net divides to feed multiple destinations, the difference in delay down each path can occasionally be significant. The Elmore model is readily applied to each section of such a net to obtain a good delay estimate at the start of a simulation, but the performance of a net-level simulation is reduced by the greater number of circuit nodes that require modelling.

4.6.5 Landauer Limit and Reversible Computation

In theory, if a computer does not destroy any information, it can be run with no energy. A computation that does not destroy information is called a **reversible calculation**, since the input data can be recreated from the output data. Conventional computer programs are not structured in this way. For example, once the average value of a list has been computed, the memory holding that list is typically overwritten with new data and used for something else.

There are theoretical limits on the energy that an irreversible computation requires. However, the current technology is a long way from these limits in two respects:

1. We use too much energy representing and communicating bits.

2. We use von Neumann-based computation, which moves data to a centralised ALU, a design that does not scale well (Section 6.4).

Consider electrical computers:

- If a computer is built using a network of standard components (such as transistors) and the interconnection pattern expresses the design intent, then the components must be at different spatial locations. The computer will have some physical volume.

- If the components are connected using electrical wires, these nets have capacitance, resistance and inductance that stop them behaving like ideal conductors. The smaller the volume, the less wire we need and the better the nets (and hence, computer) will work.

- If transistors are used that need a swing of about 0.7 V on their gates to switch them reliably between off and on, then the nets need to move through at least that much potential difference.

As explained (Section 4.6.2), the capacitance of the nets is our main enemy. Given a prescribed minimum voltage swing, the energy used by switching a wire between logic levels can be made smaller only by reducing its area and hence, capacitance. Hence, smaller computers are always better.

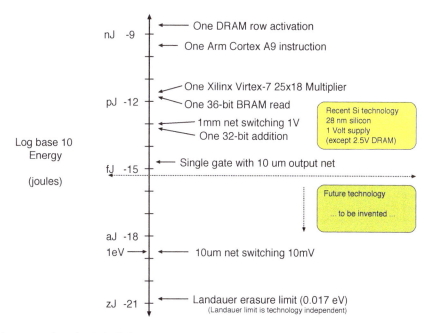

Figure 4.27 Dynamic energy use for various technologies

Landauer worked out the minimum energy use per bit [2], in theory, for a computer that deletes data as it goes (e.g. erasing the old contents of a register when new data are loaded). Computing more efficiently than this requires major low-level design changes to ensure that information is never deleted, taking us towards **reversible computing**. Reversible logic (e.g. Toffoli logic) can get below the Landauer limit. Some standard algorithms, such as encryption and lossless compression, are mainly reversible. The trick is to code in a way that does not delete intermediate results during a computation. Such techniques may be in wide use within two decades. In irreversible computing, the traditional approach of wasting the energy of each transition can be countered using techniques like regenerative braking in electric vehicles. In one approach, the logic runs on AC and returns charge to the power supply using resonant circuits. Switching transistors close only when they have no voltage across them and open only when they have no current flowing.

Figure 4.27 shows ballpark figures for dynamic energy use in today's (2020) sub-28-nm silicon technology. We see that contemporary computers are about six orders of magnitude above the Landauer limit in terms of energy efficiency, so a significant amount of improvement is still possible before we have to consider reversibility. If we make the wantonly hopeful assumption that Moore-like growth continues (Section 8.2), with technology doubling in performance every 18 months, we could intersect the reversible computing limit in about 2050, since $1.5 \times \log_2(10^6)$ is roughly 30 years.

4.6.6 Gate Delay as a Function of Supply Voltage

The FO4 delay is often used to represent the performance of digital logic technology. The **FO4 delay** is the delay through an invertor that feeds four other nearby invertors (fanout of four). This is illustrated in Figure 4.28. The FO4 depends on the implementation technology and the PVT parameters (Section 8.4.4). The variation with supply voltage is particularly important and is exploited for DVFS (Section 4.6.8) and VCOs (Section 4.9.5). The combinational delay of a particular design can also be expressed in a technology-independent way by quoting it in units of FO4 delay. Note the ITRS roadmap in Table 8.2 instead uses FO3 (fan-out of 3) instead of FO4 metric.

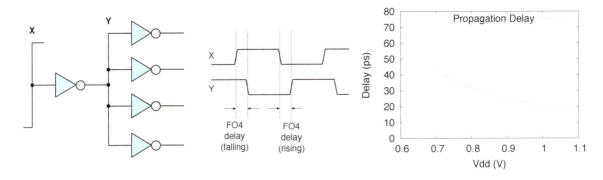

Figure 4.28 Fanout 4 (FO4) delay specification (left) and CMOS logic propagation delay versus supply voltage (right)

As noted earlier, the gate threshold voltage V_T for FETs in a CMOS design is the voltage at which they nominally switch from off to on. The lowest possible supply voltage to a logic system is bounded by the threshold voltage. Above this voltage, the logic delay is roughly inversely proportional to the supply voltage. Accordingly, to operate faster, we need a higher supply voltage for a given load capacitance. The **CMOS speed law** embodies the main shape of the delay versus supply voltage plot:

$$\text{Gate delay} \propto \frac{C \times V}{(V - V_T)^2} \tag{4.1}$$

This plot is sketched on the right in Figure 4.28.

4.6.7 SPICE Simulation of an Invertor

The CMOS speed law can be demonstrated using a low-level simulation. The predominant simulator for analogue electronics is SPICE (Simulation Program with Integrated Circuit Emphasis). SPICE can be used in a stand-alone form for small circuits or can be invoked through mixed-signal simulations (Section 8.3.7) in which digital electronics interact with analogue electronics. Figure 4.29 is a complete demonstration of the use of `hspice`. A standard CMOS invertor, composed of two MOSFETs, is simulated at two supply voltages.

Figure 4.30 shows two output responses for different supply voltages. The curves for the output load capacitor are fairly typically exponential when charging or discharging. The shape is not a true $1 - \exp(-t/CR)$ curve due to non-linearity in the MOSFETs. However, it is pretty close. If the FETs had the same on-resistances at the two supply voltages, although the swing of the output in the two plots would be different, the delays before they cross the half-supply level would be identical. The difference arises because the on-resistance is lower when the gate voltage is lower (i.e. when it is closer to the transistor threshold voltage).

4.6.8 Dynamic Voltage and Frequency Scaling

We will look at four techniques for saving power in the 2-D space defined in Table 4.2.

Table 4.2 Design space for dynamic power-saving techniques

	Clock	Power
On/Off	Clock gating	Power supply gating
Variable	Dynamic frequency scaling (DFS)	Dynamic voltage scaling (DVS)

As Figure 4.28 shows, the CMOS delay is broadly inversely proportional to the supply voltage; hence, as the clock frequency is increased, then, over a limited range, the supply voltage can be adjusted roughly proportionally to the clock frequency so that the timing closure can still be met (Section 8.12.16). At a single supply voltage, the speed of a gate can be altered at design time by choosing its transistor geometries. Standard cell buffers are typically available with several **cell drive strengths** (Section 8.4.1).

The fCV^2 formula means that power consumption is quadratic in supply voltage (Section 4.6.2). Building on these observations, dynamic voltage and frequency scaling (DVFS) enables a circuit to operate efficiently at different speeds with different powers. Under DVFS, as the performance needs change, the clock frequency for a system or subsystem is moved between pre-programmed

```
// spice-cmos-inverter-djg-demo.hsp
// Updated 2017 by David J. Greaves
// Based on demo by David Harris harrisd@leland.stanford.edu
// Declare global supply nets and connect them to a constant-voltage supply
.global Vdd Gnd
Vsupply Vdd Gnd DC `VddVoltage'
/////////////////////////////////////////
// Set up the transistor geometry by defining lambda
.opt scale=0.35u  * Define lambda // This is half the minimum channel length.
// Set up some typical MOSFET parameters.
//http://www.seas.upenn.edu/~jan/spice/spice.models.html#mosis1.2um

.MODEL CMOSN NMOS LEVEL=3 PHI=0.600000 TOX=2.1200E-08 XJ=0.200000U
    +TPG=1 VTO=0.7860 DELTA=6.9670E-01 LD=1.6470E-07 KP=9.6379E-05
    +UO=591.7 THETA=8.1220E-02 RSH=8.5450E+01 GAMMA=0.5863
    +NSUB=2.7470E+16 NFS=1.98E+12 VMAX=1.7330E+05 ETA=4.3680E-02
    +KAPPA=1.3960E-01 CGDO=4.0241E-10 CGSO=4.0241E-10
    +CGBO=3.6144E-10 CJ=3.8541E-04 MJ=1.1854 CJSW=1.3940E-10
    +MJSW=0.125195 PB=0.800000

.MODEL CMOSP PMOS LEVEL=3 PHI=0.600000 TOX=2.1200E-08 XJ=0.200000U
    +TPG=-1 VTO=-0.9056 DELTA=1.5200E+00 LD=2.0000E-08 KP=2.9352E-05
    +UO=180.2 THETA=1.2480E-01 RSH=1.0470E+02 GAMMA=0.4863
    +NSUB=1.8900E+16 NFS=3.46E+12 VMAX=3.7320E+05 ETA=1.6410E-01
    +KAPPA=9.6940E+00 CGDO=5.3752E-11 CGSO=5.3752E-11
    +CGBO=3.3650E-10 CJ=4.8447E-04 MJ=0.5027 CJSW=1.6457E-10
    +MJSW=0.217168 PB=0.850000
/////////////////////////////////////////
// Define the invertor, made of two MOSFETs as usual, using a subcircuit.
.subckt myinv In Out N=8 P=16 // Assumes 5 lambda of diffusion on the source/drain
m1 Out In Gnd Gnd CMOSN l=2 w=N
+ as=`5*N' ad=`5*N'
+ ps=`N+10' pd=`N+10'
m2 Out In Vdd Vdd CMOSP l=2 w=P
+ as=`5*P' ad=`5*P'
+ ps=`P+10' pd=`P+10'
.ends myinv


/////////////////////////////////////////
// Top-level simulation net list
//   One instance of my invertor and a load capacitor
x1 In Out  myinv         // Invertor
C1 Out Gnd 0.1pF         // Load capacitor
/////////////////////////////////////////
// Stimulus: Create a waveform generator to drive In
// Use a  "Piecewise linear source"  PWL that takes a list of time/voltage pairs.
Vstim In Gnd PWL(0 0 1ns 0   1.05ns `VddVoltage'  3ns VddVoltage   3.2ns 0)
/////////////////////////////////////////
// Invoke transient simulation (that itself will first find a steady state)
.tran .01ns 6ns // Set the time step and total duration
.plot TRAN v(In) v(Out)
.end
```

Figure 4.29 SPICE description and setup for two transistors arranged as a CMOS invertor simulated with a two-step input

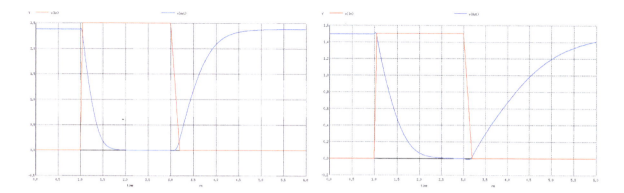

Figure 4.30 Plots of the invertor when running from V_{CC} supplies of 2.5 V (left) and 1.5 V (right). Red is the input stimulus and blue is the simulated output

frequencies. Simultaneously, the supply voltage is adjusted to be the lowest that reliably works at the chosen clock frequency. Overall, this gives a cubic power cost. The dynamic power is proportional to clock frequency and supply voltage squared, so when the supply voltage is also increased roughly linearly with clock frequency, there is a cubic factor in the power cost. However, the energy use for a given computation will grow only quadratically, since the task will be completed more quickly, so the cubic power is expended for less time. DVFS obtains peak performance under heavy loads, yet avoids the cubic penalty when idle.

DVFS is commonly used in laptop computers and cell phones, because the computational load varies greatly according to what the user is doing. A process called the **CPU governor** chooses an appropriate clock frequency, typically based on measuring the operating system halt time. Each processor will **halt** when there are no runnable jobs in the operating system job queue. Halting is commanded by an explicit halt instruction and processing resumes on the next hardware interrupt. The operating system has an idle task that has the lowest static priority, so that it runs when there is no user work to run. The task body contains a halt instruction. The **system load average** is computed by the operating system based on timestamping when a core halts and again when it resumes after the halt instruction. This load average, or a variant of it, is the main input to the governor daemon.

DVFS Worked Example
As an example, consider a subsystem with an area of 64 mm^2 and average net length of 0.1 mm containing 400 000 gates/mm^2. Assume an average toggle rate of $a = 0.25$. The CV^2 energy of a complete cycle is expended at half the toggle rate. The effective net capacitance is 0.1 mm × 1 fF/mm × 400K × 64 mm^2 = 2.5 nF. Table 4.3 gives the typical power consumption for a subsystem when clocked at different frequencies and voltages. It is important to ensure that the supply voltage is sufficient for the clock frequency in use: too low a voltage means that signals do not arrive at D-type inputs in time to meet the setup time. A factor of four increase in clock frequency has resulted in a nearly tenfold increase in power.

Table 4.3 Example of static and dynamic power use for a three-level DVFS configuration. (The static current was estimated using $\beta V^{0.9}$, where β was chosen to give an approximate 1:3 ratio of static to dynamic power at the middle supply voltage)

Supply voltage (V)	Clock frequency (MHz)	Static power (mW)	Dynamic power (mW)	Total power (mW)
0.8	100	40	24	64
1.35	100	67	68	135
1.35	200	67	136	204
1.8	100	90	121	211
1.8	200	90	243	333
1.8	400	90	486	576

DVFS Shortcomings

DVFS was very popular throughout the first decade of the 21st century, when CMOS geometries of 45 to 90 nm were widely used. These had a very low leakage. For a predictable hard real-time task, DVFS could be arranged to finish just in time. For instance, a video decoder would clock at just the right speed for each frame to be ready to display on time. Computing faster and halting is worse due to the quadratic cost of running fixed-sized jobs faster. In today's technologies, DVFS is less attractive for two reasons. First, the higher static power means it can be better to compute as fast as possible and then switch off using power gating (Section 4.6.10). Second, the range of voltages where the logic will operate correctly is much lower, so getting a significant energy saving from DVFS is not possible.

4.6.9 Dynamic Clock Gating

DVFS involves adjusting the clock frequency and supply voltage to a subsystem. Both of these are typically controlled by feedback loops that contain low-pass filters. Hence, there is inertia in the adjustment and changes must be performed with a granularity of at least 1 to 10 ms. Turning off the clock and turning off the power to a subsystem are two further power-saving techniques. These are purely digital and can be done orders of magnitude more quickly. We will discuss power gating in Section 4.6.10. Here we discuss automatic clock gating.

Clock distribution trees (Section 4.9.5) consume a considerable amount of power in a SoC. The clock might use 10 per cent of the energy in an active subsystem. A region of logic is **idle** if all the flip-flops are being loaded with their current contents, either as a result of synchronous clock enables or just through the nature of the design. This is very common, but such a region still consumes 10 per cent of its power because the clock is turned on. An idle period is some number of adjacent idle clock cycles, which can last a single clock cycle or thousands. Considerable savings can be made by turning off the clocks during idle periods.

Figure 4.31 shows three circuits that effectively disable the clock to a subsystem. Figure 4.31(a) shows a synchronous clock-enable structure using an external multiplexer. This multiplexer is part of the flip-flop in reality and is implemented with lower overhead than shown. However, such a circuit does not stop the clock input to the flip-flop or save the dynamic power consumed by the clock net. Instead of using synchronous clock enables, current design practice is to use a clock gating insertion tool that asynchronously gates the clock. One clock-control logic gate can serve a number of neighbouring flip-flops, such as a state machine, broadside register or some number of these. Hence, the clock net in that region will consume no dynamic power when gated off.

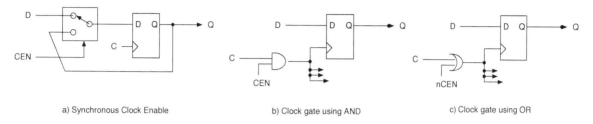

a) Synchronous Clock Enable   b) Clock gate using AND   c) Clock gate using OR

Figure 4.31 Clock enable using (a) a multiplexor, (b) an AND gate and (c) an OR gate

Figure 4.31(b) shows gating with an AND gate whereas Figure 4.31(c) has an OR gate. A problem with the AND gate is that if the clock enable (CEN) changes when the clock is high, there is a glitch on the clock net. A similar problem with the OR gate solution arises if CEN changes when the clock is low. Hence, care must be taken not to generate glitches on the clock as it is gated. Transparent latches in the clock-enable signal prevents these glitches, as shown in Figure 4.32. The transparent latch delays any changes during the clock enable so that they are applied only during a safe phase of the clock.

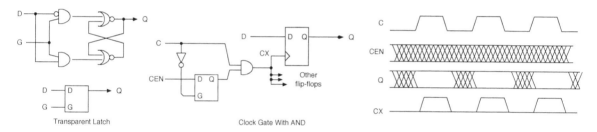

Transparent Latch   Clock Gate With AND

Figure 4.32 Illustrating a transparent latch and its use to suppress clock gating glitches

Compared with synchronous clock enables, in combinational clock gating, care must be taken to match the clock skew when crossing in and out of a non-gated domain. Delay buffers may have to be inserted to avoid a **shoot-through** by building out the non-gated signal paths as well. A shoot-through occurs when a D-type is supposed to register its current D-input value, but this has already changed to its new value before the clock signal arrives.

The question now arises of how to generate a clock-enable condition. One could use software to control complete blocks using additional control register flags, as is the norm for power gating (Section 4.6.10). However, today's designs use fast automatic detection on a finer-grained basis. Synthesis tools automatically insert additional logic for clock-required conditions. A clock edge is required if any register can change its state on that clock edge.

Figure 4.33 shows a basic technique for deriving a clock-required expression. It uses a so-called mitre pattern, in which the difference between D-inputs and Q-outputs for a set of flip-flops is computed. If there is a difference, a clock is needed for that group of flip-flops. The amount of such mitre logic needs to be constrained, otherwise there will be no net energy saving. The increase in area generally

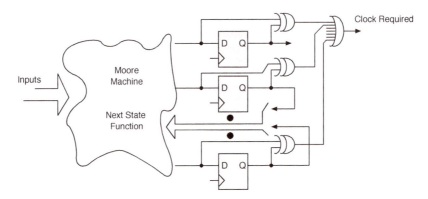

Figure 4.33 Using XOR gates to determine whether a clock edge would have any effect

increases the net length, costing further energy. It is critical to choose carefully which flip-flops are included in a gated group. The tools use heuristic search algorithms.

A **mitre** is the characteristic shape of a bishop's hat and a joint in woodworking (e.g. at the corners of picture frames). It is where two planes form a prismatic edge.

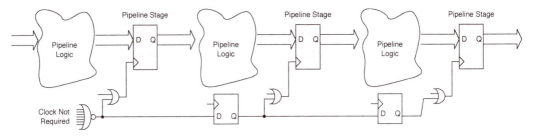

Figure 4.34 Clock-needed computations forwarded down a pipeline

An analysis of a design structure can enable clock-gated domains to share information constructively. For instance, as sketched in Figure 4.34, activity in one region may depend on activity in another region the clock cycle before. Another technique is to use a counter to implement a retriggerable monostable state. This is helpful if the last useful clock cycle is bounded to occur within a statically determined time horizon of an event detected by a mitre construction. In each clock cycle, all registers will be being reloaded with their current data after the settling time.

4.6.10 Dynamic Supply Gating

A SoC design that serves multiple different products can have large functional blocks in silicon that are never used during the lifetime of a product. Within a single product, not all the subsystems are typically in use at once. For instance, for the SoC for a tablet computer, whether the Bluetooth interface is being used is independent of whether the MPEG compression accelerator is active. Cryptographic coder blocks for various ciphers may be present, but only one is likely to be in use at once. Hence, the ability to independently turn the various subsystems within a chip off and on is very useful for saving energy. Each subsystem may support a set of **sleep modes**, which always includes fully off and fully active, but which may also include standby or data retention modes. The fully off mode is supported using dynamic supply gating, also known as power gating. Dark silicon constraints imply that, for all future chips, most of the area must be mostly powered off (Section 8.2).

Figure 4.35 shows the general principle of power gating. In essence, a large transistor serves as an on/off switch for a subsystem. This will be designed as a low-leakage transistor at the expense of switching speed. Its channel width will be ratioed to be the same as the sum of those components connected to the rail it feeds, or slightly more. The extra transistor can be either an N-channel device at the ground side, in which case it is called a **footer**, or a P-channel device at the power supply side, in which case it is called a **header**. The detailed circuit shown on the right indicates how a footer power gate is configured. Footers are most commonly used because N-type transistors have better on-resistance for a given area.

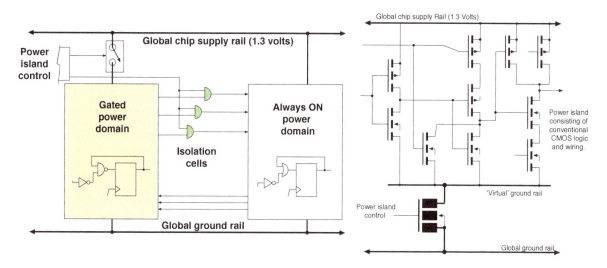

Figure 4.35 Power gating in general (left) and an actual power gate circuit (right)

Power gating implicitly introduces a transistor stacking effect such that, in sleep mode, the drain of the header or footer settles to an intermediate voltage, effectively making the gate-source voltage negative for the transistors in the block. This further reduces the leakage. As a downside, the gating transistors increase the on-resistance, which negatively impacts performance when the logic is active.

Output nets from a gated-off region cannot be allowed to float, since they can give rise to large short-circuit currents (Section 4.6.2). Hence, special **domain isolation cells** are inserted into the signal paths. These cells are designed to tolerate floating inputs and produce a definite logic zero when their source is turned off. Dynamic power gating typically requires some sequencing. The power controller will use several clock cycles to perform an ordered power-up (power-down) of a region and enable (disable) isolation gates. Additionally, a gradual turn-on over tens of milliseconds avoids creating noise on the global power rails. Isolation cells on the input to an off region are normally not required, but these outputs could be set to an appropriate logic level if parasitic paths through protection diodes are a problem in a particular technology.

Originally, powering off or on was controlled by software or top-level input pads to the SoC. Any state held in registers in a powered-off region is normally lost. This is fine for programmer-controller power phasing, since the programmer will know that the subsystem needs reinitialisation. Today, dedicated microsequencer hardware can control a hundred power islands within a single subsystem. Automatic power gating often uses the AMBA P or Q protocols described in Section 3.7.5.

Common practice is to power off a whole chip except for one or two RAMs and register files. This is **partial power gating**. It was particularly common before flash memory was invented, since a small battery was used to retain the contents using a lower supply voltage (known sometimes as the CMOS RAM data-holding voltage). Today, most laptops, tablets and PCs still have a second, tiny battery that maintains a small amount of running logic when the main power is off or the battery removed. This runs the **real-time clock (RTC)** and might be needed for secret retention of the secure enclave (Section 4.9.1). If logic is run only at a low speed it can be run on a lower voltage. Likewise, for **data retention**, a lower voltage is needed on SRAM storage cells than is normally used for normal reading and writing operations. These reduced voltages can be provided by using a power-switching transistor, half on, half off, as a linear voltage regulator. Linear regulators dissipate energy as heat and so are far less efficient than adjusting the standard switched-mode power supply to a lower voltage, but the overall power is still reduced . Another technique that dynamically alters a subsystem from active to standby levels of performance is **dynamic body bias**.

Dynamic Body Bias

A conventional MOSFET is principally controlled by the potential difference between its gate and its substrate. The active transistor layer sits on top of the silicon wafer. The wafer is doped as P-type and is normally connected to the ground potential. N-type transistors can use the substrate P-doping or sit inside wells with stronger doping. P-type transistors sit inside N-wells that are normally connected to a VDD supply potential. In **body biasing**, a voltage offset applied to the transistor substrate can change the effective threshold voltage of the transistor. This is achieved by removing the normal 'tub-ties' that connect the well to the supply rail, instead connecting a low-current voltage generator. The system can then adjust the leakage current of all transistors in the well, either statically or dynamically. When a subsystem is not active (all nets are stable), the body bias can be adjusted to enter low leakage mode. If a signal must be conveyed quickly or a result delivered, the bias can be adjusted quickly in advance. The potential across the well/substrate boundary can be quickly discharged with large transistors. When activity ceases, it is not important how quickly the body bias builds up again, which is done using low-current switched-capacitor invertors. Unfortunately, body bias does not work effectively in FinFET technologies (Section 8.2.1) since, due to their geometry, the substrate potential has less effect compared with the drain and source potentials.

Thermal Throttles

In the past, chips were often **core-bound** or **pad-bound**. Pad-bound meant that a chip had too many I/O signals for its core logic area, and the number of I/O signals puts a lower bound on the perimeter of a chip. Today's VLSI technology allows I/O pads in the middle of a chip, so being pad-bound is uncommon. Core-bound still arises and is preferable. If core-bound, the chip dimensions are governed by the area of the content. Today's VLSI is commonly **power-bound**, meaning that the area must be inflated for heat dissipation.

A **power throttle** measures the temperature of a SoC and reduces the clock frequency and perhaps the power supply voltage if it is becoming too hot. As computed in Section 4.4.1, the thermal time constant for a chip and its heat spreaders and sinks is of the order of seconds. Hence, temperature-based throttles are much slower to respond than clock gating or load-based DVFS. In a multi-socket environment, dynamically moving the work between chips helps even out the power dissipation. Relocating a task every second has very little impact on cache performance, since the vast majority of cache-line lifetimes are orders of magnitude shorter. A commercial implementation for processing blades in a server farm is Intel's **running average power limit (RAPL)**, which provides a temperature- and power-aware API for the operating system governor. An alternative approach is **computational sprinting**: short bursts of processing are allowed to far exceed the heat removal capacity. Much of the workload of a portable computer, like displaying a web page, is exceptionally bursty in demand terms, but accurate calibration of the thermal capacities enables the workload to be met without expensive heat-removal structures.

4.6.11 Future Trends for Energy Use

Table 4.4 Summary of the properties of four power-saving techniques

Technique	Clock gating	Supply gating	DVFS
Control	Automatic	Various	Software
Granularity	Register or FSM	Larger blocks	Macroscopic
Clock tree	Mostly free runs	Turned off	Slows down
Response time	Instant	2 to 3 cycles	Instant (or ms if PLL adjusted)

Energy can be saved by intelligent control of the power supply and clock frequency. Table 4.4 summarises the principal aspects. The term **dark silicon** refers to having a large proportion of a chip switched off at any one time (Section 8.2). This is expected to be the mainstream way forward as levels of integration grow, although certain application scenarios can warrant the use of pumped liquids or other esoteric forms of heat-extraction technology. One approach for using dark silicon is to put the inner loops of frequently used algorithms in hardware known as **conservation cores** [3]. Custom accelerators can be generated using a high-level synthesis (Section 6.9) of the standard software kernels in application-specific hardware coprocessors, and these can be put on the chip in case they are needed.

Other power-saving approaches are to use advanced fluid-based cooling or to move away from silicon FETs. Laptops have used simple fluid pipe cooling for decades, but heavy-duty water cooling is returning for server-grade computing, going full circle back to the 1960s when water-cooled mainframes were common. Increasing use of the third dimension with die-stacking (Section 8.9.1) and multi-chip modules is greatly reducing interconnect energy use, but concentrates the power into a smaller space. The biggest breakthrough is likely to come from a shift away from silicon FETs to something that operates reliably with a lower voltage swing. For instance, if logic could run from a

0.1-V supply instead of a 1.0-V supply, it would use 1 per cent of the power (Section 4.6.5). An optical interconnect using lithographically printed light guides could also be made to work, especially for inter-chip interconnections.

4.7 Designing for Testability and Debug Integration

Testing and debugging are related subjects that overlap since some mechanisms can be used for both purposes. Both benefit from additional circuitry in a SoC that plays no part in normal operation. An overhead of 5 per cent by area is not uncommon. This consumes hardly any power when not in use. The goal of production testing is to rapidly check that each unit manufactured operates as designed. Production testing will be discussed in Section 8.8. First, we will consider debugging the applications running on a SoC.

4.7.1 Application Debugging

A SoC contains numerous programmable components that run software or that are set up and controlled by software. However, software always has bugs. Although many programming errors can be investigated with a virtual platform or ESL model (Chapter 5), this is not always sufficient or appropriate. Many bugs arise from obscure and unexpected interactions that are different on the virtual platform or do not occur at all. Hence, silicon hardware resources need to be devoted to debugging. Indeed, today's complex SoCs typically can have a considerable amount of logic for debugging. Given adequate power gating (Section 4.6.10), there is little energy overhead from having the debug infrastructure present yet switched off. The area overhead is not a cost problem either, except perhaps for large trace buffers (Section 4.7.2).

Any debug infrastructure needs to be unobtrusive. A so-called **heisenbug** is a bug that disappears when debug monitoring is turned on. This is most unhelpful. Making the debug infrastructure as independent of the mainstream functionality as possible minimises the occurrence of heisenbugs. Hence, having dedicated resources for the debug infrastructure is a good approach.

The three main aspects of a debug infrastructure are **tracing**, **triggering** and **single stepping**. All are accessed via a **debug access port (DAP)**. Tracing refers to storing information in a trace buffer. Triggering determines when to start and stop tracing. Single stepping enables a subsystem or whole SoC to be halted and manually advanced one clock cycle or instruction at a time. Traces are often stored in compressed form. One form of compression relies on the program code being correctly loaded and reliably fetched during execution. Given an off-line copy of the machine code, the processor execution can be replayed forward or backward inside a debugger just from knowing what values were deleted from the registers when their contents were overwritten. However, if the problem being debugged is in the instruction stream, such an inference will be wrong and the uncompressed visualisation will be misleading.

A considerable amount of static meta-information is also available via the DAP. This includes the chip version number and can include a **debug reflection API**, which allows the inventory and arrangement of the debug infrastructure to be accessed by software. Hence, a generic debugger can configure itself to show structure diagrams and human-readable register and bit-field names. The textual names and many further details can typically be fetched into the debugger over the Internet based on looking up the IP block kinds and version numbers stored in the on-chip ROM.

The single-processor debug primitives available are generally the same whether debugging the real hardware or an emulated model. For instance, the GNU `gdb` program is normally used to debug a program running as a separate user-space program on the same machine that the debugger is running on, but by using the `target remote` command, it can attach to the real hardware or another machine using a TCP socket. The standard techniques accessible through a debugger include:

1. **Pause and step**: A core can be stopped, stepped one instruction or allowed to resume normal execution. A single step is often facilitated by a core run mode that executes one instruction and then interrupts or pauses. This enables the debugger to run on the core being debugged.

2. **Processor register access**: Any of the programmer's model registers within a core can be read or changed by the debugger.

3. **Remote reads and writes**: A debugger can cause a load or store operation, either directly on a main system bus or as though it were issued by a nominated core. That core may be running or halted. There is minimal interruption to the running core, but there is some small overhead from the additional debug traffic. This operation may cause a pipeline stall, so it is not completely unobtrusive. More serious can be side effects from particularly fragile bugs. A remote operation can cause the re-arbitration of interconnect components, page faults and cache misses. It can upset the read and write queues in a DRAM controller. Not only does re-arbitration switch between initiators, which has its own overhead, but the arbitration decision after the debug cycle may not return to the original initiator. A sequential consistency bug can change or disappear in such situations.

4. **Watchpoints and breakpoints**: A debugger can use hardware registers to store addresses of interest. There might be four or eight such registers available centrally or per core. When a load or store address matches an address in a **watchpoint register**, an event is generated. Likewise, when the program counter matches a value in a **breakpoint register**, an event is generated.

5. **Tracing** and **cross-trigger state machine**: See Section 4.7.2.

A SoC typically has a single logical DAP. Figure 4.36 shows a basic overall setup suitable for a microcontroller or single-core SoC. The TCP connection from the debugger connects to a USB 'dongle' that makes the net-level connection to the SoC. JTAG is illustrated (Section 4.7.3). This has a one-bit data path and so can be slow. Faster alternatives use parallel data. The DAP connects to the one core and is also shown as being able to initiate its own transactions on the primary interconnect. In this simple single-core system, the breakpoint and watchpoint registers are in the CPU core or perhaps inside a **performance management unit (PMU)** coprocessor attached to the core (Section 2.7.9). The

DAP can pause and single step the core as well as inspect and modify its registers. When a watchpoint, breakpoint or other event occurs, the programmable options include to count it in a PMU register, to interrupt the core or to pause the core so that the debugger can take over.

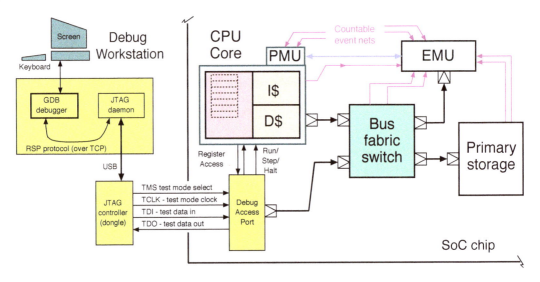

Figure 4.36 Debugging hardware for a single-core SoC. A debug access port is connected via JTAG and USB to a debug workstation

Many non-core IP blocks also generate events, and it can be useful to count them. Wires (net-level flags) connect the IP block to the counter for each such event (shown in pink). These could be routed to the PMU of one of the cores, but an alternative implementation uses a dedicated **event-monitoring unit (EMU)**. This can count events such as shared L2 misses, bus transactions and DRAM activations.

4.7.2 Multi-core Debug Integration

As noted, if a SoC has one processor, the debug interface connects directly to that core. Although the per-core debug primitive set has not greatly changed in the multiprocessor SoC (MPSoC) era, we inevitably have multiple instances of that set. Additionally, other IP blocks typically now have debug interfaces as well.

Figure 4.37 shows two additional main components of an advanced SoC debugging solution. These are event trace logging and cross-triggering. It is implied that all the facilities shown in Figure 4.36 still exist, such as the ability of the DAP to initiate transactions in every address space. To support trace logging, the cores are given an additional port that delivers a stream of trace events to dedicated event busses (green). The port supports various levels of detail, from off, to just interrupts and branches, and to traces that contain sufficient data for a complete programmer-view replay. The streams from the different cores are combined or thinned out with trace event funnels and programmable event filters. The funnels provide multiplexing as well as some smarter functionality, such as sharing a single timestamp for data from different inputs that have the same timestamp or generating an explicit overload token rather than tacitly dropping data if there is a temporary overload. A compressor performs run-length encoding of consecutive identical events or for lossless algorithms, like Lempel–Ziv, that exploit repeated patterns. Overall, the event bandwidth must not overwhelm the event destination, which is either an on-chip SRAM event buffer or a dedicated high-performance bus bond-out. A **bond-out**, in this sense, is a set of pads that may be disconnected in mass production packages (Section 8.9) but made available for external connection in a higher-cost test and development package. Off-chip trace buffers are commonly used by industrial or automotive controllers. For these, a wide parallel DAP dedicates most of its pins to data. Alternatively, a multi-gigabit serialiser can be used to export the data rapidly (Section 3.8).

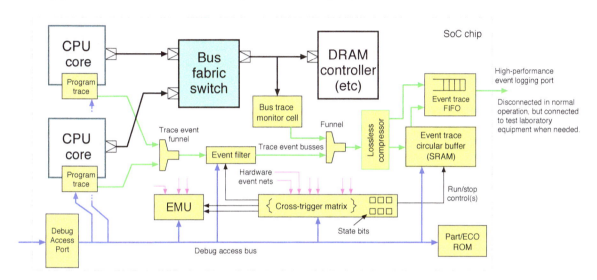

Figure 4.37 Typical additional event-stream debug resources for a modern MPSoC. Operational data busses are black. Event-stream busses are green. Debug-access busses are blue. The pink arrows denote event-monitoring nets from miscellaneous IP blocks that either do not have their own counters or need to be made available for cross-triggering

It is easy to collect too much event trace data from CPU cores. Each core might average 10 bits per instruction executed. Data can, instead, be collected from system busses. The figure shows a bus trace monitor connected to the DRAM controller input. This should generate two orders of magnitude less data than a CPU core at normal cache hit rates. Moreover, data from reads may not need to be logged if the memory is working properly, since the data will be the same as what was earlier written, though the data may have been written outside the temporal window being captured. An event filter may be programmed to record events corresponding only to narrow address windows, thereby extending the effective temporal window.

For the on-chip trace buffer, because only a finite pool of trace memory is available, a circular arrangement based on address wrapping is used so that the oldest data are constantly being overwritten. Hence, data up to a point of interest can be captured by stopping the trace just after that point. The recent history is then preserved in the buffer. It is also possible for traces to be stored in the main DRAM of the SoC or for periodic dumping of the SRAM trace buffer to the main memory under operating system control, but these intrusive mechanisms may mask the feature being investigated.

Debug infrastructure should normally be created with the assistance of an automated tool within the SoC design system, perhaps as part of the interconnect synthesis. This will not only ensure the correct wiring of the debug components, but can also be used to create meta-information files that cross-reference physical addresses with textual names. This meta-information can be imported into the debugger. Some of the meta-information may be aggregated in the single ROM shown on the bottom right of Figure 4.37. The ROM also gives the part number and ECO variant (Section 8.10). Typical sizes are 4 to 200 bytes of information. Alternatively, each IP block commonly has an identifier hard-coded into the first register of its internal debug space. A major work item that can be handled via such a holistic approach is proper crossing between the power and clock domains. If a component is in a standby mode or powered off, it will not respond to a transaction on its debug port. The debugger must either avoid issuing such a request or else go through the necessary power phase/mode changes needed for the request to be handled.

A simple system uses one state bit for the run/pause state of each core and one state bit for whether tracing is on or off. These state bits are driven by a configuration matrix whose inputs are the watch and break events and other events from the PMU and other subsystems. Such a simple system is inadequate for detecting complex patterns defined by sequences of events or for dynamically adjusting the event filter predicates.

As needed originally for the PMU, significant events generated by each IP block are available as net-level flags. At the cost of a small amount of wiring, these can be pooled as inputs to a central programmable matrix to form a generic **cross-trigger state machine**. Additional state flip-flops are provided that can be set and reset by outputs of the matrix. Their outputs are just fed back as further inputs to the matrix. Hence, a state machine can be programmed to match a user-specified sequence of events. Additionally, a user program can be instrumented to generate specific events by accessing an otherwise-unused watchpoint address. As well as programmable state flags, additional resources such as counters can be provided, again with both their input and output connections being programmable in the matrix, or just read out over the debug bus.

4.7.3 Debug Navigation and JTAG

There are typically several different ways of connecting to the DAP of a SoC. They vary in their cost, intrusiveness and security. A DAP may be selectively accessible to one of the cores on the SoC. This is often the primary core, which is the first to boot, or it could be a dedicated tiny processor that just manages booting, debug and initial DVFS and DRAM configuration. Designs need to be secure against two attacks: IP theft and data access. The debug channel provides an obvious backdoor that needs hiding from reverse engineering and malicious applications. Security can be enforced physically by wiring dedicated pins on the SoC directly to an unpopulated socket on the circuit board. Alternatively, security can be provided cryptographically and wrapped up into secure boot mechanisms. Most SoCs support a number of boot methods, e.g. by strapping a combination of pins to supply or ground. These same techniques can be extended to providing access control levels for the debug channels (Section 9.1.1).

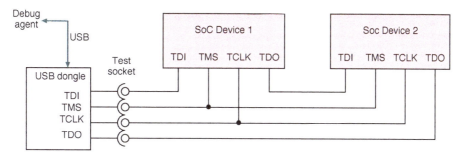

Figure 4.38 JTAG interface chaining at board level to create a top-level node in the debug device tree

One of the oldest and most common DAPs is the **Joint Test Action Group (JTAG)** port, standardised as IEEE 1149. This uses four wires per chip (Table 4.5).

Table 4.5 JTAG signal list

TDI	In	Test data in: serial bits from test agent or previous device
TMS	In	Test mode select: frame data and addresses
TCK	In	Test clock: clocks each bit in and out
TDO	Out	Test data out: to next device or back to agent

There can be numerous chips at the circuit board level, each with a DAP. Figure 4.38 shows how two can be linked into a daisy chain using JTAG wiring. JTAG is a serial bus that provides access to test registers in a SoC. There can be any number of bits in a register and there can be any number of chips in the daisy chain. One of the test registers is defined as a bypass register that then provides access to the next chip in the chain. A protocol is defined using the values on the TMS pin to address any of the test registers in any chip in the daisy chain. The old content of that test register is then shifted out and new content is shifted in. New content will be ignored for a read-only register. Certain test registers are predefined to hold the manufacturer and device numbers so that debugger software can dynamically adapt to the physical ordering and presence of different SoCs at the board level. In an advanced debug architecture, one of the JTAG test registers will be used to generate an address on the internal debug access bus (bottom blue line in Figure 4.37) and another for data reads and writes to that address. However, JTAG is typically limited to just a few Mbps and hence, high-performance parallel or USB-based DAPs are now additionally provided.

4.7.4 Additional DAP Facilities

The original purpose of JTAG was for making boundary scans for board-level product testing, as explained in Section 4.7.5. A SoC typically has a hundred or more bond pads. In a **boundary scan**, a virtual connection is made to each pad that carries an I/O signal using a shift register structure that is accessed via just a few bond pads. SoCs do not always support boundary scanning, but this debug port is increasingly used for other chip-level product tests and manufacture purposes. Some of these are:

- **Redundancy strapping**: Parts of a defective die are hidden to make a lower-specification product or to substitute with a standby instance (Section 8.8.4).

- **Voltage and speed grading** a part: Ring oscillators or other silicon process instrumentation is accessed for calibration and installation of DVFS tables (Section 4.6.8).

- Installing the **MAC address**, PKI **secret key** or other data that need to be different in each SoC manufactured.

- General **BIOS and file system flashing**: Boot ROM, embedded applications and other low-level code stored in flash memory are installed.

- Accessing **built-in self-test (BIST)** mechanisms (Section 4.7.6).

4.7.5 Boundary and General Path Scans

SoCs contain IP blocks from different IP vendors. Each came with a production test programme. Production testing of wafers and chips is discussed in Section 8.8. Test vectors are applied to the bond pads of the whole chip. However, for integrated IP blocks, it can be useful to apply a per-block test programme in the same way to each block inside a chip. Moreover, it is sometimes helpful to be able to run a chip-level production test when the SoC is attached to a circuit board. Scan path testing provides these mechanisms. It was the original motivation for the JTAG definition.

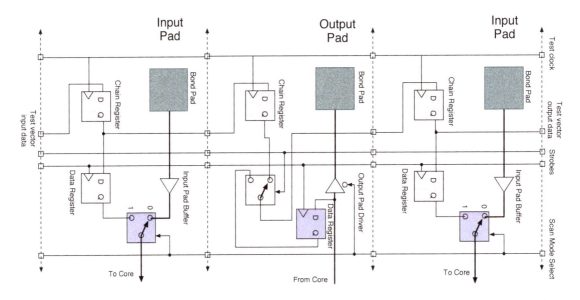

Figure 4.39 Basic structure of the additional logic required in input and output pads for boundary scanning. Serial data are shifted from one pad to the next using the test clock. The result from the previous test vector is shifted out as a vector is shifted in. The two strobe signals are used to apply the test vector to the input pads and to sample the data at the output pads

Figure 4.39 shows a fragment of a boundary scan path. The path is inserted into the electronics of each input and output pad. When the scan mode select net is low, the scan logic has no effect, but in scan mode, the boundary scan logic takes over from the input pads. The scan logic uses a shift and store approach. Two flip-flops are added to each pad. One flop in each pad is a stage in the chain for a shift register. A complete word of length equal to the number of instrumented pads is shifted in from the DAP controller. Such a word is called a **test vector** (Section 8.8.2). Then, on the `strobe` signal, data are captured from the output pads and new data applied to the input pads. The captured data are shifted out as the next vector is shifted in. The second flop in each pad, the data register, keeps the applied test vector stable during the shifting.

Clearly, boundary scan can be applied to appropriate IP blocks in a SoC. This might be suitable for hard macrocells (Section 8.4.2), such as a custom processor core. However, with increased standardisation of on-chip busses, such as the AXI standard, boundary scanning of IP blocks is less commonly used. A variant can be used for BIST access. A **general scan path** is similar to a boundary scan path, but the scan path is threaded through all of the flip-flops within the IP block. This allows the cycle-by-cycle observation of a component, but the component cannot be used at full speed during this mode and there is a significant overhead in the additional wiring. General scan path logic is typically inserted by running a logic synthesiser (Section 8.3.8) in a special mode. This additional logic is called a **logic built-in self-test (LBIST)**.

4.7.6 BIST for SRAM Memories (MBIST)

Figure 4.40 shows an SRAM component with a BIST/ECC wrapper around it. **Built-in self test (BIST)** circuits are used in hardware subsystems that cannot easily be tested in other ways. BIST for memory is called **MBIST**. For instance, full access to the data memory of a **trusted compute module** or a **secure enclave** (Section 4.9.1) might be completely denied from outside the silicon for security. If each RAM has its own BIST, the RAMs can be tested in parallel during the production test. Serial testing could be the only option if the RAM is tested using code on one of the cores or if external test vectors under a wafer probe are used. Under normal operation, the self-test wrapper acts as a bus protocol target for externally commanded reads and writes. However, in self-test mode, which will be selected over the DAP, the wrapper will run memory tests that write and then read back standard patterns such as 0/F/5/A and 'walking ones'. The results will be readable over the debug bus.

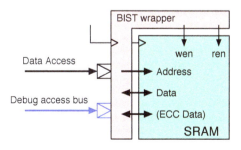

Figure 4.40 A static RAM with self-test wrapper around it. An error correction wrapper has a similar structure, but then the SRAM data bus will be wider than the external data bus. Both wrappers are often logically present, in which case a single wrapper may implement both functionalities

Error-correcting code (ECC) memory has a similar structure. Rather than building and operating a RAM out of completely reliable technology, other design points are used. A RAM that is clocked a little too fast or run on a slightly low voltage or exposed to atomic radiation will suffer the occasional error. Provided the actual error rate is within the design margin, data can be corrected upon readout or a periodic 'scrub'. Like a refresh for DRAM, scrubbing is the process of periodically reading out each word and writing back a corrected version if necessary. The ECC wrapper extends the word width for writes by appending additional parity check or correction digits. On reading back, if the bits do not match, the data are corrected where possible or else an error response is returned to the transaction. Statistics on the rate of corrections are readable over the debug interface. The debug interface may also be used to program the **scrub rate**. Since a data access port supports handshaking, contention for a RAM location is simply solved using arbitration. The same ECC techniques are also commonly used for DRAM, but DRAM is off-chip and has a separate production test.

4.8 Reliability and Security

SoCs are sold into diverse markets that differ in their reliability and security requirements. A SoC may need to be ultra-reliable for healthcare and avionics applications. It may need to be robust under high or low temperatures or able to withstand high radiation levels in outer space. Often, a SoC needs to be secure against reverse engineering, either in protecting its own intellectual property or when serving as a gateway device for financial transactions or valuable copyright-protected materials, such as digital video projection.

4.8.1 Physical Faults, Performance Degradation, Error Detection and Correction, and Pre- and Post-silicon Mitigation Techniques

Faults are classed as hard or soft. A **hard fault** occurs consistently and arises from a manufacturing fault or a failure. On the other hand, a **soft fault** happens at random during an execution and is not re-encountered on a re-execution. A **single-event upset (SEU)** is a soft fault that arises from external interference, such as a cosmic ray hitting the silicon chip, power supply noise or intense **radio-frequency interference (RFI)** originating from a nearby transmitter or faulty heavy-duty switch gear. Some hard faults are manufacturing faults arising from dislocations in the silicon crystal lattice or dirt in the processing steps. Chips with this sort of fault should be discarded during the production test.

Hard faults also arise from damage during use. Damage can be caused by an **electrostatic discharge (ESD)** in which a charged object, typically a human, touches signal wiring. All chip I/O bond pads have protection diodes that handle everyday electrostatic discharges, but certain clothes or floor materials can lead to excessive charge that can flow into the core circuitry and burn out the miniature structures. Lightning storms can cause the same problem, either from a direct strike or by inducing voltages in the cabling between components. Discharges can also enter via the mains electricity grid and power supply.

Hard faults can occur due to wear. A flash memory may no longer erase owing to the build-up of residual charge (Section 2.6.8). The flow of electricity through a silicon chip structure causes gradual **electromigration**. As explained in Section 8.4.5, metallic materials can be moved by an electric current from where they were placed during manufacture. Eventually, a component may no longer function correctly, leading to a hard fault.

4.9 Hardware-based Security

Building on the history of time-sharing mainframes, the basic principles of information security on a SoC remain access control lists and virtualisation. These traditionally relied on VM and partitioning of the ISA into user and supervisor mode instructions. However, the need for multiple roots of trust for authenticated financial and cell phone transactions together with copyright in multimedia streams raises new requirements for digital rights management and copy protection. Players of online games need assurance that other players are not using a version in which gunshots always hit. Traditional virtualisation applies only to user-mode instructions, so further hardware support has been added to most ISAs, where it was lacking, to fully virtualise the platform to the extent that multiple complete operating systems can be run at once.

Low-cost hardware platforms typically run without VM. Instead, a limited form of hardware protection is offered by a **memory protection unit (MPU)**. An MPU is programmed or hardwired to divide the physical memory space into a small number of protected regions, e.g. 8. Each region has access control privileges, which include the standard read, write and execute privileges. As with the standard page fault used by conventional VM, an exception is raised for a privilege violation. An MPU can be programmed only in supervisor mode and all interrupts, including an MPU fault, are run in supervisor mode. I/O devices may be guarded from user-mode code if they are configured or hardwired to take note of the security-level indication in the bus transaction. In an AXI interconnect, this is communicated in the 3-bit `AWPROT` field, which defines four levels of security for each piece of code or data.

The classical approach to virtualising a SoC fully so that multiple so-called **guest** operating systems can run at once is to run each operating system in user mode and to emulate all instructions that fault on a privilege violation. Such a fault is handled by a small and trusted **virtual machine monitor (VMM)**, which is also known as as a **hypervisor**. This requires the ISA to ensure that any **behaviour-sensitive instruction** raises such a fault [4]. A behaviour-sensitive instruction is one whose result might be different if run in user mode instead of supervisor mode. If the result is different but no fault is raised, then the VMM cannot intervene to emulate the expected behaviour. Nearly all major ISAs that previously had instructions of this nature have recently been altered to facilitate virtualisation. If such alterations are not possible, an alternative is to rewrite parts of the operating system to avoid such sequences. This can be folded into the automated code rewriting that is often used as part of the emulation of privileged instructions using hotspot detection and other JIT techniques.

4.9.1 Trusted Platform and Computer Modules

A **trusted platform module (TPM)** is a secure subsystem that was originally implemented as a separate chip on PC motherboards. The module is tightly delineated using a separate piece of silicon. **Tamper-proof** protection might also be implemented, in which secrets held are destroyed if an attempt to open or probe the circuit is detected. This secret repository is called a **secure enclave**. Intrusion avoidance and detection are typically implemented with additional metal layers on the wafer or around the package. A TPM can also check for repeated similar inquiries, repeated resets or a slow clock frequency. A TPM typically contains a non-volatile store, a random number generator and a low-throughput cryptographic processor. Together, these provide the following typical services:

- **Platform identifier**: This is rather like the MAC address of a network card, but cannot be faked. It is often used for software licensing.

- **RSA key-pair generator**: This is used in **public key encryption (PKI)** (Section 9.1.1). A key pair comprises a public key and a private key. The private key is kept entirely within the TPM, which prevents it from being cloned or shared maliciously.

- **Authentication**: A one-way hash function is combined with a key also held in the TPM to produce an unfakable digital signature for a body of data streamed to the TPM.

- A **key/value store with access control**: Small amounts of data, such as high scores in a game or a PIN, are saved under a string key and updated, deleted or retrieved only with authenticated commands.

- **Random number generation**: This is a source of the random nonce values required in many secure protocols. The values are produced by pieces of logic that have truly random behaviour, generally based on metastable resolutions (Section 3.7.2) or the amplification of random electron movements. (This differs from a **physically unclonable function (PUF)**, which uses random variations arising during manufacturing to implement a function that behaves consistently on any particular device, but which varies randomly between devices.)

If a TPM has only a low-speed connection to the main processor, high-throughput encryption is achieved using the TPM to generate session keys, perhaps once per second. These are installed in the main crypto-processors or as part of the secondary storage interface for encrypted file systems.

However, having a separate chip is expensive and contrary to the SoC philosophy. The data passing in and out of such chips is communicated on the bus nets. Such chips have exposed power connections that can create a **side channel**, which is an unintentional communication path that allows secrets to escape. Supply connections have been attacked using **differential power analysis (DPA)**, electron-beam scanning and physical probing. Some poor designs have been triggered into revealing their secrets using runt clock pulses on their interfaces. In DPA, a test is run millions of times. The supply current waveform is accurately recorded and averaged. In the same way that a safe cracker with a stethoscope can successfully find the dial settings where each hidden tumbler hits the next,

DPA can detect at what bit positions a tentative key fails to match. Designs attempt to mitigate this by using a PRBS (Section 3.8) to induce random wait states and a random number generator to permute address and data bits to a RAM each time power is applied.

4.9.2 Trusted Execution Mode

Rather than having physical security around a trusted enclave, as with a physical TPM chip, an alternative is to emulate this behaviour on a SoC core that has a dedicated security mode, which supports a **trusted execution environment (TEE)**. This mode has exclusive access to a region of **curtained memory** and certain peripherals that cannot be accessed from other processing modes, including any supervisor mode. This is one of the motivations for the TrustZone architectural enhancements from Arm, which has a new processing state called **hypervisor mode**. Each interrupt source can be programmed to either interrupt into hypervisor mode or behave as normal. Hence, hypervisor mode can service page faults by emulating the page walk of a guest operating system and serve as a basis for efficient VMM provision. For high performance, hardware assistance for page walking of the guest VM mapping may also be provided.

4.9.3 Capability-based Protection

An alternative to virtual memory that can also serve as a basis for VMMs is provided by **capability architectures** [5, 6]. All data in registers or memory locations under a capability architecture is either plain data or a capability. A hidden tag bit on all values marks which form is held. The ISA makes it impossible to create a capability from plain data. On system reset, one register is loaded with a comprehensive **almighty capability** that can access any location for reading, writing or executing. ISA instructions refine a capability into one that has fewer permissions or covers a smaller region of memory. There is no restriction on executing the refine operation but there is no inverse instruction or equivalent sequence of instructions.

Recent research has shown that a capability ISA can be implemented for a low hardware cost [7]. Efficiency can be similar to that of simple MPUs. This is being explored commercially by Arm in the Morello project. An existing ISA was changed so that all I/O and memory accesses must use the capability protection mechanism. This immensely improves security compared with MPU-based solutions, for which programmers must exercise considerable discipline to make sure there are no side channels. Most code can be recompiled without change, especially if conventional pointers are supported within a memory region defined by capabilities stored in implied segment registers rather than forcing all memory access to be made directly via a capability. A small amount of additional code refines the capabilities at boot time and in dynamic memory allocations (stack and heap). This leads to a very promising, highly secure design point, although there is a memory overhead in storing tag bits.

4.9.4 Clock Sources

Most electronic products use a sound wave inside a quartz crystal as a clock source. Ultra cheap products, like a musical greeting card, instead use an R/C oscillator, but this typically has only 10 per cent accuracy. One semitone is 6 per cent, so these cards are often well out of pitch. Figure 4.41

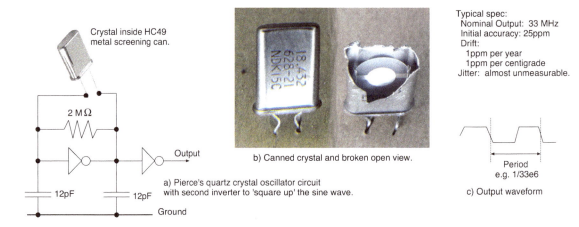

Figure 4.41 Crystal oscillator circuit (left), canned crystal and contents (centre), and specification and output waveform (right)

shows a typical circuit that exploits the piezoelectric effect of a crystal to make it resonate. An invertor becomes an inverting amplifier using a resistor to bias it into its high-gain nearly linear region. The oscillation frequency is set by the reciprocal of the thickness. Above 20 MHz or so, a crystal cannot be cut thinly enough, so a 3rd of 5th overtone is forced with an external L/C tank circuit.

4.9.5 PLL and Clock Trees

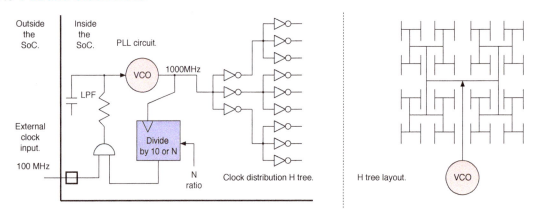

Figure 4.42 Clock multiplication using a PLL (left) and clock distribution layout using a fractal H-tree (right)

For higher clock frequencies of around 1 GHz, which are commonly needed for CPU cores, the crystal oscillator frequency is multiplied up on-chip using a **phase-locked loop (PLL)**. A PLL is shown on the left of Figure 4.42. A **voltage-controlled oscillator (VCO)** generates a clock whose frequency depends on the average voltage on its control input. By dividing down the generated frequency by a constant factor, e.g. 10 as shown, the frequency can be made the same as that of the board-level clock of a crystal under locked operation. A simple AND gate can serve as a phase comparator. If the VCO output is a little too fast, the output from the divider will overlap less with the high cycle of the external clock input, resulting in a reduced average voltage on the AND gate output. The resistor and capacitor form a **low-pass filter (LPF)**. This helps provide inertia and stability. The VCO reduces its output frequency and remains phase and frequency locked to the external input. Dynamic frequency scaling (Section 4.6.8) can be implemented by changing the division ratio with a larger division factor leading to a higher system clock rate for a fixed external reference.

A clock tree delivers a clock to all flops in a domain with sufficiently low skew. Too much skew (difference in arrival times) leads to a shoot-through, such that a flip-flop output has already changed while it is still being used to determine the next state of a companion (Section 4.6.9). Skew in delivery is minimised using a balanced clock distribution tree, so that each path from the VCO to the clock input of a flip-flop has the same net length and the same number of buffers. Inverters are used as buffers to minimise **pulse shrinkage**. In most technologies, a buffer propagates the zero-to-one transition faster or slower than the opposite transition. If a chain is composed of non-inverting stages, the effects will accumulate systematically, resulting in duty-cycle distortion in which the pulse width of one phase of the clock shrinks. One layout that ensures a balanced structure is the binary H-tree, shown on the right of Figure 4.42. An inverter can be placed at every (or every other) point where the clock net splits two ways. The flip-flops are wired to the ends of every line making up the smallest H pattern.

If the H is balanced, the clock distribution delay does not require further consideration. However, if unbalanced clock timing is needed for clock skewing (Section 4.9.6) or to compensate for delays in clock gates, a more detailed delay model is needed beyond the simple lumped-element delay model of Section 4.6.4. The resistance of each net segment produces a delay down that segment that depends on the loading of the segment. A full SPICE simulation is always possible, but the **Elmore delay** model provides a reasonable approximation to real behaviour. The total capacitive load on a segment is simply summed and used along with the resistance of that segment to model its delay. The delay to a point on the net is the sum of the delays thereby calculated from the source. Both forking and non-forking nets can easily be computed with the Elmore model. For a homogeneous non-forking net, the Elmore delay degenerates to a simple sum of an arithmetic progression and gives the same answer for any resolution of a lumped-element model. That answer is quadratic in length and gives the delay as $L^2RC/2$ where R and C are the resistance and capacitance per unit length. This contrasts with the linear derating with length used in simpler models (Section 4.6.4).

4.9.6 Clock Skewing and Multi-cycle Paths

Although the golden principle of synchronous logic design has served us well for decades, today, with the support of advanced EDA tools, the principle can be deliberately violated. The principle is that all registers in a clock domain are clocked at exactly the same time and that all their inputs have properly settled in advance of the setup time before the next clock edge (Section 4.4.2). Both clock skewing and multi-clock paths can increase performance more than is allowed under the golden rule.

Clock skewing is the process of deliberately offsetting the delivery of a clock edge to a register or group of registers within a clock domain. The default design approach is to aim for zero skew, but it is

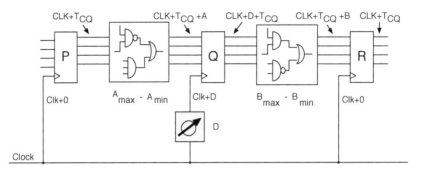

Figure 4.43 Clock skewing. The delivery of the clock edge to some D-types is delayed or advanced to balance out timing margins either side

valid to deliver the clock late to a group of registers if there is a long combinational path on their input and shorter paths on all of their outputs.

Figure 4.43 shows the most basic setup. The clock to the broadside register Q is made earlier or later by changing the structure of the clock distribution network (typically an H-tree; Section 4.9.5). The amount of offset is D. There are multiple paths through the combinational logic, so, even in this very simple scenario, there is a range of arrival times at the D-inputs. These add on to the clock-to-Q time T_{CQ}. All inputs must be stable before the setup time of Q, T_{SU}. Likewise, adjusting D alters the time of arrival at registers fed by Q, but it is their hold time that is likely to be violated. A shoot-through (Section 4.6.9) without violating the set and hold times is even possible if D is unreasonably large.

The maximum amount of clock advance allowable (most negative D) is governed by $T_{CQ} + A_{max} + T_{SU} < T + D$. This inequality ensures that the setup time into register Q is met. The maximum amount of clock retard allowable (most positive D) is governed by $T_{CQ} + B_{min} - D > T_{hold}$. This inequality ensures the hold time into register R is met. Of course, in realistic scenarios, every register could be given a controlled skew to its clock, and the combinational paths of data, as the data move between the registers, would follow a more complex path. Nonetheless, deliberate clock skew remains a valuable tool.

Timing **slack** is the difference between the arrival of data at the end of a path and the required arrival time defined by the clock period, design constraints and timing margins. Positive slack means that the path has met its constraints. Negative slack means that the path has failed to meet its constraints. For any non-trivial subsystem or clock domain, there is a huge number of delay paths. These are explored in parallel by a **static timing analyser (STA)** (Section 8.12.1), which creates lengthy report files.

Timing slack is often reported in two ways: the **worst negative slack (WNS)** and the **total negative slack (TNS)**. As the terms suggest, WNS is the slack of the one path with the largest timing violation and TNS is the sum of the slack of all paths that violate their timing constraints. A third value that is often reported is the **number of violating paths (NVP)**. These values are a quick way to estimate how much more timing optimisation is necessary (for negative slack) or possible (for positive slack). A slack graph is a histogram of the timing slack. It has the general form shown in Figure 4.44. The plot is a good visual representation of how much more optimisation is necessary. Timing optimisation and

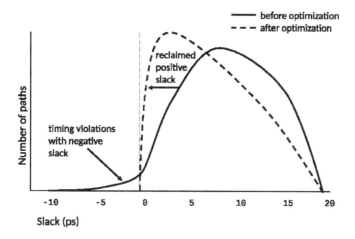

Figure 4.44 Basic form of a timing slack graph

automated algorithms strive to reduce the negative slack to zero. In addition, it is generally sensible to reclaim power and area using optimisations that strive to reduce the positive slack to zero as well.

A **multi-cycle path** is a combinational logic path that intentionally takes more than one clock cycle to convey a signal between two registers in a common clock domain. Figure 4.45 illustrates the typical structure, which has no unusual features, except that the combinational delay through the logic block is large with respect to the clock period $T = 1/f$.

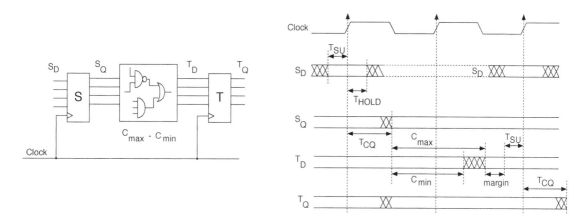

Figure 4.45 Schematic (left) and timing diagram (right) of a typical multi-cycle path. The delay through logic block C ranges from C_{min} to C_{max} with both limits being between one and two clock periods

The maximum clock frequency is more than doubled when a multi-cycle path is used, since the register timing overheads are encountered only every other clock cycle. It is given by the inequality $T_{CQ} + C_{max} + T_{SU} < 2T$. This is based on 'multi' meaning exactly 2, which is the normal case. Depending on design style, there is also a minimum clock frequency. If a multi-cycle path is to act as an extra stage of pipeline delay, the period must be no longer than given by $T_{CQ} + C_{min} > T + T_{hold}$.

Generally speaking, logic that has a minimum operating frequency should be avoided, since it cannot be single-stepped and can be harder to debug. A multi-cycle path becomes a single-cycle path at low frequencies. Often, multi-cycle paths are used where design is intrinsically tolerant to any amount of pipelining, which is where the data are self-qualifying using a valid net or paddable justification symbol (Section 3.7.4).

The difference between inertial and transport delays is described in Section 8.3.5. Multi-cycle paths can potentially be designed on the transport principle, meaning that more than one value can actively progress through the delay structure. This requires much tighter understanding of the precise delay structure in the logic path and can be avoided in many applications. Additionally, it is possible that register T becomes metastable in clock cycles where its output should not be used. This does not cause a functional problem but could occasionally slightly increase energy use.

4.10 Summary

For many electronics products, the most important task is SoC design. As much logic as possible should normally be included on the primary ASIC. This chapter has presented many of the low-level considerations and techniques in SoC design. Whenever a basic equation defines the behaviour, this equation has been presented. A potential design will deploy some combination of techniques. However, a system architect will rarely view the overall problem mathematically. Instead they will make instinct-directed design decisions while being tacitly aware of the basic shapes of the underlying curves. It is important to be able to get rapid feedback of the energy, area, cost and performance of a potential design without having to invest too much effort in that particular design point. Techniques for generating high-level models of the system will be presented next, in Chapter 5. Design exploration is the process of experimenting with major and minor design variations to optimise these key metrics. This will be covered in Chapter 6.

The reader has now seen formulae and techniques that cover the main quantities used in the high-level design of a SoC. They should have become familiar with parallel speedup, queuing delay, electricity use, thermal management, test structures, security and clock distribution.

4.10.1 Exercises

1. If an accelerator multiplies the performance of one quarter of a task by a factor of four, what is the overall speedup?

2. The server for a queue has a deterministic response time of 1 µs. If arrivals are random and the server is loaded to 70% utilisation, what is the average time spent waiting in the queue?

3. If the server is still loaded to 70% but now has two queues, with one being served in preference to the other, and 10% of the traffic is in the high-priority queue, how much faster is the higher-priority work served than the previous design where it shared its queue with all forms of traffic?

4. If a switched-on region of logic has an average static to dynamic power use of 1 to 4 and a clock gating can save 85% of the dynamic power, discuss whether there is a further benefit to power gating.

5. What is the minimum information that needs to be stored in a processor trace buffer to capture all aspects of the behaviour of a program model given that the machine code image is also available?

6. A 100-kbit SRAM mitigates against a manufacturing fault using redundancy. Compute the percentage overhead for a specific design approach of your own choosing. Assuming at most one fault per die, which may or may not lie in an SRAM region, how do the advantages of your approach vary according to the percentage of the die that is an SRAM protected in this way?

7. Assuming an embarrassingly parallel problem, in which all data can be held close to the processing element that operates on it, use Pollack's rule and other equations to derive a formula for approximate total energy use with a varying number of cores and various clock frequencies within a given silicon area.

8. Consider a succession of matrix multiplications, as performed by **convolutional neural networks (CNNs)** and similar applications in which the output of one stage is the input to the next. Is FIFO storage needed between stages and if so, could a region of scratchpad RAM be sensibly used or would it be better to have a full hardware FIFO buffer?

References

[1] André M. DeHon. Location, location, location: The role of spatial locality in asymptotic energy minimization. In *Proceedings of the ACM/SIGDA International Symposium on Field Programmable Gate Arrays*, FPGA '13, pages 137–146, New York, NY, USA, 2013. Association for Computing Machinery. ISBN 9781450318877. doi: 10.1145/2435264.2435291. URL https://doi.org/10.1145/2435264.2435291.

[2] R. Landauer. Irreversibility and heat generation in the computing process. *IBM J. Res. Dev.*, 5(3):183–191, July 1961. ISSN 0018-8646. doi: 10.1147/rd.53.0183. URL https://doi.org/10.1147/rd.53.0183.

[3] Ganesh Venkatesh, Jack Sampson, Nathan Goulding, Saturnino Garcia, Vladyslav Bryksin, Jose Lugo-Martinez, Steven Swanson, and Michael Bedford Taylor. Conservation cores: Reducing the energy of mature computations. In *Proceedings of the 15th International Conference on Architectural Support for Programming Languages and Operating Systems*, ASPLOS XV, pages 205–218, New York, NY, USA, 2010. Association for Computing Machinery. ISBN 9781605588391. doi: 10.1145/1736020.1736044. URL https://doi.org/10.1145/1736020.1736044.

[4] Gerald J. Popek and Robert P. Goldberg. Formal requirements for virtualizable third generation architectures. *Commun. ACM*, 17(7):412–421, July 1974. ISSN 0001-0782. doi: 10.1145/361011.361073. URL https://doi.org/10.1145/361011.361073.

[5] Henry M. Levy. *Capability-Based Computer Systems*. Digital Press, 2014. ISBN 148310740X.

[6] M. V. Wilkes and R. M. Needham. *The Cambridge CAP Computer and Its Operating System*. Elsevier, January 1979. URL https://www.microsoft.com/en-us/research/publication/the-cambridge-cap-computer-and-its-operating-system/.

[7] Jonathan Woodruff, Robert Watson, David Chisnall, Simon Moore, Jonathan Anderson, Brooks Davis, Ben Laurie, Peter Neumann, Robert Norton, and Michael Roe. The CHERI capability model: Revisiting RISC in an age of risk. In *Proceedings of the International Symposium on Computer Architecture*, pages 457–468, June 2014. ISBN 978-1-4799-4394-4. doi: 10.1109/ISCA.2014.6853201.

Chapter 5

Electronic
System-Level
Modelling

A SoC combines hardware and software and communicates with the outside world via various interfaces. An **electronic system-level (ESL) model** of a SoC can simulate the complete system behaviour. This includes running all the software that the real SoC will run in a largely unmodified form. An alternative name for an ESL model is a **virtual platform**. In some SoC design flows, creating the ESL model is the first design step. A process of **incremental refinement** then gradually replaces high-level components with lower-level models or actual implementations. Ultimately, all of the system is implemented, but a good ESL methodology enables an arbitrary mix of high- and low-level modelling styles that interwork. A typical use case is when all the design is present in high-level form except for one or two subsystems of current interest for which greater modelling detail is needed to answer a specific design question.

In this chapter, we present the main aims of and approaches to ESL modelling. We review the SystemC modelling library and its transaction library and discuss how high-level models can be calibrated to give useful insights into power and performance.

The performance of an ESL model must be good enough to execute large programs in a reasonable time. This typically means achieving at least 1 per cent of real system performance. An ESL model is normally accurate in terms of memory layout and content, but many other hardware details are commonly neglected unless they are of special relevance to the test being run. This is the principal means of achieving a high-performance simulation.

By default, an ESL model simulates the system from the point of power-up or reset. Another way to apply an ESL model to complex software is checkpoint and replay. This is useful if a significant amount of software must run before the point of interest is approached. A checkpoint is chosen, such as after the boot or operating system start. At the checkpoint, the entire state of the model is saved to a checkpoint file. Information could be captured from the real system in principle, but the ESL model may not be identical to the real system and minor discrepancies may arise. Moreover, instrumenting the real system may be tricky (especially if it does not exist yet). Since the checkpoint serves as the basis for a number of experiments, the time invested in generating it is amortised.

To conduct an experiment, the ESL model is loaded with the checkpoint data and modelling rolls forward from that point. The model may be switched to a greater level of detail than used for preparing the checkpoint, either globally or just for some subsystems. For instance a high-level model of an I/O block may be switched to an RTL model.

5.1 Modelling Abstractions

The modelling system should ideally support all stages of the design process, from design entry to fabrication. However, we cannot model a complete SoC in detail and expect to simulate the booting of the operating system in a reasonable time. A model that is a million times slower than the real hardware would take 115 days to simulate a boot sequence that lasts 10 seconds! An ESL virtual platform must support a number of levels of modelling abstraction and a way to interwork between them. Most ESL models are built on top of some form of **event-driven simulation (EDS)** (also known as

discrete-event simulation). An EDS simulator defines various types of discrete event and the simulation is a progression of events in the time domain. Detailed variations of EDS are discussed in Section 8.3.4. The main variation in modelling detail is the type of event predominantly used: examples range from the change in state of an individual digital net to the delivery of a complete Ethernet packet. At the highest level, events are replaced with flow rates, giving a **fluid-flow model**, which essentially traces the progression of a set of simultaneous differential equations.

An overall taxonomy of modelling levels is as follows:

1. **Functional modelling**: The output from a simulation run is accurate.

2. **Memory-accurate modelling**: The contents and layout of memory are accurate.

3. **Cycle lumped** or **untimed TLM**: Complete transactions between IP blocks, such as the delivery of a burst of data, are modelled as atomic events. No timestamps are recorded on transactions. Cycle counts are accurate at the end of a program run; however, individual cycles are not modelled. Typically a sub-model will do a quantum of work and then update the cycle count.

4. **Stochastic** or **loosely timed TLM**: The number of transactions is accurate, and even though the order may be wrong, each is given a timestamp based on standard queuing models. Thus, an overall runtime can be reported. Formulae from queuing theory (Section 4.3.1) can be used to incorporate the time spent waiting in queues instead of modelling the queues themselves. Synthetic traffic injectors, characterised by a mean rate and burst size and other numeric parameters, replace real applications, although traces from real runs can also be replayed from a file.

5. **Approximately timed TLM**: The number and order of transactions are accurate and the degree to which they overlap or interfere is measured.

6. **Cycle-accurate simulation**: The number of clock cycles consumed is accurate and the work done in each clock cycle is accurately modelled. A simulation of synthesisable RTL gives such a model, if the combinational nets are evaluated only when needed.

7. **Net-level EDS**: The netlist of the subsystem is fully modelled and the ordering of net changes within a clock cycle is accurate.

8. **Analogue and mixed-signal simulation**: Voltage waveforms for certain nodes are modelled.

Before explaining these levels in greater detail, two further terms are worth defining:

1. With **programmer-view accuracy**, the model correctly reflects the contents of programmer-visible memory and registers. The **programmer's view (PV)** contains only architecturally significant registers, such as those that the software programmer can manipulate with instructions. Other registers in a particular hardware implementation, such as pipeline stages and holding registers to

overcome structural hazards (Section 6.3.2), are not part of the PV. These are typically not present in a PV model. If a PV model also has a notion of time, it is denoted PV+T. Similarly, PV+ET denotes the modelling of energy and time use.

2. The term '**behavioural modelling**' has no precise definition, but generally denotes a simulation model that is different from the real implementation. For instance, a handcrafted program may be written to model the behaviour of a component or subsystem. More specifically, it can denote a model that expresses the behaviour of a component using an imperative thread of execution, as in software programming. Such a thread performs successive reads and writes of registers, whereas an RTL implementation makes all the assignments in parallel on a clock edge. In Section 5.3, we implement behavioural models of hardware components using the SystemC library.

As mentioned in Chapter 1, the starting point for a SoC for some classes of application may be a software program that generates the same output as the SoC should generate. This is the **functional model**. For an IoT device, the model would serve the same responses over the network. For an RF transmitter subsystem, it might write the analogue waveform to be fed to the real antenna to a file on the modelling workstation. The output generated by this highest of models is shown in yellow on Figure 1.10. Although such models represent none of the structure of the SoC implementation, they define the basic behaviour required and provide reference data that can be used to evaluate both the SoC-based solution and the reset of the ecosystem.

A SoC typically contains a large amount of memory. The next refinement can be to determine the number of different logical memory spaces there should be in the SoC and to plan their detailed layout. The software in the functional model should be partitioned into that representing hardware and that remaining as software running inside the SoC. This model will have a number of arrays, which, ultimately, will be held in one or more SRAM and DRAM components in the real hardware. In a **memory-accurate model**, the contents of each array in the model are the same as the contents of the real memory in the final implementation. Manually counting the frequency of operations on the arrays or the number of iterations of the inner loops of this model gives a preliminary estimate of the amount of processing power and memory bandwidth needed in the SoC. A simple spreadsheet analysis of these figures can be used as a first estimate of the final power consumption and battery life. Using an **assertion-based design (ABD)** approach (Section 7.2.2), the first assertions can be written about the contents of the memory.

In ESL modelling, the next refinement is to generate a **transaction-level model (TLM)**. In mainstream computer science, the term **transaction** is related to properties of atomicity, plus commits and rollbacks. In ESL modelling, the term means less than that. Rather, a transaction simply means that one component invokes an operation on another component. Using object-oriented programming, the components can be modelled as instances of classes and the transactions implemented as method invocations of one component or another. A transaction could be as simple as changing the value of one net, but more commonly a transaction represents hundreds or thousands of nets changing value. Moreover, many of the real nets or interconnect components do not need to be represented at all.

This is the primary reason that a TLM model runs so much faster than a net-level simulation. TLM models can optionally include time, power and energy. TLM modelling is discussed in Section 5.4.

A **cycle-accurate model** for a subsystem models all state bits in registers and RAMs for the subsystem. The state bits are updated once per clock cycle to reflect their new value on that clock edge. The values for combinational nets do not have to be computed if a static analysis shows that they are not participating in the next-state function. If they are computed, there is no representation of when in the clock cycle they changed or whether they glitched. To increase performance, a cycle-accurate model will typically use a simple **two-value logic system** or a **four-value logic system** rather than the richer logic of Verilog or VHDL (Section 8.3.3). A **cycle-callable model** is a cycle-accurate model of one clock domain. It essentially consists of a subroutine that can be called by a thread in a higher-level simulator that causes the model to advance by one clock cycle. For instance, a cycle-callable model of a counter would just be a subroutine that increments the counter value.

Lower-level models represent all the flip-flops and busses of the real implementation. These are based on RTL implementations of the components. RTL synthesis does not greatly affect the number of state bits or their meaning, although there may be some optimisation of the state encoding, as mentioned in Section 4.4.2. RTL synthesis does, however, instantiate many combinational gates and it can also **bit blast** (implement a bus or arithmetic operator in terms of its individual bits, Section 8.3.8), so an EDS simulation post-synthesis runs much more slowly than before RTL synthesis. The simulation is slower not only because of the 10× to 50× increase in the number of nets, but also because the timing of combinational nets within the clock cycle is accurately represented.

As discussed in Section 8.3.7, an even lower-level simulation is possible, in which the voltage waveform on a net is simulated rather than just being treated as a digital value. This is required for analogue and mixed-signal systems but is not normally required for digital logic.

5.1.1 ESL Flow Diagram

ESL flows are most commonly based on C++. The SystemC TLM library for C++ is also typically used (Section 5.3). In SoC design, C/C++ tends to be used for behavioural models of peripherals, for embedded applications, for the operating system and for its device drivers. The interface specifications for the hardware-to-software APIs are then in `.h` files, which are imported into both the hardware and software strands. These three forms of C++ file are shown across the top of Figure 5.1. To create the embedded machine code for an SoC-level product, the software strand is compiled with a compiler appropriate for the embedded cores (e.g. `gcc-arm`). As explained in Chapters 6 and 8, the behavioural models of the hardware are converted by various means into the RTL and gate-level hardware for the real SoC. This is illustrated in the diagonal right-to-left downwards trajectory in the figure. On the other hand, the fastest ESL models are typically generated by the left-to-right downwards trajectory. This takes the hardware models and the embedded software and links them together so that the entire system can be run as a single application program. This is possible only if suitable coding guidelines are followed. Instead of simulating millions of times slower than real time, this hybrid model can run even faster than real time, such as when a high-performance modelling

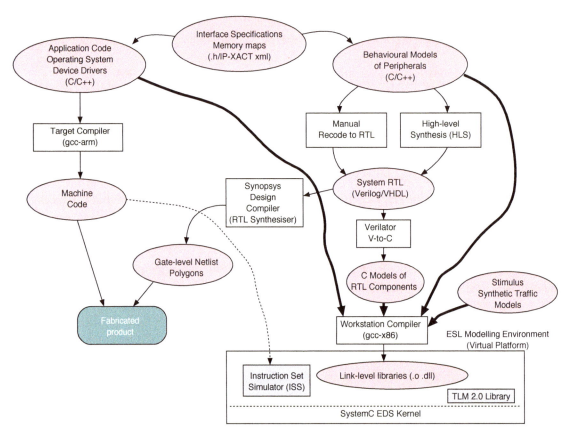

Figure 5.1 Overall setup of a generic ESL flow. The heavy lines show the fastest technique, which avoids using an instruction set simulator (ISS) through native cross-compiling of the embedded firmware and direct linking with behavioural models of the hardware

workstation has a more powerful processor than the embedded SoC cores. The hybrid program may rely on a threads package, typically provided by the SystemC EDS kernel, but it is coded so that context switches are minimised.

A simple yet stark example of the potential performance gain is to consider a network packet being received by a device driver and transferred over the bus to memory. This will involve tens of thousands of transitions at the gate outputs of the real implementation. Using a net-level simulation, the simulation for each gate transition might require the modelling workstation to execute 100 instructions. However, with a suitable ESL coding style, the packet reception transaction can be modelled with a simple method call between one component and another that takes fewer than 100 instructions in total. With careful memory management, the data transferred by the transaction does not even need to be copied; a pointer to its buffer is all that needs to be conveyed in the transaction.

Figure 5.1 also shows two flow variations:

1. An **instruction set simulator (ISS)** may be used to interpret the machine code of the embedded cores. The typical structure of an interpreting ISS is illustrated in Section 5.5. However, the best ISS

implementations, like JIT compilers for JavaScript, spot frequently used execution paths in the inner loops of the interpreted machine code and cross-compile this code to native machine code for the modelling workstation. Hence, the performance can again approach faster than real-time speed.

2. If an RTL model differs greatly from the initial high-level model or if a high-level model does not exist, the RTL design can be projected back to a C++ model using standard tools. One of the first to do this was VTOC from Tenison EDA. Today, the public-domain Verilator tool is often used. Some IP providers make C++ models directly available. For instance, Arm provides many C++ models generated from internal RTL using the Carbon tool chain.

5.2 Interconnect Modelling

Interconnect models are used to study the behaviour of an interconnect and for performance trade-offs before the actual interconnect is designed. They also serve to provide realistic delay estimates during ESL modelling of a complete SoC. Another quite useful role for a detailed interconnect model is to replicate a problem in a production version and then carry out mitigation studies. Both packetised networks-on-chip (NoCs) and conventional circuit-switched interconnects convey discrete events that encounter queueing and arbitration, so the same modelling techniques largely apply to both.

An interconnect can be modelled at a high level using queuing theory or in more detail by modelling individual contention events. The stochastic queuing formulae presented in Section 4.3.1 reflect the emergent behaviour that occurs when a large number of uncorrelated event generators share interconnect components. However, real designs can convey a large amount of unexpectedly correlated traffic and queuing theory then gives the wrong answer. For instance, the queuing formula for an $M/M/1$ system gives an inflated result for systems that are actually closer to $M/D/1$ due to deterministic behaviour in the server or when the events it potentially serves cannot all arrive at once due to secondary mechanisms.

In more detail, a taxonomy of interconnect modelling, in order of increasing detail, is:

1. **High-level static analysis**: A fluid-flow model populates a spreadsheet (or equivalent) using the traffic flow matrix defined in Section 3.5.1. If the routing protocol is followed, then for each point of contention, the utilisation and service disciplines are known and hence, the buffer occupancy and transit delay can be computed from the standard stochastic formulae. This approach is suitable for an initial design, and it can also generate simplistic delay values, which are added to the 'sc_time &delay' field in a loosely timed TLM model.

2. **Virtual queuing**: A virtual platform propagates transactions across an interconnect without queue models or delay. However, the routing protocol is followed and hence, the dynamic level of traffic at each contention point is accurate to the timescale within which transaction ordering is maintained

(e.g. the TLM quantum). A delay penalty based on stochastic formulae is then added to the transaction `delay` field. This style of modelling is demonstrated in detail in Section 5.4.5.

3. **TLM queuing**: High-level models of switching elements contain queues of transactions. Coding based on blocking TLM (Section 5.4.1) is then typically required.

4. **Cycle-accurate modelling**: The model is accurate to the clock cycle, either using TLM or RTL-level simulation, as described in Section 5.2.2.

5.2.1 Stochastic Interconnect Modelling

There is a wealth of material in the networking domain that models interconnects for various forms of random traffic. Many of the models based on a Markov process [1] are excellent analytical tools for detailed mathematical studies. A Markov process is one in which the current state of the system is sufficient to predict its next behaviour. The system operates as a chain of operations each modifying the current state of the system and no further history is required. Markov models work well when traffic sources are uncorrelated and the applied load is independent of the round-trip latency. Many aspects of wide-area networks such as the Internet can be accurately studied in this way. Many factors affect network behaviour, e.g. packet arrival rates and times at the various ingress points and packet departure rates at the egress points. Traffic levels can be regarded as stationary or slowly varying with a daily and weekly pattern. Even for a NoC, this sort of information is typically available, or at least some meaningful approximation can be found. Hence, Markov models are useful for high-level dimensioning and provisioning studies. Given sufficiently accurate traffic models, e.g. in terms of packet length distribution, the effects of arbitration policies and other features of an interconnect can be explored.

Despite their advantages, stochastic sources and Markovian fabric models are often not helpful for a particular issue with a production chip. Compared with cycle-accurate modelling, problems include:

- broad-brush correlations in traffic patterns (such as responding to a request) may not be captured adequately

- local effects may be neglected at a particular contention point

- the order of transactions will be incorrect under loose timing (see later)

- a deadlock may be missed.

5.2.2 Cycle-accurate Interconnect Modelling

The most detailed and lowest level of interconnect modelling is cycle-accurate modelling. **Aliasing traffic** occurs when a link carries multiple flows. The term is especially relevant if traffic shares a NoC virtual channel. The behaviour of an interconnect with respect to event interdependence and various other aliasing effects cannot be effectively investigated at any higher level of abstraction, because, at a contention point, the traffic shape can entirely change the performance characteristic. As an example, if two packets arrive at a switching element such that each arrival requires arbitration, then there will be a delay resulting in an increase in overall latency. However, if the same two packets arrive one after the other, no such delay is observed. Any store-and-forward network distorts the shape of the traffic from that received at the ingress to that which it displays at the egress.

To model an entire interconnect at a cycle-accurate level, each of the individual sub-models must operate at a cycle-accurate level. The end points can be modelled using a **bus functional model (BFM)** or plugged into a real system, e.g. Arm's mesh generators [2, 3]. Quite often it is not necessary to integrate actual end-point devices for performance analysis or problem-solving. The input stimuli can be either traces, obtained from real-world systems, or more popularly synthetic scenarios, as described in Section 3.5.1. A second and detailed analysis phase can use more accurate end-point models or RTL-level simulations.

If multiple clocks or clock edges are used, sub-cycle accuracy modelling is occasionally needed, since a cycle-accurate model may still be insufficient to capture the subtleties of a problem. There may be behavioural differences between RTL and the model, and it is not trivial to get the model right. Such models are stabilised over generations of a product.

As stated at the start of this chapter, a virtual platform ideally supports interworking between different levels of abstraction. If a behavioural subtlety has been identified, only the localised subsystem needs to use a low-level model. This is joined to the remainder of the ESL model using transactors (Section 5.4.8).

5.3 SystemC Modelling Library

SystemC is a free library for C++ for hardware modelling. It was initially promoted by OSCI, the Open SystemC Initiative, and is now available from Accelera and standardised as IEEE-1666 [4]. Each hardware component is defined by a C++ class that may instantiate lower-level components. SystemC neatly supports any mixture of TLM and net-level modelling and it can be used for simulation and synthesis. It was originally designed as an RTL-equivalent means of representing digital logic inside C++. The next sections cover these basic aspects and then Sections Section 5.4 and Section 6.9 move on to uses for ESL and synthesis.

The SystemC core library includes the following essential elements:

- A module system with inter-module channels: C++ class instances are instantiated in a hierarchy, following the circuit component structure, in the same way that RTL modules instantiate each other.

- A kernel that runs in user space: It provides facilities for the system time, pausing a simulation and name resolution. It implements an EDS event queue that roughly follows the detailed semantics of VHDL (described in Section 8.3.4). Event notifications and threads are provided. The threads are not pre-emptive, which allows user code to take a lightweight approach to data structure locks, but there may be problems running SystemC on multi-core workstations. Threads run inside components either using a lightweight trampoline style, returning the thread to the kernel without blocking, or by blocking the thread inside the component, which requires a per-thread stack.

- The compute/commit signal paradigm, as well as other forms of channel for connecting components together: The compute/commit operation, described in Section 8.3.6, is needed inside a zero-delay model of a clock domain to avoid shoot-through (Section 4.6.9), which occurs when one flip-flop in a clock domain changes its output before another has read the previous value. If propagation times are unknown, as is the case when writing new code or porting to a new fabrication technology, a zero-delay model is preferable to a model that embodies an arbitrary and inaccurate non-zero delay.

- A library of arbitrary fixed-precision integers: Hardware typically uses many busses and counters with different widths that wrap accordingly. SystemC provides classes of signed and unsigned variables of any width that behave in the same way. For instance, a user can define an `sc_int` of 5 bits and put it inside a signal. Being signed, it will overflow when it is incremented beyond 15 and wrap to -16. The library includes overloads of all the standard arithmetic and logic operators for these types.

- Plotting output functions that enable waveforms to be captured to a file and viewed with a standard waveform viewer program such as gtkwave, as shown in Section 5.3.3.

A problem with SystemC arises from the lack of a reflection API in the C language. A reflection API, as found in Python for instance, enables a program to inspect its own source code. This is very useful for reporting runtime errors and other types of static analysis, such as when an expression may need to be recomputed due to its free variables having changed value. To overcome this, SystemC coding sometimes requires the user to annotate a structure with its name as a string, but the C preprocessor can help minimise the amount of double-entry of identifiers needed. Another problem is that hardware engineers are often not C++ experts, but if they misuse the library, they can be faced with complex and advanced C++ error messages.

One of the major benefits of SystemC is the intrinsic excellent performance of anything coded in C++. Moreover, it is a standard adopted by the entire electronic design automation (EDA) industry. General-purpose behavioural code, including application code and device drivers, is modelled and/or implemented in this common language.

First Example: A Binary Counter

SystemC enables a component to be defined using the SC_MODULE and SC_CTOR macros. Figure 5.2 gives an example component definition. The example is a leaf component since it has no children. It uses behavioural modelling to express what it does on each clock edge. Each of these SC macros is expanded into a C++ class definition and its constructor along with some code that registers each instance with the runtime SystemC kernel. Modules inherit various attributes appropriate for an hierarchic hardware design, including an instance name, a type name and channel binding capability.

```
SC_MODULE(mycounter) // An example of a leaf module (no subcomponents)
{
    sc_in  < bool      > clk, reset;
    sc_out < sc_int<10> > myout;

    void mybev()  // Internal behaviour, invoked as an SC_METHOD
    {
        myout = (reset) ? 0: (myout.read()+1); // Use .read() since sc_out makes a signal
    }

    SC_CTOR(mycounter)        // Constructor
      { SC_METHOD(mybev);      // Require that mybev is called on each positive edge of clk
        sensitive << clk.pos();
      }
}
```

Figure 5.2 A 10-bit binary counter with synchronous reset, coded as a SystemC class

The `sensitive` construct registers a callback with the EDS kernel that says when the code inside the module should be run. However, an unattractive feature of SystemC is the need to use the `.read()` method when reading a signal.

5.3.1 SystemC Structural Netlist

A **structural netlist** or **gate-level netlist** is a circuit diagram showing the connections between components (Figure 5.3 and Section 8.3.1).

A SystemC templated **channel** is a general purpose interface between components. We rarely use the raw channels. Instead, the derived forms – `sc_in`, `sc_out` and `sc_signal` – are mostly used. These channels implement the compute/commit paradigm required for **delta cycles** (Section 8.3.6). This avoids indeterminacy from racing in zero-delay models. The fragment in Figure 5.4 illustrates the compute/commit behaviour. The `sc_signal` is an abstract (templated) data type that has a current value and a next value. Signal reads get the current value, and the next value is written. If the EDS kernel blocks when there are no more events in the current time step, the pending new values are committed to the visible current values. Hence, the value read from the signal changes from 95 to 96.

Other channels provided include a buffer, FIFO and mutex. Users can overload the channel class to implement channels with their own semantics as needed. Note that a rich set of non-standard channels is not a good basis for reusable IP blocks that are widely interoperable. Hence, designers should minimise the number of new channel types. However, it is not possible to get high performance from a model that invokes the EDS kernel for every change of every net or bus.

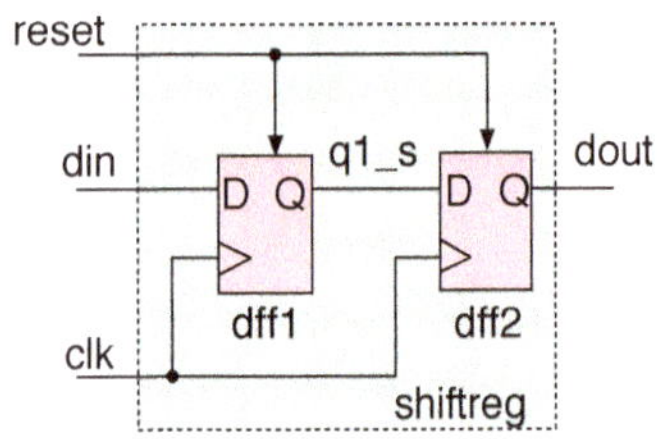

```
//Example of structural hierarchy and wiring between levels:
SC_MODULE(shiftreg)  // Two-bit shift register
{   sc_in  < bool >  clk, reset, din;
    sc_out < bool >  dout;

    sc_signal < bool > q1_s;
    dff dff1, dff2;      // Instantiate FFs

    SC_CTOR(shiftreg) : dff1("dff1"), dff2("dff2")
    {   dff1.clk(clk);
        dff1.reset(reset);
        dff1.d(din);
        dff1.q(q1_s);

        dff2.clk(clk);
        dff2.reset(reset);
        dff2.d(q1_s);
        dff2.q(dout);
    }
};
```

Figure 5.3 Schematic (left) and SystemC structural netlist (right) for a 2-bit shift register

```
int nv;                    // nv is a simple C variable (POD, plain old data)
sc_out    < int > data;    // data and mysig are sc_signals (non-POD)
sc_signal < int > mysig;   //
...
     nv += 1;
     data = nv;
     mysig = nv;
     printf("Before nv=%i, %i %i\n'', nv, data.read(), mysig.read());
     wait(10, SC_NS);
     printf("After  nv=%i, %i %i\n'', nv, data.read(), mysig.read());
...
Before nv=96, 95 95
After  nv=96, 96 96
```

Figure 5.4 Compute/commit behaviour

5.3.2 SystemC Threads and Methods

SystemC enables a user module to have its own thread and stack. However, the memory footprint is lower if the user code operates in a trampoline style using only non-blocking upcalls from the kernel. As shown in the subsequent examples, the constructor for a component typically uses one or other of these coding styles, depending on its needs and complexity. Code can block, either by making a blocking system call, such as a read, or a SystemC call, such as wait(sc_time), or by entering a lengthy or infinite loop. There may be multiple threads active, using, perhaps, a mixture of these two styles. The constructor selects the thread for each upcall using either:

- The SC_THREAD macro if an upcall is allowed to block and retain the thread forever.

- The SC_METHOD for an upcall that will not block but always returns once the instantaneous work is complete.

For efficiency, designers should use SC_METHOD whenever possible. SC_THREAD should be reserved for when an important state must be retained in the program counter from one activation to the next or for when asynchronous active behaviour is needed. This choice of programming styles is also the basis for two main programming TLM styles introduced later: blocking and non-blocking (Section 5.4.1).

The earlier counterexample of Figure 5.2 used SC_METHOD. Figure 5.5 is an example that uses SC_THREAD. It is a data source that provides a stream of increasing numbers using a net-level four-phase handshake (Section 3.1.3).

```
SC_MODULE(mydata_generator)
{ sc_out < int  > data;
  sc_out < bool > req;
  sc_in  < bool > ack;

  void myloop()
  { while(1)
    { data = data.read() + 1;
      wait(10, SC_NS);
      req = 1;
      do { wait(10, SC_NS); } while(!ack.read());
      req = 0;
      do { wait(10, SC_NS); } while(ack.read());
    }
  }

  SC_CTOR(mydata_generator)
  {
    SC_THREAD(myloop);
  }
}
```

Figure 5.5 Sample code using SC_THREAD

SystemC supports all standard ISO time specifications from femtoseconds to seconds using a library type SC_TIME. For instance,

$$sc\_time\ ten\_nanoseconds(10,\ SC\_NS)$$

defines a variable called ten_nanoseconds initialised to the eponymous value. A SystemC thread can then block for this time using wait(ten_nanoseconds). All standard arithmetic overloads are supported for the SC_TIME type.

Waiting for an arbitrary Boolean expression to become true is hard to implement in a language such as C++ because it is compiled. It does not have a reflection API that enables a user expression to be re-evaluated by the EDS kernel. Yet, we still want a reasonably neat and efficient way of blocking a thread on an arbitrary event expression coded in C++. The original solution was the delayed evaluation class. For instance, one would write:

```
waituntil(mycount.delayed() > 5 && !reset.delayed());
```

The `delayed()` suffix used neat overloading tricks to construct the abstract syntax tree of the expression on the runtime heap rather than compile the expression natively. Hence, the kernel could deduce its support (the set of conditions for which the expression needs to be re-evaluated) and evaluate it when needed. This was deemed to be too unwieldy and removed. Today, we write a less efficient spin, viz.:

```
do { wait(10, SC_NS); } while(!((mycount > 5 && !reset)));
```

Moreover, within SystemC, there is no direct equivalent to the continuous assignment of Verilog. However, the fully supported sensitivity list `always @(*)` or `always_comb` can be reproduced with an `SC_METHOD` where the user manually lists the supporting nets. Performance is enhanced by putting the continuous assignment behaviour in a method and remembering to call that method whenever the support is changed in other parts of the model. However, such manual coding is liable to programming error and is fragile when edited. Fortunately, for TLM models in SystemC, very little continuous assignment is needed, with the exception being, perhaps, just interrupt wiring.

5.3.3 SystemC Plotting and its GUI

SystemC supports the dumping of a waveform plot to the industry-standard **Verilog Change Dump (VCD)** files for later viewing with visualisers such as gtkwave, ModelSim from Mentor Graphics and many other tools from the major EDA vendors. A VCD file stores net names and a list of changes in value to those nets with associated timestamps. The nets are held in a tree structure that typically represents the originating design hierarchy. In SystemC, traces like the one shown in Figure 5.6 can be

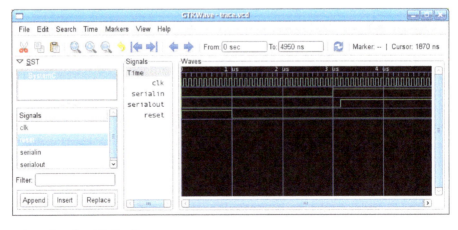

Figure 5.6 An example waveform view plotted by gtkwave

generated by passing the nets to be traced to `sc_trace` calls, as in the top-level fragment in Figure 5.7. Again, due to the lack of a reflection API in C++, for the correct signal names to be shown, the nets need to be named when instantiated or else (re)named when passed to `sc_trace`.

```
sc_trace_file *tf = sc_create_vcd_trace_file("tracefilename");

// Now call:
// sc_trace(tf, <traced variable>, <string>);

sc_signal < bool  > serialin("serialin"); // A named signal
sc_signal < bool  > serialout;           // An unnamed signal
float fbar;
sc_trace(tf, clk);
sc_trace(tf, serialin);
sc_trace(tf, serialout, "serialout");     // Give name since not named above
sc_trace(tf, fbar, "fbar");               // Give name since POD form

sc_start(1000, SC_NS);                    // Simulate for 1 microsecond (old API)
sc_close_vcd_trace_file(tr);
return 0;
```

Figure 5.7 Naming nets

5.3.4 Towards Greater Modelling Efficiency

One approach for conveying more data per kernel operation is to pass more detailed data types along the SystemC channels, which is a step towards transactional modelling. A record containing all the values on a bus can be supplied as the `sc_channel` template type. The channel requires various methods to be defined, such as the equality operator overload shown in the fragment in Figure 5.8.

```
sc_signal < bool > mywire; // Rather than a channel conveying just one bit

struct capsule
{ int ts_int1, ts_int2;
  bool operator== (struct ts other)
  { return (ts_int1 == other.ts_int1) && (ts_int2 == other.ts_int2); }

  int next_ts_int1, next_ts_int2; // Pending updates
  void update()
  { ts_int1 = next_ts_int1; ts_int2 = next_ts_int2;
  }
  ...
  ... // Also must define read(), write() and value_changed()
};

sc_signal < struct capsule > myast; // We can send two integers at once
```

Figure 5.8 Equality operator overload

This can be rather heavy. For instance, the `value_changed` operator must be defined so that positive edges can be used, as in Figure 5.9, but this is rarely used.

```
void mymethod() { .... }
SC_METHOD(mymethod)
sensitive << myast.pos(); // User must define concept of posedge for his own abstract type
```

Figure 5.9 Positive edge

5.4 Transaction-level Modelling

As mentioned earlier, SystemC was originally intended for detailed net-level modelling of hardware, but today its main uses are:

- **Architectural exploration:** Making a fast and quick, high-level model of a SoC to explore performance variations against various dimensions, such as bus width and cache memory size (Chapter 6).

- **Transaction-level ESL models (TLM) of systems:** Handshaking protocols between components and net-level modelling of hardware are replaced with subroutine calls between higher-level models of those components.

- **Synthesis:** RTL is synthesised from SystemC source code using either the RTL constructs of SystemC or a high-level synthesis (Section 6.9).

Two coding styles were recommended by OSCI. These are called 1.0 and 2.0. The 1.0 standard is slightly easier to understand but the 2.0 standard is now more widely used and interoperable. We present them both since 1.0 illustrates some significant concepts. Each standard supports both so-called blocking and non-blocking transactions, but the 2.0 library supports interworking between the blocking and non-blocking styles and adds many further features such as back channels. With release 2.0, SystemC implemented an extension called `sc_export`, which allows a parent module to inherit the interface of one of its children. This is vital for the common situation where the exporting module is not the top-level module of the component being wired up. Moreover, the same binding mechanisms used in the structural netlist of Section 5.3.1 to connect wires between components can be used to connect TLM calls.

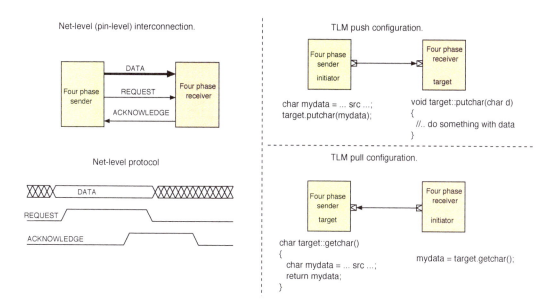

Figure 5.10 Three views of the four-phase transactional protocol from Section 3.1.3 operating between a sender and a receiver. The views are for a net-level connection, an untimed TLM push and an untimed TLM pull

Figure 5.10 is an example of a transactional protocol for a simplex data flow implemented at net level and TLM level. The two variant TLM implementations show that the TLM initiator can be the source or sink of the data.

5.4.1 OSCI TLM 1.0 Standard

The TLM 1.0 standard is essentially a coding style that uses the conventional C++ concepts of multiple inheritance: an SC_MODULE that implements an interface just inherits it using the C++ inheritance mechanism. Figure 5.11 shows the definition of a component called fifo_device, which has two interfaces, read and write. The former has one callable method whereas the latter has two. The interfaces are defined as the C++ virtual classes shown on the left. A net-level implementation of the interfaces typically has data busses and handshake nets to qualify the data on the data busses and implement flow control. The handshake nets do not appear in the TLM equivalent. They are replaced with the acts of calling and returning from the methods in the interfaces.

The left-hand code box in Figure 5.12 shows the SystemC module definition. It does not use the SC_MODULE macro because that macro is incompatible with the additional interface declarations; hence, there is an explicit call to the sc_module constructor that registers instances with the kernel.

The example module is a target for TLM calls. The right-hand code box gives the definition of another module, called fifo_writer, which initiates calls to a FIFO module. It also shows instantiation of the module and binding of its TLM-style interfaces. The net-level implementations of these interfaces might use about 25 wires, but all the details have been modelled using simple method invocations. The net-level modelling of the write transaction might involve change in state for 10 sc_signals as well as

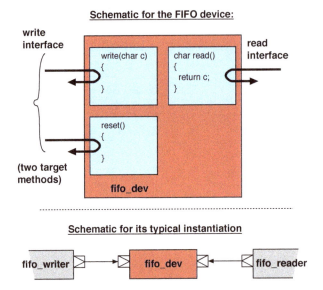

Figure 5.11 Schematic of a FIFO device (top) and its typical instantiation (bottom)

```
//Define the interfaces:                        SC_MODULE("fifo_writer")
class write_if: public sc_interface            {
{ public:                                        sc_port< write_if > outputport;
  virtual void write(char) = 0;                  sc_in < bool > clk;
  virtual void reset() = 0;                      void writer()
};                                               {
                                                   outputport.write(random());
class read_if: public sc_interface               }
{ public:
  virtual char read() = 0;                        SC_CTOR(fifo_writer) {
};                                                  SC_METHOD(writer);
                                                    sensitive << clk.pos();
//Define a component that inherits:              }
class fifo_dev: sc_module("fifo_dev"),         }
public write_if, public read_if, ...
{                                                //Top level instances:
  void write(char) { ... }                       fifo_dev myfifo("myfifo");
  void reset() { ... }                           fifo_writer mywriter("mywriter");
                                                 // Port binding:
  ...                                            mywriter.outputport(myfifo);
}
```

Figure 5.12 SystemC module definition of an interface (left) and FIFO writer (right)

10 upcalls into the the behavioural model of the FIFO buffer from the EDS kernel. In the free OSCI SystemC kernel, each upcall is a computed jump, which tends to result in a pipeline stall on modern processors. The TLM implementation, however, does not need to enter the EDS kernel at all and there are no computed jumps. Although TLM is three orders of magnitude faster, its disadvantage is that it does model any concept of time. Moreover, it is not directly possible to dynamically model energy in

terms of the number of nets changed. Also, note that all notions of the system clock and clock tree are missing at this level of modelling. These shortcoming are mitigated in Section 5.4.3 and Section 5.6.7.

A callable TLM method may contain thread-blocking primitives. A blocking method must be called with an SC_THREAD, whereas non-blocking can use the lighter SC_METHOD. Method names should be prefixed with either b_ or nb_, respectively. This shows whether they can block and reduces the likelihood of programmer error if a blocking entry point is invoked with an SC_METHOD. Moreover, the standard defines different handshaking models for the two forms. These naming and handshaking principles were retained in TLM 2.0. Namely:

- For a **blocking** method, hardware flow control signals are implied by the thread call and return of the method. The call event implies that the handshake to send arguments has taken place and the return implies that the handshake for communicating the result has taken place.

- For a **non-blocking** method, two separate methods must be defined, one for sending the arguments and the second for returning the result. The methods themselves return a Boolean completion status flag and the initiator must repeatedly invoke each method until it returns true. Hence, thread blocking is replaced with caller spinning. An example is presented later under the approximately timed TLM heading (Section 5.4.6).

TLM 1.0 had no standardised or recommended structure for payloads. Different houses could adopt their own models of standard bus structures, leading to incompatible IP block models at SoC assembly time. There was also the problem of how to have multiple instances of the same type of interface on a component, e.g. for a packet router. This design pattern is not often needed in software, and hence, there is no support for it in high-level languages like C++, but it is a common requirement in hardware designs. A workaround was to add a dummy formal type parameter to the interface specification that is given a different concrete type in each instance of an interface. That was really ugly.

Another problem was having to choose between blocking and non-blocking coding. Since any particular method is either blocking or non-blocking, the initiator and target had to agree on which style was being used to make calling possible. Alternatively, the target had to provide both forms. In TLM 2.0, all of these issues are hidden using TLM sockets, which have lightweight library code that solves all these issues.

5.4.2 OSCI TLM 2.0 Standard

Although there was a limited capability in SystemC 1.0 to pass threads along channels, and hence, make subroutine calls along infrastructure originally design to model nets, this was made much easier in SystemC 2.0. TLM 2.0 (July 2008) tidied away the TLM 1.0 interface inheritance problems by providing **TLM convenience sockets**, listed in Table 5.1. It also defined the **TLM generic payload** to promote compatibility between IP block vendors. Further, it defined memory/garbage ownership and transport primitives with timing and fast backdoor access to RAM models.

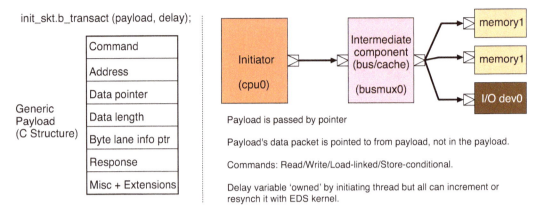

init_skt.b_transact (payload, delay);

Generic
Payload
(C Structure)

| Command |
| Address |
| Data pointer |
| Data length |
| Byte lane info ptr |
| Response |
| Misc + Extensions |

Payload is passed by pointer

Payload's data packet is pointed to from payload, not in the payload.

Commands: Read/Write/Load-linked/Store-conditional.

Delay variable 'owned' by initiating thread but all can increment or resynch it with EDS kernel.

Figure 5.13 TLM 2.0 generic payload structure (left) and interconnection of three IP blocks showing passthrough and demultiplexing (right)

In TLM 2.0, rather than having application-specific method names, the focus is on generic bus operation. Individual functions are achieved by dispatching on the address field in the same way as the real hardware. That is, there are different addressable registers/methods in the target IP block for the different functions, such as reset and write. Figure 5.13 illustrates the general setup. A generic payload is a record in memory that is passed by reference as an argument to method calls that are made via the sockets. The right shows three IP blocks: an initiator, a passthrough and a target. The initiator thread runs code in both of the other two blocks as its calls and returns. Each block can inspect and modify the generic payload. The fields of a generic payload can be set up with code such as in Figure 5.14.

```
// Filling in the fields or a TLM2.0 generic payload:
  trans.set_command(tlm::TLM_WRITE_COMMAND);
  trans.set_address(addr);
  trans.set_data_ptr(reinterpret_cast<unsigned char*>(&data));
  trans.set_data_length(4);
  trans.set_streaming_width(4);
  trans.set_byte_enable_ptr(0);
  trans.set_response_status( tlm::TLM_INCOMPLETE_RESPONSE );

// Sending the payload through a TLM socket:
  socket->b_transport(trans, delay);
```

Figure 5.14 Setting up a generic payload

The sockets themselves can handle any type of payload, but C++ strong typing ensures that all interconnected sites agree. Formats for cache lines, USB request blocks (URBs), 802.3 network frames and audio samples are common examples. The generic payload can be extended on a custom basis and intermediate bus bridges and routers can be polymorphic about this, as they do not need to know about all the extensions. The generic payload encompassed some advanced features, such as burst transfers and byte laning, but the command field uses an enumeration that ranges over just read and write. That command set is woefully inadequate given the rich set used by a modern SoC interconnect (Section 3.1), so non-standard extensions are always needed in real use.

As a worked example, consider a small SRAM connected as a bus target. This is an SC_MODULE defined as a class. The first step is to define the target socket in the .h file:

```
SC_MODULE(cbgram)
{
    tlm_utils::simple_target_socket<cbgram> port0;
    ...
```

Here is the constructor:

```
cbgram::cbgram(sc_module_name name, uint32_t mem_size, bool tracing_on, bool dmi_on):
  sc_module(name), port0("port0"),
  latency(10, SC_NS), mem_size(mem_size), tracing_on(tracing_on), dmi_on(dmi_on)
{
  mem = new uint8_t [mem_size]; // Allocate memory to store contents
  // Register callback for incoming b_transport interface method call
  port0.register_b_transport(this, &cbgram::b_transact);
}
```

The constructor will register various callbacks with the socket. In this case, there is just the blocking entry point called b_transact. This is defined as follows:

```
void cbgram::b_transact(tlm::tlm_generic_payload &trans, sc_time &delay)
{
  tlm::tlm_command cmd = trans.get_command();
  uint32_t    adr = (uint32_t)trans.get_address();
  uint8_t *  ptr = trans.get_data_ptr();
  uint32_t    len = trans.get_data_length();
  uint8_t *  lanes = trans.get_byte_enable_ptr();
  uint32_t    wid = trans.get_streaming_width();

 if (cmd == tlm::TLM_READ_COMMAND)
    {
      ptr[0] = mem[adr];
    }
  else ...
  trans.set_response_status(tlm::TLM_OK_RESPONSE);
}
```

This is the minimal C++ code required for a working implementation. The instantiator will connect the initiator to the target using the bind method provided by all convenience ports. Calls to the bind method establish the interconnection topology between the socket instances. The coding style is identical to that for a SystemC structural netlist, as in Section 5.3.1. Following the instance naming of Figure 5.13, the required code is:

```
busmux0.init_socket.bind(memory0.port0);
busmux0.init_socket.bind(memory1.port0);
busmux0.init_socket.bind(iodev0.port0);
```

Table 5.1 lists the set of convenience sockets defined by TLM 2.0. The problem of multiple instances of one type of port is solved by the multi-sockets. These sockets can be bound more than once, as shown in the fragment above. Passthrough sockets enable a generic payload reference to be passed on to a further TLM call. This directly reflects the behaviour of interconnect components as they forward a flit. An initiator specifies which binding to a multi-port is used by supplying an integer to an overload of the subscription operator:

```
int n = ...;  // Which binding to deliver message to
output_socket[n]->b_transport(trans, delay);
```

As well as the blocking transport method, sockets can invoke and register a non-blocking equivalent. The sockets map calls from one form to the other if the required target is not registered. In addition, there is a reverse channel so that a target can invoke a method on an initiator. This is especially useful for operations such as cache snoop and line invalidate (Section 2.4) where a shared L2 needs to remove entries in an L1 but each L1 is configured as an initiator that operates on the L2.

Table 5.1 List of TLM 2.0 convenience socket types

simple_initiator_socket.h	A version of an initiator socket that has a default implementation of all interfaces. It allows the registration of an implementation for any of the interfaces to the socket, either unique interfaces or tagged interfaces (carrying an additional ID).
simple_target_socket.h	A basic target socket that has a default implementation of all interfaces. It also allows the registration of an implementation for any of the interfaces to the socket, either unique interfaces or tagged interfaces (carrying an additional ID). This socket allows only one of the transport interfaces (blocking or non-blocking) to be registered and implements a conversion if the socket is used on the other interface.
passthrough_target_socket.h	A target socket that has a default implementation of all interfaces. It also allows the registration of an implementation for any of the interfaces to the socket.
multi_passthrough_initiator_socket.h	An implementation of a socket that allows multiple targets to be bound to the same initiator socket. It implements a mechanism that allows the index of the socket the call passed through in the backward path to be identified.
multi_passthrough_target_socket.h	An implementation of a socket that allows multiple initiators to bind to the same target socket. It implements a mechanism that allows the index of the socket the call passed through in the forward path to be identified.

5.4.3 TLM Models with Timing (TLM+T)

A TLM model does not need to refer to the system clock. As discussed, the TLM calls between behavioural models of IP blocks do not need to invoke the EDS kernel at all. So if timing and performance indications are wanted, mechanisms are needed that periodically interact with the kernel. Moreover, given the non-pre-emptive scheduling of SystemC, a single thread can hog the modelling resources such that other parts of the system cannot make progress. To study system performance, however, we must model the time taken by a real transaction in the initiator and target and over the bus or NoC.

There are two defined methods for annotating timings in TLM modelling with SystemC. **Loosely timed TLM** has less overhead and sometimes less accuracy than **approximately timed TLM**. Both use the SystemC EDS kernel with its `tnow` variable defined by the head of the discrete event queue, as explained in Section 8.3.4. This remains the main time reference, but we do not aim to use the kernel very much, perhaps entering it only when inter-thread communication is needed. This reduces the context swap overhead. To make good use of the caches on the modelling workstation, the aim is to run a large number of ISS instructions or other operations before context switching.

Note, in SystemC, we can always print the kernel `tnow` with:

```
cout << ``Time now is : `` << simcontext()->time_stamp() << `` \n'';
```

5.4.4 TLM with Loosely Timed Modelling

The naive way to add timing annotations to TLM modelling is to block the SystemC kernel in a transaction until the prescribed time has elapsed. For instance:

```
sc_time clock_period  = sc_time(5, SC_NS);  // 200 MHz clock

int b_mem_read(A)`
{
   int r = 0;
   if (A < 0 or A >= SIZE) error(....);
   else r = MEM[A];
   wait(clock_period * 3);   // <-- Directly model memory access time: three cycles, say
   return r;
}
```

Although this is accurate, it has an enormous overhead compared with untimed TLM due to the frequent scheduling decisions required by the EDS kernel. The preferred alternative is **loosely timed coding**, which is very efficient. You may have noticed in the SRAM example of Section 5.4.2 that the `b_transact method` has a second parameter, `delay`. There needs to be an instance of such a variable for each loosely timed thread and easy mutable access to it is needed at all sites where that thread might be held up. Hence, it is passed by reference as an additional argument in each TLM call. The coding then augments the `delay` variable instead of delaying the thread. So a target routine that models an action that takes 140 ns on average is coded as:

```
//The leading ampersand on delay is the C++ denotation for pass-by-reference
void b_putbyte(char d, sc_time &delay)
{
  ...
  delay += sc_time(140, SC_NS); // It should be increment at each point where time would pass...
}
```

The `delay` variable records how far ahead of kernel time its associated thread has advanced. A thread using this timing style, in which a model runs ahead of the event queue, is using **temporal decoupling**. At any point, any thread can **resync** itself with the kernel by performing:

```
// Resynch idiomatic form:
  wait(delay);
  delay = 0;
// Note: delay has units sc_time so the SystemC overload of wait is called, not the O/S POSIX wait
```

On calling `wait(delay)`, the current thread yields and the simulation time advances to where or beyond the current thread has progressed. All other threads will likewise catch up.

However, a loosely timed thread needs to yield only when it is waiting for a result delivered from another thread. To prevent threads from getting too far apart in terms of modelled time, a limit is imposed by a so-called **quantum keeper**. Every thread must encounter a quantum keeper at least once in its outermost loop. The code for the quantum keeper can be very simple. It operates with respect to a setting called the **global quantum**. The amount that the thread has run ahead of global time is limited to an integer multiple of the global quantum. The integer is typically 1, in which case the code is just a conditional resync:

```
void quantum_keep(&delay) { if (delay > global_q) { wait(delay); delay = 0; } }
```

If a thread needs to spin while waiting for a result from some other thread, it must also call `wait` using code such as:

```
while (!condition_of_interest)
{
  wait(delay);
  delay = 0;
}
```

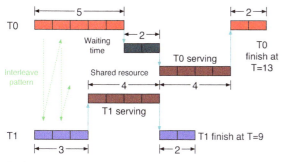 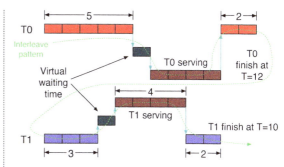

Cycle-accurate or approximately-timed, interleaved operation. Large-quantum loose timing: T0 run entirely before T1.

Figure 5.15 Illustration of modelling artefacts relating to model interleaving and timing arising from loosely timed TLM. In a cycle-accurate or approximately timed model (left), two threads, T0 and T1, can access a shared resource. One blocks while the resource is busy. With loose timing (right), the average contention delay is added to the response times of all customers. With a large quantum, one thread may run entirely before the other

Loose timing, especially with a large quantum, does not preserve relative transaction ordering between threads. Figure 5.15 shows two threads contending for a shared resource. With an accurate model (left), the simulator rapidly switches context between the modelled threads or uses separate simulator threads for the parallel behaviour. The interleave pattern is sketched in green. However, an accurate model will maintain transaction order and allocate a queuing delay to the thread that queues in reality. On the other hand, a loosely timed TLM model may gloss over contention details and just add the average amount of delay, denoted as the virtual queuing time, to each contender. Computation of the average delay is presented in the next section, but note that the average result for T0 and T1 in the figure is correctly maintained. Moreover, with a large quantum, the whole of the work by T0 may be completed before T1 has started to work, so the shared resource may serve T0 before T1, whereas in reality it would serve T1 first.

Hence, an interleaving that is different from reality will sometimes be modelled. Although this may sound bad, it can be beneficial in terms of evaluating the robustness of a system-level design against race conditions. Many components are designed to tolerate alternative transaction interleaving. However, any target susceptible to RaW hazards or similar (Section 6.3) may deliver a different result that is wrong. Given that order is correctly preserved within a loosely timed thread and that the interleaving of such threads tends to model situations that race in the real world (such as two cores storing to the same location), the ability to easily explore different interleavings of the same test is useful. The degree of interleaving is directly adjustable via the quantum.

Generally, we can choose the quantum according to our current modelling interest:

▪ A **large time quantum** results in a fast simulation because there are fewer EDS kernel calls.

▪ A **small time quantum** makes the interleaving of transactions more accurate.

Other approaches to loosely timed simulation exist. The Zsim simulator [5] uses a hybrid approach, called **bound weave**. The simulation period defined by the quantum setting is partitioned into two phases. In the first phase, no contention between parallel threads is modelled. They proceed without a delay penalty, but a log is kept of each access to a shared resource, which includes the operation performed and the relative timestamp from the previous operation. In the second phase, the logs from each thread undergo an accurate EDS analysis so that precise times can be allocated to each event. Zsim was designed for simulating multi-core software and also some hardware aspects of the platform, such as the cache structure. Due to the typically low density of potentially and actually interfering loads and stores, a considerable speedup can be achieved. If transactions have run out of order and there are consequences, the quantum can be subdivided and run again. Overall, this gives very accurate results for such systems and mostly avoids the need for detailed modelling of parallel cache activity.

5.4.5 Modelling Contention under Loosely Timed TLM

If more than one client wants to use a resource simultaneously, we have contention. Real queues are used in hardware, either in FIFO memories or through flow control applying backpressure on the source to stall it until the contended resource is available. An arbiter allocates a resource to one client at a time (Section 4.2.1). Using loosely timed TLM, contention such as this can be modelled using real or virtual queues:

1. In a low-level model, the real queues are modelled in detail. The entries in the queues are TLM payloads and the finite durations of the queue and enqueue operations are modelled. This style is also ideal for approximately timed, non-blocking TLM.

2. A higher-level, blocking TLM model may queue transactions by blocking the client thread until a transaction can be served or forwarded. This still enables alternative arbitration policies to be explored, but may not be ideal for initiators that support multiple outstanding transactions.

3. In the highest level of modelling, a transaction can be run straight away. The ordering effects of the queue are not modelled. However, the estimated delay spent in the queue can be added to the client's delay account. This is **virtual queueing** and is ideal for loosely timed, blocking TLM models.

SystemC provides a TLM payload queue library component to support style 2. With a virtual queue (style 3), although the TLM call passes through the bus/NoC model without suffering a delay or experiencing the contention or queuing of the real system, we use standard queueing theory to provide an appropriate estimated amount of delay. Delay estimates are based on dynamic measurements of the local utilisation ρ at the contention point. These are used in the appropriate waiting time formula, such as for $M/D/1$ (Section 4.3.1):

$$T_Q = \frac{\rho^2}{2(1-\rho)\mu}$$

The utilisation is calculated with the standard running average formula, with response time $\alpha \approx 0.05$, for the most recent transaction spacing:

$$\rho_{n+1} = (1-\alpha)\rho_n + \frac{\alpha(T_n - T_{n-1})}{\mu}$$

```
vqueue::b_transact(pkt, sc_time &delay)
{
    // Measure utilisation and predict queue delay based on last 32 transactions
    if (++opcount == 32)
    {   sc_time delta = sc_time_stamp()+delay-last_measure_time;
        local_processing_delay += (delay_formula(delta/32)-local_processing_delay)/16;
        logging.log(25, delta);                    // record utilisation
        last_measure_time = sc_time_stamp()+delay;
        opcount = 0;
    }

    // Add estimated (virtual) queuing penalty
    delay += local_processing_delay;

    // Do actual work
    output.b_transact(pky, delay);
}
```

Figure 5.16 Essence of the code for a virtual queue contention point. A number of clients send work using `vqueue::b_transact`. The work is done straight away by `output.b_transact`, but the virtual time spent in the queue is added to the loosely timed delay

Alternatively, it can be calculated as the average time between the last 32 transactions, as shown in Figure 5.16. In the figure, the delay formula function knows how many bus cycles per unit time can be handled, and hence, it can compute the queuing delay. The same approach can be applied to a server with an internal queue or backpressure.

As well as subsuming queues, a single multi-socket can model traffic that is conveyed in parallel over several physical busses that allow for the spatial reuse of bandwidth. It can also model traffic serialised in the time domain over a single bus. In all cases, the precise details are not implemented. For a parallel bus, an array of utilisation metrics is maintained and the appropriate equations are used.

5.4.6 Non-blocking TLM coding

The blocking coding style is very lightweight, but at the cost of numerous assumptions. Examples include not separating out the queuing time and service times for a transaction and relying on the properties of independent random variables that do not hold if there are correlations. However, real designs inevitably have correlated traffic patterns. Although loose timing can be an oversimplification, it remains generally suitable for architectural exploration since it does show whether one design is better than another and it provides a quantitative indication of how much. However, if greater accuracy is required from a TLM model, non-blocking coding with approximate timing should be used.

Non-blocking TLM coding is normally used with approximate timing rather than loose timing. Like loose timing, the non-blocking style separates the interconnect busy time from the server busy time, but, in addition, pipelined TLM paths are modelled in detail. New requests are initiated while outstanding results are still to be returned. As with the blocking TLM style, there is a precise start and end point to a transaction, but two or more further timing reference points are used to delimit the end of conveying arguments and the start of conveying the result. The method calls take an additional argument called `phase`, which ranges over four values in sequence: `BEGIN_REQ`, `END_REQ`, `BEGIN_RESP` and `END_RESP`. Moreover, the time delay argument to the method call is used differently. It is not there to support loose timing, as it is just an additional delay that can be used to model the communication overhead in the interconnect, if that delay is not explicitly modelled in another component.

With approximate timing, threads are kept in lockstep with the SystemC kernel. The titular approximations disappear if the models are correctly parametrised with the number of clock cycles taken in the real hardware. Moreover, all queues and contention are modelled in detail. However, detailed figures for clock cycles are not normally known unless RTL is available.

5.4.7 Typical ISS Setup with Loose Timing and Temporal Decoupling

Figure 5.17 is a typical loosely timed model showing just one CPU of a MPSoC. For each CPU core, a single `SC_THREAD` is used that passes between components and back to the originator and only rarely enters the SystemC kernel. As needed for temporal decoupling, associated with each thread is a variable called `delay`, which records how far it has run ahead of the kernel simulation time. A thread yields only when it needs an actual result from another thread or because its delay has exceeded the quantum. As the thread progresses around the system, each component increments the delay reference parameter in the TLM call signature, according to how long it would have delayed the client thread under approximate timing. Every thread must encounter a quantum keeper at least once in its outermost loop. It is also possible to quantum keep at other components, as shown. Moreover, if an interconnect component is modelling actual queues or is locked while waiting for another thread to complete, the model will be forced to enter the EDS kernel from those components.

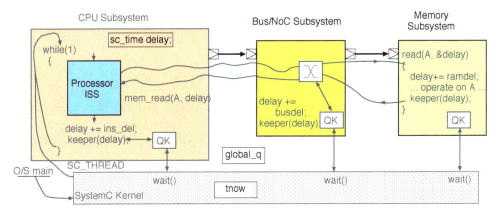

Figure 5.17 Typical setup of a thread using loosely timed modelling with a quantum keeper for one core of an MPSoC. In reality there would be multiple interconnect components between the initiator and its final target

5.4.8 TLM Transactors for Bridging Modelling Styles

An aim in ESL modelling is to replace parts of a high-level model with lower-level models that have greater detail, if necessary. TLM models in SystemC can interwork with cycle-accurate C models generated from RTL using so-called **TLM transactors**. TLM models in C++ can also interact with RTL models using a combination of transactors and various **programming language interface (PLI) gateways** supported by mainstream RTL tools.

A transactor converts the representation of a component from hardware to software. There are four forms of transactor for a bus protocol. Either of the two sides may be an initiator or a target, giving the four possibilities. The initiator of a net-level interface is the one that asserts the command signals that take the interface net out of its starting or idle state (e.g. by asserting a REQ or command_valid net). The initiator for a TLM interface is the side that makes a subroutine or method call and the target is the side that provides the entry point to be called.

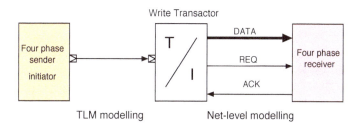

Figure 5.18 Mixing modelling styles using a target-to-initiator transactor. An initiator-to-target transactor, not shown, would receive net-level transactions and make method calls on a TLM target

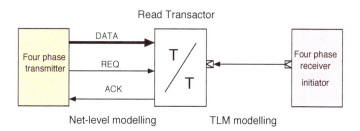

Figure 5.19 Mixing modelling styles using a mailbox paradigm transactor

Figures 5.18 and 5.19 show example transactor configurations. A net-level implementation of a four-phase asynchronous port interworks with a TLM component. The code for these two transactors is very simple. The following two methods work:

```
// Write transactor 4/P handshake
b_putbyte(char d)
{
  while(ack) do wait(10, SC_NS);
  data = d;
  settle();
  req = 1;
  while(!ack) do wait(10, SC_NS);
  req = 0;
}
```

```
// Read transactor 4/P handshake
char b_getbyte()
{
  while(!req) do wait(10, SC_NS);
  char r = data;
  ack = 1;
  while(req) do wait(10, SC_NS);
  ack = 0;
  return r;
}
```

5.4.9 ESL Model of the LocalLink Protocol

Figure 5.20 shows two TLM modelling styles for the LocalLink protocol. The timing diagram is reproduced from Figure 3.5. If the start-of-frame net is deleted and the end-of-frame signal is renamed DLAST, the protocol becomes the essence of AXI4-Stream. Both modelling styles are coded using blocking transactions with data originating from the initiator (the push rather than the pull paradigm). Hence, neither needs to represent the `src_rdy` or `dest_rdy` signals. Both are represented at a high level and bound using the simple arrangement shown in Figure 5.20(c).

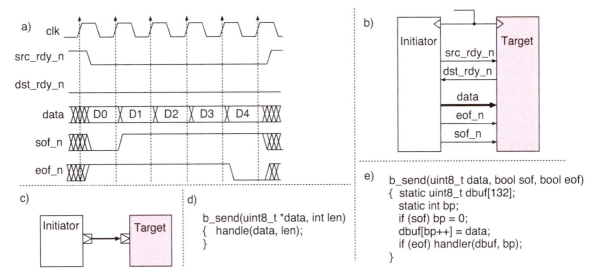

Figure 5.20 Five views of the LocalLink protocol (also of AXI4-Stream). (a) Timing diagram. (b) Net-level wiring. (c) TLM abstract view. (d) Blocking TLM target code, big step. (e) Blocking TLM, small step

The code fragment in Figure 5.20(d) is a large-step operation. The whole multi-word transaction is conveyed as a single TLM call. The fragment in Figure 5.20(e) shows small-step operation in which the method signature represents the framing signals and each word is conveyed in a separate transaction. Choosing which modelling style to use depends on the level of interest in the interface timing. The large-step style gives higher simulation throughput but lower event resolution.

5.5 Processor Modelling with Different Levels of Abstraction

An **instruction set simulator (ISS)** is a program that interprets or otherwise manages to execute machine code as part of an ESL model. An ISS will always be PV accurate, but hidden registers that overcome structural hazards or implement pipeline stages are typically not modelled. An ISS is typically not cycle-accurate, meaning it cannot give a completely accurate report of the number of clock cycles needed, and, if it is connected to a memory system model, it may not initiate its transactions at the same time as a real implementation. An ISS may not model time, or it may just give an estimate of time based on the mix of instructions it executed and pre-loaded tables of how many cycles these instructions take on a particular real implementation. However, for heavily pipelined and out-of-order processors, such tables may not be public or they may not have a simple form. Moreover, the actual execution time is heavily dependent on the rest of the memory system.

Processor manufacturers sell ISS models of their cores for customers to incorporate into ESL models. A number of open-source models are available from projects such as Gem5 [6] and QEMU [7]. It is quite easy to implement a home-brewed low-performance ISS as a SystemC component, which will connect to TLM models of the caches. The general structure is to define a class that contains the main register file and a method called step(), which is called to execute one instruction. With the increasing use and availability of formal specifications for an ISA, it is also possible to generate such an ISS from the instruction specification using macros. The class definition starts with something like:

```
SC_MODULE(mips64iss)
{ // Programmer's view state:
  u64_t regfile[32];   // General purpose registers (R0 is constant zero)
  u64_t pc;            // Program counter (low two bits always zero)
  u5_t  mode;          // Mode (user, supervisor, etc.)
  ...
public:
  void reset();        // Power-on reset
  void step();         // Run one instruction
  int irq;             // Polled each cycle to check for an interrupt
  ...
}
```

The fragment in Figure 5.21 of a main step function evaluates one instruction, but this does not necessarily correspond to one clock cycle in hardware (e.g. fetch and execute are operating on different instructions due to pipelining or the multiple issue). It also shows the main structure for the MIPS instruction set.

5.5.1 Forms of ISS and Their Variants

Table 5.2 Typical relative performance of different virtual platform processor modelling approaches compared with real time. Figures assume a high-performance modelling workstation and a SoC with just one core

Index	Type of ISS	I-cache traffic modelled	D-cache traffic modelled	Relative performance
(1)	Interpreted RTL	Y	Y	0.000001
(2)	Compiled RTL	Y	Y	0.00001
(3)	V-to-C C++	Y	Y	0.001
(4)	Handcrafted cycle-accurate C++	Y	Y	0.1
(5)	Handcrafted high-level C++	Y	Y	1.0
(6)	Trace buffer/JIT C++	N	Y	20.0
(7)	Native cross-compile	N	N	50.0

```
void mips64iss::step()
{
  u32_t ins = ins_fetch(pc);
  pc += 4;
  u8_t opcode = ins >> 26;      // Major opcode
  u8_t scode = ins&0x3F;        // Minor opcode
  u5_t rs = (ins >> 21)&31;     // Registers
  u5_t rd = (ins >> 11)&31;
  u5_t rt = (ins >> 16)&31;

  if (!opcode) switch (scode) // decode minor opcode
  {
    case 052: /* SLT - set on less than */
      regfile_up(rd, ((int64_t)regfile[rs]) < ((int64_t)regfile[rt]));
      break;

    case 053: /* SLTU - set on less than unsigned */
      regfile_up(rd, ((u64_t)regfile[rs]) < ((u64_t)regfile[rt]));
      break;
      ...
  ...

void mips64iss::regfile_up(u5_t d, u64_t w32)
{ if (d != 0) // Register zero stays at zero
    { TRC(trace("[ r%i := %11X ]", d, w32));
      regfile[d] = w32;
    }
}
```

Figure 5.21 Main step function

Various forms of ISS are possible, modelling more or less detail. Table 5.2 lists the main techniques with indicative performance compared to real-world execution.

An interpreted RTL ISS is a cycle-accurate model of the processor core (1). These are commonly available. Using that model under an EDS interpreted simulator produces a system that typically runs one millionth of real-time speed. Using natively compiled RTL (2), as is currently a common practice for commercial RTL simulators from the main EDA vendors, is 10× faster but hopeless for serious software testing.

A fast cycle-accurate C++ model of a core can be generated using tools such as Carbon, Tenison VTOC or Verilator (3). Such a model has intermediate performance. These tools model less detail than compiled RTL. They use a two-valued logic system and discard events within a clock cycle. A handcrafted model (4) is generally much better, requiring perhaps 100 workstation instructions to be executed for each modelled instruction. The workstation clock frequency is generally about 10× faster than the modelled embedded system, so such a system runs only 10× slower than real time.

Abstracting further and dispensing with cycle accuracy, a handcrafted behavioural model (5) performs well but is generally throttled by the overhead of modelling instructions and data operations in the model of the system bus.

A just-in-time (JIT) cross-compilation of the target machine code to native workstation machine code (6) gives excellent performance (say 20× faster than real time) but the instruction fetch traffic is no longer fully modelled. Instruction counts and bus cycles are not accurate. Techniques that unroll loops and concatenate basic blocks, as used for trace caches in processor architecture and high-performance JavaScript, can be used. Finally, cross-compiling the embedded software using the workstation native compiler (7), as shown in Figure 5.1, exposes the unfettered raw performance of the workstation for CPU-intensive code and has the best performance.

With all these techniques, performance degrades as the number of cores to be modelled decreases. On the other hand, performance should increase with the number of cores on the modelling workstation. Recently, a number of approaches have been developed that provide the original non-pre-emptive SystemC semantics on multi-core modelling workstations. Perhaps due to a lack of foresight, the original SystemC semantics preserved the strict serialisation of threads, although this cannot easily be enforced for generic C++ code running on cache-coherent platforms. The main alternative approaches are to adopt a strict additional coding discipline for all thread-shared variables or to preprocess the SystemC so that it appropriately guards and instruments sections of code that are likely to race. Adopting a strict coding style is not overly troublesome in most circumstances. For instance, it can be done by providing monitor-style mutual exclusion locks on TLM transaction targets.

5.5.2 Using the C Preprocessor to Adapt Firmware

Ideally, the ESL model would be able to run the unmodified machine code of the target platform. This is clearly not possible with the natively compiled approach (7) just described; however, the source code can be used if minor modifications are made to the parts that interact with the I/O devices, namely the device drivers. For the DMA controller of Section 2.7.5, the access to device registers could be changed as follows:

```
#define DMACONT_BASE        (0xFFFFCD00) // Or other memory map value
#define DMACONT_SRC_REG    0
#define DMACONT_DEST_REG   4
#define DMACONT_LENGTH_REG 8             // These are the offsets of the addressable registers
#define DMACONT_STATUS_REG 12

#ifdef ACTUAL_FIRMWARE
  // For real system and lower-level models:
  // Store via processor bus to DMACONT device register
  #define DMACONT_WRITE(A, D)    (*(DMACONT_BASE+A*4)) = (D)
  #define DMACONT_READ(A)        (*(DMACONT_BASE+A*4))
#else
  // For high-level TLM modelling:
  // Make a direct subroutine call from the firmware to the DMACONT model
  #define DMACONT_WRITE(A, D)    dmaunit.completer_write(A, D)
  #define DMACONT_READ(A)        dmaunit.completer_read(A)
```

```
#endif
// The device driver will make all hardware accesses to the unit using these macros
// When compiled natively, the calls directly invoke the behavioural model
```

This change uses the C preprocessor to conditionally replace loads and stores to device registers to simple read and write transactions in a behavioural model of the device. This gives the fastest possible model since no aspects of the interconnect are modelled. Similar modifications would redirect the loads and stores to a TLM model of the interconnect or to a transactor connected to a net-level model of the interconnect. This is slower but accurately models bus traffic.

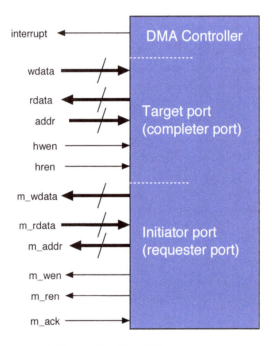

Figure 5.22 Block diagram of one channel of a DMA unit. (Repeated from Figure 2.34)

Figure 5.22 reproduces the DMA controller from an earlier chapter. A suitable behavioural model of (one channel of) the DMA controller has the two parts shown in Figure 5.23. On the left is the target for programmed I/O that updates the PV registers. On the right is the DMA active behaviour that copies blocks of data. This is exceptionally succinct in TLM form!

Ideally the interrupt output would be driven with an RTL-like continuous assignment. This is relatively expensive in SystemC (Section 5.3.2), so a suitable coding style is to place the interrupt driving code in a subroutine that is invoked (and inlined by the compiler) at all points where the supporting expressions might change, which are the assigns to busy and int_enable.

```
// Behavioural model of
// target side: PIO register r/w
uint32 src, dest, length;
bool busy, int_enable;

u32_t status() { return (busy << 31)
          | (int_enable << 30); }

u32_t completer_read(u32_t a)
{
  return (a==0)? src: (a==4) ? dest:
    (a==8) ? (length) : status();
}
void completer_write(u32_t1 a, u32_t d)
{
  if (a==0) src=d;
  else if (a==4) dest=d;
  else if (a==8) length = d;
  else if (a==12)
  { busy = d >> 31;
    int_enable = d >> 30; }
}
```

```
// Bev model of bus mastering portion
while(1)
{
  waituntil(busy);
  while (length-- > 0)
    mem.write(dest++, mem.read(src++));
  busy = 0;
}
```

Interrupt code:

```
interrupt = int_enable&!busy;
```

Figure 5.23 Behavioural model of (one channel of) the DMA controller

5.5.3 ESL Cache Modelling and DMI

A real SoC contains caches that improve performance. Perversely, including the cache in an ESL model may reduce performance, especially if it is caching a type of memory that is easy to model, such as SRAM. This is because, in the model, all levels of the memory hierarchy are actually held in workstation memory that has homogeneous access time.

Depending on the need, we may want to measure the hit ratio in the I or D caches, or the effect on performance from the misses, or neither, or all such metrics. So a cache can be modelled at various levels of abstraction

◾ not at all, since caches do not affect functionality

◾ using an estimated hit ratio and randomly adding a delay to main memory transactions accordingly

◾ fully modelling the tags and their lookup (while providing backdoor access to the main memory for the data)

◾ modelling the cache data RAMs as well (which is needed for detailed power modelling).

The backdoor access to the next level of store is possible in TLM 2.0 using a **direct memory interface (DMI)**. This enables an initiator to get direct access to an area of memory inside a target. It can then access that memory using a direct pointer rather than via TLM calls. A DMI conveys meta-information about how long an access would take in reality and that information is used by the initiator from time to time to correct for timing, such as adding the latency of access to a loosely timed delay. Of course, this leads to under-reporting of metrics delivered by the interconnect, such as the operation count and energy used.

An instruction cache (I-cache), when modelled, may or may not be accessed by an emulator or ISS. For instance, the ISS may use backdoor access to the program in main memory, or it might use JIT techniques, in which commonly executed inner loops of emulated code are converted to the native machine code of the modelling workstation. Hence, an advanced ISS may result in misleading instruction fetch traffic.

5.6 ESL Modelling of Power, Performance and Area

The three primary non-functional parameters of a SoC are power, performance and area (PPA). An ESL model of a complete SoC contains a complete list of the IP blocks making up the SoC and a full description of the module hierarchy. An ESL model can accurately reflect the power-gated and clock domains of the final SoC. Moreover, if each IP block is annotated with its predicted eventual area, the ESL model can provide valuable geometric information, even though there were no place or route steps (Section 5.6.6). Many of these area figures will be accurately known from previous tapeouts of the same IP block. However, they may need scaling for a new VLSI geometry or process.

The number of transactions between IP blocks in a functioning ESL model is the same as the number of transactions on the real SoC. Likewise, the number of power-gating mode changes is also accurately reflected, so annotating each of these with the energy used enables the ESL model to give preliminary indications of the power. When estimating static energy use, the time a domain spends being powered up is as important as the power it consumes when active. A TLM+T model can give sufficiently accurate performance figures, but previous tapeouts or gate switching estimates are needed for the power computation. Where RTL is available for an IP block, it can serve as a valuable source of PPA information for an ESL model.

5.6.1 Estimating the Operating Frequency and Power with RTL

RTL implementations of an IP block may be too slow to include in an ESL model, but static and dynamic analyses of the RTL can generate useful metrics that can be back-ported to the ESL model. RTL simulations can give accurate power figures, especially if a full place-and-route analysis is performed. Advanced ESL flows aim to provide rapid power indications during the early architectural exploration phases. Once back-ported, many architectures can be explored based on the same leaf metrics.

RTL synthesis is relatively quick, but produces a detailed output that is slow to simulate and otherwise process for a large chip; hence, pre-synthesis energy and delay models are desirable. A place-and-route analysis gives accurate wiring lengths but is highly time-consuming for a design point, so that this approach is not really compatible with the goals of an ESL model. A simulation of a

Table 5.3 Product space of power and area estimates for an RTL implementation

	Without simulation	Using simulation
Without place and route	Fast design exploration Area and delay heuristics needed	Can generate indicative activity ratios that can be used instead of a simulation in further runs
With place and route	Static timing analyser will give an accurate clock frequency	Gold standard: only bettered by measuring a real chip

placed-and-routed design can give very accurate energy and critical path figures, but is likewise useless for 'what if' style design exploration.

Table 5.3 defines the space for RTL power and area modelling. The slowest but most accurate design point is at the bottom right. Power estimation using simulation post-layout is typically based on a scalar product in a spreadsheet:

$$E_{dynamic} = V^2 \sum_i C_i s_i$$

The capacitance of each net C_i can be accurately extracted from the layout. The number of discharges s_i is read from a file that contains the number of changes on each net during a net-level simulation. A Switching Activity Interchange Format (SAIF) file format records this information and also supports some aspects of a static power computation (e.g. when a logic value is degraded by a pass transistor (Section 8.5.1) and hence, incurring a higher short-circuit current). VCD files may also be used, but the temporal information is ignored (Section 5.3.3).

RTL can also be used for estimating power through a static analysis instead of a simulation. After RTL synthesis, we have a netlist and can use approximate models (based on Rent's rule, Section 5.6.6) for wire lengths, provided the hierarchy in the ESL model has a sufficient depth (perhaps five or more levels). This requirement can typically be satisfied by any full-SoC model. The natural hierarchy of the RTL input design can be used. Alternatively, a clustering/clique-finding algorithm can determine a rough placement for the floor plan (Section 8.6) without a full place-and-route analysis.

Unsynthesised RTL, such as the fragment in Figure 5.24, tends to reflect the following metrics accurately:

▪ number of flip-flops

▪ number and bit widths of arithmetic operators

▪ size of RAMs (likely to be explicit instances in an ASIC anyway).

Random logic complexity can be modelled in gate-equivalent units. These might count a ripple-carry adder stage as 4 gates, a multiplexor as 3 gates per bit and a D-type flip-flop as 6 gates. These cell counts can give a prediction for the static power use that is sufficient to assist with architectural exploration. Inaccuracies arise from power gating, level-dependent variations of static power (the

```
module CTR16(
  input mainclk,
  input din, input cen,
  output o);

  reg [3:0] count, oldcount;          // D-types

  always @(posedge mainclk) begin
      if (cen) count <= count + 1;    // ALU
      if (din) oldcount <= count;     // Wiring
      end

  assign o = count[3] ^ count[1];     // Combinational

endmodule
```

Figure 5.24 Example RTL fragment used in a static analysis

pass transistor effect) and synthesis variations, such as state re-encoding (Section 4.4.2) and cell drive strength selection (Section 8.4.1).

However, the following dynamic quantities are not manifest in the RTL and instead, require heuristic estimates:

- dynamic clock gating ratios

- flip-flop activity (number of enabled cycles and number of flipping bits)

- number of reads and writes to RAMs

- glitch energy in combinational logic.

There are also techniques for estimating the logic activity using balance equations. The balance equations range over a pair of values for each net, consisting of:

- **average duty cycle**: the fraction of time at logic one

- **average toggle rate**: the fraction of clock cycles during which a net changes value.

Consider an XOR gate with inputs toggling randomly. If the inputs are uncorrelated, the output is also random and its toggle rate can be predicted to be 50 per cent (cf. entropy computations in information theory). However, if we replace it with an AND or OR gate, the output duty cycle will be 1 in 4 on average and its toggle rate will be given by the binomial theorem, and so on.

Overall, a synchronous digital logic subsystem can be roughly modelled with a set of balance equations (simultaneous equations) in terms of the average duty cycle and expected toggle rate on each net. D-types make no difference. Inverters subtract the duty cycle from unity. Other forms of logic can be modelled with similar equations.

Is this a useful technique? Such models need statistics for the input nets. The accuracy can, however, be predicted statically. First, a tool computes the partial derivatives with respect to the input assumptions. If they are all very small, our result holds for all inputs. Such techniques are also used inside logic synthesisers to minimise the glitch energy.

5.6.2 Typical Macroscopic Performance Equations: SRAM Example

It is important to have an accurate model of each SRAM within an ESL model. Because of the simple internal structure of an SRAM, a generic TLM template with only a few parameters can be adapted to each instance. Most SRAMs are generated by **memory generator** tools from an EDA vendor (Section 8.3.10). The compiler also generates a data sheet that contains the necessary values for the component. Table 5.4 lists the normal parameters for a RAM compiler together with selected values.

Table 5.4 Normal parameters for a RAM compiler together with selected values

Parameter	Value
Fabrication geometry	22 nm
Organisation	64Kx64
Nominal VDD	1.0 V
Number of banks	1
Read/write ports per bank	1
Read ports per bank	0
Write ports per bank	0

The CACTI cache modelling tool from HP Labs [8] is widely used to create ESL metadata for memory. It can generate energy, area and performance figures for SRAM, caches of various organisations and DRAM. Version 7.0 added support for die-stacked devices. The program reads a set of basic process properties from configuration files for known geometries, such as dielectric constants and sheet resistivities for 22 nm. It then models the layout of a memory in detail, comparing various numbers of banks, bit lines and word lines to find the best configuration given the user's expressed importance weighting for static power, dynamic power, area and access time. Being coded in C++, the tool can easily be invoked from the constructor of a memory model. It takes under a second to run for a simple SRAM, so could be invoked each time the supply voltage is adjusted, but the results will typically be cached.

For example, Figure 5.25 plots CACTI outputs for SRAMs of different sizes, implemented in 22 nm technology. The full set of build scripts and results for this CACTI run is included in the `cacti22` folder.

Instead of conducting a considerable amount of performance sweeping, CACTI-like optimisers can be replaced with simple formulae, based on the same implementation architecture and underlying physical parameters. For instance, for a single-ported SRAM in 45 nm, the following equations broadly hold for a wide range of capacities and read bus widths:

Area: $\qquad 13000 + \dfrac{5}{8} \times \text{bits}$ $\qquad$ µm^2

Read energy: $\qquad 5 + (1.2 \times 10^{-4}) \times \dfrac{\text{bits}}{8}$ $\qquad$ pJ

Leakage (static power): $\quad 82$ $\qquad$ nW/bit

Random access latency: $\; 0.21 + 3.8 \times 10^{-4} \times \dfrac{\sqrt{\text{bits}}}{\text{supply voltage}}$ $\quad$ ns

The area is essentially 34λ on a side where $\lambda = 22.5$ nm in 45 nm (Section 8.2). As shown in the code fragments of Figure 5.26, these equations can then be installed directly in the constructor of an ESL model, allowing the RAM to be re-evaluated if the supply voltage is changed.

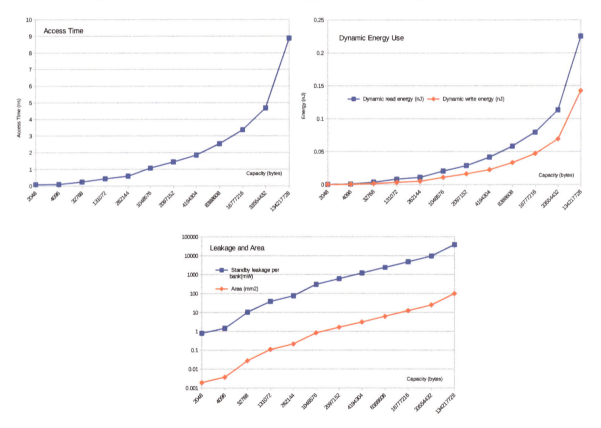

Figure 5.25 Performance and overheads for various sizes of a single-ported 32-bit data width SRAM implemented in 22 nm, as modelled by CACTI 7.0. The tool gives the access time, read and write dynamic energy use, and static power and area use for each size

```
void sram64_cbg::recompute_pvt_parameters() // Called in constructor and when Vcc is changed
{
  m_latency =  sc_time(0.21 + 3.8e-4 *sqrt(float(m_bits)), SC_NS);

  pw_power leakage = pw_power(82.0 * m_bits, PW_nW);
  set_static_power(leakage);

  set_fixed_area(pw_area(13359.0 + 4.93/8 * m_bits, PW_squm));

  m_read_energy_op = pw_energy(5.0 + 1.2e-4 / 8.0 *m_bits, pw_energy_unit::PW_pJ);
  m_write_energy_op = 2.0 * m_read_energy_op; // rule of thumb!

  // NB: Might want different energy when high-order address bits change

  pw_voltage vcc = get_vcc();
  m_latency = m_latency / vcc.to_volts();
  cout << name () << ":" << kind() << ": final latency = " << m_latency << "\n";
}




void sram64_cbg::b_access(PW_TLM_PAYTYPE &trans, sc_time &delay)
{
  tlm::tlm_command cmd = trans.get_command();

  // Log wiring power consumed by transaction arriving here.
  // Also set which nets modelled by the TLM will be active after this operation:
  // For a write none (except a response ack) and for read the payload data.
  trans.pw_log_hop(this,  (cmd==tlm::TLM_READ_COMMAND ? PW_TGP_DATA: PW_TGP_NOFIELDS) |
          PW_TGP_ACCT_CKP,  &read_bus_tracker);

  if (cmd == tlm::TLM_READ_COMMAND)
    {
      // Log internal transaction energy for read
      pw_module_base::record_energy_use(m_read_energy_op);
      ...
    }
  else if (cmd == tlm::TLM_WRITE_COMMAND)
    {
      // Log internal transaction energy for write
      pw_module_base::record_energy_use(m_write_energy_op);
      ...
    }
}
```

Figure 5.26 TLM+TE model of an SRAM. Constructor and blocking transport methods

5.6.3 Typical Macroscopic Performance Equations: DRAM Example

A DRAM channel is some number of DRAM die (e.g. 16) connected to a set of I/O pads on a controller. The channel data width is typically 16, 32 or 64 bits. The capacity might be 16 Gbytes. DRAM power generally comes from a different budget from the main SoC since it is normally off-chip. However, when die-stacked, thermal management of the combination must be considered. A major contribution to DRAM energy use is the static power of its **physical layer (PHY)**, which is the set of I/O pads both on-SoC and on-DRAM that drive the high-performance PCB or interposer conductors between the pieces of silicon. PHY power can be minimised if the traces are short, which is the motivation for multi-chip modules and die-stacking. Micron released a multi-channel DRAM package, the Micron **hybrid memory cube (HMC)**, whose structure is like that in Figure 5.27. One or more vertical stacks of DRAM chips are mounted on a controller chip using **through-silicon vias**. The device is shared by a number of hosts, each linked by a SERDES channel (Section 3.8) that typically runs for several inches over the main circuit board. Generic devices of this nature are being standardised by JEDEC and developed by the **high bandwidth memory (HBM)** group of companies.

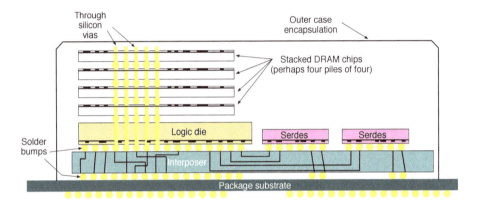

Figure 5.27 A die-stacked DRAM subsystem in the style of the Micron HMC and HBM. Several DRAM chips are piled on top of an upside-down (flip-chip) controller chip, interconnected into a 3-D structure using **through-silicon vias**. There could be several stacks. A passive interposer (ceramic PCB) wires the logic die using a parallel interconnect to SERDES chips (also upside-down) for serial connection over the circuit board to the hosts

The high-performance PHY of a DRAM subsystem consumes power. The PHY drives data over a circuit board at GHz rates, both in the controller and in the devices themselves. PHY power is largely static and can be significantly minimised by either die-stacking or automatically entering low-power standby modes when possible. Dynamic energy use is directly related to the principal DRAM operations. In summary, energy use comprises:

- **Controller static power**: The on-SoC controller logic and any associated mini-cache (Section 2.6.6).

- **DRAM static power**: Each die takes about 100 mW when idle but may enter a sleep mode if left unused for a millisecond or so, reducing this to about 10 mW. Some DRAMs self-refresh while in a sleep mode, so they can remain in it indefinitely.

- Each **row activation** consumes dynamic energy in the row lines of the addressed page.

- Each **column activation and data transfer** consumes on-chip energy at both ends as well as considerable energy in driving the PCB conductors. The figures in Table 5.5 show that reads and writes consume roughly the same amount of energy and, strangely, differ between the 4-Gb and 8-Gb devices as to which takes more.

- Each **row closure** (writeback, deactivate or precharge) consumes dynamic energy, principally in the devices.

- **Refresh operations** consume energy like an activate command, again, principally in the devices.

The DRAMsim3 tool [9] is freely downloadable along with configuration files for a large variety of DRAM devices. The latest release includes HMC models. The DRAM models in the tool can run various free-standing exercises. It can model DRAM as part of an ESL model such as Prazor or Gem5. The simulator supports several page-closing policies and can report statistics for an access pattern, such as throughput achieved and energy used. A TLM+E model of a DRAM chip includes energy figures like those computed by DRAMsim3. They can accumulate the dynamic energy for each operation.

Table 5.5 Example performance data from collated DRAMSim4 data sheets for a variety of DDR4 devices, showing their closed page, random access time and dynamic energy for several major operations (total energy for 8 devices making up a 32-bit data bus). Only two significant figures are accurate. Note: $V_{DD} = 1.2 V$ and $t_{CL} = t_{RCD} = t_{RP}$

Device type (capacity, word size and speed)	t_{CL} (cycles)	Clock frequency (MHz)	Access time (ns)	Activate (pJ)	Read (pJ)	Write (pJ)
DDR4_4Gb_x4_1866	13	934.6	32.1	4006.1	5752.3	6985.0
DDR4_4Gb_x4_2133	16	1063.8	33.8	3754.0	5775.4	7219.2
DDR4_4Gb_x4_2400	17	1204.8	31.5	4063.7	5418.2	7330.6
DDR4_4Gb_x4_2666	19	1333.3	31.5	4104.0	6048.0	7488.0
DDR4_8Gb_x4_1866	13	934.6	32.1	5156.5	5341.4	4930.6
DDR4_8Gb_x4_2133	16	1063.8	33.8	5270.0	4692.5	4331.5
DDR4_8Gb_x4_2666	19	1333.3	31.5	6105.6	4608.0	4089.6
DDR4_8Gb_x4_2933	21	1470.6	31.3	6632.4	4595.7	4021.2
DDR4_8Gb_x4_3200	22	1587.3	30.2	7136.6	4644.9	4015.9

Table 5.5 shows data computed from configuration files for a variety of DDR4 devices. Being double data rate, the clock frequency is half the listed number of transfers per second. The access time quoted is the absolute minimal possible, starting from a closed page and includes $t_{CL} + t_{RCD} + BL/2$, where the burst size $BL = 8$. In reality, the achieved access time is considerably more, since there are several more pipeline stages in the controller and there are random overheads arising from having to close a page or cross clock domains. The data sheets provide an indicative current use for each of the main operating phases. In TLM, the energy for each major operation is computed by multiplying together the current, supply voltage V_{DD}, clock period and number of cycles spent in that phase. DDR4 devices also have a second rail called V_{PP} of typically 2.5 V, which also delivers some energy, but this can be neglected in a rough model, since the supply currents specified by most manufacturers are an upper bound. Also, as mentioned above, there is a considerable static power overhead for the high-performance data PHY, which should be modelled using phase/mode analysis, as the device is taken in and out of standby modes by its controller.

5.6.4 Macroscopic Phase and Mode Power Estimation Formula

IP blocks of any significant complexity support various power modes. These include off, sleep, idle, run, etc. They may set their own operating mode or be commanded externally using something like the Arm Q-channel protocol (Section 3.7.5). Most blocks consume a fairly predictable average amount of power in each of their power phases or modes, certainly for static power use. The clock frequency and supply voltage are also subject to step changes, which enlarges the discrete phase/mode operating space. If the blocks in an ESL model can correctly switch between energy states, a simple technique for estimating energy use is based on the percentage of time spent in each state.

Table 5.6 Phase/mode example: supply rail voltage and current and total power consumption for 3320C-EZK USB line driver devices

Operating mode	Rail 1		Rail 2		Rail 3		Total power
	(volts)	(mA)	(volts)	(mA)	(volts)	(mA)	(mW)
Standby	3.3	0.018	1.8	0.0007	3.3	0.03	0.16
L/S mode	3.3	6.3	1.8	11	3.3	5	57
H/S mode	3.3	29	1.8	22	3.3	59	155

For instance, the Parallella board shown in Figure 5.28 has two 3320C USB line drivers (highlighted with red boxes). They use three supply rails and have three operating modes. The current consumed by each rail depends on the mode. The documented nominal currents are shown in Table 5.6, along with the total power consumption. The actual power depends on the traffic activity, but for many line transceiver circuits that contain a significant amount of analogue electronics, the variation is not great. The TLM POWER2 library [10] for SystemC uses constant power figures for each phase and mode. For any component that changes mode each time it goes busy or idle, using a constant for each phase and mode gives a reasonable model for both static and dynamic power. However, this approach is not suitable for components whose dynamic power use is not correlated with an explicit phase or mode change.

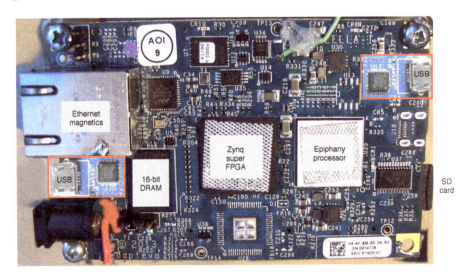

Figure 5.28 A Parallella single-board computer. The two 3320C USB driver devices and connectors are highlighted in red boxes

5.6.5 Spreadsheet-based Energy Accounting

A basic approach for estimating power consumption uses a spreadsheet that lists each register, gate and IP block in the design. The total power used by a component can be computed with the average number of operations per second performed by the component, its static power use and its energy use per operation. Figure 5.29 illustrates the basic parts of such a spreadsheet. For each RAM or ALU present, the energy per operation must be known. For RISC-style processors, the energy per instruction is roughly the same over most instruction types and it is not generally needed to know the precise mix of instructions used to obtain a sufficiently accurate power estimate. For random logic for miscellaneous registers and gates, the energy use for each component depends linearly on the activity ratio (toggle rate). Initial guesses in the spreadsheet are typically set close to the worst case, which is conservative but often wildly out. Hence, SAIF-based or other dynamic trace information must be fed in to get an accurate result (Section 5.6.1). Given the chip package structure and cooling arrangements, the same spreadsheet can compute the likely junction temperature.

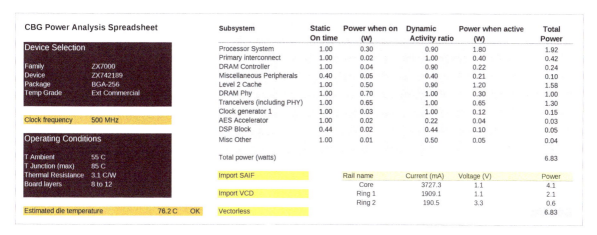

Figure 5.29 Example power estimation spreadsheet. The inventory of instantiated components is annotated with clock frequencies and activity ratios to generate an approximate total power use in watts

5.6.6 Rent's Rule for Estimating Wire Length

As explained in Section 4.6.8, energy use today is dominated by wiring capacitance. Hence, reliable indications of net length and net toggle rate are needed to compute energy use. The activity ratio-based, phase/mode spreadsheet just presented does not take the physical layout into account. An ESL model does not include place-and-route data (Section 8.7.1), but the design hierarchy is accurately reflected in the high-level model and the number of transactions between subsystems will also be accurate. The area of each subsystem can be reliably estimated from the RTL or previous implementations. A floor plan (Section 8.6) may provide additional guidance.

Knowing the average net length and the average activity ratio is not sufficient to get the average power, due to the non-uniform distribution of events (all the activity may occur on the longer nets, for instance). Hence, it is better to have a more detailed model when forming the product. Rent's rule provides the answer.

If the physical area of each leaf cell is known, the area of each component in a hierarchic design can be estimated using the sum of the parts plus the percentage swell (e.g. 5 per cent). In the 1960's, E. F. Rent, working at IBM, first popularised a rule of thumb pertaining to the organisation of computing logic, specifically the relationship between the number of external signal connections (terminals) to a logic block and the number of logic gates in the logic block:

$$\text{Number of terminals} = k \times \text{Number of gates}^{\rho}$$

It has been formalised, justified and enhanced over the decades [11], so is largely accurate and can be applied to circuits ranging from small digital circuits to mainframe computers.

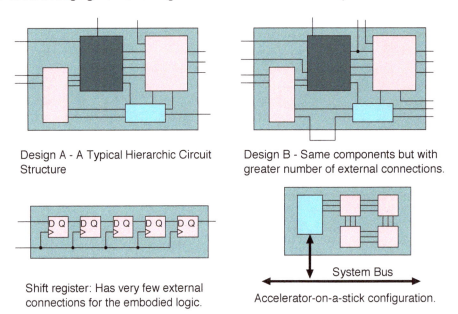

Design A - A Typical Hierarchic Circuit Structure

Design B - Same components but with greater number of external connections.

Shift register: Has very few external connections for the embodied logic.

System Bus

Accelerator-on-a-stick configuration.

Figure 5.30 Two similar designs with different Rent exponents (top) and two non-Rentian design points (bottom)

Rent's rule is basically a simple power law that gives the number of terminals for a subsystem as a function of the number of logic gates in the subsystem. Figure 5.30 shows that designs with very similar functionality can have small variations in the Rent coefficient. Circuits like the shift register are definite outliers. There is no increase in external connectivity regardless of length, so these have a Rent exponent $\rho = 0$. A circuit composed of components that do no have any local wiring between them is the other extreme possibility, having a Rent exponent $\rho = 1.0$. However, the rule of thumb is that for most general subsystems, the Rent exponent is between about 0.5 and 0.7. The values apply also to certain accelerator-on-a-stick structures in which data are copied in and out over a comparatively narrow access bus but the accelerator has a significant amount of logic (Section 6.4).

Also the degree of unfold in an accelerator (Section 4.4.2) affects the Rent exponent; unfolding an algorithm for faster execution uses more logic but the accelerator would, by default, still have the same number of external connections.

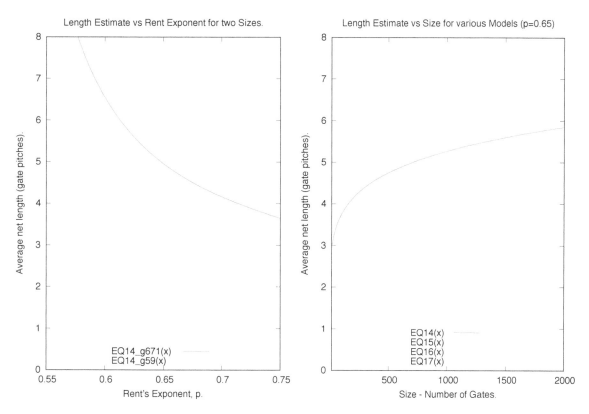

Figure 5.31 Left: average net length in systems composed of 59 and 671 gates for various values of rent exponent. Right: average net length for subsystems of different sizes for rent exponent of 0.65 using four improved equations presented in [12]

Figure 5.31-left plots variation in expected average net length for subsystems of two different sizes, showing the sensitivity to exponent value. Clearly, there is not a huge variation for designs once *p* is above 0.6, which is the normal region. Numerous improvements have been explored for Rent's basic model. For example, Hefeida and Chowdhury [12] present four equations, numbered 14 to 17, which are plotted in Figure 5.31-right. Again, there is not a great deal of variation between the models. It is not surprising that the general shape of the right-hand plot looks broadly like a square-root function of the number of gates.

For a single level of design hierarchy, the random placement of blocks in a square with area defined by their aggregate areas gives a particular net length distribution. Generalisations of Rent's rule can model the real-world wire length distribution by assuming that a good placement is always used in practice. Careful placement reduces the net length by a Rent-like factor (e.g. by a factor of 2). If we know the area of each leaf cell in a hierarchic design, even without placement, we can follow the trajectory of the net up and down the hierarchy and apply Rent-like rules. This is illustrated in

Figure 5.32. Hence, we can estimate the length of a signal by sampling a power law distribution whose maximum is the square root of the area of the lowest-common-parent component in the hierarchy.

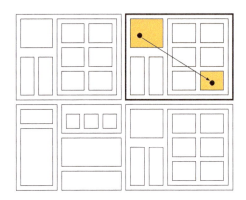

Figure 5.32 Lowest common parent of the end-point logic blocks. The distance between two end points is always roughly the same for any sensible layout of a design, so a detailed layout, like the one shown, is not required

5.6.7 Dynamic Energy Modelling in TLM

The TLM POWER3 library [13] modified the TLM POWER2 approach by capturing dynamic power use by logging energy quanta for each TLM transaction or other event. Dynamic power use in a TLM model has two components: the energy associated with the explicitly modelled transactions between IP blocks and the energy of intensive internal computation that is not correlated with visible transactions. Most I/O blocks use very little of the second form of power. For other devices, such as CPU cores, the internal power use can also be readily allocated to discrete events, such as the fetch, decode and execute of each instruction.

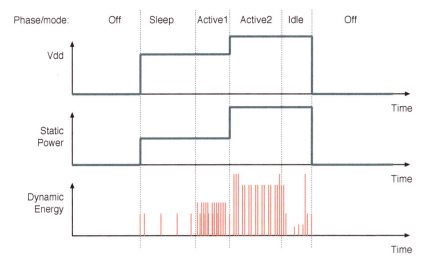

Figure 5.33 Example of a transactional energy modelling plot. Static power depends on the power mode, whereas the dynamic power depends on internal and external activity events

Overall, electrical consumption modelling in TLM is best handled using a hybrid of power and energy quanta, as illustrated in Figure 5.33. The static power is modelled with an average power annotation of the current phase or mode, which uses energy in proportion to how long the block is in that phase or mode. In contrast, the dynamic energy is modelled by accumulating the energy associated with discrete events, many of which are transactions. The Cambridge TLM POWER3 library for SystemC supports this hybrid approach. It also uses Rent's rule and the lowest-common-parent approach to estimate the wiring length between components. To compute this distance, it gets from the SystemC kernel database a list of the instantiated modules in the design hierarchy and relies on user annotations of how much area each leaf component requires. It then counts the bit transitions in the generic payload to estimate the dynamic power use for the nets of the real SoC.

5.6.8 ESL Modelling of DVFS and Power Gating

The SystemC database of instantiated modules has a tree form, with the root being the pad ring of the SoC. The clock, voltage and power-gated domains are commonly tightly coupled with the module instance tree. It is logical to record the supply voltage and power status for each subsystem at the root of the appropriate subtree. The TLM POWER3 library takes this approach and invokes a callback on all components in the subtree whenever the supply voltage is changed. The user-provided power and performance equations can be recomputed during this callback. However, it is not as necessary to have a callback for a clock frequency change if most of the dynamic energy use is associated with a transaction, since the transaction spacing will be adjusted accordingly by the delay values, whether loosely or approximately timed.

```
+--------------------------+--------------------------+--------------------------+--------------------------+
| MODULE  NAME             |        STATICO ENERGY    |       DYNAMIC1 ENERGY    |         WIRING2 ENERGY   |
+--------------------------+--------------------------+--------------------------+--------------------------+
Standalone modules:
| ...top.coreunit_0.core_0 |     9.997983e-05J  0.77% |     3.25128e-05J   0.25% |   1.35116151e-07J  0.00% |
| Memory 0 (DRAM)          |     0.00866173075J 66.65%|     0.004199797373J 32.32%|  1.32334593e-07J  0.00% |
| the_top.uart0            |                0J  0.00% |        8.84e-07J   0.01% |        2.746e-12J  0.00% |
Customer Accounts:
| anonymous                |     0.00866173075J 66.65%|     3.25128e-05J   0.25% |   2.6745349e-07J   0.00% |
| busaccess_0              |                0J  0.00% |     0.00420136352J 32.33%|              0J   0.00% |
+--------------------------+--------------------------+--------------------------+--------------------------+
| TOP LEVEL++              |     0.00876171058J 67.42%|     0.004233876323J 32.58%|  2.6745349e-07J   0.00% |
+--------------------------+--------------------------+--------------------------+--------------------------+
Each line is for a separately-traced subsystem. These lines may be neither disjoint or complete.
The TOP LEVEL figure is simply another line in the table that relates to the highest module found.
Total energy used: 12900 uJ  (12995854356318 fJ)


+--------------------------+--------------------------+--------------------------+--------------------------+
| MODULE  NAME             |        STATICO POWER     |       DYNAMIC1 POWER     |         WIRING2 POWER    |
+--------------------------+--------------------------+--------------------------+--------------------------+
Standalone modules:
| ...top.coreunit_0.core_0 |         0.01W    75.38%  |   0.00325193592W 24.51%  | 1.35143409e-05W   0.10%  |
| Memory 0 (DRAM)          |     0.866347818W 67.35%  |   0.420064464W   32.65%  | 1.3236129e-05W    0.00%  |
| the_top.uart0            |             0W    0.00%  | 8.84178339e-05W 100.00%  |  2.74655e-10W     0.00%  |
Customer Accounts:
| anonymous                |     0.866347818W 99.62%  |   0.00325193592W  0.37%  | 2.67507446e-05W   0.00%  |
| busaccess_0              |             0W    0.00%  |   0.420221111W  100.00%  |           0W      0.00%  |
+--------------------------+--------------------------+--------------------------+--------------------------+
| TOP LEVEL++              |     0.876347818W 67.42%  |   0.423473047W   32.58%  | 2.67507446e-05W   0.00%  |
+--------------------------+--------------------------+--------------------------+--------------------------+
Each line is for a separately-traced subsystem. These lines may be neither disjoint or complete.
The TOP LEVEL figure is simply another line in the table that relates to the highest module found.
Average power used: 1290 mW  (1299847614895725 fW)
```

Figure 5.34 Example reports generated by the TLM POWER3 library. The energy use between two checkpoints is shown in the upper table and power consumption in the lower table. A total for the whole device is given, along with subtotals for parts of the design hierarchy specifically selected by the user

Figure 5.34 shows an example of an output from the TLM POWER3 library for the Parallella platform modelled in Section 5.7. The tool gives totals for phase/mode static power use, dynamic power use inside components and the wiring power collected from the transaction activity and estimated wiring length.

5.7 Case Study: Modelling the Zynq Platform (Prazor)

The Prazor/VHLS virtual platform is a simulator implemented in SystemC using TLM 2.0 sockets. It can model a number of CPU architectures, including x86_64, Arm-7, MIPS and OpenRISC.

5.8 Summary

In this chapter, we have presented the main aims and approaches for ESL modelling. Very few design houses use the full ESL approach that we have advocated. Although they may start off with an ESL model of a SoC and use it for architectural exploration, it will later be maintained only as a virtual platform for software development. All major EDA companies offer ESL modelling platforms and IP vendors, such as Arm, provide compatible ISS products and **fast models** of their IP blocks that are portable over a number of platforms. The principal trade-off is accuracy versus efficiency, with a loss of accuracy arising from the incorrect interleaving of transactions from different initiators. Another use is to produce accurate performance and energy reports. Some products concentrate almost entirely on providing an accurate software development platform, such as gem5, QEMU and various Android simulators. Others focus on integrating with mainstream RTL simulators.

The reader should have mastered the core concepts and constructs of the SystemC modelling language, both for its original purpose for net-level modelling and as an ESL modelling framework. A number of detailed modelling styles have been presented.

5.8.1 Exercises

1. Estimate the number of CPU instructions executed by a modelling workstation when net-level and TLM models alternatively simulate the transfer of a frame over a LocalLink interface.

2. Using the additional materials from the `four-phase` folder, perform a net-level simulation of the source and sink. Then code in SystemC a net-level FIFO to go between them and modify the test bench to include it. Finally, write and deploy a transactor to the TLM-1 style sink that is also provided.

3. If access to the real hardware is not yet possible, discuss how development, debugging and performance analysis of device driver code can be facilitated by a virtual platform. What might be the same and what might be different?

4. In the additional materials `toy-esl` folder, work through the four SystemC TLM coding examples in which processors access memory. (Note, for ease of getting started and debugging, this material does not use TLM 2.0 sockets. It essentially does the same thing as the Prazor system, but at a much more basic level.)

5. A NoC switching element is modelled using SystemC TLM. What mechanisms exist for capturing the queuing delay if passthrough TLM sockets are to be used in the NoC element model?

6. Assuming a typical Rent value, using a spreadsheet or simple program, tabulate the average wiring length versus number of hierarchy levels crossed for a transactional interface in a typical SoC. Which of the following do you need to assume: total number of hierarchy levels, average number of child components to a component, variation in area of a component, Rentian exponent, average number of connections to a component and percentage of local nets to a component? Obtain a numerical figure for the partial derivatives of the result with respect to each of your assumptions. Which is the most important?

7. To what extent can a simple spreadsheet or static analysis determine the average activity ratio for a net or subsystem? What further information is needed? Given activity numbers, what further information may be needed to generate an idealised mapping of subsystems to power domains? What other considerations should be applied to determine a practical power domain mapping?

8. Give simple examples where out-of-order transaction processing arising from the loosely timed modelling approach causes and does not cause functional accuracy errors. Are transaction counts likely to be wrong under loose timing?

References

[1] Sumit K. Mandal, Raid Ayoub, Michael Kishinevsky, and Umit Y. Ogras. Analytical performance models for NoCs with multiple priority traffic classes. *ACM Trans. Embed. Comput. Syst.*, 18(5s), October 2019. ISSN 1539-9087. doi: 10.1145/3358176. URL https://doi.org/10.1145/3358176.

[2] Arm Ltd. Corelink CMN-600 coherent mesh network. https://developer.arm.com/ip-products/system-ip/corelink-interconnect/corelink-coherent-mesh-network-family/corelink-cmn-600, 2020.

[3] Arm Ltd. Arm CoreLink NI-700 Network-on-Chip Interconnect, Technical Reference Manual. https://developer.arm.com/documentation/101566/0100/Introduction/About-the-CoreLink-NI-700-Network-on-Chip-Interconnect, 2020.

[4] *IEEE Standard for Standard SystemC Language Reference Manual.* IEEE, 2011. Std 1666-2011.

[5] Daniel Sanchez and Christos Kozyrakis. Zsim: fast and accurate microarchitectural simulation of thousand-core systems. *ACM SIGARCH Computer Architecture News*, 41:475, 2013. doi: 10.1145/2508148.2485963.

[6] Nathan Binkert, Bradford Beckmann, Gabriel Black, Steven K. Reinhardt, Ali Saidi, Arkaprava Basu, Joel Hestness, Derek R. Hower, Tushar Krishna, Somayeh Sardashti, Rathijit Sen, Korey Sewell, Muhammad Shoaib, Nilay Vaish, Mark D. Hill, and David A. Wood. The Gem5 simulator. *SIGARCH Comput. Archit. News*, 39(2):1–7, August 2011. ISSN 0163-5964. doi: 10.1145/2024716.2024718. URL https://doi.org/10.1145/2024716.2024718.

[7] The Software Freedom Conservancy. QEMU the fast processor emulator. https://www.qemu.org/, 2020.

[8] N. Muralimanohar, R. Balasubramonian, and N. Jouppi. Optimizing NUCA organizations and wiring alternatives for large caches with CACTI 6.0. In *40th Annual IEEE/ACM International Symposium on Microarchitecture (MICRO 2007)*, pages 3–14, 2007. doi: 10.1109/MICRO.2007.33.

[9] Shang Li, Zhiyuan Yang, Dhriaj Reddy, Ankur Srivastava, and Bruce Jacob. DRAMsim3: a cycle-accurate, thermal-capable DRAM simulator. *IEEE Computer Architecture Letters*, PP:1, 2020. doi: 10.1109/LCA.2020.2973991.

[10] Matthieu Moy. Mini power-aware TLM-platform. https://matthieu-moy.fr/spip/?Mini-Power-Aware-TLM-Platform, 2010.

[11] D. Strooband, H. Van Marck, and J. Van Campenhout. An accurate interconnection length estimation for computer logic. In *Proceedings of the 6th Great Lakes Symposium on VLSI*, pages 50–55, 1996. doi: 10.1109/GLSV.1996.497592.

[12] Mohamed S. Hefeida and Masud H. Chowdhury. Improved model for wire-length estimation in stochastic wiring distribution. *arXiv preprint arXiv:1502.05931*, 2015.

[13] David J. Greaves and M. Yasin. TLM POWER3: Power estimation methodology for SystemC TLM 2.0. In *Proceedings of the 2012 Forum on Specification and Design Languages*, pages 106–111, 2012.

Chapter 6

Architectural
Design Exploration

As already mentioned in Section 1.4.2, the algorithms and functional requirements for an application are implemented using one or more pieces of silicon. Each major piece of silicon contains one or more custom or standard microprocessors. Some of the silicon has a custom design for a high-volume product, some of it has a design common to different devices in a product line, some of it has a standard design and some of it has a third-party design.

The result of architectural design is a mapping of the design into physical components. Certain electronic requirements, such as high voltage, microwave radio frequencies and optimum memory bit density, are still fulfilled with optimised silicon (or GaAs) processes, but today, almost everything else is either a standard part or can be mapped onto a single System-on-Chip (SoC). If an architectural design requires more than one chip, the process is known as **design partition**. Beyond the fundamental properties of silicon, a design partition must take into account non-technical aspects, such as the stability of requirements, the design lifetime, ease of reuse and other market forces, such as whether a third-party source is required by the target customers.

When designing a subsystem, the architect must choose what to have as hardware, what to have as software and whether custom or standard processors are needed. When designing the complete SoC, they must think about sharing the subsystem load over the chosen processing elements. Estimates of the instruction fetch and data bandwidth for each element and subsystem are needed when deciding how much memory to instantiate and where each class of data and instruction will be stored. The envisioned system data flow between subsystems is another important consideration in terms of bus capacity, how busses should be interconnected and whether a network-on-chip (NoC) is justified (Section 3.4).

The design specification will include must-have and desirable targets. The architect will have to guarantee that all must-have goals are achieved and that most of the desirable goals have been addressed. As a must-have example, if an I/O port has to receive data from a pre-existing standard or communication protocol, then it must run at x MHz, where x might be 12.5 MHz for a 100-Mbps serial link that has been deserialised by a factor of 8 to give bytes. To increase profitability, a desirable target could be that its area should be less than y mm^2, though this is not always an obligation. Respecting each constraint is part of the daily work of the whole design team, but the chosen design partition must first be suitable. Achieving this is called **design closure**.

In this chapter, we review the major influences on architectural design. These arise from functional requirements, including technology limitations such as power, area (Section 8.2) and mixing constraints (Section 6.1). Choosing which pre-existing IP blocks and complete chips to use is also important. Engineers use modular designs to manage scaling and future reuse. The microarchitecture of new subsystems must take into account structural hazards (Section 6.3). Communications between subsystems must be carefully designed (Section 6.4.1) to be adequate but not over-engineered. **Architectural exploration** is the process of trying out different design partitions and microarchitecture details at a high level. These issues are discussed in Section 8.2 whereas ESL methods are presented in Chapter 5. This chapter also has a section on modern design languages (Section 6.8), which are far more expressive than conventional RTL.

6.1 Hardware and Software Design Partition

A number of separate pieces of silicon are combined to form the final product. The principal reasons for using more than one piece of silicon are (see also Section 8.4):

- **Modular engineering**: No design team can create the complete product as one module. This is infeasible to do, both in terms of staff management and the capacity of tools. A test program for each subcomponent, known as as **unit test**, is also a must-have for quality control and yield management. Design lifetime, revision control, component sourcing and portable reuse all benefit from a modular approach.

- **Size and capacity**: For CMOS technology, a silicon chip measuring between about 6 and 11 mm on a side is the sweet spot (Section 8.11.1).

- **Technology mismatch**: Ultra-high frequency logic can be better implemented on **GaAs** than on silicon; hence, a separate chip must be used. Analogue electronics may need to switch high voltages and hence, require thicker oxide layers, or the analogue electronics may use very large transistors for high currents and hence, not be a cost-effective use of state-of-the-art fabrication lines (Figure 8.32). Processes that are ideal for DRAM are different from those that are ideal for flash, SRAM and general-purpose logic.

- **Supply chain and costs**: The costs associated with an in-house custom chip are very different from those for a standard part. Standard parts are generally mature products and available at a lower price per unit area of silicon, compared with in-house designs. A standard part has a larger market than a bespoke part, so that non-recurring expenses (NRE) are amortised differently (Section 8.11).

- **Isolation**: Sensitive analogue signals for audio and radio frequencies need shielding from general-purpose logic. This can be achieved by isolating the power supply and floor plan (Section 8.6.1). However, because of the need for different types of transistors, a separate integrated circuit (IC) is commonly used for the **analogue front end (AFE)**.

- **Risk**: Using existing chips that are known to work (and whose suppliers can be sued) has a lower risk than developing chips in-house. Chips larger than $1\,cm^2$ are high risk, especially for new fabrication geometries.

Many functions can be realised in software or hardware. In general, a software implementation has lower development costs and is easier to change post tapeout (Section 8.7.7), so this tends to be the default approach. The principal reasons for implementing a function in hardware are:

- for physical I/O using line drivers or physical media interfaces

- to reduce energy use

- for real-time uses where jitter or throughput requirements rule out a software implementation.

Hardware implementations do not have an instruction fetch and decode overhead. A hardware implementation is often more parallel than a software version. Hence, it can clock at a lower frequency and it has a lower V^2 overhead (Section 4.6.8). Dedicated data paths in hardware are more efficient than multiplexed paths, but ALU and RAM energy use tends to be the same. These comparisons are developed further in Section 6.4.

If a function is to be implemented on a programmable processor, the next question is whether a custom or off-the-shelf processor should be used. Another possibility is to use a custom coprocessor for the high-performance data path but not for control or data management. The principal functions that benefit from non-standard processor data paths are:

- bit-oriented operations

- highly compute-intensive SIMD

- other algorithms with custom data paths

- algorithms that might be altered post tapeout.

The following functions are best implemented in software on standard cores:

- highly complex, non-repetitive functions

- low-throughput computations of any sort

- functions that might be altered post tapeout

- generally, as much as possible.

6.1.1 Design Partitioning Example: A Bluetooth Module

Radio communications much above VHF (above 150 MHz) use high-frequency waveforms that cannot be directly processed by an **analogue-to-digital convertor (ADC)** or a **digital-to-analogue convertor (DAC)**. Figure 6.1 shows the typical structure of a wireless link for digital signals. Only simplex communication is shown, but many applications require bidirectional communication. This is typically achieved using **time-division duplexing**, in which the two ends alternate between sending and receiving, sharing the same antenna and radio spectrum.

Heterodyning is used. This is implemented in the analogue mixers that multiply two waveforms. A sine wave carrier is used for the frequency conversion, as this exploits the
$\sin(A) \times \sin(B) = -\cos(A+B)/2$ half of the standard identity for converting frequency upwards. The other half is used for converting downwards. The high-frequency circuity is almost always on a different chip to separate it from the digital signal processing (DSP) of the baseband logic.

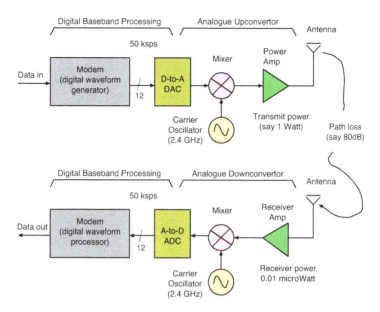

Figure 6.1 Typical wireless link for digital communications, showing the transmitter (top) and receiver (bottom) for a simplex link

Many digital radio systems use **quadrature modulation**. A local oscillator generates two outputs with a 90° phase shift between them. Each feeds its own mixer, which is coupled to its own ADCs or DAC. This creates a radio signal with different data in the upper and lower sidebands, which requires less energy per bit transmitted.

Figure 6.2 shows an early implementation of a Bluetooth USB dongle with an ISSC chipset. This uses three pieces of silicon on a small PCB. On the front side there is an IS1601 AFE and an IS1002 baseband processor along with an antenna track at the left end. On the reverse is an FT24C04 serial EEPROM and a 16-MHz crystal. The crystal serves as a clock for the digital logic and a frequency reference for the RF carrier. Three pieces of silicon were used, mainly because the three sections require wildly different types of circuit structure:

1. The analogue IC has amplifiers, oscillators, filters and mixers that operate in the 2.4-GHz band. This was too fast for CMOS transistors and so bipolar transistors with thin bases were used (certainly in early versions). The module amplifies the radio signals and converts them using the mixers down to an intermediate frequency of a few MHz, which can be processed by the ADC and DAC components of the digital circuit.

2. The digital circuit has a small amount of low-frequency analogue circuitry in its ADC and DACs and perhaps, in its interface logic. A USB interface requires signal amplification and clock recovery (Section 3.8). Additional analogue line drivers may be present on the silicon, e.g. an audio headset, microphone and phone interface, but these will be powered permanently off in this deployment. Overall, the baseband chip is mostly digital, with random logic implementations of the modem functions and a microcontroller with local RAM. The local RAM holds a system stack, local variables and temporary buffers for data being sent or received.

3. A flash ROM chip (Section 2.6.8) is a standard part. It is a non-volatile memory that can hold firmware for the microcontroller, parameters for the modem and encryption keys, and other end-application functions.

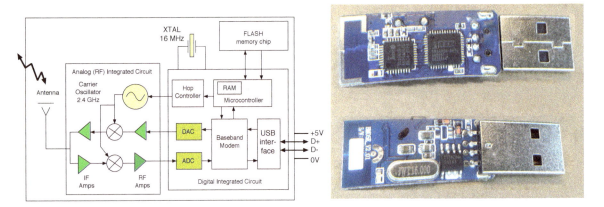

Figure 6.2 Block diagram and photographs of a first-generation Bluetooth USB dongle

In the early 2010s, due to advances in technology, a complete Bluetooth module could be implemented on one piece of silicon, but this still presented major technical challenges due to the diverse requirements of the various subsystems. Figure 6.3 demonstrates yet further integration. The three-chip Wi-Fi solution on the left had been replaced by 2013 with the single-chip solution shown on the right.

6.2 Design Space Exploration

Design space exploration (DSE) is the process of evaluating a succession of different designs while trying to understand which decisions lead to a good design and then finally selecting a design that meets each requirement, or exceeds them if possible. DSE can be manual or automated. DSE applies at the microarchitecture level, such as in the optimisation loops of high-level synthesis (HLS) tools (Section 6.9), but more typically the term refers to system-level architecture design, which is called **architectural exploration**.

System design goals were discussed in Section 4.1. These include performance (or throughput), battery life (or energy use) and manufacturing costs. The goals for just the silicon cost alone are usually called **power, performance and area (PPA)** (Section 5.6). Numeric values of these goals form the **objective metric vector**, which quantifies the quality of a design point. The design space can be approximately formalised as another vector whose component members are each design decision, such as what and how many cores, how many DRAM channels, clock frequency and so on. In practice, a linear vector is a poor approximation of a real design space, which is a very large, if not infinite, tree. The tree structure arises since many design decisions are predicated by others: you can only choose a DRAM clock frequency if you are using DRAM! However, it is sensible to review conventional

Figure 6.3 Two PCIe 802.11 Wi-Fi modules for a laptop. Their shielding lids have been removed. The older unit, on the left, has a three-chip set from Broadcom. It is physically nearly twice the size of the newer unit, shown on the right, which has been magnified 2×. The new unit uses a Qualcomm QCA9565 device that has a higher throughput and also includes Bluetooth. The only other active part needed is the 40-MHz crystal oscillator to the left of the chip. As can be seen at top right, to give a lower-cost lower-performance product, the second of the two diversity antenna sockets, labelled 'ALT', was not fitted

multi-objective optimisation, since it certainly applies within regions of the design space, even if optimisation in general is better left to gut instinct honed by years of design experience.

In formal multi-objective optimisation, the design vector V is processed by an evaluation function to give an objective vector M based on the individual metrics: $M = E(V)$. Ideally, the value of each metric should be as large as possible. If a design does not work, zero is reported for all its metrics. Preferably, evaluation functions are quick to run. This is the motivation of the ESL models in Chapter 5. An overall figure of merit for a design can be given by a **scalarisation function**, $S(M) = m$, which returns the scalar merit m. This is also known as the **goodness**. Again, we seek as high a goodness as possible. However, performing DSE based on M instead of m is more intelligent and potentially faster since function S throws away useful information.

Multi-variate optimisation is also known as **hill climbing**. A hill-climbing algorithm starts with one or some number of manually created seed reference designs, $V_0, V_1, \ldots, V_n$. To find the best design point, these vectors are refined or otherwise mutated to create further vectors. Frequently, there are numerous equally good or best design points. These are said to be members of a Pareto-optimal set. For a **Pareto optimal solution**, any attempt to improve one of the objective functions is compromised by a decrease in one or more of the others. The members of the set all have the same value of m. An optimisation algorithm would then return a number of results, and the engineer would have to decide which to use.

One problem with hill-climbing algorithms is that they can get stuck in **local maxima**, which are design points where a small change to any component of the design vector leads to a worse design. A bad algorithm will return a false maximum because it has not explored sufficiently far away from a seed point to find a better maximum. Hill-climbing algorithms include simulated annealing, genetic algorithms, gradient ascent, ant colony optimisation and particle swarm optimisation. Simulated annealing starts with only one of the V_i seeds and is run for each in turn, with the best result being selected, whereas the others use all the seeds at once.

If there are various local maxima with scalar metric values m_i, the ratio of the smallest to the optimal solution is sometimes called the **locality gap**:

$$\text{Locality gap} = \max_i \left(\frac{m_{\text{optimum}}}{m_i} \right)$$

Baseline code for **simulated annealing** is presented in Figure 6.4. Simulated annealing is a blind search in that it looks at m instead of M. It is named after the equivalent process in metalworking. To avoid local maxima, simulated annealing uses a state variable called 'temperature', which starts at a high value, perhaps based on knowledge of the locality gap, and is gradually decreased during the process. A new trial design point is created by perturbing the current point such that the step size is larger at higher temperatures. If the new point is better than the current one, it is adopted. Moreover, if the new trial point is worse than the current point, it is also adopted with a probability proportional to its temperature. When we get below a threshold temperature, only improvements are accepted: this is the so-called **quench phase**. Rather than running simulated annealing for each seed in turn, **particle swarm optimisation** runs agents in parallel, iterating over a set of successively improving designs.

A **gradient ascent** uses M instead of m to implement a multi-dimensional quantised variant of Newton–Raphson iteration. A number of **orthogonal perturbations** δ_i are made to the current design point V. Walsh functions are sometimes used as a basis; these are like binary versions of a Fourier sine/cosine basis. An estimate of the partial derivative of M with respect to each perturbation vector is computed:

$$D_i = \frac{M(V) - M(V + \delta_i)}{|\delta_i|}$$

A motion vector is then created from the weighted sum of each derivative and V is replaced with $V - \alpha D$, where α is a fractional parameter selected to trade off the speed of convergence with stability and overshoot.

In manual DSE, engineers typically use a **genetic algorithm** (whether they know the formal name or not!). Genetic algorithms are also commonly automated. Two existing design points are cross-bred to create a new design point. If this is better than either of its parents, it replaces the weaker parent in the working set. Cross-breeding is simply a matter of taking some random fields from the first parent and the complementary fields from the other parent.

```
temp    := 200                // Set initial temperature to a high value
ans     := first_guess        // This is the design vector (or tree)
metric := metric_metric ans   // We seek the highest-metric answer

while (temp > 1)
{
   // Create new design point, offsetting with delta proportional to temperature
   ans' := perturb_ans temp ans

   // Evaluate (scalar) objective function (figure of merit) for new design point
   metric' := metric_metric ans'

   // Accept if better probabilistically
   accept := (metric' > metric) || rand(100..200) < temp;
   if (accept) (ans, metric, temp) := (ans', metric', temp * 0.99)
}
return ans;
```

Figure 6.4 An iteration for hill climbing using simulated annealing to find a design point with the highest scalar metric

Constructive Algorithms

The main alternatives to hill climbing are constructive algorithms. A **constructive algorithm** generates an output design without iterating. Hence, such algorithms are fast, but tend to deliver inferior results. They often use little more intelligence than the greedy principle from computer science. At each step, a **greedy algorithm** always takes the best-looking current option without considering subsequent steps. The output design can be measured to given an initial indication of performance. It can also be used to generate a seed point for incremental transform-based improvement.

One example is a constructive placer used to generate a seed design for a place-and-route run (Section 8.7.1). A naive constructive placer first sorts the nodes into decreasing order of connectivity. The component with the highest connectivity is placed in the middle of a 2-D area. Using a **force-directed approach**, it then places each component in turn into a site, whether occupied or not, to minimise the wiring distance to already-placed components. If the site is occupied, a partial row or column is shoved aside, so that the extremity of the row or column now lies in empty space. The shove-aside cost has order $\sqrt{n}$, so the total constructive placement cost is $n\sqrt{n}$.

NP-Hard Algorithms

An **NP-hard algorithm** has no known solution method, other than trying every possible solution and assessing which is best. The measurement cost is polynomial in time complexity and trying each solution is factorial or exponential in complexity. However, in a fictional world where every solution can be tried non-deterministically (i.e. in parallel), the time cost would reduce to the polynomial checking cost, hence, the name *NP*.

In nearly all circumstances, individual optimisations applied to a subsystem are non-composable, so that the global optimisation of a system is NP-hard. A **non-composable optimisation** is one where applying a transformation on one subsystem prevents or diminishes the effect of another optimisation on a neighbour. A good example is sub-expression computation. Suppose a logic signal is needed in two subsystems and the information to generate it is present in both. Is it better to compute it twice or to compute it in one and send the result to the other with additional wiring? There are no known algorithms for solving such problems perfectly, apart from exponential trial and error. Indeed, even the general problem of minimising the logic within a subsystem while ignoring wiring length is NP-hard. Although that problem is well solved heuristically by Espresso (Section 8.3.8), once net length and energy **design intents** (Section 8.3) are added, even the heuristics become complex.

6.2.1 DSE Workflows

A three-step approach to DSE, starting at the top-level, is as follows:

1. The overall requirements are manually broken down into tasks.

2. The tasks are allocated to subsystems.

3. The subsystems are designed.

A number of **use cases** are defined in the system specification. A use case may correspond to one or more tasks. All use cases must be supported, but an **exclusivity matrix** identifies tasks that do not need to be supported concurrently. A device may have phases of operation, such as start-up, firmware upgrade and showtime, that are exclusive. Moreover, certain application combinations might be precluded due to the overall load or other reasons, such as providing satellite navigation and video-conferencing at the same time on a mobile phone.

The output of one task is frequently the input to another. These dependencies are defined in the **task dependency matrix**, which controls which tasks can be performed in parallel and limits the available parallelism (Section 4.2).

For a particular task, the three main digital resources that need to be provided are: (1) the input and output bandwidth, (2) storage for intermediate results and (3) a number of arithmetic operations. On-chip storage in SRAM always offers the highest throughput, but storage capacity limitations mean that nearby DRAM must be used. It is important for the DRAM system to offer sufficient read and write bandwidth. On the other hand, DRAM capacity is typically a limiting factor only for cloud-scale algorithms, such as search completions on Google or product suggestions during online shopping on Amazon. Secondary storage capacity is rarely a restriction at the moment, due to the capacity of SSD and SD cards. (Magnetic spinning media and tape are also relevant, but not for most SoC projects.) A typical approach for quantifying the requirements of a task is to take an implementation in C and compile it for a simple processor. A combination of static analysis and running the program then gives a naive preliminary indication of the key resources needed.

Finally, the designer needs to consider the power supply and heat extraction. Power density restrictions affect modern system designs and require dark silicon (Section 8.2). If parts of the system are in different chips, the energy for communicating between those parts goes up, but it is significantly easier to get heat out.

Although some IP blocks have higher licensing costs than others, to a first approximation, the cost of a square millimetre of silicon on a SoC is the same, regardless of what it is used for. The three important baseline figures per square millimetre of area are:

1. **Computation density**: Each integer-arithmetic ALU has a silicon area proportional to its precision in bits. To evaluate a design without regard to a particular silicon geometry, the area can be expressed in units of square lambda (λ^2) (Section 8.2). A 32-bit ripple carry adder needs about 128 two-input gate equivalents and each gate needs about $1000\lambda^2$ (Section 8.2.1). A faster adder, such as the synthesis-friendly Kogge-Stone design, requires four or more times the area. The growth in area with increasing precision is logarithmic.

2. **Communication density**: If a logic gate is implemented using polysilicon and metal layer 1, then metal layers 2 and 3 are available for wiring and data busses. A wiring pitch of 15λ is easily achievable, allowing several bits of a bus to pass over a single gate. However, longer busses made of fine wires (6λ pitch) suffer badly from increased resistance and delay (Figure 3.2). A lower pitch and hence, lower data flux are needed for longer distances or on higher metal layers where lower fabrication precision is achieved. Some busses need to turn a corner, which can use significant area for wide busses. This problem arises mainly at the meeting point of blocks that have already been physically optimised or have a hardened layout (Figure 6.5). The local net width and spacing rules may have to be adjusted manually, or else the nets may need to be manually assigned to a broader set of metal layers.

3. **Storage density**: An SRAM cell requires six transistors and, like a simple gate, also uses about $1000\lambda^2$ of silicon. However, support circuitry also requires space, which is a non-negligible overhead for RAM smaller than 64 kbytes. A D-type flip-flop typically counts as six gate equivalents, and hence, uses about $6000\lambda^2$.

For technology-independent DSE, the logic delay can be conveniently expressed using scalar multiples of the FO4 delay (Section 4.6.6). It is then possible to estimate the delay using pre-synthesis RTL by analysing the complexity of the right-hand expressions and making assumptions about the degree of sub-expression sharing that the logic synthesiser may make (Section 8.3.1). Appropriate factorisation and reuse of sub-expressions is obviously beneficial for locally derived results, but with today's technology, sending the result of a 32-bit addition a significant fraction of a millimetre across a chip may use more power then recomputing it locally. This can influence the microarchitecture design (Section 6.2.4).

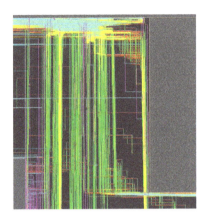

Figure 6.5 Screenshot from a place-and-route tool, showing how the wiring avoids a region of hardened layout (grey area on the right). Some area is required to route these interconnections

6.2.2 C Functional Models

As presented in Section 5.1, designing a subsystem for a SoC often starts with a **functional model** of the intended system coded in C/C++. This model embodies the required behaviour of the hardware implementation. It is an **executable specification** (Section 7.9) of the system, although its structure is likely to be unsuitable for direct implementation or HLS (Section 6.9).

As well as defining the functionality, a C/C++ model can directly provide an initial estimate of the computational resources required. Detailed profiling of the program will reveal its computational load, whereas a manual inspection of the compiled binary will indicate the size of coefficient ROMs. The number of load and store operations is not likely to be informative, most likely because a different control-flow structure will be needed for the hardware implementation (Section 6.2.3). However, the number of ALU and floating-point operations is very valuable, along with the number of DRAM activations, if the functional model uses the same memory layout in terms of DRAM use. Profiling with a test load can be performed in four ways:

1. Run the functional model on a workstation and use a C profiler (e.g. gprof) to find the number of calls of each subroutine. The program can be manually factored into more subroutines than strictly required to obtain finer detail.

2. For all loop bodies, instrument each line of code that performs an arithmetic operation to increment the global statistics counters, then export the counts to a spreadsheet after each run.

3. For a simple in-order processor, cross-compile the functional model. Instrument the code to take note of the global clock tick register in the counter/timer block or PMU (Section 2.7.9). Run the model on any real hardware available and export the timing information to a spreadsheet. Some PMUs may break down the number of instructions.

4. Run the functional model on a virtual platform with the ISS (Section 5.5) in a mode that reports the number of each type of instruction. Cache activity logs are also useful for memory-bound computations.

Profiling should be run with different sizes of test load to provide information about the start-up overhead of the main algorithm so that it can be factored out. The scaling factor should be determined, which ideally would be linear. The functional model is also a good resource for becoming familiar with the overall problem domain and for capturing data input and output files from test runs. These files can be later replayed against ESL and RTL models of the system, once it is developed.

Table 6.1 lists the ROM requirements for an MP3 decoder. The constant data entries in a C implementation of the decoder were examined with the `objdump` utility. The last entry in the `.rodata` segment ends at virtual address 0x2350, so about 9 kbytes of ROM are needed before any mirroring (Section 6.9.1). Table 6.2 reports instrumented figures for the MP3 decoder when generating 16-bit stereo sound from a 128 kbps input stream. However, the decoder supports various sub-modes of operation (level 1/2 or level 3) and for both levels, the MP3 dynamically switches between operational modes depending on the content (transient sounds versus pitched sounds). It also supports many different bit rates, sample rates and other parameters. Therefore, many experiments are needed to determine the average and 99th percentile computational load. The worst-case load is best found by (or at least cross-checked against) a static analysis of the source code.

Table 6.1 Determining the ROM needs of an MP3 decoder by disassembling a segment `.rodata`

Label	Start address (hex)
g_drmp3_pow43-0x120	0x0000
g_drmp3_pow43>	0x120
g_scf_partitions.6678>	0x0c40
...	
_end_of_static	0x2350

Table 6.2 Statistics logged during one second of a profile run of MP3 stream decoding. The numbers of integer ALU operations exclude loop control and array subscription operations

Event type	Number of operations
Input bytes	16 392
Output frames	44 352
DCT operations	154
Floating-point adds and subtracts	874 965
Floating-point multiplies	401 255
Integer adds and subtracts	162 107
Integer multiplies	88 704

The instrumented figures should be checked against simple analytic estimates. For instance, we should expect a data expansion ratio of about 10 to 1. This should correspond to the ratio of input and output data bits. We know that MP3 uses overlapping **discrete cosine transforms (DCTs)** with 576 samples per sound granule (or 192 for occasional short granules) and so the number of transforms per second should be $44\,100 \times 2/576$ for stereo sound at 44.1 kbps, and so on.

The computational load indicates the number of ALUs needed given a target system clock rate. The tabulated figures sum to under 10 MOPS (million operations per second). This shows that MP3 audio decoding is a taxing operation for low-clock-rate embedded CPUs, but not a problem for a single core of a tablet- or laptop-grade processor. However, the reference implementation uses floating-point arithmetic and is certainly not appropriate for a low-energy implementation suitable for embedding in a spectacle stem or hearing aid.

6.2.3 Functional Model Refactoring to ESL

Although a software functional model can directly provide useful ALU operation count and ROM size metrics, it generally requires manual refactoring in a number of ways before data movement and parallelism metrics can be explored. A suitably refactored model can serve as an **electronic system level (ESL)** model (Chapter 5). Typical refactoring operations include:

- **Disabling unused options**: The program will typically include many options that are irrelevant. These include conditional compilation options for alternative operating systems (e.g. Android and Windows). They may include support for different output variations. The MP3 example supports 10 audio device drivers whereas only raw PCM output was required. There may be options to exploit various SIMD instruction sets, such as SSE2 or Arm NEON. For instance, an **Advanced Encryption Standard (AES)** encoder/decoder would typically check whether the target processor has AES instructions. If not, it would use everyday instructions instead. All non-essential code should be deleted.

- **Splitting off management functions**: Most data-intensive applications that are acceleration targets contain dedicated code for starting, stopping and configuring options. These are likely to be retained in the software and need new mechanisms for interconnection to the accelerated data paths. Section 6.4.2 discusses manual co-design factoring of control functions to convey parameters via a programmed I/O (PIO) register bank. Similar mechanisms are needed if exceptions are raised or for access to the file system.

- **Splitting off coefficient computations**: The functional model may compute large tables of constants when it starts, such as sine waves and window functions. For a hardware implementation, these are placed in ROM or else RAM that is initialised by the host processor.

- **Static allocation**: Hardware implementations often use statically allocated memory pools or dedicated SRAM. The software version makes dynamic allocations on the stack and heap. To convert to static form, the size of each resource needs to be analysed from the system specification and for all available test loads. If a resource is to remain in DRAM, a base address in the PIO configuration bank can be used, written by the host at start-up time.

- **Changing the thread library**: A portable program that can run on Windows and Linux is already likely to use a shim layer to abstract the threading primitives of each substrate. It may be useful to replace or augment the abstraction to use the SystemC threading system (Section 5.3) so that the functions performed by the various threads can be placed in separate hardware components.

- **Changing the control flow**: The control-flow graph of the software implementation is likely to be irrelevant for hardware acceleration. In software, various subsystems are likely to be interconnected using method calls. In the MP3 example, the main IDCT decoder was invoked as a subroutine of the Huffman decoder, whereas for DSE experiments, other paradigms need to be explored, such as running each component in its own thread and using FIFO channels with a mailbox design (Section 6.3.4). To exploit greater parallelism than present in the functional model, finer-grained work units need to be identified. The **loop-splitting transform** takes a loop with no loop-carried dependencies (Section 6.9.1) and creates two or more similar loops that share out the original loop range. Each new loop needs to be wrapped up as a method with a signature suitable for running as an autonomous thread.

- **Changing the precision**: A software implementation will use the predefined native word sizes of the C language (8, 16, 32 and 64). Energy efficiency in hardware is achieved using custom field widths. Changing the definition of all variables to use an arbitrary- precision library (Section 5.3) can be done using global edits of the source code. The widths themselves can then be adjusted during DSE or automatically by some synthesis back ends. A custom data encoding can be explored by overloading all the standard operators in C++.

Rather than using two's complement or IEEE floating-point arithmetic, a hardware implementation can often benefit from using **custom data encoding**. For certain functions, especially those with many probability computations, values are commonly stored as logarithms. Multiplication can then be replaced with addition. Although logarithms cannot express negative numbers directly, it is simple to add an additional sign bit. For instance, a 6-bit field could use the most significant bit to hold the sign. All zeroes would represent 0, and the remaining values would represent geometric values of the form 1.5^j. Unity is represented with $j = 0$. All arithmetic operations on these values can be directly implemented in small ROMs of $2^{12} = 4096$ entries, or just 1024 entries if the sign bit is handled in logic. Higher-precision temporary results are typically maintained to avoid an **underflow** (Section 6.8.1) during accumulation operations (running sums) or when necessary. A ROM implementation can easily support **saturating arithmetic**, as commonly required in DSP applications. In saturating arithmetic, an overflow is replaced with an underflow. For instance, in 8-bit two's complement encoding, `127+2` will return 127 (`0x7f`) instead of -127 (`0x81`). Applications for which a custom numeric representation can produce a significant energy saving include neural networks, low-density parity check decoding and the Viterbi algorithm.

After all these changes, the C/C++ program should still work, producing the same output as it did before, but it is likely to be less efficient. This does not matter, of course.

6.2.4 Microarchitecture of a Subsystem

The **microarchitecture** of a subsystem is equivalent to its **data path**, as it is the layout of data busses between its **functional units (FUs)**, such as register files and ALUs (Section 6.8.1).

Once tasks have been allocated to subsystems, the microarchitecture for each subsystem must be designed. Whether the subsystem is based on a processor or custom hardware, one of the most influential aspects is how data moves in and out. DMA (Section 2.7.5) is often the obvious choice, but in reality the main difference between DMA and PIO on a simple core is the instruction fetch overhead of the simple core, since the memory bandwidth, bus bandwidth and energy for data movement are essentially unchanged.

If custom hardware is to be used, the microarchitecture can either be designed manually or created using HLS (Section 6.9) or similar tools. In both cases, the microarchitecture is dominated by the layout of data in memory. Most arithmetic operations are comparatively cheap. Multiplying or dividing by powers of two is free for integer arithmetic and requires a small adder for floating point. Likewise, the absolute value function and negation functions are free, or virtually free, for floating-point arithmetic. On the other hand, multiplying large mantissa numbers, such as 64-bit integers when both arguments are variable, is expensive and should be avoided if possible. Division should also generally be avoided, by, for instance, multiplying by the reciprocal. Single-precision floating-point multiplication requires only a 24-bit multiplier, so does not have a significant cost.

In modern silicon, energy costs are more troublesome than area costs, and energy use primarily arises from going off chip, from moving data a long distance over the chip or from considerable use of multiplexing. Recall that the most powerful component in a software implementation is the memory system. Knuth's classic book on algorithms, *The Art of Computer Programming* [1], extensively uses arrays, which were seen as a low-cost atomic operation, but this does not hold for modern hardware. GPU architectures achieve high performance using a constrained memory model. Random accesses from processing elements (PEs) to flat memory space is banned (Section 6.9.1). High-performance processors use energy-hungry cache structures to give the illusion of random access, whereas low-energy approaches use scratchpads (Section 2.3) where memory layout optimisations are performed at compile time.

A principal issue in microarchitecture design is avoiding the three main forms of hazard (Section 6.3). Mirroring data over multiple memories and using dual-port memories are solutions, but this is resource-expensive (Section 2.6.5). Allowing components to operate asynchronously using FIFO buffers (Section 6.3.4) can reduce busy waiting and stalls, but having many small memories, FIFO buffers and so on can be area-expensive due to the lack of statistical sharing of the available storage (Section 4.3.3).

Finding a suitable microarchitecture for a subsystem requires considerable effort. If it proves to be difficult, despite rapid feedback from a high-level virtual platform (Chapter 5), it is often sensible to start again and consider a different algorithm or data layout. Many problems involve the manipulation of sparse arrays. Graph algorithms are the main example. There are two adjacency list projections for a graph algorithm: edge centric and node centric. Typically a graph has more edges than nodes. In an **edge-centric graph**, the iteration is over the edges, which may be streamed past an array of PEs. In contrast, for a **node-centric graph**, the iteration is over the nodes. Nodes vary in arity and the data flow is, thus, irregular. For several mainstream problems, such as finding the single-source shortest path, the classical algorithm devised by Dijkstra, which is optimal on a single-core processor, is unsuitable for attaining a parallel speedup. Using an alternative algorithm is often much better than trying to make small improvements to the microarchitecture.

6.2.5 Interconnect Optimisation

Minimising the energy required for communications is generally one of the top concerns in SoC design. Thus, it is important to consider the design and optimisation of an interconnect.

The goodness metric for interconnect design includes the usual silicon area, net length and energy costs. These can be based on the same high-level parametric formulae embedded in an ESL model of the canvas parts. These formulae were obtained from fitting curves to RTL synthesis data for each part in isolation. Also included in a cost model for NoC-based designs are throughput, QoS and HoL penalties. Incorporating these aspects is more difficult, since it is easy to form a metric with a very 'bumpy' surface that performs badly in a hill-climbing search. For instance, it is unclear whether the scalar reduction to goodness should give a positive or negative credit to aspects of the design that provide more throughput than is needed.

Fortunately, the goodness metric needs to designed only once for any interconnect tool flow. Its behaviour can be extensively analysed from hill-climbing traces for benchmark designs. The end user then benefits from a fast solution. Machine learning techniques can be used.

Two approaches for seeding an automated interconnect generation process are agglomerative clustering and the Steiner tree approach, as presented in Section 3.9. **Agglomerative clustering** is a constructive algorithm (Section 6.2) that starts by placing each source and destination in its own set and then successively combining sets by interconnecting them with switching elements. It uses only radix-3 elements, so local or global optimisations are also applied to conglomerate simple elements into higher arity elements, if available.

If hill climbing uses only mutations that consist of the smallest possible changes in any dimension, then it is a **local search**. Making large changes to a design point can lead to *hunting* by the algorithm and poor convergence. An exploration based entirely on local searches in the vicinity of working solutions cannot find the optimum solution if the optimum is disconnected from all seed points. However, before its quench phase, simulated annealing (Section 6.2) based on local searching can follow paths through non-working design points.

Fortunately, local searches are extremely effective for solving **facility location problems** [2]. Classically, in a facility location problem, the location of a new parcel sorting office has to be chosen due to the closure of an existing one. The aim is to minimise the cost of conveying parcels between a fixed set of customers. If switching elements are treated as facilities and the aim is to minimise the net length while avoiding obstacles, then the topology generation problem is very similar to facility location problems. Hence, it can be solved well by a local search.

When optimising an interconnect, several local change operations can be utilised, although some are suitable only for NoC-based solutions. Each preserves operational correctness. Some of these are as follows:

- switch_vc: In this change operation, virtual circuit (VC) assignments are twiddled to arrive at a different solution. The choice of VC and which traffic entry to twiddle the VC on are based on heuristics, such as traffic criticality and HoL conflicts.

```
1: procedure switch_vc
2:    for each route from src to dst do
3:       for e in the route do
4:          VC_set[v][src] = e
5:    Compute edge-set intersection for each pair of VCs
6:    random_shuffle(edge-intersection < threshold)
7:    merge_vcs(pick lowest selected VC)
```

- switch_route: In this change operation, part of a static route is modified, based on element port utilisation, to distribute traffic evenly across ports. Prohibited edges are checked to prevent a cycle from causing a deadlock (Section 3.4.3).

```
1: procedure switch_route
2:    for each route from src to dst do
3:       for each unconsidered edge e in the route do
4:          Tag e as considered
5:          src_r = source(edge e)
6:          tx_p = least_utilised_port(src_r)
7:          if path_exists(tx_p, dst) then
8:             p = shortest_path(from tx_p, dst)
9:             Save alternative candidate for route
10:               break
11:          else
12:               continue
13:    Update all the route vectors from the candidate
```

- switch_end_point_port: An end point is rewired to a a different hub or switching element in the vicinity to generate another solution.

- switch_router: A switching element is interchanged with another in the vicinity and all the connections moved to the new one.

- switch_path_based_on_traffic: An entire path is switched to an alternative to generate a new solution.

- switch_end_point_vc: A VC at an end point or protocol-converting bridge transmit port is switched to a new one, while ensuring that deadlocks do not occur due to this change.

- merge_vc: Two transmit VCs from a protocol-converting bridge are merged. That is, one of the VCs is chosen to represent both of them as a new solution. Deadlock constraints are honoured, as in switch_end_point_vc and switch_vc above.

- `merge_end_point_ports`: Multiple routes originating from a common bridge transmit port are merged to generate a new solution.

```
1: procedure merge_end_point_ports
2:    For all bridges, compute average and peak rates for the system
3:    random_shuffle(bridges where average and peak < threshold)
4:    for bridges do
5:       Merge all the routes across all ports
6:    Update the route vectors
```

6.3 Hazards

The design and optimisation of a microarchitecture typically attempt to maximise the utilisation of a minimal number of FUs, such as register files and ALUs (Section 6.8.1). In today's SoCs, having a larger number of FUs is not a severe problem provided they have low static-power dissipation (Section 4.6.1). However, minimising the overall distance of data movement is also a primary aim. Using more silicon makes nets longer. As well as average utilisation, the performance of a subsystem depends on its clock frequency and degree of parallelism. The clock frequency can be increased using more pipelining (Section 4.4.2), but this can also increase the **hazard penalty**, which is the cost of recovering from or avoiding a hazard. Hazards cause stalls or misspeculation, both of which reduce the throughput of a subsystem.

- A **pipeline stall** is essentially a clock gating step (Section 4.6.9) at a certain stage in the pipeline beyond which the content of **architectural registers** is not updated.

- A **misspeculation** occurs when the wrong data are processed. No results can be committed to primary state registers or RAM until the speculation guard is qualified (i.e. the true result is known).

Both situations arise from hazards and have a penalty. A good design avoids hazards and minimises the penalty incurred from each remaining hazard. The main forms of hazard are:

- **Write-after-write (WaW) hazard**: One write must occur after another otherwise the wrong answer persists.

- **Read-after-write (RaW) or write-after-read (WaR) hazard**: The write and read at a location must not be accidentally permuted.

- **Other data hazard**: Part of a pipeline stalls if an operand simply has not arrived in time for use.

- **Control hazard**: When it is not yet clear whether the results of an operation should be committed (but the computation can still start speculatively).

- **Name alias hazard**: When it cannot be determined in advance whether two subscripts to an array (of RAM address bus values) are going to be equal.

- **Structural hazard**: There are insufficient physical resources to do everything at once.

Sometimes a hazard can be classed in more than one way. For instance, if the address to a register file has not yet arrived, there is a data hazard on the address, but this could be regarded as a control hazard for the register file operation (read or write). However, changing the classification does not alter the associated penalty!

A structural hazard occurs when an operation cannot proceed because a resource is already in use. Structural hazards may occur for the following reasons:

- memories and register files have insufficient ports

- memories, especially DRAM, have variable latency

- there are not enough mirrorable FUs (Section 6.8.1) for all the arithmetic in the current clock tick

- when a resource is not fully pipelined, i.e. it cannot accept new work when it is busy.

A **fully pipelined** FU can start a new operation on every clock cycle. Such components have a fixed latency (pipeline delay). They are common, and they are the easiest components to form schedules around. Two non-fully pipelined FU forms are:

1. Those that have a **re-initiation interval** greater than unity. For example, the component might accept new data every third clock cycle but still have a fixed latency.

2. Those with a pair of handshake wires that kick off processing and inform the client logic when it is busy or ready, respectively. This arrangement is used for computations that are performed better with variable latency, such as wide-word multiplications and divisions.

Synchronous RAMs, and most complex ALUs, excluding division, are generally fully pipelined and have a fixed latency. An example of a component that cannot accept new input data every clock cycle (i.e. it is not fully pipelined) is a sequential long multiplier, as described in Section 6.9. The adjective 'flash' is sometimes used for a combinational (or single-cycle) implementation of an FU. For example, a **flash multiplier** operates in less than one clock cycle and uses quadratic silicon area. (Although, in theory, $n \log n$ area is possible for enormous multipliers.)

6.3.1 Hazards From Array Memories

A structural hazard in an RTL design can make the RTL non-synthesisable (Section 8.3.2). Consider the following expressions. They make liberal use of array subscription and the multiplier operator. The structural hazard sources are numbered:

```
always @(posedge clk) begin
    q0 <= Boz[e3]              // 3
    q1 <= Foo[e0] + Foo[e1];   // 1
    q2 <= Bar[Bar[e2]];        // 2
    q3 <= a*b + c*d;           // 4
    q4 <= Boz[e4]              // 3
    end
```

1. The RAMs or register files Foo, Bar and Boz may not have two read ports.

2. Even with two ports, can Bar perform the double subscription in one clock cycle?

3. Read operations on Boz may be a long way apart in the code, so the hazard is hard to spot.

4. The cost of providing two **flash multipliers** for use in one clock cycle, which then lie idle much of the rest of the time, is likely not warranted.

RAMs have a small number of ports but when RTL arrays are held in RAM, it is easy to write RTL expressions that require many operations on the contents of a RAM in one operation, even from within one thread. For instance, we might need to implement three operations on a RAM:

$$A[x] \; <= \; A[y + A[z]]$$

Moreover, this requires a combinational read port on the RAM, which is normally not feasible for more than a few kilobytes.

Because it is a very low-level language, RTL typically requires the user to schedule port use manually. To overcome hazards automatically, stalls and holding registers need to be inserted. The programmer's original model of the design must be stalled when ports are reused in the time domain and require extra clock cycles to copy data to and from the holding registers. This is not a feature of standard RTL, so it must be done either by hand or automatically using the put/get paradigm of Bluespec (Section 6.8.5) or general HLS (Section 6.9). The put/get approach makes the sending (putting) of arguments asynchronous to the getting of results, as on a split-port bus (Section 3.1.3). In contrast, HLS uses a compile-time static schedule that understands static pipeline delays and stalls the entire schedule if any component is not ready.

6.3.2 Overcoming Structural Hazards using Holding Registers

One way to overcome a structural hazard is to deploy more resources. These will suffer correspondingly less contention. For instance, we might have three multipliers instead of one. This is a **spatial solution**. For RAMs and register files, we need to add more ports to them or mirror them (i.e. to ensure the same data are written to each copy). An **architectural register** holds data that are part of the algorithm or programmer's view state. On the other hand, in a **temporal solution**, a holding register is inserted to overcome a structural hazard (by hand or by a design-entry language compiler). Sometimes, the value that is needed is always available elsewhere in the design and needs forwarding. Sometimes, an extra sequencer step is needed.

For example, say we know nothing about e0 and e1:

```
always @(posedge clk) begin
   ...
   ans = Foo[e0] + Foo[e1];
   ...
   end
```

We can load a holding register in an additional cycle:

```
always @(posedge clk) begin
   pc = !pc;
   ...
   if (!pc) holding <= Foo[e0];
   if (pc)  ans <= holding + Foo[e1];
   ...
   end
```

Alternatively, we may be able to analyse the pattern for e0 and e1:

```
always @(posedge clk) begin
   ...
   ee = ee + 1;
   ...
   ans = Foo[ee] + Foo[ee-1];
   ...
   end
```

Then, apart from the first cycle, we can use a holding register to **loop forward** the value from the previous iteration (Section 6.9.1):

```
always @(posedge clk) begin
   ...
   ee <= ee + 1;
   holding <= Foo[ee];
   ans <= holding + Foo[ee];
   ...
   end
```

Although these examples used memories, other FUs, such as fixed- and floating-point ALUs, also have structural hazards. A good design not only balances structural resource use between clock cycles but also critical-path timing delays. These example fragments handled one hazard and used two clock cycles. They were localised transformations. If there is a large number of clock cycles, memories and ALUs, a global search and optimisation procedure is needed to find a good balance for the load on structural components.

6.3.3 Name Alias Hazards

A **name alias hazard** arises when an analysis tool cannot tell whether two references are to the same storage location. There are three possible situations: definitely different, definitely the same and cannot tell. The third of these raises problems in the static optimisation of hardware or software structures. Expanding blocking assignments in RTL can lead to name aliases.

Suppose we know nothing about *xx* and *yy*, then consider:

```
begin
   ...
   if (g) Foo[xx] = e1;
   r2 = Foo[yy];
```

To avoid name alias problems, this must be compiled to non-blocking pure RTL as:

```
begin
   ...
   Foo[xx] <= (g) ? e1: Foo[xx];
   r2 <= (xx==yy) ? ((g) ? e1:  Foo[xx]): Foo[yy];
```

Quite commonly, we do know something about the subscript expressions. If they are compile-time constants, we can check their equality at compile time. Suppose that at the ellipsis (...) we had the line $yy = xx+1$;. It is then 'obvious' that xx and yy cannot be the same value. The compiler can then determine that the array subscripts will never alias and it can eliminate the conditional expression construct. Many other patterns in the preceding code can guarantee that these variables are unequal. A sufficiently rich set of rules, built into the tool, can make this deduction, and many others like it, for a large number of typical program structures. However, no set of rules can be complete due to the decidability of the halting problem. Limited domains for which the problem is solvable are discussed in Section 6.9.1.

6.3.4 FIFO Buffers and Dual-port IP Blocks

Flow control between accelerated sub-tasks is known as **orchestration**. Often the most efficient data layout for one sub-task is different from that for another that shares the data. Further, the order in which data are generated by a sub-task may not be ideal for the consumer. If a major reorganisation of the layout is required, there can be little alternative to storing the data in memory and reading the data back with a different pattern. This should ideally be done in SRAM on-chip and the top-level design should be chosen to minimise the SRAM size. If done off-chip in DRAM, one of the two access patterns is bound to be DRAM-unfriendly. In that case, the layout used is typically the best for the readout, if data are often read more than once. If only temporal decoupling is required, FIFO buffering can be used.

Figure 6.6 shows three possible initiator/target configurations for a device with two transactional ports, such as a FIFO buffer or a task in a multistage accelerator. We assume that there is flow control at each port (e.g. using the standard synchronous interface (Section 3.1.3) or credit (Section 3.4.4)). The arrows show the flow from initiator to target. For simplex ports, the data do not always flow in the same direction as the arrow. For duplex and half-duplex ports, the data flow in both directions, so cannot possibly flow only in the direction of the arrow.

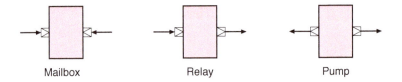

Mailbox   Relay   Pump

Figure 6.6 Mailbox, relay and pump paradigms: three initiator/target configurations possible for dual-ported IP blocks

A dual-ported component that is an initiator on both sides has a **pump pattern**. A component that is a target on both sides has a **mailbox pattern**. The memory used for data follows the mailbox pattern, as do all FIFO, LIFO and RAM components, but the memory can be nominally inside a proactive wrapper that makes one of the other paradigms visible externally.

FIFO Buffers and Combinational Paths

A synchronous FIFO buffer cannot be bubble-free without also having a combinational path.

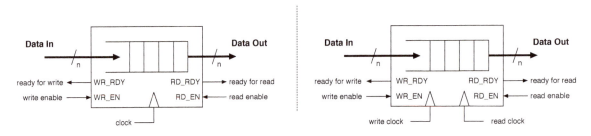

Figure 6.7 Schematic symbols of a FIFO buffer following the mailbox pattern: synchronous (left) and clock-domain crossing (right)

A **FIFO buffer** is a first-in, first-out queue. Although a FIFO buffer helps decouple timing constraints between coupled subsystems, thereby boosting performance, long combinational paths can arise if care is not taken. A long combinational path reduces the allowable clock frequency. A FIFO buffer has an internal storage limit (its capacity), but the interface is independent of that. A hardware FIFO buffer follows the mailbox pattern in that it has two target ports. Figure 6.7 shows the schematic symbols for two such FIFO buffers, one synchronous and one asynchronous, with the latter being suitable for clock-domain crossing (Section 3.7.1).

Except for a credit-controlled FIFO buffer (Figure 3.32), each of the two ports has a pair of standard synchronous handshake nets (Section 3.1.3). Some FIFO buffers provide further status output signals, such as half or nearly full. For a clock-domain crossing FIFO buffer, these will be timed according to one of the clock domains. The signals can be output twice, synchronised for each domain. Table 6.3 shows that synchronous FIFO buffers can be:

1. **Fully registered**: The effect of a read or write is visible at only the opposite port a clock cycle later.

2. **Bypass**: The input data appear straight away at the output of an empty FIFO buffer.

3. **Pipelined**: Does not support a simultaneous enqueue and dequeue operation when full.

4. **Bubble-free**: Simultaneous read and write operations are always possible.

A fully registered FIFO buffer is the only synchronous variation with a local handshake that fully isolates combinational paths between the coupled subsystems.

Table 6.3 Synchronous delay and combinational paths for basic FIFO types

Type	Data latency	Ready latency	Combinational paths
Fully registered	1	1	None
Bypass	0	1	WR_EN → RD_RDY
Pipelined	1	0	RD_EN → WR_RDY
Bubble-free	0	0	Both directions
Asynchronous	Several	Several	None
Credit-controlled	1	n/a	None

Figure 6.8 shows a circuit for a one-place synchronous FIFO buffer. (One place means that the capacity is 1. For multi-place FIFO buffers, the data may be either shifted internally or held in dual-ported RAM as a circular queue with in and out pointers.) The dashed paths show the optional signal paths, called **bypass** and **pipeline**, defining a total of four behaviours. Using either optional signal provides a speedup in terms of latency, for the forward and reverse paths, respectively. If a FIFO buffer is installed to assist with timing closure, having either path can extend the critical path. In other words, their use can remove clock cycles but can also restrict the clock frequency. If both paths are present and there is combinational logic in both the read and write initiators, as shown, a combinational loop is created.

A **bubble** is strictly a clock cycle when nothing happens due to a delay in the ready signal propagating backwards, but the term can sometimes be applied to the equivalent forward path delay. For a large FIFO buffer, the presence of bubbles when full is insignificant, since under normal conditions, it should not be full and fullness will be associated with other, perhaps more major, system-level problems.

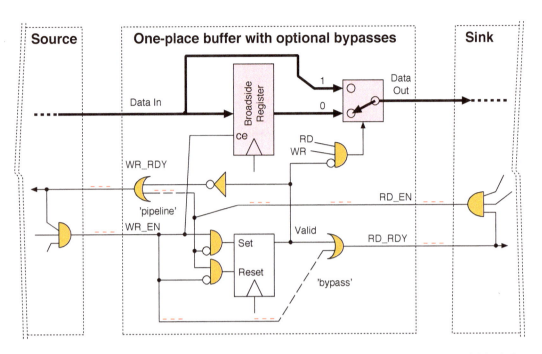

Figure 6.8 A generic schematic of a one-place synchronous FIFO buffer. A synchronous set/reset flip-flop records whether there are valid data in the broadside register. The dashed lines show optional latency-reducing wiring. The output multiplexer is needed only if the dashed bypass wire is installed. Also illustrated are typical patterns of combinational path wiring in the client source and sink. The red annotations show a potential combinational loop

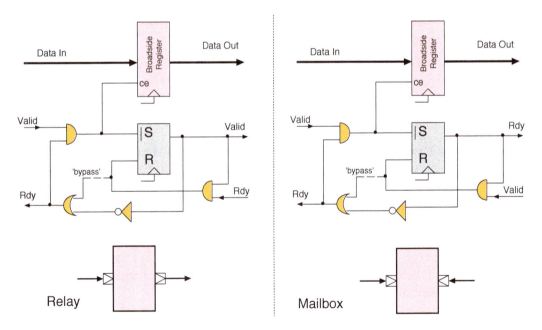

Figure 6.9 Relay and mailbox paradigms for a one-place synchronous FIFO buffer. If there are no combinational paths, the only differences are the net names

However, for the minimal FIFO buffers of size one (a single-place queue), which are potentially desirable for re-timing a standard synchronous handshake, bubbles reduce the throughput to 50 per cent, since only either a queue or a dequeue is possible in any one clock cycle. For this reason, FIFO buffers with a combinational reverse path are preferable for single-place queues. FIFO buffers with at least two places should be used if combinational paths must be prevented in both directions. Alternatively, credit-based flow control (Section 3.4.4) can be used to eliminate the ready signals entirely.

Figure 6.9 shows that the mailbox and relay paradigms, under the standard synchronous handshake, are equivalent except for the net names.

6.4 Custom Accelerators

A **hardware accelerator** implements a task in hardware that would otherwise be performed in software. Perhaps the first hardware accelerator added alongside the integer execution units (ALUs) of early computers was the **floating-point unit (FPU)**. However, accelerators can serve many different purposes and sit elsewhere within the architecture. Examples include cryptographic processors for security, motion predictors for MPEG video compression, network packet filters in firewall applications and **neural processing units** and similar inference engines for AI libraries such as Tensorflow [3]. Custom hardware is always much more energy efficient than general-purpose processors. Thus, frequently used algorithms should be implemented in silicon. Nine reasons why this is better are:

1. Pollack's rule states that energy use in a von Neumann core grows with the square of its IPC (Section 2.1.1). However, a custom accelerator, using a static schedule, moves the out-of-order overheads to compile time. Hence, closer to linear growth is achievable.

2. Von Neumann SIMD vector extensions (Section 2.1.2) greatly amortise the fetch and decode energy, but a custom accelerator does better. Spatio-parallel processing uses less energy than equivalent temporal processing (i.e. at higher clock rates) due to V^2 power scaling (Section 4.6.8).

3. Paths, registers and FUs can have appropriate widths rather than being rounded up to general word sizes.

4. A dedicated data path will not have unnecessary additional components in its route, such as unused multiplexors, that just slow it down.

5. Operator fusion: For instance, a custom accelerator can implement a fused accumulate rather than renormalising after each summation (Section 6.8.1).

6. A custom accelerator with combinational logic uses zero energy recomputing sub-expressions whose support has not changed. Moreover, it has no overhead when determining whether the support (input values) has changed.

7. A custom accelerator has zero instruction fetch and decode energy. Any controlling microsequencer or predication control uses close to zero energy.

8. Data locality can easily be exploited on a custom accelerator. The operands are held closer to FUs, giving **near-data processing (NDP)**.

9. Asymptotic limit studies indicate that custom accelerators have potential for massively parallel processing [4].

The performance of von Neumann cores is easily surpassed with custom hardware, especially for algorithms with data-dependent control flow that has only localised effects. The computer, as originally designed by Babbage as a 'universal machine', suffers considerable overhead from being fully programmable. This is sometimes called the **Turing tax**. The dynamic scheduling of today's advanced out-of-order cores is up to two orders of magnitude less energy efficient than custom hardware [5, 6]. For example, when performing 32-bit addition on an out-of-order core, up to one hundred times the energy of the addition is consumed in deciding whether to do it, selecting the operands and storing the result in a temporary register. Super-scalar cores achieve an effective IPC of three on average, at best. SIMD extensions (Section 2.1.2) can give another factor of three or four when appropriate, but parallel hardware is limited only by its power supply, heat extraction and off-chip data bandwidth.

6.4.1 Accelerator Communication

SoC interconnects were the subject of Chapter 3. A mainstream SoC interconnect essentially supports data movement between cores and main memory for load/store and instructions via caches. A SoC uses two forms of PIO:

- **Port-mapped I/O (PMIO)** uses a special address space outside of normal memory that is accessed with instructions such as `in` and `out`.

- **Memory-mapped I/O (MMIO)** relies on I/O devices being allocated addresses inside the normal von Neumann address space, which is primarily used for programs and data. Such I/O is done using instructions such as `load` and `store`.

PMIO was very useful on A16 microprocessors since valuable address space was not consumed by the I/O devices, but A32 architectures generally provide no PMIO instructions and hence, use MMIO. The distinction is irrelevant these days, but mentioned for completeness. However, accelerators can be connected to CPU cores in other ways, outside of mainstream MMIO, PMIO and DMA.

As defined above, hardware accelerators improve the performance of code nominally running on a general-purpose CPU core. When externally accelerated, this core becomes known as the **host processor**, although it may be relegated to just running management functions. Communication paradigms between the host and the accelerator vary according to their degree of decoupling. The principal paradigms are:

1. Extend the CPU with a **custom data path** and custom ALU, as shown in Figure 6.10(a). The new facility is accessed using a **custom ISA extension**, which is a new instruction in the **instruction set architecture (ISA)** (Section 2.1.1 and Section 2.1.3). This does not provide any parallelism but is appropriate for operations that can be completed in the time for a single instruction (e.g. two or three clock cycles in a pipelined core), such as the specialised arithmetic for a **cyclic redundancy check (CRC)**.

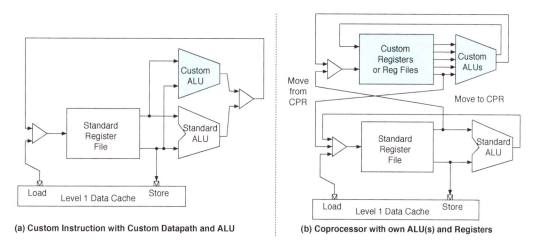

(a) Custom Instruction with Custom Datapath and ALU   **(b) Coprocessor with own ALU(s) and Registers**

Figure 6.10 A custom ALU inside a CPU core implemented in two similar ways: (a) as a custom instruction or (b) as a coprocessor

2. Add a tightly coupled **custom coprocessor**, as shown in Figure 6.10(b). This has fast data paths for load/store operands from and to the main CPU. The main CPU still generates the address values for load/store operations. This is a typical structure of a FPU. Such a coprocessor has its own register file and can perform some operations, like computing cosines and logarithms, without intervention from the core.

3. An accelerator or high-performance peripheral can request instant attention from the main CPU using a **fast interrupt (FIQ)**. Such an interrupt has a dedicated register file, so no context save and restore are needed, and the operating system will return from a fast interrupt without invoking the scheduler. Such an interrupt does not normally change the readiness of processes to run, but when it does, it can change a scheduler flag (semaphore/mutex etc.) and force an early end of the slice so that the scheduler is invoked.

4. More advanced dedicated inter-core wiring is used in some architectures. Some Arm cores support fast signalling between cores with the special signal event (SEV) and wait-for event (WFE) instructions. Again, these are faster to use than **inter-core interrupts (ICIs)** sent through a generic interrupt controller (GIC) (Section 2.5).

Devices inspired by the Transputer [7] integrate synchronisation and message-passing primitives into the instruction set. This supports low-overhead **remote procedure calls** between cores. Figure 6.11 shows fast access to a specialised NoC that enables one core to send part of its register file to another core. The routing could be based on which cores are currently idle using additional signalling nets (not shown). If the receiver's program counter can be set from the message, this provides automatic invocation of a predefined handler.

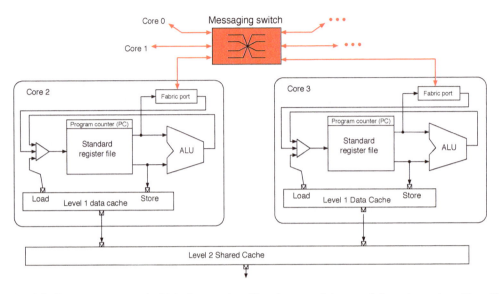

Figure 6.11 A specialised inter-core message-passing fabric allows cores to rapidly exchange a packet composed of several successive registers with each other

5. The accelerator can be connected to the main system bus as a **custom peripheral unit**, as shown in Figure 6.12. Operands are transferred in and out using PIO or pseudo DMA. Under **pseudo DMA** (Section 3.1), the host processor generates memory addresses or network traffic and the accelerator simply snoops or interposes on the data stream.

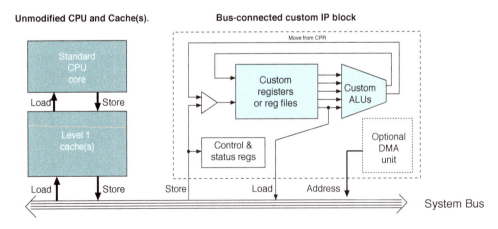

Figure 6.12 A custom function implemented as a peripheral IP block, with optional DMA (bus master) capability

6. As paradigm 5, but with the new IP block having bus master capabilities so that it can fetch data itself (DMA), with polled or interrupt-driven synchronisation with the main CPU. A key design

decision is whether such an accelerator operates on virtual or physical addresses and whether it is cache-consistent with the cores. The Xilinx Zynq platform allows accelerators to be configured in either way (Section 6.5).

7. Use an FPGA or bank of FPGAs without a conventional CPU at all. A CPU in a supervisory role is normally a more sensible use of silicon.

6.4.2 Multiple Sub-tasks

Figure 6.13 shows a typical accelerated subsystem that connects to a high-performance data input, such as an AFE (Section 2.7.6). It has several sub-tasks. This subsystem does not require DRAM access for intermediate results. It is managed by a host processor that makes PIO operations (Section 2.7) on a file of status and control registers. The management overhead is typically small and the same processor has the capacity to do many other functions.

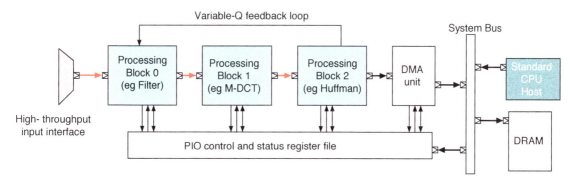

Figure 6.13 Example of a hardware accelerator receiving data from a specialist interface. It uses DMA for data transfer to the main memory. PIO is managed by the host processor

6.4.3 Custom Accelerator Example I

The following code embodies the CRC algorithm used in the Ethernet and many other applications. The generating polynomial is

$$G(x) = x^{32} + x^{26} + x^{23} + x^{22} + x^{16} + x^{12} + x^{11} + x^{10} + x^8 + x^7 + x^5 + x^4 + x^2 + x^1 + 1$$

The code make intensive use of bit-level operations and so does not work efficiently on general-purpose CPU cores.

```
// Generating polynomial:
const uint32_t ethernet_polynomial_le = 0xedb88320U;

// Bit-oriented implementation: processes a byte array
unsigned ether_crc_le(int length, u8_t *data, int resetf)
{
    unsigned int crc = (resetf) ? 0xffffffff: 0;        /* Initial value */
    while(--length >= 0)
      {
```

```
    unsigned char current_octet = *data++;
    for (int bit = 8; --bit >= 0; current_octet >>= 1) {
      if ((crc ^ current_octet) & 1) {
        crc >>= 1;
        crc ^= ethernet_polynomial_le;
      } else
        crc >>= 1;
    }
  }
  return crc;
}
```

The code is structured to take 8 bits at a time and uses one iteration of the inner loop per input bit. Many other implementations are possible. For instance, by using two identical 256-word ROMs with 32-bit words, 8 bits can be processed in one clock cycle using the code:

```
unsigned char c = crc >> 24;
crc = (crc << 8) ^ crc32_rom[*data++] ^ crc32_rom[c];
```

A single ROM cannot be used since it must be consulted in two places per clock cycle. A 16-bit implementation would give twice the throughput but requires ROMs that are 256× larger. A 32-bit version following that scheme would require infeasibly large ROMs. The function can instead be implemented with XOR gates. The expected number of gates for a 32-bit input, 32-bit output random XOR function is $32^2/2 = 512$ with a critical path of 5 two-input gates. However, the number required in reality is about 452 and the critical path can be reduced with higher fan-in XORs [8].

The best position for such an accelerator is close to where the data are already moving. This is a common design pattern and is known as a bump-in-wire accelerator (Section 6.4.4). Hence, for data that are being handled by a core and are in its register file or data path, this is best implemented as a **custom ISA extension** using a new instruction (Section 6.4.1). An additional register file or decoupled operation, as in a coprocessor, is not appropriate for a 32-bit CRC, but would be useful for a more complex function.

Related design decisions arise when accelerating Advanced Encryption Standard (AES) [9] and various secure hashes, such as SHA (Section 9.1.1). Like CRC, these apply many XOR gates to streaming data while updating a small amount of additional state held in accumulating registers. AES operates in 10 to 14 rounds, which must be performed on a data block of 16 bytes in succession. The encryption key, once loaded, is expanded using a simple ancillary algorithm to give a different 128-bit number for each round. Additional storage can be usefully provided to hold the expanded key, but the nature of this needs to be considered when virtualising (Section 4.9), such as whether it needs to be saved and restored over operating system context swaps.

The main consideration for a AES coprocessor is whether to sequence the rounds using program control by the main core or whether the coprocessor proceeds asynchronously using its own sequencer. Any increase in the interrupt latency or the possibility of a mid-block data cache miss or TLB miss are also significant considerations. For AES, the sequencer runtime is likely to be comparable in cycles to TLB miss processing etc., so would not significantly increase latency if made uninterruptible. Moreover, it does not access memory during operation, assuming the expanded key is held in registers, so the duration is not extended by cache misses. However, most major architectures, including Arm and Intel, sequence the rounds using the main core.

6.4.4 FPGA Acceleration in the Cloud

Historically, many hardware accelerator projects have ultimately been unsuccessful for one of these reasons:

- The hardware development takes too long and general-purpose CPUs meanwhile make progress and overtake them (their development teams are vastly more resourced).

- The overhead of copying the data in and out of the accelerator exceeds the processing speedup.

- The hardware implementation is out of date, such as when the requirements or a protocol standard is changed.

A **field-programmable gate array (FPGA)** is a semiconductor device that is rapidly programmable to take on the role of an ASIC. FPGAs are discussed in detail in Section 8.5.2. They dominate the recent history of reconfigurable computing and have successfully displaced fetch-execute operations for a variety of tasks, especially those with a low-complexity control flow (i.e. those with a simple flow chart). The FPGAs used have a fine-grained reconfigurable structure due to their heritage in hardware circuits. There is an argument for having wider busses as the lowest programmable feature. Likewise, having simple ALU slices instead of lookup tables (LUTs) is common. These changes amortise the programming overhead to some extent. The result is called a **coarse-grained reconfigurable array**.

Today, FPGAs are available as a resource in several cloud compute environments, currently based on everyday fine-grained FPGA. However, we expect that specialised devices will be produced for the cloud. These may be coarser grained, may have less esoteric I/O support and may be adapted to simplify time sharing and virtualisation. Cloud environments use large devices. Until fairly recently, FPGAs have not had hardened DRAM controllers, and consequently, they have been short of DRAM bandwidth. However, the devices used in cloud acceleration have two or more DRAM channels.

By connecting FPGA accelerators where the data are moving already, the overhead of copying data in and out of the FPGA can often be mitigated. Microsoft have produced several generations of blades for their data centres, and recent versions have placed the FPGA in series with the blade's network connection, thereby enabling copy-free pre- and post-processing of data. For instance, an index hash can be computed for database fields as the data are read in. This is sometimes called a **bump-in-wire accelerator**.

Figure 6.14 illustrates the structure of a server blade with an FPGA. A conventional blade typically has two standard CPUs, each with two DRAM channels. It has an Ethernet NIC that connects to the so-called **top-of-rack Ethernet hub**, which serves many tens of blades. It typically also has an SSD or hard disk for local data storage, or at least for booting and paging. With the FPGA extension, all secondary storage and network traffic is passed through the FPGA. An FPGA is programmed with a backstop that gives the processors transparent access to its resources when the FPGA is not being used.

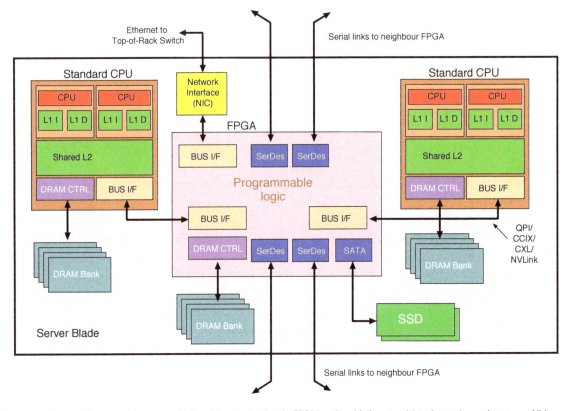

Figure 6.14 Representative bump-in-wire server blade architecture that has the FPGA in series with the network interface and secondary storage (disk drives or SSD)

The other notable feature is a local interconnect between FPGAs using SERDES channels (Section 3.8). A cluster of FPGAs can be joined together with inter-blade wiring. For example, eight blades may be placed in a ring or **hyper-ring**, which is a standard ring, unidirectional or bidirectional, but with a small number of longer distance links (called chords) that decrease the mean diameter and increase the sectional bandwidth. Commonly, all the FPGAs in a cluster use one blade or core as their **host CPU**. The remaining CPUs operate independently, executing unrelated tasks. This is explained by Caulfield et al. in 'A cloud-scale acceleration architecture' [10].

The interconnect standard used between the processors and the FPGA is often coherent [11, 12], such as the Intel **quick path interconnect (QPI)** standard. This replaced the older front-side busses and is cache-consistent. Other protocols used include CCIX, CXL and NVLink (Section 3.8.2).

6.5 Super FPGAs

An FPGA devotes a large area of silicon to programmable components and programmable circuit-switched wiring (Section 8.5.1). Although programmable structures use at least an order of magnitude more silicon than custom VLSI and deliver up to an order of magnitude lower clock frequencies, it is very attractive to combine FPGAs with standard CPU cores, memory and other IP blocks. The high degree of parallelism in the **programmable logic (PL)** mitigates the lower clock frequency whereas the optimisation inherent in the standard parts leads to an acceptable overall silicon budget. The energy used by a board-level interconnect is also avoided with a single-chip approach. Before super FPGAs, it was sometimes a good design point to devote FPGA area to implementing standard processors and IP blocks. This could give a smaller overall **bill of materials (BoM)** for the final product, despite the somewhat extravagant use of silicon. A processor implemented in PL is known as a soft core. If an IP block is new and NRE (Section 8.11) are not warranted, implementing it as an FPGA is the obvious choice.

Recently, a new generation of so-called super FPGAs has emerged. The chips have both a large number of standard IP blocks as well as a large area of PL in FPGA form. A good example is the Zynq range from Xilinx [11]. Figure 6.15 shows the typical block diagram for such a component. All members of the family will have the same **hardened architecture**, which is non-programmable, but the amount of PL available varies from part to part. The PL is at the top of the figure. It connects to the hardened IP blocks using nine AXI bus ports (Section 3.1.5). A number of clock and reset generators as well as interrupt signals can be connected between the two parts.

Significant components of the hardened logic are two Arm A9 processors with a shared L2 cache, the double-data-rate (DDR) DRAM controller and an on-chip SRAM scratchpad memory of 256 kbytes (Section 2.3). Rather than using a NoC, the device has several bus switching elements. These mostly have three or four inputs and three or four outputs. The DRAM controller has four target ports and operates out-of-order using a small local cache and write buffer, as per Section 2.6.6.

Not shown on the figure are the numerous I/O pads. These are mostly multifunctional, with a pin having three to five different programmable uses. As well as being usable for multistandard generic input and output to the PL (i.e. with different logic levels, drive strengths and slew rates), the pins can be routed to specific hardened IP blocks. As well as DRAM, these include many of the standard blocks described in Section 2.7, such as Ethernet, UART, USB and others. These IP blocks are all transaction targets, but many are also initiators. They are represented on Figure 6.15 as the I/O peripheral block (IOP) at centre right.

The multiple AXI ports between the hardened logic and PL are of three different types. The four left-hand ports give high throughput access to the DRAM and scratchpad. They can be 32 or 64 bits wide. The four right-hand ports are primarily for PIO. These allow software on the Arm cores to target register files implemented in the PL. The reverse direction allows soft cores and other controllers, implemented in the PL, to perform PIO on the hardened peripherals.

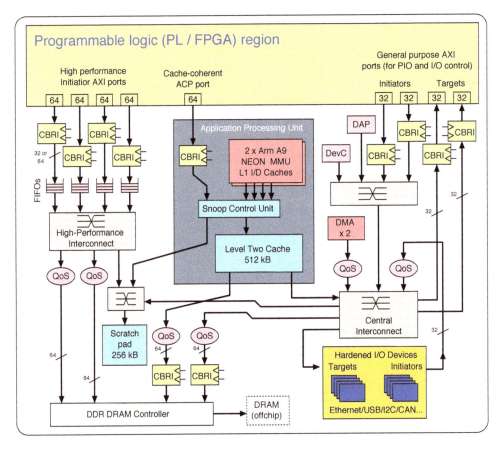

Figure 6.15 Simplified block diagram of a super FPGA, like the Xilinx Zynq devices

The device operates with a global, flat address space that covers all peripherals and memory. The central AXI port allows the PL to initiate transactions on the whole space. Moreover, these transactions are cache-coherent with the shared L2 cache (which is physically mapped, of course). Although limited bandwidth is available through this single AXI port, compared with the four on the left, the lack of a need for software-enforced consistency can be beneficial for some applications, such as anything that does a considerable amount of fine-grained random access to data structures that are simultaneously being accessed by the Arm cores.

Key parameters for recent Zynq parts are given in Table 6.4. Logic is primarily implemented in the LUTs. The equivalent number of two-input gates for each LUT varies according to the design, but can be around 15. These parts support a larger number of gigabit transceivers (Section 3.8), Ethernet ports and CCIX off-chip cache-coherent interconnects (Section 3.8.2). Two or four SERDES ports can be paralleled to form a higher-bandwidth logical port using the hardware support in the **Interlaken protocol**.

Table 6.4 Key parameters for a range of super-FPGA parts available from Xilinx in 2018

Device name	VU31P	VU33P	VU35P	VU37P	VU11P	VU13P
System logic cells (k)	962	962	1907	2852	2835	3780
CLB flip-flops (k)	879	879	1743	2607	2592	3456
CLB LUTs (k)	440	440	872	1304	1296	1728
Maximum distributed RAM (Mb)	12.5	12.5	24.6	36.7	36.2	48.3
Total block RAM (Mb)	23.6	23.6	47.3	70.9	70.9	94.5
Ultra RAM (Mb)	90.0	90.0	180.0	270.0	270.0	360.0
HBM DRAM (GB)	4	8	8	8	–	–
Clock management tiles	4	4	5	3	6	4
DSP slices	2880	2880	5952	9024	9216	12 288
PCIe ports	4	4	5	6	3	4
CCIX ports	4	4	4	4	–	–
150G Interlaken	0	0	2	4	6	8
100G Ethernet with RS-FEC	2	2	5	8	9	12
Maximum single-ended I/O	208	208	416	624	624	832
Multi-standard Gbps SERDES	32	32	64	96	96	128

6.6 Asymptotic Analysis

In this section, we present four analytic studies that justify abstract design decisions based on relatively crude assumptions about their effects. Asymptotic analysis is a widely used sanity check for a theory or formula. It is also known as 'taking it to the limit'. An **asymptotic analysis** considers the behaviour of a model when its parameters are taken to extreme values. Such values are commonly well outside the design space of a sensible or even feasible product, but the procedure gives insight into the structure of the design problem and the accuracy of the model. For instance, if the capacity of a cache is set to zero or to the size of main memory, then a model or formula should report its capacity miss ratio as one or zero at these extremes, respectively. This result arises regardless of implementation technology or fabrication process.

A model that gives inaccurate results in numerical terms can still be very useful for DSE, provided it has the correct **partial derivative polarity**. For instance, a model might be parametrised with double the correct activation energy for a DRAM row. In basic terms, if changing a design parameter makes some things better and other things worse, the model is still useful for exploration provided it correctly distinguishes between metrics that are improving and those that are deteriorating. The power and energy reported by a model with twice the activation energy would be out according to how often the DRAM traffic crosses pages, but these could still reflect the complex shape of the merit surfaces and indicate the presence of sweet spots and false maxima.

Although this section uses equations and spreadsheets to evaluate composite system behaviour, it should be emphasised that the same elemental formulae can be embedded in ESL models of system components. The composite behaviour is then represented by the ESL model as a whole and automatically recomputed when tests are run on different ESL architectures.

In the following sections, we present four examples with non-linear effects:

1. Using a memory hierarchy: Instead of an enormous fast cache, there is a fast L1 and a large L2 to get the same hit rate at almost the same latency but with far less energy use (Section 6.6.1).

2. Using multiple cores when you can: A high-performance core (Intel Nehalem style) consumes far more power than a set of simple cores with similar total throughput (Section 6.6.2).

3. Using a multi-access NoC instead of a switched NoC that has spatial reuse (Section 6.6.3).

4. Using more static power at the expense of being able to run a task at a higher clock rate (Section 6.6.4).

6.6.1 Illustration 1: Hierarchical Cache

For a given CMOS technology, it is possible to design circuits with different trade-offs of delay and energy use. By varying the transistor size and doping, this is possible even for a single supply voltage. Hence, a cache with a given silicon area can have a small capacity and fast response times or a large capacity and slower responses. (Reliability and the use of ECC is another potential dimension but not explored here.) Two points in a fictional design space are called L1 and L2. These differ by 10 to 1 in access times and area (although 3 or 4 to 1 may be all that is possible in many technologies). Their respective performance is tabulated in Table 6.5 using arbitrary units for area and energy. The access time reciprocally decreases with the square root of capacity on the assumption that the bit-line capacitance is the dominant factor whereas the energy of access is just proportional to capacity. Clearly, the ratio between these two power laws could be adjusted in a further exploration, but this is a reasonable starting point. A formula that models the hit ratio for a given cache size must pass through the origin and asymptotically approach 100 per cent. Any formula with broadly the correct shape and intercepts can be used. The spreadsheet used $s/(512+s)$ but could equally have used $1 - \exp(-s/512)$ to illustrate the same point.

It is now possible to show that having two caches with different speed/power ratios is a good design point. Table 6.6 tabulates 4 two-level caches that use L1 technology backed by L2 technology. The most obvious distinction between having one or two caches is clear from the bottom line of each table. For the largest cache considered, the energy for L1 alone is roughly 10 times that for L2 alone, but for L2 alone, the average access times is 10 times higher. For a composite design, where an L1 of size 4096 is prefixed onto the front side of the largest L2, the average access time drops until it is only slightly worse than if the whole cache were made of L1 technology. However, the energy used by the combination is vastly lower. This was based on the L2 having zero leakage, so its power use decreased in direct proportion to its access rate. However, even if 30 per cent of its energy use is static power, the bottom-line energy would increase by only 150 units, with the total still remaining less than the 262 arising from making the whole cache from the low-power L2 technology. Although not shown here, we could also explore a higher density for L2 in a similar framework.

Table 6.5 Basic parameters for two caches with different speed/power ratios but the same technology and bit density, versus cache size

Cache Size	L1					L2				
	Energy	Area	Hit rate	Access time	Mean time	Energy	Area	Hit rate	Access time	Mean time
1	0.01	0.001	0.002	0.0	200	0.001	0.001	0.002	0.1	200
2	0.02	0.002	0.004	0.0	199	0.002	0.002	0.004	0.1	199
4	0.04	0.004	0.008	0.0	198	0.004	0.004	0.008	0.2	198
8	0.08	0.008	0.015	0.0	197	0.008	0.008	0.015	0.3	197
16	0.16	0.016	0.030	0.0	194	0.016	0.016	0.030	0.4	194
32	0.32	0.032	0.059	0.1	188	0.032	0.032	0.059	0.6	188
64	0.64	0.064	0.111	0.1	178	0.064	0.064	0.111	0.8	178
128	1.28	0.128	0.200	0.1	160	0.128	0.128	0.200	1.1	160
256	2.56	0.256	0.333	0.2	133	0.256	0.256	0.333	1.6	134
512	5.12	0.512	0.500	0.2	100	0.512	0.512	0.500	2.3	101
1024	10.24	1.024	0.667	0.3	67	1.024	1.024	0.667	3.2	69
2048	20.48	2.048	0.800	0.5	40	2.048	2.048	0.800	4.5	44
4096	40.96	4.096	0.889	0.6	23	4.096	4.096	0.889	6.4	28
8192	81.92	8.192	0.941	0.9	13	8.192	8.192	0.941	9.1	20
16 384	163.84	16.384	0.970	1.3	7	16.384	16.384	0.970	12.8	18
32 768	327.68	32.768	0.985	1.8	5	32.768	32.768	0.985	18.1	21
65 536	655.36	65.536	0.992	2.6	4	65.536	65.536	0.992	25.6	27
131 072	1310.72	131.072	0.996	3.6	4	131.072	131.072	0.996	36.2	37
262 144	2621.44	262.144	0.998	5.1	5	262.144	262.144	0.998	51.2	51

Table 6.6 Some composite design examples

L1 size	L2 size	L2 energy	Composite energy	Composite area	Composite mean time
64	262 144	233.0	233.6	262.2	45.8
128	262 144	209.7	211.0	262.3	41.2
1024	262 144	87.4	97.6	263.2	17.4
4096	262 144	29.1	70.1	266.2	6.3

6.6.2 Illustration 2: big.LITTLE

Using smaller circuitry is the best way to improve the performance of a computer. However, for a given geometry, performance can be increased in three orthogonal ways: increasing the IPC of individual cores (i.e. increasing their complexity, c), clocking faster (i.e. increasing the DVFS voltage, v) or using more cores, n. Approximate power laws for performance and power are summarised in Table 6.7. Pollack's rule (Section 2.1.1) suggests that performance increases with the square root of complexity. With voltage scaling (Section 4.6.8), there is a cubic growth of power when the clock frequency is increased in proportion to the voltage (although the energy use for a fixed-size task grows only quadratically). Simply having more cores generally results in a sub-linear improvement due to inter-core communication overheads, so 0.9 is used for the exponent here. The bottom line of the table considers the power/performance ratio and shows that the throughput can be doubled for the smallest increase in power by altering the third parameter – the number of cores.

The big.LITTLE architecture from Arm was motivated by Pollack's rule. Most computer systems have bursty application loads. Halting the cores saves dynamic energy whereas clock gating reduces the clock tree energy while halted. New work interrupts the processor, which takes it out of the halt state. However, static power use is proportional to the complexity of the core, as is dynamic energy use by

Table 6.7 Power laws for performance delivered and power used in terms of three independent parameters

Metric	Core complexity (c)	DVFS voltage (v)	Number of cores (n)
Performance delivered	$c^{0.5}$	$v^{1.0}$	$n^{0.9}$
Power used	$c^{1.0}$	$v^{3.0}$	$n^{1.0}$
Increase in power for double performance	4	8	2.16

ungated portions of the system. Hence, having a complex core that spends a long time halted uses more energy than running the same work on a simple core that spends proportionately less time halted. The big.LITTLE technology makes it easy to shift work between cores of different sizes as the measured load varies [13].

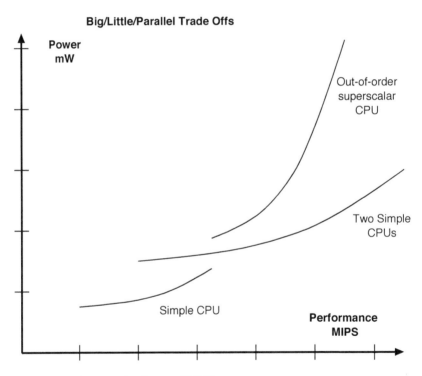

Figure 6.16 Relative performance of simple and complex CPU cores with DVFS

Figure 6.16 illustrates three systems that vary in power and performance. Each system traces a line as the supply voltage is varied. Importantly, having two smaller CPUs is clearly the best of the three designs. Moreover, one of the two cores could be switched off entirely to encompass the single simple CPU.

This shows it is better to write a parallel program if you can and then use multiple simple cores. However, exploiting two cores in parallel is possible only with certain workloads. Three forms of parallel speedup are well known from classical imperative parallel programming:

- **Task-level parallelism**: Partition the input data over nodes and run the same program on each node. If there is no inter-node communication, this is called an **embarrassingly parallel problem**, since there is no excuse for sub-linear performance scaling.

- **Programmer-defined thread-level parallelism**: The programmer uses constructs such as `pthreads`, Cilk or C# `Parallel.for` loops to explicitly denote local regions of concurrent activity that typically communicate using shared variables. SIMD vector instructions are another from of programmer-defined parallelism.

- **Instruction-level parallelism**: The imperative program (or local region of) is converted to data flows. All ALU operations can potentially be run in parallel, but operands remain prerequisites for results and load/store operations on a given mutable object must respect program order. This is the behaviour of a super-scalar core that achieves an IPC of greater than one (Section 2.2).

The multi-core approach is applicable only for the first two approaches. Legacy code with a complex control flow, such as a PDF viewer, can be significantly accelerated only using the third approach. Alternatively, a PDF viewer could be refactored, or perhaps even the file formats amended, to suit parallel programming. For the PDF example, the key step is to establish the page and word layout as soon as possible so that each word, letter or line can be rendered in parallel. However, older code might not be structured so that it can establish where the next letter is to be placed until it has completed rendering the current letter. In the paper 'Brawny cores still beat wimpy cores, most of the time' [14], Hölzle argues that:

> Slower, but energy-efficient 'wimpy' cores only win for general workloads if their single-core speed is reasonably close to that of mid-range 'brawny' cores.

6.6.3 Illustration 3: NoC Topology Trade-off

Figure 3.20 shows a 2-D unidirectional torus NoC composed of radix-3 elements. A related common variant is a bidirectional torus, which requires radix-5 elements and correspondingly greater complexity. A very efficient radix-5 element was designed by IBM in 2014 [15]. Nonetheless, the complexity of either torus is much greater than an equivalent multi-access network. As explained in Section 3.3.1, a **multi-access network** has a shared medium that is forwarded between participants with minimal logic. Broadside registers can be freely inserted for timing closure, but the overall logic cost may be much lower, as explored here.

All network topologies have throughput that is **bisectional**. This means that the average bandwidth between all sources and destinations either side of any partition of the topology is bounded by the bandwidth of the links cut by that line. Figure 6.17 shows several NoC designs that use a multi-access shared medium. A slotted ring and counter-rotating ring have constant bandwidth if cut with a horizontal line. Hence, their throughput can be expected to degrade reciprocally in proportion to the number of end points connected. Although this is, indeed, the case for rings, if there is a mix of local and global traffic, the sectional bandwidth may be less important.

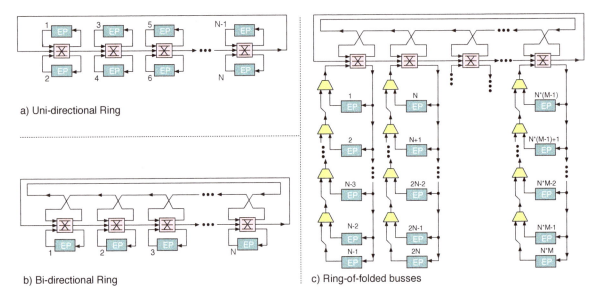

a) Uni-directional Ring

b) Bi-directional Ring

c) Ring-of-folded busses

Figure 6.17 Three multi-access NoC topologies

A slotted ring of folded busses can exploit traffic locality if flows between stations on the same bus do not need to use the ring. The ring can be bidirectional, as shown, or unidirectional. The arcs of the ring typically use wider busses than are used for folded bus links. With appropriately dimensioned VCs on the rings, it is easy to ensure that traffic does not arrive at a folded bus faster than the bus bandwidth. For instance, a ring might use four times the data width of folded busses and four VCs that are directly mapped to the word lanes on the ring.

A folded bus has a significant advantage over a ring because it is possible to stall the transmit half globally while allowing the receive half to continue. For a bus layout, a clock enable net connected to the transmit logic of all stations must be added. For a tree layout, the reverse channel already exists, which means that it is always possible to instantly and losslessly insert a slot at the fold point for a folded bus. In keeping with the multi-access principle, no FIFO structure is required.

On the other hand, and again assuming there is no queue or buffer at the connection point, a bridge between two rings can deadlock, as follows. A slot flit (or phit) can move between rings without additional buffering only if the destination ring has an empty slot at the moment it needs to be read off the source ring. If not, the source ring must be stalled. Since slots move in both directions between the rings, there is a chance that both need to be stalled. No further progress can then be made, resulting in a deadlock. In essence, all four turns are in use (Section 3.4.3). Since both rings at the connection point need to transfer data to the other one, a straightforward slot swap is a possible solution. Neither then needs to stall. However, this works only if the rings have the same word widths, there are no multicasts, there are no bandwidth-limiting VCs and destinations are released for busy slots. Most designs will fail for nearly all of these aspects.

Using a hardware construction language (Section 6.8.3), it is relatively easy to generate multi-access ring, bus and mesh NoC structures and to capture the total gate count used. The resulting throughput using balanced traffic assumptions is readily calculated from the sectional bandwidth formulae. Alternatively, the resulting hardware can be simulated to measure the achieved throughput under various traffic models, such as those with greater amounts of local traffic than remote traffic, based on the assumption that some care was put into the overall layout.

In Figure 6.18, the gate counts and balanced throughput figures for eight designs were captured in a spreadsheet and the effective throughput per clock cycle, per gate input are plotted. The gate input metric was directly measured from the hardware designs. For CMOS combinational gates, it relates to half the transistor count. For D-types, a figure of 12 inputs was used, based on a D-type being equivalent to about six 2-input gates.

All FIFOs modelled could hold up to two 136-bit flits. Being multi-access, the ring and bus designs have no FIFO storage in the network fabric, but a transmit and a receive FIFO were added to each station and included in the gate count. For the torus NoC designs, one FIFO was used per output port of each switching element and there was further arbitration and credit counter overhead as well. But FIFOs were then not included at each ingress and egress port, since the fabric FIFO was deemed sufficient.

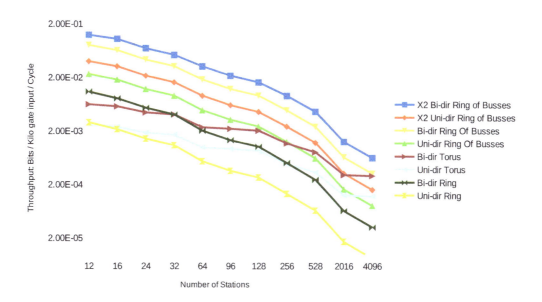

Figure 6.18 Comparison of various multi-access and switched NoC designs in terms of throughput (136 bit words per clock cycle) per gate input as the number of end points (stations) is increased.

The baseline networks modelled are a unidirectional and a bidirectional slotted ring and a unidirectional (radix-3 element) and bidirectional (radix-5 element) torus. The bidirectional rings are designed not to deliver two flits at once to a given destination by using two logical channels, as discussed in Section 3.3.1. Then hybrid networks were modelled where each slotted ring station connects to a number of client stations using a local folded bus, following the pattern on the right of Figure 3.20. A fat ring, with twice the bandwidth (×2) on each link was also included in the study.

As expected, the multi-access networks degrade reciprocally in performance as the number of stations is increased, owing to bandwidth sharing. However, they start off at a much higher throughput per gate input owing to their intrinsic simplicity. The crossover points for several of the different approaches can be seen in the plot. Their precise locations will, of course, depend greatly on many design details.

For the largest configuration plotted, the unidirectional torus has twice the overall bandwidth of the bidirectional fat ring, and the bidirectional torus has eight times more throughput. But the throughput per gate input can be seen not yet to have crossed over with this number of stations (4096). This demonstrates the significant complexity of hop-by-hop flow control, compared with multi-access techniques. For this reason, a recent 4-core chip from IBM uses counter-rotating rings with a bus width of 128 bytes [16]. However, the downside of multi-access is that destinations must always be ready to receive the bandwidth they were provisioned to receive in the network design or else a higher-level transport protocol, using responses, must be relied on. All modern SoC protocols support retry, but their design intent may have been that it would rarely be used.

6.6.4 Illustration 4: Static and Dynamic Power Trade-off

The principles of **dynamic voltage and frequency scaling (DVFS)** were explained in Section 4.6.8 by assuming that all the transistors in a design have the same leakage. For 90-nm technology, the static leakage is low so there is considerable scope for DVFS. With sub-45-nm geometries, performance can be traded off for greater leakage but supply voltages have considerably less freedom and are always about 1 V. Dynamic body bias, available in some technologies, results in further runtime differences (Section 4.6.10) and is another possibility.

With DVFS using low-leakage logic, the energy use is generally lowest by computing slowly at a lower voltage and finishing just in time. However, for sub-45 nm, there is reduced freedom in the choice of voltage. Generally, transistors are turned off less for lower voltages; hence, there is a higher static leakage current. So, with modern geometries, it can now be better to operate quickly within the voltage/frequency band that works and then powering off until next deadline. Low-leakage large but slow transistors are still required for power gating.

It is now possible to fabricate transistors with different speeds using methods other than just altering the channel width. Transistor thresholds can be adjusted by using different doping levels or ion implantation, to produce either low-leakage transistors or fast transistors. The variations can be made globally or in local regions, such as the output cells of a subsystem. If these are mixed on a single chip, the faster transistors are commonly used for critical-path routes (Section 4.4.2). The rest of the logic is then made from low-leakage transistors (Section 4.6.3).

The problem can be formulated using example coefficients to demonstrate the basic trade-off. Design exploration using ESL models gives the coefficients for a specific application and architecture. The R program in Figure 6.19 captures the essence. Two implementation technologies and two levels of parallelism are considered, to give a total of four cases. A simple linear model of frequency versus supply voltage was used, but the more accurate reciprocal formula from Section 4.6.6 could be used instead. The two levels of leakage were selected as being roughly 5 and 30 per cent of the average dynamic energy.

```
# Unfold=1 is the baseline design. Unfold=3 uses three times more silicon.
static_dynamic_tradeoff <- function(clock_freq, leakage, unfold, xx)
{
  op_count <- 2e7;

  # Model: Pollack-like unfold benefit
  execution_time <- op_count / clock_freq / (unfold ^ 0.75);

  # Model: Higher supply needed for higher clock and leakage resistance slightly increasing with Vdd
  vdd <- 1 + 0.5 * (clock_freq/100e6);
  static_power <- leakage * vdd ^ 0.9 * unfold;

  # Integrate static power and energy
  static_energy <- static_power * execution_time;

  # Use CV^2 for dynamic energy
  dynamic_energy <- op_count * vdd ^ 2.0 * 5e-10;
}
```

Figure 6.19 Trading off Aesop's hare versus the tortoise for increasingly leaky technology. In a hard real-time computation, we know the number of clock cycles needed but should we do them quickly and halt (Hare) or do them slowly and finish just in time (Tortoise)?

Figure 6.20 plots the static, dynamic and total energy for the four configurations. Of key significance is the design point with the lowest total energy. For the higher leakage system, this can be seen at a clock frequency of around 200 MHz, with not much dependence on the unfold factor. For the low-leakage technology, the lowest frequencies have the lowest energy use while still being able to meet the deadline.

6.7 Virtual Platform Examples

As mentioned in Section 1.4.3, partitioning a design into hardware and software components is known as **co-design** and if this is performed by an automatic tool, it is known as **co-synthesis**. Co-synthesis is still not mature, so all SoCs are developed using manual co-design. An ESL model (Chapter 5) based on a virtual platform is generally the tool of choice for manual architectural exploration.

6.7.1 The Prazor/Zynq Virtual Platform

Two well-known software simulators are QEMU [17], which is used by the **software development kit (SDK)** for the standard phone model in the Android operating system, and Gem5 [18], which is often used for Arm system modelling. EDA companies sometimes offer proprietary enhancements to these

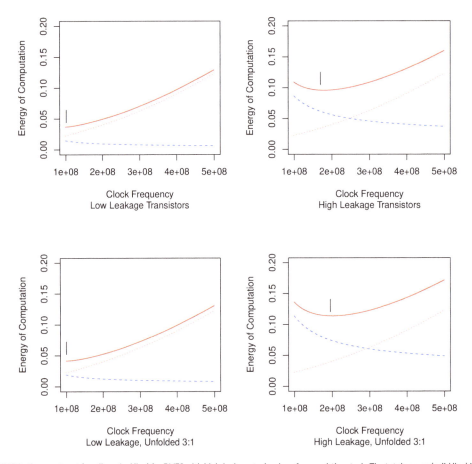

Figure 6.20 Shift in the sweet spot (small vertical line) for DVFS with high-leakage technology for a real-time task. The total energy (solid line) is the sum of the static energy (dashes) and dynamic energy (dots)

public-domain platforms that provide enhanced accuracy, for instance, per-cycle timing or energy use. However, these tools are not set up for interworking with RTL-level SystemC models or RTL simulators.

The Prazor virtual platform (ESL simulator) is implemented using SystemC and supports interworking between RTL-level SystemC and high-level SystemC models using TLM 2.0 sockets. Any mix of heterogeneous cores can be included in the system model. The ISAs provided are x86_64, Arm-32 (including Thumb2), MIPS and OpenRISC-32, but others can be added. Prazor uses the TLM_POWER3 library [19] to generate energy profiles for an overall system.

In the MPEG worked example, we show how to run a C implementation of the compression algorithm on a real and Prazor Arm core to obtain the baseline computational complexity and energy use and then explore accelerations by a variety of hardware accelerators.

6.7.2 Co-design Worked Example: MPEG Video Compression

MPEG compression is typically a **hard real-time problem**. It can be done better offline, if the raw video is in secondary storage, but that use case tends to be reserved as a mastering step in producing feature films. Hard real-time compression has recurring sub-problems, each of which must be solved before a specific deadline. The deadlines could be generated by the system timer in a real-time operating system, but are more likely to be generated by the frame-ready event from a camera.

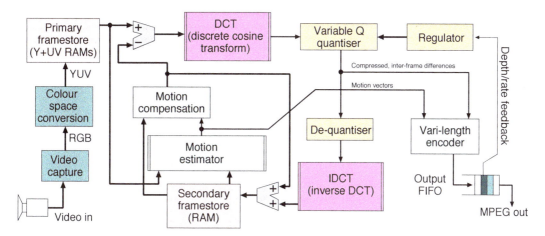

Figure 6.21 Block diagram for an MPEG compression subsystem. The input is a real-time video stream and the outut is an MPEG transport stream (without sound). The DCT, IDCT and motion estimators are highly compute intensive

MPEG compression is implemented on all smartphones. To prevent the phone from getting too hot to hold and to ensure that the battery lifetime is not severely impacted, the compression relies on special coprocessors or separate hardware accelerators. As shown in Figure 6.21, MPEG compression of a live stream involves the following steps:

1. Capturing the real-time video, frame by frame, in a RAM frame store in YUV format. The luminance (Y) and chrominance (U and V) are then processed separately as parallel streams.

2. Applying the **discrete cosine transform (DCT)** to each channel.

3. Quantising the DCT values. The least significant bits are removed, giving rise to a large number of zero values. The division ratio is controlled by a regulator using negative feedback based on the current data output rate.

4. Variable-length encoding of the resulting stream. The zeros produced by the quantiser are represented concisely.

5. Regenerating the compressed image in a secondary frame store by de-quantising the transmitted data and applying IDCT.

6. Computing motion vectors by comparing blocks in the primary and secondary frame stores that are largely similar, but perhaps displaced by a few pixels.

7. Subtracting the identified moving patches from the primary frame store output so that these zones contain just a few residual variations. This compresses much better in the DCT. Hence, mainly the inter-frame differences and post-motion compensation are compressed. Every *n*th frame is a so-called **key frame**, which is compressed in isolation to allow a recovery from transmission errors.

For a battery-operated device, which of these tasks should be done in hardware and which in software?

A mobile phone can have an internal USB bus with the camera device connected to the main SoC via USB. This is a standard IP block and no bespoke hardware is then required. This opens the potential for a fully software implementation. However, only the forward-facing low-quality camera is likely to be connected by USB. The most common camera interface is a bespoke parallel 8-bit bus operating at 10 to 40 MB of data per second. This can be connected only to special hardware. A camera typically generates alternating chrominance and luminescence bytes, rather than RGB, so the bulk of the colour-space conversion occurs inside the camera. A matrix multiply on the chrominance channels produces a rotation as the final tint correction. Although the whole task is classed as hard real time, the camera interface is especially so, with bursty asynchronous data occurring only after quantisation. Given that bespoke hardware is required for the hardware interface, it is a small additional overhead to implement a complex multiplication in hardware before storing the data in the frame store.

The primary frame store needs to be accessed in raster scan order when writing and 8 × 8 tile order when reading. Storing eight lines could potentially be sufficient if motion estimation was not needed (e.g. for the motion JPEG or **audio video interleave (AVI)** formats). A more reasonable design is to store two whole frames, using double buffering, with one being read while the other is loaded. For motion estimation, we require a third copy for comparing the motion vectors.

Next, the amount of processing power needed for each of the remaining steps is estimated. Profiling a software functional model (Section 6.2.2) rapidly identifies the tasks that require the most effort. It is worthwhile targeting these with hardware acceleration. The DCT, IDCT and motion prediction blocks are the largest consumers of ALU operations. The variable-length encoding unit can also be implemented in hardware, since it is comparatively easy to do so, though it does not fit well on a general-purpose CPU.

The discrete cosine transform (DCT) performs a 2-D Fourier transform on a tile of pixels from the image, giving the mean intensity and coefficients for various horizontal and vertical frequencies. In JPEG compression, many of these frequencies have very little energy, so that it can be replaced by zero without subjectively degrading picture quality. However, MPEG also exploits inter-frame correlations.

```csharp
//Output bit-to-byte buffer
void putbits(uint val, uint no_of_bits)
{
  buffer |= val << (int)no_of_bits;
  buffer_bits += no_of_bits;
  while (buffer_bits >= 8)
  { yield_byte((byte)(buffer & 0xFF));
    buffer_bits -= 8;
    buffer_bits >>= 8;
  }
}

// Send a DC component
void putDC(sVLCtable [] tab, int val)
{
  uint absval, size;
  absval = (uint) Math.Abs(val);
  /* Compute dct_dc_size */
  size = 0;
  while (absval!=0)
  { absval >>= 1;
    size ++;
  }
  // Generate VLC for dct_dc_size (B-12 or B-13)
  putbits(tab[size].code, tab[size].len);
  // Append fixed-length code (dc_dct_differential)
  if (size!=0) // Send val + (2 ^ size) - 1
  { if (val>=0) absval = (uint)val;
    else absval = (uint)(val + (1 << (int)size) - 1);
    putbits(absval, size);
  }
}

void putDClum(int val)
{
  putDC(DClumtab, val);
}

void putDCchrom(int val)
{
  putDC(DCchromtab, val);
}

void putAC(int run, int signed_level, int vlcformat)
{
    // ...
}
```

```csharp
/* Generate variable-length codes for an intra-coded
   block (6.2.6, 6.3.17) */
void putintrablk(Picture picture, short [] blk, int cc)
{
  /* DC Difference from previous block (7.2.1) */
  int dct_diff = blk[0] - picture.dc_dct_pred[cc];
  picture.dc_dct_pred[cc] = blk[0];

  if (cc==0) putDClum(dct_diff);
  else putDCchrom(dct_diff);

  /* AC coefficients (7.2.2) */
  int run = 0;
  byte [] scan_tbl = (picture.altscan ? alternate_scan:
                      zig_zag_scan);
  for (int n=1; n<64; n++)
  { // Use appropriate entropy scanning pattern
    int signed_level = blk[scan_tbl[n]];
    if (signed_level!=0)
    {
      putAC(run, signed_level, picture.intravlc);
      run = 0;
    }
    else run++; /* count zero coefficients */
  }

  /* End of Block -- normative block punctuation */
  if (picture.intravlc!=0) putbits(6,4); // 0110 (B-15)
    else putbits(2,2); // 10 (B-14)
}

// Return difference between two (8*h) sub-sampled
//          blocks
// blk1, blk2: addresses of top left pels of both blocks
// rowstride:  distance (in bytes) of vertically
//          adjacent pels
// h:          height of block (usually 8 or 16)
int sumsq_sub22(byte [] blk1, byte [] blk2,
      int rowstride, int h)
{
  int ss = 0, p1 = 0, p2 = 0;
  for (int j=0; j<h; j++)
  {
    for (int i=0; i<8; i++)
    { int v = blk1[p1+i] - blk2[p2+i];
      ss += v*v;
    }
    p1+= rowstride; p2+= rowstride;
  }
  return ss;
}
```

Figure 6.22 Code fragments for an MPEG encoder, coded in C# for Kiwi HLS. The putintrablk routine takes the 64 values from the quantised DCT and transmits them using the variable-length coding and with a run-length encoding of zero values in the routines it calls. The sumsq_sub22 function is one of many used during motion estimation to compute differences between macro blocks

An MPEG compressor must search for regions in the current frame that can be modelled as regions shifted from the previous frame. Searching for shifts much greater than 10 pixels is generally not useful, but even just computing all possible correlations within an X and Y region of ± 10 pixels would require $20^2 = 400$ comparisons. Each comparison needs to operate on a block of several hundred pixels to determine similarity, so naive searching is infeasible. Hence, the so-called **block-matching algorithm** used for motion estimation has to be designed with care. An exhaustive rectangular search is not used in practice. Instead, successive 2-D approximation techniques are used. For instance, all eight compass points can be explored with an offset of 16 pixels and the neighbours of the best of those are then explored with an offset of eight pixels, and so on. Also, only the luminance channel needs to be examined for motion, since the colour channels will experience the same movement. A popular implementation was **optimised hierarchical block matching** [20]. However, various other techniques can be used (e.g. diamond search patterns and those based on nearby motion vectors). A further saving is typically achieved in the earlier parts of the search by operating on subsampled images. These have been reduced by 2-to-1 in each direction, thereby reducing the work by a factor of four.

Figure 6.22 shows various fragments of MPEG encoder code, adapted from the source code for the GNU Avidemux editor. These can be run as regular software on an embedded processor or converted to hardware using HLS (Section 6.9). Additionally, the CPU-intensive primitives used in motion estimation are commonly coded in assembler and use SIMD extensions (Section 2.1.2), if available. The different individual subsystems can each be implemented in various ways, so there is a large potential design space.

In common with many compression techniques, both lossy and lossless, decompression is much simpler than compression, as it is simply a matter of following instructions generated by the compressor and does not require expensive correlation search operations. The output from many compression algorithms can be decoded by the same decompressor.

Many architectures and implementations for MPEG and MP4 compression have been published, with [21] notably providing a detailed discussion of energy and cycle use, but see also [22, 23].

6.8 Design-entry Languages

As well as low-level coding in RTL and SystemC, higher-level design-entry systems are increasingly being used. These are especially useful when complex algorithms must be implemented in hardware accelerators. Graphical tools that support high-level structural design and automatically generate interconnects are commonly used. These tend to be based on IP-XACT and are discussed in Section 6.8.2. The currently popular textual languages are Chisel (Section 6.8.3) and Bluespec (Section 6.8.5). Both of these require the designer to understand clock cycles. One difference is that Bluespec can automatically allocate work to clock cycles, whereas this is manual in Chisel, like RTL. With HLS (Section 6.9), clocking need not appear in the design language, although better quality designs require the designer to have some understanding of hardware mapping.

Verilog and VHDL focus more on simulation than logic synthesis. The rules for translation to hardware that define the synthesisable subset were standardised after the languages had been defined. These languages are verbose when expressing module structure. Manually connecting an AXI bus to a component requires tens of lines of code. Many of these lines contain details that can easily be generated by a macro in a higher-level language. RTL is precise: the number of state variables, the size of registers and the width of busses are all explicit.

Perhaps the major shortcoming of conventional RTL is that the language gives the designer no help with concurrency. That is, the designer must keep track of all aspects of handshaking between logic circuits and shared reading of register resources. This is ironic since hardware systems have much greater parallelism than software systems. An RTL model cannot express whether a register has a live value in it or is idle. The assignment of an X to a register is ignored during synthesis when the register is read. Compiler optimisation is limited to minimising the combinational logic, since sequential logic minimisation and state re-encoding are not allowed.

Higher-level designs should have few redundant expressions and should be amenable to substantial automatic DSE by the compiler flow. Advanced compilers can generate **data paths** and **schedules**, including re-encoding and repipelining to meet timing closure and power budgets (Section 4.4.2). A design where the language expresses which registers contain live data can be more freely folded in time, by the compiler, to generate different designs, for instance using more silicon and fewer clock cycles.

Verilog and VHDL have enabled vast ASICs to be designed by hand, so in that sense they are successful. However, better languages are needed to meet the following EDA aims:

- To speed up design processes and reduce the time to market.

- To understand pipelined RAMs and ALUs.

- To allow richer behavioural specifications.

- To readily allow time/space folding experiments.

- To give the compiler greater freedom and hence, more scope for optimisation.

- To facilitate the implementation of a formal specification.

- To facilitate proof of conformance to a specification.

- To allow rule-based programming (i.e. a logic-programming sublanguage).

- To allow seamless integration with bus standards.

- To be aware of clock and power domains and able to deploy domain-crossing mechanisms or at least flag designs that wantonly cross domain boundaries.

- To compile into software as well as into hardware.

Higher-level tools normally output RTL, so that RTL behaves like an assembly language for digital hardware. A **hardware construction language (HCL)** (Section 6.8.3) does nothing other than print out a netlist. It is a low-level language whose main purpose is to alleviate the tedious manual entry of regular netlists for complex busses that traverse multiple levels of design hierarchy. Other than HCLs and similar elaboration techniques, the primary higher-level design styles with data-dependent control flow can be divided into either:

- **Behavioural**: These use imperative software-like code. Threads have stacks, pass between modules and make subroutine calls on user-defined and primitive methods.

- **Declarative, functional and logical**: These have constraining assertions about the allowable behaviour, but any ordering constraints are implicit (e.g. SQL queries) rather than being based on program counters. A **declarative program** can be defined as an unordered list of definitions, rules or assertions that simultaneously hold at all times.

Designing is undoubtedly easier with a higher-level design language in which a serial thread of execution works on various modules than the forced parallelism of expressions found in RTL-style coding. Ideally, a new thread should be introduced only when there is a need for concurrent behaviour in the design. However, the semantics of an imperative language need to be expressed declaratively when proving the correctness of a design and the same constructions can, to a large extent, be used to convert one form of design expression into the other. Hence, a good entry language should allow an arbitrary mix of design styles. The tool can hide these conversions from the user. For safety-critical applications, a declarative style normally enables the safety rules to be directly expressed in the language, which is an advantage. Using declarative expressions normally gives the compiler much greater freedom for design optimisation. However, all advanced tools have a history of being difficult to use, so adoption is slow. Two particular problems are:

1. Unexpected changes: Sometimes when an engineer makes one small change to one aspect of a design, this has a massive effect on the rendered RTL, either changing many net names or changing its entire shape. This makes debugging hard.

2. Unexpected size: The art of engineering is creating a design that is cost-effective and performant. Compilers for higher-level design languages, especially early C-to-gates flows (Section 6.9), sometimes unexpectedly generate very large designs, whereas a good tool leaves the engineer fully in charge of the cost/performance trade-off.

A further problem with declarative designs is that RAM is a vital component in all hardware systems and it is intrinsically imperative. So a convert-to-imperative step must exist at some point in the design flow. For long-running applications, memory has to be recyled, which requires explicit memory management or some form of hardware garbage collection [24]. Both automatic parallelisation and memory release can be severely limited if memory array subscripts cannot be distinguished when performing compile-time optimisations. This is the **name alias problem** (Section 6.3.3).

6.8.1 Functional Units

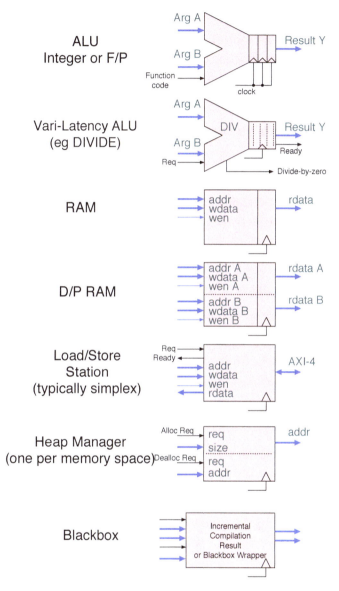

Figure 6.23 Typical examples of FUs deployed by higher-level design languages, especially HLS

Higher-level design-entry languages almost always generate synthesisable RTL (Section 8.3). The RTL has a mix of the operators and gates supported by the back-end logic synthesiser, such as integer addition, and structural component instances known as FUs. A **functional unit (FU)** is a standard component designed to be used in many designs and often instantiated multiple times in a single design, such as those in Figure 6.23. The main examples are integer ALUs, floating-point ALUs and static RAM. A single port on a multi-ported bus fabric, NoC or DRAM controller can also usefully be modelled as an FU. Some FUs are instantiable only once per chip, such as a power controller for global on/off and PSU health monitoring. Application-specific FUs are also possible. These exploit the FU framework to wrap up custom logic and esoteric physical devices, such as ADCs, DACs and SERDESs (Section 3.8).

As well as the specification of the function to be performed by the FU, such as multiplying or adding, a block that performs a function in some number of clock cycles can be characterised using the following metrics:

- **Precision**: This is the word width in bits.

- **Referentially transparent (stateless)**: This Boolean indicates whether the unit always yields the same result for the same arguments. An FU that is stateless is called a **mirrorable FU** and can be replicated as often as desired. Examples are ROMs and ALUs. In contrast, RAM has state and cannot simply be replicated to increase the read or write bandwidth since the replicas will diverge.

- **EIS (an end in itself)**: This Boolean indicates that the FU has unseen side effects, such as being non-volatile or turning on an LED. Such an FU cannot be deleted by logic trimming even if it appears that none of its outputs are used.

- **Fixed or variable latency**: This flag denotes whether the FU has fixed or variable latency. There is also an integer value, which is used for budgeting, that is the precise pipeline delay if fixed or an average if variable.

- **Initiation interval (II)**: This integer gives the minimum number of cycles between operation starts. A unit whose initiation interval is one is said to be **fully pipelined** (Section 6.3).

- **Energy**: This real number indicates the energy per operation. For example, an SRAM might use 5 pJ for each read or write.

- **Gate count or area**: This estimate of the area is used to make physically aware predictions of the floor plan and wiring length. It is typically given in square microns or, for a FPGA, the number of LUTs and DSP blocks.

In today's ASIC and FPGA technology, combinational adds and subtracts of up to 32-bit words are typical. However, RAM reads, multiplies and divides are usually allocated at least one pipeline cycle, with larger multiplies and all divides being two or more. For 64-bit words and for FPUs and RAM larger than L1 (e.g. 32 kbytes), it is common for the latency to be two or more cycles, but with an initiation interval of one.

Functional Unit Chaining

Naively instantiating standard FUs can be wasteful of performance, precision and silicon area. Generally, if the output of one FU is to be fed directly to another, then some optimisation can be made. Many sensible optimisations involve changes to the state encoding or algorithm that are beyond the possibilities of the back-end logic synthesiser. A common example is an associative reduction operator (Section 6.9.1), such as floating-point addition in a scalar product. In that example, we do not wish to denormalise and round-and-renormalise the operand and result at each addition. This adds overheads such as:

- It increases the processing latency in clock cycles or the gate delay for the critical path.

- It requires modulo scheduling (Section 6.9) for loops shorter than the reduction operator's latency.

- It uses considerable silicon area.

For example, in 'When FPGAs are better at floating-point than microprocessors' [25], Dinechin et al. report that a fixed-point adder of width greater than the normal mantissa precision can reduce or eliminate underflow errors and operate with less energy and fewer clock cycles (Figure 6.24).

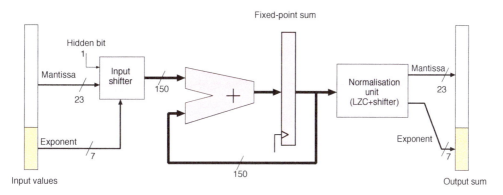

Figure 6.24 Fixed-point implementation of a floating-point accumulator

Their approach is to denormalise the mantissa on input to each iteration and renormalise at the end when the result is needed. This architecture can accept a new input word every clock cycle, whereas six or more standard floating-point adders would otherwise be needed to get that level of throughput, and these would be liable to underflow. If a non-zero number is added to a floating-point accumulator and its value does not change, a complete **underflow** occurs. For instance, with a 3-digit base-10 mantissa, 1.23 + 0.001 will underflow, giving 1.23.

At the expense of one or two additional clock cycles, the adder can be internally pipelined to give low-complexity high-frequency operation, saving one or two carry bits to the next clock cycle. Typical running-average use cases require an input value stream with a high bandwidth, but the output is generally used in a decimated form (i.e. only every 10th or so result is looked at). (See also Figure 6.51 and the related exercise.)

Static Versus Dynamic Scheduling

High-throughput hardware with highly pipelined FUs (Section 6.8.1) requires careful scheduling to balance data-dependencies while achieving high FU utilisation (Section 6.9). A **static schedule** is computed at compile time. The runtime manifestation is the set of output functions from the controlling sequencer, which requires negligible runtime energy. A **dynamic schedule** is computed at runtime. Dynamic scheduling of instructions is performed in out-of-order CPUs (Section 2.2) and can dominate the actual computation energy. The downside of static scheduling is a lack of flexibility, which is required if there are variable-latency FUs. Some operations are intrinsically or better implemented with a variable latency. Examples are division and reading from cached DRAM. This means a static schedule cannot be completely rigid and must be based on expected execution times.

In multithreaded source code, as compiled by Kiwi HLS (Section 6.9), threads can compete for shared resources, such as global mutexes or a frame store written to by all threads. Such structural hazards can be managed by a global schedule or else treated as variable-latency operations. Decoupling is possible through FIFO channels (Section 6.8.4), but if these block, again the static schedule is disrupted.

A **systolic array** is a mainstream example of global static scheduling. Such an array has a number of identical **processing elements (PEs)** that operate in lockstep. Array elements communicate directly with their neighbours, passing data on at regular intervals, like a heartbeat, hence, the name. As well as PE-to-PE links, global nets and busses distribute commands and scalar values that are needed to sequence load/compute/unload phases and distribute coefficients and other constants. The input data and intermediate results to be processed are frequently multi-dimensional and, in the standard approach, a further dimension is defined as the time sequence of values held in a particular register. PEs are normally in a 1-D or 2-D pattern. Data are often allowed to move a distance of at most one PE per clock cycle. To compile an algorithm for a systolic array, a mapping between the multi-dimensional value set and the PE pattern is required. The mapping must observe causality, meaning that not only must no value be read before it is computed, but also that the value has had time to move the required distance through the PE structure. The dimensions of the data are commonly much larger than the available PE dimensions, so a compile-time **strip-mining** process is also applied, in which the dimensions are folded so that each PE handles more than one datum according to a static schedule.

Schemes for dynamically adapting a static schedule include a simple **pipeline stall**, or having a number of static schedules and switching between them, on the fly. Another approach is the **server farm** paradigm, in which PEs locally use an efficient static schedule but work is dynamically allocated to them. Figure 6.25 shows the basic abstraction. The rich Bluespec library contains a **completion buffer** and other flexible structures for easy creation of pools of servers for dynamic load sharing. The unit of dynamic work can be small or large. For instance, to match DRAM access time variability, it may be better if the unit is coupled to either a DRAM burst transfer or a DRAM row activation.

6.8.2 Accellera IP-XACT

IP-XACT is a set of XML schemas that describe IP blocks, their interfaces and structural designs [26]. It was first standardised as IEEE-1685 in 2009. Its primary aim is to help automate the design process in terms of block configuration, interconnect, test program generation and documentation, especially if blocks are from diverse IP suppliers. It describes the hardware interfaces of a block, register layouts

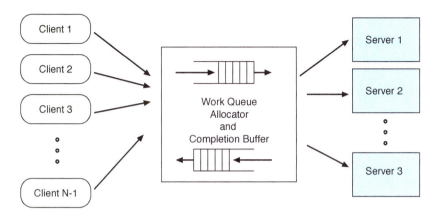

Figure 6.25 Dynamic load balancing using the server farm paradigm

and non-functional attributes. There is also a mechanism for vendor-specific extensions, which is used heavily by real-world tools.

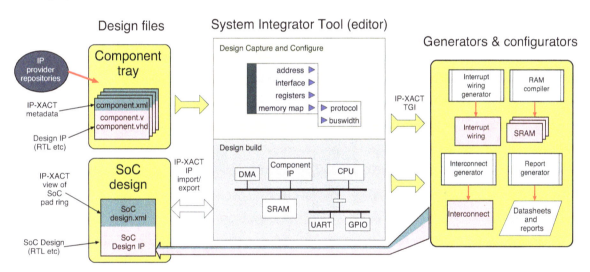

Figure 6.26 Generic setup of a system integrator tool. This is the IP-XACT reference model for design capture and synthesis. A central interactive editor enables a system to be created from externally provided IP blocks by invoking generator and configurator tools

In a generic IP-XACT tool flow, a number of EDA tools process and generate the relevant XML documents. The tools are classed as editors, generators, checkers or automation assistants. The primary tool is a **system integrator**, which is typically GUI-based. It includes an editor and can invoke the other tools. The editor is a high-level design environment for creating and amending the block diagram of a SoC. The general setup is illustrated in Figure 6.26. IP blocks are each provided with accompanying electronic XML data sheets. The editor is used to deploy the blocks on a canvas. Numerous plug-ins are invoked via a **tightly coupled generator interface (TGI)**. These check design rules, generate inter-component wiring, run reports on power, area, latency etc. and launch compilers to generate implementation details. Interconnects, interrupts and the debug infrastructure can typically be generated. A plug-in for designing a high-level interconnect topology might also be used.

One algorithm for automatic topology synthesis was presented in Section 3.9. Each generated sub-assembly should be described with fresh IP-XACT meta-information, in the same way that leaf IP blocks were. Thus, a hierarchical design flow is possible.

IP blocks should be imported from the IP vendor via a revision control and licence/purchasing interface. Documentation in IP-XACT form should be supplied in the delivery package. The package typically also contains test programs and human-readable documentation. The system integrator can represent each available block in an inventory or component tray. An IP block is described with the `component` schema, which gives its name and version number and lists its `ports`. (The typewriter font is used for schema elements.) Ports must conform to an interface standard defined in further files. There may be various versions of a component referred to in the document, each as a `view` element, relating to different versions of a design. Typical levels are gate, RTL and TLM. Each view typically contains a list of filenames as a `fileSet`. These files implement the design at that level of abstraction in the appropriate language, like Verilog, C++ or a **property specification language (PSL)** (Section 7.4).

Extensions allow arbitrary additional material to be embedded. These may include a schematic icon for the GUI rendition of the block, the formal specification of a bus protocol, the bus abstraction definition (Section 7.5) and non-functional data such as energy and area estimates. The programmer's view address space of registers inside each block can also be described, as shown in Figure 6.27. This uses the `register` and `memoryMap` or `addressBlock` elements. Bit fields within a register can be named and given access types, such as read only, write once or self-resetting.

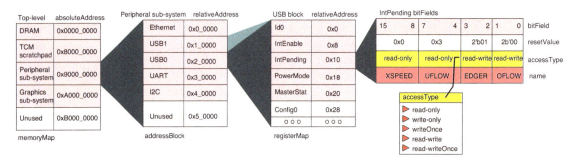

Figure 6.27 IP-XACT structures for documenting the memory map and register field definitions, plus the access type supported for each bit field

The basic unit of an interconnect is the bus, but this can be described in various forms. Hence, interfaces are always described at two levels. The high level is the bus definition, which names the interface and describes how it can be connected to other interfaces. There may be several bus abstraction files, which define implementations of the bus at lower levels. The two most common forms, respectively, encompass the TLM (Section 5.4.8) and net-level definitions of the interface. All forms of connection can be generated from the same high-level wiring diagram.

For each `port` of a `component`, there is a `busInterface` element in the document. This may have a `signalMap`, which maps the formal net names in the interface to the names used in a corresponding `bus abstraction` specification of the port. Simple IP-XACT wiring generation tools use the signal map to determine how the nets on one interface are connected to the nets on another instance for the same formal port on another component. The bus instance name may be in the IP-XACT design or it may be given a name based on the instance names of the components connected by the wiring generator.

Figure 6.28 illustrates the automatic generation of a passive interconnect using IP-XACT. A passive interconnect has point-to-point or multipoint wiring. Five IP-XACT XML files are required to describe this connection, but only one is not shared over other similar connections. The example bus is a standard synchronous interface (Section 3.1.3) with end-of-packet indication using DLAST. Components with the interface are either data sources or data sinks, which have nets in opposite directions. The bus is defined generically by its **bus definition** IP-XACT file. For net-level output, the relevant implementation is in the RTL **bus abstraction** file.

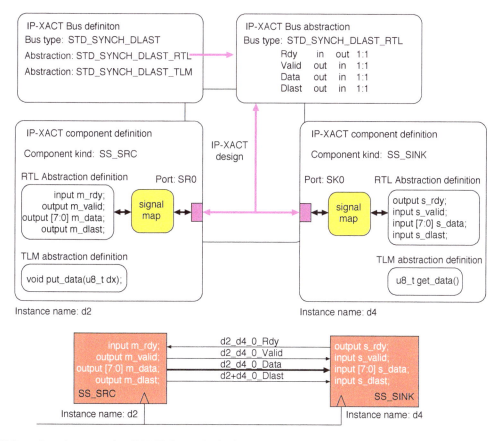

Figure 6.28 Generating an interconnect from IP-XACT: abstract view (top) using five IP-XACT XML files and synthesised wiring (bottom)

The overall high-level design is described in an IP-XACT design document. This lists the component kinds and instance names. It describes the wiring between the ports with a simple connectivity matrix. We have two component kinds in the example, so there must be two **component** IP-XACT documents. The busInterface element gives the port kind and port instance name.

The logic generated is shown at the bottom of the figure. It looks quite simple considering the number of XML files involved. However, often an hierarchical output (a netlist with a structure) is needed, in which case multiple nets need to cross tediously in and out of modules. This can be exceptionally verbose and error-prone if manually entered in RTL. Interrupt wiring and the debug infrastructure can also be generated and configured in a similar way.

Test benches following the **OVM/UVM** coding standard can also be rendered (Section 8.8.1) by suitable generators. Leaf IP blocks tend to be supplied with their own test benches that follow this standard. Address base offsetting may be used if an IP block is embedded in another, but this makes test programs fail. However, if the offsetting is documented in IP-XACT, automatic compensation for compliant test programs can be implemented. Additional test benches can also be created automatically for composed subsystems.

IP-XACT Generators

As well as wiring generators, there are various other synthesis plug-ins, such as RAM compilers (Section 8.3.10). Busses tend to have many variations in terms of address and data width, presence of sideband signals and maximum number of outstanding transactions. Active interconnect components, such as multiplexers and NoC elements, also need to be configured, such as FIFO depth and number of ports. Many of the components required are synthesised on demand by interconnect generator tools. When invoked, these tools generate not only the IP blocks but also the complete suite of IP-XACT documents required for integration.

An interconnect generator can be automatically triggered if the ports that need to be connected are defined with incompatible types in their `bus definitions`. The system integrator will not make a direct connection but can perform a pattern match on the available interconnect or glue logic generators to find a suitable adaptor and run it. This may cross clock domains or power domains or may adjust the bus width.

Standard arithmetic operators, such as floating-point ALUs or fast Fourier transform (FFT) units, can also be generated by **core generators**. Again, the GUI for these generators may be accessible via the system integrator API and again the generator outputs the necessary meta-files in IP-XACT form.

Another class of generators manages memory maps and produces C header files for inclusion in device drivers. Hence, header files in RTL and C are always synchronised with the machine-generated documentation in PDF or word-processor formats.

Design checkers can perform a static analysis of the SoC as a whole. Simple checks based on output-to-output and disconnected input rules can be applied. If IP-XACT extensions have gate counts, or area and power use estimates, the design checkers can sum over the component inventory to give system-wide totals.

Example System Integrator Tools

SoC system integrator tools are often based on the Eclipse IDE or other generic frameworks that were primarily designed for the integrated debugging and development of software. As well as being interactive, they can also be run as batch processes using TCL scripting or perhaps Python or Ruby. A number of broadly similar system integrator tools are available from different vendors. These vary according to how much automation they provide and how well they support software co-design and the generation of ESL virtual platforms. Examples are Platform Designer from Intel [27], SDSoC/Vitis from Xilinx [28] and Socrates from Arm [29]. Figure 6.29 shows the manual deployment of IP blocks and a point-to-point interconnect using an IP-XACT-based GUI tool. Clock, reset and interrupt interconnect will be configured one net at a time, but large numbers of nets are connected with a single mouse click for bus connections.

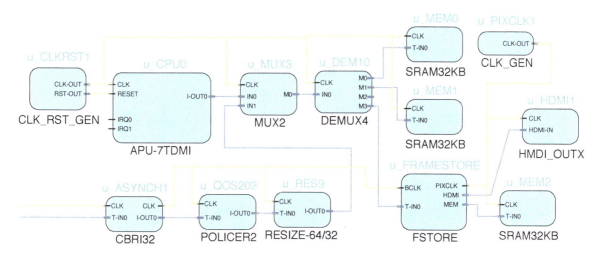

Figure 6.29 Example of high-level manual wiring between subsystems with wiring configured using a GUI

The Arm tool allows IP blocks to be configured for evaluation before they are licensed. It drives two main interconnect mesh generator tools: the CMN-600 Coherent Mesh Network Generator from Arm [30] and a companion tool for non-coherent interconnects [31].

Figure 6.30 is a screenshot from Socrates after running the Network-On-Chip Synthesis Engine (NoC-SE), which generated the NI-700 mesh. The various blobs in red are ingress interfaces; those in green are egress interfaces; the 'H' and remainder in purple are NI-700 routing elements. Those with two colours are **power and clock domain convertors (PCDCs)** (Section 3.7.1 and Section 4.6.10). Those with a small arrow inside are bus resizers. The three scattered light blue circles are performance management units (Section 2.7.9). In grey are unroutable areas (UAs) and the blue large boxes are various external IP clusters named CPU, DDR and so on.

6.8.3 Hardware Construction Languages

A **hardware construction language (HCL)** is a program that prints out a circuit diagram, which is called **elaboration**. There are two principal differences between RTLs and HCLs:

1. An HCL is far more expressive than the limited facilities supported by the **generate** statements found in VHDL and Verilog (Section 8.3.1). HCLs can concisely and elegantly describe

multi-dimensional structures with arbitrary hierarchy and localised variations and parametrisations.

2. HCLs support very little **data-dependent control flow**. An elaborate time thread has no meaning at runtime. Indeed, functional and declarative expressions are typically used in HCLs so that the notion of threading at elaborate time may not exist. To achieve data-dependent effects, explicit rendering of multiplexors is usually used, although sometimes there is syntactic support for multiplexors so that `if` like structures can be used.

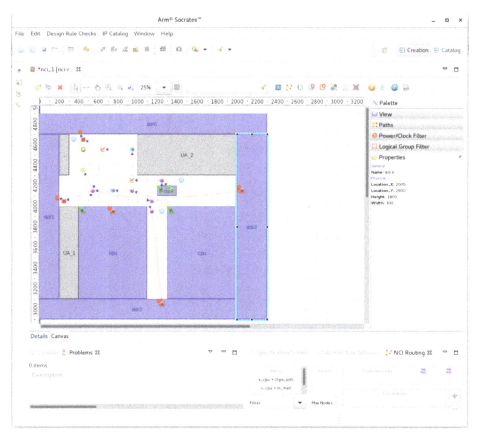

Figure 6.30 Screenshot of the connectivity matrix editor within Arm Socrates

HCLs have much in common with new paradigms for rendering **computation graphs** in cloud and machine learning orchestration. Generative approaches for programming supercomputers, such as DryadLINQ from Microsoft, also elegantly support the rendering of large static computation trees. These can be split over multiple processing nodes or blades. They are agnostic as to what mix of nodes is used: FPGA, GPU or CPU. If FPGA accelerators are used (Section 6.4), synergies may be possible.

Two mainstream HCLs are Lava and Chisel. Lava was implemented in the language Haskell in 1998 [32] but many derivatives are used for niche applications today (e.g. Cλash [33]). Functional programming languages, like Haskell, have vast expressive power for concisely describing common operations, such replication, mapping and scalar reduction (Section 4.4.2). Application scenarios include adders, multipliers, NoCs (Section 3.4), FFTs (Section 6.9.1) and anything that has a repetitive structure at small or large scale.

Chisel HCL

Chisel HCL [34] is a HCL embedded as a **domain-specific language (DSL)** in the Scala language. Scala is a very powerful general-purpose language that embodies all of the power of functional programming (proper closures etc.) as well as popular imperative features, such as objects and assignment to variables. However, Chisel does not allow general Scala programs to be converted to hardware, as that requires HLS (Section 6.9).

The output from Chisel is RTL or SystemC. The latter is mainly used to increase the speed of simulation in a virtual platform or otherwise. For one component to include another, a Chisel module generator invokes the generator for the child. This potentially results in compile-time flattening of the hierarchy, although there is an option to preserve the hierarchy. As well as quickly generating a large amount of hardware, two further elegant aspects of Chisel are its wiring bundles and automatic bit-width determination for busses and registers that are not specified. As with system integrator tools based on IP-XACT, the bundle mechanism easily allows busses to be run up and down the module hierarchy without the need for manual configuration of every net direction at each level.

Validly tagged data are one of the most fundamental paradigms in hardware. A register or bus is either in use or idle. Standard RTL has no widely used coding standard for representing this and bus qualifiers must be manually entered alongside the data carrying part of any bus or register. This is easier if user-defined data types are supported by the hardware language, especially if all users follow the same conventions. Chisel nurtures this convergence by providing a standard library that includes the maybe/option type for validly tagged data as well as prototypes for FIFO buffers and SRAM. Future tool chains may expect such conventions to be followed, e.g. for compiler-based logic optimisation.

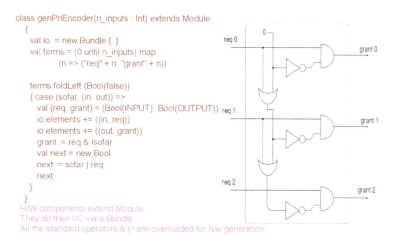

Figure 6.31 An example Chisel module: a static-priority arbiter, showing Chisel source code (left) and the circuit generated (right) when `n_inputs` *is 3*

Figure 6.31 shows a Chisel example in Scala and schematic form. The Scala class has no methods and does all of its work in its constructor. The constructor extends the Chisel base `Module` and generates a combinational priority encoder whose number of inputs is passed to the constructor at elaboration time. The input and output contacts are generated by the call to `map`. Then, for each input and output pair, an anonymous function is folded. A scalar, which is carried between each fold, is the combinational net that indicates whether any stage with a higher priority than the current is active.

Figure 6.32 is a Chisel example using synchronous logic and a `when` block. The clock net is not manifest in the low-level Chisel code. The `Reg()` primitive references an implicit clock, while the surrounding scope sets the clock domain name and the resets. This example goes beyond Lava-like HCL. It demonstrates how multiplexers are inferred. There are two possible sources of input to the register. Note that the register width does not have to be specified. The Chisel width determiner deduces that no logic will ever connect to bits higher than bit 7 and so creates an 8-bit register in the output RTL.

```
1 class CTR8_SLD extends Module      10  when (io.load)
2 {                                   11  {
3   val io = new Bundle               12    reg0 := io.DIN
4   {                                 13  }
5     val DIN  = UInt(INPUT, 8)       14  .otherwise
6     val load = Bool(INPUT)          15  {
7     val Q    = UInt(OUTPUT, 8)      16    reg0 := reg0 + 1
8   }                                 17  }
9   val reg0 = Reg(UInt())            18  io.Q := reg0
                                      19 }
```

Figure 6.32 An 8-bit counter with a synchronous load using sequential logic and a `when`/`otherwise` clause: Chisel source code and schematic symbol

Although Chisel supports advanced structural elaboration and reduces the amount of typing compared with using RTL directly, it retains the RTL semantics. Hence, the designer must allocate work to clock cycles. Moreover, to achieve high utilisation with pipelined FUs, manual sequencing and scoreboarding are required, which again is left to the design engineer.

6.8.4 Handel-C

Parallel thread communication via shared variables is widely recognised to be a poor communication paradigm, despite being the mainstay of parallel programming on multi-core computers. Using shared variables to communicate between threads is a low-level model of computation:

▫ The user must abide by self-imposed protocol conventions, and hence, the method is error-prone.

▫ Quite rich mutex and semaphore semantics must be supported by the tool chain.

▫ Cache and sequential consistency are necessary.

▫ It has become (unfortunately) the primary parallel communications paradigm in today's chip multiprocessors (CMPs).

▫ Thus, it is generally better avoided (so say many at least)!

The main disadvantage of shared variables is too much freedom of expression. Arbitrary user protocols are commonly coded, although the compilers are in complete ignorance of their semantics. Accordingly, the optimisations deployable by the compiler are severely limited. The primary alternative is inter-thread communication by **message passing**.

```
// Generator (src)          // Processor              // Consumer (sink)
while(1)                     while(1)                  while(1)
{                            {                         {
  ch1 ! (x);                   ch2 ! (ch1? + 2)          $display(ch2?);
  x += 3;                    }                         }
}
```

Figure 6.33 Three communication processes expressed using Handel-C

Using channels makes concurrency explicit and allows synthesis to re-time the design.

A mainstream example of message passing being compiled to hardware is the Handel-C language. Its compiler converts a variant of the Occam programming language to RTL. Figure 6.33 illustrates the essence of this design style. Three sequential processes are composed in parallel and communicate via channels. Handel-C has two message communication primitives: c!v is used to write a value v to channel c and c? is used to read it. Each channel has a bounded storage capacity that is nominally established when it is declared. The read and write primitives are blocking, so the thread blocks when reading an empty channel and when writing to a full channel. Richer concurrent structures are possible using the keywords SEQ and PAR, which enable threads to fork and join.

This coding style encourages the writer to exploit thread-level parallelism, yet the compiler has massive freedom to optimise. If static analysis shows that a thread never blocks on any channel, where helpful, its work can instead be redistributed and inlined in other threads. Other channels may be reduced to combinational logic between the program counters of communicating threads. The minimal required channel capacity can often be determined at compile time by static analysis phases that balance the load by allocating work to clock cycles while avoiding **accidental serialisation** or a **deadlock**. Accidental serialisation occurs when a program that was written for a parallel platform mostly runs sequentially due to structural hazards relating to commonly used resources (Section 6.3).

6.8.5 Bluespec System Verilog

Using guarded atomic actions is an old and well-loved design paradigm in computer science. Recently, Bluespec System Verilog has successfully raised the level of abstraction in hardware design using this paradigm [35].

Like Chisel and Lava, Bluespec benefits from having an advanced elaboration language for rendering structure. Early versions were very powerful, being directly embedded in Haskell, whereas an easier-to-use and slightly restricted subset was used for the commercial variant of the language. The elaboration language, however, is an orthogonal aspect. What is significant is the basic unit that is rendered by the elaboration stage.

Bluespec essentially has two types of entity that can be rendered: modules and rules. Modules can be defined by the user or built in. They can instantiate instances of other modules in a classical hardware structural hierarchy (Section 8.3.1). Modules are not regarded as having net-level connections (although when rendered as RTL, they do, of course). Instead, they support TLM-style method entry points (Section 5.4), which can be invoked from a parent module. Methods are grouped into interfaces and made accessible to the parent module. An interface can also be passed into a module so that the module can make use of interfaces defined in other parts of the structure.

The second type of entity is a rule. As well as containing instances of smaller modules, a module may have one or more rules. A rule makes method calls on the interfaces of the instantiated modules and on methods of interfaces passed in from above. Leaf methods may not be re-entrant in the sense that they may be in use by only one rule at a time. For example, a hardware broadside register of *n* bits has a `read()` method and a `write()` method. Any number of rules can use the read method at once, but the write method can be called by only one rule in any one clock cycle.

Compared with the other design languages covered in this section, Bluespec sits between RTL and HLS with regard to clock cycles. For performance reasons, a designer using Bluespec normally takes a keen interest in what is done in what clock cycle, but the compiler has the final say and the rate of progress of a design is sometimes slower than expected. This is because of the Bluespec **scheduler**. If methods cannot be called more than once per clock cycle, any rules that wish to call the same method must do so in turn. Rules are always exercised at most once per clock cycle under the default compilation semantics. Moreover, the mainstream Bluespec compiler generates only a static schedule and reports starvation for rules that manifestly can never fire under a static schedule. To achieve dynamic scheduling, the user must instantiate stateful arbiters so that different rules are arbitrated at runtime. The intention was that a compiler can direct scheduling decisions to span various power/performance implementations for a given program. However, designs with an over-reliance on shared variables suffer RaW and WaR hazards if the schedule is altered. There are other compilers that insert their own dynamic schedulers.

Figure 6.34 has three Bluespec rules that demonstrate contention. This example looks pretty much like RTL, so it understandable by experienced RTL engineers. The rule `countone` attempts to increment the register `rx` while it is less than 30. The expression (`rx < 30`) in the rule definition line is called its **explicit guard**. For this rule, whatever its starting value, it should count to 30 and stop. A standard Bluespec semantic is that a rule can fire at most once per clock cycle; hence, this rule can increment the register at most once per clock cycle. The second rule, `counttwo`, attempts to add 2 to the same register when it is above 20. Clearly, both rules can fire if the register is between 21 and 29. However, only one rule is allowed to write to the register in a single clock cycle. The Bluespec scheduler will detect this condition, and give one rule static priority over the other. The decision will be reported to the user in a compilation log file. Annotations can be added to control the relative priority if the user has a preference. Either way, one rule will always fire at the expense of total

```
module mkTb1 (Empty);             // This module has no externally callable methods

   Reg#(int) rx <- mkReg (23);    // Create an instance of a 23-bit register called rx

   rule countone (rx < 30);       // A rule named 'countup' with an explicit guard
      int y = rx + 1;             // This is short for int y = rx.read() + 1;
      rx <= rx + 1;               // This is short for rx.write(rx.read() + 1);
      $display ("countone: rx = %0d, y = %0d", rx, y);
   endrule

   rule counttwo (rx > 20);       // A competing rule, also guarded
      rx <= rx + 2;               // This increments twice each cycle
      $display ("counttwo: rx = %0d", rx);
   endrule

   rule done (rx >= 40);          // A third rule
      $finish (0);
   endrule

endmodule: mkTb1
```

Figure 6.34 A Bluespec example in which three rules compete to act on a simple broadside register

starvation for the other rule in this interval. Once above 29, the second rule is the only one that can fire, and the count sequence will go up in 2s until it reaches 40, when the final rule will exit the simulation. In real hardware, the RTL generated from the final rule will be ignored during logic synthesis, since real hardware cannot exit, and the second rule will continue until the register goes negative at 2^{22}.

This small example is easy to analyse by inspection, but, in general, rules that interfere may be far away from each other, perhaps in different source files. However, the compiler will analyse all possibilities and generate what it deems to be an appropriate static prioritisation. If the user does not like the compiler's decisions, additional guard conditions and annotations can manually steer the schedule towards the preferred behaviour. If a round-robin service is desired (Section 4.2.1), an additional state has to be added, either manually or via the extensions available in some Bluespec compilers.

Figure 6.35 demonstrates inter-module wiring in Bluespec. As mentioned, modules are interconnected using method calls. A method call must be completed in a clock cycle, so access to any pipelined unit requires two transactions on different methods, called put() and get(). (For commonly used paradigms, like put/get, Bluespec offers type-class mechanisms that ease their interconnection, but our simple example does not show that.) As with IP-XACT, the interface definition is shared by the initiator and the target. The net declarations in the hardware are determined from the definition and the reciprocal net directions between initiator and target. The example shows Bluespec source code for the initiator and the net-level schematic of the target. For each method, there is a handshake net in each direction together with parallel data busses for each argument and the result.

```
interface Pipe_ifc;
   method Action put(int arg);
   method int get();
endinterface
```

```
module mkTb2 (Empty); // Testbench

   Reg#(int) x         <- mkReg ('h10);
   Pipe_ifc   thepipe <- mkPipe;

   rule fill;    // explicit guard of (true) is implied
      thepipe.put(x);
      // This is short for   x.write(x.read() + 'h10);
      x <= x + 'h10;
   endrule

   rule drain;
      let y = thepipe.get();
      $display ("    y = %0h", y);
   endrule
endmodule
```

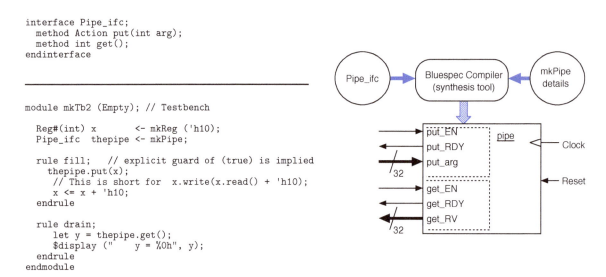

Figure 6.35 Bluespec definition of an example interface, the `Pipe_ifc` (top left), the definition of a component that has an instance of a component that has that interface and two rules to operate on it (bottom left) and a net-level schematic symbol for the instantiated component showing handshake nets. The symbol for the Tb2 component has no external nets (apart from clock and reset) since it has an empty interface

The fill and drain rules in Figure 6.35 do not use explicit guards but remain guarded by the **implicit guards** of all methods they invoke. These are the _RDY nets of each method. The compiler generates a composite guard for any rule as a conjunction of its explicit guard, the implicit guards of any methods called in the explicit guard and the implicit guards of all methods in the rule body. When it is holding off a rule to avoid starving another, the scheduler adds a further clause in the conjunction. An annotation or a command-line option can select a non-strict compilation mode for a rule. In that case, the implicit guards of code that is not going to be run when the rule fires, due to being surrounded by an if statement whose guard does not hold, can be excluded from the expression for the rule guard. The RDY signals from each method indicate the implicit guard of the method. When a rule exercises a method, it multiplexes its arguments on to the method argument bus and drives the _EN signal for the method high, using an input to a disjunction for each method that collects the fire signals for all rules that invoke the method.

Bluespec was intended to be declarative, both in the elaboration language for the design structure and with the guarded atomic action paradigm for its rules. Declarative programming is not ideal in all situations. A behavioural sublanguage based on a finite-state machine (FSM) is also available for when an imperative expression is best. This is converted into declarative rule form as a preprocessing step during elaboration. The let-bind structure, illustrated in both the above examples for variable y, also helps with imperative-like coding. However, the principal components in real hardware are the register and the SRAM. Both of these are imperative and suffer RaW-like hazards (Section 6.3), which makes the order of firing rules important. Within a rule, we have atomicity, but large designs need to use multiple rules and these are best coupled with FIFO-like structures to avoid RaW hazards. Alternatively, we can use a highly defensive programming style that tolerates any rule ordering. As with Handel-C, due to the clean semantics of the language, advanced compilers have the potential to explore a wide implementation space, well beyond that dictated by direct translation according to the programmer's model. Like Chisel, it has good support for **validly tagged data** in registers and busses. Hence, compiler optimisations that ignore dead data are possible. However, the put/get paradigm for access to pipelined RAMs, ALUs and other FUs (Section 6.8.1) forces a slightly verbose programming style that could be simplified with such a compiler.

6.9 High-level Synthesis

The holy grail of **high-level synthesis (HLS)** is to convert arbitrary software to hardware automatically. There are two principal reasons for attempting this:

- **Engineer productivity**: Section 6.8 mentioned time to market and the related benefits of higher-level design expression. HLS grants access to a very rich design expression environment. Fragments of existing code can be readily compiled to hardware and new code can be created quickly. HLS is particularly adroit at using complex pipelined FUs (Section 6.8.1), which are very difficult to deploy in any programming style where the pipeline must be manually constructed by the user.

- **Power and performance**: When accelerating common big-data applications, HLS can target FPGA to generate custom coprocessors and networks of interconnected accelerators. Equally, for portable devices, longer battery life is possible when intensive processing is performed using specialised logic instead of software on a general-purpose core. The improved performance due to hardware accelerators was covered in Section 6.4.

Although it has been a research topic for decades, HLS is now seeing industrial traction. The advantages of using a general-purpose language to describe both hardware and software are becoming apparent. Algorithms can be ported easily and tested in software environments before implementation in hardware. There is also the potential benefit that software engineers can be used instead of building hardware, as they are normally cheaper to employ than ASIC engineers!

A wide variety of HLS tools are available. They vary in their purpose and capabilities. Most accept C, C++ or SystemC as input languages, but there are also tools for Python, C# and other less popular languages. Figure 6.36 illustrates a typical tool flow. The HLS compiler generates RTL that is then synthesised for ASIC or converted to an FPGA bit stream. A colloquial name for such a tool used to be a **C-to-gates compiler**. All generate RTL and some can generate SystemC as an additional output. An advantage of using SystemC as the input is the predefined library of multi-bit words, but these are also available in other ways, such as through the various portable C libraries that have been verified to compile tidily on a given tool. The RTL subset of SystemC (Section 5.3.2) can also be seamlessly used to combine HLS with RTL coding styles if certain operations, such as interface protocols, need to be clock-aware in their coding. Some tools are dedicated to generating highly optimised hardware implementations of algorithmic kernels. Others support a complete software ecosystem, including multithreading and transparent access to the file system, like Kiwi (Section 6.9)

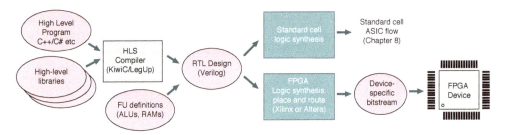

Figure 6.36 Basic steps of an HLS tool chain for ASIC or FPGA

HLS Synthesisable Subsets and Flow

Although the ideal is to convert arbitrary legacy programs to hardware, this does not work very well in general. Existing code tends to need refactoring to suit the **synthesisable subset** supported by the HLS tool. At a very minimum, the boundary of what is to be put in hardware needs to be defined, typically using the instance of a class or a particular subroutine. New code is likely to be written with knowledge of how well the chosen tool copes with a particular language construct. Typical subset restrictions include the following:

▪ The program must be finite-state and single-threaded.

▪ All recursion must be bounded or else is not allowed at all.

▪ All dynamic storage allocation is outside infinite loops (or de-allocated again in the same loop).

▪ Only Boolean logic and integer arithmetic can be used (although many tools now support floating-point and custom precision as well).

▪ There is limited string handling.

▪ There is very limited standard library support.

▪ Which loops have runtime bounds has to be explicit.

The classical HLS tool is a compiler that operates much like a software compiler, but there are many differences. It includes parallelism detection algorithms, which facilitate the creation of large circuits, but these are not always required. Hence, it needs guidance regarding the time/space trade-off. Moreover, it can benefit significantly from **profile-directed feedback**, which gives a clear indication of how often each region of code is executed. It is pointless producing high-performance hardware for control-flow arcs that are seldom used, such as start-up code or error handlers. A software compiler takes advantage of caches to move frequently used data to higher-bandwidth storage cells, but the HLS compiler makes these decisions at compile time, dispensing with all but the last-level cache. Mainstream HLS tools use a static schedule (Section 6.8.1), although, as discussed, these schedules can suffer when interacting with variable-latency FUs, such as DRAM and for divides.

A compiler normally has an extensive library of mathematical functions and common I/O routines. There is also a library of **execution substrates** or **shells**, which can easily host the generated RTL simulation, FPGA evaluation boards or cloud server blades.

Although some HLS tools can process multithreaded code, they essentially repeat the compilation flow separately for each thread. Resource sharing between threads needs to use the server farm paradigm using an array of processing elements (PEs). Each PE is from a separate HLS thread run (Section 6.8.1). The internal steps of an HLS compiler for a single thread take an imperative program and convert it to a **custom data path** with an optional **sequencing FSM** when required. The steps are:

1. **Lexing and parsing**: This is the same as any high-level language (HLL). Lexing is the process of recognising the syntactic tokens in an input file, such as keywords and composite symbols like >=. Parsing forms an **abstract syntax tree** from these tokens, provided the input is grammatically correct. Otherwise, it reports a syntax error.

2. **Type and reference checking**: Again, this is like any HLL. Errors are reported if an integer is added to a string, if an invoked primitive is unsupported or if a variable is not initialised.

3. **Trimming**: Unreachable code is deleted. Register widths are reduced if it is manifest that the value stored is bounded. Constants are propagated between code blocks. Identity reductions are applied to operators, such as multiplying by unity.

4. **Loop unwinding**: Parallelism is easily increased by loop unwinding, subject to loop-carried dependencies (Section 6.9.1).

5. **Strength reduction**: An operator may be replaced with a lower area operator where possible, such as replacing a multiplication by -1 with a subtraction from 0.

6. **Reassociation**: A sequence of associative operators is typically parsed with a linear association, whereas a tree-like structure results in shorter delays and better FU utilisation. For instance $a + (b + (c + d))$ is replaced with $(a + b) + (c + d)$.

7. **Binding**: Every storage element and PE, such as a variable, an add operation or a memory read, is allocated a physical resource. The compiler must select an inventory of FUs, such as RAMs and ALUs, to instantiate.

8. **Address mapping**: Memory layouts and loop nest ordering are optimised. Arrays of structs can be permuted to structs of arrays (Section 6.9.1). Polyhedral address mapping is applied to loop nests (Section 6.9.1).

9. **Scheduling**: Each physical resource can be used many times in the time domain. A static schedule is generated to assign work to clock cycles. This is typically a scoreboard of what expressions are available at what clock offset for a basic block (Section 6.9).

10. **Sequencer generation**: A controlling FSM that embodies the schedule and drives multiplexor and ALU function codes is generated.

11. **Quantity surveying**: The number of hardware resources and clock cycles used can now be readily computed.

12. **Optimisation**: The binding and scheduling phases may be revisited to ensure they better match any user-provided target metrics. Iterative strategies, as outlined in Section 6.2, are used.

13. **RTL output**: The resulting design is printed to a Verilog or VHDL file and optionally as SystemC. IP-XACT documentation is also written by some tools.

Simple Worked HLS Example

```
// A simple long multiplier with
// variable latency
int multiply(int A, int B)
{
  int RA=A;
  int RB=B;
  int RC=0;
  while(RA>0)
  {
    if odd(RA) RC = RC + RB;
    RA = RA >> 1;
    RB = RB << 1;
  }
  return RC;
}
```

```
module LONGMULT8b8(clk, reset, C, Ready, A, B, Start);
  input clk, reset, Start;
  output Ready;
  input [7:0] A, B;
  output [15:0] C;
  reg [15:0] RC, RB, RA;
  reg         Ready;

  reg xx, yy, qq, pp; // Control and predicate nets
  reg [1:0] fc;
  reg [3:0] state;
  always @(posedge clk) begin
      xx = 0; // default settings.
      yy = 0;
      fc = 0;

      // Predicates
      pp = (RA!=16'h0);    // Work while pp holds
      qq = RA[0];          // Odd if qq holds

      if (reset) begin     // Sequencer
          state <= 0;
          Ready <= 0;
          end
      else case (state)
          0: if (Start) begin
              xx = 1;
              yy = 1;
              fc = 2;
              state <= 1;
          end

          1: begin
              fc = qq;
              if (!pp) state <= 2;
          end
          2: begin
              Ready <= 1;
              if (!Start) state <= 3;
          end

          3: begin
              Ready <= 0;
              state <= 0;
          end

      endcase // case (state)
      RB <= (yy) ? B: RB<<1;    // Data path
      RA <= (xx) ? A: RA>>1;
      RC <= (fc==2) ? 0: (fc==1) ? RC+RB: RC;
      end

  assign C = RC;
endmodule
```

Figure 6.37 A very basic worked HLS example showing the input source code (left) and generated RTL (right) for a 32-bit multiplier as a variable-latency FU with start and ready handshake nets

As a simple worked example of HLS, we consider long multiplication implemented in C, as shown on the left of Figure 6.37. Following a strictly **syntax-directed approach**, with no search of the solution space for minimum clock cycles, minimum area or maximum clock frequency, we use a simple one-to-one mapping of ALUs to the source code text. As can be seen in the generated RTL, shown on the right, each register has a multiplexer that ranges over all expressions stored in it. Figure 6.38 (left) shows the resulting data path. The compilation output could serve as a primitive FU to be instantiated by further runs of the HLS tool (right). The accompanying documentation would describe its input, output and handshake nets in XML using an IP-XACT schema. For such a simple algorithm, there is no performance benefit compared to in-lining its compilation within a parent, but keeping it separate means its input and output busses are an easy-to-find structure during debugging.

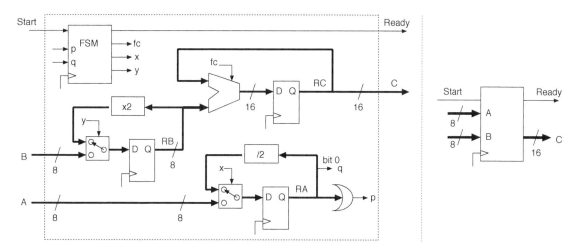

Figure 6.38 Long multiplier output from HLS showing the internal data path and sequencer (left) and the schematic symbol (right). The result is used as an FU in a higher-level design

Pipelined Scheduling: One Basic Block

The simple multiplier example just considered had no multi-cycle FUs. Indeed, it could be considered as a design exercise for a generic variable-latency FU for use at a higher level.

Now, suppose that we wish to compute $Y := Y \times Y + 1.0/\sqrt{X \times X + Z \times Z}$ and suppose the FUs chosen include a 1.0/SQRT unit that takes 5 cycles, an ADD FU that takes 4 cycles and a SQUARE FU that takes 3. None of the FUs are pipelined and hence, they have an initiation interval equal to their latency, such as our simple multiplier (Section 6.3). Note that a multiply may be faster than an add in floating-point arithmetic (as there is no exponent denormalising step and a 24- versus a 32-bit mantissa) and that the reciprocal of a square root may be cheaper to compute than a square root.

Figure 6.39 shows one possible computation schedule. The squaring operation for input Y has slack, as it can be shifted between offsets 4 and 10 if we want to use the same FU for X as Y. If the assignment to Y is inside a loop, then Y would have a loop-carried dependency (Section 6.9.1). The loop can be reissued earlier if the dependency occurs later in the loop body schedule, thus increasing the loop rate. In general, each sub-expression can be migrated between its earliest and latest times

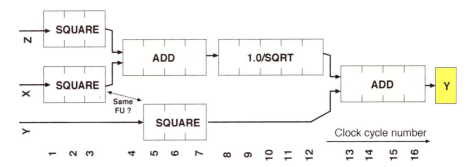

Figure 6.39 An example of a static schedule for a basic block containing a single assignment

within a schedule. There are knock-on effects regarding the sharing of FUs for different sub-expressions and the commencement of subsequent basic blocks.

If the SQUARE unit is now fully pipelined, the same SQUARE unit could be used for X and Z with only a single cycle extension to the schedule. One operation starts the cycle after the other. The earliest start time for the squaring of Y is now 2.

After some loop unrolling, we have an expanded control-flow graph that has larger basic blocks than the original HLL program. In classical HLS, each basic block of an expanded graph is given a time-domain static schedule.

A good heuristic for scheduling is to start the operations that have the largest processing delay as early as possible. This is called a **list schedule**. Finding an optimum schedule is NP-hard and integer linear programming packages are often deployed to find an optimum trade-off for the schedule and resource use.

The result for this example was stored in only one output variable. A basic block schedule typically contains multiple assignments, with sub-expressions and FUs being reused in the time domain throughout the schedule and shared between output assignments. To avoid RaW hazards within a basic block, all reads to a variable or memory location must be scheduled before all writes to the same variable. The name alias problem means we must be conservative in this analysis when considering whether array subscripts are equal (Section 6.9.1). This is undecidable in general theory, but often doable in practice (Section 6.9.1). Indeed, many subscript expressions are simple functions of loop induction. We need to understand their patterns to increase performance. An **induction variable** in a loop is simply the variable that is stepped at each iteration.

Modulo Scheduling

Earlier in Section 6.9, we discussed the shortest possible schedule, but sometimes a longer schedule is acceptable and preferable if it uses less silicon. For example, the high-level expression of a basic block may contain arithmetic operators, such as 9 additions and 10 multiplies for a 10-stage finite-impulse response filter. However, we may wish to render this in hardware using fewer FUs. For instance, to do this in three clock cycles of at least three times the streaming sample rate, three adders and four multipliers should be sufficient, as these would meet the required number of basic operations per second, assuming they can each compute a new result every clock cycle. However, such FUs are often pipelined and the output from one may not be ready in time to be the input to the next. Streaming hardware designs with a low **initiation interval (II)** are surprisingly complex and difficult to find when the available ALUs are heavily pipelined. Floating-point ALUs tend to have a multi-cycle delay (a latency of four to six cycles is common for adds and multiplies in a FPGA). However, such problems are always solvable with the minimal number of FUs, given sufficient pipelining. In our example, the pipeline II is 3, but the latency is more than 3. The design issue is then to minimise the latency and the number of additional holding registers. These two aims are, at least, compatible.

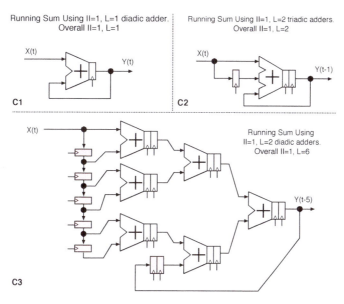

Figure 6.40 Various circuits that compute a running sum. The everyday circuit C1 can be used if the adder has a latency of 1. However, if the adder has a latency of 2, more complex circuits are needed, namely C2 and C3

Figure 6.40 tackles a simpler example: compute the running sum of streaming data with an II of 1 and no oversampling. Circuit C1 is the obvious answer for integer arithmetic, but for floating-point arithmetic, an adder with a latency of 1 is rarely good due to its very long combinational paths. If an adder with a latency of 2 and three inputs is available, then solution C2 is feasible. However, if the adders have only two inputs, the fairly complex design of C3 must be used. Since single-precision floating-point adders generally have a latency of at least 3, C3 is unlikely to be realised in practice.

In general, a scheduler or planner will produce a static mapping of operations to FUs. The creation of the schedule can be formulated nicely as an **integer linear programming** problem, as demonstrated in 'ILP-based Modulo Scheduling and Binding for Register Minimization' [36]. The aim is to find a set of integer values that simultaneously make a set of simple inequalities hold over sums of the variables. The schedule will use some number of FUs and have a duration that is some integral number of initiation intervals before it repeats. The result is called a **modulo schedule**. A schedule that uses the fewest number of FUs will generally be preferred over a schedule that is as short as possible, since additional complexity arising from schedule length is likely to be less than the area and energy costs of additional FUs. Per-FU utilisation is also bound to be be lower if more FUs are used for the same system throughput. Once the schedule is computed, it is then fairly simple to render a sequencer circuit and the additional holding registers as needed. Integer linear programming problems occur in many fields, so there are many general-purpose solver packages.

Pipelined Scheduling between Basic Blocks

Programs do not consist of just one basic block. They typically have loops and data-dependent control flow. Due to the high level of pipelining inherent in an efficient hardware implementation of a single basic block, multiple basic blocks, even from one thread, will be executing at once. Frequently, an inner loop consists of one basic block repeated, and so it is competing with itself for structural resources and data hazards. This is **loop pipelining**. If an outer loop has to be pipelined, all loops inside it must be pipelined too. The inter-block scheduling problem grows exponentially with a base equal to the average control-flow fanout, but only a finite part needs to be governed by the maximal block length.

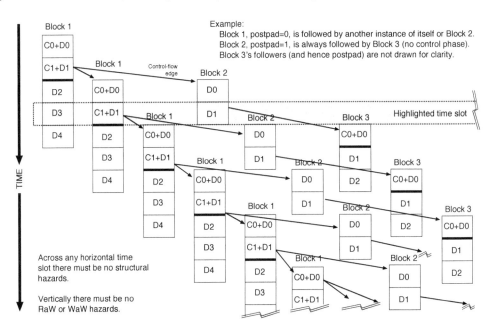

Figure 6.41 Fragment of an example inter-block initiation and hazard graph. Block 1 may be followed by itself or by block 2. Each block schedule contains both C (control flow) predicate evaluation and D (data) computation operations

Each block has its own static schedule of determined length (Figure 6.41). The shortest possible schedule arises from commencing each operation as soon as all of its arguments are ready and instantiating a fresh FU to compute the operation, if no free one is available. This results in an **as-soon-as-possible schedule**. The early part of the schedule generally contains control-flow predicate computation to determine which block will run next. This can take several cycles (if predicates depend on synchronous RAM contents) or be null if the block is the initialisation code for a subsequent loop (i.e. the basic block ends on a branch destination rather than on a conditional branch). The later part of a block contains data reads, data writes and ALU computations. Data operations can also occur in the control phase, but if resources are tight (typically memory read bandwidth), the control work should be given a higher scheduling priority and hence, remain at the top of the schedule. At most one control section will be running at any time per thread. However, a number of data sections from successors and from predecessors may still be running.

In the highlighted time slot in Figure 6.41, the D3 operations of the first block are concurrent with the control and data operations (C1+D1) of a later copy of itself when it has looped back or with the D1 phase of block 2, if it has exited from its tight loop.

Each time offset in a block schedule needs to be checked for structural hazards (Section 6.3) against the resource use of all other blocks that are potentially running at the same time. As well as avoiding structural hazards, the schedule must not contain RaW or WaW hazards. So a block must read a datum at a point in its schedule after any earlier block that might be running has written it. If this can occur at the same time, forwarding logic must be synthesised.

It may be necessary to add a 'postpad' to relax the schedule. This is a delay beyond what is needed by the control-flow predicate computation before following the control-flow arc. This introduces extra space in the global schedule allowing more time and hence, generally requiring fewer FUs.

Ensuring sequential consistency (Section 4.5) imposes a further constraint on scheduling order, since for certain blocks, the order of operations must be (partially) respected. For instance, if a packet is stored in a shared memory and then signalled ready with a write to a flag or pointer in the same RAM, the signalling operation must be last. (This is not a WaW hazard since the writes are to different addresses in the RAM.) Observing these limits typically results in an expansion of the overall schedule.

The HLS of multithreaded programs or those with parallel annotations (Section 6.9.1) takes into account whether the various user threads operate in lockstep, like a systolic array (Section 6.8.1), or asynchronously. Compilers such as **Kiwi HLS** [37] target heterogeneous threads. As well as using conventional auto-parallelisation, this tool comprehends the parallel programming constructs of the input HLL. For Kiwi, this is C#, which has a rich set of operators that are commonly used for database and big data applications. Each thread undergoes classical HLS to generate a static schedule for that thread, but in the resulting hardware, the threads interact dynamically using arbiters, mutexes and FIFO queues.

6.9.1 Discovering Parallelism and Shared Variables in Iterations

HLS compilers attempt to discover instruction-level parallelism in a user program. The program may be manually annotated with parallel markup. For example, in C++ OpenMP, we write:

```
\#pragma omp parallel for
```

In C#, we can map a delegate using:

```
Parallel.For(0, matARows, i => ...)
```

Similar primitives exist in other libraries and languages, such as Cilk for C++ or CUDA and OpenCL for GPU. Data-sharing patterns between potentially parallel elements always need to have the correct degree of isolation to achieve high performance. The programmer must always pay attention to the values read and written by a loop body. If one body reads a value written by another, the order of scheduling is likely to make a difference. However, commutable effects, such as increment, summation and bit set, can be detected by compilers and rearranged to remove obstacles to parallelism.

A loop can be at the top level or nested inside another. The way that outer loops influence inner loop bounds and the way that successive iterations of a single loop influence each other typically follow one of a number of named design patterns. If the loop bounds of one loop are set by the value of an outer loop variable, the inner loop is said to be **polyhedral** (Section 6.9.1). The way that data and control interact between one loop body and another affects which loop bodies can be run in what order or in parallel with each other. A **natural loop** has a single entry and exit point. A **bounded loop** has its limits determined before entry. If a loop variable evolves linearly, the variables and expressions in the body that depend only linearly on the loop variable are termed **induction variables** and **induction expressions**, respectively, and can be ignored for loop classification, since their values are always independently available in each loop body with minimal overhead.

```
public static int associative_reduction_example(int starting)
{
  int vr = 0;
  for (int i=0;i<15;i++) // or also i+=4
    {
      int vx = (i+starting)*(i+3)*(i+5); // Mapped computation
      vr ^= ((vx&128)>0 ? 1:0);          // Associative reduction
    }
  return vr;
}
```

Figure 6.42 An iteration that performs associative reduction (in vr)

For a single loop, the well-known **map-reduce paradigm** describes a factorisation of the loop body into a part that can be computed in isolated parallel silos followed by an associative reduction operator that gives the same answer under any bracketing (the associative principle). Figure 6.42 illustrates a basic map-reduce paradigm. The variable i is the induction variable and vr is the **scalar accumulator**. Common associative operators are addition, multiplication, maximum and bitwise OR. The example uses XOR.

A **loop-carried dependency** means that parallelisation of consecutive loop bodies is not possible. In Figure 6.43, the output from one iteration is an input to the next iteration. This breaks the map-reduce paradigm, despite there still being a scalar reduction in the result. Often such a loop body can be split into a part that is and a part that is not dependent on the previous iteration, with at least the independent part being run in parallel. This occurs in the example. Here, xf1() is free of the loop dependency, so the available parallel speedup is given by Amdahl's rule based on the relative partition of work between xf1() and xf2() (Section 4.2).

```
double loop_carried_example(double seed, double arg0)
{
  double vr = 0.0, vd = seed;
  for (int i=0;i<15;i++)
  {
      double vd = xf1(i*arg0);     // Parallelisable
      vd = xf2(vd + vd) * 3.14;    // Non-parallelisable
      vr += vd;
  }
  return vr;
}
```

Figure 6.43 An iteration that has a loop-carried data dependency (through variable vd)

```
static int [] foos = new int [10];
static int ipos = 0;
public static int loop_forwarding_example(int newdata)
{
  foos[ipos ++] = newdata;
  ipos %= foos.Length;
  int sum = 0;
  for (int i=0;i<foos.Length-1;i++)
    {
      int dv = foos[i]^foos[i+1];  // Two adjacent locations are read
      sum += dv;                   // Associative scalar reduction in sum
    }
  return sum;
}
```

Figure 6.44 A loop where data fetched in one iteration (foo[i]) can usefully be forwarded to a subsequent iteration

A value read from an array in one iteration can be **loop forwarded** from one iteration to another. This can overcome structural hazards and optimises memory bus bandwidth. Given the code of Figure 6.44, an HLS compiler should use only one read port on the array foo[], making one access per clock cycle. It will deploy a holding register to forward the value read in the current iteration to the next.

Data-dependent control flow and loop exit conditions also complicate auto-parallelisation. Figure 6.45 gives a generic example. Typical loops have various special cases at their boundaries. It is important to ensure that this seldom-executed boundary code does not degrade the performance of the majority of iterations. Careful coding, perhaps using predicating and bounded loops, can help, but the HLS compiler should ideally always automate the process. DRAM access mechanisms inevitably round data fetched up to the next burst size multiple (Section 2.6.6). The predicated approach advances the loop variable to its *a priori* bounded end value, but implements a mechanism to discard unwanted side effects beyond the true end, such as not storing the result. How early in a loop body

```
public static int data_dependent_controlflow_example(int seed)
{
  int vr = 0;
  int i;
  for (i=0;i<20;i++)
    {
      vr += i*i*seed;
      if (vr > 1111) break; // Early loop exit
    }
  return i;
}
```

Figure 6.45 A loop that has data-dependent control flow (the loop exit depends on variable vr)

the exit condition can be determined is an important consideration and compilers do this at the start of the block schedule (as illustrated in Figure 6.39).

Memory Banking and Wide Data

Whether computing on standard CPUs or FPGA, DRAM memory bandwidth is often the main performance bottleneck. The design space for DRAM banks was introduced in Section 4.5. Since the data transfer rate per bit for a read or write port is fixed, two ways to increase memory bandwidth are to use **multiple banks** or **wide memories**. Multiple banks (aka channels) can be accessed simultaneously at different locations, whereas memories with a wider word are accessed at just one location at a time (per port). Both yield more data for each access. Both also may or may not need lane steering or a crossbar routing matrix, depending on the application and allowable mappings of data to processing units. The performance of GPUs can be increased by not using lane steering . In this case, the data are partitioned with close association to PEs, which avoids combinational delays in the routing matrix and improves the clock speed, but this is unsuitable for some algorithmic kernels (e.g. FFT, Section 6.9.1).

There are some important binding decisions for memory:

- Which user arrays should have their own RAMs? Which should share? Which should be put into DRAM?

- Should a user array be spread over RAMs or DRAM channels to increase the bandwidth?

- How are data to be packed into words in the RAMs?

- Should extra copies of a ROM be freely deployed to increase the read bandwidth?

- Should data be mirrored in RAMs, as this requires additional work when writing to keep the copies in step (Section 4.5)?

■ How should data be organised over DRAM rows? Should data even be stored in DRAM more than once with different row alignments?

It is informative to consider the best data layout for several standard algorithms. As well as considering mapping and the interleaving of a logical address space over various DRAM channels, two paradigms pertain to layout within an address space. An **array of structs** is the most common layout in HLLs, especially object-oriented languages. All fields of a class are adjacent in an on-heap record. The alternative, a **struct of arrays**, requires fewer page activations if a loop examines only certain fields within the data, which is common.

Example 1: Data Layout for the Burrows–Wheeler Transform

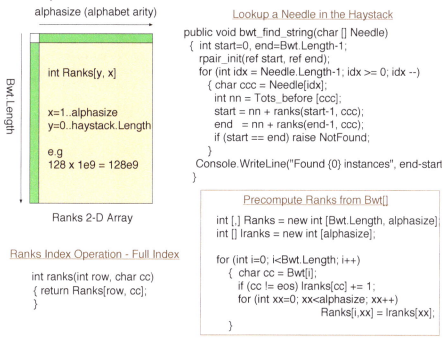

alphasize (alphabet arity)

int Ranks[y, x]

x=1..alphasize
y=0..haystack.Length

e.g
128 x 1e9 = 128e9

Bwt.Length

Ranks 2-D Array

Lookup a Needle in the Haystack

```
public void bwt_find_string(char [] Needle)
{ int start=0, end=Bwt.Length-1;
  rpair_init(ref start, ref end);
  for (int idx = Needle.Length-1; idx >= 0; idx --)
  { char ccc = Needle[idx];
    int nn = Tots_before [ccc];
    start = nn + ranks(start-1, ccc);
    end  = nn + ranks(end-1, ccc);
    if (start == end) raise NotFound;
  }
  Console.WriteLine("Found {0} instances", end-start
}
```

Ranks Index Operation - Full Index

```
int ranks(int row, char cc)
{ return Ranks[row, cc];
}
```

Precompute Ranks from Bwt[]

```
int [,] Ranks = new int [Bwt.Length, alphasize]
int [] Iranks = new int [alphasize];

for (int i=0; i<Bwt.Length; i++)
{ char cc = Bwt[i];
  if (cc != eos) Iranks[cc] += 1;
  for (int xx=0; xx<alphasize; xx++)
          Ranks[i,xx] = Iranks[xx];
}
```

Figure 6.46 Lookup procedure when searching for a string using the BWT. A haystack has been transformed and stored in Bwt []. *An index* Ranks [] *is computed for it. Looking for the string in* Needle *is then very fast*

The **Burrows–Wheeler transform (BWT)** of a string of length m characters is another string of the same length and alphabet. In accordance with the definition of a transform, it preserves information and has an inverse. The BWT has various useful properties. It can be used as a pre-step for lossless compression since the BWT of a string usually compresses much better under many simple schemes. It also encodes all substrings of the original string in sorted order, so a needle of length m can be searched in a haystack string of length m with $\mathcal{O}(m \log n)$ cost [38].

The code in Figure 6.46 follows [39]. It efficiently finds perfect string matches of the contents of the Needle [] array in the BWT of a haystack, which is stored in Bwt []. The code in the inset at the bottom right has pre-computed an index. The Tots_before [] array is very small and easily fits in BRAM

(Section 8.5.2) on an FPGA. The array Ranks is large. It is 2-D, indexed by character and contains integers ranging up to the haystack size (requiring more bits than a character from the alphabet).

However, for big data, such as the billion bases in a genome, the Ranks array may be too big for the available DRAM. The solution is to decimate the Ranks array by some factor, such as 32, and then store only every 32nd row in memory. If the search string is not in a stored row, the contents of the relevant row are interpolated on the fly. This requires that the original string is stored, but this may be useful for many other related purposes anyway.

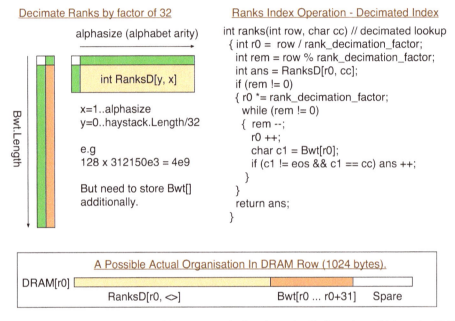

Figure 6.47 Compacted Ranks array for BWT, redefinition of the ranks () routine for an interpolated lookup and a sensible layout in a DRAM row

The decimation is illustrated in Figure 6.47. Access patterns to the RanksD [] array do not have spatial or temporal locality, especially at the start of the search when start and end are well separated. If only one bank channel of DRAM is available, then random access delays dominate. (The only way to get better performance is task-level parallelism. Multiple needles could be searched for concurrently, which at least overcomes the round-trip latency to the DRAM, but not the low performance intrinsic to not having spatial locality.) However, one good idea is to store the BWT fragment in the same DRAM row as the ranking information. Then only one row activation is needed per needle character.

For what factor of decimation is the interpolator not on the critical path? This will depend mainly on how much the HLS compiler chooses (or is commanded via pragmas) to unwind it. In general, when aligning data in DRAM rows, sometimes a pair of items that are known to be needed by both can be split into different rows. In this case, storing everything twice may help, with one copy offset by half a row length from the other, since then it is possible to address the copy manually due to the good alignment.

An interesting research question is whether HLS compilers should attempt to replicate the information as suggested.

Example 2: Data Dependencies in the Smith–Waterman Algorithm

The Smith–Waterman algorithm [40] matches two very similar strings to find the alignment with the minimum edit distance. The strings are typically a whole DNA genome and a variant or a fragment thought to have come from it. A quadratic algorithm based on dynamic programming is used. Entries in a 2-D array have a score that depends on the three immediate neighbours with lower index, as shown in Figure 6.48. Zeros are inserted for negative subscripts at the edges. The entry with maximum score is then found.

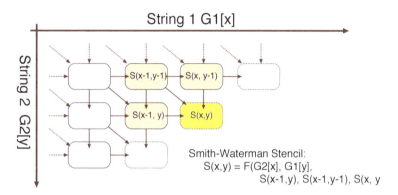

Figure 6.48 Data dependencies (slightly simplified) in the Smith–Waterman alignment-finding algorithm

A naive implementation is a pair of nested `for` loops that iterate over each dimension. However, acceleration is achieved by computing as many scores in parallel as possible. There is no simple nesting of two `for` loops that can work. Instead, items on the anti-diagonal frontier must be computed in parallel. This is a simple example of polyhedral address mapping.

Polyhedral Address Mapping

A set of nested loops where the bounds of inner loops depend on linear combinations of surrounding induction variables defines a **polyhedral space** or **polytope**. This space is scanned by a vector consisting of the induction variables. Under a polyhedral mapping, the loop nesting order may be changed and **affine transformations** are applied to many of the loop variables with the aim of exposing parallelism or repacking the array subscripts to use less overall memory. Affine transformations include linear scaling, translations, axis interchanges and other rotations.

Overall, a useful transformation is one that compacts sparse access patterns into a packed form or partitions array read subscripts into disjoint sets so that they can be served in parallel by different memories. If data dependencies are sufficiently determined, thread-future reads can be started at the earliest point after the supporting writes have been made to meet all the RaW data dependencies.

Although the input code may have been written without much thought for automatic parallelisation, there is often a structure that can be usefully mined and exploited. The pattern of array subscriptions is extracted by the compiler and matched against standard decidable theory schemas. If a **decidable subscript pattern** is found, then the compiler can be completely sure which data dependencies and anti-dependencies exist and, more importantly, definitely do not exist. A **data dependency** is present in the normal case when an array location has to be written before it is read. An **anti-dependency** occurs when an array location cannot be updated with a fresh value because one or more reads of the old value must first take place. If neither such dependency exists, the work can be performed in parallel without an interlock.

Standard decidable theories include integer linear inequalities (**linear programming**), **Presburger arithmetic** (one operand of a multiplication must be constant) and the **octagon domain** (the maximum difference between two subscripts is constrained by a natural number). Although these schemas vary in expressivity and their provers can sometimes take hours to run, they can all rapidly handle the common cases, such as determining that `A[x]` is always a different location from `A[x+1]`, which is the basic requirement for doing work in parallel. Determining at compile time whether two array subscript expressions are equal is called the **name alias hazard** (Section 6.3.3).

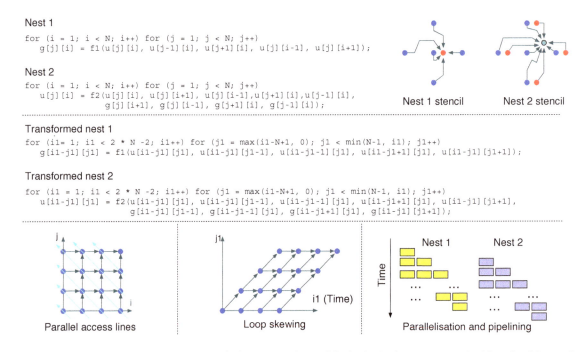

Nest 1
```
for (i = 1; i < N; i++) for (j = 1; j < N; j++)
    g[j][i] = f1(u[j][i], u[j-1][i], u[j+1][i], u[j][i-1], u[j][i+1]);
```

Nest 2
```
for (i = 1; i < N; i++) for (j = 1; j < N; j++)
    u[j][i] = f2(u[j][i], u[j][i+1], u[j][i-1], u[j+1][i], u[j-1][i],
                g[j][i+1], g[j][i-1], g[j+1][i], g[j-1][i]);
```

Nest 1 stencil   Nest 2 stencil

Transformed nest 1
```
for (i1= 1; i1 < 2 * N -2; i1++) for (j1 = max(i1-N+1, 0); j1 < min(N-1, i1); j1++)
    g[i1-j1][j1] = f1(u[i1-j1][j1], u[i1-j1][j1-1], u[i1-j1-1][j1], u[i1-j1+1][j1], u[i1-j1][j1+1]);
```

Transformed nest 2
```
for (i1 = 1; i1 < 2 * N -2; i1++) for (j1 = max(i1-N+1, 0); j1 < min(N-1, i1); j1++)
    u[i1-j1][j1] = f2(u[i1-j1][j1], u[i1-j1][j1-1], u[i1-j1-1][j1], u[i1-j1+1][j1], u[i1-j1][j1+1],
                g[i1-j1][j1-1], g[i1-j1-1][j1], g[i1-j1+1][j1], g[i1-j1][j1+1]);
```

Parallel access lines   Loop skewing   i1 (Time)   Time   Nest 1   Nest 2   Parallelisation and pipelining

Figure 6.49 *Affine transformation examples, adapted from [41]. Nest 1 runs after nest 2, but by skewing the access pattern of each loop, there is increased parallelism available within each nest and pipelining becomes possible. Nest 2 commences just after nest 1 has produced its first diagonal output*

Polyhedral mappings must sometimes be designed to facilitate streaming input and output data so that an efficient pipeline can be established. For big data, at least one of the loop bounds is commonly an iteration over a file streamed from secondary storage. For example, in Figure 6.49, the kernel code from a standard image-processing de-noiser is presented in abstract form. This is taken from [41]. The data generated in `g[i,j]` from the first loop nest is the input to the following process, which is nest 2. Both the inner and outer loop bounds are transformed. As with the Smith–Waterman example, skewing the inner loop in each nest increases the locally available parallelism. Each item on the anti-diagonals, as highlighted at bottom left, can run simultaneously. Moreover, by suitably matching the loop structures of the two nests (in this case they are identical), nest 2 can commence operation as soon as the first data have been generated by nest 1. Hence, a cut-through pipeline is created.

As well as enabling successive pipeline stages to mesh efficiently, loop structures are commonly modified for two other reasons. The first is to minimise the storage footprint by converting to (largely) **in-place form**. Here, the memory locations that contained the input data are used for the output data. The second relates, as always, to optimising DRAM row activation patterns, such as using a nest of six for loops for array multiplication instead of the textbook three.

Example 3: The Perfect Shuffle Network, an FFT Example

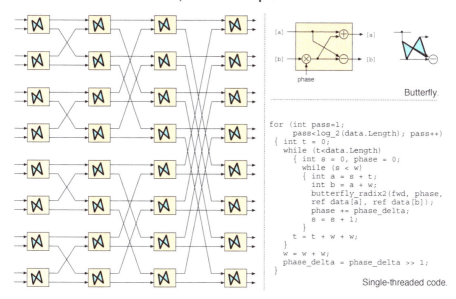

```
for (int pass=1;
        pass<log_2(data.Length); pass++)
{ int t = 0;
  while (t<data.Length)
    { int s = 0, phase = 0;
      while (s < w)
      { int a = s + t;
        int b = a + w;
        butterfly_radix2(fwd, phase,
        ref data[a], ref data[b]);
        phase += phase_delta;
        s = s + 1;
      }
      t = t + w + w;
    }
    w = w + w;
    phase_delta = phase_delta >> 1;
}
```
Single-threaded code.

Figure 6.50 Shuffle data flow for an FFT (left), elemental butterfly (top right) and code (bottom right)

Not all algorithms are amenable to polyhedral mapping, despite their data movements having a regular structure, such as a **fast Fourier transform (FFT)**. Figure 6.50 shows a 16-point FFT, but typically applications have hundreds or thousands of points. For an N-point FFT, $\log_2(N)$ passes are required, each with $N/2$ elemental computations known as butterflies. The butterfly operator has two operands (which are, generally, both complex numbers) and delivers two results. Internally it contains a rotation and two arithmetic operators (top right), but the details are unimportant for the current purposes. The successive passes can be done in place on one array. The operands are passed by reference to the butterfly (bottom right).

This pattern of data movement is known as a shuffle. It is also used in many switching and sorting algorithms. From the data dependencies in the figure, it is clear that a parallel speedup (Section 4.2) of $N/2 = 8$ is potentially available, since each of the eight butterflies in a pass is independent of the others. However, the downside of shuffle computations for acceleration is that **no packing of the data** (structural partitioning of the data array) into spatially separate memories **works well for all of the passes**. What is good at the start is poor at the end. Generating a good parallel implementation for large FFTs remains a challenge for HLS tools and is perhaps best tackled using a hybrid system of local and shared scratchpads that behave like a CMP cached memory. The compile-time knowledge of the eviction pattern eliminates the need for an associative lookup at runtime.

6.10 Summary

SoCs contain a number of processors, memories and I/O devices. In the simplest architecture, all the CPUs would be identical. There would be a single flat address space to span all the memory and every I/O device would be mapped into that same address space. A generic interrupt controller could enable any I/O device to interrupt any core with either a static mapping or a load-based distribution algorithm (Section 2.5). This approach is simple, flexible and homogeneous but is typically not good enough in terms of power, performance and area (PPA).

The performance of von Neumann cores is easily improved with custom hardware, which has no fetch-execute overhead. Moreover, the fetch-execute overhead of today's advanced out-of-order cores is up to two orders of magnitude less energy efficient [5, 6]. For example, for 32-bit addition, up to 100× the energy of the addition is consumed in deciding whether to do it, selecting the operands and storing the result in a dynamically renamed register.

More transistors in VLSI are now produced in the form of **dark silicon**, which is switched off most of the time (Section 8.2). Thus, implementing standard kernels as custom hardware cores is attractive due to the power saved. In the **conservation cores** approach [42], the inner loops of mature computations, such as several popular Android applications, were to be implemented in silicon on future mobile phones.

Accelerators can be tightly coupled with a conventional core or can be a separate bus-connected IP block. The choice depends on whether the processor core has something better to do while the accelerator is running and whether there is sufficient data bandwidth for them to share a single bus connection to main memory. Whether the data are likely to be in or needed in a given L1 data cache greatly influences the trade-off.

Design exploration takes place on multiple levels. These span the system architecture and design partition, the interconnect and the microarchitecture of subsystems. Automatic interconnect generators, HLS and modern design languages are starting to automate the second and third of these. For the first – the top-level architecture – experimental automated co-synthesis tools have been developed, but these have not yet seen industrial traction.

Whether using manual design partition and co-design, or automatic **co-synthesis**, design starts with a top-level specification. This may be directly executable [43], but preferably it dictates as little as possible about the final system structure, so that there are maximal opportunities for exploration and optimisation. The task dependency graph must be partitioned over storage and execution resources to meet PPA objectives. Design partition then determines storage locations, the degree of replication, whether hardware or software is used at each point and how the different subsystems communicate.

Automated co-synthesis procedures were briefly mentioned in Section 1.4.3. They can potentially be used at both the partitioning stage and in the design of individual subsystems. The partitioning stage uses high-level heuristics [44], but these are in their infancy. A good solution would render system architects redundant, so from an employment perspective, we are perhaps glad that automated co-synthesis is immature. However, these tool flows can help with the automatic design of hardware/software interfaces in terms of register layout, device driver header files and code stubs. The automatic implementation of a subsystem starts with its specification and typically uses a heuristic-driven sequence of **stepwise refinements**, each of which preserves the specified behaviour. Refinement is complete when the subsystem exists as a fully imperative implementation [45]. A typical refinement step is that if A is specified to be the same as B and one of them is already known, then an assignment is made from the known to the unknown. There are many alternative algorithms for generating logic from formal specifications, such as those based on SAT solvers [46] and interface automata [47].

From this chapter, the reader should understand the principles that motivate the partition of a design over pieces of silicon and over PEs within those chips. These include technology constraints as well as engineering and commercial considerations, such as design portability and economies of scale. Memory bandwidth dimensioning is nearly always a key consideration. The asymptotic analysis examples of Section 6.6 emphasised that simple equations that capture general trends can steer the architect to a good design. The in-depth study of three options for RTL design entry should motivate RTL engineers to exploit higher-level design expression languages, both for their clarity of design intent and their flexible time/space trade-off exploration.

There is no single best design flow for design exploration. Hopefully, this chapter has discussed a sufficient diversity of techniques. The exercises give further food for thought.

6.10.1 Exercises

1. Consider the design of a high-quality digital movie camera. Sketch a feasible top-level block diagram, remembering to include a viewfinder and audio subsystem, but you may ignore autofocusing. How many circuit boards, SoCs and processors should it have? To mitigate against the camera shaking, what are the relative costs of implementing a vision stabiliser using voice-coil prism hardware compared with an electronic/software-only implementation.

2. An algorithm performs a task that is essentially the same as completing a jigsaw puzzle. Input values and output results are to be held in DRAM. Describe input and output data formats that might be suitable for a jigsaw with a plain image but no mating edge that can falsely mate with the wrong edge. The input data set is approximately 1 Gbyte. By considering how many DRAM row activations and data transfers are needed, estimate how fast this problem can be solved by a

uniprocessor, a multi-core PRAM model (Section 2.3) and a hardware accelerator. State any assumptions.

3. Two processes that run largely independently occasionally have to access a stateless function that is best implemented using about 1 mm^2 of silicon. Two instances could be put down or one instance could be shared. What considerations affect whether sharing or replication is best? If shared, what sharing mechanisms might be appropriate and what would they look like at the hardware level?

4. Consider the following kernel, which tallies the set bit count in each word. Such bit-level operations are inefficient using general-purpose CPU instruction sets. If hardware support is to be added, what might be the best way of making the functionality available to low-level software?

```
for (int xx=0; xx<1024; xx++)
{
    unsigned int d = Data[xx];
    int count = 0;
    while (d > 0) { if (d&1) count ++;   d >>= 1; }
    if (!xx || count > maxcount) { maxcount = count; where = xx; }
}
```

5. Data loss can be avoided during a transfer between adjacent synchronous components by using a bidirectional handshake or performance guarantees. Explain these principles. What would be needed for such components to be imported into an IP-XACT-based system integrator tool if the tool allows easy interconnection but can also ensure that connections are always lossless?

6. What is a fully pipelined component? What is the principal problem with an RTL logic synthesiser automatically instantiating pipelined ALUs? A fully pipelined multiplier has a latency of three clock cycles. What is its throughput in terms of multiplications per clock cycle?

7. A bus carries data values, one per clock cycle, forming a sequence X(t) as illustrated in Figure 6.51. Also shown is a circuit that computes a value Y(t-3). It uses two adders that have a pipeline latency of 2 and an initiation interval of 1. The circuit was designed to compute the running sum of bus values. Check that it does this or else design an equivalent circuit that works but uses the same adder components.

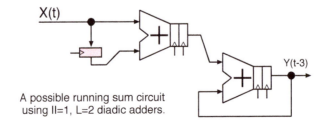

X(t)

Y(t-3)

A possible running sum circuit
using Il=1, L=2 diadic adders.

Figure 6.51 A circuit intended to compute the running sum of streaming data values

8. Does **strength reduction** help save area, energy or both? Give an expression that can benefit from three different strength reduction rules.

9. Is a NoC that uses store-and-forward elements with cut-through routing a multi-access NoC? Does multi-access lead to more or fewer chances of deadlocking?

10. Does either of the following two loops have dependencies or anti-dependencies between iterations? How can they be parallelised? See reference [48].

```
loop1:  for (i=0; i<N; i++)  A[i] := (A[i] + A[N-1-i])/2
loop2:  for (i=0; i<N; i++)  A[2*i] = A[i] + 0.5f;
```

References

[1] D. Knuth. *The Art of Computer Programming*. Addison-Wesley, Reading, Mass, 1968. ISBN 0-201-03801-3.

[2] Holger Hoos and Thomas Stützle. *Stochastic Local Search: Foundations & Applications*. Morgan Kaufmann Publishers Inc, San Francisco, CA, USA, 2004.

[3] Tensorflow: An end-to-end open source machine learning platform. https://www.tensorflow.org, 2020.

[4] André M. DeHon. Location, location, location: The role of spatial locality in asymptotic energy minimization. In *Proceedings of the ACM/SIGDA International Symposium on Field Programmable Gate Arrays*, FPGA '13, pages 137–146, New York, NY, USA, 2013. Association for Computing Machinery. ISBN 9781450318877. doi: 10.1145/2435264.2435291. URL https://doi.org/10.1145/2435264.2435291.

[5] M. Qasaimeh, K. Denolf, J. Lo, K. Vissers, J. Zambreno, and P. H. Jones. Comparing energy efficiency of CPU, GPU and FPGA implementations for vision kernels. In *2019 IEEE International Conference on Embedded Software and Systems (ICESS)*, pages 1–8, 2019. doi: 10.1109/ICESS.2019.8782524.

[6] Jeremy Fowers, Greg Brown, Patrick Cooke, and Greg Stitt. A performance and energy comparison of FPGAs, GPUs, and multicores for sliding-window applications. In *Proceedings of the ACM/SIGDA International Symposium on Field Programmable Gate Arrays*, FPGA '12, pages 47–56, New York, NY, USA, 2012. Association for Computing Machinery. ISBN 9781450311557. doi: 10.1145/2145694.2145704. URL https://doi.org/10.1145/2145694.2145704.

[7] INMOS Limited. *Transputer Reference Manual*. Prentice Hall International (UK) Ltd, GBR, 1988. ISBN 013929001X.

[8] Giovanni Patane, Giuseppe Campobello, and Marco Russo. Parallel CRC realization. *IEEE Transactions on Computers*, 52:1312–1319, 2003. doi: 10.1109/TC.2003.1234528.

[9] Federal Information Processing Standards Publication. Announcing the advanced encryption standard (AES). https://nvlpubs.nist.gov/nistpubs/FIPS/NIST.FIPS.197.pdf, 2001.

[10] A. M. Caulfield, E. S. Chung, A. Putnam, H. Angepat, J. Fowers, M. Haselman, S. Heil, M. Humphrey, P. Kaur, J. Kim, D. Lo, T. Massengill, K. Ovtcharov, M. Papamichael, L. Woods, S. Lanka, D. Chiou, and D. Burger. A cloud-scale acceleration architecture. In *49th Annual IEEE/ACM International Symposium on Microarchitecture (MICRO)*, pages 1–13, 2016. doi: 10.1109/MICRO.2016.7783710.

[11] Louise H. Crockett and Ross A. Elliot. *The Zynq Book: Embedded Processing with the Arm Cortex-A9 on the Xilinx Zynq-7000 All Programmable SoC*. Strathclyde Academic Media, Glasgow, United Kingdom, 2014. ISBN 978-0-9929787-0-9.

[12] Andrew Putnam, Adrian M. Caulfield, Eric S. Chung, Derek Chiou, Kypros Constantinides, John Demme, Hadi Esmaeilzadeh, Jeremy Fowers, Gopi Prashanth Gopal, Jan Gray, Michael Haselman, Scott Hauck, Stephen Heil, Amir Hormati, Joo-Young Kim, Sitaram Lanka, James Larus, Eric Peterson, Simon Pope, Aaron Smith, Jason Thong, Phillip Yi Xiao, and Doug Burger. A reconfigurable fabric for accelerating large-scale datacenter services. In *Proceeding of the 41st Annual International Symposium on Computer Architecture*, ISCA '14, pages 13–24. IEEE Press, 2014. ISBN 9781479943944.

[13] Arm Ltd. big.LITTLE Technology: The Future of Mobile: Making very high performance available in a mobile envelope without sacrificing energy efficiency. https://img.hexus.net/v2/press_releases/arm/big.LITTLE. Whitepaper.pdf, 2013.

[14] Urs Hölzle. Brawny cores still beat wimpy cores, most of the time. Technical report, Google, 2010.

[15] Dongkook Park, Aniruddha Vaidya, Akhilesh Kumar, and Mani Azimi. MoDe-X: Microarchitecture of a layout-aware modular decoupled crossbar for on-chip interconnects. *IEEE Transactions on Computers*, 63: 622–636, 2014. doi: 10.1109/TC.2012.203.

[16] A. Agrawal, S. K. Lee, J. Silberman, M. Ziegler, M. Kang, S. Venkataramani, N. Cao, B. Fleischer, M. Guillorn, M. Cohen, S. Mueller, J. Oh, M. Lutz, J. Jung, S. Koswatta, C. Zhou, V. Zalani, J. Bonanno, R. Casatuta, C. Y. Chen, J. Choi, H. Haynie, A. Herbert, R. Jain, M. Kar, K. H. Kim, Y. Li, Z. Ren, S. Rider, M. Schaal, K. Schelm, M. Scheuermann, X. Sun, H. Tran, N. Wang, W. Wang, X. Zhang, V. Shah, B. Curran, V. Srinivasan, P. F. Lu, S. Shukla, L. Chang, and K. Gopalakrishnan. 9.1 a 7nm 4-core AI chip with 25.6TFLOPS hybrid FP8 training, 102.4TOPS INT4 inference and workload-aware throttling. In *2021 IEEE International Solid-State Circuits Conference (ISSCC)*, volume 64, pages 144–146, 2021. doi: 10.1109/ISSCC42613.2021.9365791.

[17] The Software Freedom Conservancy. QEMU the fast processor emulator. https://www.qemu.org/, 2020.

[18] Nathan Binkert, Bradford Beckmann, Gabriel Black, Steven K. Reinhardt, Ali Saidi, Arkaprava Basu, Joel Hestness, Derek R. Hower, Tushar Krishna, Somayeh Sardashti, Rathijit Sen, Korey Sewell, Muhammad Shoaib, Nilay Vaish, Mark D. Hill, and David A. Wood. The Gem5 simulator. *SIGARCH Comput. Archit. News*, 39(2):1–7, August 2011. ISSN 0163-5964. doi: 10.1145/2024716.2024718. URL https://doi.org/10.1145/2024716.2024718.

[19] David J. Greaves and M. Yasin. TLM POWER3: Power estimation methodology for SystemC TLM 2.0. In *Proceedings of the 2012 Forum on Specification and Design Languages*, pages 106–111, 2012.

[20] Changsoo Je and Hyung-Min Park. Optimized hierarchical block matching for fast and accurate image registration. *Signal Processing: Image Communication*, 28:779–791, 2013. doi: 10.1016/j.image.2013.04.002.

[21] Andrew Kinane, Daniel Larkin, and Noel O'Connor. Energy-efficient acceleration of MPEG-4 compression tools. *EURASIP Journal on Embedded Systems*, 2007:1–18, 2007. doi: 10.1155/2007/28735.

[22] Shih-Hao Wang, Wen-Hsiao Peng, Yuwen He, Guan-Yi Lin, Cheng-Yi Lin, Shih-Chien Chang, Chung-Neng Wang, and Tihao Chiang. A software-hardware co-implementation of MPEG-4 advanced video coding (AVC) decoder with block level pipelining. *VLSI Signal Processing*, 41:93–110, 2005. doi: 10.1007/s11265-005-6253-3.

[23] Luz Garcia, Victor Reyes, Dacil Barreto, Gustavo Marrero, Tomas Bautista, and Antonio Nuñez. Analysis of MPEG-4 advanced simple profile (ASP) architectures using a system-level design methodology. In *XX Conference on Design of Circuits and Integrated Systems, Proceedings of DCIS*, 2005.

[24] David F. Bacon, Perry Cheng, and V.T. Rajan. A real-time garbage collector with low overhead and consistent utilization. *ACM SIGPLAN Notices*, 38(1):285–298, 2003.

[25] Florent Dinechin, Jérémie Detrey, Octavian Creţ, and Radu Tudoran. When FPGAs are better at floating-point than microprocessors, January 2008. LIP research report RR2007-40.

[26] *IEEE Standard for IP-XACT, Standard Structure for Packaging, Integrating, and Reusing IP within Tool Flows*. IEEE, 2014. Std 1685-2014 (Revision of Std 1685-2009).

[27] Intel Corporation. Platform designer (formerly called QSys). https://www.intel.com/content/www/us/en/programmable/support/support-resources/design-software/qsys.html, 2020.

[28] Xilinx Inc. SDSoC development environment. https://www.xilinx.com/products/design-tools/software-zone/sdsoc.html.

[29] Arm Ltd. Arm Socrates user guide version 1.5 (9th release). https://developer.arm.com/documentation/101399/0105/Introduction/About-Socrates, 2020.

[30] Arm Ltd. Corelink CMN-600 coherent mesh network. https://developer.arm.com/ip-products/system-ip/corelink-interconnect/corelink-coherent-mesh-network-family/corelink-cmn-600, 2020.

[31] Arm Ltd. Arm CoreLink NI-700 Network-on-Chip Interconnect, Technical Reference Manual. https://developer.arm.com/documentation/101566/0100/Introduction/About-the-CoreLink-NI-700-Network-on-Chip-Interconnect, 2020.

[32] Per Bjesse, Koen Claessen, Mary Sheeran, and Satnam Singh. Lava: Hardware design in Haskell. In *Proceedings of the 3rd ACM SIGPLAN International Conference on Functional Programming*, ICFP '98, pages 174–184, New York, NY, USA, 1998. Association for Computing Machinery. ISBN 1581130244. doi: 10.1145/289423.289440. URL https://doi.org/10.1145/289423.289440.

[33] Bahram N. Uchevler, Kjetil Svarstad, Jan Kuper, and Christiaan Baaij. System-level modelling of dynamic reconfigurable designs using functional programming abstractions. In *International Symposium on Quality Electronic Design*, pages 379–385. IEEE, 2013. doi: 10.1109/ISQED.2013.6523639. URL https://doi.org/10.1109/ISQED.2013.6523639.

[34] Jonathan Bachrach, Huy Vo, Brian Richards, Yunsup Lee, Andrew Waterman, Rimas Avižienis, John Wawrzynek, and Krste Asanović. Chisel: Constructing hardware in a Scala embedded language. In *Proceedings of the 49th Annual Design Automation Conference*, DAC '12, pages 1216–1225, New York, NY, USA, 2012. Association for Computing Machinery. ISBN 9781450311991. doi: 10.1145/2228360.2228584. URL https://doi.org/10.1145/2228360.2228584.

[35] M. Arvind. Bluespec: A language for hardware design, simulation, synthesis and verification. In *Proceedings of the First ACM and IEEE International Conference on Formal Methods and Models for Co-Design*, MEMOCODE '03, page 249, USA, 2003. IEEE Computer Society. ISBN 0769519237.

[36] P. Sittel, M. Kumm, J. Oppermann, K. Möller, P. Zipf, and A. Koch. ILP-based modulo scheduling and binding for register minimization. In *28th International Conference on Field Programmable Logic and Applications (FPL)*, pages 265–2656. IEEE, 2018. doi: 10.1109/FPL.2018.00053.

[37] David J. Greaves and S. Singh. Kiwi: Designing application specific circuits with concurrent C# programs. In *Proceedings of the 8th ACM/IEEE International Conference on Formal Methods and Models for Codesign*, MEMOCODE '10, pages 21–30, USA, 2010. IEEE Computer Society. ISBN 9781424478866. doi: 10.1109/MEMCOD.2010.5558627. URL https://doi.org/10.1109/MEMCOD.2010.5558627.

[38] T. Bell, M. Powell, A. Mukherjee, and D. Adjeroh. Searching BWT compressed text with the Boyer-Moore algorithm and binary search. In *Proceedings of the Data Compression Conference*, pages 112–121, 2002. doi: 10.1109/DCC.2002.999949.

[39] Paul T. Draghicescu, Greg Edvenson, and Corey B. Olson. Inexact search acceleration on FPGAs using the Burrows–Wheeler transform. Technical report, Pico Computing Inc, 2012.

[40] T. Smith and M. Waterman. Identification of common molecular subsequences. *Journal of Molecular Biology*, 147 1:195–197, 1981.

[41] Wei Zuo, Yun Liang, Peng Li, Kyle Rupnow, Deming Chen, and Jason Cong. Improving high level synthesis optimization opportunity through polyhedral transformations. In *Proceedings of the ACM/SIGDA International Symposium on Field Programmable Gate Arrays*, FPGA '13, pages 9–18, New York, NY, USA, 2013. Association for Computing Machinery. ISBN 9781450318877. doi: 10.1145/2435264.2435271. URL https://doi.org/10.1145/2435264.2435271.

[42] Ganesh Venkatesh, Jack Sampson, Nathan Goulding, Saturnino Garcia, Vladyslav Bryksin, Jose Lugo-Martinez, Steven Swanson, and Michael Bedford Taylor. Conservation cores: Reducing the energy of mature computations. In *Proceedings of the 15th International Conference on Architectural Support for Programming Languages and Operating Systems*, ASPLOS XV, pages 205–218, New York, NY, USA, 2010. Association for Computing Machinery. ISBN 9781605588391. doi: 10.1145/1736020.1736044. URL https://doi.org/10.1145/1736020.1736044.

[43] Norbert E. Fuchs. Specifications are (preferably) executable. *Softw. Eng. J.*, 7(5):323–334, September 1992. ISSN 0268-6961. doi: 10.1049/sej.1992.0033. URL https://doi.org/10.1049/sej.1992.0033.

[44] Imene Mhadhbi, Slim Ben Othman, and Slim Ben Saoud. An efficient technique for hardware/software partitioning process in codesign. *Scientific Programming*, 2016:1–11, 2016. doi: 10.1155/2016/6382765.

[45] Ralph-Johan Back and Joakim von Wright. Correctness and refinement of statements. In *Refinement Calculus*, pages 269–298. Springer, 1998. ISBN 978-0-387-98417-9. doi: 10.1007/978-1-4612- 1674-2_17.

[46] David J. Greaves. Automated hardware synthesis from formal specification using SAT solvers. In *Proceedings of the 15th IEEE International Workshop on Rapid System Prototyping*, pages 15–20, 2004. doi: 10.1109/ IWRSP.2004.1311089.

[47] David J. Greaves and M. J. Nam. Synthesis of glue logic, transactors, multiplexors and serialisors from protocol specifications. *IET Conference Proceedings*, pages 171–177(6), January 2010. URL https://digital-library.theiet.org/content/conferences/10.1049/ic.2010.0148.

[48] J. Liu, J. Wickerson, and G. A. Constantinides. Loop splitting for efficient pipelining in high-level synthesis. In *24th Annual International Symposium on Field-Programmable Custom Computing Machines*, pages 72–79. IEEE, 2016. doi: 10.1109/FCCM.2016.27.

Chapter 7

Formal Methods and
Assertion-based Design

SmallCheck says: 'If a program does not fail in any simple case, it hardly ever fails in any case.' [1].

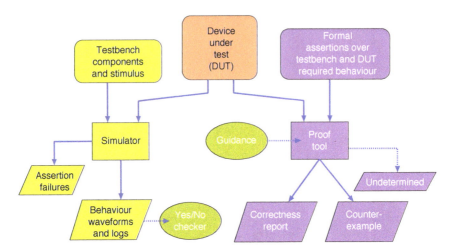

Figure 7.1 Comparing simulation (left) with a formal proof of correctness (right)

A formal proof of correctness for a system or component requires a formal specification of what it is supposed to do or not do. Figure 7.1 illustrates the principal difference between simulation and formal correctness for a **device under test (DUT)**. A simulation requires models of the surrounding components or stimulus. These determine what is fed into the DUT during the simulation. The simulator writes logs containing the console output, waveforms and other data. A checker can examine the logs and yield a pass or fail based on the observable output. An **assertion** is a statement that is either true or false. An assertion is normally expected to hold universally, but it can have a **guard condition** that qualifies where or when it is required to hold. An assertion checker may be built into a simulator for dynamic validation (Section 7.3.1). A major shortcoming of simulation is that any run can feasibly simulate only a small amount of the possible input behaviour and hence, the possible behaviour of the DUT. For instance, if a DUT has 200 flip-flops, it is not possible for a simulation to enter every one of the 2^{200} possible states in the lifetime of the universe. Hence, simulations are far from perfect and hardly ever catch rare errors:

> An error which occurs once in many millions of clock cycles will never randomly be encoun-
> tered in simulation but is likely to be hit within a few seconds of powering up the real silicon.
> – David J. Greaves.

However, a component rarely needs to operate correctly over all possible inputs. When a component is integrated into a system, and hence, composed with other components, the possible behaviour of each component is limited, since certain inputs will not be generated under certain circumstances. A component design specification typically has numerous associated don't-care input conditions for which any behaviour is allowable (Section 8.3.8). For a formal proof of correctness, the simulator and the concrete stimulus are replaced with a proof tool and **environmental constraints**, which model the behaviour of the other system components and are typically given in the form of **assumptions**, which together specify the full range of possible input stimulus patterns.

Parts of the test bench used for a simulation can often be reused for a formal proof. A proof tool does not require a clear distinction between the DUT and its test bench provided both are expressed in a language that the tool can understand, because it can treat the combination of the test bench and the true DUT as a composite DUT. This technique increases code reuse and is sometimes preferred by engineers since it is often easier and more useful to implement behaviour directly in a thin test bench (known as a shim) than to specify that behaviour as environmental constraints.

Unlike a simulator, a formal tool attempts to prove that an assertion holds over all possible test bench and stimulus patterns. Such input sequences may be infinite, but inductive techniques can often cope with these. As well as assertions, which can be checked during a simulation, a larger class of properties involving future behaviours, like the absence of a deadlock, can also be proved.

Using formal techniques has become mainstream in hardware design. The synthesisable subsets of Verilog and VHDL are described in [2] and [3], respectively. They have the same set of core semantics, as presented in Section 8.3. These languages and core ideas were extended to the **property specification language (PSL)** [4] and **System Verilog Assertions (SVA)** [5], which also share a common core set of concepts. They both define formal semantics for temporal logic expressions that are widely used in various ways, for example, to define the allowable transactions on standard busses.

In many industries, a formally verified result may be *required* by the end customer. As explained later, the requirement is typically in the form of **test coverage metrics** with separate quotas being applicable for dynamic simulations and formal proofs (Section 7.1.1). Another form of semi-formal quality assurance is based on dynamic coverage checks (which log that the flow of control has passed a point or that a property was held).

7.1 Formal Languages and Tools

As defined in Section 6.8, the two main styles of programming languages are imperative and declarative. Many programming languages are imperative. In an **imperative language**, a sequence of commands successively changes the values of variables, so that the order of commands matters. For instance, the value read from a variable depends on whether it has already been written to. In contrast, for a **declarative language**, the order of the statements does not matter. For instance, the clauses of a legal contract can be listed in any order without affecting what is and what is not allowed under that contract. Declarative languages are typically used to express properties that need to be proven. Everyday mathematics can be thought of as a declarative language. Axioms (such as $1 + 1 = 2$) and theorems (such as $\forall x \, \exists y$ such that $y > x$) can be listed in any order, although to prove a theorem, some axioms and earlier theorems are generally needed.

For digital systems, assertions are naturally phrased in terms of digital conditions. For mixed-signal simulations (Section 8.3.7) that include continuous quantities such as voltage and pressure, Boolean predicates over analogue variables are used. A **predicate** is any function that returns true or false. For certain proofs, these may be augmented using the rules of linearity or metric spaces, such as

$x > y \wedge y > z \implies x > z$. (In formal languages, it is common to use $\wedge$ and $\vee$ instead of && and || to denote logical AND and OR. We call these connectives conjunction and disjunction, respectively.)

All subsystems in a SoC evolve over time, as the values of registers and memory locations change and interfaces carry ordered sequences of values and handshake transitions. Hence, a **temporal algebra** is nearly always required to relate values at one time to those that immediately follow or will occur some time later. Formal languages for hardware description, indeed, have a large vocabulary of temporal operators. These include various 'before' and 'until' operators as well as the the suffix implications we present for PSL in Section 7.4.

Formal proof engines are either automatic or manual. An **automatic prover** requires no input from the engineer in proving correctness or generating a counterexample, though many of them do benefit from various command-line hints and heuristic weights. The most important type of automatic proof tool is a **model checker**, which starts from the reset state and considers all possible next states arising from all possible input values. Hence, it essentially performs a breadth-first search of the state space. Some tools are, indeed, directly implemented in this way using an enormous bit map stored in gigabytes of main memory to check whether a state has already been visited. Other tools implement **bounded model checking**, which considers only a limited number of steps from the reset state (e.g. 20 to 100).

The manual alternative is a **theorem prover**, although these generally contain a significant amount of automation to assist with repetitive steps and to suggest or explore possible next steps in the proof. A theorem prover has a database of axioms, logic rules and already derived theorems. The primary operation is to apply an inference rule to existing results to generate a new theorem with the intention of eventually generating the theorem the user set out to prove. A theorem prover ensures that whatever sequence of operations is selected, it is impossible to create an incorrect theorem. However, it is certainly possible to generate vast numbers of irrelevant or useless theorems. Hence, manual assistance is nearly always required to guide the system to the desired result. However, as said, the semi-automatic application of rules is commonly supported (where the automation is called a **tactic**). Previous proofs can be saved as tactics for replay in the current proof.

In practice, proving theorems requires considerable effort and only a small percentage of formal work is conducted this way. Theorem-proving teams are often quite small, even in a very large semiconductor house. Hence, this approach is practically applicable only for a few well-defined problems. A mainstream example is the floating-point data path in an FPU (Section 6.4). Such circuits are less amenable to automatic model checking due to the many XOR gates (which means that there is no good sort order in BDD-based checking, for instance). However, once correctness is demonstrated, it is exhaustive – an actual proof!

A **binary decision diagram (BDD)** is a compact representation of the truth table used inside many formal tools. Comparing functions for equivalence is instant using BDD representations. Many other useful operations are also quick, such as the logic functions for conjunction (AND), disjunction (OR) and negation (NOT) applied between or on a BDD. Existential checks, such as whether a function is satisfiable under certain conditions, have the same cost as a conjunction. Their main disadvantage is that their compactness depends on their **sort order**, which is an ancillary total ordering of all the variables in an expression. It is relatively easy to find a good sort order for a function, but this may not be a good sort order for another function. Conjunctions and disjunctions require the operands to be in the same sort order. Hence, BDD packages often spend the majority of their time making heuristic-based searches for a good sort order or rearranging a BDD from one order to another.

7.1.1 Verification Coverage

Digital computers are, theoretically speaking, finite-state machines (FSMs). Across even a large set of simulations, only a subset of the states will be entered. Thus, only a subset of the possible set of state-to-state transitions will be executed. The number of states entered can be expressed as a percentage of the total number of states to give a **test coverage** metric for a simulation trace or test program. The ideal coverage is 100 per cent. However, state-based test coverage is seldom used. The main alternatives are fault coverage and functional coverage.

The **fault coverage** is the percentage of stuck-at faults discovered by a set of simulations. It is often used for production test programs, and so is explained in Section 8.8. In basic terms, a **stuck-at fault** occurs when a net is permanently at logic one or zero, regardless of its driving logic. The denominator for this metric is twice the number of nets, since a net can be stuck either high or low.

There are many similar ways of defining **functional coverage**. These may be expressed in terms of high-level design goals but are not necessarily easy to automate. For a simulation, common coverage measures reported by tools include:

1. **Lines or statements**: How many lines of code were executed? In general software, a common coverage metric is the percentage of the lines of code that were executed. The same metric readily applies to RTL simulations.

2. **Branches**: How many branches of conditional statements were executed?

3. **Expressions**: How many of the possible values of a sub-expression were hit? For arithmetic, this is generally unrealistic to measure, but for a Boolean expression with logical operators, the 2^n growth of possibilities in terms of number of inputs is more feasible to explore.

4. **Path coverage**: If there are unavoidable correlations between conditional branches, only some of the paths through block-structured behavioural RTL or software can possibly be taken. Such correlations arise when a succession of `if` statements apply to a set of similar supporting inputs. A set of simulations is likely to execute fewer still paths. Tools can check for obvious correlations and determine a denominator for pairs or triples of successive conditional branches. Hence, a valuable coverage metric can be reported, although decidability implies the denominator may be too high, giving a coverage lower than the true value.

5. **Toggle coverage**: How often did a state bit transition from zero to one or from one to zero?

Measuring the number of hits of each coverage point indicates how well a simulation test bench explored the design space. Typically, each point will be expected to be hit many times overall.

These measures can also be used to produce **formal cover properties**, which can be used as reachability checks. Formal coverage is normally computed by a model checker and differs from a simulation, since demonstrating that a cover is reachable says nothing directly about the quality of the other assertions. However, a formal trace for a cover can identify the minimum number of cycles that must be searched before that point is exercised. Once we have these minimum depths, there are various ways of using them to gauge the usefulness of the undetermined results, which are, otherwise, so hard to quantify.

Several standard types of coverage metric are used to ensure that a set of assertions cover an acceptable amount of the design space:

- **The PSL `cover` directive (Section 7.4)**: This keeps activation statistics for each assertion. Assertions in the form of an implication that have low or zero activations of their antecedents (the expression on the left-hand side of the implication operator) do not contribute.

- **COI coverage**: How much of the design is included in the driving logic of at least one assertion? The **cone of influence (COI)** of a net or variable encompasses the nets and variables that it depends on. These are known as its **sequential support** or **combinational support**. For a combinational net, the COI extends backwards to flip-flop outputs. The sequential support extends through D-types and can easily be very large, such as a complete clock domain. The COI is important when repipelining a design (Section 4.4.2).

- **COI reachability**: If an assertion is explored only for N clock cycles by the model checker, how does that compare with the number of cycles required to affect the state elements in its driving logic?

- **Proof core**: Some elements in the COI of an assertion may not actually be required to reason about the assertion's correctness. How much of the design state is actually required by at least one assertion?

COI coverage is used at early stages to help direct the work to areas of the design for which no check currently exists.

COI reachability is useful during model checking, as it can identify properties that the tool is struggling to explore to a meaningful depth. Attention can then be brought to bear on these, for example, by using divide-and-conquer techniques (such as case splitting and assume-guarantee methods) or by **overconstraining** the environment or the design to reduce the state space being explored. Alternatively, helper properties may be devised that are more easily proven and which help the model checker to exclude irrelevant states.

Achieving 100 per cent coverage in every part of a design is, typically, impossible, and so **coverage targets** are set. It is often best to set these at the beginning of a project, so that they are not negatively influenced during design work as deadlines approach and difficult areas are revealed. Medical, defence and aerospace applications generally require much higher percentage coverage than commercial products and contracts. Safety standards may require a minimum coverage level. Meeting coverage targets does not mean that the design has been completely verified, but any missing coverage is a strong indication that something has been left unchecked. Scaling of formal checking is a practical problem. Today's tools certainly cannot check a complete SoC in one pass. An incremental approach based around individual subsystems is used in practice.

7.1.2 Property Completeness

How can a designer determine whether adding a new assertion improves the proof? When should they stop adding assertions? As we have said, a design team should set good coverage targets beforehand, but they also need confidence that all parts of the design have been observed.

Once a design has met its verification targets, using **design mutations** can be useful for detecting further behaviour that is not covered by the existing properties. In this technique, the DUT is changed or mutated, such by as forcing a sub-expression to be stuck at zero or one or by altering an operator from addition to subtraction. If the set of verification properties is truly complete, then one would expect that this mutation will cause a related property to fail. If the mutated DUT does not affect the verification then this may indicate an area of the DUT that is not fully checked by the verification properties.

In practice, there can be false positives, in particular if the mutated element is not functional but rather a performance optimisation. For example, if a DUT is permitted, but not required, to merge some transactions, then the absence of a property that fires when the merging logic is broken is not a functional failure. In fact, a reasonable verification property is something like: 'If transactions are merged then the conditions for merging exist' and not 'When the conditions for merging exist then transactions must be merged.' However, if a design is mature and few coverage holes are expected, mutation may be a useful technique.

7.1.3 When Is a Formal Specification Complete?

When is a formal specification complete?

- Does it fully define an actual implementation (this is overly restrictive)?

- Does it exactly prescribe all allowable and observable behaviours?

By 'formal' we mean a machine-readable description of what is correct or incorrect behaviour. A *complete* specification could describe all allowable behaviours and prohibit all remaining behaviours, but most formal definitions today are not complete in this sense. For instance, a definition that consists of a list of safety assertions and a few liveness assertions could still allow all sorts of behaviours that the designer knows are wrong. A complete specification can be defined as one that describes all observable behaviours. Such a specification does not restrict or proscribe the internal implementation in **black box** terms since this is not observable.

7.2 Assertions

An **assertion** is a statement about whether a property holds. As mentioned earlier, assertions may be true or false. An assertion about the **current state** of a system can vary as the system changes state. This is called a **state property**. Many assertions have a **guard condition**, which identifies when the property is expected to hold, which can be always, at some point in the future or at certain clock edges.

We will describe three main forms of assertion: procedural assertions, safety assertions and liveness assertions. In assertion theory, a procedural assertion is just a specific form of safety assertion. Indeed, there are techniques for mapping any number of safety and liveness assertions into just one safety assertion [6], but this typically adds additional state that needs to be checked. For a non-specialist, it is easier to handle safety and liveness separately, and, if it is helpful, to allow the tools to automate any such mappings. However, as we discuss in Section 7.9, if a tool does not explicitly support liveness, a liveness assertion can be expressed as a safety assertion.

Immediate Assertions

In imperative software languages, programmers are used to embedding procedural assertions at critical points. For instance, in C++, the `assert.h` header is commonly used (Figure 7.2).

```
assert(x<4);
x := x + 1000;
assert(x<1004);
```

Figure 7.2 Examples of imperative or procedural safety assertions in a software language such as C++. These conditions must hold when reached by the program's flow of control

These are called **procedural assertions** or **immediate assertions**. VHDL has an equivalent statement using its `assert`, `report` and `severity` keywords. Similarly, in System Verilog, the `expect` statement provides the same functionality. However, most VHDL and Verilog coders today use the equivalents in the **property specification language (PSL)** whereas System Verilog users use **System Verilog Assertions (SVA)**. These are described shortly in Section 7.4.

Safety Assertions

A **safety assertion** states a property that must always hold. It embodies the essence of a declaration, such as a declaration of human rights. However, in electronics it is likely to be less grand such as, for an indicator panel: 'Never is light A on at the same time as light B' (with the word order following the syntax illustrated below). An example that conveys the concept of real-world safety is: 'Never are both the inner door and outer door of the airlock open at the same time unless the ship is surrounded by a breathable atmosphere.'

Another word for a safety declaration is a **system invariant**. An assertion that holds at all times is often called a **concurrent assertion** to distinguish it from an immediate or procedural assertion. The keywords **always** and **never** are used to introduce a concurrent safety declaration. The following examples of equivalent safety assertions show that a list of safety assertions is the same as a conjunction of their predicates:

```
always S1, S2;          // A list of safety predicates could be separated by commas.
always S1; always S2;   // Or they could be listed as separate statements.
always S1 && S2;        // Or they could use a single `safety' keyword and a conjunction.
never !S1;              // The opposite of `always' is `never'.
never !S2;              // So `always S2' can be written as `never !S2'.
```

These examples demonstrate a **guarded safety assertion**, which holds only under certain conditions. In hardware, a guard condition could be a state predicate, a clock edge or a combination of these:

```
whenever (P1) P2;       // The `whenever' construct guardedly asserts that P1 implies P2.
always  !P1 || P2;      // Implication can be expanded to when P1 does not hold, P2 must.
```

Liveness Assertions

A **liveness assertion** is a property that needs to be fulfillable at some later time. A guarded example is: 'If the emergency button is pressed, eventually at least one of the doors will become unlocked.' Liveness properties normally use keywords such as **eventually** or phrases such as **it will always be possible to**. The door unlocking example is a liveness assertion despite not having a subordinate 'if' clause.

If a safety property is contravened, the trace of events forms a **counterexample** and that trace will have a specific finite length. It is sometimes claimed that a liveness failure cannot have a counterexample with a finite trace. However, many liveness failures can have a trace that ends in a deadlock, which is a finite trace if we consider that the world stops at the deadlock. Likewise, if a trace enters a livelock and it is clear that the system will never return to normal operation, there is a finite number of steps before the livelock.

Liveness assertions are not the same as reachability assertions. A **reachable assertion** specifies that a future state or sequence is possible under at least one forward path but is not guaranteed to be possible under all other intermediate paths.

The opposite of liveness, roughly speaking, is a **deadlock**, as introduced in Section 3.4.3. For instance, in older motor cars, it used to be easy to lock the car keys in the boot (or trunk in the USA), since a key was not needed to lock the boot. However, the only way to reopen the boot is to use the key, which is impossible if the only key is in the boot. Hence, this is a deadlock. Modern motor cars have a wireless link to the key, which detects whether the key is in the boot. The system, thus, disallows a route that leads only to a deadlock, which is known as **deadlock avoidance**.

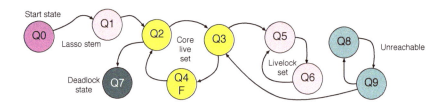

Figure 7.3 FSM transition diagram with liveness, fairness and deadlock indications

Temporal logic defines at least three distinct forms of liveness: simple liveness, progress and liveness with fairness. Figure 7.3 illustrates an FSM with 10 states. State Q0 is the initial state, entered on reset. In reality, the edges would be guarded with conditions for when they might be taken, but the edge conditions are not important as long as they at least hold sometimes. The states can be classified into five classes:

1. **Unreachable**: States Q8 and Q9 are unreachable since there is no normal route to them. However, extraordinary events, such as a **single-event upset (SEU)** (Section 8.2.1), could possibly cause entry to such a state. For safety-critical systems, an exit arc should be provided wherever practical, such as raising an interrupt or, as shown, ensuring there is an arc back to normal operation: Q8 → Q9 → Q3.

2. **Start-up stem**: Certain states are used only at system start-up. In the figure, the start-up stem consists of Q0 and Q1. In formal phraseology, this is known as the **lasso stem**.

3. **Live set**: For most systems, there is a **core live set**. Each state is reachable, in some number of steps, from every other state in the set. In the figure, this is the subset Q2, Q3 and Q4. These form the loop of the lasso. They represent the main runtime behaviour of the system.

4. **Deadlock**: A deadlock state has no successor. In the figure, Q7 has no successor, so if the system ever enters this state, nothing further will happen.

5. **Livelock set**: Often there is a small set of states that are tantamount to a deadlock in that no useful progress occurs if any of them are entered. The system, from then on, stays in the livelock set, transitioning between them, but not doing anything useful and never returning to the core live set. In the figure, Q5 and Q6 form a livelock set.

A livelock set is, technically speaking, a live set, since each member is reachable from all others. However, from the designer's point of view, a livelock set is dead. This distinction commonly needs to be communicated to formal tools. One way to do this is with a **fairness annotation**. In the figure, the letter 'F' on Q4 shows that it has been denoted as a member of the fair set. If fairness markers are used, then they define the live set. Hence, the core live set is now constrained to be the {Q2, Q3, Q4} subset and not the {Q5, Q6} subset. Every state in the fair set needs to be reachable by all others in that set. In the example, any or all of Q2, Q3 or Q4 could be marked as fair to achieve the required effect.

A common real-world design pattern for a server uses an **eternal process loop**. This is an infinite loop whose first statement makes a blocking dequeue from a work FIFO buffer. It then performs that work (known as dispatching the action) before returning to the head of the loop for the next work item. In this pattern, a fairness annotation for the head of the loop is sufficient to ensure that no work item holds up the server indefinitely.

7.2.1 Predicate and Property Forms

As defined earlier, a **predicate** is any function that returns true or false. Predicates are used in properties and properties are used in assertions. The most simple form of predicate directly uses the Boolean state of the target digital system. For instance in 'Never is light A off when light B is on', two predicates are combined to form a property using the 'when' keyword and the whole becomes an assertion when 'never' is prefixed. More complex predicates have numeric values. For instance: 'The value in register X is always less than the value in register Y.' For digital systems, the registers have finite states and such predicates can readily be converted to a Boolean form by bit blasting (Section 8.3.8). Many tools take this approach, but it is somewhat crude and can become overly verbose for complex arithmetic expressions because the laws and identities of mathematics provide, ultimately, a simpler route.

A **state property** is a Boolean expression involving state predicates. It interprets variables in just the current state. For instance: 'Light A is off and register $X \leq 12$.' A **path property**, on the other hand, relates successive state properties to each other. For instance: 'Light A always goes off before light B comes on.'

An assertion can use assertion variables. An **assertion variable** does not exist outside the formal context, and it is used just in a single assertion. It has local scope, so that it does not clash with any other assertions that use the same variable name or any other concurrently running instances of the assertion. In formal logic, variables are commonly either universally or existentially quantified, such as x and y, respectively, in $\forall x \, \exists y$ such that $y > x$. However, in hardware, especially when checked with dynamic validation, assertion variables are frequently bound in the antecedent of an implication and used in the consequent.

Typically, for an interconnect component or network, an important requirement is **data conservation**: the data that go in come out the other side. Similar devices, such as a demultiplexer, essentially filter the output data using some sort of routing predicate, such as addresses within a given range. Such predicates are intrinsically already in formal form! The conservation of data is a symbolic path property. The use of assertion variables for data conservation by a FIFO device is explored in Section 7.6.4.

In **black-box testing**, assertions can range only over the externally visible behaviour of the DUT, i.e. the behaviour of its output terminals. In principle, a black-box test is portable over any implementation of a device, since the testing does not rely on how the internal state is held. If an implementation has a variable input-to-output latency, the black-box specification must be coded in a form that supports **temporally floating ports**. It cannot simply say: 'The word that goes in port A in the current clock cycle will come out of port B three cycles later.' For example, a FIFO buffer allows any amount of time delay. On the other hand, in *white-box testing*, the internal state variables of the DUT can be inspected.

Some specifications prescribe that there are no combinational paths between various inputs and outputs. This is easy to check with a variant of a static timing analyser (Section 8.12.1). Others specify that there are no sequential dependencies. For instance, for the standard synchronous handshake, as used in the AXI bus standard (Section 3.1.5), the ready signal is normally not allowed to wait for the valid signal, since the connected component could be waiting in the reverse direction, which would result in a deadlock. Such causality is a liveness property checked by a model checker.

7.2.2 Assertion-based Design

Assertion-based design (ABD) is a SoC design approach that encourages assertions to be written as early as possible, preferably *before* coding or implementation starts. Many assertions can be applied equally as well to a high-level behavioural model of a SoC as to the final implementation. For instance, in a memory-accurate model (Section 5.1), it may be that several memory locations or registers should only ever have zero, except for one of them, which has a non-zero value. This is the safety invariant. Typically, these registers can hold mutual exclusion locks. There are no such locks in a single-threaded functional model of the SoC, but once the first threaded model is created, they will be present.

Hence, ABD recommends:

1. Writing assertions when capturing the high-level design *before* detailed coding starts.

2. Writing further assertions as coding and development take place. The high-level assertions are applied to ESL, RTL and net-level implementations.

3. Using the same assertions in product testing.

4. Potentially embedding some of the assertions as runtime monitors in the product for reporting, automatic shutdowns or as a fail-safe.

Assertions can be locally coded, reused from previous designs or be associated with a bus standard or IP block. SoC designs always use a module hierarchy. Assertions are supplied along with each IP block as part of IP delivery. For a protocol or bus standard, all IP blocks that conform to that standard can share the assertions that embody that standard. These may be supplied as **formal verification IP** in a verification IP (VIP) block (Section 7.5).

7.2.3 Regression Testing

If a test of SoC that has passed begins to fail again after some change, the system is said to have regressed. Regression testing seeks to identify such regressions. If an ABD methodology is followed, then as the SoC project evolves, the number of assertions and tests that can be run increases. A **test suite** is a named mixture of formal and simulation-based tests of a design. RTL simulations are discussed in Section 8.3.3. Non-functional tests, such as measuring total area or delay using static timing analysis (Section 8.12.1), can also be included. When a designer implements or modifies a particular subsystem, they will manually create or run the relevant test suite that concentrates on that component.

A test of a single subsystem in isolation is called a **unit test**. It is common to have a number of separate unit tests for different aspects of a subsystem. Running each of these sequentially or in parallel is also a unit test for that subsystem. Unit tests can be quite thorough and vary greatly in complexity. A unit test that triggers just the **built-in self-test (BIST)** logic of a subsystem (Section 4.7.6) will be very short. However, unit tests that model complex interaction with the surrounding components can be time-consuming to create. Instead, the team will rely on whole-system tests, which exercise the whole SoC in some specific or limited way, perhaps involving device drivers and other software.

A full regression test typically runs overnight on a server farm. The suite should be as extensive as possible, but usually cannot include every possible test. For a nominated time zone, it is typically run during the seven-hour window between the last check-in of engineering work at midnight and the quick team meeting at the start of the next working day. As well as having limited time, it could be limited by the availability of software licences for EDA tools and the available budget for CPU time.

A SoC design is held in a **revision control system**, which tracks which engineer made which edit to the design. A regression suite manager can generate reports and logs of passed and failed tests. Each failed test is associated with a module instance, so that a regression can be attributed to an engineer based on the nearest edit in both the revision history and the design hierarchy. Thus, an automated email can be sent to the engineer and it can be logged as a bug.

7.3 Simulation with Assertions

Assertions can be checked both with formal tools and by simulations. The latter is known as **dynamic validation**. Simulation is less thorough than a formal method, since it considers only one possible next step from the current state. Some formal tools are limited in the number of steps that they can consider (Section 7.1), whereas simulation is far less constrained in terms of path depth. Assertions and rules can also be used to create a simulation stimulus for **directed random validation** (Section 7.3.2).

7.3.1 Simulations and Dynamic Validation

Using a proof tool to check a property is commonly called **static validation** since it does not execute the system. Instead, it statically 'stares' at the source code. On the other hand, **dynamic validation** runs a simulation, or performs some other form of execution, while checking properties. A dynamic validation run considers only one state trajectory and, unlike a formal proof, can never guarantee that all possible state trajectories will satisfy all the required properties. A safety property violation can be reported as soon as it is encountered. However, dynamic validation cannot prove that safety is never violated.

Dynamic validation tends not to be as useful for checking liveness properties since any simulation has a finite length and a liveness property may not be satisfied until after the stopping point. However, simulations are normally orders of magnitude longer than the typical temporal extent of a liveness assertion, so most liveness assertions are checked at least once during a run. Liveness properties are often phrased in implication form, such as: 'After every A there will be a B.' So, a dynamic validation run can check that there has been coverage of the property, if there is at least one occurrence of A followed by a B. It can flag a warning at the stopping point if there is an A that has not yet been followed by a B.

7.3.2 Automated Stimulus Generation: Directed and Constrained Random Verification

Any simulation of a subsystem needs **stimulus** sequences for its inputs. The clock and reset inputs are generally straightforward, and can be stimulated with generic behavioural models, as shown in Section 7.3.2. Other inputs require application-specific waveforms. A **directed test** uses handcrafted input waveforms to examine a specific behaviour. Directed tests are normally designed to be easy to analyse in terms of their expected output, but they tend to lack the levels of parallel activity found in real-world use cases. Even if a large number of directed tests are available, systems may still have hidden defects that are found only when there is a specific ordering or overlapping of the directed tests.

Hence, it is very common also to use **undirected testing**, which invokes a random sequence of feasible activities. This is especially useful for **dynamic equivalence validation** if there are two or more implementations of the DUT, such as a high-level model and an RTL model. A typical example is a processor core, which can be tested with a random, yet valid, instruction stream. The stream is padded at both ends with NOP (no operation) instructions so the pipeline is idle at the start and end of the test. The effect on the register file and caches can then simply be compared between the two models.

It is generally not sensible to perform random tests with totally unconstrained inputs. In the processor instruction stream example, only valid instructions should be fed in. Implementations of a model from different parts of the design flow almost always vary in terms of their behaviour for don't-care input values due to design optimisations. Hence, **constrained random verification (CRV)** is used. CRV uses a formal description of the allowable input values and sequences. With some CRV tools, the reactive behaviour of external components can also be specified, such as a given input being the disjunction of two outputs delayed by two clock cycles, or whatever. System Verilog has native support for CRV, so a hardware engineer can easily include such test-bench behaviour as part of a CRV test.

Arm's weak memory coherency model is formally specified in the Cat language. The Diy7 tool from the University of Cambridge and Inria [7] can generate an almost infinite set of short, random, concurrent programs that act as litmus tests for exercising the concurrency model and checking the outcomes. This is another form of CRV. These programs can be run on real silicon or in a RTL and ESL simulation to validate dynamically that each implementation conforms to the specification. Arm reports having found silicon errata using this technique.

System Verilog has several constructs that enable a collection of variables to be set to constrained random values. A variable can be declared with the `rand` modifier as part of its type. New random values are assigned with a call to the `randomize()` system function and constraints are specified using the `constraint` and `with` keywords. If the variables are over-constrained, such that no setting can be found, the `randomize()` call returns zero instead of one.

The following example shows a System Verilog class definition. The three fields are randomised. Moreover, there is a constraint on the relative order of the start and stop values and that the index field must be between the pointers:

```
class region_ptr;
  rand bit [31:0] index;
  rand bit [31:0] start_index, stop_index;
  constraint index_sanity { stop_index >= start_index; index >= start_index; index < stop_index; }
endclass
  ...
  region_ptr rp0 = new;
  testno = 0;
  while (testno < test_max) begin
    rp0.randomize() with { start_index > 32'h1000; index-start_index >= 32'h100; };
  ...
  end
```

When instantiated, each call to the `randomize` method will assign new random values to the fields that satisfy all the constraints. Using the `with` qualifier, additional constraints can be passed in to each `randomize` call so that specific regions of interest can be explored as required. By altering the constraints, different phases of the test program can be successive explored and so on.

The problem of generating a vector of constrained random variables is not straightforward. A naive approach can waste an inordinate amount of time generating and discarding vectors. If a linear range is required, the well-known modulo technique is typically used, such as `random()%100`, which returns a number in the range 0 to 99. For complex sets of constraints, the most straightforward approach is to convert the constraints to a **Boolean satisfiability problem (SAT)** by bit blasting (Section 8.3.8). A **SAT solver** finds solutions to such problems (Section 7.6.1). There are various SAT algorithms, but many of them can be seeded with a set of random starting values and they will converge on a nearby solution. Hence, a randomly seeded SAT run often generates a fresh result. Previous solutions can be readily stored in RAM and automatically avoided if regenerated.

Since formal specifications for many standard interfaces are widely available as formal VIPs (Section 7.5), CRV forms the basis for streams of synthetic data corresponding to all sorts of protocols. The following example from Specman Elite [8] generates streams of IEEE 802.2 logic-link layer frames:

```
struct LLCHeader { v: int( bits:2); O: int(bits 14); }

struct frame {
  llc: LLCHeader;
  destAddr: uint (bits:48);
  srcAddr: uint (bits:48);
  size: int (bits:32);
  payload: list of byte;
  keep payload.size() in [0..size];
}
```

An hierarchy of specifications and constraints is supported. One can compose and extend a specification to restrict its possible behaviours. For instance, the following construct ensures that the frames generated have zero payload size:

```
// Subclass the frame to make it more specialised:
extend frame { keep size == 0;  };
```

7.3.3 Simulation versus Formal Checking

It is sometimes stated that simulations are effective in finding many early bugs in a design. This may simply be because designers tend to simulate before making formal checks. Often, early bugs are just low-hanging fruit, which both simulation and formal checking are good at finding! The key difference between formal checking and simulation is that a formal approach explores all possible next states, albeit slowly, whereas a simulation explores a single path more rapidly. A simulation can be partly formal, using bus monitors for dynamic validation and CRV (Section 7.3.2) to create a stimulus.

Simulation is effective at finding bugs that can be observed only in system states that take many cycles to reach. Compared with model checking, which tends to explore each clock cycle exhaustively before progressing to the next, a simulation can rapidly execute many clock cycles and reach such **deep states**. However, this may require the careful generation of a random stimulus or even a manually constructed stimulus. If a stimulus can be created that is expected to reach such buggy deep states, then it may also be possible to create constraints that describe the corresponding set of states and use these to begin model checking from a constrained non-reset state. Although such an analysis will not provide an exhaustive proof, it is often a very effective **bug-hunting** technique.

Once the early low-hanging bugs are fixed, a formal proof may be more effective at finding the remainder. These tend to lurk in unusual corner cases, where particular alignments or conjunctions of conditions are not handled correctly.

A simulation is generally easier to understand. A simulation measures performance. It can produce a golden output that can be compared against a stored result to give a pass or fail. Alternatively, it is common to compute a CRC or other hash digest of the main outputs (Section 9.1.1) using a few additional lines of RTL. The digest is compared with a known good value at the end of the simulation to likewise give a pass or fail.

The benefits of formal techniques in theory (and challenges in practice):

▪ We capture what the system is supposed to do.

▪ They are theoretically complete (but how can we define or determine this?) (Section 7.1.3).

▪ They are scalable (but tools are limited in practice).

▪ Rare corner situations in the exponential state space (unusual conjunctions of events) are covered.

Although extensive simulation is time-consuming, it may not be exhaustive. Nonetheless simulations are needed for:

▪ performance analysis and general design confidence

▪ generating some **production test vectors** (Section 8.8.2).

Most formal tools fail to span the hardware/software divide adequately, which means that if a property relies on complex or custom interactions between the hardware and software, then proving correctness may be difficult. The general approach for fully certified systems, like the CakeML stack [9], is to use layers of proven abstractions, with the principal abstraction being that the hardware correctly implements the ISA semantics of the programmer's model. Hence, the proof that the program is correct assumes that the hardware is correct, which is verified independently. Alternatively, for very small microcontroller applications, both the ISA description and the program can be converted to a single formal representation [10].

In practice, simulation and formal tools symbiotically feed each other in the verification flow:

▪ If a counterexample is found by a formal method, it is often output in a form that can constrain the simulation stimulus. This means that the simulator can rapidly reproduce the bug. Engineers find it easier to analyse bugs with a familiar simulator. For instance, the net waveforms and design hierarchy may be presented in a more readable form.

A bug found by a simulator can be used for a new regression test associated with the bug to ensure that the fix remains fixed. Also, the state trajectory can be extended into those corners that are hard to reach in a simulation.

- Given the scalability issues of formal checking, bugs that require many cycles of activity before they occur may be difficult or impossible to find using model checking, but may be found during long simulation runs. In some cases, triaging a simulation trace can reveal the key events that led to the bug. For example, a bug may occur whenever a transaction of type A is initiated before an in-flight transaction of type B completes on the interconnect. Such events can be expressed as cover properties, which guide the model checker in a semi-exhaustive bug-hunting mode. The model checker searches for the first event (start of transaction B) and, once found, it uses the generalised state for that as the initial state of a new exhaustive search. In this way, a model checker can reach deeper states than with an exhaustive search from the reset. If a deep bug has taken large amounts of simulation to discover, this technique can be useful for finding related bugs. The technique is also applicable to post-silicon debugging, where complete traces are not available, but a few key state values can be extracted. These then form the cover points and used to reproduce a complete failure trace with a formal approach.

7.4 Property Specification Language

The **property specification language (PSL)** was defined by a consortium of EDA companies working within the Accellera trade body and finally standardised as IEEE 1850 [4]. It has several concrete syntaxes for embedding in different languages, such as Verilog, VHDL and SystemC. Each concrete syntax is a 'sugaring' of standard temporal algebra constructs, as the original name for PSL was 'Sugar'.

The core of PSL is a **linear-time temporal logic** algebra designed for RTL engineering. In a linear-time temporal algebra, path properties relate a state to its successors and predecessors. Each state has just one successor. PSL also defines an optional branching extension, which goes beyond this core by allowing a state to have multiple successors. This results in **branching-time temporal logic**, which is a form of combinational tree logic. Branching time is required if an assertion explicitly ranges over all possible futures. The core of the linear-time language is compatible with dynamic validation whereas the optional branching extension requires a suitable formal proof engine (model checker or theorem prover).

Consider the two PSL examples in Figure 7.4. The assertions start with a label that is a textual name, which is reported in any failure messages alongside the conventional line number and file name of the failing assertion. The rd_or_wr_1 assertion fails on any clock cycle where both the read and write nets hold. This is a state property inside a safety assertion. The req_grant_2 assertion uses temporal operators and is a path property. It states that on any clock edge where the req net holds, the grant net will hold in one of the clock cycles starting two, three or four cycles later.

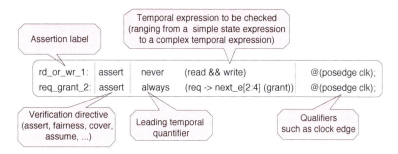

Figure 7.4 Two simple PSL assertions

The verification directive comes after the assertion label. In our examples, it is `assert`. Three further directives are worth highlighting. They each have the same syntactic form as the `assert` directive:

- The `cover` directive defines a property that should be included in coverage reports (Section 7.1.1). In dynamic validation, the number of times it is encountered is reported, with a warning if this is zero. For a static proof, it can be reported whether the property holds in the reachable trajectory space, which is the set of all paths taken between all reachable states.

- The argument to an `assume` directive is assumed to always hold true in any static verification run. This directive must be used carefully, since anything false that is assumed, or any pair of assumptions that contradict each other, in theory, would allow any result at all to be proved (technically, this is an implication with an invalid antecedent). However, the tools typically issue a warning if they detect a completely incompatible set of assumptions.

- The argument to a `fairness` directive defines a point in the live set that is assumed during liveness property checking (Section 7.2).

After the verification directive comes the property to be checked. This tends to start with a leading temporal quantifier but many forms are possible, including `always`, `eventually`, `in the next step`, `in at least one possible future` and various forms of `before` and `until`. These can be nested inside each other, leading to complicated expressions that are very hard to understand. Many of them can be expressed in terms of others, so most of them are not strictly needed. The choice of which to support primitively is a language design issue. PSL includes about 31 in its core set, with a further 16 in the optional branching extension. It also provides the sequence implication operators, `|->` and `|=>`, which we will cover shortly.

In most simple cases, an assertion is a simple safety or liveness assertion. It has a leading temporal quantifier, as in the two examples above, which used `always` and `never`. The `always` quantifier introduces a safety property. The following expression must hold every time the qualifying expression holds. The `never` directive behaves the same as an `always` quantifier but with a negated argument. The `eventually!` directive introduces a liveness property that relates to the future. It is suffixed with a bang sign to indicate that it is a so-called strong property that cannot be (fully) checked in a simulation. A liveness assertion does not always start with `eventually!`, as that keyword can be in the consequent of an implication or it can be expressed without the keyword at all, using arbitrary repetition followed by a match.

Finally, there is a sensitivity guard, such as a clock edge and any enable signals to denote at which time or under what conditions the assertion should be expected to hold. The assertion is ignored at other times. The enable signals can equally well be factored into the property expression. A `report` clause is a string that is printed on success or failure.

7.4.1 PSL Four-level Syntax Structure

Since PSL is embedded in the concrete syntax of several other languages, the details vary from one embedding to another. However, all implementations use roughly the same abstract syntax, which has four principal layers:

1. **Modelling layer**: This is the lowest level. Essentially, it is the surrounding language. It is used in particular for creating state predicates that range over the nets and variables of the host language. However, other auxiliary structures are sometimes needed to support verification or constrain a stimulus, such as for the FIFO example in Section 7.6.4. Note that PSL cannot understand non-Boolean constructs in the DUT. Hence, scalar values must be reduced to Booleans and any predicates, such as comparing scalars with each other or constants, must be defined in this layer. Hence, the primary and essential purpose of this layer is to create state predicates that the temporal logic can range over. For instance:

```
reg [7:0] temperature;
wire temp_low = temperature <= 8'd2;
wire temp_ok = temperature < 8'd99;
```

A new form added to the host language by the modelling layer is **non-deterministic choice** using the `union` keyword. This binary operator allows a simulator to randomly choose one of two values as part of CRV (Section 7.3.2). For example:

```
reg [7:0] temperature;  // Explore a random-walk in 1-D
always @posedge(clk) temperature <= (temperature + 1) union (temperature - 1);
```

This construct is more powerful in a formal proof since the tool will explore every possible combination of non-deterministic choices for the design.

2. **Boolean layer**: All high-level languages and RTLs have their own syntax for Boolean operators and this can be used within the modelling layer. However, Boolean combinations can also be formed using the Boolean layer. The concrete syntax of this layer is typically identical to that of the surrounding language to avoid confusion, which means the Boolean layer is commonly not needed.

3. **Temporal layer**: This is used to define named sub-expressions and properties that use all the temporal quantifiers and operators. The following example defines two SERES sequences and then defines a property with them using a sequence implication. These terms are defined later in this chapter.

```
wire en = ifc_req && ifc_ack; // Conjunction of standard synch fwd and rev handshakes

// Sequence definitions
sequence s0 is { (en && ifc_dfirst); (en[*1 to 100]); (en && ifc_dlast) };

sequence s1 is { (en && ifc_dfirst); (en[*1 to 100]); (en && ifc_aborted) };

// Property definition uses previously defined sequences s0 and s1
property p1 is ifc_end_of_reset |=> {s0; s1};

demo1: assert always p1 @(posedge clk);
```

4. **Verification layer**: This implements the declarative language. It includes the main keywords, such as `assert` and `cover`.

7.4.2 Extended Regular Expressions and SERES

One of the most distinctive features of PSL are **Sugar extended regular expressions (SERES)**, which are a form of regular expression. As said, Sugar was the original name for PSL. These are also known as *sequences*.

Table 7.1 The three principal regular expression operators and concise derived shorthands

Syntax	Fundamental	Description
{A;B}	Core	Semicolon denotes sequence concatenation
{A[*]}	Core	A postfix asterisk denotes arbitrary repetition
{A|B}	Core	Vertical bar (stile) denotes alternation
{A[+]}	Derived	One or more occurrences of A
{A[*n]}	Derived	Repeat *n* times
{A[=n]}	Derived	Repeat *n* times non-consecutively
{A[->n]}	Derived	As =n but ending on the last occurrence
{A:B}	Derived	Fusion concatenation (last of A occurs during first of B)

There are three primary operators for everyday regular expressions in computer science: concatenation, alternation and arbitrary repetition (Table 7.1). Accordingly, these are the three core constructs in SERES, but with catenation being interpreted in the time domain, advancing one token for each event detected by the sensitivity clause. A SERES is defined inside curly braces. Like everyday regular expressions, a large number of syntactic shorthands are built on top of the core operators, such as {A[+]}, which is short for {A;A[*]}. Both mean one or more occurrences of A. Likewise, {B[3]} is short for three consecutive occurrences of B, so is short for {B;B;B}. As a third example, {C[->3]} is short for skipping to the third next occurrence of C, but with gaps allowed, which maps to {C;1[*];C;1[*];C}. In these examples, A, B and C could be Boolean expressions from the modelling layer, or any other PSL property, including nested SERES and expressions with further temporal quantifiers such as `eventually!`. Variants of the repetition operator accept ranges. For instance, `{D[2:4]}` is short for the alternation `{D[2]|D[3]|D[4]}`. The repetition counts and ranges must be compile-time constants for most of today's tools (i.e. they cannot depend on quantified variables).

Table 7.2 Summary of the main SERES temporal conjunction and sequencing dyadic operators

Operator	Syntax	Description
Simple conjunction	A & B	A and B finish matching at once
Length-matching conjunction	A && B	A and B occur at once with common duration (length matching)
Simple conjunction	A within B	A occurred at some point during B
Strong positive sequencing	A until B	A held at all times until B started
Weak positive sequencing	A before B	A held before B held
Sequence implication	A |=> B	Whenever A finishes, B immediately starts
Fusion implication	A |-> B	The same, but with the last event of B coincident with the first of A

The disjunction (OR) of a pair of sequences is supported by the SERES alternation operator, but there are numerous forms of conjunction and sequencing that combine a pair of SERES. These may be nested for more complex combinations. Table 7.2 shows three conjunction and four sequencing operators. The conjunction operators take two operands and, in essence, run two matching sub-operations in parallel. The various operators differ in terms of the truth function that combines the output of the sub-operations. The sequencing operators again run two sub-operations, but instead of being in parallel, they run one after the other. See [4, 11] for full details, but we will shortly use some of these in our examples. For convenience, as shown in Table 7.3, PSL defines some simple path-to-state macros, many of which resemble similar built-in primitives in VHDL.

Table 7.3 Some built-in primitive macros in PSL

Macro function	Description
rose(X)	X changed from zero to one
fell(X)	X changed from one to zero
stable(X)	X did not change
changed(X)	X did change
onehot(X)	X is a power of 2
onehot0(X)	X is zero or a power of 2

7.4.3 System Verilog Assertions

PSL was lightly modified to become the language **System Verilog Assertions (SVA)** [5]. For instance, `##n` is used in a sequence instead of `next[n]` to wait for *n* sensitivity events (typically, clock cycles). Moreover, `A[*]` in PSL, which stands for any number of occurrences of `A`, must be written more verbosely as the consecutive range `A[*0:$]`, meaning a repeat count in the range zero to infinity, where the dollar sign denotes infinity (or end of the simulation). The choice of temporal quantifiers and operators selected for SVA is slightly different from PSL, but the core language has similar expressibility. SVA does not have an optional branching extension, but it provides better support for assertion variables. We will use SVA examples, rather than PSL, in the rest of this chapter.

If an SVA assertion fails, rather than simply creating a log entry or stopping the simulation, a System Verilog **action block** enables the result of an assertion to trigger further System Verilog code, so that assertion handlers or recovery actions can be implemented more easily in System Verilog. Additionally, the sensitivity language for System Verilog, which is normally just used for detecting clock edge and reset conditions, is extended to range over complex temporal logic expressions using the SVA syntax.

7.5 Formal Interface Protocol Checkers

A **formal VIP block** is supplied by an IP block vendor in the same way as a regular IP block, but instead of providing an instantiable subsystem, it provides a set of verification conditions or test vectors. A VIP is often coded mainly in System Verilog, following UVM (Section 8.8.1). VIPs are available for all widely used bus standards, including DRAM, AXI, Ethernet, PCIe, USB, SATA, SD card and HDMI. As well as formal specifications, such an IP block can include test bench components, such as **synthetic data sources** that create an endless stream of traffic conforming to a protocol.

A bus usually conforms to a well-established protocol, and investment in a formal specification of the protocol is normally worthwhile. When verifying a SoC interconnect, the interface protocols provide a good layer of abstraction, which can be used to verify the properties of the interconnect. IP blocks connected via a standard protocol can be treated as black boxes. For example, reasoning about interconnect properties relating to the correct delivery of packets from one location to another does not require information about the detailed behaviour of the connected IP blocks. With appropriate models of the connected blocks, including fairness assumptions, constraints on the types of packets, etc., it should be possible to verify the significant behaviour of the interconnect without knowing the functionality of the IP block.

Several families of commercial products have formal **protocol checkers (PCs)**. These check properties derived from the protocol specification. There are two main types of PC: interface PCs and system PCs. An **interface PC** inspects transactions at an interface in isolation and ensures that each one conforms to the protocol specification. These may track some state at a single interface. For example, a response received at the interface may be deemed illegal based on the known history of requests at that interface.

A **system PC** ensures that the transactions at an interface are consistent with the known system state. For example, a cache coherency protocol may require that an IP block does not respond to a read request with valid data if it has received an invalidation request. System PCs model more complex dependencies for transactions that interface with checkers.

Formal PCs can be configured in one of two main modes. These reflect whether the IP is a producer or a consumer. In practice, this involves determining which properties of the PC are assumed and which are asserted. It is a form of verification based on assumptions and guarantees. If an IP block has been verified against a formal PC in producer mode, then it can be assumed that one can verify the interconnect with the same PC in consumer mode with the IP block being absent or treated as a black box. Alternatively, if both the producer and consumer are present in full, then the PC will be configured with all properties as assertions. In this situation, any assumptions would potentially over-constrain the design and mask bugs.

Bus Monitor and Interface Checker Example

The upper diagram in Figure 7.5 illustrates a bus PC that connects to a classical system bus. The lower diagram shows multiple interface checkers, as might be used with a modern switched SoC bus. In either case, the checkers monitor the net-level transitions during a simulation run. The checker can report protocol violations, keep statistics regarding data movement and check coverage for each form of transaction that can potentially be conveyed.

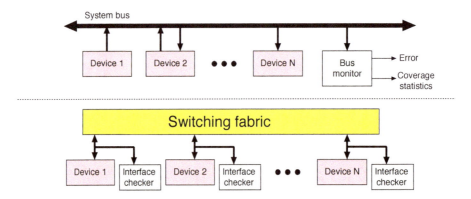

Figure 7.5 Dynamic validation: Monitoring bus operation with an RTL checker (top) or interface PCs (bottom)

There are numerous potential implementation forms and uses for such checkers:

▪ They can be implemented formally in PSL or SVA for dynamic validation in a proof of correctness.

▪ They can be compiled from a formal specification to an RTL-level FSM, again for dynamic validation. This is useful if SystemC or an old simulator (e.g. a Verilog interpreter) is being used that does not natively support PSL or other temporal logic. All temporal logic constructs can be compiled to a hardware FSM that can detect property satisfaction and violation.

▪ They can be compiled to RTL, synthesised into silicon and used at runtime to provide assurances in a safety-critical application.

When used for dynamic validation, coverage and error outputs are updated as execution progresses. Safety and liveness properties differ in how they can be reported:

▪ For a safety property, violations can be indicated immediately, as soon as an illegal state or sequence is detected.

▪ For a liveness property, the monitor can indicate whether it has been tested at least once and also whether there is a pending antecedent that is yet to be satisfied.

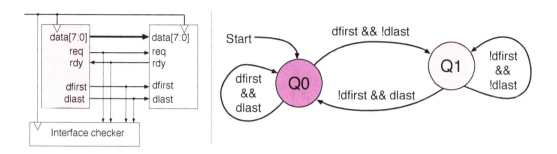

Figure 7.6 Framed standard synchronous connection, with interface checker instance (left) and allowable protocol transitions (right). Only allowed qualified edges are shown. Any other qualified transitions are protocol errors

The left-hand side of Figure 7.6 is an example of a simple concrete interface checker. The two components communicate using the framed standard synchronous interface from Section 3.1.3. An interface checker monitors the protocol. Under the protocol, byte-wide data are transferred only on clock cycles where both `req` and `rdy` hold. The `dfirst` and `dlast` nets convey an additional packet framing protocol. The state machine for the framing protocol is show on the right-hand side of the diagram. In a cycle where both `dfirst` and `dlast` hold, a single-byte frame is transferred. Otherwise, these two nets denote the first and last bytes of a frame, respectively. There are three protocol constraints, C1 to C3. In natural language, they can be expressed as:

- C1: It is illegal to start a frame while one is in progress.

- C2: It is illegal to end a frame that has not started.

- C3: It is illegal to transfer a byte that is not part of a frame.

Figure 7.7 shows a suitable fragment of a VIP block in the form of an RTL PC that can be connected to any such interface. This is fairly easy for an experienced RTL engineer to write. The checker uses only Verilog 2000 constructs. It indicates which constraint was violated with a warning message and an error code stored in a local variable that can be traced in a waveform viewer.

Figure 7.8 is an alternative to an RTL checker. It uses SVA, which does not have the various `until` and `before` operators of PSL, so some temporal expressions are a little more verbose. The upper assertion, `sva_transaction`, allows multi-word frames, using sequence implication (Table 7.2). `dfirst` must be followed by a `dlast` after zero or more cycles without another `dfirst`. However, this assertion does not detect C3 errors (bytes outside any frame). The lower assertion, `good_Q0`, relates to behaviour after a reset or the end of a previous frame. It insists that the only actions allowable at those points are an idle cycle or a cycle where `dfirst` holds.

```
module framed_standard_sync_monitor(
              input reset,
              input clk,         // Clock input. ALL CONNECTIONS ARE INPUTS!
              input req,         // Request signal
              input rdy,         // Ready signal, for the reverse direction
              input [7:0] data,  // Data bus
              input dfirst,      // First word of packet indicator
              input dlast);      // Last word indicator
  bit q1; integer error_flag;
  always @(posedge clk)
    if (reset) q1 = 0;
    else begin
    error_flag = 0;
    if (req && rdy && !q1) begin
      if (dfirst && !dlast) q1 = 1; // Frame start
      else if (dlast && !dfirst) begin
        $display("%m: %1t: C2: End outside of frame.", $time);  error_flag = 2;
        end
      else if (!dlast && !dfirst) begin
        $display("%m: %1t: C3: Byte outside a frame.", $time); error_flag = 3;
        end
      end
    else if (req && rdy && q1) begin
       if (!dfirst && dlast) q1 = 0; // Frame end
       else if (dlast && dlast) begin
         $display("%m: %1t: C1b: One-word frame during existing frame.", $time); error_flag = 1;
         end
       else if (!dlast && dfirst) begin
         $display("%m: %1t: C1a: Frame start during existing frame.", $time); error_flag = 1;
         end
       end
    end
endmodule
```

Figure 7.7 Example of a PC for the framed interface implemented using an RTL state machine

```
  wire en = req && rdy;

  // The transition from Q0 -> Q1 -> ... -> Q1 -> Q0:
  sva_transaction: assert property (@(posedge clk)
    ( (en && dfirst && !dlast) |=> (!en || (!dfirst && !dlast))[*0:$] ##0 (en && !dfirst && dlast) ) )

  // Forbid any exit from Q0 except with dfirst:
  good_Q0: assert property (@(posedge clk)
    ( (en && dlast) || reset |=> (!(en && dfirst))[*0:$] ##0 (en && dfirst) ) )
```

Figure 7.8 Comparable example of the PC implemented with SVA. The ##0 form is an idiomatic marker that merely separates successive SERES components

7.6 Equivalence Checking

Often we have two versions or implementations of a subsystem or component that we need to check are equivalent. The two implementations can be expressed in a common language or different languages. When different, either the designs can be converted to a common language with translators or extractors, or else the checker tool can directly read in the various designs and map them internally. Several equivalence checking tasks are illustrated in Figure 8.1, which is a physical flow diagram. An example translator is the netlist extractor used to mask polygons in Section 8.7.6.

There are two categories of tools for equivalence checking: those that compare only combinational logic and those that can compare behaviour across flop boundaries. The former is known as **Boolean equivalence checking** or **logical equivalence checking (LEC)** whilst the latter is **sequential equivalence checking (SEC)**. A special case of SEC is **X-propagation checking**, which is commonly used to ensure that RTL don't-care values do not affect the observable behaviour of a system. These three techniques are described in the following sections.

7.6.1 Boolean Equivalence Checking

A **Boolean equivalence problem** can be expressed as follows: Do two functions produce the same output? Boolean equivalence checking compares two implementations of a combinational structure modulo the input conditions that are specifically denoted as don't-care. It is a LEC problem. If synthesis is constrained not to introduce any state re-encoding or D-type migration (Section 4.4.2), the next-state function of two implementations should be identical and hence, LEC can form the basis of SEC. Otherwise, more advanced techniques must be used, as in Section 7.6.2. For instance, if a logic synthesiser is used with state re-encoding disabled, the two versions for equivalence checking are:

▪ the RTL input to the logic synthesiser

▪ the gate-level netlist, output by the tool, post-synthesis.

A basic method for LEC, illustrated in Figure 7.9, is to create an **equivalence mitre** of the two designs using a disjunction of XOR gate outputs. Then, a negation of the mitre is fed into a **SAT solver** to see if it can find any input conditions that produce a one on the output. Applying a SAT solver is a matter of trying all input combinations, so has exponential cost in theory and is NP-complete. However, specialist SAT solvers, such as zChaff [12], have various mechanisms that can discover the hidden structure in most real-world problems, so that they are normally quite quick at finding an answer, taking hours instead of multiples of the lifetime of the universe. If a SAT solver reports that there are no input combinations such that the mitre indicates there is a functionality difference, then the designs are equivalent.

In practice, synthesis tools may optimise the driving logic in ways that alter the combinational behaviour. The main example is the exploitation of don't-care conditions. Often a don't-care state can be readily captured and expressed as another Boolean function of the input. The Boolean function is called the **don't-care predicate**. It can be inferred from synthesisable RTL from the reachable state

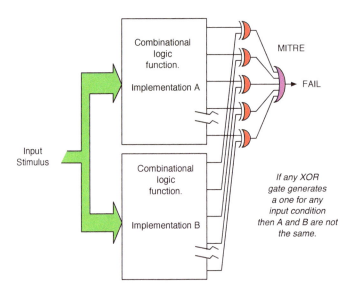

Figure 7.9 A mitre compares the outputs from a pair of supposedly equivalent combinational components

space (Section 7.1.1) and from RTL sites where an X is assigned to a net or from conditions not covered in case statements. The input to a SAT solver is normally given in **conjunctive normal form (CNF)**, which is a list of clauses expressing a product of sums, such as $(a+\bar{b}).(c).(\bar{a}+d)$. Hence, the negation of the don't-care predicate can be appended to the SAT solver input as additional CNF clauses so that the FAIL output will not be satisfied in a don't-care situation. However, in practice, the reachable state space is a subset of that apparent from RTL analysis due to unknown additional input pattern constraints.

Commercial equivalence tools are highly integrated with each other, so that changes made for power or timing optimisation or for an **engineering change order (ECO)** are often sufficiently well documented that false negatives can be avoided. Alternatively, they can highlight the specific changes that have been made deliberately. For instance, a logic synthesis tool (Section 8.3.8) can provide hints about potential differences between the RTL and gate-level designs. The widely used Formality tool embodies a wide variety of solver engines under a uniform user interface [13]. It includes ECO highlighting (Section 8.10).

7.6.2 Sequential Equivalence Checking

Whilst Boolean equivalence checking is useful for ensuring that synthesised logic has preserved the behaviour of the original RTL, it is limited in that it cannot check behaviours that evolve over multiple clock cycles. As mentioned, if a logic synthesiser makes a change to the state encoding, there will no longer be logical equivalence for the next-state functions. Indeed, the number of such flip-flops may be different, as would be the case with a mapping to one-hot encoding.

Determining whether two implementations of a sequential subsystem have the same observable behaviour is called **sequential equivalence checking (SEC)**. For example, two implementations of the same functionality could be implemented in a pipelined style, but with different functionality in each stage or with different numbers of pipeline stages.

In formal terms, two implementations of a sequential function are said to **bisimulate** each other if they have identical observable behaviour. Bisimulation tools find a minimum-complexity FSM that produces the required behaviour. Any actual implementation has a nominal mapping from its state encoding to the states in the minimal model. A model checker is a general-purpose tool that can reason about such multi-cycle behaviour. Accordingly, engineers commonly use their favourite model checker tool for SEC problems, instead of a bespoke tool.

Figure 7.10 is an SEC example. It shows two implementations of a two-bit shift register. They have equivalent observable behaviour (ignoring any glitches) but differ greatly in the amount of internal state and how it is used. This is in contrast to simply adding a pipeline stage, as illustrated in Figure 4.14, where the behaviour of the existing state is largely unchanged. Note, when implementing longer shift registers, the design based on multiplexers (right) would use more logic and less power than the design based on shifting (left), since fewer nets toggle on each clock edge.

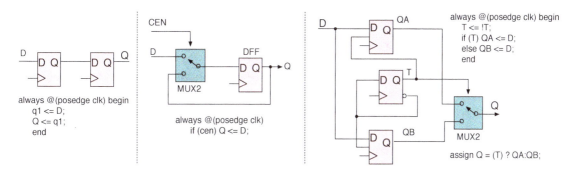

Figure 7.10 A two-bit shift register (left) with a conventional design. By using a clock-enabled flip-flop (centre), an alternative implementation is possible (right). The state encoding is totally different, but the observable black-box behaviour is identical

The question we wish to answer with SEC is: Does each pair of designs follow the same state trajectory? However, there are several possible notions of sameness:

1. There is a one-to-one mapping of flip-flop outputs between the two designs such that the members of a mapped pair always agree.

2. For each symbol in the alphabet enumerated by all possible states of one design, there is a corresponding symbol in the alphabet enumerated by the other, and these symbols always agree.

3. For an observable subset of the state (e.g. the Moore output nets for an interface) and a set of functions of the state (e.g. the Mealy outputs at the interface), the output symbols in the subset (i.e. at the interface) always agree.

4. Under **stuttering equivalence**, one design becomes out of step with the other due to the different number of allowed idle symbols on an interface, but the trajectory of non-idle symbols remains identical. (For a standard synchronous interface (Section 3.1.3), the idle symbol is conveyed on any clock cycle where there is no conjunction of `valid` and `ready`.)

5. Any of the above, but when inputs are wired to an external FSM (i.e. when interfacing with a reactive automaton).

For the first notion of sameness above, a mitre arrangement, similar to that used in Boolean equivalence checking, can be used, but with each part of the mitre also including clocked elements instead of only the combinational logic sections. Many commercial tools provide SEC-specific commands for creating such a check.

One useful application of simple mitre-based SEC is verifying that clock gating conditions are correct (Section 4.6.9). When introduced to a design, clock gating should not affect the design behaviour, only its energy use. When testing for behavioural changes, the two designs to be compared should be identical except that the clock enable conditions in one design should all be tied to their active value whereas those in the other are left under the control of the clock gating logic. An SEC analysis should then identify a stimulus that is handled differently with and without the clock gating.

Most other situations are more complex due to state re-encoding or because they are from different design flows. However, the two versions should have the same set of ports (same port signature). If the two designs have different throughputs or latency, some work is required to design an appropriate shim before model checking. Some EDA tools support conditional fields that specify the time and state requirements for each pair of comparison points. For example, a tool may have conditions such as when an output in one design matches the other design's output with a difference of five cycles, but only if the valid flag is high one cycle before. In SVA, if the two design instances are called `spec` and `imp`, this could be expressed as a comparison property of the form:

```
(spec.validOut ## 1) |-> ( ##5 (imp.dataOut == $past(spec.dataOut, 5))
```

Typically, we are interested only in the observable behaviour at outputs under some stimulus constraints. This is point 5 above.

7.6.3 X-propagation Checking

A specific form of SEC is known as **X-propagation checking**. Recall that HDLs use the symbol X as a logic value. It represents an unknown in a simulation and don't-care in logic synthesis. As explained by Turpin in 'The dangers of living with an X' [14], the semantics of X in RTL can be dangerous because RTL bugs can be masked, especially if a formal tool treats the buggy condition as a don't-care. In X-propagation checking, the sequential equivalence of a design is checked against itself. One might think that every design is trivially equivalent to itself. However, although a silicon implementation of a

DUT may have only 1's or 0's in its registers, a simulation state may also contain X-values. Such simulation states are abstractions of multiple possible real-world states.

There are two distinct sources of uncertain values in typical logic designs:

1. X-values arise in simulation and reality from a register that is not reset. Such registers are used to optimise the area, power and layout of a design. The value of such a register can be zero or one after a system reset. It may be useful to verify that these non-reset values do not unduly influence the observable behaviour of the DUT. Uninitialised memory is also a common source of X-values. A simulation propagates such X-values through expressions and assignments, whereas a formal approach can separately analyse all possible actual values. The way that a simulation propagates X-values through everyday logic gates follows common sense and is spelled out in Figure 8.15.

2. X-values may be introduced to a DUT externally because it is very common for don't-cares to appear in protocol and interface specifications. For example, the standard synchronous interface (Section 3.1.3) conveys a sequence of valid and idle symbols. A valid symbol is any word on the data bus on any clock cycle where `valid` and `ready` both hold. However, the data bus can have any value during an idle symbol (as it is a don't-care). Any action taken that is based on that value is unjustified.

X-propagation checking of a design ensures that replacing a don't-care with a real logic value does not have any consequences for output values that are not don't-cares. (Don't-care values on inputs are, of course, allowed to affect the values of don't-care outputs because, um…, we don't care about them.) An effective way of ensuring this is to express it in the formal specification of the interfaces of the DUT. The property to check is that if no *unknown* values were passed in as *valid* data, then no output values, qualified as *valid*, are *unknown*. In short, for either an input or output port, the formal specification is essentially: 'If `valid`, the data are not X.'

A model checker can be used for X-propagation checking by taking two instances of a DUT, feeding them with very similar input values and checking for divergence in their output using a mitre. The DUT is assumed to behave deterministically if operating correctly. This is normal for mainstream digital logic, with the exception of certain niche applications such as PUF generators (Section 8.8.2). Hence, any divergence between the two instances arises either from uninitialised registers or from inappropriately acting on don't-care values passed in.

X-propagation Example
Figure 7.11 shows a minimal concrete example that uses a simple DUT with a data bus of just one bit. The bus has a `valid` qualifier. For further clarity, we assume that any reverse-direction `ready` handshake net is always asserted and so is not shown. Two instances of the DUT are mitred for X-propagation checking using the illustrated **formal glue** shim logic placed around the instances.

Interface specifications should be reusable over all such port instances. Our DUT has the same signature and protocol for its output as for its input, so there is only one interface specification to consider. The X-propagation rules for an interface specification are:

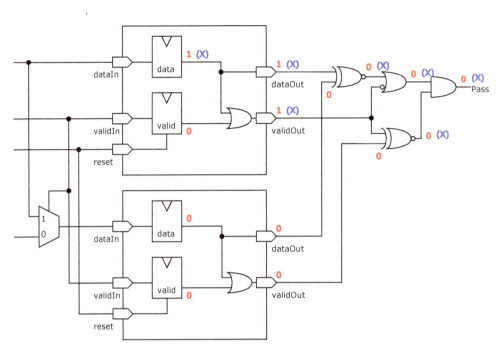

Figure 7.11 An X-propagation mitre around two instances of a simple DUT. The equivalence comparison is modified to ignore mismatches on the data bus if the valid output from the upper instance does not hold. A counterexample, as found by a model checker, is denoted in red. The alternative values that would be encountered in a simulation are in blue

1. By convention, `reset` is not allowed to be unknown.

2. The value of `valid` is not unknown (unless `reset` holds).

3. The value of `data` cannot be unknown when `valid` holds (unless `reset` holds).

The input and output shim structures are constructed to reflect these rules. Both instances of the design have their `reset` inputs tied together. This ensures that the value of `reset` in both is either one or zero and reflects the first rule. The second rule is a property that is a guarantee of the environment for an input and must be honoured by the DUT for an output. Accordingly, the `validIn` inputs to both instances are also tied together to reflect proper environment behaviour. (The model checker will not generate don't-care values for free inputs.) The third rule is honoured on the input side using the multiplexor for the `dataIn` input. This ensures the two instances receive the same data when `validIn` holds, whereas they can be different when it is false.

For the output signals, due to the determinacy of the design, we expect to see lockstep values except where a deviation is allowed. For the output, the third rule is expanded as: when `validOut` is high, `dataOut` is not allowed to be unknown. The XNOR gates that compare the outputs between the two instances follow the classical mitre pattern. They generate true logic values while the two DUTs match; hence, the Pass output should be at a constant logic one. The subtlety is that the data match can be ignored if either of the `validOut` qualifiers does not hold. It does not matter which is selected, since if the other disagrees, this disagreement generates a failure.

The X-propagation check is conducted by applying a model checker to the whole assembly, which consists of the two instances and the input and output shims. In model checking, the verification condition is that the `Pass` output always holds. All the inputs on the left are free and all possible sequences of values are explored to see if any sequence leads to a counterexample. The failure is any situation where `validOut` holds while the two `dataOut` values differ.

The example DUT is manifestly poorly designed. Its `validOut` output is a function of the value in the data register, which is updated every clock cycle, whether or not the `validIn` qualifier holds. Our experiment will find this fault. The red annotations in the figure show a possible counterexample on a cycle after `validIn` was held low. During that cycle, to model the arrival of an X-value, the model checker was free to provide different values on the two `dataIn` ports. As a result, the data registers now hold different values. Since the outputs of the two DUTs are different, a counterexample has been found. In a white-box approach, similar mitre logic, as applied to the DUT output, can also be applied between corresponding registers or nets inside the DUT. This may find a counterexample more quickly.

Note that at this point, if we were just simulating the DUT, there would be an X-value at `dataOut`, as shown with the blue annotations. The simulation state is an abstraction of the two states we see in Figure 7.11. In this instance, the simulator would also propagate an X-value to `validOut`. Hence, even without the mitre, a simulation would demonstrate the propagation of an X-value to an output.

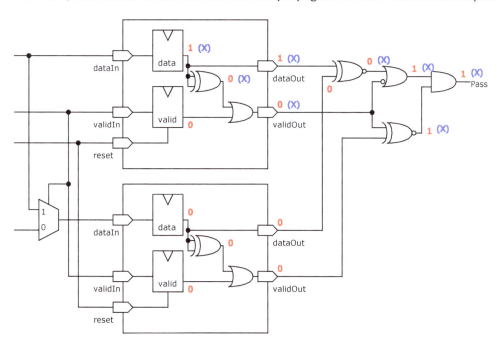

Figure 7.12 An alternative DUT. The circuit produces a false negative under X-propagation simulation. The blue annotations show CRV simulation values, whereas model checker values, in red, correctly indicate that the DUT has passed the test

The modified DUT in Figure 7.12 demonstrates the limitation of CRV. It has an additional XOR gate. The modification, as illustrated, makes no sense in a real design, but real designs commonly contain logic that essentially has this structure, especially if there are test mode multiplexers (Section 8.8.2). As shown with the blue values, an X-propagation test using an CRV simulation would propagate an X-value to `validOut` if the data register has an X-value. However, no failure is reported when using a model checker for formal SEC. This is correct, since the output of the XOR gate can never be one, as the data cannot influence the `validOut` signal.

7.6.4 Model Checking the Items in a Data Path

The correctness of many components depends on various forms of **data conservation**, which means that the data that entered subsequently come out again. The data values are opaque, which means that there is no structure or meaning to any particular value. Hence, they are represented symbolically (i.e. with a variable) in a formal specification. Two approaches to proving correctness are: (1) to write assertions using language extensions that include **assertion variables** and (2) as in X-propagation, a shim of **formal glue** coded in RTL can be placed around such a component.

We consider a LIFO stack example. Using temporal logic for the first approach, we need to write that for all times t, if a value SD is pushed into the FIFO buffer, then the same value is popped out at future time t':

$$\forall t\ \text{Push}(t, SD) \implies \exists t'\ \text{Pop}(t') = SD$$

This can be coded in SVA using an assertion variable:

```
(Push, SD=dataIn) 1[0:\$] (Pop && (SD==dataOut))
```

The assertion variable SD is given a value and then `dataOut` is checked against it later. However, this is not sufficient, since this would also describe a FIFO buffer or allow the same data to come out any number of times. Hence, the current number of items in the DUT must be included in the specification. For most engineers, the second approach, using an RTL shim, is easier to use than advanced assertions. In fact, unlike an SMT tool, which typically has a theory of natural numbers as an installed library, the problem cannot be expressed in PSL or SVA without also manually spelling out the behaviour of an up/down counter in bit-blasted form.

Figure 7.13 is a suitable shim for demonstrating the correctness of a LIFO stack. It forms what is known as a **stable oracle**. It can model ∀-style universal quantification. This formal glue harness around the LIFO DUT could be simulated, using CRV (Section 7.3.2) or otherwise, but it serves as a complete check of data conservation during model checking.

The test runs as follows. The first push operation where the externally driven `SampleNow` input is asserted is checked in detail. The value pushed is stored in the shim broadside register SD, which acts as an assertion variable. Flip-flop QA is then set, which enables the shim's up/down counter to track further pushes and pops before the datum of interest is popped. When that datum emerges, the

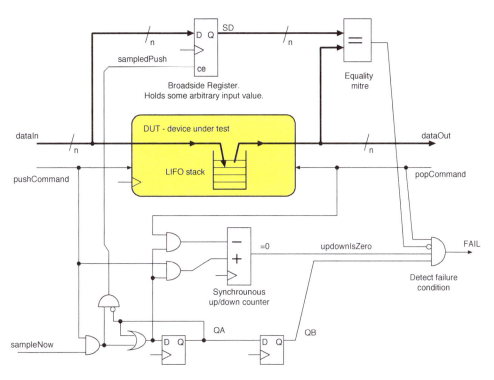

Figure 7.13 A formal glue shim around a data path component (a LIFO stack). This enables symbolic verification using a basic model checker. All inputs on the left are unconstrained, as is the pop input on the right. No stimulus pattern should make the FAIL output hold

up/down counter will again be zero and, at this time, the word coming out is mitred against the held SD value. If they disagree, the test has failed, as flagged by the FAIL output. This would be checked with LIFO_CORRECT_1:

```
LIFO_CORRECT_1: assert property (@(posedge clk) !FAIL)
```

Alternatively, LIFO_CORRECT_2 could be used, but would be harder to trace in a waveform viewer:

```
LIFO_CORRECT_2: assert property (@(posedge clk) !(QB && updownIsZero && dataOut!=SD))
```

The shim checks just one datum in any simulation run, since there is only one first time when SampleNow is asserted during a push. However, in model checking, all possible data values at all possible time offsets and interleavings of push and pop are checked. That is the nature of model checkers. Rather than a complex temporal logic assertion, the complexity is in the RTL shim and the simple never assertion is all that is applied to the FAIL output. This output should never hold for a working DUT. To avoid spurious errors arising from FIFO overflows or under-runs, the push and pop inputs can be ANDed with the not-full and not-empty outputs found on real-world FIFO buffers. Overall, this harness enables a symbolic condition (i.e. one containing quantified free variables) to be checked by a simple model checker that accepts only temporal logic assertions over Boolean predicates.

To provide some help with symbolic assertions (those containing quantified variables), SVA supports local variables inside property definitions. Unlike a variable or register defined in the surrounding RTL, there is a fresh instance of local variables declared in a property for each activation of the property. There are concurrent activations if the property is spatially used more than once or lasts multiple clock cycles. A single-use site starts fresh instances more frequently. After declaration, the variable must be assigned a value before it is used. The assignment is typically in the antecedent to a sequence implication:

```
property data_conserve; @(posedge clk)
  logic [31:0] SD; // Local variable
  (sampledPush, SD = dataIn) |=>  ##[1:$] (popCommand && updownIsZero && SD == dataOut);
endproperty
```

Such an assignment before use is a limitation of several current tools, but, in theory, a variable can be read before assignment using **variable unification**, as in logic programming languages such as Prolog. With unification, there is no distinction between write and read operations; rather, the value is the same at each use site.

7.7 Connectivity Checking

When assembling a SoC design, it is important to ensure that the connections between blocks are implemented correctly. There are potentially thousands of such connections, each with their own conditions for being active, varying latencies and dynamic read/write behaviours, so they can be a rich source of bugs. A formal application known as a **connectivity checker** can be used to verify that an implementation meets its specification. Some tools can generate a specification from an implementation. This can be used for a regression test or to generate an initial specification from a known good design, which can be refined to provide a specification for a new design.

Such tools vary in how the connectivity specification is provided, but typically they have a format that can express:

- source to destination points for a connection

- dynamic conditions, including temporal expressions, under which the connection is active

- permitted latencies between the end points

- default values for points when not connected.

These specifications are used to create assertions, which can be used by a standard HDL model checker to ensure that the implementation has the required connectivity.

7.8 Checking the Security Policy

With the increasing importance of ensuring security in devices of all kinds, there is growing interest in techniques for verifying **security requirements**. A general approach is emerging. It begins by taking known high-level attack models and characterising their dependencies and impact at the device level. Each of these can be used to identify **secure assets** and **secure modes** of operation and the ways that these are expected to interact. For example, a policy may state that a specific register cannot be read unless the device is in a secure execution mode. A requirements analysis could demonstrate that this is adequate protection against a specific attack model. If these secure assets and secure modes can be mapped to HDL elements and state, it is possible to use formal security-checking applications to ensure that any secure data are visible only in accordance with the policy.

Tools with this capability typically express security policies in terms of assets and the conditions under which they can hold secure data. In the register read example, the register content may be specified as always secure, but the security level of the read data port for the encompassing register file may vary according to the processing mode of the subsystem. With this information, a model checker can look for a counterexample where non-secure data at the read port are influenced by secure data in the register. The technique for detecting such **taint traces** is basically similar to that for X-propagation (Section 7.6.3).

Such policy checks may require extra information to cope with timing, pipelining or more complex interactions. For example, there may be some latency, so that if secure register data are read during secure execution mode, the data may still be visible at the read port exactly one cycle after a switch to non-secure execution mode. Although it would usually be forbidden for the read port to hold secure data during that cycle, other control logic might be able to ensure that the secure data are not propagated to non-secure observers. In such special cases, additional logic or conditions on the secure status of the data may be required.

Work on standardising the documentation of this style of security policy is currently being undertaken by the Accellera IP Security Assurance Working Group [15]. Their current white paper [16] proposes a standard notation for sharing security policies between IP vendors and SoC developers that is very close to the style of the policy described above.

7.9 Summary

ABD in SoC design often focuses on safety and liveness properties of systems and the formal specifications of the protocols at the ports of a system. However, there are many other useful properties we may wish to ensure or reason about, such as those involving counting and data conservation. These are less well embodied in contemporary tools.

PSL deals with concrete values rather than symbolic values. Many interesting properties relate to symbolic data (e.g. specifying the correct behaviour of a FIFO buffer). Using PSL, all symbolic tokens must be wrapped up in the modelling layer, which is not the core language. SVA is essentially the same, although its support for assertion variables increases its expressivity. SVA does not have an `eventually!` E construct, so liveness must be expressed using constructs such as `1[0:$]` E.

Formal methods are taking over from simulation, with the percentage of bugs being found by formal methods growing. However, there is a lack of formal design entry. Low-level languages, such as Verilog, do not seamlessly mix with automatic synthesis from a formal specification and so the double-entry of designs is common.

If a bug has a one in ten million chance of being found by simulation, then it will likely be missed, since fewer than that number of clock cycles are typically simulated over all the development simulation runs. However, for a clock frequency of just 10 MHz, the bug might show up in the real hardware in one second!

Many specifications of the functionality required or for operational safety are expressed in plain English. In natural language terms, an **executable specification** is one that is sufficient for an implementation team to start work without further significant design decisions being needed. In a formal specification, an executable specification is one that can be run as a program to generate some output [17]. Manual inspection of that output gives confidence that the specification is correct. This is very helpful if the team has little experience with the specification language. A principal objection to executable specifications, raised in [18], is that 'executable specifications can produce particular results in cases where a more implicit specification may allow a number of different results'. However, this is only to be expected. For example, Prolog is the most widely used executable logic language. A user can take the first answer a Prolog program generates or instead ask the system to enumerate every possible answer, even if there is an infinite number of them.

As mentioned at the start of this chapter, there are two main styles of mechanised proof tool: automatic and manual. Automatic proof tools nominally require no manual input. The main example is a model checker. Their grander descendant, checker tools based on **satisfiability modulo theories (SMT)**, have expanded the application space for automatic proofs by combining various knowledge domains for sets, integer formulae, linked lists and so on. Well-known general-purpose model checkers are SMV [19] and Spin. Yices and Z3 are SMT solvers.

Industrial SoC design mostly uses fully automated provers, whereas research into specification and verification often uses manually guided provers. The latter may make suggestions about proof steps but their main role is to check whether the result has been derived without a false step. Manual proof tools include HOL, Isabelle, ACL2 and Coq.

EDA formal tool packages include Cadence JasperGold, Mentor QuestaFormal and Synopsys VCFormal.

7.9.1 Exercises

1. Define the following classifications of programming languages and systems: declarative, functional, imperative, behavioural and logic. What class are the following languages: Prolog, SQL, Verilog, C++, Specman Elite, PSL and LISP?

2. The synchronous subsystem in Figure 7.14 has three inputs: clock, reset and start. It has one output called Q. It must generate two output pulses for each zero-to-one transition of the start input (unless it is already generating pulses). Give an RTL implementation of the component. Write a formal specification for it using PSL or SVA. Speculate whether your RTL implementation could have been synthesised from your formal specification.

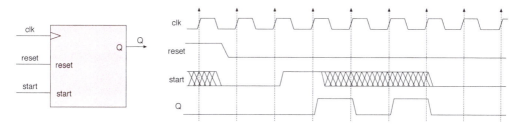

Figure 7.14 A pulse generator: schematic symbol and timing waveforms

3. Create a formal glue shim like the one in Figure 7.13 to check the correctness of a FIFO component.

4. Create a similar formal proof of the correctness of a RAM, showing that writes to different locations do not interfere with each other.

5. Prove the equivalence of the two designs in Figure 7.10 by naming each state in each design and defining a minimal FSM whose states are each labelled with the list of states in each input design that they model.

6. Implement the checker described in the `bus-checker` folder of the additional material.

References

[1] Colin Runciman, Matthew Naylor, and Fredrik Lindblad. SmallCheck and Lazy SmallCheck: Automatic exhaustive testing for small values. In *Proceedings of the First ACM SIGPLAN Symposium on Haskell*, Haskell '08, pages 37–48, New York, NY, USA, 2008. Association for Computing Machinery. ISBN 9781605580647. doi: 10.1145/1411286.1411292. URL https://doi.org/10.1145/1411286.1411292.

[2] *IEEE Standard for VHDL Language Reference Manual.* IEEE, 2019. Std 1076-2019.

[3] *IEC/IEEE International Standard – Verilog(R) Register Transfer Level Synthesis.* IEEE, 2002. IEC 62142-2005, First edition, 2005-06, Std 1364.1.

[4] *IEEE Standard for Property Specification Language (PSL).* IEEE, 2010. Std 1850-2010.

[5] *IEEE Standard for System Verilog – Unified Hardware Design, Specification, and Verification Language.* IEEE, 2018. Std 1800-2017 (Revision of Std 1800-2012).

[6] Armin Biere, Cyrille Artho, and Viktor Schuppan. Liveness checking as safety checking. *Electronic Notes in Theoretical Computer Science*, 66(2):160–177, 2002.

[7] Jade Alglave, Luc Maranget, Susmit Sarkar, and Peter Sewell. Fences in weak memory models. In *Proceedings of the 22nd International Conference on Computer Aided Verification*, CAV'10, pages 258–272, Berlin, Heidelberg, 2010. Springer-Verlag. ISBN 364214294X. doi: 10.1007/978-3-642-14295-6_25. URL https://doi.org/10.1007/978-3-642-14295-6_25.

[8] Cadence Design Systems Ltd. Specman Elite: Verification automation from block to chip to system levels. https://www.cadence.com/content/dam/cadence-www/global/en_US/documents/tools/system-design-verification/specman-elite-ds.pdf, 2020.

[9] Ramana Kumar, Magnus O. Myreen, Michael Norrish, and Scott Owens. CakeML: A Verified Implementation of ML. *SIGPLAN Not.*, 49(1):179–191, January 2014. ISSN 0362-1340. doi: 10.1145/2578855.2535841. URL https://doi.org/10.1145/2578855.2535841.

[10] David J. Greaves. Model checking a CAN network of PIC CPUs. https://www.cl.cam.ac.uk/research/srg/han/Lambda, 2006.

[11] Doulos Global Training. The designer's guide to PSL. https://www.doulos.com/knowhow/psl, 2021.

[12] Yogesh S. Mahajan, Zhaohui Fu, and Sharad Malik. Zchaff2004: An efficient SAT solver. In Holger H. Hoos and David G. Mitchell, editors, *Theory and Applications of Satisfiability Testing*, pages 360–375, Berlin, Heidelberg, 2005. Springer Berlin Heidelberg. ISBN 978-3-540-31580-3.

[13] Synopsys Inc. Formality equivalence checking. https://www.synopsys.com/implementation-and-signoff/signoff/formality-equivalence-checking.html, 2020.

[14] Mike Turpin. The dangers of living with an X (bugs hidden in your Verilog). In *Synopsys Users Group Meeting*, 2003.

[15] IP Security Assurance Working Group. https://www.accellera.org/activities/working-groups/ip-security-assurance, 2021.

[16] Brent Sherman, Mike Borza, James Pangburn, Ambar Sarkar, Wen Chenand, Anders Nordstrom, Kathy Herring Hayashi, Michael Munsey, John Hallman, Alric Althoff, Jonathan Valamehr, Adam Sherer, Ireneusz Sobanski, Sohrab Aftabjahani, and Sridhar Nimmagadda. IP security assurance standard whitepaper. Technical report, Accellera, 2019.

[17] Norbert E. Fuchs. Specifications are (preferably) executable. *Softw. Eng. J.*, 7(5):323–334, September 1992. ISSN 0268-6961. doi: 10.1049/sej.1992.0033. URL https://doi.org/10.1049/ sej1992.0033.

[18] Ian Hayes and C. B. Jones. Specifications are not (necessarily) executable. *Softw. Eng. J.*, 4(6):330–338, November 1989. ISSN 0268-6961. doi: 10.1049/sej.1989.0045. URL https://doi.org/10.1049/sej.1989.0045.

[19] Kenneth L. McMillan. The SMV system. In *Symbolic Model Checking*, pages 61–85. Springer, 1993. ISBN 978-1-4615-3190-6. doi: 10.1007/978-1-4615-3190-6_4. URL https://doi.org/10.1007/978-1-4615-3190-6_4.

Chapter 8

Fabrication and Production

In this chapter, we discuss the back end of the SoC flow, including RTL simulation and synthesis and chip layout and testing. This is sometimes called the **physical flow**. The design and manufacture of SoCs are generally separate processes, carried out by different companies. Devices are normally made at a **foundry**. There are various possible interfaces with foundry services, but we will consider the most basic flow, in which the SoC house sends a file in GDS format (**graphical database system**) containing a layout and also a purchase order to the foundry and receives back packaged or unpacked dies (Section 8.9). In this chapter, we also cover aspects of design verification not covered in Chapter 7 (on formal methods) and we cover production testing.

The design flow in electronic design automation (EDA) is partitioned at the RTL level between the front end and the back end. The main tool that bridges the two halves is a logic synthesiser (Section 8.3.8), but other tools such as a floor-plan layout editor and verification flows cross the gap. The principal distinction between them is that the front end is largely technology-independent whereas the back end is based around a particular fabrication technology and specific chip instance. We do not expect to be able to reuse any of the back-end effort in another design, whereas the front-end IP is portable and parameterisable.

The mainstream approach in a physical SoC flow is called **semi-custom design**, which uses a **standard cell library**, as described in Section 8.4.1. A cell library defines individual gates, flip-flops and other components such as I/O pads and clock generators. Static RAMs from a **memory generator** (Section 8.3.10) are also treated as cells.

Figure 8.1 shows the main back-end stages of a physical SoC flow. Later, we will add the design verification checks to this diagram (Figure 8.45). The articulation point between the front and back ends is **synthesisable RTL**, which is discussed in Section 8.3. The diagram shows a linear progression of steps. However, design decisions made at one step alter the feasibility and performance of subsequent steps, so an iterative approach has to be used. The degree of iteration is greatly reduced with modern EDA tools since the tool for each step can anticipate what might happen in the next step using heuristic estimators. Such tools are said to be **physically aware**. For example, if a signal needs to be delivered to several points around a chip, different buffering approaches would use different numbers and types of buffers, which would vary in their power, performance and area. These three metrics are collectively known as the *PPA* power, performance and area (PPA) parameters for a design. The chip, as a whole, will have targets for the sums of each of these metrics. **Physical design closure** is the process of adjusting these aspects of the design details so that the global targets are met.

As well as the succession of operations on the primary data structures representing the circuitry, the left of the figure shows a parallel cascade of plans that map logic and I/O connections to named zones. A zone is a floor plan area or a clock or power domain. Together these combine to document the high-level layout of the chip. The tools at each step consult the plans.

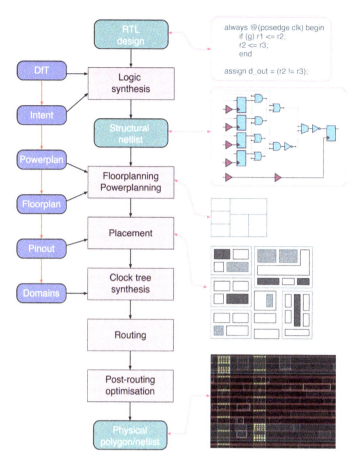

```
always @(posedge clk) begin
    if (g) r1 <= r2;
    r2 <= r3;
    end

assign d_out = (r2 != r3);
```

Figure 8.1 Back-end stages in the synthesis and physical design of a SoC, showing representative diagrams for five of the stages. The red track on the left is the physical intent flow

8.1 Evolution of Design Closure

The design of a chip was much simpler in the early days of **very large-scale integration (VLSI)**. The first microprocessors in the 1970s integrated a few thousand logic gates and operated at low frequencies. For instance, the Z80 microprocessor was fabricated from 18 mm^2 of 4-µm NMOS silicon and clocked 7000 transistors at 4 MHz. Devices used one layer of metal wiring with all net crossings implemented using a polysilicon FET gate layer for wiring in the orthogonal direction. Manufacturing design rules were soon established. Initially, only very simple rules were needed, mostly regarding the minimum distance between polygon features. A chip was guaranteed to work if all the design rules were obeyed. Nowadays, SoCs that integrate hundreds of millions of logic circuits with clocks of frequencies above 1 GHz are not unusual.

A design has must-have and nice-to-have parameters. For example, it may be mandatory for the main clock to be at least x MHz so that it can connect to an existing interface or communication protocol. It may be nice to have a total area of less than y mm^2. Meeting the area target will increase profitability, with more dies possible on a single wafer, but it is not always an obligation. The role of the back-end design team is to satisfy all the constraints, which is called **design closure**. As well as meeting all the other design rules, this principally comprises **power closure** and **timing closure** (Section 8.12.16).

Miniaturisation has been possible thanks to many improvements in the processing of silicon materials. However, miniaturisation generates a virtuous circle of increasingly dense faster transistors that consume less and less power. The downside is that electronic chips have become more and more sensitive to power supply noise, electric field coupling between conductors and temperature variations. SoC design engineers must consider all possible process variations and external sensitivities to guarantee the proper functioning of the whole system.

Therefore, designers need to close designs that are increasingly more complex. The dimensions of the elementary components are continuously decreasing and have now reached a few nanometres. Moore's law predicted that the number of transistors on a silicon chip should double every two years, which has largely held true for the last few decades. This is mapped in the **International Technology Roadmap for Semiconductors (ITRS)** and discussed in Section 8.2.

The challenges of design closure are met using advanced **computer-aided design (CAD)** tools and sophisticated **electronic design automation (EDA)** flows. As the transistors and nets have become ever smaller, the EDA flow has evolved from a simple concatenation of sequential tasks to an iterative flow with complex interdependencies. The stages of the back-end EDA flow (Figure 8.1) are described in the subsequent sections of this chapter. In short, they are:

- **Logic synthesis**: The RTL code is translated into circuits realising Boolean functions and sequential elements. These are mapped into a netlist of technology cells, which is the gate-level **structural netlist**. This netlist is a circuit diagram showing the connections between components (Section 8.3.1). It is optimised before and after technology mapping to reduce the area and power and to increase performance (Section 8.3.8).

- **Design for testability (DfT)**: Various test structures (e.g. scan chains) are inserted into the synthesised netlist (Section 4.7.5).

- **Floor planning**: Various nodes of the hierarchic RTL representation of a SoC are assigned to a polygon map representing areas of the chip. Large objects, such as SRAMs, analogue IP blocks and CPU cores, are placed in logic areas and I/O pins are spread over the chip or at its periphery according to the package that is to be used (Section 8.3.12 and Section 8.6).

- **Power planning**: As part of floor planning, the power supply arrangement for the device is determined, taking into account the position of power-gated regions and any on-chip voltage regulators. The arrangement may have to ensure that power rails do not swap metallisation layers (Section 8.6.1).

- **Placement**: Zones of the chip that are to be populated with logic (typically, standard cells) have a placement grid sketched out in accordance with the power-gating plan. The technology cells are then placed on the grid according to design constraints (e.g. no overlaps) (Section 8.7.1).

- **Clock tree insertion**: The clock within each clock domain must be suitably buffered so as to meet performance goals but without over-engineering, which would waste power. (Section 8.7.2).

- **Routing**: The wires that connect the gates in the netlist are routed (Section 8.7.3).

- **Post-routing optimisation**: Any issue that limits performance or prevents targets from being achieved must be fixed. Further enhancements are made to enhance manufacturability (Section 8.7.5).

- **Sign-off checks**: The SoC design is exhaustively verified to ensure that all design rules are respected, that it is logically correct and that the performance will be met. Separate sign-offs are required for functionality (Section 8.7.8), timing (Section 8.12), power and the test program (Section 8.8.2).

- **Tapeout, data preparation and photomask generation**: A SoC design drawing is converted into photomasks for photolithography (Section 8.7.8).

8.1.1 Physically Aware Design Flows

The aim of an EDA flow is to convert a conceptualised idea into polygons that respect all the timing and electrical constraints to ensure that the SoC works. EDA flows are becoming more and more complex, and moreover, the number of timing and electrical constraints is increasing.

The timing and electrical constraints represent the performance and low-power criteria of a working SoC. As discussed in Chapter 6, the power, performance and area (PPA) metrics for a SoC result from very complex interactions at many levels of the design flow. Front-end design engineers must write efficient RTL code and use the most efficient specialist cells available in the target technology, such as ALU bit slices. Choosing the best data layout, algorithm and interconnect technology is always critically important. However, back-end engineers can also apply their expertise by significantly improving the major metrics. For an RTL input file, a logic synthesiser can produce a very large number of possible outputs, depending on additional synthesis intent settings (Section 8.3.8). As well as optimising the floor plan and power plan, back-end engineers control the regeneration strategy to buffer or pipeline long nets across the die. They may promote long nets to less resistive metal layers to reduce propagation times. Other advanced techniques for the back end include **clock skewing** (Section 4.9.6) to balance up slack time in logic paths.

Modern SoC designers are aware that the constraints need to be defined increasingly earlier in the EDA flow, since these have increasing global influence on the design of the SoC as a whole. There is more flexibility to address a constraint if it is addressed earlier in the flow, but it is also more difficult to predict the convergence of a constraint when it is addressed earlier. For example, inserting a pipeline stage into a huge logic function within the RTL code can have a much greater impact on the performance of the whole SoC than a manual correction during post-routing optimisation. Moreover, even if the design engineers use advanced EDA tools, it is very difficult for them to predict what will work. For example, before the chip logic is synthesised, placed and routed, it is hard to predict whether a change in RTL coding will help to achieve the target performance.

In the same way that they are **timing-aware**, modern EDA tools are **power-aware** and are driven by a **power intent file**. This file commonly uses the **universal power format (UPF)** defined by Synopsys and standardised as IEEE-1801 [1]. It contains an abstract description of how the SoC power supplies are to be structured, with details of the external supply roots, voltage levels, which components can be switched off and which components must always remain on.

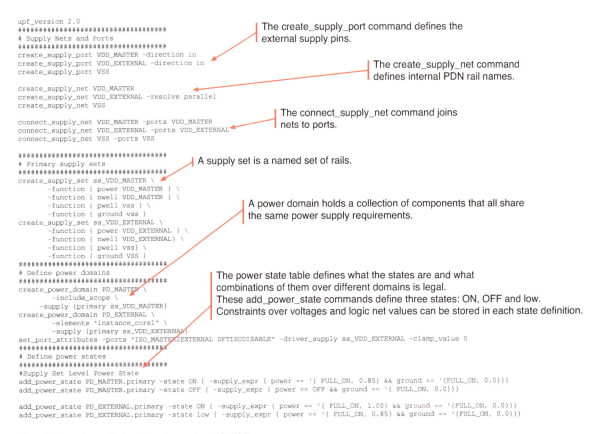

Figure 8.2 A small example of a universal power format (UPF) file

Figure 8.2 shows a minimal UPF example. UPF commands are embedded in the tool command language (TCL). The example defines three main power rails, two power domains and three power states. There is no `set_scope` command, so it uses a hierarchy with just one level. In general, the format is hierarchic. It defines a tree of domains in which a node takes on its parent's properties unless explicitly changed. The `set_retention` command defines signals for gate control inputs to volatile memories while neighbouring domains power down. Commands such as `set_level_shifter` control the instantiation of level shifters between domains.

The synthesis and placement steps automatically insert an appropriate number of power-gating switches and isolation cells at the required boundaries in the logical hierarchy and between physical regions. Since CAD tools are iterated to fix any timing violations to hit performance targets, it is a must that they are power-aware because they update the number, location and properties of these cells.

Area Dependencies

As electronic chips become smaller, more chips can fit on a silicon wafer. Moreover, the cost per chip is lower. A yield and cost trade-off is presented in Section 8.11.1. As manufacturing and lithography process improve, the size of transistors and nets decreases. Recent technology nodes require explicit consideration of delay propagation along some non-clock nets, since this is no longer negligible for the finest wires available (Section 4.6.4). Clock networks, of course, are always subjected to very detailed modelling.

PPA targets normally involve a trade-off between maximising performance, minimising power consumption and minimising area. For example, should an adder be a ripple-carry adder or use look-ahead? The propagation delay is smaller in a look-ahead adder than for ripple carry, but the additional logic of a look-ahead adder requires more silicon area (Section 8.3.8).

Back-end EDA flows have seen major changes in the last 30 years and are still changing. CAD tools are evolving as CMOS manufacturing technology is downscaled, leading to new challenges, such as signal integrity, leakage power and reliability. We highly recommend that design engineers working on high-performance designs use a physical back-end design flow rather than the older non-physical synthesis flows. A **physical synthesis flow** includes net length estimates at all stages prior to routing, if they are known. The flow revolves around a floor plan, instead of using only the physical data available within the technology libraries. Thanks to the floor plan, tools can anticipate an approximate location for each cell and can estimate more accurately the wiring length between cells. They can also use the gate density and routing congestion to estimate how much space must be left for net routing beyond the area used by logic. A **floor-plan-aware** approach generally accelerates design closure and meets PPA targets.

Formerly, an RTL designer performed the principal logic synthesis, while the back-end team only placed and routed the cells. Today, logic synthesisers are still used by RTL designers to get quick feedback on the impact of an RTL change. However, to meet the PPA objectives, the principal synthesis is now handled by the back-end team.

Introducing the physical constraints into the flow sooner gives better results for signal timing, area and also design time. Physically aware flows give a more accurate view of the issues that the designer would have encountered later in older flows. Thus, design engineers no longer need to use multiple long iteration loops.

Physically aware logic synthesisers are distinct from place-and-route tools, but these are becoming ever more closely integrated and the emergence of a single tool is widely predicted. Note that some modern SoCs are so complex that in some cases a non-physical synthesis flow will provide better results than a physical synthesis flow.

8.2 VLSI Geometry

The feature size of a **VLSI circuit** is historically called λ, as popularised by Mead and Conway [2]. It is essentially the smallest separation between different mask polygons so that the features remain reliably isolated during fabrication. It is half the drawn gate width, so for a 45 nm geometry, $\lambda = 22.5$ nm.

Table 8.1 Representative microprocessors

Year introduced	Microprocessor	No of transistors	Geometry
2007	Dual-core Intel Itanium 2	1.6 billion	90 nm
2010	8-core Intel Nehalem	2.3 billion	45 nm
2010	Altera Stratix IV FPGA	2.5 billion	40 nm
2015	Intel CPU	circa 10 billion	19 nm
2020	Nvidia's GA100 Ampere	54 billion	7 nm

The mainstream VLSI technology from 2004 to 2008 was 90 nm (Table 8.1). This had low leakage and very high wafer yields. Now, the industry is commonly using 14 nm or smaller, taking us into the so-called **deep submicron era**. The definition and usefulness of λ are more complex for these advanced technology nodes, but it still remains a useful unit for speaking about the size of gates, RAM cells and wiring pitch. As λ has decreased, the number of transistors per square millimetre has increased, and slightly larger chips have also been routinely made. Progress has roughly tracked *Moore's law*, with examples plotted in Figure 8.3.

In 1971, Robert Dennard presented a seminal workshop paper (now lost) that first predicted that as transistors get smaller in VLSI, their power density would remain constant. The consequence is that power use is proportional to area, as both voltage and current scale (downward) with length. This became known as the **Dennard scaling rule** [3]. The rule held for many decades and was greatly assisted by a move from 5 V logic swings down to around about 0.9 V, with a corresponding quadratic energy saving (Section 4.6.8). This relation meant that no new heat extraction technology was needed as VLSI capabilities improved. However, as Horowitz pointed out in 2007 [4], once the supply voltage was 1 V, with the silicon CMOS threshold voltage V_T being in the range 0.4 to 0.6 V, depending on device construction, logic cannot be run at much lower voltages without greatly increasing the leakage (static power) (Section 4.6.3).

The end of Dennard scaling is generally considered to have occurred in about 2006. Although geometry scaling has continued to enable more and more logic to be integrated on a single chip, this logic cannot all be in operation at once while a cheap metallic heat spreader (Section 4.4.1) or ethanol heat pipe is still used as the main cooling component. This limitation is often called the **power wall**.

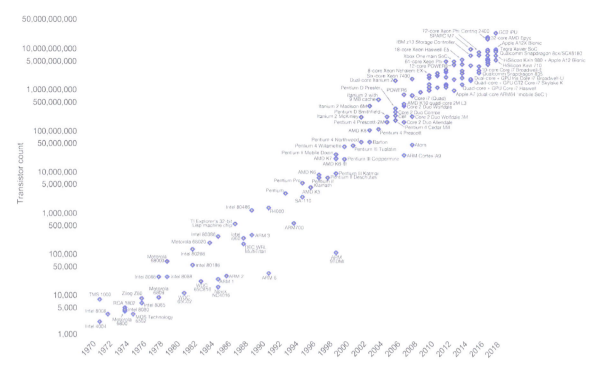

Figure 8.3 Technology scaling scatter plot (source: ourworldindata.org, Hannah Ritchie and Max Roser, 2018. From: https://ourworldindata.org/uploads/2019/05/Transistor-Count-over-time-to-2018.png (2019 version). Reproduced under the terms of the Creative Commons Attribution Share-Alike Licence, CC BY-SA 4.0 <https://creativecommons.org/licenses/by-sa/4.0>)

Transistors are still being made smaller and smaller but the sizes of the atoms is a problem. The spacing of silicon atoms is about 0.2 nm, so 7 nm technology is just tens of atoms wide. The intersection of VLSI technology and the size of an atom was historically called the **silicon end point**. The power wall and electron tunnelling through small features have turned out instead to be the limitations. These can possibly be overcome using graphene and carbon nanotubes as substrates.

Gallium arsenide (GaAs) has been a feasible alternative to silicon for decades. It has four times higher electron mobility, so a transistor of a given size switches about four times faster. Integrated circuits (ICs) using JFET technology have been built from GaAs, but it has been hard to make large low-energy chips from GaAs due to the forward current from a gate into the channel of the JFET diode. Alternatives to silicon for mainstream logic remain in their infancy.

Just making silicon chips physically smaller does not exploit today's VLSI manufacturing technology. Making a chip about 1 cm on a side still gives a good yield. The only way forward is either to use expensive and esoteric heat extraction technology or to accept **dark silicon**. If power gating (Section 4.6.10) is used to disable large regions of the die, power dissipation is no longer a problem. Domains that are switched off to save power are known as dark silicon regions. Figure 8.4 shows the amount of a typical chip that may be active at any instant, given typical SoC heat-spreader technology, as the process geometry is reduced.

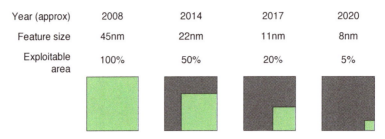

Year (approx)	2008	2014	2017	2020
Feature size	45nm	22nm	11nm	8nm
Exploitable area	100%	50%	20%	5%

Figure 8.4 Dark silicon (using data from [5, 6])

8.2.1 VLSI Evolution

As sketched in Figure 8.51, a VLSI IC is made on a **wafer** of silicon that is about 0.3 mm thick and large enough to hold hundreds of devices. The wafer is a single crystal of silicon that is nearly completely free from dislocations. In this chapter, we assume that the reader understands the fundamentals of IC manufacturing, so here we just summarise the key steps.

Nearly all digital circuits are made from **field-effect transistors (FETs)** based on **complementary oxide of silicon (CMOS)** fabrication. As sketched in Figure 8.5, the transistors are either P- or N-type according to the underlying doping of the wafer in the region where they are constructed. The doping, like all other manufacturing steps, is laid down by ion injection or photolithography from the masks for each layer using high-frequency light to cure a layer of photoresist. A traditional planar FET is formed when a strip of opposite doping, called the channel, is interrupted by a short break, called the gate. The gate consists of a very thin layer of silicon dioxide with a track of polysilicon on top. Unlike the monosilicon of the wafer, which is only lightly doped, the polysilicon is heavily doped so that it conducts electricity reasonably well, but not as well as the metal deposited on the higher levels.

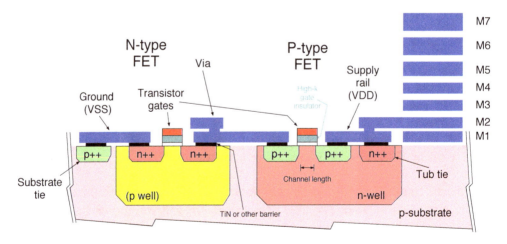

Figure 8.5 Basic layers in planar CMOS VLSI. Cross section through an invertor fabricated using planar transistors (not FinFETs) in a twin-well process and metal layers, M1 to M7 (not to scale)

CMOS uses **enhancement mode** FETs. These have no electrical connection between the gate and the channel. They are switched off when there is no potential difference between the gate and the well they are constructed in. An N-channel FET is built in a P well or on the base wafer, which has been lightly doped as P to have an excess of holes. The wafer and any well are connected to the ground supply rail using a substrate tie or P well tub tie (not shown). Hence, the ground rail is also known as V_{ss} for CMOS devices. For P-channel transistors, everything is reversed. The well is connected to the positive supply rail and they start to conduct when their gate is negative with respect to that potential.

The switching performance of a FET is inversely proportional to its channel length, which in a CMOS process is the smallest feature (e.g. 22 nm). The thickness of the gate insulation is, typically, an order of magnitude smaller and is also a critical parameter. The channel thickness does not depend on the mask, but is instead controlled by the fabrication recipe in terms of the amount of deposition and etching used. It can consist of just five layers of silicon dioxide atoms, which is about 1 nm in thickness. A downside of the thinness is the comparatively high electrostatic field. The field strength across the insulator can be 10^9 V/m when there is a 1 V gate to the substrate potential. For comparison, only three times this field strength is needed for air to break down completely and turn into a conducting spark. Even before the breakdown potential is reached, significant leakage is caused by electron tunnelling in the supposed insulator. One way to reduce the field strength is simply to use a thicker insulating layer, but this would reduce the effective capacitance of the gate, reducing its effect on the channel and so degrading the transistor. In all modern processes, rather than just using SiO_2 as the gate insulator, a layer of a high permittivity material (κ or ϵ_r), such as Al_2O_3, is added between the gate conductor (the polysilicon) and the gate insulator. This processing step is also useful when making capacitors for other purposes, especially as the storage element in DRAM.

On top of the transistor layer, there are alternating layers of metal (conductors) and silicon dioxide (insulators). Vertical holes are cut through the layers and filled with the same metal to make vias, which are conducting joints between layers. The metal layers M1 and M2 provide a local interconnection for the power and logic signals (nets). The higher layers of metal are used for longer distance nets and clock distribution. The highest layers form the **power delivery network (PDN)**.

Before 1980, aluminium was exclusively used as the metal for an interconnect. It is easy to deposit as a wafer-wide layer and can be etched selectively. Aluminium has a resistivity of $2.7 \times 10^{-8} \, \Omega\,m$. With successively finer tracks at smaller geometries, the RC time constants (Section 4.9.5) became a problem and motivated a switch to copper, which has a lower resistivity of $1.7 \times 10^{-8} \, \Omega\,m$. Copper also suffers less from electromigration (Section 8.4.5), but it requires an isolation layer, such as titanium nitride (TiN), shown in black in the figure, to stop the copper leaching into the silicon.

One of the largest problems with small-geometry transistors is their leakage. As was presented in Section 4.6.3, this is the current they pass when they are supposedly off. Smaller-geometry transistors have a lower threshold voltage V_T, but this has not fallen in proportion to the reductions in supply voltage. Figure 8.5 shows conventional planar transistors that are made below the planar surface of the starting wafer. Leakage can be reduced by switching to non-planar **FinFET** structures.

FinFET designs make greater use of the third dimension by extending the channel upwards, with the gate wrapping around the channel, which increases the contact area. The gate is then more effective in controlling the channel. A thin and short channel is needed for good performance. Extending the channel upwards gives it a fin-like shape, hence, the name, and increases the channel cross-sectional area, which reduces the on-resistance. Nonetheless, multiple FinFETs, typically, need to be wired in parallel to produce a suitable drive strength.

A FinFET has a more elaborate construction than a planar FET, but switches faster and uses less silicon area. Figure 8.6 shows the basic structure of a FinFET along with three possible layouts that have multiple FinFETs in parallel. Four in parallel have one quarter the on-resistance and switch 4× faster when driving a net of given capacitance. The second diagram shows two FETs in parallel. Each polysilicon gate line (in red) is called a *finger*, so this is a multi-finger design. Alternatively, as shown in the third diagram, the same finger can run over multiple fins. Finally, as shown in the fourth diagram, a hybrid approach can be used: two fingers such that each gate has two fins.

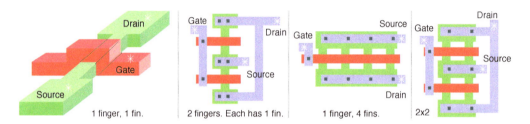

Figure 8.6 Generic 3-D structure of a FinFET (left). The gate is wrapped around the channel. To get a sufficiently low on-resistance, a number of FETs are arranged in parallel using techniques shown in the other three diagrams, which are in 2-D plan view

Figure 8.7 shows the lower layers of a section of a typical traditional standard cell design. Each row shown contains about six gates. The power rail widths are nominally 10λ, but where they abut in the two middle rows, the resultant width is 20λ. Overall, the cell height is about 80λ and hence, 8 times the width of the power rail. The total size of a simple two-input NOR gate is about $400\lambda^2$. The black squares are vertical vias. Multiple vias are used to connect to the drain or source end of the FET channel to achieve low ohmic resistance. Note also that the P-type diffusion has twice the width of the N-type. This is required to get equal on-resistances for the two types of FET given the approximately double resistivity of the P-type material at optimal doping levels.

Cells vary in complexity. A two-input NOR gate uses just four transistors in CMOS, but such small cells have inefficient area use if heavily used. So it is common to use multi-function gates, such as the AND-OR-INVERT gate of Section 8.3.8, which has four inputs and uses eight transistors in a compact layout. A D-type flip-flop is normally counted as the equivalent of 6 two-input logic gates (based on the classic dual RS latch circuit from the TTL handbook [7]). From these figures, a rule-of-thumb density for realistic logic is about 1000 to $2000\lambda^2$ per cell. An SRAM cell (six transistors) also typically uses about $1000\lambda^2$ with row and and column control and sense logic using further area.

Each chip on a wafer is individually tested during the production test (Section 8.8). Then the wafer is diced into individual chips, which are packaged singly or in **multi-chip modules (MCMs)** (Section 8.9) for soldering to the **printed-circuit board (PCB)**. However, high-energy alpha particles are common in outer space and happen sufficiently often on Earth to be a problem to small electronic components, such as the transistors in modern VLSI. A **single-event upset (SEU)** arises from a burst of radiation

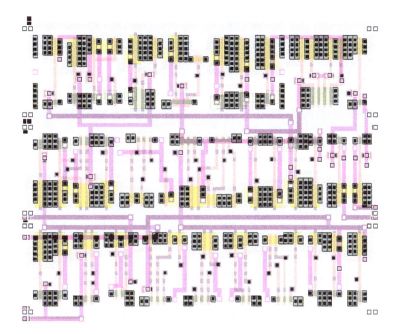

Figure 8.7 Typical first-generation standard cell layout showing three rows of cells. Power rails of alternating polarity run horizontally using the metal M1 layer (blue). This is also used for the internal wiring within the cells. N- and P-type diffusion zones are shown in green and yellow. FET gates are formed where the polysilicon (orange) crosses a diffusion layer. The violet and brown indicate metal wiring layers used for inter-cell connections. The brown layer is predominantly used for horizontal net segments and the violet for vertical segments (source: Reproduced with permission from J. Rabaey, University of California at Berkeley)

incident on the silicon. This can be detected by parity (Section 3.1.7) and corrected in memory using an **error-correcting code (ECC)** (Section 4.7.6). This is called a **soft hardware error** because the next time the circuit is used, the error will not be present.

The top layer of a chip is a thick layer of silicon dioxide known as the **passivation layer**. Although a device can work correctly without passivation, this layer provides protection against water in the atmosphere and offers **radiation hardness**. An additional layer of high bandgap dielectric may also be painted onto the top of a chip for further radiation protection. If a device is to be probed for debugging, it is better to use one where these final layers have not been added or have been removed.

8.2.2 Typical and Future Values

It is helpful to list some concrete numbers. Consider a fictional device with just standard cell logic at 22 nm. Its track capacitance will vary across layers, but might be about 0.3 fF/μm. Hence, the energy stored in a 1 mm net that is at logic one using a supply $V_{dd} = 1$ V is 0.15 pJ. This energy will be dissipated to ground when the net is discharged and an equal amount of energy will be lost in the supply network on the zero-to-one transition.

Assuming a region with a core utilisation ratio of nearly 100 per cent (Section 8.3.12) and given the $2000\lambda^2$ area for an AOI, the area needed per gate with $\lambda = 11$ nm is one quarter of a square micron. This would give a logic density for densely packed zones of about 5 million gates per square millimetre. The area of a 1000-gate subsystem would, therefore, be about 200 μm², which with a square aspect ratio would be 14 μm on a side. By Rent's rule (Section 5.6.6) or otherwise, the average net length might be one third of this, which is about 4 μm. Thus, with 0.3 fF/μm, the average net would have a capacitance of about 1 fF.

Table 8.2 ITRS roadmap projection for geometry, supply voltage, transistor properties and FO3 gate energy. Predictions are made for both high-performance (HP) and low-performance (LP) transistors (source: Reproduced with permission from the Semiconductor Industry Association)

Year of production	2015	2017	2019	2021	2024	2027	2030
Logic device technology names	P70M56	P48M36	P42M24	P32M20	P24M12G1	P24M12G2	P24M12G3
Logic industry node range label (nm)	16/14	11/10	8/7	6/5	4/3	3/2.5	2/1.5
Logic device structure	FinFET FDSOI	FinFET FDSOI	FinFET LGAA	FinFET LGAA VGAA	VGAA M3D	VGAA M3D	VGAA M3D
Device Electrical Specifications							
Power supply voltage, V_{dd} (V)	0.80	0.75	0.70	0.65	0.55	0.45	0.40
Sub-threshold slope (mV/decade)	75	70	68	65	40	25	25
Inversion layer thickness (nm)	1.10	1.00	0.90	0.85	0.80	0.80	0.80
V_T sat (mV) at I_{off} = 100 nA/μm, HP logic	129	129	133	136	84	52	52
V_T sat (mV) at I_{off} = 100 nA/μm, LP logic	351	336	333	326	201	125	125
Effective mobility ($cm^2 V^{-1} s^{-1}$)	200	150	120	100	100	100	100
R_{ext} (Ω m), HP Logic	280	238	202	172	146	124	106
Ballisticity: injection velocity (cm/s)	1.20×10^{-7}	1.32×10^{-7}	1.45×10^{-7}	1.60×10^{-7}	1.76×10^{-7}	1.93×10^{-7}	2.13×10^{-7}
V_{dsat} (V), HP logic	0.115	0.127	0.136	0.128	0.141	0.155	0.170
V_{dsat} (V), LP logic	0.125	0.141	0.155	0.153	0.169	0.186	0.204
I_{on} (A/m) at I_{off} = 100 nA/μm, HP logic with R_{ext} = 0	2311	2541	2782	2917	3001	2670	2408
I_{on} (A/m) at I_{off} = 100 nA/μm, HP logic after R_{ext}	1177	1287	1397	1476	1546	1456	1391
I_{on} (A/m) at I_{off} = 100 pA/μm, LP logic with R_{ext} = 0	1455	1567	1614	1603	2008	1933	1582
I_{on} (A/m) at I_{off} = 100 pA/μm, LP logic after R_{ext}	596	637	637	629	890	956	821
Cch, total (fF/μm²), HP/LP logic	31.38	34.52	38.35	40.61	43.14	43.14	43.14
Cgate, total (fF/μm), HP logic	1.81	1.49	1.29	0.97	1.04	1.04	1.04
Cgate, total (fF/μm), LP Logic	1.96	1.66	1.47	1.17	1.24	1.24	1.24
CV/I (ps), FO3 load, HP logic	3.69	2.61	1.94	1.29	1.11	0.96	0.89
I/(CV) (1/ps), FO3 load, HP logic	0.27	0.38	0.52	0.78	0.90	1.04	1.12
Energy per switching (CV^2) (fJ/switching), FO3 load, HP logic	3.47	2.52	1.89	1.24	0.94	0.63	0.50

The dynamic energy use depends on the clock frequency and mean toggle ratio. Assuming a busy subsystem with a high mean toggle ratio of 0.2 and a clock frequency of 500 MHz, the subsystem power consumption when running from a 1 V supply would be

$$N_{gates} \times C \times V^2 \times (t_r f/2) = 1000 \times 10^{-15} \times 1^2 \times \left(\frac{0.2 \times 500 \times 10^6}{2} \right),$$

which is 50 microwatts (50 µW). A high activity ratio reflects very busy logic. Nets in XOR-rich circuity, such as an AES encoder, essentially have random values, which change every other clock cycle on average. Most subsystems have lower activity ratios when in use and the long-term average activity ratio depends on how frequently the block is used.

Theoretically, the number of such systems on a chip that has a square of active silicon of length 1 cm could be:

$$\left(\frac{0.01}{14 \times 10^{-6}}\right)^2 \approx 500 \times 10^3$$

It would consume 25 watts if they were all active at once. A real chip will also have longer distance nets on higher metal layers, and these may use the same amount of energy again. The static power also needs to be included. This could be as much as a third again, although this depends greatly on power gating ratios and whether the transistors are fast or low leakage. The I/O pads also need to be considered. These are likely to consume a similar amount of power as the core, but generally with a higher static power component if there are a large number of LVDS connections (Section 3.8).

Heat dissipation levels in the tens of Watts require expensive cooling arrangements, as used in high-performance games consoles and cloud computing blades. In an embedded SoC, much lower average activity ratios are typically encountered and power gating is heavily used to reduce the static energy component.

The future trajectory for VLSI is predicted by market analysts and trade bodies such as the *International Technology Roadmap for Semiconductors (ITRS)* and the *International Roadmap for Devices and Systems (IRDS)*. Table 8.2 is taken from the ITRS Executive Summary published in 2015 [8]. It predicts a move from FinFET to **vertical gate all around (VGAA)** transistors where the source, gate and drain are in a vertical stack. V_{dd} is predicted to reduce to under half a volt by 2030. The bottom line shows that the energy per operation per gate is predicted to improve by a factor of 4 in roughly a decade, which implies roughly four times more transistors can be active within the dark silicon power envelope. The 2020 Update to the roadmap [9] extends the time frame to 2034 and continues to show exponential growth in the number of gates and DRAM bits per mm^2, as reproduced in Table 8.3. The ITRS projections tend to become self-fulfilling since semiconductor manufacturers often use the roadmap figures as their own target.

Table 8.3 ITRS predictions from [9] for the gate density and DRAM density for future silicon nodes, and the expected number of cores in an 80 mm^2 CMP

Year	Gate density (Mgates/mm²)	DRAM density (Mbits/mm²)	No of cores
2020	17	47	27
2022	23	58	36
2025	29	68	46
2028	37	78	58
2031	71	164	112
2034	142	329	224

Before 2000, the gate length was roughly the same as the node's feature size, λ, which is half the spacing between tracks on the M1 metal layer (Section 8.2.1). Moving towards 2010, the effective gate length could be made shorter than the M1 feature size by techniques such as over etching of the gate material during manufacture, leading to gates with length perhaps one third of the metal half pitch with the advertised feature size being somewhere in between [10]. With the advent of FinFETs and recent discrepancies between the ITRS technology node name and the actual transistor size, things have moved back the other way with the transistors being bigger than the advertised feature size. This has become confusing.

A relatively sane example is presented in Table 8.4. This gives figures for a 28-nm lithographic technology node that was implemented using a **shrink** of a cell library designed for 32 nm. In early VLSI technologies, optical shrinking of the image projected by a photomask could be used to increase the density for a known reliable design. Shrinking a layout is no longer as easy, but the approach is still useful. The design effort invested in a node can be given a longer lifetime by linearly scaling all dimensions by a small factor.

Table 8.4 Main parameters for an example CMOS lithographic node (TSMC 28 nm)

Parameter	Value
Approximate year	2010
Structure	1P8M (one poly layer, eight metal layers), HKMG (high-K metal gate)
Transistors	CMOS, high performance, low leakage
Cell structure	12 track, Tapless
M1 wiring pitch	90 nm (three times the advertised feature size!)
Gate length	28 nm = (30 nm pre-shrink) × (0.9 shrink factor)
Contacted poly pitch	130 nm (sets the maximum density of gates)
Raw gate density	2 945 000 gates/mm^2
Supply voltage	DVFS between 1.0 V and 1.8 V

The deployed cell library uses a 12-track cell height with **tapless wells**. This means the tub ties shown in Figure 8.5 are not present on every transistor, but instead placed at regular intervals, such as between cells. This increases the density. The cited gate density gives the average area per gate as about 0.4 µm^2, although some of this area is just wiring channels, depending on the core utilisation ratio. With a metal pitch of 90 nm, the cell height would be 12 × 90 nm, which is approximately 1 µm. The minimum cell width needs to be around one third of this to achieve the quoted maximum gate density.

8.3 Register Transfer Languages

A **register transfer level (RTL)** language describes what is loaded into a register on a clock edge. Verilog and VHDL are the predominant RTLs, but they include various other constructs beyond register transfer primitives. The most recent major change to the Verilog languages was System Verilog, which is not always compatible with older Verilog dialects. In this book, we use Verilog, System Verilog and VHDL synonymously. RTLs provide two main functions: simulation and synthesis. Both Verilog and VHDL support both simulation and synthesis with nearly identical paradigms. Older versions of Verilog were missing several useful features compared with VHDL, such as user-defined types to describe net-level interfaces, but these were added to System Verilog.

RTL can be generated manually by engineers using a text editor but another major source is higher-level tools, such as interconnect synthesisers (Section 6.8.2), high-level synthesis (HLS; Section 6.9), Chisel (Section 6.8.3) and Bluespec (Section 6.8.5). As Figure 8.8 shows, RTL is processed by two main EDA tools. On the left, a simulation generates waveforms and console logs. On the right, the RTL is compiled to logic gate instances from a target cell technology library using a process called **logic synthesis**. A logic synthesiser also accepts **design intents** and metrics, which influence how it optimises for speed, area, power and testability. The output from a logic synthesiser is a gate-level netlist, which is usually in structural RTL format. Hence, the output can be fed into a **gate-level simulation**, as shown by the curved blue arrow.

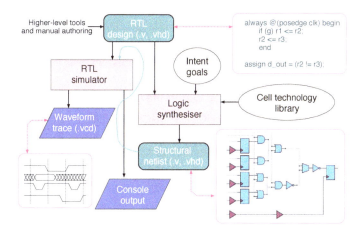

Figure 8.8 EDA tools applied to synthesisable RTL for a simulation (left) and the synthesis to a gate-level or structural netlist (right)

A number of EDA vendors provide synthesis and simulation tools for RTL. A noteworthy synthesis tool, which has been the mainstay of the industry for decades, is Design Compiler from Synopsys, but Genus from Cadence is also widely used.

The constructs available in RTL can essentially be divided into five classes:

1. **Structural netlists**: These enable an hierarchic component tree to be instantiated. They describe the net-level wiring between components (Section 8.3.1).

2. Unordered lists of assignment statements: These define **combinational logic** (Section 8.3.1). The right-hand expression describes potentially complex logic using a rich set of integer operators, including all those found in software languages such as C++ and Java. In Verilog, these statements are called **continuous assignment** statements and in VHDL they are known as **concurrent signal assignments** but their structure follows class 4 below.

3. Unordered lists of **pure register transfers** (Section 8.3.1): There is nominally one list per synchronous clock domain that is the concatenation of each smaller such list in the various component modules. Each list has the same structure as that of class 2, except that the lists of class 2 are not associated with a clock edge.

4. **Synthesisable behavioural RTL**: This uses a thread to describe behaviour. A thread may write a variable more than once (Section 8.3.1). In Verilog, a thread is introduced with the `always` keyword. In VHDL, the keyword is `process`. Both sequential and combinational logic are generated in this way.

5. The remainder of the language contains the so-called **non-synthesisable constructs**, for which there are no hardware generation rules (Section 8.3.2).

The first four classes are the **synthesisable subset**. Only constructs in these classes can be processed by logic synthesisers. The remaining constructs are ignored or generate compilation errors and warnings. All the constructs, however, are used in a simulation.

To be acceptable to logic synthesis tools, even within the four allowed classes, tight coding rules need to be followed. For instance, a continuously assigned variable must not be assigned in more than one place and a register must not be updated by more than one clock domain. Floating-point expressions cannot be synthesised. Also, compared with general-purpose languages such as C/C++, there are much tighter restrictions on what a thread can do. It cannot leave the module where it was defined and the thread blocking and synchronisation primitives are restricted to waiting for a clock edge of one clock. As languages used to describe massively concurrent systems, RTLs are very primitive. They reflect what is possible with a localised projection into hardware.

8.3.1 RTL Structural Elaboration

When an RTL file has been parsed by an EDA tool, it must be **elaborated**. Command line or TCL tool interfaces to logic synthesisers generally have separate commands to read an RTL file and to elaborate it. Often the details of an RTL design are unimportant since only the module signature is required. VHDL allows the signature (the list of input and output connections) to be held in a separate file, but Verilog does not. Elaborating RTL consists of various stages presented here. The output from elaboration is a technology-independent representation of the design using a small set of basic primitives for sequential and combinational elements.

All hardware description languages and RTLs contain further constructs for **structural elaboration**, which is the process of evaluating macro-like commands at compile time. A **generate statement** is an iterative construct that is executed (elaborated) at compile time to generate multiple instances of a component and the associated wiring. Chisel (Section 6.8.3) and Bluespec (Section 6.8.5) use powerful higher-order functional languages to achieve structural elaboration. Older RTLs support a more mundane style such as the Verilog example in Figure 8.9. The example uses a simple `for` loop and a generate variable, declared with the `genvar` keyword, which disappears during elaboration. Another process, used in some logic synthesisers to facilitate inter-module optimisations, is flattening (Section 8.3.1).

```
wire dout[39:0];
reg[3:0] values[0:4] = {5, 6, 7, 8, 15};

generate
  genvar i;
  for (i=0; i<5; i++)  begin
    MUT mut[i] (
      .out(dout[i*8+7:i*8]),
      .value_in(values[i]),
      .clk(clk),
      );
  end
endgenerate
```

Figure 8.9 Example of a generate statement in Verilog RTL (left) and the resulting structural netlist (right)

Any delay time values in RTL are ignored during synthesis. Components are synthesisable whether they have delays in them or not. So that zero-delay components can be simulated deterministically, a simulator core implements **delta cycles**. Theoretically, anything written in RTL that describes deterministic and finite-state behaviour ought to be synthesisable. However, the community wanted a simple set of rules for generating hardware from RTL, so that engineers could retain good control over circuit structures based on what they had written in RTL.

Today, one might argue that designers and programmers should not be forced into using such low-level expressions with the resulting excessively parallel thought patterns. Certainly, it is good that programmers are forced to express designs in ways that can be parallelised, but the compiler should have much more freedom regarding the details of how to allocate events to clock cycles and the state encoding.

RTL synthesis tools are not normally expected to greatly re-time a design by altering the amount of state or state encodings. Newer languages and flows (such as Bluespec and HLS) still encourage the user to express a design in parallel terms, yet provide easier-to-use constructs with the expectation that detailed timing and encoding might be chosen by the tool. However, if a design is worthy of a considerable amount of low-level handcrafting, such as for a high-performance processor microarchitecture, the ability to tightly prescribe the precise structure of the generated logic is still needed.

Structural Verilog

Figure 8.10 is an example of a structural netlist with a hierarchy. The flip-flip components have **component kind** DFFR and instance names Ff_i. This style of RTL is generated by a logic synthesiser. If fed into a logic synthesiser, it might be unprocessed, especially if marked up with a **do-not-touch macro**, or else it may be modified. For instance, the cells in the input library may be replaced with cells from the synthesis library. Alternatively, if several of these components are instantiated, each might

```
module subcircuit(
  input clk,
  input rst,
  output q2);
  wire q1, q3, a;
  DFFR Ff_1(clk, rst, a, q1, qb1),
       Ff_2(clk, rst, q1, q2, qb2),
       Ff_3(clk, rst, q2, q3, qb3);
  NOR2 Nor2_1(a, q2, q3);
endmodule
```

Figure 8.10 A structural RTL example (left) and the net-level circuit it defines (a divide-by-five Johnson counter, right)

be optimised to suit its environment (e.g. the reset input may not be used) or deleted entirely if its output is not used by anything.

Continuous Assignment

Figure 8.11 demonstrates how a combinational logic circuit can be defined using the Verilog `assign` keyword, which makes a continuous assignment of an expression to a net. The example uses 1-bit expressions, but operations on busses (known as vectors in Verilog) are also allowed. However, operators like multiply or add on wide busses are often synthesised into a circuit with too much delay. The explicit instantiation of synchronous or pipelined library components is better. The circuit as shown would be generated only if the logic synthesiser were operating in a special literal-translate mode, since straightforward logic minimisation tells us that multiplexing against the don't-care value X can always be neglected. Other optimisations are likely to be implemented using minimisation based on a Karnaugh map of the remaining single-output function with three inputs. These are influenced by the surrounding logic and the need to share sub-expressions with other parts of the local design. The choice of logic gate is influenced by whether this circuit is on the critical path (Section 4.4.2) of the encompassing clock domain.

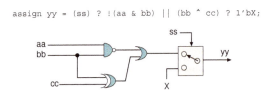

```
assign yy = (ss) ? !(aa & bb) || (bb ^ cc) ? 1'bX;
```

Figure 8.11 A combinational RTL example (top) and the naive net-level circuit it defines (bottom)

The order in which continuous assignments are listed in the source file is unimportant. Tools often insist that continuous logic is loop-free, otherwise intentional or unintentional level-sensitive latches may be formed (e.g. the RS latch of Figure 8.17). To be synthesisable, each net must be either combinationally or sequentially assigned but not both. If combinational, each bit needs to be assigned exactly once. Bit inserts to vectors are allowed on the left-hand sides (but not combinational array writes):

```
assign    d[0] = 0;              // A single-bit insert
assign    d[31:1] = e[30:0];     // A bit field insert (lhs) and field extract (rhs)
```

Pure RTL

Pure RTL is an unordered list of synchronous register transfers associated with a clock edge. In Verilog, the transfers are listed inside an `always` block. In System Verilog, the keyword is `always_ff`. It does not matter how many lists are used or which list an assignment is in. So the left and right fragments in the following are equivalent. The order of the `always` statements in the file is insignificant and the order of assignments inside the `always` block is also insignificant:

```
                                         always @(posedge clk) begin
always @(posedge clk)   a <= (b) ? c : d;      a <= (b) ? c : d;
always @(posedge clk)   b <= c - d;            b <= c - d;
always @(posedge clk)   c <= 22 - c;           c <= 22 - c;
                                         end
```

Pure RTL is not very expressive and used only in relatively simple cases. However, it is important since all the other synthesisable constructs are first converted to pure RTL or continuous assignments during the elaboration stage of logic synthesis. An engineer writing RTL sometimes needs to be aware of this, especially if they are trying to debug the output of the logic synthesiser.

Behavioural RTL

Behavioural RTL builds on pure RTL by supporting the `if`, `then`, `else`, `switch`, `case`, `default` and `break` constructs found in most block-structured high-level languages. Unlike pure RTL, a variable can be assigned more than once or not at all. If a particular flow of control does not make an assignment, the variable retains its previous value. This either involves generating a clock-enable expression for the register or instantiating a multiplexor and feedback path so that the previous value is reloaded on the clock edge. If a variable is updated more than once, the last value assigned before the thread pauses is loaded into the hardware register by the generated logic.

The following CTR16 example shows a simple use of the `if` statement. The comments show the pure RTL produced by elaboration.

```
module CTR16(
    input mainclk,
    input din,
    output o);

    reg [3:0] count;   // A 4-bit register
    reg flip;          // A single flip-flop
    always @(posedge mainclk) begin      // These two become pure RTL as:
        if (din) count <= count + 1;     //   count <= (din) ? count+1 : count;
        else flip <= !flip;              //   flip <= (din) ? flip : !flip;
```

```
        end

    // Note ^ is the exclusive-or operator
    assign o = count[3] ^ flip;
endmodule
```

Pure RTL directly corresponds to synchronous hardware, which updates all the registers on the active edge of the clock. The next-state function is evaluated based on the current contents of the registers. All the next values are committed atomically. Hence, the right-hand expressions in pure RTL are unaffected by any assignments to these variables in the list of assignments. In hardware, this is implemented using the two stages of latching inside an edge-triggered flip-flop. In an RTL simulation, this is implemented using the **compute/commit** paradigm as part of the **delta cycle** mechanism (Section 8.3.6).

However, this behaviour is totally different from that of regular imperative programming languages, such as C/C++. In these languages, the order of assignments in a list is important. Writing a value affects the values read by the right-hand expressions of subsequent writes. This software-like programming paradigm is arguably more useful for expressing complex behaviour than pure RTL, which is better at describing hardware-like constructs, such as shift registers. Each RTL provides mechanisms for accessing both programming styles. Verilog provides two assignment operators whereas the behaviour of VHDL and SystemC depends on the type of variable being assigned.

In Verilog, all registers can be assigned with the non-blocking operator <=, as seen in pure RTL. They can also be assigned with the blocking operator =. Blocking assignments have an immediate effect, as subsequent reads of the assigned variables by the same thread see the new value. It is possible to use both assignments for a single variable, but this is generally discouraged since the resulting behaviour is hard to follow. The names 'blocking' and 'non-blocking' are also a bit obscure since they relate to the behaviour arising when delays are included in the right-hand expressions, but these are seldom if ever used in practice. In VHDL and SystemC, assignments to variables behave as expected, using the Verilog blocking semantic. However, assignments to **signals** follow the compute/commit paradigm. The detailed operation is presented in Section 8.3.6.

Here is a concrete example:

```
always @(posedge clk) begin              always @(posedge clk) begin
    if (k) foo = y;                          foo <= (k) ? y: foo;
    bar = !foo;                              bar <= !((k) ? y: foo);
    end                                      end
```

In Verilog, the behavioural code on the left uses blocking assignments. It is equivalent to the pure RTL code on the right, which uses non-blocking assignments. One of the elaboration steps in a logic synthesiser makes this transformation.

The value stored in the hardware version of the left-hand side is the last value assigned by the thread before the thread pauses to wait for the next event. (As mentioned in Section 5.3.1, a SystemC `sc_signal` is implemented with a current and a next value and it is necessary to use the `net.read()` method to read the value of a SystemC signal because C++ does not allow a read operator to be overridden.) For logic to be synthesisable, registers must be assigned by exactly one `always` block.

The case statement in Verilog differs from that in C/C++ in a number of syntactic ways: (1) The case tags do not have to be constant. (2) There is no fall-through from one branch to the next. (3) An explicit `begin/end` block is required to place more than one statement in a branch. Aside from these details, there are some subtler coding issues regarding logic minimisation. The following two fragments have the same behaviour (ignoring simulation details where `e1` has the unknown value `X` and further relevant differences between the `===` and `==` comparison operators):

```
case (e1) // synthesis PPP
    1 : y <= e2;
    2 : y <= e3;
default : y <= 32'bx;
```

```
if  (e1==1) y <= e2;
else if (e1==2) y <= e3;
else y <= 32'bx;
```

Both fragments assign the don't-care value `X` to the output in the default branch. This is good coding practice since it can grant significant design space to the logic minimiser, which can choose an implementation that meets the design intent. Most logic synthesisers check for pragmas inside the comment containing PPP. Two widely used pragmas are `full_case` and `parallel_case`.

The `full_case` annotation has no effect if a default clause is present, but manually writing the default clause is laborious and error-prone if many nets are updated in the case statement, rather than just the one shown. A `full_case` pragma tells the logic synthesiser that no cases beyond those listed are important and it is allowed to do what it likes in the remaining situations.

A logic synthesiser converts a `case` statement to a series of `if` statements as part of its elaboration, as in the above example. The command with the first matching tag is executed. To preserve this behaviour when converting to pure RTL during logic synthesis, the negation of all previous guards must be AND'ed with the guard of the current command. Our example shows simple integer case tags. These are manifestly disjoint, but Verilog allows more complex tags in its `casex` and `casez` variants that include wild cards. With these, more than one branch can match. Also, as said, the case tags do not have to be constants. If they are expressions, it is possible for several case tags to have the same value. Again, more than one can match simultaneously. The `parallel_case` annotation allows the logic synthesiser to consider each case condition in parallel and non-deterministically merge the effects of more than one matching branch. This is not a nice programming style. However, the advantage is that for a high-arity case statement (one with many tags), less combinational logic is chained together during the elaboration, resulting in a shorter critical path (Section 4.4.2). Essentially, the `parallel_case` pragma is an assertion by the engineer to the logic synthesiser that the case branches are mutually exclusive even though this cannot be statically determined (except possibly by reachable state space formal methods; Section 7.1.1).

One downside of advanced or RTL coding styles arises when debugging a design or tool. If the RTL is very abstract, it is more complex to match one line of RTL code with the output generated by the synthesis tool. It is not uncommon for a back-end engineer to perform manual reverse engineering to tie up a gate or net with its high-level origin.

Structural Flattening

Parts of a module instantiation tree can be collapsed into an equivalent single module instance by **flattening**. The resulting module has the same signature as the root module in the tree, but the contents of each instantiated component are directly included in the new module. Several consecutive levels of the hierarchy can be flattened at once. A fully flattened netlist has one component definition with no child instances or instances only of components that are leaf cells. A **leaf cell** is one that is not defined in the RTL. Leaf cells are either primitives in the RTL, such as the Verilog bufif0 cell, which defines a tri-state buffer, or else provided by an external cell library. Figure 8.12 shows structural RTL before and after flattening as well as a circuit diagram showing the component boundaries.

Hierarchic Netlist

```
module MOD1(output b, input a);
  wire c;
  INV inv1(c, a);
  MODX modx1(b, c);
endmodule


module MOD2(output q, input s, input r);
  wire c;
  INV inv2(c, s);
  MODY mody1(q, c, r);
endmodule


module MODTOP(output rr, input aa, input bb);
  wire l, m;
  MOD1 m(l, aa);
  MOD1 n(m, bb);
  MOD2 o(rr, l, m);
endmodule
```

Equivalent Flattened Netlist

```
module MODTOP (output rr, input aa, input bb
  wire l, m;
  wire m_c, n_c, o_c;

  INV m_inv1(m_c, aa);
  INV n_inv1(n_c, bb);
  INV o_inv2(o_c, l);
  MODX m_modx1(m_c, l);
  MODX n_modx1(n_c, m);
  MODY o_mody1(rr, o_c, m);

endmodule
```

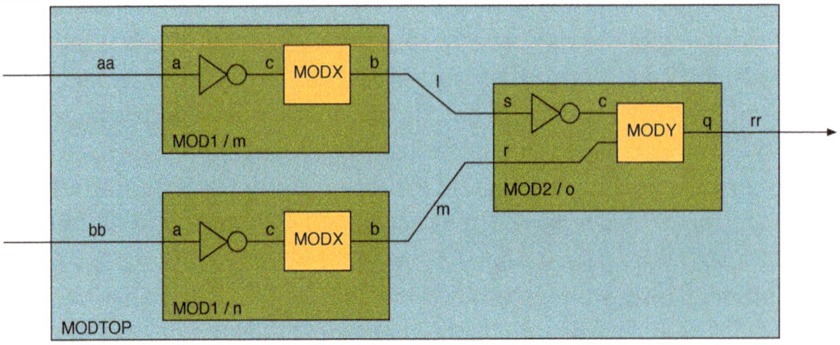

Figure 8.12 Example RTL fragment, before and after flattening. For many designs, the flattened netlist is often bigger than the hierarchic netlist owing to multiple instances of the same component. Here it was smaller

Some tools intrinsically flatten a design during analysis, for instance, to get a total gate count. Moreover, an engineering team may sometimes make an explicit flattening decision and synthesise several layers of hierarchy as one unit. This can be useful for capturing higher-level aspects of SoC partitioning, e.g. after several rounds of experimental synthesis and prototyping the floor plan. Flattening can also provide a more compact result since inter-module optimisation may remove functionality that will not be used, such as redundant outputs, tied-off inputs or other behavioural constraints arising from the composition.

8.3.2 Unsynthesisable RTL

Not all RTL is officially synthesisable, as defined by the language standards. However, commercial tools tend to support larger subsets than the official standards. The example shows RTL with event control in the body of a thread. This defines a state machine for a simulation and is synthesised as such by some tools. The state machine requires a register for a program counter that was not in the source code.

```
input clk, din;
output reg [3:0] q; // Four bits of state are defined here

always begin
    q <= 1;
    @(posedge clk) q <= 2;
    if (din) @(posedge clk) q <= 3;
    q <= 4;
    end
```

Since the thread can pause at two places, one bit of state is required to indicate in which of the two states the machine sits. Does the output q ever take on the value 4? No, the thread loops to the top after that assignment and the new value of 1 is stored straight away.

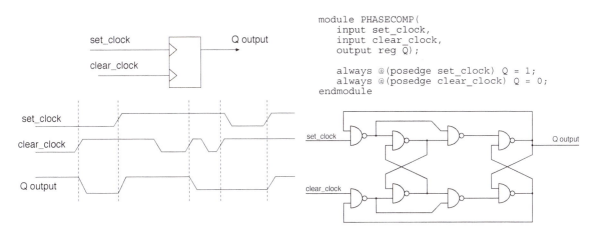

```
module PHASECOMP(
    input set_clock,
    input clear_clock,
    output reg Q);

    always @(posedge set_clock) Q = 1;
    always @(posedge clear_clock) Q = 0;
endmodule
```

Figure 8.13 Schematic symbol, Verilog model, timing diagram and possible implementation for a dual-edge-triggered RS flop

As a second non-synthesisable example, consider the dual-edge-triggered flip-flop of Figure 8.13. This useful component is used as the phase comparator in phase-locked loops (PLLs; Section 4.9.5). The output is set by the positive edge of one input and cleared by the positive edge of the other. Compared with a simple AND-gate comparator, this component is not sensitive to the duty cycle of the inputs and operates over a full 360° of phase difference instead of the 180° of an AND gate. A suitable Verilog model is often needed in mixed-signal simulations Section 8.3.7 and is easily coded (top right of figure). Here a variable is updated by more than one thread. However, although it can be modelled in Verilog and has a net-level equivalent, such structures are *not* supported in Verilog synthesis. A handcrafted circuit for the edge-triggered reset-set (RS) flop is used in practice. The implementation at bottom right has eight NAND gates in a relatively complex arrangement. We do not expect general-purpose logic synthesis tools to create such circuits. This circuit was handcrafted by experts in previous decades.

A third common use of non-synthesisable RTL code is for test benches, which generate stimulus to exercise the device under test (DUT). They commonly use delays to space out events, whereas logic synthesisers ignore all delay annotations in the source RTL. To generate a clock and reset signal in the top level of a simulation, RTL like the following Verilog is typically used:

```
// Typical RTL test bench for stimulus generation

// Set the time in seconds for each clock unit
`timescale 1 ns

reg clk, reset;
initial begin clk=0; forever #5 clk = !clk; end   // Clock source 100 MHz
initial begin reset = 1; # 125 reset = 0; end     // Power-on reset generator
```

A final common use of non-synthesisable RTL is for abstract models of components. For instance, only a tiny percentage of the content space of a DRAM chip may be accessed in a simulation run. A simulation model that has a directly indexed array to store the whole of a DRAM chip's content may break various simulation tools, whereas an associative structure that is totally different from the real implementation may be able to simulate the chip properly. Alternatively, ESL to RTL hybrid models that use transactors to build SystemC models (Section 5.4.8) can be used to avoid writing abstract component models in low-level RTL.

As a form of summary or cheat sheet, Figure 8.14 shows synthesisable Verilog fragments as well as the circuits typically generated. However, logic synthesisers cannot be expected to synthesise into hardware the full set of constructs of a rich RTL. Inevitably, there are problems with:

- unbounded loops

- recursive functions

- library functions, which may access file or screen I/O.

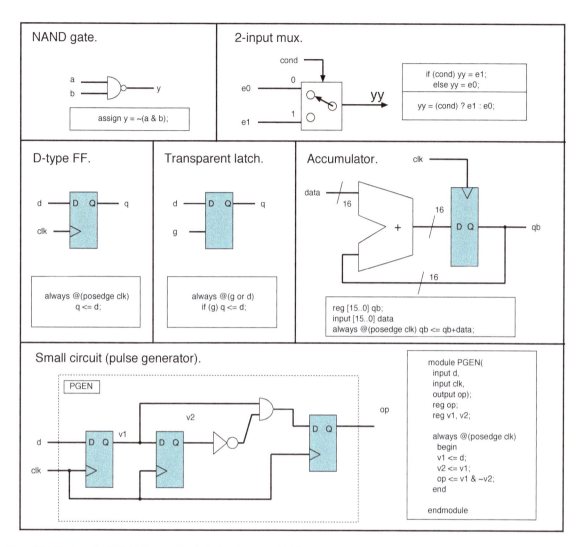

Figure 8.14 Simple synthesisable Verilog examples, including a transparent latch

8.3.3 RTL Simulation Algorithms

A digital simulator takes a binary view of the voltage on each net, as it should be either a one or a zero. A cycle-accurate simulation (Section 5.1) typically uses just these two states, giving a so-called **two-value logic system**. A minimum of two additional states is needed to simulate the majority of everyday logic gates. This gives a **four-value logic** system whose behaviour with six common gates is illustrated in Figure 8.15. In a four-value logic system, each net (wire or signal), at a particular time, has one of the following logic values:

- 0 = logic zero

- 1 = logic one

- Z = high impedance: not driven at the moment

- X = uncertain: the simulator does not know.

Note that Z behaves as an X in most input contexts, but a pass transistor (Section 8.5.1) or transmission-gate two-input multiplexor will output a Z when the selected input is a Z. Note also that the meaning of the symbol 'X' depends on the tool applied. It means 'uncertain' during simulation and 'don't-care' during logic synthesis. The don't-care in logic synthesis enables logic minimisation (Section 8.3.8).

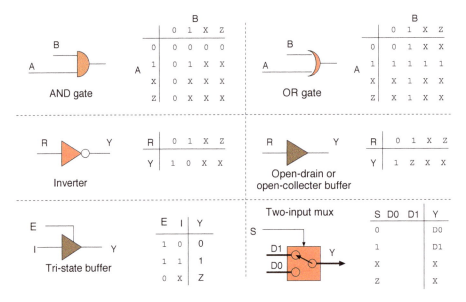

Figure 8.15 Four-value logic-level encoding and its behaviour for six common gates

The four-value system is insufficient for modelling configurations like the bus keeper of Section 4.6.2 and other configurations, such as an SRAM write (Section 2.6.4) in which a gate with a light drive capability is intentionally overwhelmed by a gate with larger output transistors. Verilog and VHDL use more complex logic systems. Verilog uses a hard-coded seven-level drive-strength system. There are three strengths for each of logic zero and one, and another for high impedance. Each net is modelled as being in a range of values delimited by two values from the seven-value range, leading to 28 possible values. This enables a net-resolution function to be applied when a net is driven by more than one source. For instance, if one and zero have the same drive strength, then this will resolve to an X, but the stronger will win when the strengths are not matched. Weak effects, such as those from pull-up resistors or due to signal degradation in pass transistors, can also be modelled. VHDL originally supported a pluggable logic modelling system, but most modern tools use a coding called std_logic that has two drive strengths and distinguishes between unknown and uninitialised values.

8.3.4 Event-driven Simulation

The principal algorithm for simulating RTL is **event-driven simulation (EDS)** augmented with **delta cycles**. Another name for EDS is **discrete-event simulation**. A faster alternative is cycle-accurate simulation (Section 5.1), as implemented by tools such as Verilator (Section 5.5.1). EDS uses an **EDS kernel**, which maintains an **event queue** together with behavioural models of the components being simulated. Figure 8.16 shows an example event queue. The kernel maintains a pointer to the current event, which is the event at the head of the queue. It also maintains the simulation time `tnow`, which is the time when the last event was removed from the queue. In a hardware simulation, an event is a change in the value of a net at some simulation time. An event queue is in ascending order, and newly generated events are inserted so as to preserve this property.

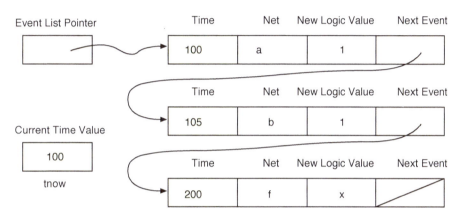

Figure 8.16 EDS event queue, which is a linked list, sorted in ascending temporal order

On start-up, the simulator must first elaborate the module hierarchy and any `generate` statements (Section 8.3.1), so that each individual net in multiply instanced components is stored in memory as a net name and current value. Current values are normally all initialised to X, denoting 'don't know'. For each component instance, a record or object is allocated to maintain its local state. The simulator then generates a sensitivity matrix that records which models are sensitive to changes on which nets. This could be every input to a model, but for sequential circuits, such as the 10-bit counter of Figure 5.2, this could be just the clock and any asynchronous reset inputs. The simulator then enters the main simulation loop. The loop takes the next event from the head of the queue and dispatches it, which means changing the net to that value and chaining to the next event. All component models that are sensitive to changes on that net then run, potentially generating new events that are inserted into the event queue in order. When the queue is empty, nothing further will happen and the simulation is over. Initial events are typically created by the clock and reset generators, as described in Section 8.3.2.

8.3.5 Inertial and Transport Delays

Two types of delay need to be modelled. Consider a simple two-input NOR gate model with a 250 ps delay. The behavioural code inside the model, in SystemC-like syntax, is something like this:

```
SC_MODULE(NOR2)
{  sc_in < bool > i1, i2; sc_out < bool > y;
   void behaviour()
   {  y.write(!(i1.read() || i2.read()), SC_TIME(250, SC_PS));
   }
   SC_CTOR(NOR2) { SC_METHOD(behaviour); sensitive << i1 << i2;
}
```

This model is run when either of its inputs changes. This causes a new event to be placed in the event queue 250 ps later, which results in a pure **transport delay** because multiple changes on the input within 250 ps will potentially result in multiple changes on the output that time later (Figure 8.17). This is unrealistic. A NOR gate made of transistors will not respond to rapid changes on its input. It will decisively change its output only when the inputs have been stable for 250 ps. In other words, it exhibits inertia. To model **inertial delay**, the event queue insert function must scan for any existing scheduled changes to a different value before the one about to be inserted and delete them. This involves little overhead, since ordered insertion involves scanning down the event queue anyway.

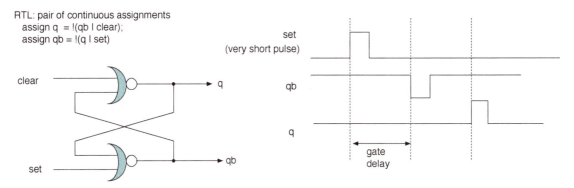

Figure 8.17 Behaviour of a runt pulse in an RS latch when modelling with transport delay

8.3.6 Compute/Commit Modelling and the Delta Cycle

VHDL, Verilog RTL and SystemC all support the **compute/commit** paradigm, which is also known as the **evaluate/update** paradigm, using **delta cycles**. To model the edge-triggered behaviour of D-type flip-flops, RTL simulators must not immediately commit the new value of a register once it has been computed. Instead, they must hold the new value as a **pending update** in a separate variable. The pending updates can be committed only when all customers of the current value have read this existing value. For a clock domain, they must all be committed at once, in the same way that real hardware copies the value from the first latch inside the flip-flop to the second.

Accordingly, as well as the event queue, RTL simulators maintain a set of pending updates as another data structure. Non-blocking assigns in Verilog and signal assigns in VHDL and SystemC are added as new pending updates to the set, replacing any existing pending update for the same left-hand side. These assigns do not go via the event queue. The EDS kernel is enhanced so that it periodically empties the pending update set by committing the updates it contains. If moving to the next event on the event queue would increase the `tnow` value, that is, the next event on the event queue has a time greater than the one just processed, then the pending set is emptied. When delta cycles are modelled, as introduced shortly, `tnow` can increase by such a small amount that its numerical value does not actually change, but this must be treated like an advance, in that it causes a commit of pending updates.

The following fragment of code will not correctly simulate without the pending update mechanism. If the new assignment is made to A before it is read for the assignment to B, this would be a **shoot-through** (Section 4.6.9) and the old value of A would be lost entirely.

```
// Example: Swap data between a pair of registers
reg [7:0] A, B;
always @(posedge clock) begin
      A <= B;
      B <= A;
      end
// e.g. If A=3 and B=42 then B becomes 3 and A becomes 42.
```

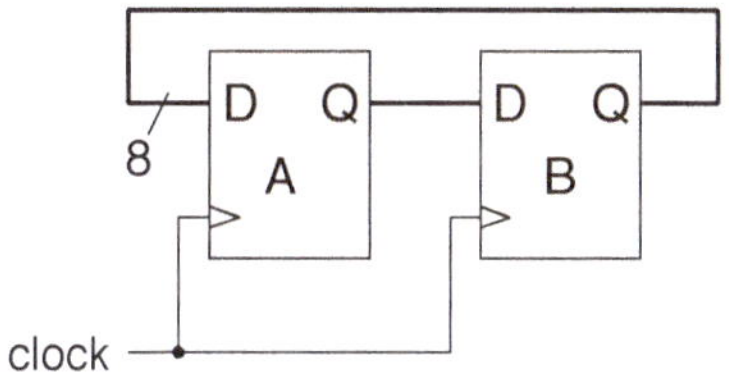

Figure 8.18 RTL code fragment and logical function for swapping data between a pair of registers

Generic RTL is coded without knowing the target technology, since during the early stages of design exploration, the target technology may be uncertain. To ensure the correct behaviour of synchronous edge-triggered hardware, the clock-to-Q propagation delay of D-types must be greater than their hold time (Section 4.4.2). Rather than requiring arbitrary delay values to be inserted in a technology-neutral model, RTL simulators provide the delta cycle mechanism, which supports zero-delay models. A **zero-delay model** does not model the clock-to-Q propagation time. Instead, it changes its output directly after the clock event. Moreover, no setup or hold-time parameters are stored for reporting timing violations. Gates likewise have a zero propagation delay.

The committed pending updates are sometimes to nets that models are sensitive to. This is certainly the case for gated clocks and resets, but is also likely for signals that feed combinational logic. Hence, new events and new pending updates are often created as a result of committing a batch of pending updates. With zero-delay models, much of this new work is at the current simulation time. However, when triggering a commit of pending updates, this new work is treated as an infinitesimally small progression into the future, which does cause them to be committed. This is called a delta cycle.

Hardware simulators commonly support the compute/commit or **signal** paradigm for non-blocking updates. The signal has **current** and **next** values.

8.3.7 Mixed Analogue and Digital Simulation

The real world is analogue and not all electronics is digital. For standalone modelling of analogue electronics, a simulator such as SPICE is often used (Section 4.6.7). SPICE-like simulators can operate in numerous ways, but commonly they first solve the **nodal simultaneous equations** defined by Kirchhoff's laws over the analogue circuit netlist to get a DC operating point and then they apply

Euler's method with a dynamic time step in a numerical integration using piecewise linear approximations. EDA vendors provide various gateway mechanisms between simulator tools to enable digital **co-simulation**. This enables an EDS-based RTL simulator to interwork with analogue models. The demand for such **hybrid system modelling** is growing with the prevalence of IoT controller devices in fuel pumps, engine management systems, cooling plants, etc. These are known as **cyber-physical systems**.

Figure 8.19 shows the main components of one example, a hybrid power and automatic braking system for a motor car. The analogue components of such systems are defined by a few differential equations and it is possible to simulate them alongside the controlling SoC using the modest **analogue and mixed signal (AMS)** extensions now commonly found in RTL simulators and within SystemC. In this example, the main analogue state variables could be the road and flywheel velocities, assuming the clutch decouples these to some extent, and also the fuel and battery charge levels. Velocity is the integral of acceleration, and the fuel level is the integral of fuel consumption. The battery level is the integral of the difference between the charge in and out. The SoC model can be either RTL or ESL, so that the embedded software that couples the user interface to the drive system responds realistically.

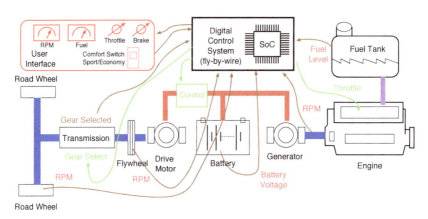

Figure 8.19 Hybrid automobile transmission system

SystemC defines three AMS modelling formalisms: TDF, LSF and ELN. In the **timed data flow (TDF)** model, components exchange analogue values with each other periodically at some sampling rate, such as every 10 µs. By the sampling theorem, this would be sufficient to convey signals of up to 50 MHz bandwidth without aliasing artefacts. A TDF model defines a method called `processing()`, which is invoked at the appropriate rate as the simulation time advances. A so-called cluster of models share a static schedule of when they should communicate. This sets the relative ordering of the calls to the `processing()` methods of each TDF instance in the cluster. The periodic behaviour of TDF allows it to operate independently of the main SystemC event-driven kernel used for digital logic.

The SystemC **linear signal flow (LSF)** library provides a set of primitive analogue operators, such as adders and differentiators, which enable all the basic structures in differential equations to be constructed in a self-documenting and executable form. The advantage of constructing the system from a standard operator library is that reflection is possible. In general programming, reflection means that a program can read its own source code. Thus, other code can analyse the structure and perform analytic differentiation, summation, integration and other forms of analysis, such as a sensitivity analysis, to determine a good time step. This would not be possible for an implementation with ad hoc coding.

The SystemC library of **electrical linear networks (ELN)** provides a set of standard electrical components that enable SPICE-like simulations to be run. The three basic components (resistors, capacitors and inductors) are, of course, available. Further voltage-controlled variants, such as a transconductance amplifier (voltage-controlled current generator), enable most FET and other semiconductor models to be readily created.

The current flowing in an ELN network of resistors can be represented as a set of **nodal equations**, and solutions can be found with a suitable simultaneous equation solver. Euler's method is typically used to model time-varying components, such as capacitors and inductors, since Euler's method is a simple approach for solving **finite-difference time-domain (FDTD)** problems. For instance, to simulate the capacitor charge on the left in Figure 8.21, a time step `delta_t` is selected that is, typically, about 1 per cent of the time constant. The iteration on the bottom right is then executed.

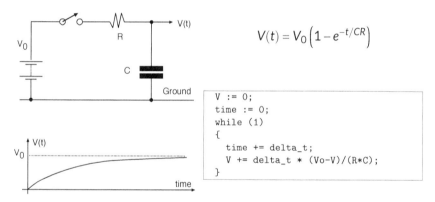

$$V(t) = V_0\left(1 - e^{-t/CR}\right)$$

```
V := 0;
time := 0;
while (1)
{
    time += delta_t;
    V += delta_t * (Vo-V)/(R*C);
}
```

Figure 8.20 Capacitor charging circuit

The error in Euler's method decreases quadratically with shrinking time step, but an overly small time step results in a slow simulation for a complex finite-element simulation. However, this is not a problem in situations where part of a complex SoC or plant controller is run alongside a plant model that has just a few state variables, like a car transmission system, because there are orders of magnitude difference in the time constants (e.g. a 100-MHz clock versus the 1 ms shortest inertial time constant). Simulating the analogue subsystem inside the RTL simulator then makes sense. Moreover, most plant control approaches use closed-loop negative feedback, and the controller is just as good at managing a slightly errored plant model as the real model.

The extensions to RTL to support AMS include:

■ As well as digital net declarations, analogue variables can be declared in a component module to represent voltage potentials, current flows, or other plant state variables. A new type of formal parameter, the `electrical` contact, enables analogue wiring to pass between components in a structural netlist.

- A new type of **analogue procedural block** can appear in a module alongside standard behavioural code for digital models (the `initial` and `always` blocks in Verilog).

- Digital signal values can be set (write operations) from any context outside an analogue procedural block, as normal.

- Analogue potentials and flows can receive contributions (write operations) only from inside an analogue procedural block.

- An `analog initial begin ... end` statement sets up initial analogue variable values, such as the initial charge in a battery or fuel levels in a tank.

- A new sensitivity enables analogue behaviour to trigger actions in either the digital or analogue domain. For instance, the Verilog AMS `cross` keyword can be used in contexts where `posedge` and `negedge` would normally be used. Hence,

```
always @(cross(fuel_level - 1.0))
begin low_fuel_alarm <= (fuel_level < 1.0); end
```

updates the low-fuel signal each time the `fuel_level` crosses the value 1.0.

Here are two examples for a three-cell battery and a simple resistor:

```
// Three 1.5 cells in series make a 4.5-V battery
module Battery4V5(input voltage anode, output voltage cathode);
  voltage t1, t2;
  analog begin
    V(anode) <+ 1.5 + V(t2);
    V(t2) <+ 1.5 + V(t1);
    V(t2) <+ 1.5 + V(cathode);
  end
endmodule


module resistor (inout electrical a, inout electrical b);
  parameter real R = 4700;
  analog V(a,b) <+ R * I(a,b);
endmodule
```

Under the ELN formalism, the SystemC initialisation and simulation cycles are extended to solve the nodal flow equations. Nodal equations are generally solved iteratively rather than using direct methods such as Gaussian elimination or using matrix inverses. Iterative methods tend to be more stable and are fast when the state has advanced only slightly from the previous time step. When the kernel dequeues a time-advancing event from the event queue, the simulation time is advanced. The analogue part of the simulator maintains a time quantum beyond which the nodal equations need to be recomputed. This quantum is dynamically adjusted depending on the behaviour of the equations. If the equations are 'bendy', meaning that linear extrapolation using Euler's method over the quantum will lead to too much error, the time step can be reduced, otherwise it can be gradually enlarged at each step. Overall, two forms of iteration are needed. The first is iteration at a time step to solve the nodal equations to a sufficient accuracy. The second is between time steps. In a simple implementation, once the simulation time has advanced beyond the Euler quantum, the analogue subsystem is re-solved. If the extrapolation errors are too great, the simulator must go back to the last time step and simulate forward again using a smaller analogue quantum. This mechanism is also the basis for SPICE simulations (Section 4.6.7). Each analogue variable that is the argument to a `cross`, or other analogue sensitivity, is then examined to see if new digital domain work has been triggered. If so, new events are injected on the discrete event queue for the current simulation time.

An interesting problem attributable to Zeno

A common problem with mixed simulation configurations is that the Euler quantum can get exponentially smaller and a significant amount of time is wasted simulating artefacts of no interest. The classic example was phrased by Zeno as a race between Achilles and a tortoise (Figure 8.21):

> 'In a race, the quickest runner can never overtake the slowest, since the pursuer must first reach the point whence the pursued started, so that the slower must always hold a lead … and so you can never catch up,' the tortoise concluded sympathetically.

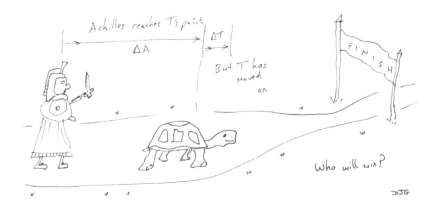

Figure 8.21 Zeno wondered whether Achilles could ever catch the tortoise, but we know that the sum of a geometric progression often converges

A more typical problem in a hybrid system simulation is the infinite bouncing frequency that occurs when a ball is dropped. Effective simulation of either system requires a solution to the Zeno paradox. A **Zeno hybrid system model** makes an infinite number of discrete transitions during a finite time interval. Below is AMS-style code for such a ball drop. Figure 8.22 is the corresponding time plot. Although a pen-and-paper analysis clearly shows that the ball will stop bouncing at a definite time, its approach to that time is infinitely detailed.

```
// AMS simulation of a ball bouncing -> infinite bouncing frequency!
module ballbounce();
  real height, velocity;

  analog initial begin height = 7.0; velocity = 0.0; end

  analog begin // We want auto-time step selection for this FDTD
     height   <+ -velocity;      // Falling downwards
     velocity <+ 9.8;            // Acceleration due to gravity
  end

  // We want discrete event triggered execution here
  always @(cross height) begin
     velocity = -0.75 * velocity; // Inelastic bounce
     height = 0.000001;           // Hmm, some fudge here!
  end
endmodule
// NB: The syntax above may not work in all AMS tools
```

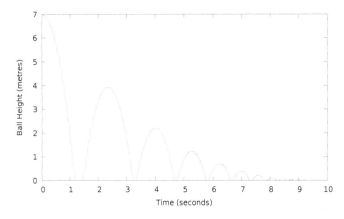

Figure 8.22 Hybrid model simulation of a bouncing ball dropped from 7.0 m. It stops completely at 9.366 s

A brute-force approach to solving Zeno models is to set a minimum time quantum below which detailed modelling will be ignored. Sadly, this is insufficient for modelling many behaviours of real interest, especially those with close to discontinuous behaviour and critical inflection points, such as the positive feedback used inside a common Schmitt trigger. A **Schmitt trigger** is a single-input voltage comparator with hysteresis. Having hysteresis means that its output turns from zero to one when the input voltage is above a hardwired upper trigger level, but does not return to zero until the input has fallen below a slightly lower trigger level. When the input voltage is between these trigger levels, it exhibits a memory effect that is useful for rejecting noise on the input. Research into Zeno suppression is ongoing, but solutions involve recognising patterns in the automatic quantum adjustment and flagging these as an unmodelled Zeno episode with X-values in the traces.

8.3.8 Logic Synthesis

Logic synthesis is the process of converting synthesisable RTL into a structural netlist. As Figure 8.8 showed, apart from the RTL, the synthesiser needs a cell library specification and intent metrics. Using a physical flow, a **floor plan** may also be provided that gives or allocates the area(s) available and specifies the location of some inputs and outputs. There may also be technology-specific information, such as the wiring resistance for each layer of metallisation.

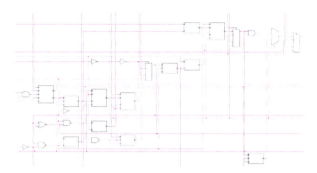

Figure 8.23 Fragment of a synthesised netlist rendered in a schematic viewer

Logic synthesis is an under-constrained optimisation problem. Anyone who has solved **Karnaugh maps** by hand will recall that more than one set of cubes can be used to generate a given output. The process of choosing which cubes to use and finding which sub-expressions are useful when generating several output functions becomes exponentially complex. Iteration and hill climbing must be used. The Espresso algorithm [11] expresses the on-set and the off-set for a logic function using lists of cubes. It iterates, expanding the cubes to their maximum valid size and then contracting them down to a minimum size again. Two iterations are commonly sufficient. Additionally, a logic synthesiser will sometimes re-encode a state so that, for instance, an output function is simple to decode and can be generated quickly after the clock edge (Section 4.4.2).

A logic synthesiser is generally structured into three phases:

1. **Elaboration**: The RTL input is translated into an internal representation, based on Boolean functions. In this form, the tool implements basic logic optimisation, removes redundant logic and may apply standard optimisation algorithms, such as constant folding and common sub-expression sharing, which are technology independent. **Constant folding** is the process of performing work at compile time that does not require any runtime values, such as adding constants together or discarding multiplexor input expressions that will never be used.

2. **Mapping**: The tool converts the optimised internal representation into target technology cells. It will insert testability structures, such as scan chains and boundary-scan cells (Section 4.7.5). If the intent specifies the power domains, the tool will insert level shifters and isolation cells where domains are crossed (Section 4.6.10) and power-gating cells as required (Section 4.6.10). After this phase, the designer can get a first estimation of PPA for a power- and DfT-aware design. If automatic clock gating is used (Section 4.6.9), the clock gates and their enabling expressions are inserted.

3. **Technology-based optimisation**: The netlist is optimised to meet the PPA constraints better. The drive strength of logic cells may be upsized or downsized, or the cells may be cloned or merged if better sub-expression-sharing opportunities exist. If a physical synthesis flow is floor-plan-aware, repeaters are inserted since the tool can estimate net lengths. The tool can also resize gates when splitting and distributing them along long wires. Such optimisations are iterated until the PPA targets are achieved. Sometimes the tool cannot find any way to close the design. If the PPA targets are not achieved, the designer must look at the RTL code and see how it can be written differently, or else revise the PPA constraints.

```
module TC(input clk, input cen);            module TC(input clk, input cen);
  reg [1:0] count;                            wire u10022, u10021, u10020, u10019;
  always @(posedge clk) if (cen) count<=count+1;   wire [1:0] count;
endmodule                                     input cen;   input clk;
                                              CVINV  i10021(u10021, count[0]);
                                              CVMUX2 i10022(u10022, cen, u10021, count[0]);
                                              CVDFF  u10023(count[0], u10022, clk, 1'b1, 1'b0, 1'b0);
                                              CVXOR2 i10019(u10019, count[0], count[1]);
                                              CVMUX2 i10020(u10020, cen, u10019, count[1]);
                                              CVDFF  u10024(count[1], u10020, clk, 1'b1, 1'b0, 1'b0);
                                            endmodule
```

Figure 8.24 Baseline RTL elaboration example showing synthesisable RTL input (left) and structural netlist output that uses generic gates (right)

Figure 8.24 shows example input and output for the RTL elaboration phase. The RTL input was converted to an implementation technology that included invertors, multiplexers, D-type flip-flops and XOR gates. For each gate, the output is the first-listed terminal. For a two-bit counter, there is no difference between the various types of adders, but for wider words, the synthesiser would have to decide which carry structure to use. The RTL elaboration phase can be implemented with three steps:

E1: Convert behavioural code to pure RTL. Each variable is assigned only once.

E2: Convert each assignment that is made to a multi-bit vector to a list of assignments, one for each bit of the vector.

E3: Convert the right-hand side of each bit assignment to a network of gates and other cells.

As with the simulator, a logic synthesiser elaborates `generate` constructs before starting synthesis. It also does some flattening (Section 8.3.1) to facilitate inter-module optimisation, but it may need to preserve aspects of the design hierarchy because this contains some information about how long nets are likely to be. Moreover, module instance names need to be associated with labels in the floor plan in a physical synthesis flow.

In step E1, all points where variables are assigned are scanned. The assignments on the left-hand side are collated. This results in exactly one input expression for each register, regardless of how many times it is assigned. As was described in Section 8.3.1, control flow constructs lead to multiplexer expressions. Reads of nets already given blocking assignments are elaborated accordingly.

In step E2, for each register that is more than 1 bit wide, separate assignments must be created for each bit. This procedure is colloquially known as **bit blasting**. The process removes all arithmetic operators and leaves only Boolean operators, which can then be directly implemented in gates. This is trivial for bitwise logic operations, such as an XOR of two words, but for adders, the type of adder must be chosen. Well-known adding techniques formed from simple gates use ripple carry, look-ahead or Kogge–Stone structures. A cell library may contain specialist adder cells. A recoding optimisation step may convert them to carry-save adders etc.

Multiplication is more complex due to its quadratic logic cost. Only small multipliers can sensibly be generated from standard gates inside a logic synthesiser. Therefore, the asterisk operator should be applied only to arguments if the sum of the argument bit widths is less than about 16. Beyond that, the engineer should manually instantiate a multiplier component. However, if one operand is a constant, standard compiler **strength reduction** techniques are deployed and much larger operands can safely be synthesised. For instance, multiplying by any constant that only has a few bits different from a power of two can be turned into that number of adders. Indeed, multiplying by a power of two is just a shift, implemented by wiring without gate cost. Synthesis of RTL containing a division should generally be avoided for all but tiny bit widths unless the denominator is a constant. Figure 8.25 shows a practical division example. For all the arithmetic operators, instantiating a generic functional unit (Section 6.8.1) may be preferable during elaboration, with these then being expanded or replaced during the technology mapping phase.

```
reg [31:0] q, n;
...
q = n / 10;
return q;
```

```
reg [31:0] q, n;
...
q = (n >> 1) + (n >> 2);
q += (q >> 4);
q += (q >> 8);
q += (q >> 16);
return q >> 3;
```

Figure 8.25 Essence of logic synthesised for integer division of the 32-bit value n by the constant 10 using just adders, based on 8/10 being 0.11001100 recurring. A logic synthesiser can create similar bespoke divide circuits for any constant denominator

Figure 8.26 shows a component that is commonly used, both as a technology-independent gate at the output of elaboration and in cell technology libraries. This is the four-input **AND-OR-INVERT (AOI)** gate. It includes a fair amount of useful functionality in a structure that is directly realisable in CMOS with a maximum of two transistors in series between the supply and output. Degenerate forms of it with one input tied off to either logic level are also widely useful. Because it inverts on every path from input to output, **pulse shrinkage** is minimised (Section 4.9.5).

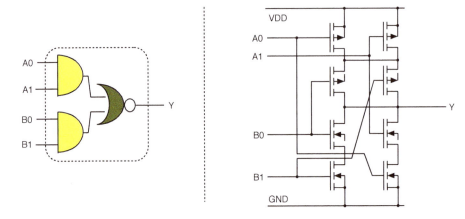

Figure 8.26 AND-OR-INVERT gate, logical function (left) and actual circuit when realised in CMOS (right)

In the third elaboration step, E3, a gate-level circuit is generated for each of the bits assigned to each register. A very wide selection of circuits and cells in a cell library can achieve a given function. Wherever the RTL assigns don't-care X values, an even wider choice of circuits becomes available and the tool is better able to select a design that best meets the design intents. The tool minimises the logic using multi-output versions of classic algorithms such as Quine–McCluskey and Espresso. The classic algorithms give the implementation with the lowest logic cost for a single-output function, but since a different logic function is typically needed for each D-type input, algorithms that make the best use of shared sub-expressions will give a lower aggregate complexity. As shown in brown in Figure 8.45, an equivalence checker (Section 7.6) is commonly used to compare a synthesised gate-level circuit with the pre-synthesis RTL.

Liberal use of the X don't-care designation in the source RTL allows the synthesis tool freedom to perform this logic minimisation.

8.3.9 Arrays and RAM Inference in RTL

RTLs support bits, bit vectors (words) and arrays of bit vectors (RAMs). Arrays in the RTL can be synthesised to structural instances of SSRAM (Section 2.6.4) or else to register files made of flip-flops. With some tools, certain patterns of array use are defined to trigger **RAM inference**, which instantiates a RAM in the generated netlist. A typical pattern is shown in Figure 8.27. There are two essential rules for inferring synchronous RAM:

1. One expression must be clearly recognisable as the address for each port.

2. The data read out must be registered by the required number of pipeline broadside registers to match the latency of the target technology without using (peeking at) any of the data in that pipeline.

```
module SSRAM(
  input clk,                  // Synchronous reads and writes
  input ren,                  // Read enable (optional)
  input wen,                  // Write enable
  input [14:0] addr,          // Address input
  input [31:0] wdata,         // Write data in
  output reg [31:0] rdata);   // Read data out
  reg [31:0] myram [32767:0]; // 32k words of 32 bits each
  always @(posedge clk) begin
    if (ren) rdata <= myram[addr];
    if (wen) myram[addr] <= wdata;
  end
endmodule
```

Figure 8.27 Typical RTL coding style for RAM inference. Data out is registered once without otherwise being used and the same subscript expression is used in both the read and write contexts

RAM inference is mainly used by logic synthesis tools for field-programmable gate arrays (FPGAs). ASIC designs, however, normally require the RTL to contain explicit structural instances that have been generated by a RAM compiler (see below). This is because ancillary fabrication information needs to be collected for an ASIC, including, perhaps, per RAM licence fees.

Collating assignments to arrays with dynamic subscriptions is more problematic than for scalars. The **name alias problem** is that at compile time it is not always possible to determine whether a pair of subscripts are going to be the same or different at runtime, and hence, for blocking variable assigns, the tool cannot look up the already assigned values. Instead, it must generate a multiplexer to forward undecidable assigns. Reads also present a problem. The infix array subscript operator in RTL, denoted with square brackets, $A[s]$, cannot be directly translated into a read of synchronous SRAM. Synchronous SRAM, as in Figure 8.27, requires the address to be presented the cycle before. Moreover, a structural hazard (Section 6.3) is raised by expressions such as $A[s1] + A[s2]$, which require the SRAM to be read at two locations at once, which is impossible if it has a single port. These problems are overcome in higher-level tools by using automatically generated schedules, as in HLS (Section 6.9) and Bluespec HDL (Section 6.8.5).

8.3.10 Memory Macrocell Compiler

An average SoC may have about 75 per cent of its area devoted to RAM, which, typically, is generated by a **memory compiler**. The input parameters are:

- **Size**: Word width and number of words

- **Port description**: Each port has an address input. It can be read only, read-write or write only. For a read-write port, the old data from the addressed word are typically read out as well as being replaced with a fresh value. Depending on the number and combination, there are three main forms of SRAM. The two main flavours are single-ported (SP_SRAM) and dual-ported (DP_SRAM; Section 2.6.5). There is also **two-port SRAM (TP_SRAM)**, which exclusively dedicates one port to write operations and the other to read operations. This type of memory is particularly suitable for an area-optimised FIFO buffer in a clock-domain crossing context (Section 3.7.1).

- **Clocking information**: This is the frequency and latency for synchronous RAM or the access time and write-pulse width for asynchronous RAM.

- **Resolution**: What to do on write/write and write/read conflicts between ports.

The outputs from a RAM compiler are a data sheet for the RAM, RTL and ESL simulation models and a list of the polygons required for the fabrication masks. There are similar generators for FIFO buffers and masked ROM.

Sometimes self-test modules are also generated along with the RAM. Built-in self-tests (BISTs) were discussed in Section 4.7.6. For example, Mentor's MBIST Architect^{TM} generates an RTL BIST with the memory. Arm/Artisan's generator generates a wrapper that allows a RAM to self-repair by diverting access from a fault row to a spare row as a form of **redundancy zapping** (Section 8.8.4).

8.3.11 Conventional RTL Compared with Software

The word **behaviour**, when applied to a style of RTL or software coding, tends to simply mean that a sequential thread is used to express the sequential execution of the statements. Despite the apparent power of this form of expression, there are severe limitations in the defined synthesisable subsets of Verilog and VHDL.

Compared with multi-threaded software, the limitations include, for instance, that each variable must be written to by only one thread and that a thread is unable to leave the current file or module to execute subroutines or methods in other parts of the design. RTL is statically allocated (i.e. no user data are stored on a stack or heap). Threads do not leave their starting context and all communication is through shared variables that denote wires. There are no thread synchronisation primitives, except to wait on a clock edge. RTL requires the programmer to think in a massively parallel way and leaves no freedom for the execution platform to reschedule the design.

Software, on the other hand, uses far fewer threads. The writer puts them just where they are needed for asynchronous behaviour to exploit parallelism where it needs to be explicit. The threads may pass from one module to another and thread blocking is used to control the flow of the data.

An RTL **behavioural model** is a short program, generally containing unsynthesisable constructs, that serves to replace a complex hardware subsystem, such as a DRAM DIMM (Section 2.6.6). A behavioural model produces the same useful result but executes much more quickly because it does not model the values of all the internal nets and pipeline stages (which provide no benefit until converted to actual parallel hardware). In some instances, an RTL model of a subsystem may not be available due to IP copy protection, although RTL simulators can, typically, read encrypted RTL.

RTL is not as expressive for algorithms or data structures as most software programming languages. In a concurrency model, everything executes in lockstep. The programmer has to keep track of all this concurrency. They must generate their own bespoke handshaking and flow control between components. Moreover, except for the occasional use of don't-cares, Verilog and VHDL do not express when a register is **live** with data. Hence, automatic refactoring and certain correctness proofs are impossible without additional annotation. More advanced RTLs, such as Bluespec (Section 6.8.5), have addressed many of these issues. If a programmer wants to use conventional software paradigms, HLS (Section 6.9) can be applied to (stylised) software to produce RTL.

8.3.12 Synthesis Intent and Goals

The logic synthesiser chooses a design based on sets of guiding metrics that are known as the synthesis intent. Four common optimisation targets are:

▪ **Area**: Achieving the smallest area normally means using the lowest number of gates and careful optimisation when factorising logic functions into sub-expressions that are to be shared by more than one output function. Using very small technology cells obviously helps meet area targets. However, small cells have a higher wiring density. The design can then become **wiring or metal limited** instead of **transistor limited**, so that more care is required in designing the wiring between gates than in how many transistors are deployed. Thin wires are possible, leading to high-resistance tracking with greater RC delays. Fewer tracks of greater thickness occupy the same area in a wiring layer and may be better. Another alternative is to compute the same expression in several places. For instance, it takes less energy to compute a 32-bit addition than to communicate the result a distance of 1 mm.

▪ **Performance**: A performance intent specifies that a subsystem must meet a target clock frequency, such as 500 MHz, or it may specify various logic paths that must meet target delays, such as 150 ps between input P and output Q. Performance targets are evaluated by determining the critical paths using static timing analysis (Section 8.12.1). They may be met by adjusting circuit structures. Cell libraries often provide cell variants with different propagation delays and drive strengths. These differ in their consumption of area and power. Hence, timing targets can also be met by selecting appropriate cells taking into account the expected net load capacitance and track resistance.

With FinFET technology nodes (Section 8.2.1), starting with 14 nm and below, the propagation delay in nets is as important as the propagation delay through the logic cells. This is why physically aware synthesis tools that estimate the net delay are critical.

▪ **Energy**: Static energy use is greatly affected by whether low- or high-leakage cells are used, but is largely correlated with area for a given technology. Power gating helps (Section 4.6.10). Dynamic power is affected by the detailed logic design, but not a great deal. Glitches in certain combinational logic structures, especially those containing many XOR gates, can consume a significant amount of energy. This can be reduced by adding redundant cubes during logic minimisation, but this is not always feasible for CRC generators and fast adders. Clock gating

(Section 4.6.9) is one of the best methods for reducing dynamic power. It is best implemented automatically inside the logic synthesiser, based on power intent pragmas.

▪ **Testability**: A production test of some logic structures may require many test vectors (Section 8.8.2). This is a problem if the depreciation of the testing equipment while in use is similar to the cost of the die being tested. Logic circuits with few outputs or which include fail-safe mechanisms, such as majority voting, can be hard to test. They can be made more accessible by asking the logic synthesiser to avoid them or to perform scan-chain insertion (Section 4.7.5). Alternatively, they can be tested using additional dedicated test modes invoked with a test input pin that is strapped off under normal operation.

▪ **Floor plan**: An additional intent in physical synthesis is to fit a specific **floor plan**, which describes the shape of the available silicon area. This may not be a rectangle or it may have masked-out regions into which other circuits will later be inserted. For multi-chip and die-stacked designs (Section 8.9.1), the vias between devices determine where inter-chip connections must be situated. The position of the I/O and the general shape of the silicon region affect the buffering strategies for signals that need to pass through the region. It may be pointless to factorise a logic expression such that a term can be used for two purposes if the two purposes are physically separated.

The **core utilisation ratio** is the percentage area taken up by cells within a region of a SoC. Early VLSI had very few metal layers, so cell rows had to be spaced well apart. Perhaps twice as much area was devoted to wiring channels than for active logic cells, and the core utilisation ratio was about 33 per cent. Since many metal layers are available today, wiring can freely run over the top of cells, using separate layers from the metal that forms part of the cell itself. The core utilisation ratio is now well above 80 per cent. Further layers on top carry long-distance nets, clocks and power supplies. However, a wider cell in which the wiring contacts are spread out more can sometimes be preferable to a dense cell. A wider cell may have much more drive strength and does not need several repeaters, helping to reduce the propagation delays.

Figure 8.28 illustrates the relationship among utilisation ratio, core area and performance. The highest utilisation ratios occur for low-frequency operations. The convex hull of best performing points is plotted as the black dashed line. It switches back and forth among the utilisation ratios in the vicinity of 84 per cent at low frequencies. Some lines kink back on themselves beyond the best design point. Moreover, the area significantly increases as the frequency increases, since higher drive strengths and hence, bigger cells are needed, which results in higher manufacturing costs.

Several standard cell architectures are usually developed for a process node (Section 8.4). They vary in cell height. The **cell height** is usually counted as the number of equivalent routing tracks in the first horizontal routing layer. The **cell width**, on the other hand, varies from cell to cell, according to complexity. Note that for standard cell systems, the term **horizontal** is used to denote the direction of the power rails, as illustrated in Figure 8.7. A flipped row has its ground at the top, as in the middle row in that figure. In reality, rows of cells in different subsystems are often run in orthogonal directions,

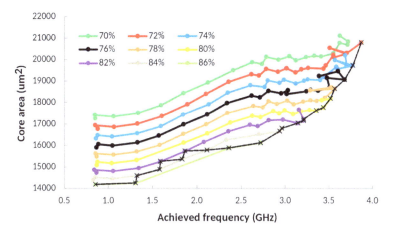

Figure 8.28 Scatter plot of area versus operating frequency for a design (Arm Cortex-A9 Falcon) on a common process node and cell library for different core utilisation ratios. The best performers are highlighted with black crosses (and joined together with the black dashed line)

with 'horizontal' for one being at right angles to 'horizontal' for another. The direction makes no difference to functionality, and may be chosen to assist with the design of the PDN or whatever.

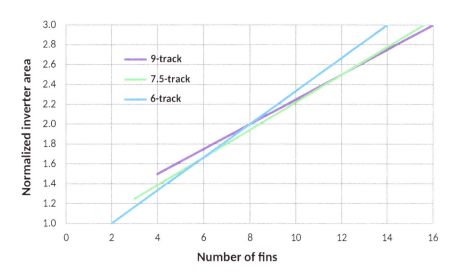

Figure 8.29 FinFET invertor area versus number of fins for different cell heights at a process node

For a given cell height, there is an equivalent maximum FET width or maximum number of FinFET fins in modern processes. As an example, a 6-track height has two fins per FET finger, a 7.5-track has three fins and 9-track four fins at maximum. Increasing the cell drive strength is achieved by increasing the number of fins proportionally. The cell area increases with the number of FET fingers. A taller cell quickly becomes more area efficient than a smaller cell as the number of fins is increased. In the example shown in Figure 8.29, it is clear that the 6-track cell (blue line) is more area efficient for a low drive strength whereas it is the least area efficient for higher drive strength cells with more fins.

The high drive strength and better area efficiency of taller cells results in better area usage when operating at higher frequencies where the need for a higher drive strength is more common. However, many nets are short in some kinds of subsystem, and then the higher drive strength is not needed for the cells that drive these shorter nets. Thus, a taller cell may be wasteful. Moreover, the area of a block of logic is dominated by the more complex cells. Flip-flops are more complex than typical gates, and the flip-flop area could be 40 per cent of the block area. Complex cells tend to have a lower fraction of their area devoted to transistors that drive their output net (or nets), hence, being taller is less beneficial for such cells.

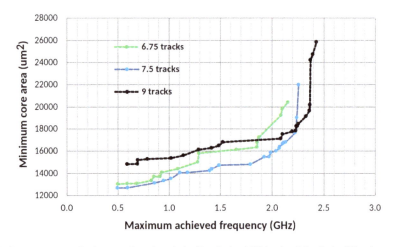

Figure 8.30 Scatter plot of area versus operating frequency for a given design (Arm Cortex-A9 Falcon) and standard cell libraries on a common process node that vary in cell height, measured in track equivalents

The complex effects of changing the cell height is demonstrated in Figure 8.30. This shows how the core area for a given RTL processor design varied with target frequency for different cell heights for a given process node. For each library, the design was synthesised for different area and performance intents. As just explained, it is often assumed that a smaller cell architecture will deliver a smaller block area at low frequency intent, but this is clearly not always true (the blue line is below the green line throughout). Smaller cells have fewer horizontal routing tracks so that routing may become more difficult and not enable a high core utilisation rate. A lower utilisation rate may counteract the advantage of the smaller cell area. But taller cell architectures do generally deliver better high-frequency results. Hence the best choice of cell architecture also depends on the design type, as characterised by the ratio of gates to flip-flops and the net length distribution.

8.4 Chip Types and Classifications

There are different types of chip manufacturer based on where their silicon is manufactured and how they sell it. Manufacturers can broadly be classified as:

1. Integrated device manufacturers (IDMs) or vertical market chip makers, such as Samsung and Intel, which design, manufacture and sell chips, and sometimes the products they go in

2. **Fabless** manufacturers, such as NVIDIA and Xilinx, which design and sell chips but outsource manufacturing to **foundries**

3. Foundry companies, which own the fabrication equipment and associated IP, such as cell libraries, and manufacture chips designed and sold by their customers under their customer's brand.

The world's major foundries famously include SMC and TSMC, but IDMs may also offer foundry services if they have spare capacity or older processes no longer suitable for their new products. Each foundry offers a number of process nodes, introducing a new one every year or so while still continuing to offer the older ones at reduced prices. A **process node** is a manufacturing geometry (e.g. 14 nm) together with all the ancillary information, such as the resistivity of the various materials, wafer size and transconductance of the transistors. Each parameter is characterised at the various PVT corners (Section 8.4.4).

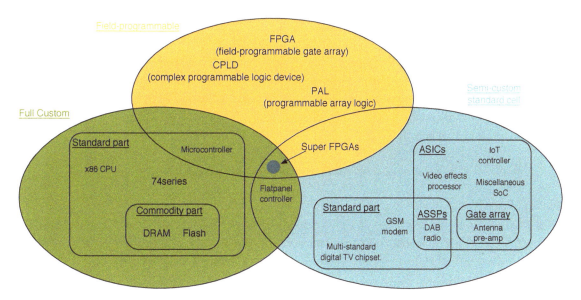

Figure 8.31 A broad-brush classification of digital ICs into full-custom, semi-custom and field-programmable classes with some example device roles

Figure 8.31 illustrates ways of classifying ICs. The outer ellipses represent the three main design approaches for physical silicon: full custom, semi-custom and field-programmable. Many chips include a combination of all three design techniques. Within each outer ellipse, there are possible subdivisions into standard parts and **application-specific integrated circuits (ASICs)**.

Electronic equipment designers prefer to use a standard part if one is already available and the resulting **bill of materials (BoM)** is acceptable, but build their own ASIC or use FPGAs (Section 8.5.2) if this is cheaper when the **non-recurring expense (NRE)** is adequately amortised over the production volume (Section 8.11). A standard part could be an **application-specific standard part (ASSP)**. If a standard part is not suitable, the choice between full custom, semi-custom and field-programmable approaches has to be made, depending on performance, production volume and cost requirements. These terms are defined as follows:

- In a **full-custom design**, detailed, manual design effort is put into the circuit details, including transistor sizes and the physical layout. This should achieve the preferred optimum compromise of speed, density and power consumption for a given target technology. It is used for devices that will be produced in very large quantities, e.g. millions of parts, if the design cost is justified. Processor ALU, register files and related data paths are often full custom, as are multiplier circuits. SRAM and DRAM also use full-custom designs for the bit cells, line drivers and sense amplifiers.

- In a **semi-custom design**, logic gates are taken from a cell technology library (Section 8.4.1). Each cell has a fixed design that is repeated each time it is used, both within a chip and across any devices that use the library, which simplifies the design process. Performance and area margins conservatively enable portable use. Hence, for instance, the drive power of the cell is not optimised for each instance, but two or three variants of a cell may be made. These vary in their delay and load derating factors (Section 4.6.4).

- For **field-programmable** devices, specialised standard parts are customised with programmable wiring for a specific function. The programming is done quickly without expensive equipment. This results in **NRE** of close to zero, but device performance is significantly degraded. Compared with a semi-custom chip, up to 50 per cent more area is used and a reduction of the clock frequency by between 3× and 15× is typical.

Semi-custom chips for general-purpose VLSI designs are built using a library of logic cells.

Standard Parts

A **standard part** is essentially any chip that a chip manufacturer is prepared to sell to someone else along with a data sheet and supporting EDA models. The design may previously have been an ASIC for a specific customer that is now on general release. Many standard parts are general-purpose logic, memory or microprocessor devices. These are frequently full-custom chips designed in-house by an IDM and specifically optimised to make the most of an in-house fabrication line, perhaps using optimisations not made available to others who use the line, such as a foundry. Other standard parts include graphics controllers, digital TV chip sets, GPS receivers and miscellaneous useful chips needed in high volumes. These are all ASSPs.

Other standard parts are completely generic. This class notably includes most memory devices and devices with a long history, such as the 74-series ICs. These parts are interchangeably made by a variety of semiconductor houses. Equipment manufacturers do not particularly mind which supplier is used, since cost is the most important factor. For such devices, futures can be purchased on commodity stock exchanges or spot markets, especially for flash and DRAM. Customers usually seek at least a **second-source supplier** for non-commodity parts, so that production can continue if the primary supplier has a financial or technical problem. Another option is to put the IP for the product into secure escrow.

Application-Specific Integrated Circuits

An **application-specific integrated circuit (ASIC)** is a custom chip designed for a specific application. The costs of developing and using an ASIC are compared with the costs of using an existing or field-programmable part. An existing part may not perform the required function exactly, requiring either a design specification change or some additional *glue logic* to adapt the part to the application. The other main reasons for designing an ASIC include protecting valuable design or algorithm IP, avoiding licensing costs, minimising customs duty, and simplifying and protecting the supply chain for a product. These reasons are important in their own right and can be more significant than cost savings relating to the BoM.

Mixing a variety of technologies on a single silicon chip can be cost-effective but may require extra masks and typically involves compromises in performance compared with building the circuit with a process that is appropriately optimised. More than one ASIC may be needed if application-specific functions are physically distant, require different technologies or are just too big for one chip. In some cases, an ASIC is used to split the costs and risks or because part of the system will be subsequently reused. Circuit structures that motivate the use of multiple different chips with different fabrication recipes are:

▪ power consumption limitations (power above 5 W needs special attention)

▪ die size limitations (chips above 11 mm on a side might have significantly higher costs per mm^2)

▪ special considerations:

  - special static, dynamic or non-volatile RAM needs

  - analogue IP blocks that need low noise supplies or shielding structures

  - very high-frequency operation, perhaps needing GaAs instead of silicon

  - heavy current or high voltage output capabilities for load control, e.g. solenoids and driving a motor/

Silicon fabrication lines are, typically, priced per wafer. Hence, the customer is charged per unit area of silicon processed. Applications that switch heavy load currents need large-area transistors. It is wasteful to build these on a high-performance low-geometry fabrication line. Therefore, power output stages are, typically, put onto a separate chip and fabricated by an older and hence, larger-geometry, fabrication line, although a standard part is often sufficient.

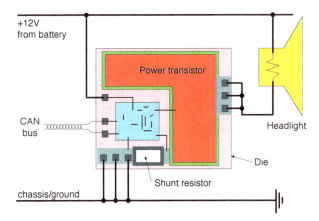

Figure 8.32 SoC application diagram for an automotive headlight controller. A heavy load is connected to a controller-area network (CAN) bus

Applications such as the car headlight controller of Figure 8.32 would be made on an old-technology line. This device has nearly all of its silicon area devoted to one transistor, which controls the heavy load. Another large component on the chip is a small-value current-sensing resistor, which is used for fault detection. Although there are many thousands of transistors in a network interface and embedded application controller (if not hard-coded), these can be made in a very large geometry process, since only low performance is required. The silicon area for the controller will still amount to a small fraction of the total die.

8.4.1 Semi-custom (Cell-based) Design

There are two forms of semi-custom design: standard cells and gate arrays. Gate arrays are discussed in Section 8.5). Standard cells are far more common for SoC applications. Both are masked ASICs. This means that they are application-specific designs needing fabrication masks. At least some of a mask embodies the design and the mask is used only for that device. Masked ROMs (Section 2.6.2) are specific for an application. They have one mask that embodies the data to be stored but do not have custom logic.

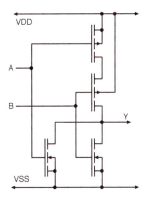
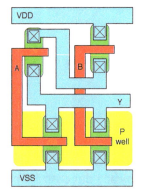

Figure 8.33 Two-input NOR gate, circuit schematic (left) and several layers of a standard cell layout (right). Blue is the bottom layer of metal, red is polysilicon, green is channel diffusion and yellow is the P well in which the N-channel FETs are constructed

Standard cell designs use a set of well-proven logic cells from a target technology library, also known as the **cell library**. Figure 8.33 shows a schematic and physical layout of an elementary standard cell. Cells share a common height so that when they are adjacent to each other in rows on the chip, the power supply rails join up and run without interruptions from cell to cell. Cells vary in width according to their complexity and have predefined coordinates for each contact where inter-cell wiring must be connected. All the N-type transistors are in the half of the cell adjacent to the VSS, so that a shared P well of diffusion can be put down with low resolution in an early fabrication step. Likewise, the P-type transistors, which conduct when their gate is low, are at the top.

As well as logic gates and registers, a basic cell library contains level shifters, clock buffers, power domain isolation cells (Section 4.6.10) and **I/O pads** of various sorts (Section 4.8.1). The output pads buffer the on-chip signals generating the much greater drive power needed to drive PCB traces. Input pads provide protection against static electricity and board-level fault conditions. There are also various specialist cells for clock generation and distribution.

The internal structure of a cell can be flipped horizontally if this helps in reducing the wiring. Similarly, a whole row of cells can be flipped vertically, for the same reason. The wiring generator will correctly swap over the supply connections. The domain supply will come from one of the upper layers of metal. Upper layer masks cannot be deposited with high accuracy and so are more suitable for heavy-duty purposes, such as a supply PDN.

Standard cells are defined with different drive strengths to match the output load they need to drive. The drive strength affects the output drive transistor width or the number of transistors connected in parallel within the cell. For example, INV_X4 refers to an invertor with four-finger FETs. As explained in Section 4.6.4, an output load consists of the sum of the input capacitances of the driven cells and the capacitances of the wires used to interconnect the cells. Usually a multi-drive cell has similar timing performance to a single-drive cell if the output load is increased by the same multiple. Moreover, the power used by a multi-drive cell is increased from that for a single-drive cell by, approximately, the same multiple.

Figure 8.34 shows a cell from the human-readable data book for a standard cell library. The cell is a four-input NAND gate. The machine-readable version has hundreds of parameters for each cell. Slightly odd functions, such as !(a.b + c.d), which is known as AND-OR-INVERT (AOI), are also available, since such patterns are commonly generated in logic synthesis and have a compact circuit (Section 8.3.8). A data sheet gives the logic function, the structural RTL that needs to be generated to instantiate it, and detailed timing figures. As also explained in Section 4.6.4, the timing model includes an intrinsic delay and derating per output load unit. These figures are different for each input and for each polarity of output transition. The illustrated device has twice the normal drive strength; hence, its delay derating factors are likely to be about half those for a $1\times$ version of the cell. A more detailed data sheet may indicate the static and dynamic energy use.

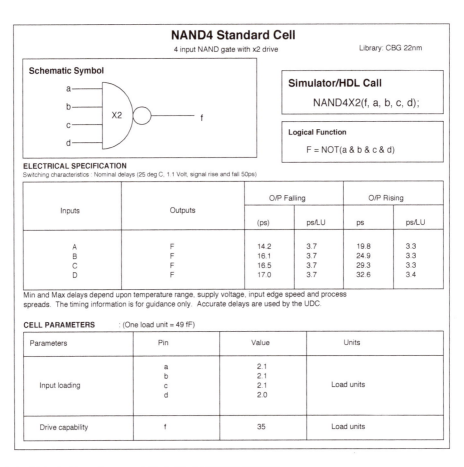

NAND4 Standard Cell

4 input NAND gate with x2 drive

Library: CBG 22nm

Schematic Symbol

a
b
X2
c
d
f

Simulator/HDL Call

NAND4X2(f, a, b, c, d);

Logical Function

F = NOT(a & b & c & d)

ELECTRICAL SPECIFICATION

Switching characteristics : Nominal delays (25 deg C, 1.1 Volt, signal rise and fall 50ps)

Inputs	Outputs	O/P Falling		O/P Rising	
		(ps)	ps/LU	ps	ps/LU
A	F	14.2	3.7	19.8	3.3
B	F	16.1	3.7	24.9	3.3
C	F	16.5	3.7	29.3	3.3
D	F	17.0	3.7	32.6	3.4

Min and Max delays depend upon temperature range, supply voltage, input edge speed and process spreads. The timing information is for guidance only. Accurate delays are used by the UDC.

CELL PARAMETERS   : (One load unit = 49 fF)

Parameters	Pin	Value	Units
Input loading	a	2.1	Load units
	b	2.1	
	c	2.1	
	d	2.0	
Drive capability	f	35	Load units

Figure 8.34 Typical cell data sheet from a human-readable version of a standard cell library

8.4.2 Standard Cell Data

For each cell in a library, a number of different machine-readable data types are needed. These are split over a number of files and cover the functionality, layout, schematic symbol, timing analysis, power analysis, noise analysis and variability analysis. The main file forms are:

- **Symbol**: The logic symbol shows the contacts (external connections) to the cell. It gives their directions and names, as well as the preferred layout as a schematic view. There may be a simple set of port connection constraints, which stop outputs from being connected to each other in a schematic GUI.

- **Schematic**: The internal cell circuit is a transistor-level description of the cell. It is needed for a SPICE simulation (Section 8.4.3) and occasionally needs to be inspected for other purposes.

- **Liberty**: A Liberty (`lib`) file contains the main machine-readable data sheet for each cell (Section 8.12.6). It repeats the name and direction of each contact, but also contains all the electrical features. It is used for the timing, power, variability and signal integrity analyses. The pin-to-pin timing is given, including setup and hold-times for edge-sensitive logic. Many parameters are provided for the nine PVT positions (Section 8.4.4). Much of the data will have been generated by SPICE simulations of each cell. The Liberty file also documents the various drive waveforms with the different transition times used during characterisation.

- **RTL**: An RTL model or truth table defines the logical function of the cell, which is needed both for the logic synthesis and a net-level simulation. Continuous assignment suffices for a logic gate. For a more-complex component, such as a PLL, a behavioural model is needed.

- **LEF**: A **library exchange format (LEF)** file contains an abstract or physical representation of the cell sufficient for placement and routing. The primary information is the cell size and locations of the contacts within the cell, along with rules that restrict what is put above or nearby.

- **DEF**: A **design exchange format (DEF)** file contains the complete physical view of the cell used for the tapeout. This builds on the abstract view by listing the polygons required on all affected layer masks. The upper wiring levels are normally not affected and can be used for power or signal wiring over the cell.

For complex cells, the production test requirements, including the required test coverage, are also provided. Further data are also needed, but these may need to be combined with per process information from fabrication for them to be usable. Such data include electromigration (Section 8.4.5) and IR-drop analyses.

Supercells or Hard Macros

Within a semi-custom design, a mechanism is needed to support islands of full-custom design. Thus, a full-custom component is treated as a **supercell**, also known as a **hard macro** or **hard layout macro**. For the semi-custom design tools, a supercell is no different from an everyday logic gate; it is just much larger and has many more net-level connections and may use more metal layers. Memory, CPU cores, PLLs (Section 4.9.5) and SERDES (Section 3.8) are the main examples of supercells.

8.4.3 SPICE Characterisation

Before a cell library can be used, it must be characterised. The main tool is analogue simulation, typically performed with SPICE (Section 4.6.7). Selected results are verified using measurements of real silicon. The amount of data generated is huge. A set of Liberty files can sometimes be terabytes in size. Characterising a library may require several thousands of CPU hours, so a CPU farm must be used. CMOS processes have transistors with different threshold voltages (multi-V_T) and different channel lengths. A library usually targets one threshold voltage and one channel length, so there can be as many libraries as different threshold voltages and channel lengths. Some cells use a mix of threshold voltages. Modern circuits often use a mix of different V_T libraries to optimise the PPA. Cells with the lowest V_T corresponding to the fastest transistors are used for the most critical paths in terms of timing, thus defining the maximum performance of the circuit. Other V_T values and channel lengths are used to reduce the static power leakage, since a higher V_T or longer channel transistors have a lower leakage current.

8.4.4 PVT Variations

The electrical features of manufactured silicon devices vary from wafer to wafer, across the wafer from die to die, and across the die (local variations). This is known as **process variation**. Two further forms of variation occur during operation. These arise from the supply voltage used and the operating temperature. These three dimensions of variation define the principal **process, voltage and temperature (PVT)** space. Each of these has a nominal, minimum and maximum value. Example ranges are shown in Table 8.5. The nominal value is also called the typical value when it is measured instead of being applied. Correct operation is required under all possible variations of these parameters. The limits of the principal PVT values basically define a cuboid space, which has eight corners. A ninth point is the nominal operating point in the centre of the cube. The silicon is characterised at all nine points.

Table 8.5 Example of process, voltage and temperature (PVT) ranges

Parameter	Values
Process variation	0.9 to 1.1
Supply voltage range	0.85 to 1.1 V
Temperature range	0 to 70°C

The slow and fast process variation limits correspond to a given standard deviation from the average, usually 3σ for a Gaussian distribution. In reality, process variation can be split into further dimensions. Rather than just a line between fast and slow, non-systematic variations must be explored, such as where the P and N resistances vary in opposite directions, as discussed in Section 8.12.4. Variations of the net resistance and the dielectric constant for the insulator between conductors also need to be taken into account. A manufacturing foundry provides specific models of the resistance and capacitance of the different metal layers composing the metal stack of the process. Variation outside this range can occur, but devices that fail should be spotted during the production test.

Two points of special interest are the fast corner and the slow corner. The slow point is at the highest temperature with the lowest supply voltage on the slowest silicon. The fast point is the opposite corner. For a quick verification, a simulation of just these two corners can be used. An all-corner simulation is needed prior to sign-off (Section 8.7.7).

8.4.5 Electromigration

Electric currents move metallic materials from where they were placed during manufacture, which is called *electromigration*. The atoms move along the line of a strong current density, which is a thermally activated physical mechanism. The magnitude depends on the line temperature, which is fixed by the global temperature of the circuit and the heat dissipated by Joule heating along the line. Thus, the resistance of the metal line varies over the lifetime of the circuit, which significantly impacts its timing behaviour and can lead to non-functionality.

A standard cell library uses the maximum electromigration conditions for temperature (e.g. 100°C) and lifetime (e.g. 10 years). These conditions apply when a circuit is in continuous operation. Circuit lifetime can exceed the electromigration lifetime if the circuit is in standby mode for a significant amount of time. The temperature may also vary during the circuit lifetime, typically for automotive applications. In this case, the electromigration specification has an equivalent average temperature and lifetime accounting for the different lengths of time at each temperature.

The electromigration limit of a metal line depends on its width and length. Foundries provide mathematical models for calculating the electromigration limit under three different characterisations: average (DC), root mean squared (rms) and peak current. For each net, it is necessary to check that none of the three types of current will exceed the electromigration limits of the conductors deployed.

A significant DC current flows only in the PDN. The signal nets and vias conveying logic values experience only bidirectional currents, which arise from the rise and fall transitions as they charge and discharge the associated capacitance. This results in a net-zero DC current. So, only rms and peak electromigration limits apply to signal nets.

A DC current can simply be estimated from:

$$I_{DC} = C_{load} V_{dd} F$$

where C_{load} is the output load, V_{dd} the power supply voltage and F the frequency. If $I_{EM\,DC}$ is the maximum electromigration DC limit of the output conductor, it is possible to determine the maximum load and frequency product limit:

$$C_{load} F = \frac{I_{EM\,DC}}{V_{dd}}$$

The maximum output load can then be determined once the operating frequency has been set. The same process can be applied to the rms and peak currents. The most limiting condition of the DC, rms and peak currents fixes the maximum $C_{load} F$ product.

For high-frequency switching currents, a larger voltage can develop due to the parasitic inductance of a conductor than to the IR drop because of conductor resistance. Multiple wires, spread out in parallel, have a lower total inductance than a single wire with the same cross-sectional area. The asymptotic limit of this approach is a **ground plane**, commonly used on PCBs, which has the theoretical minimum inductance. Moreover, it is no longer possible to widen the routing wires at advanced process nodes, as this blocks too many routing opportunities. Thus, the effective electromigration limit can be increased by using several narrow wires in parallel, connected together with via arrays, thus enabling the current to be shared over the different branches.

8.4.6 Waveform-based Cell Characterisation

As already mentioned, characterisation data for standard cells are nearly always obtained from a SPICE simulation. This is done by applying a signal to the input pin and measuring either the output voltage or current signal. Alternatively, the current in the power supply or the input pin capacitance can be measured. Running SPICE requires a supplied or extracted SPICE netlist for the cell. This is a translation of the schematics into the long-established format used by SPICE. A SPICE simulation for an invertor was presented in Section 4.6.7.

Manufacturing foundries provide SPICE model cards for each type of transistor for different V_T values and channel lengths. An **extraction deck** is also provided. This has the resistive and capacitive components of each wire extracted from the layout of the cell. (The term *deck* is an old-fashioned name for a computer file, dating from the days of punched cards.) The resistance and capacitance are based on the size of the nets and the spacing between them. When used in a physical implementation of a circuit, each standard cell is abutted to other standard cells. Routing nets may fly over the cells and may add capacitive components that modify the electrical features of the cell. Since SPICE FET models account for proximity effects, it is necessary to extract the cell netlist from a realistic environment. To avoid the need to consider all possible cases of neighbour cells and routing over the cell, the cell netlist is extracted for the worst-case and best-case configurations, which are then associated with the worst-case and best-case timing corners.

The **slew rate** of a logic net is the rate of change of its voltage when switching between logic values. It can be expressed in volts per picosecond. As presented in Section 4.6.4, historically, the signal applied to the input pin of a cell was a simple signal: a linear voltage ramp ranging from 0 to the power-supply voltage V_{dd}. Net transition times cannot be measured from 0 to 100 per cent of the output signal given the non-linear shapes; instead, they are measured between selected low and high ratios, typical values being 20–80 per cent or 30–70 per cent. The low and high ratios are usually picked to maximise the accuracy of the timing analysis compared to a SPICE simulation. The output current waveform depends on the derivative of the output voltage across the output load and hence, the slew rate.

For more advanced process nodes, using a linear segment input signal has proven to be inaccurate, as it is not sufficiently representative of the actual voltage waveform. Thus, the linear input signal has been replaced by a driver waveform corresponding to the output signal of a selected cell, usually an invertor or a buffer, under different net length loading conditions. There are as many driver waveforms as different input transition times used to build the lookup tables (LUTs), each waveform corresponding to an input transition time. The driver waveform for a transition time is obtained by adjusting its output load, the transition time still being measured between the low and high voltages. Figure 8.35 shows how the measured gate delay increases as the input transition times become longer. The plotted lines are parallel under heavy output load conditions, which shows that that a slow input waveform interacts only non-linearly with output load derating for light output loads.

The **Miller effect** is the amplification of the capacitance from the output of an inverting voltage amplifier back to its input. John Milton Miller identified this effect while working on vacuum tubes in 1920, but it also applies to CMOS logic gates. Any parasitic capacitance between the input and output

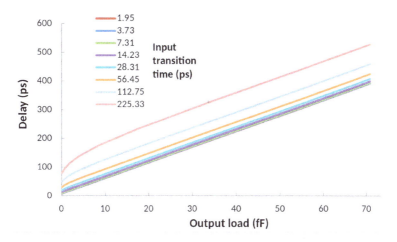

Figure 8.35 Delay versus output loading capacitance for various input transition rates

of an inverting gate is amplified because the input and output are switching in opposite directions, as shown in Figure 8.36. As transistors have shrunk, the Miller capacitance has become more significant because the distance between the drain and gate has decreased and because the switching time has decreased. The Miller capacitance also distorts waveforms and must be factored into delay models.

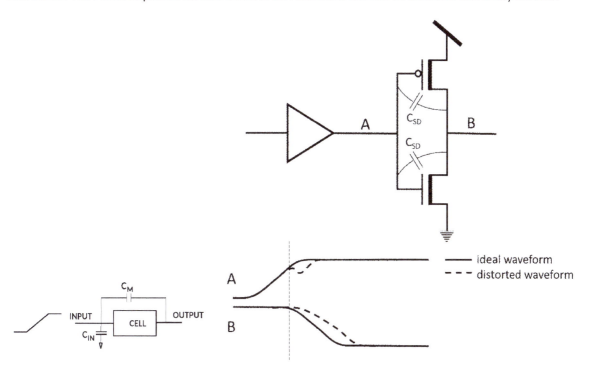

Figure 8.36 Input capacitance is augmented or diminished due to the Miller effect. It is augmented by the opposite-moving plate potentials arising from an inverting configuration, which is the common case

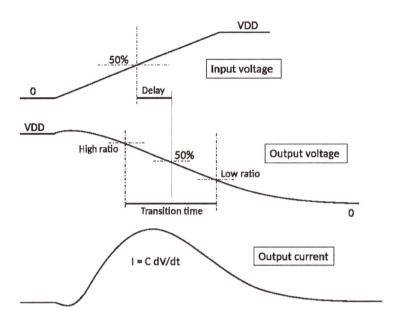

Figure 8.37 Real-world gate, with a linear slew input waveform, showing the timing behaviour of V_{in}, V_{out} and I_{out}

Figure 8.37 shows real-world timing waveforms, illustrating the Miller effect and limited slew input signals. To increase timing accuracy, the output current and voltage waveforms are sampled and stored in LUTs in the Liberty file (Section 8.12.6) for each input transition time and output load. The cell timing accuracy is not improved, as the timing measurement still depends on the delay and the output transition time for an input transition time and output load. These waveforms are used to improve the timing accuracy in the wires, which are modelled as distributed RC networks.

8.4.7 Noise Characterisation

For digital logic to remain digital, noise levels must be kept under control. If the noise level exceeds the noise margins (Section 2.6.3), the logic will behave in analogue ways, meaning zeros and ones may not be adequately distinguished. There are two main forms of circuit noise in digital electronics:

1. **Signal crosstalk** arises when two nets run together for a long distance in parallel. Because of the stray capacitance, if one experiences a noise voltage then the other makes a transition. Inductive coupling is a potential issue too. Both effects are exacerbated if the transition has a high slew rate, since they are proportional to the rate of change of voltage and current in the conductor, respectively.

2. **Power supply noise** arises when the current that gates draw from the supply or dissipate into the ground rail changes. This is mostly due to the inductance of the power rails, but resistance is also important, especially in power-gating transistors (Figure 4.35). In CMOS, the dynamic current is always greater than the static current and it also varies much more, as its name suggests. The

supply current changes when a gate driving a long net charges and discharges its capacitive load, looking much like the output current in Figure 8.37. Both the resistive and inductive elements of the supply network develop noise proportional to the output slew rate. For the resistive element, this is because the net output current depends on the slew rate. For the inductive element, this is intrinsic since $V = L\,dI/dt$. Power supply noise is reduced by arranging the power supply structures in a grid and adding **decoupling capacitors** between the rails to reduce locally the effective supply impedance (Section 8.6.1). Such capacitors can be fabricated in VLSI using reverse-biased diodes, which can be built in a high-walled trench to increase their effective plate area while not consuming too much real estate.

If the ground potential of a gate rises as its output switches from one to zero, this so-called **ground bounce** causes the effective voltage on its input contacts to decrease. In the worst case, the gate experiences a one-to-zero glitch on some inputs. For CMOS VLSI, the supply rail is the voltage reference for the P-type transistors, and so there is a similar effect for the supply rail too. The level of general activity in nearby cells causes a slightly different effect, called **supply droop**, which comprises lower-frequency variations in the operating voltage that cause the supply to be reduced for a period of several gate switching times.

The noise characterisation for a cell includes several types of sampled data: (1) the static voltage transfer curve, (2) the output impedance as a function of the input and output voltages, (3) the output voltage waveform for a few selected input transition times under various output load values and (4) the output voltage waveform in response to an input triangular signal of fixed height (voltage) and width (time). The output impedance of a cell alters how susceptible its output network is to crosstalk. The triangle simulates a rail bounce. At all points, the instantaneous derivative of the transfer function is critical, since if this is greater than unity in absolute terms, noise will be amplified by the cell.

8.5 Gate Arrays

In standard cell designs, cells from the library can freely be placed anywhere on the silicon and the number of I/O pads and the size of the die can freely be chosen. Clearly, this requires that all the masks used for a chip are unique to that design and cannot be used again. On the other hand, a **gate array** is a piece of silicon with a predefined component layout such that a particular design can be implemented using custom wiring between the available components.

Silicon vendors offer a range of chip sizes for gate array designs. Each size of chip has a fixed layout and the location of each transistor, resistor and I/O pad is common to every design that uses that size. A particular design is fabricated on the smallest array on which it can fit, but, nonetheless, a fair percentage of the logic cells are not used. This can lead to a low density of active silicon, especially if many **hard IP blocks** are present as macrocells that are unused.

Gate arrays can be mask-programmed or field-programmed. For mask-programmed devices, the custom wiring is implemented using two or three layers of custom metal wiring. Therefore, only two or three custom masks are needed for a new design. Fixed-pin arrangements also amortise design efforts in packaging design and characterisation. Mask-programmed arrays were popular in the 1990s but today tend to be used only for niche applications, such as for ultra-high frequencies (above 20 GHz), perhaps using GaAs instead of silicon as the semiconductor. Figure 8.38 shows the metal layers of an example of a mask-programmed gate array. The regular layout is clear. The bond pads can be seen around the edge. The white patches are areas of wasted silicon.

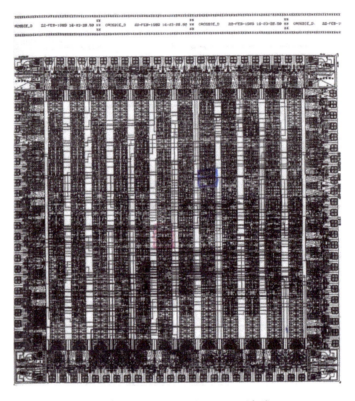

Figure 8.38 Metal layers in a mask-programmed gate array (ECL codec for fibre optic ring network [12])

On the other hand, FPGAs are used very widely today and account for more than one fifth of the semiconductor market by revenue. The programming in an FPGA is purely electronic and takes place at device power-up time. Both the logic elements and the wiring are programmable in an FPGA. The wiring is programmed using pass-transistor multiplexers.

8.5.1 Pass-transistor Multiplexers

A **transmission gate**, also known as a **bilateral switch**, acts like an electromechanical relay. When closed, it can carry an analogue or digital signal in either direction and when open, the contacts are isolated. Figure 8.39 shows a circuit and typical symbols. A pair of FETs connect terminals P and Q together when the S input is high, but when S is low, neither conducts. Two transistors are used since each has a region of poor conduction where the other has good conduction. The poor conduction region for the N-FET is where the input voltage (on either P or Q) is high, since the potential difference between the gate and the ends of the channel is close to zero. When enabled, such circuits are very fast at conveying signals between the two terminals since the transistors are essentially already on when the signal arrives.

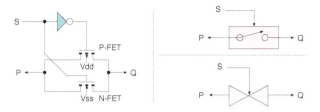

Figure 8.39 Transmission gate or bilateral switch: internal wiring (left) and schematic symbols (right)

It is common to remove one of the FETs from a transmission gate. This gives a **pass-transistor** configuration. A P-FET requires more area for the same on-resistance as an N-FET, so, generally, it is the P-FET that is removed to save the most area. A pass transistor is a cheap (in terms of area) and efficient (in delay terms) form of programmable wiring, but, compared with a logic gate, it attenuates rather than amplifies the signal. A good quality logic one voltage fed into a pass transistor comes out degraded. Such a signal must not be used as the control input to a further pass transistor since this will approximately double the degrading, but it can be passed through another pass transistor without problem provided that the transistor has the full logic one voltage on its gate.

Hence, subject to wiring constraints, a pass transistor is a high-performance low-area input channel for a multiplexer. Figure 8.40 compares two types of pass-transistor multiplexer with an active logic two-input multiplexer. If wide busses are to be multiplexed, the logic driving the gates of each bit line does not need to be replicated. The structure is easy to lay out, as the gate net crosses the channel diffusion regions of multiple bit lanes. Moreover, multiple gates can cross the same channel diffusion line, creating a succession of pass transistors in series, as shown on the right. An alternative structure, which has a lower on-resistance and hence, lower delay, at the expense of control logic, is to use a pass transistor per input and use a controlling binary-to-unary decoder. Again, for large words, the decoder area is amortised over all bit lanes.

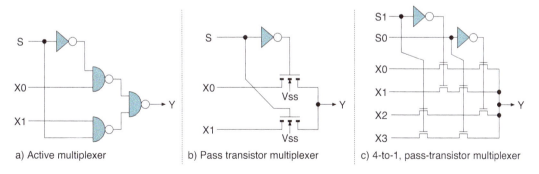

a) Active multiplexer b) Pass transistor multiplexer c) 4-to-1, pass-transistor multiplexer

Figure 8.40 An active multiplexer (a) needs more silicon area than a pass-transistor multiplexer (b), but restores logic levels rather than degrading the signal. Larger pass-transistor multiplexers (c) are efficient and easy to lay out

8.5.2 Field-programmable Gate Arrays

As already stated, over 20 per cent of chip sales revenue is now from field-programmable logic devices. These chips can be programmed electronically on the user's site to provide the desired function. **Programmable array logic (PAL)** and **complex programmable logic devices (CPLDs)** are forms of programmable logic that are fast and small. They are used for high-performance glue logic to create interfaces between standard parts. Field-programmable devices are normally volatile (with programming being required after every power-up), reprogrammable or one-time programmable, which depends on how the programming information is stored inside the device, such as in RAM cells or in any of the ways used for ROM, such as electrostatic charge storage (e.g. flash).

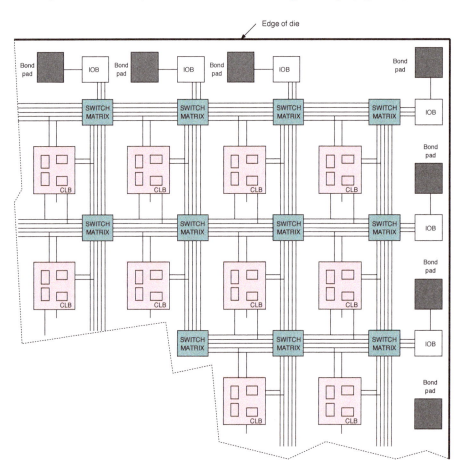

Figure 8.41 FPGA, showing the I/O blocks around the edge, the interconnection matrix blocks and the configurable logic blocks. Recently, the regular structure has been broken up by custom blocks, including RAM and multiplier (aka DSP) blocks

The most important field-programmable devices today are **field-programmable gate arrays (FPGAs)**. An FPGA mainly consists of an array of **configurable logic blocks (CLBs)** and programmable wiring structures, as shown in Figure 8.41. Not shown is a fair amount of hidden logic and configuration memory, which are used just for programming it. Also, some I/O pins are dedicated to programming.

Figure 8.42 shows the basic structure of a minimal CLB and an **I/O block (IOB)**. This CLB contains two D-types and two **lookup tables (LUTs)**. A bypass multiplexor per D-type enables it to be ignored for combinational logic use. The LUT required in this example is a 32 × 1 SRAM. It can implement any logic function with five inputs. The CLB contains two such LUTs with additional steering logic allowing local feedback to replace inputs from the inter-CLB wiring. Modern structures allow the flexible sharing of LUT RAM between up to four D-types. The RAM can be **fractured** in various ways to implement, for instance, two functions of five inputs or one function of six inputs.

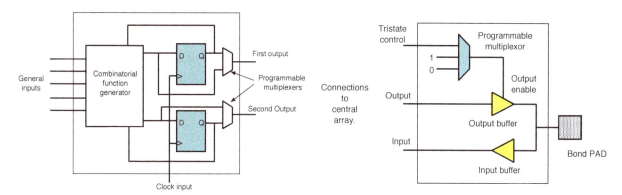

Figure 8.42 CLB (left) and an IOB (right) for a simple FPGA

The IOB illustrated can be programmed to be an input, an output or a tri-state output. Modern IOBs use 20 or so programming bits to alter fine-grained aspects (such as the slew rate and logic levels) as well as pull-up and series-termination resistors. Also, many IOBs are switchable between general-purpose use and direct wiring to a hard I/O macro block such as an Ethernet MAC or a SERDES (Section 3.8).

Much of the area of an FPGA has programmable wiring. A switch matrix is implemented using pass-transistor multiplexers (Section 8.5.1). The matrix supports only a limited fraction of the possible interconnection patterns between its terminals, but this tends to be mitigated by additional programmable multiplexers to select which fabric nets are fed as inputs into the CLBs. Dedicated, low-skew or low-delay wiring for clock nets or for fast ripple-carry adders is available in most FPGAs. Most also contain a **long line** for sending signals long distances without switching, which helps to overcome the 2-D planar limitations (Section 3.4).

The first FPGA devices were developed in about 1990. These were devices like the Xilinx XC2064, which had 64 logic blocks. However, capacities have grown enormously, following Moore's law. Key statistics for some contemporary devices are listed in Table 6.4. Modern FPGAs have several million flip-flops, many megabytes of on-chip RAM and a good assortment of peripheral devices, such as 3 and 75 Gb/s serial transceivers (Section 3.8). These FPGAs allow the LUT RAM to be used as user RAM and also provide two other forms of dedicated RAM block. The so-called block RAMs can be configured to act with many different word widths, different numbers of words and be single- or dual-ported . They even have a FIFO mode. UltraRAM is a recent architectural addition. It has a higher density and uses internal error correction (Section 4.7.6).

As well as RAM, fast paths for adder carry chains were soon added to FPGA architectures. Multiply–accumulate blocks, called **digital signal processing (DSP)** blocks, were another another important addition because implementing multipliers from LUTs is highly inefficient.

Figure 8.43 shows the DSP block from a Xilinx Virtex family FPGA. A DSP block like this mainly contains a multiplier that delivers a 48-bit result and an adder for summing intermediate results from long multiplication. The output from one block has a high-performance programmable connection to the summation input of a neighbour. The multiplier operands are two's complement 25- and 18-bit operands. For a 32- or 64-bit multiplier, an appropriate number of these need to be combined using long multiplication implemented in user wiring but exploiting the fast summation path. Single-precision floating-point arithmetic has a 24-bit unsigned mantissa; hence, 25-bit signed operation means the full mantissa can be multiplied with two DSP blocks.

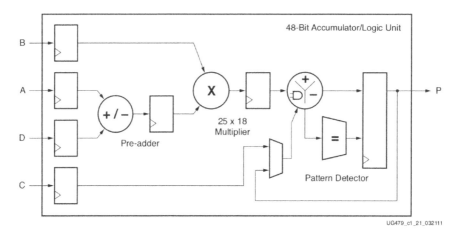

Figure 8.43 The DSP block in the Xilinx Virtex 7 family (©Xilinx Inc). The main functions offered are multiply–accumulate and multiply–sum for long multiplication of wider words than supported by the 25 × 18 base unit

The logic density can be 10–20 per cent of that of masked ASIC, leading to considerably larger dies for the same functionality [13]. Hence, there are much greater per unit costs (Section 8.11.1). Moreover, compared with standard cell logic, FPGAs tend to be slow, achieving perhaps one third of the clock frequency of the equivalent masked ASIC. The slowness arises from the longer nets spanning the larger die area and because the signals pass through programmable wiring junctions and the pass-transistor resistance increases the time constant.

FPGAs have a number of key use cases:

- **Low-volume ASIC replacement**: Due to the high NRE (Section 8.11) of a masked device and the very low NRE for implementing an FPGA, FPGAs are preferred to ASICs for low-volume production runs. For instance, television and sound recording equipment, such as mixing desks and effects processors, have production runs of just thousands. If the silicon cost for an FPGA is around £1000 and the NRE for an equivalent SoC is several million, an equipment manufacturer will generally opt to use an FPGA for their products.

- **ASIC prototyping**: If a new IP block must interface with a real-time peripheral, an FPGA implementation of the logic is generally used for functional verification. Examples include printers, scanners, modems and radio-frequency links. Because the achievable FPGA clock frequency is generally lower than the ASIC equivalent, a degree of manual reorganisation of the logic is sometimes needed, such as using a wider bus from the AFE (Section 2.7.6) to the main logic. However, this will be structured so that as much RTL as possible is identical with that in the ASIC version. The ASIC prototype may also contain a greater amount of instrumentation that captures details to trace buffers.

- **ASIC emulation**: Aside from RTL simulation, ASIC emulation can have either a hardware or software approach. ESL software models and Verilog-to-C flows are increasingly popular, as discussed in Section 5.1.1, but FPGA-based emulation boxes are also still used. These are described in Section 8.5.4.

- **Algorithm acceleration**: FPGAs are increasingly seen as computing elements in their own right, alongside CPUs and GPUs. Cloud computing, such as Amazon Web Services, offers FPGA blades to rent by the minute (Section 6.4). Energy savings of two orders of magnitude are often seen when a suitable application is accelerated on FPGA. Due to the massively increased parallelism, commonly the execution speed can also increase, although this is hampered by the order of magnitude reduction in the clock frequency compared with a CPU (e.g. 200 MHz instead of 2 GHz).

8.5.3 Structured ASIC

If an FPGA-based product has a considerable product uptake, one way to reduce production costs is to replace the FPGA with a **structured ASIC**, which closes the gap between ASICs and FPGAs. The design is prototyped on FPGA and early customer shipments likewise. However, the FPGA vendor offers a turnkey cost reduction path. For example, two implementations of the same design (Xilinx EasyPath in 2005) cross over at 6250 units:

Device	NRE	Unit cost
Spartan-3 FPGA	0	$12
EasyPath E3S1500	$75 000	hphantom0$1

It is also possible to sell a customer a cost-reduced FPGA device that has partially failed its production test. This is acceptable provided the faults are known to be irrelevant for the customer's application. However, the option of going from FPGA to ASIC may be preferred since the die will be significantly smaller (e.g. 1/30th the size [13]).

8.5.4 FPGA SoC Emulators

As well as the manual development of FPGA prototypes, FPGAs can be used as part of a turnkey EDA accelerator. Such tools aim to simulate a complete SoC at above one tenth the target clock frequency, but with minimal manual intervention and little or no manual modification to the RTL. Examples are *Protium* from Cadence Design Systems and *Veloce* from Mentor Graphics.

The SoC RTL is refactored by a compiler that is part of the SoC emulator. It is then automatically partitioned and placed on a number of physical FPGAs, which are the companion part of the emulator package. The partition is made invisible by the compiler and may involve multiplexing a number of design nets on a single inter-FPGA net. FPGAs do not easily support a significant amount of clock gating (as few special nets are optimised for clock distribution), so a processing step converts from a gated clock to a clock-enable form. The number of clock and power domains will, typically, be reduced as well.

The idea is that the FPGAs are largely hidden from the RTL engineer, although, in reality, RTL engineers are fully familiar with FPGAs and able to compensate for where the idealised flow breaks down. A SoC uses licensed IP blocks from third parties. Automated substitution of alternative IP blocks tends to work effectively for RAM and ALUs, but a DRAM likely uses different parts and channel structure. Other IP blocks correspond to hardened macros on the FPGAs in the emulator, so automatic substitution can be applied. If an IP block is supplied in synthesisable form, it can be synthesised in the FPGA programmable fabric. Many FPGAs contain Arm cores, as do many SoCs, but more than likely, there will be differences in the Arm core version provided.

Despite these shortcomings, FPGA emulation provides a high-performance platform that can be useful for real-time or near real-time whole-system evaluation. Such emulators are often leased by the day and can be cloud-based, so it is easy for a manager to make a cost trade-off against slower virtual platforms that may also be running in the cloud. An emulator has workflow management tools, such as a job queue, so that various teams can exploit it back to back. A cloud-based emulator can consecutively run different tests for companies with competing products!

8.6 Floor and Power Planning

The floor plan of a SoC depends on many factors, including the location of important I/O pads for power supplies, DRAM banks, low-noise analogue devices, multi-chip stack/MCM vias and so on. The shape of hard macros cannot be changed, so these must be considered first. Subsystems that run from the same clock or in the same power-gating domain ideally need to be adjacent.

8.6.1 Power Planning

In a **power plan**, each subsystem is allocated to a supply rail and power-gating domain (Section 4.6.10). The power plan depends strongly on the power intent files supplied to the logic synthesiser, but the precise details vary according to the EDA tool vendor.

Figure 8.44 shows the main ingredients of a power supply design. The illustrated device uses four external power supplies and internally generates two further supplies. The two main supplies are 3.3 V for the I/O pad ring and 1.1 V for the main core logic. It is common to require a higher supply voltage to drive signals off-chip than for the core, but even when a common voltage is used, the two supplies are always fed in separately so that heavy switching currents in the I/O supply do not induce voltages drops in the inevitable supply wiring inductance that would couple noise into the core logic (Section 8.12.10). The core logic is run as low as possible due to the V^2 energy effect (Section 4.6.1).

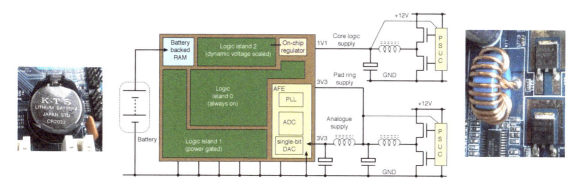

Figure 8.44 Power and floor plan for a simple SoC along with the external supply, which uses battery-backed RAM (left) and buck regulators (right). PSUC: power supply controller

Both main supplies are from an external 12-V rail. The main power supply can more efficiently generate 12 V than 3.3 V since the current is correspondingly lower for the same power and the Schottky rectifier diodes will drop the same voltage, more or less, regardless of the current delivered, hence, will waste less power. The MOSFETs in the buck regulators are, however, highly efficient as they have a very low on-resistance of far less than 1 Ω.

The device has a small amount of analogue electronics in its AFE (Section 2.7.6), which is highly sensitive to supply noise. Hence, its supply and ground are kept separate and have additional filtering external to the device package.

The fourth external supply is for the battery-backed RAM. Since RAM is volatile, a battery backup is one way to preserve the contents during a system power-down. The RAM is powered from the main supply during normal operation, so the battery needs to supply only a minimal retention voltage to overcome static leakage in the RAM cells (Section 4.6.10).

Each subsystem or IP block is allocated to a power island in the power intent file. The power and floor plan then typically arranges each island as a contiguous region that tessellates with the others. Three core islands are illustrated in our simple example. Island 0 is permanently connected to the 1.1-V core supply. Island 1 is power-gated off or on (Section 4.6.10). Island 2 has its supply voltage adjusted by an **on-chip regulator**, either for data retention or for DVFS (Section 4.6.8). An on-chip regulator is, typically, a linear regulator instead of a switching regulator because linear regulators do not require inductors or large capacitors. Although linear regulators are inefficient, wasting energy as heat, there is still an overall energy saving since a lower current drops the same potential ($P = VI$) compared with having the island permanently on the full supply voltage.

If flash or dynamic body bias (Section 4.6.10) is used, additional supplies need to be created on-chip using switched-capacitor invertors. Flash requires voltages of up to 10 V or so to drive electron tunnelling. In this context, an **invertor** is an electronic circuit that produces a higher voltage from a lower voltage. Transformers are commonly used in general electrical situations, but on-chip inductors and transformers of any significant capacity cannot easily be implemented. It is easier to make on-chip capacitors.

A **switched-capacitor invertor** uses one or more capacitors connected to a mesh of diodes and transistors. An oscillator or clock alternately connects the capacitors in parallel to the local low-voltage supply and then in series to generate the required higher voltage. While in series, the charge is coupled into another **tank capacitor**, which provides smoothing. The purpose of smoothing is to maintain the potential while the charge-ferrying capacitors are in the alternate state.

A power plan must be strongly coupled with the chip package design, particularly with respect to supply pin positioning and any on-chip or in-package decoupling capacitors. A **decoupling capacitor** is simply a capacitor between the power and ground that acts as a local energy source for when a sudden heavy demand arises. It prevents the power supply voltage drooping as a result of the supply resistance and inductance. An on-chip capacitor is made from a reverse-biased diode with as large a junction area as possible. This is achieved in the same way as for DRAM bit cells by exploiting the third dimension. The diodes are built in a high-walled trench that increases their effective plate area without consuming too much real estate.

8.7 Flow Steps

As shown in Figure 8.45, the two main flow steps in a back-end flow, after logic synthesis, are placement and routing. Power plane and clock distribution networks must also be synthesised, along with localised optimisations. As we will see, a back-end flow involves an enormous amount of **design verification** and **closure checking**. The term 'closure' refers to repeatedly making modifications until all **must-have** design conditions are met.

8.7.1 Placement

Placement is the process of assigning (x, y, z) coordinates to each part. The active layer of silicon is planar, so $z = 0$ for components on-chip, but is higher for the metallisation layers for wiring. Normally, the goal of placement is to minimise the total length of conductor needed to wire up the design. The module hierarchy of a design is referred to when looking for closely interconnected cliques of components that could become neighbours (but this information is lost if there is too much flattening). Placement can be performed by software or manually, or with any level of human participation in between. Clearly, for a design with millions of gates, a completely manual approach is impractical.

The layout view of a cell contains all the front-end and back-end layers required to generate the masks for silicon manufacturing. The physical implementation of a logic block consists of placing the cells within a floor plan and connecting them together (routing) with metal wires. The full layout view

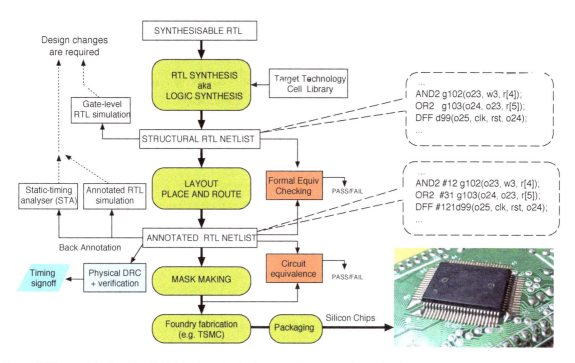

Figure 8.45 Macroscopic back-end flow highlighting the verification flow paths. Figure 8.1 is a detailed flow diagram

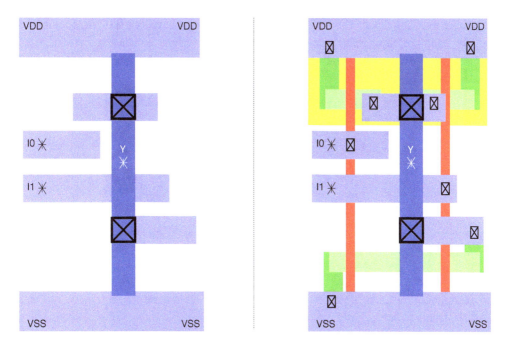

Figure 8.46 Standard cell polygons for a two-input NOR gate. The abstract view (left) identifies the power connections (top and bottom strips) and the input and output contact sites (denoted with asterisks) on the M1 and M2 metal layers, respectively (shades of blue). The full polygon set (right) is required for final design rule checking and tapeout. In reality, the right-hand polysilicon layer (red) could be under the M2 output strip but is here shown displaced for clarity

is not required, as a simplified abstract view with only the metal shapes in the cells is used by the router. Figure 8.46 shows both views of the same cell.

Each cell is identified by its boundary, which defines its width and height. Cells are horizontally abutted to the left and right boundaries of adjacent cells. The width of a cell is a multiple of a repetitive pitch. For advanced process nodes, this is usually the FET gate pitch. It is also called the *contacted poly pitch*. Cells are abutted in a row and generally flipped vertically from row to row. Each row is delimited by the shared power-supply (VDD) and ground (VSS) rails.

Cells occupy the lower layers of a chip and have exclusive use of the active semiconductor layers. The lowest metal layer, M1, is mainly used by a cell for its input and output contacts as well as some internal wiring. The M2 layer is used in many cells as well. Hence, a cell has routing constraints and obstacles. The constraints arise from the contact sites. The obstacles arise from a cell's use of layers also used for inter-cell routing.

Cell are normally placed to minimise the inter-cell net length, which is the principal aim of placement. Figure 8.47 shows a placed row of cells, and Figure 8.7 shows several horizontal rows. A constructive algorithm (Section 6.2.0) may be used to create an initial placement, which is then, typically, optimised using simulated annealing (Section 6.2). Depending on the manufacturing process, some cells cannot be abutted without violating the design rules. This can be solved by adding an attribute to the edge of the cell that would violate a design rule with respect to another abutted cell. An input file is then created to indicate to the placer the additional spacing required between the two specified edge attributes. For example, say a cell has edge attribute A and another cell has edge attribute B. A rule could be that attribute A must be spaced two contacted poly pitches from attribute B.

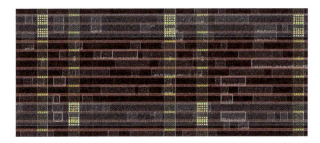

Figure 8.47 A placed horizontal strip of standard cells showing the polygons significant for routing, as rendered in a layout editor. The power and ground rails are a distinctive feature

The logic block area must be as small as possible to minimise the circuit area. This results in a reduction of the manufacturing cost since more circuits can be fitted onto the silicon wafer. An implementation aims to achieve the maximum utilisation rate for a given performance. The utilisation rate is equivalent to the active cell density, which is the total active cell area divided by the floor-plan area. The inactive area is filled by inactive cells called filler cells or it may be used to add decoupling capacitors. A logic block requires specific finishing inactive cells at the end of rows and columns and at inner or outer corners, depending on the shape of the floor plan.

8.7.2 Clock Tree Insertion

A SoC with millions of transistors may use only a handful of different clocks, so an individual clock must often be distributed to thousands of flip-flops or other clocked primitives, such as an SRAM or CPU core. The use of H-trees and PLLs for clock distribution was covered in Section 4.9.4. Many clocks need to be clock-gated (Section 4.6.9), so the H-tree structural hierarchy must be suitable for accepting the clock gate inputs at appropriate points. The delay through the gates must be suitably matched against paths that have no gates to avoid shoot-throughs (Section 4.6.9).

Physical distances are needed when generating a clock tree, so clock tree synthesis takes place after placement and before or as part of routing. A routing tool works best when there is no existing wiring on the metal layers it will use. Hence, clock trees should be routed before general logic nets. Long-distance clocks mostly use the lower middle layers, such as M4 and M5. Once the clock is designed, the router can further use these layers as it wishes, typically for longer-distance data nets and busses. Rather than using a dedicated tool, clock tree routing is generally implemented as a sequence of commands for a generic router, e.g. scripted using TCL.

In an advanced flow, rather than attempting to deliver the clock to every point at once, deliberate clock skewing (Section 4.9.6) may be used to maximise timing margins. If many registers would nominally toggle together at the same time, then light clock skewing is performed automatically by the tool to reduce the supply rail noise. A parameter sets the maximum skew value as a percentage of the fastest clock, usually 15 per cent. Manual edits can also implement more extreme clock skewing among consecutive registers of a pipeline. This is needed if the combinational logic is not properly balanced over the stages. A trial-and-error approach may be necessary to meet timing and supply noise targets simultaneously.

8.7.3 Routing

Once the cells are placed, their pins are interconnected using a succession of metal segments across the metal stack. Routing is the process of determining the route for the conductors that make up the design: it joins up all the required contacts. Normally, power supplies are given their own layers (for circuit boards and chips). A minimum of two layers of signal routing are needed. A heuristic that allocates mostly *x* direction sections on one layer and *y* direction sections on the next layer is generally used, since conductors cannot cross each other within one layer. Routing uses a regular pitch grid for each metal layer, as metal wires follow routing tracks. The metal segments are connected together with process vias, called cuts in a routing environment. Figure 8.48 shows the resulting wiring, and Figure 8.49 is a close-up.

Routing is difficult, since inserting a conductor can block the route for another. Finding the optimum routings and placements for a design has a complexity of at least NP-hard. Hence, heuristic approaches are always used, along with fairly sophisticated algorithms, such as a greedy algorithm, plus much trial and error. Some routers use a **shove-aside** approach, which moves already routed conductors sideways a bit to introduce room for the latest conductor. The most recent routers first

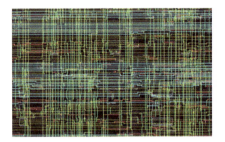

Figure 8.48 Snapshot from a place-and-route tool, showing hundreds of interlaced wires that are routed with several metal layers, both vertically and horizontally

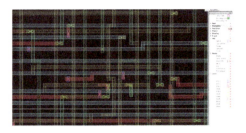

Figure 8.49 Enlargement of Figure 8.48, showing several wires routed with several metal layers (one colour for each layer), vertically and horizontally. Vias are marked with an X

place all the conductors by neglecting shorts and then iteratively swap layers and fragment conductors by inserting vias until no shorts remain.

Physically aware routing is timing driven. The RC components of the connecting wires are extracted, including the via resistances. The timing across logic paths is then calculated by accounting for the delay due to additional wires. Place-and-route is repeated to achieve the best possible timing and to reach the targeted operating frequency of the logic block.

It is desirable to have some interplay between the routing and the placement stages. Older EDA tools did not automatically consider this. If routing is *impossible* for the given number of layers and with the given placement, then either the routing or the placement needs to be changed. If a routing tool fails, it is common to adjust the placement manually (using a mouse and interactive tools) or just to run it again with new seeds for the random number generators.

8.7.4 Timing and Power Verification

Once the system has been placed and routed, the length and type of each conductor is known. As explained in Section 4.6.4, the detailed timing of every gate is affected by the stray capacitance of the conductor it drives. In modern nodes, the resistance of the conductor is also important, since this affects the delay along the net and the quality of the signal arriving at the cell. All this information is extracted from the layout, typically in IEEE **standard parasitic exchange format (SPEF)**.

Accurate delay information is used for three principal purposes:

1. It can be used by a logic simulator to check the functionality of the chip or system with the modified timing. This is known as **back annotation**. It is possible that the new delays will prevent the system from operating at the target speed.

2. The parasitic information can be used in **static timing analysis (STA)** (Section 8.12.1), not to simulate the circuit, but rather to walk over it summing delay paths from outputs back to inputs to flag possible timing errors.

3. It can be used to provide accurate estimates of the dynamic energy use for power sign-off.

It is sometimes convenient to generate behavioural models for additional, fictional components, which are instantiated in the simulation. These monitor sequences of events on their inputs and flag illegal or incorrect cases. An extreme example is a **yes/no test wrapper**, which is a complex test component connected around the bulk of the signals to a chip or complex module. It simply outputs 'yes' or 'no' at the end of the simulation. These wrappers can be quite easy to write using the behavioural constructs of a modern HDL.

After back annotation and parametric variation, the component delay may have increased by a factor of up to 2.

8.7.5 Post-route Optimisation

A router is successful when all nets are routed without conflicts. However, the solution is not necessarily optimal. For instance, the route for a net might include a complete loop, which is clearly redundant and can be detected and eliminated by checking for any points where a net crosses itself on another layer.

Another approach to optimisation is to randomly select a small group of routed nets, delete their routes and then ask the router to reconnect them, which might generate a better solution. Some optimisations have no cost or benefit but lead to a higher yield, such as removing unnecessary layer swaps. As mentioned, a common baseline approach is to use alternative metal layers for primary routing in the x and y directions and never to use diagonal nets. Such rules give a better chance of obtaining a feasible routing result, but can be relaxed during optimisation.

8.7.6 Layout versus Schematic Check

Once the mask polygons have been created in GDS-II form, a **netlist extractor** uses the polygons to rebuild a transistor-level netlist. The same tool can convert an RTL netlist into a transistor-level netlist. Then, as shown in green on the right-hand side of Figure 8.45, both transistor-level netlists are compared to ensure that there is electrical equivalence. This is called a **layout versus schematic check**.

8.7.7 Sign-off and Tapeout

The four major milestones in the physical flow are **RTL freeze**, **sign-off**, **tapeout** and **samples back**. These are allocated dates spaced over 2 months and are entered into Pert and Gantt charts from the outset of the project. The RTL freeze is mandated when the SoC RTL design is mature. System designers are then no longer able to modify the RTL. The physical flow team starts work while further design verification of the RTL takes place in parallel. Only in exceptional circumstances, such as a significant bug being found, will the chief engineer allow an RTL change after the freeze.

When the physical flow is complete, we have a **release candidate**. Because of the huge expense of a set of masks (Section 8.11), before the release candidate is sent to a foundry, a rigorous quality assurance process ensures that it meets the targets for functionality, clock frequency, power use, IP block licences, testability and bond pad placement for the package. Once every aspect of the design has been signed off by an appropriate engineering manager, it can be sent to a foundry for mask-making and to manufacture a prototype. A large-valued purchase order is also raised or ratified for the work, which should ideally hit a pre-agreed slot in the manufacturer's work cycle.

Mask-making is called 'tapeout' because the first ever integrated circuit masks were formed of opaque sticky tape manually applied to large sheets of Mylar film. The term can also be applied to the final rendering of the GDS-II files, which also used to be sent as a tape in the post.

The first devices from fabrication are sent back as quickly as possible to the designers. These are **engineering samples**. Some of the final stages of processing may not have been completed, such as passivation coatings for protection against oxidisation, reverse engineering and SEU (Section 8.2.1), and testing may not have been run, so there may be some yield failures. The engineers will install the chips on circuit boards that have been prepared in the meantime and switch them on. Hopefully, everything will work first time. That should happen, given conservative design rules and extensive pre-production verification.

8.8 Production Testing

There are two main stages of SoC testing after manufacture: wafer probing (Section 8.8.3) and packaged-device testing (Section 8.8.4). Both are fully automated by robotic handling machines and can share many aspects of a common test program (Section 8.8.2). **Device speed binning** and **redundancy zapping** (Section 8.8.4) are also performed in post-fabrication testing (Section 4.7.4).

The main test program consists of a sequence of stimuli that must be applied to the device and it contains the expected results. It may be a concatenation of individual test programs for various subsystems. If the actual results do not match the expected results, then a fault has been detected. The main test program aims to check all aspects of SoC functionality. The percentage of nets actually checked is known as the **fault coverage**. A fault simulator checks the fault coverage of the test program. The level of fault coverage required is often a contractual parameter between a foundry or assembly house and the designer. A good test program will achieve 98 to 99.5 per cent fault coverage in a few seconds of testing. Military, aerospace and medical standard equipment may need to have 100 per cent coverage. Of course, a poor test program may not find all faults. Without 100 per cent coverage, a test program has the potential to deliver a false positive, indicating that a faulty chip is usable. However, a large number of manufacturing errors, such as uneven exposure during processing, dislocations in the silicon substrate crystal or caused by dirt particles, are likely to impact on the behaviour of several nearby nets or transistors. Hence, with slightly less than 100 per cent coverage, most fabrication faults are likely to be detected.

Parts of the test program can also be applied when the device is on a circuit board via a JTAG boundary scan (Section 4.7.5), although this is not commonly needed. Certain production tests are impossible in situ on a PCB once the device is soldered on. Pad capacitance and leakage tests cannot be run due to board loading effects. The same goes for supply current use and the reverse breakdown voltage of protection diodes. Instead of testing every device shipped, however, such tests are, typically, conducted under a **window lot discipline**, in which between 100 and 300 samples are selected at random. Wafers from the various processing corners, such as FS, SS and TT (Section 8.12.4), are always sampled. The results are tabulated alongside the resistance of conductors on each layer and the frequency of test oscillators fabricated along die scoring lines and extreme corners of the circular wafer that can contain only a partial chip (Figure 8.51).

8.8.1 Universal Verification Methodology and Open Verification Methodology

During IP block development, a large number of simulations and assertions will, typically, have been used. Most IP blocks purchased from third parties are supplied with test programs. All of this material can potentially be used as a basis for a production test program.

The **universal verification methodology (UVM)** is an industry-wide methodology with a supporting library of building blocks for the systematic creation of documentation and verification harnesses for IP blocks. It is very much based on the **open verification methodology (OVM)** but was augmented by and has been standardised by the **Accellera** trade body and as IEEE-1800 [14]. Most of the resources that are freely available are coded in System Verilog and SystemC, but the methodology can be implemented in any RTL-like language, such as Chisel (Section 6.8.3).

A UVM-conforming IP block always has a prescribed set of unit tests. Every aspect follows a strict coding style, which dictates the file structure and naming scheme for the various components. It defines standard method names in the UVM **application program interface (API)**. These are then invokable by an off-the-shelf UVM driver provided by an EDA vendor or used for multiple projects in a design house.

The UVM API defines methods for instantiating an IP block as the **device under test (DUT)**, for instantiating a corresponding **test agent** and for interconnecting these components at their interfaces. Automatic wiring generation or automatic TLM binding is required. Further API components cause the agent to run a test program on the DUT and to collect and log the results. The agent may, typically, apply a set of canned test vectors (Section 8.8.2) or it may contain behavioural code that exercises various sequences. A third test possibility, present from the earliest days of OVM, is directed random sequence testing (Section 7.3.2). These different testing techniques can be freely mixed together within the framework. The overall aim is that, whatever the complexity of the IP block, the process of fully testing is turnkey. In other words, no fiddly manual setup is needed to run the tests provided. Design houses can also add their own tests under the same framework.

UVM emphasises **verification reuse**. If an IP block is embedded in a subsystem, the interfaces to the IP block are less accessible. However, it is still desirable to run existing tests on that IP block in situ. For tests based on programmed I/O (PIO), only the base address of a register file may need adjusting in the test program. For tested based on scan chains (Section 4.7.5), the routing of test multiplexors and offset in the bit stream may need to be adjusted. OVM tooling aims to automate these steps.

Device register files contain a mixture of read/write and read-only bits. Other common patterns exist, such a the {set, reset, read} register triple. The set and reset registers are always read back as zero but any ones written set or clear bits in the read register, which may be read only. UVM tooling should understand the documentation for these design patterns, using IP-XACT or otherwise, and cleanly integrate with tools that generate documentation and C header files for register files. The same principles apply to RAM blocks accessible by PIO or a path scan.

8.8.2 Test Program Generation

A test program generator works out a short sequence of tests for a subsystem that can reveal **stuck-at faults** (Section 7.1.1), which occur when a net is stuck permanently at either logic zero or one. For digital logic, various functional problems can arise, including short circuits and open circuits for supply and logic nets and transistors that do not work. Stuck-at faults cover all such possibilities and, consequently, most of the other faults in a SoC or subsystem.

If there are n nets, $2n$ individual faults could occur. Although faults tend not to occur in isolation, the baseline model is that just one of these faults will occur. If a test program detects p stuck-at faults, then its coverage is defined as $100 \times p/2n$. A manufacturing fault will quite often affect more than one net, which can compensate for a fault coverage of less than 100 per cent.

A test program for a chip (or PCB card) consists of a list of **test vectors**, generated from a simulation or otherwise. Since testing can take up a major part of the overall manufacturing time, the test program must be as short as possible to hit the required fault coverage. The test program is applied to a set of test probe points. These are, typically, the I/O pads of a chip or the **bed of nails** that a circuit board is pushed onto. For a hard macro inside a SoC, such as a CPU core, it encompasses a boundary scan of the macro.

The length of each test vector is equal to the number of probe points. Typically, each element of a vector holds one of these ASCII characters:

1   Apply a logic one to this probe point
0   Apply a logic zero to this probe point
z   Apply high impedance to this probe point
H   Expect logic one at this probe point
L   Expect logic zero at this probe point
x   Don't care what happens at this point
c   Clock this pin midway through the cycle
p   Power pin or other signal not driven by the test program

Typically, other symbols enable special pulses or varying power supply voltages to be applied. The nature of these special signals is specified in separate tables included with the test program. The vectors are applied in sequence at some clock rate (e.g. 10 million vectors per second). There may be 10^5 to 10^7 test vectors for a SoC. If any of the H or L points do not match, the DUT has failed.

For example, the pinout and one part of the test program for a 74' series logic device is shown in Figure 8.50. Spaces are allowed in the vectors for clarity. For the first gate, pins 1 and 2 are inputs and 3 is the output. The four vectors fully test the first gate. A better program is obvious. It would simultaneously test the other three gates. For sequential devices, generating a short program is tricky and often must be assisted with DfT mechanisms such as **test modes**.

```
              000 000 0 001 111 1
              123 456 7 890 123 4
            [ 00H 00H p H00 x00 p ]
            [ 01H 00H p H00 x00 p ]
            [ 10H 00H p H00 x00 p ]
            [ 11L 00H p H00 x00 p ]
```

Figure 8.50 Pin connections for a 7400 quad NAND gate device and part of a test program

Test Modes

For some designs, a very long test program is needed to test some functions. For example, the leap-year circuitry in a digital watch might need four years of clock pulses before being exercised. Therefore, the throughput of the testing station is low. For other designs, the observability of an internal state can be low. This occurs when there is a significant amount of internal state and few outputs. For example, a credit card PIN checker need have only one output net, saying good or bad. Many different test sets may have to be presented before the effect of every part of the internal logic is felt at the output net. This either leads to low fault coverage or long test programs.

Testability can be increased at the design stage using a **design for testability (DfT)** methodology. This involves:

1. Adding test outputs for different states of the internal nets. These may not be bonded in the final package for security or cost reasons but are accessible by a wafer probe.

2. Adding test inputs, which are tied off to one logic level during normal operation. These are used during testing to shorten the length of count sequences or cause more of the internal state to be accessible to the existing pins.

3. Exploiting the JTAG or other debug infrastructure (Section 4.7).

4. Running software on internal CPUs during the production test.

Certain subsystems are difficult to test thoroughly because they have random or deliberately obfuscated details. A **physically unclonable function (PUF)** delivers a consistent response on a given SoC but varies randomly between devices. A **random number generator** returns a random number every time it is queried. These devices are common in smart cards and also as subsystems in general-purpose SoCs. They are used as the basis of cryptographic protocols. Physical implementations of both types of device amplify random effects within the circuitry and give unpredictable outputs that cannot be included in a standard test program. Instead, multiple samples must be taken and a statistical analysis is used to check that the variations are sufficiently random.

Fault Simulators

A standard EDA tool that determines the fault coverage of a test program for a design is called a **fault simulator**. Its outputs are the fault coverage percentage and a list of stuck-at faults not detected by the test program. It is a variant of a normal simulator that has been augmented to keep a running set of the faults that have been detected at the current point in the simulation. At the end of the simulation, the list contains any faults undetectable by the test program. An engineer can inspect this and manually determine what additional tests are needed.

Automatic Test Generation

Another EDA tool is an **automatic test program generator**. This synthesises a good test program for a subsystem by analysing the structure of the design. For largely combinational regions and the next-state functions of sequential logic, the maximum possible fault coverage can be fairly accurately determined by a static fault coverage analysis. An algorithm uses the set of detectable faults present in the inputs of a gate to determine the set of detectable faults at the output of the gate. Repeated application gives the externally observable faults. For sequential logic, a test program generator automatically produces sequences of operations that manipulate the state of the subsystem, resulting in a state trajectory that may be totally unlike any normal operational behaviour, but which gives good fault coverage. Additional RTL can be fed into the logic synthesiser or the tool can be given DfT directives that assist the test program generation. The synthesiser then modifies how sub-expressions are shared in the logic design, adds more logic or alters the test mode behaviour.

Today, these tools cannot automatically scale to cover a whole SoC, so the resulting program must be applied through a boundary scan of the target subsystem. Third-party IP blocks, such as a USB or SATA controller, likewise have a subsystem test program that is applied through a block boundary scan or run on an internal CPU during the production test.

8.8.3 Wafer Probe Testing

Figure 8.51 shows the typical layout of dies on a silicon wafer. Before dicing, the individual chips are tested using a wafer probe (Figures 8.52 and 8.53).

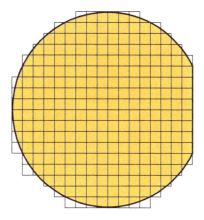

Figure 8.51 A wafer (6 to 10 inches diameter) is diced into chips (1 cm on a side or so)

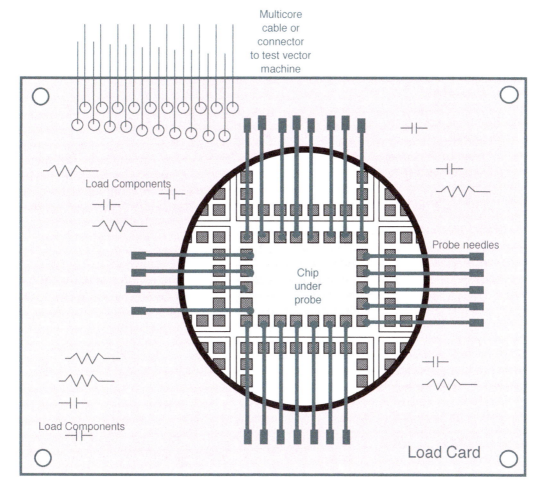

Figure 8.52 Load card with wafer probe pins for testing a chip before the wafer is diced

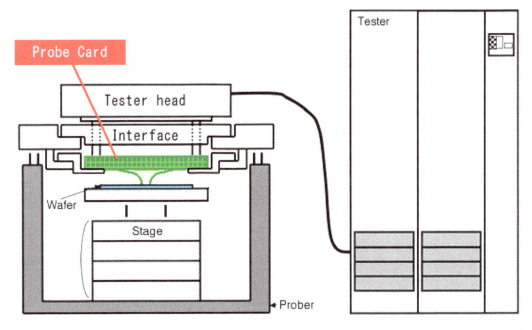

Figure 8.53 General configuration of a wafer probe testing machine. The robotic staging system delivers wafers to and from conveyor systems as well as stepping the probes over the wafer

8.8.4 Packaged Device Testing

Diced chips need to be packaged. Today, several pieces of silicon are often placed in one package as a **multi-chip module (MCM)** (Section 8.9.1). Decoupling capacitors may also be included in the package to overcome the inductance of power supply traces. Although the dies are separately tested with a wafer probe, the packaging may suffer faults and the dies can be damaged during handling. Hence, functional testing is also needed for a packaged assembly.

A package adds capacitive load to the signal nets and hence, final performance characterisation is best done on the packaged assembly. Often a single base product is sold in a number of temperature and clock frequency grades or with different DVFS parameters (Section 4.6.8). The maximum clock frequency at different supply voltages and temperatures is determined using a variety of proprietary algorithms. Military and aerospace products need to operate over a wide temperature range and higher reliability is also required. Increased reliability is also required for medical products, such as pacemakers and healthcare equipment. Measurements of a packaged device are combined with the per wafer process measurements described above.

Voltage and **speed grading** (or *binning*) is the process of assessing the performance of a component using measurements made after manufacture. Silicon process variations result in a spread of performance at the nominal supply voltage. Each device can be labelled accordingly using automated inkjet printing as the component exits the measuring station.

Another process typically performed during production test is **per device programming**. The behaviour of a device is modified indelibly or its properties are recorded on it. This is colloquially known as **zapping** the device. Physically, this can done by melting fusible straps (aka links) with a heavy current. Alternatively, floating-gate charge storage is used to program an unerasable field-programmable ROM (Section 2.6.7). There are four main reasons for doing this:

1. **Redundancy mapping** or **column sparing**: For devices with an array of similar elements, such as memories and FPGAs, the yield can be increased by using an additional complete row or column. If the production test identifies a single failed cell, its complete row or column is disabled and replaced with the redundant one.

2. **Downgrading**: A SoC with four CPU cores could be marketed as a device with only three if there is a fabrication fault in one of the cores. The fourth core is permanently hidden from the programmer's view and physically powered down. This can also be used when marketing healthy cores to address a different price/volume point.

3. **Recording a unique identifier**: This includes the address for the **media access controller (MAC)** or other unique information, such as a serial number or secret PKI key.

4. **DVFS mapping**: The appropriate LUT for supply voltage versus clock frequency can be enabled or the thermal overload temperature for an on-die **thermal monitor** can be recorded.

8.9 Device Packaging and MCMs

Chips can be connected directly to the main PCB of a device. This is used for small chips in ultra-low cost products, such as a digital thermometer. More commonly, the chip is mounted in a so-called package soldered to the circuit board.

In one common form of chip package used for mid-range chips, the silicon die has bond pads around the edge and it is welded to a copper sheet glued onto a small PCB made of high-quality fibreglass. The tracks on this **substrate** PCB are connected to the pads on the chip using **bond wires** that are contact welded at each end, both to the chip and the copper trace on the circuit board. This cold welding simply uses an appropriate mechanical force applied by an automated bonding machine to fuse the material together. The bond wires are very fragile, so the whole assembly is encapsulated in moulded plastic. At the bottom of the PCB, the contacts are in a square grid. Solder bumps are used to connect this PCB to the main PCB of the system. Several decoupling capacitors (Section 8.6.1), with a combined capacitance of about 1 μF, are also often installed on the substrate PCB, either inside or outside the plastic cover.

An alternative approach is to mount the device the other way up. This is called a **flip chip** arrangement. It was pioneered by IBM and more or less exclusively used by IBM for many decades before recently becoming mainstream. The advantage of a flip chip is its shorter wiring distance (less inductance) and the ability to put the bond pads throughout the chip instead of having just one (or perhaps two) rows around the perimeter. The disadvantage is that heat extraction through the back of the chip is no longer straightforward and a plastic surround would be useless. Instead, a heavy-duty metal casing is normally placed on top, pushing lightly against the back of the die, to provide a thermal dissipation path. This configuration is preferable for fluid-cooled heat management, since the fluid can pass through dedicated channels bored in the metal casing.

8.9.1 MCMs and Die-stacking

Recently, **multi-chip modules (MCMs)** have become popular. An MCM contains several pieces of silicon arranged in a plane or in 3-D with inter-chip wiring. MCMs typically use a silicon, ceramic or glass substrate instead of the fibreglass substrate of mid-range chips as mentioned above. However, otherwise they are essentially the same. A finer interconnect can be reliably fabricated with these higher-quality substrate materials. The substrate is typically now called an **interposer**. Chips that are designed to be side by side can be interconnected with very short bond wires without the signals passing through the interposer. These are sometimes called 'chiplets'.

Rather than suffering the low yield that can arise when producing enormous chips, an MCM can combine chiplets that have been individually tested. As shown in Figure 8.54, the chiplet long dimension makes maximum use of one mask reticule dimension while allowing a large number of short bond wires to join between abutting chiplets.

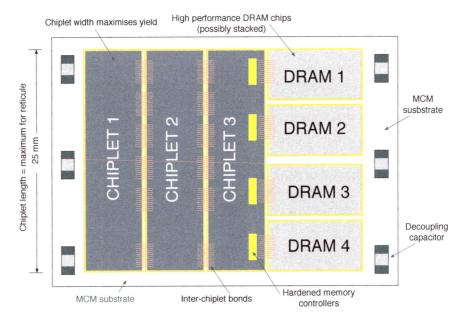

Figure 8.54 An FPGA composed of several chiplets with broadside inter-chiplet bonding, connected closely to several DRAM chips in an MCM

In **die-stacking**, one chip is placed upside down on top of another (Figure 5.27). The lower chip, which is typically larger, mates with the upper chip using a matching bond pad. The inter-chip connections can be made with solder balls that are melted during assembly. Stacking more than one chip is possible using **through-silicon vias**, which behave like the vias between metal layers within conventional VLSI. A square hole is etched and filled with molten metal (copper, aluminium or an exotic, low melting point alloy) to form a connection in the third dimension.

The technology for chip packaging and interconnect is currently evolving rapidly. As with all scaling gains in the last 70 years of computing, each time components are brought closer together, the stray capacitance of the interconnect is reduced, which enables faster and lower-energy computing.

New devices are often proven using a **multi-project wafer (MPW)**. Designs from a number of companies and research institutions share a single reticle and mask set. The **reticle** is the area exposed by one set of masks and this is stepped in the x and y directions to form a repeating pattern over the wafer. A number of different chips can thereby be fabricated simultaneously. The cost of the mask set is shared over the designs, as is the cost per wafer. MPWs are a standard part of chip design, as it is very rare for a company to build a full mask set on the first run unless the timescales are very tight and the confidence level is high. For instance, Europractice [15] produces MPWs and publishes the costs and dates of runs for a variety of technology nodes on its website. It places MPW designs with most of the main foundries. Many nodes are run four times per year. Prices are quoted in thousands of euros per mm^2. For instance, the 2021 price list quotes a run on the UMC 40 nm node at about €70 000 for a 16 mm^2 chip.

8.10 Engineering Change Orders

Hopefully, no logic design errors will be discovered in the manufactured silicon. After a significant error is found and understood, it must be corrected as quickly and cheaply as possible. Often a temporary fix is required, either to satisfy urgent customers or to understand better the nature of the problem to increase confidence that a long-term fix will work.

A variety of fixes are possible with different trade-offs of time and cost:

- A complete **respin** is the slowest and most expensive solution. The fix is made at the RTL level or above and all the back-end manufacturing steps below this level are repeated. A complete respin requires (nearly) a completely new set of masks. A respin should aim for zero or minimal disruption of the floor plan, so that at least some of the previous engineering effort put into the back-end flow can be reused.

- A less costly and quicker solution is a manual mask-level **engineering change order (ECO)**. The fix is implemented by changing a few masks, with the remainder left unchanged. This may be done manually or by re-synthesis. A **metal respin**, also sometimes known as an **A1 ECO**, changes only the metal layers. Changing just metal layers M1–M3, called an **M1-2-3 respin**, is considerably less expensive than changing the 35 to 40 layers needed for a full respin. Figure 8.55 shows an example of RTL for a **sewing kit**, which can be included in a design in anticipation of mask-level ECOs. The sewing kit contains a number of disconnected standard cells with their inputs tied off. By changing the wiring, the spare cells can be incorporated into the circuit. A manual change involves editing the polygons of the changed mask or masks. The resulting ECO is a detailed list of the edits. Both netlist verification (Section 8.7.6) and design rule checking (Section 8.1) must then be performed to provide confidence in the edits.

```
module sewkit(  // TSMC 0.18u library
      intput clk,
      input n_reset);
   // verilint 630  on : Port connected to a NULL expression
   dfcfb1  DZBRB1_1(.CDN(n_reset), .CPN(clk), .D(1'b0), .Q(), .QN());
   dfcfb1  DZBRB1_2(.CDN(n_reset), .CPN(clk), .D(1'b0), .Q(), .QN());

   nd02d2  ND02D2_1 (.A1(1'b0), .A2(1'b0), .ZN() );
   nd02d2  ND02D2_2 (.A1(1'b0), .A2(1'b0), .ZN() );

   inv0d2  INV0D2_1(.I(1'b0), .ZN());
   inv0d2  INV0D2_2(.I(1'b0), .ZN() );
   inv0d2  INV0D4_1(.I(1'b0), .ZN() );
   inv0d2  INV0D4_2(.I(1'b0), .ZN() );

   buffd7  BUFFD1_1(.I(1'b0), .Z() );
   buffd7  BUFFD1_2(.I(1'b0), .Z() );

   mx02d2  MX02D1_1(.I0(1'b0), .I1(1'b0), .S(1'b0), .Z() );
   mx02d2  MX02D1_2(.I0(1'b0), .I1(1'b0), .S(1'b0), .Z() );

   nr02d2  NR02D2_1 (.A1(1'b0), .A2(1'b0), .ZN() );
   nr02d2  NR02D2_2 (.A1(1'b0), .A2(1'b0), .ZN() );

   aoi211d2 AOI311D1_1(.A(1'b0), .B(1'b0), .C1(1'b0), .C2(1'b0), .ZN() );
   aoi211d2 AOI311D1_2(.A(1'b0), .B(1'b0), .C1(1'b0), .C2(1'b0), .ZN() );
endmodule
```

Figure 8.55 Example of structural Verilog RTL that instantiates disconnected standard cells as a 'sewing kit'

- A mask-level ECO reruns the back-end compilers to automatically regenerate the polygons for a selected number of masks. This has become automated with the recent generation of back-end tools, although interlayer fabrication optimisations are increasingly making this less possible in practice. A new circuit diagram can be generated using **ECO logic synthesis**. The compiler reads in the netlist output from a previous run and uses as much of that as possible. A router can then be used in ECO mode to constrain the wiring differences to a limited number of masks.

- A cheap solution for a limited number or samples or a tiny production runs uses a **focussed ion beam (FIB)**, which can be used to edit a chip after it has been made or during manufacture.

Typically, the top layers of the chip need to be removed to get at the problem and then put back on again. Like an electron microscope, a FIB scans one or more chips in a vacuum using a focussed and steered beam of particles. The chip is imaged by measuring the beam current during the scan. Unlike normal electron beam devices, FIB tools use cathodes containing a selection of exotic metals, such as gallium and rubidium. Once a place where a change in the target device has been located, the beam current is increased from the low level used for scanning. This either cuts gaps in the existing metal tracks or deposits new conducting strips, depending on the cathode materials. Hence, this is a form of manual rewiring.

8.11 ASIC Costs: Recurring and Non-recurring Expenses

Table 8.6 Simplistic and rough estimates of recurring (RE) and non-recurring expenses (NRE) for the first production run of n wafers

Type of expense	Item	Item cost	Total cost
NRE	6 months: 10 software engineers	$100k pa	$500k
NRE	6 months: 10 hardware engineers	$250k pa	$1250k
NRE	4 months: 20 verification engineers	$200k pa	$1333k
NRE	1 mask set (22 nm)	$1500k	$1500k
RE	Per device IP licence fees	?	$?? $\times n$
RE	6-inch wafer	$5k	$5k $\times n$
Total			$4583k + 5k$\times n$

The cost of developing and selling a SoC includes **non-recurring expenses (NRE)**, which must be paid once and for all, regardless of how many chips are made. The result of this non-recurring engineering is a mask set. Masks can be used for a very long time to produce millions of chips. The other costs are the per device cost of goods and the per device IP block licence fees. These are collectively known as **recurring expenses**. Table 8.6 gives some approximate figures.

8.11.1 Chip Cost versus Area

The per device selling price depends on the **die yield**, the fraction of working dies from each wafer. The fraction of wafers where at least some of the die work is the **wafer yield**. In the 1980s and 1990s, yields for large chips were quite low, but the lattice defect density in raw silicon ingots was reduced and manufacturing techniques improved, so that in the late 1990s, the wafer yield was typically close to 100 per cent for mature 90 nm fabrication processes. However, recently the yield has fallen as the geometries have become smaller.

The die yield (often simply the **yield**) depends on the wafer impurity density and die size. It goes down with chip area because, given a uniform defect density, there is a larger chance of a defect being present in a larger chip. The fraction of devices that pass wafer probe testing (i.e. before the wafer is diced; Section 8.8.3) and fail post-packaging tests is very low. However, full testing of analogue sections or other lengthy operations are typically skipped at the wafer probe stage.

The cost of a working device grows quickly as the die size is increased. Assume that a processed wafer costs $5000 (Table 8.6). A 6-inch diameter wafer has area $\pi r^2 \approx 18000 \text{ mm}^2$. Suppose our device has area A, which can range between 2 and 200 mm^2 (including inter-die scoring lines). The number of dies per wafer is 18 000/A. The probability of a die working is the wafer yield multiplied by the die yield. We assume that the wafer yield is 1.0, otherwise we would need to factor in the wafer cost. Let us assume that of the square millimetres of processed silicon, 99.5 per cent of them are defect-free. The die yield is then:

$$P(\text{All } A \text{ squares work}) = 0.995^A$$

The cost of each working die in dollars is then given by:

$$\frac{5000}{(18\,000/A)0.995^A}$$

Table 8.7 gives typical values computed in this way. We see that the cost of a working chip rapidly grows above the traditional sweet spot of about 11 mm on a side (121 mm^2).

Table 8.7 Die yield. The cost for a working die given a 6-inch wafer with a processing cost of $5000 and a probability of a square millimetre being defect-free of 99.55 per cent

Area (mm^2)	Number of wafer dies	Number of working dies	Cost per working die ($)
2	9000	8910	0.56
3	6000	5910	0.85
4	4500	4411	1.13
6	3000	2911	1.72
9	2000	1912	2.62
13	1385	1297	3.85
19	947	861	5.81
28	643	559	8.95
42	429	347	14.40
63	286	208	24.00
94	191	120	41.83
141	128	63	79.41
211	85	30	168.78
316	57	12	427.85
474	38	4	1416.89

8.12 Static Timing Analysis and Timing Sign-off

Static timing analysis (STA) checks the delay in every valid timing path in a cell-based design against a set of timing constraints. The term 'static' indicates that there are no test vectors and no transient simulations are necessary. Instead, all the possible paths that a logic signal can take are evaluated more or less in parallel. STA is an integral part of logic synthesis, place-and-route optimisation and final design sign-off.

Because static timing analysis is exhaustive and occurs frequently during an implementation flow, it has to be very efficient. The delays for each cell are calculated, a priori, using abstract models as described in Section 4.6.4. STA traces through the paths in a design to estimate the delays and transition times as quickly and accurately as possible using the abstract timing models for cells and RC networks representing the nets. The analyser reports by how much the rank paths violate the timing constraints.

8.12.1 STA Types: Maximum and Minimum

STA includes two basic forms of analysis known as maximum and minimum. **Maximum timing analysis** considers whether signals have settled before the setup time for a clocked cell (typically, a flip-flop). As was defined in Section 4.4.2, the worst path is known as the **critical path**. On the other hand, **minimum timing analysis** considers whether any hold time will be violated. Here, an input value changes before it has been properly registered in the clocked cell.

STA can identify the maximum clock frequency that a design can run at before **over-clocking**. If there are multi-cycle paths in a niche design, it can also report the minimum clock frequency (Section 4.9.6). The results from an STA run depend greatly on the assumptions and modelling used for the components and wiring. Hence, different process corners (Section 8.12.4) yield different results. Fast corners produce faster logic and are more likely to fail in a minimum timing analysis (assuming the hold-time specifications are less than proportionally scaled) whereas slower corners are more likely to fail in a maximum timing analysis. The situation is more complex for asymmetric corners and is discussed in Section 8.12.5.

8.12.2 Maximum Timing Analysis

For both maximum and minimum STA, the two basic approaches for the final sign-off are traditional **graph-based analysis (GBA)** and the more precise **path-based analysis (PBA)**. We first consider how to find the maximum timing under GBA.

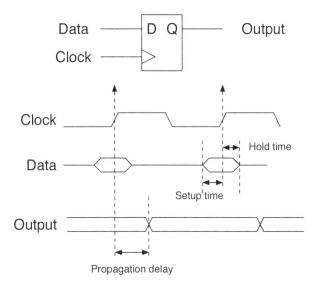

Figure 8.56 The three main timing specifications for a sequential cell, such as a flip-flop (repeated from Figure 4.13)

For maximum STA, the analyser discovers the longest event path through logic gates from one sequential element in a clock domain to another. This starts with the clock-to-Q delay of a sequential element such as a flip-flop or SSRAM (Figure 8.56). The longest path is generally the critical path, which fixes the maximum clock frequency. However, sometimes this is a false result, since this path might never be used during device operation. STA cannot detect this automatically, since that requires a full reachable-state analysis (Section 7.1.1), which is too time-consuming, but such tools are driven by configuration files that specify paths to ignore (either manually or as generated by a formal analysis).

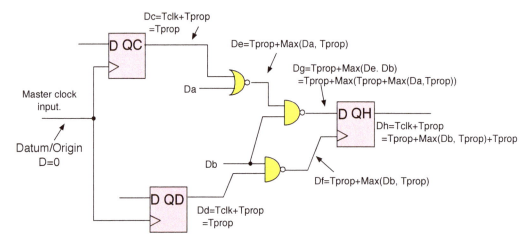

Figure 8.57 An example circuit with static timing annotations for maximum GBA analysis

Figure 8.57 shows a typical maximum timing analysis scenario using GBA. Starting with some reference point, taken as D=0, such as the master clock input to a clock domain, we compute the relative delay on the output of each gate and flop. For a combinational gate, the output delay is the propagation time for the gate added onto the maximum of its input arrival times. For an edge-triggered device, such as a D-type or JK flip-flop, there is no event path to the output from the D or JK inputs, so the output delay is just the clock delay plus the flop's clock-to-Q delay. For asynchronous flop inputs, such as preset, reset or transparent latch inputs, further input-to-output event paths must be considered. These are handled in the same way as gate inputs.

The detailed characterisation of propagation delays may not be the same for all inputs to an output, for all directions of transition or for all input slew rates. For instance, in a standard CMOS NOR gate, a pull-down uses a parallel structure, leading to matched input-to-output delays when going low, but a pull-up uses a series transistor structure and the effective substrate potential of the two transistors may not be the same, leading to a difference in the propagation delay depending on which input leads to the output making a low-to-high transition.

Having different input-to-output delays is readily handled in GBA by considering the maximum of the individual sums of input change times and propagation delays. Having different delays for each direction of slew is also comparatively easy to handle by modelling each arrival with a pair of times, one for each direction, and taking into account whether there is inverting behaviour between the input and output. For certain components, such as XOR gates, adders and toggling flip-flops, the direction of transitions dynamically changes from inverting to non-inverting, so the worst case value must be conservatively used. On the other hand, certain transitions never create an event, such as the de-assert of an asynchronous reset.

Note that for long paths of such logic, the result of a conservative analysis is likely to be significantly worse than the average case. However, designs will normally be based on worst-case margins (within a process corner), so this is acceptable. Likewise, an arrival time can be extended beyond a pair to a more complicated vector that also includes worst-case signal transition times in each direction and so on, as used in non-linear delay modelling (Section 8.12.6).

In PBA, the simplicity of using a single timing value (scalar or vector) per cell output is replaced with a separate analysis for every path through a combinational network. This converts a linear problem into a quadratic problem, but the growth is typically just a scalar increase given that the overall cost of analysis is dominated by the likely high number of disconnected combinatorial subnetworks spread over the design. A slowdown by a factor of 100 is perfectly acceptable for timing sign-off.

Providing both graph-based and path-based options helps an engineering manager balance efficiency and accuracy. The efficiency of GBA decreases the runtime of timing optimisations whereas the accuracy of PBA is required for final timing sign-off.

8.12.3 Minimum Timing Analysis

Maximum timing considers the delay between one clock edge and the next, and hence, gives the maximum clock frequency. Minimum timing is for just one clock edge and must be met regardless of clock frequency. As also shown in Figure 8.56, the data input to a sequential cell such as a flip-flop must meet the hold-time requirement. Minimum timing checks whether the data at the input of every such sequential cell is reliably captured before it changes in response to the current clock cycle. Many flip-flop designs ensure that the hold-time specification is less than the clock-to-Q propagation delay time. This enables a simple shift register to be constructed. However, some components do not meet this condition and rely on at least some combinational logic between their output and the input to another component (or indeed the same one). If a path fails to meet minimum timing, the logic value from the next clock cycle can race through the sequential cell, corrupting its state and causing a shoot-through error (Section 4.6.9).

The algorithm for minimal timing analysis can likewise use scalar or vector timing information and use GBA or PBA. The essential difference is that the minimum delay should be selected at each point where the algorithm considers the worst case. The resulting figure is then compared with the hold-time specification at the component receiving the signal.

Maximum timing defines the highest clock frequency at which the end product can operate. If a path violates maximum timing constraints, then some slower parts may fail to function properly at the desired frequency, but they will function reliably at a lower frequency, higher voltage or different temperature. On the other hand, if a path violates minimum timing constraints under any condition, some parts will fail to function reliably across some range of manufacturing tolerances and operating conditions, and nothing can be done to recover the functionality. So, minimum timing should be checked with more rigour than maximum timing.

If there is no combinational path from the output of a logic gate back to one of its inputs, a design is said to be **loop-free**. Most sequential logic is designed that way, with all loops being **sequential loops** that pass through one or more clocked elements. Level-sensitive latches, like an RS latch (Section 8.3.1), deliberately have combinational paths, of course, but these are seldom used. However, sometimes there are combinatorial paths in arbiter circuits and as a side effect of multiplexers for test modes (Section 8.8.2). In these cases, STA may not be able to distinguish properly the relevant paths for timing analysis. In other cases, certain nets are known never to change value during normal operation (e.g. a test mode control signal), and so should be ignored when checking for timing path violations. These situations need to be manually described by the designer in the scripting files read in by STA. An example of an STA driver file is given in Section 8.12.6. Examples of common sources of timing error that result in timing margins are listed in Table 8.8.

Table 8.8 Common sources of timing error

Source	Margin method
PLL clock jitter	Use clock uncertainty to reduce the clock period for maximum timing paths.
Hold constraint characterisation error	Use clock uncertainty to increase the hold-time constraints on sequential cells and reduce the risk of minimum timing failures in silicon due to shortcomings in transistor simulation modelling, RC extraction or model abstraction.
Dynamic voltage noise	Use cell delay timing derates to account for non-uniform instantaneous voltage droops on some instances in the design if those voltages are unknown.
Wire variation	Use net delay timing derates to account for non-uniform metal and via layer capacitances and resistances that are not captured in RC extraction.

8.12.4 Process Corners

Timing must be checked across the range of manufacturing tolerances, usages and environmental conditions that the end product is expected to encounter. These conditions are commonly supplied as **process, voltage and temperature (PVT)** corner models for each cell. PVT variation was introduced in Section 8.4.4, but process variations themselves also have multiple corners, which we discuss here.

Voltage corners reflect the range of on-die voltages within which the end product is specified to operate. If the product incorporates voltage and frequency scaling (Section 4.6.8), the operating voltage range may span several hundred millivolts. The voltage corners must also anticipate any voltage regulation tolerances and potential voltage overshoot due to inductance or droop due to resistance in the PDN. Thus, the voltage range for static timing analysis is always wider than the specified operating voltage range.

Similarly, temperature corners reflect the range of on-die temperatures within which the end product is specified to operate. This is determined by the environment in which the product may be used. As explained in Section 4.4.1, products intended for use in industrial, automotive or space environments are required to operate across more extreme temperature ranges than consumer products.

A process corner acknowledges the variability inherent in a semiconductor manufacturing process. It is impossible to maintain uniform values for many parameters across an entire wafer, from wafer to wafer within the same manufacturing lot, or between different lots manufactured on various pieces of equipment at different times. The parameters that vary are implant concentrations, layer thicknesses and feature dimensions. Process variations are classed as either front or back end-of-line variations.

A **front end-of-line (FEOL)** variation is a change in active component parameters, such as the gain, V_T or on-resistance of a FET. A **back end-of-line (BEOL)** variation is a change in unwanted parasitic parameters, such as net resistance and stray capacitance. Figure 8.58 is a vertical cross-sectional slice through a chip showing that FEOL affects the lowest active areas and BEOL mostly affects the metallic interconnect.

To cover FEOL variations, a foundry provides simulation models with slow transistors (S), typical transistors (T) and fast transistors (F), with the different process parameters varying within what are considered to be acceptable limits. Process corners are named with at least two letters, the first representing the process corner for the N-channel transistors and the second representing the process corner for the P-channel transistors. A special challenge are the so-called **skewed corners**, for which one type of transistor is fast and another slow. Each corner has a data file and the corner names are, typically, included in the file name. Examples of strings in model names that denote PVT corners are given in Table 8.9.

Table 8.9 Examples of process corners

String	Meaning
ss_0p9v_m40c	Slow P and N channel transistors at 0.9 V and –40°C
tt_1p0v_25c	Typical P and N channel transistors at 1.0 V and room temperature
ff_1p1v_125c	Fast P and N channel transistors at 1.1 V and 125°C

Another type of process corner is an interconnect extraction corner. An interconnect is made up of the wires and vias that are processed in the BEOL and is modelled by extracting the wire and via geometries into a netlist of parasitic resistors and capacitors, an RC netlist. As explained in Section 8.7.4, the extracted netlist is written in the IEEE **standard parasitic exchange format (SPEF)**. Foundries commonly provide at least five interconnect extraction corners to model the expected extremes of layer thickness as well as geometry width and spacing. Examples of BEOL corners are listed in Table 8.10.

Table 8.10 Examples of BEOL corners

BEOL Corner	Meaning
C_{min} or C_{best}	Narrow wires with wide spacing for the smallest capacitance component
RC_{min} or RC_{best}	Thick wires with less resistance to minimise the RC product and net delay
Typical	Wires and vias meet the target dimensions
RC_{max} or RC_{worst}	Thin wires with more resistance to maximise the RC product and net delay
C_{max} or C_{worst}	Wide wires with narrow spacing for the largest capacitance component

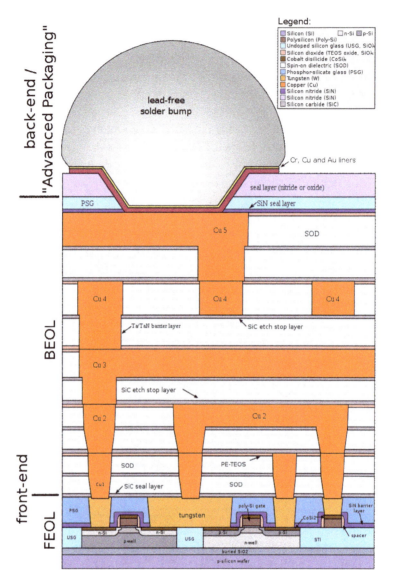

Legend:
- Silicon (Si) ☐ n-Si ☐ p-Si
- Polysilicon (Poly-Si)
- Undoped silicon glass (USG, SiO$_x$)
- Silicon dioxide (TEOS oxide, SiO$_x$)
- Cobalt disilicide (CoSi$_x$)
- Spin-on dielectric (SOD)
- Phosphor-silicate glass (PSG)
- Tungsten (W)
- Copper (Cu)
- Silicon nitride (SiN)
- Silicon nitride (SiN)
- Silicon carbide (SiC)

Figure 8.58 CMOS chip structure, highlighting layers most affected by FEOL and BEOL variations

An interconnect extraction corner also has a temperature component since resistance increases as temperature increases. So, the RC extraction temperature should match the PVT corner temperature. There is a growing need for better statistical modelling of the variations in resistance and capacitance, since net delays are becoming a larger proportion of the total path delay.

8.12.5 Early and Late Arrivals

If there are alternative timing paths between two end points or alternative timing arcs through the cells, or any kind of timing variation to account for, it is useful to distinguish between timing paths that are more pessimistic in a corner where they become faster and timing paths that are more pessimistic in a corner where they are slower. By pessimistic, we mean more likely to lead to failure of either maximum or minimum timing.

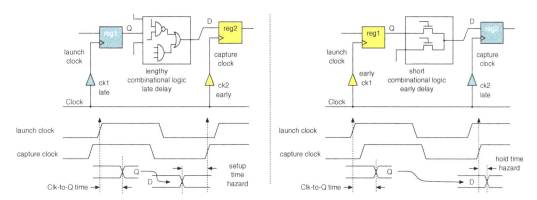

Figure 8.59 Troublesome early and late path configurations for maximum (left) and minimum (right) timing. Late path components are shaded dark

An **early path** is one that becomes more pessimistic when skewed to be faster (i.e. in a corner where the path delay is lower). Under maximum timing, as shown in Figure 8.59 (left), one form of early path is the path to a flip-flop that captures data. This is because, if that path is faster, it reduces the available clock period. Hence, it raises a setup-time risk if the combinational logic path is lengthy. Conversely, the clock delay to a flip-flop that is launching data is part of a late path, as is the combinational logic between the launching and capturing components. Similarly, a **late path** becomes more pessimistic when skewed to be slower.

Under minimum timing, the late and early paths are the other way round, as shown in Figure 8.59 (right). Hold-time violations are more likely if there is a fast path between one flip-flop and the next, a situation that arises in shift register or pass-transistor (illustrated) structures. In this situation, hold-time violations are exacerbated when the clock to a receiving flip-flop is late.

Of course, a synchronous component both launches and receives data on a clock edge, so its clock path is notionally always part of both a late path and an early path. However, typically, one or other of these paths has greater slack and is not of concern. This is where **clock skewing** can be exploited (Section 4.9.6).

Another form of variation arises between the relative performance of the P- and N-type transistors. The two types of FET are based on different diffusion steps, so their variations are not correlated. Hence, it is helpful to consider both the FS (fast N and slow P) and SF (slow N and fast P) corners. These are called skewed or asymmetric corners. Figure 8.60 (left) illustrates a typical structure with a gated clock. For this skewed SF corner, zero-to-one transitions are faster. A variation can mean that the clock to the broadside register labelled Q will arrive faster in that corner than arrivals for the D-inputs that are in the tail of the distribution for arrivals. Hence, setup times will tend to be violated. This is a maximum timing issue and can be solved by binning the whole part for a lower maximum clock frequency. However, for the logic being fed from Q, there is a minimal timing problem that cannot be solved by frequency binning. Instead, the part has to be binned for a narrower temperature range or discarded entirely.

Figure 8.60 (right) illustrates that skewed corner asymmetry tends to cancel out over longer paths of inverting logic, such as from d0 to y. However, for paths that go through just one gate, such as d2 to y, there is no cancelling. Shorter paths are also more likely to suffer hold-time violations, so this is, again, a more severe problem.

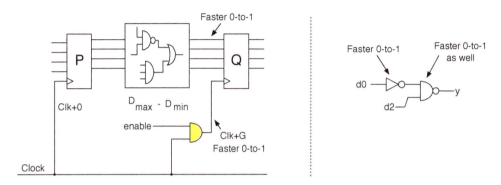

Figure 8.60 A logic structure with a gated clock that could suffer in an FS process corner (left) and a combinational logic circuit with two paths that differ in their levels of inversion

Generally, the clock path to a launching sequential element is very similar to the clock path of the receiving element. In certain cases, the difference is often just in the final section of the path. Sometimes the launcher and receiver are physically connected to the same clock net and sometimes the launcher *is* the receiver. In these cases, it is overly pessimistic to consider the general worst-case divergence between launching and capture clocks for the process corner. For the shared portion of any two clock paths, it is impossible to have fast and slow skews simultaneously. STA performs **common-path pessimism removal (CPPR)**, which discounts the variation in clock time arising from the common part of the clock distribution network that is shared between the launching and receiving components. This is labelled CPPR in a timing report.

8.12.6 Timing Models: Liberty

Abstract timing models for cells are created by running SPICE simulations to characterise them. The models are stored in text files that conform to the Liberty model format. The syntax of Liberty models was made public and is controlled by the **Liberty Technical Advisory Board (LTAB)**, which operates under the **Industry Standards and Technology Organization (ISTO)** of the IEEE. Models contain information on function, input capacitance, cell delay for each timing arc, output transition times, constraints, limitations, power and current.

Cell-level Constraints

Cell-level constraints are the timing relationships between different pins that must be met to ensure proper functioning. The most common constraints relate to the setup and hold times of sequential cells. The setup time is the minimum delay between new data arriving at the input of a sequential cell and the arrival of the clock. The hold time is the minimum delay between the arrival of the clock and any change in the valid data on the input. If the data change within the time window defined by the setup and hold times, the clock-to-output propagation delay of the sequential cell is no longer modelled accurately because the internal latches may become metastable. Metastability means that the internal voltage is not solid logic high or low but somewhere between (Section 3.7.2). Timing diagrams of setup and hold constraints for a sequential cell are shown in Figure 8.36.

Non-linear Delay Models

The simplest form of a Liberty model (Section 8.12.6) consists of LUTs indexed by the input transition time and output load. These values can be interpolated to model complex non-linear behaviour. Such models are called **non-linear delay models (NLDMs)**.

Current Source Models

Simple NLDM tables make ideal assumptions about the shape of the input waveform and the capacitive output load. However, in reality the nets are subject to charge injection due to the switching activity of nearby nets, which distorts the waveforms. The input capacitance is also a function of voltage and output switching. To model any non-ideal behaviour, a Liberty model has tables for the current indexed by input transition, output load and time. Liberty models with these tables are called **concurrent current source (CCS)** models. Such CCS models are necessary for achieving sufficient STA accuracy in modern process technologies.

A related format is called an **effective current source model (ECSM)**. If such models are supported by the EDA software, then they can be used in place of, or in combination with, CCS models. ECSM is an extension of the standard Liberty format that uses tables of voltage indexed by input transition, output load and time.

STA Constraints Example

To run an STA tool, the netlist (RTL format) and cell library data (Liberty format) are needed, along with the back annotations for the wiring delay (SPEF form) and a driver file. The de facto standard for the driver file format is **Synopsys Design Constraint (SDC)**, which, like many EDA tools, is embedded in the TCL language. An example of an SDC file demonstrating the concepts described above is shown in Figure 8.61.

Some of the most common constraints are:

- **Create clocks**: Clocks are created with a period and may be associated with an input port or an internal net. Clocks may be **free-running**, but a **generated clock** has a relationship with the frequency or phase of another clock. A generated clock is often created by a clock-divider circuit (Section 3.7.4). A **virtual clock** is not connected to any port or net. A virtual clock is often used to specify timing relationships to things beyond the design, like the I/O ports.

- **I/O timing constraints**: The timing at the ports is defined by imagining sequential cells outside the design connected to the ports. These imaginary sequential cells are assigned minimum and maximum delay, setup and hold times to complete the timing beyond the design. A driving cell and net can be assigned to input ports to represent the input waveform. A load cell or capacitance can be assigned to output ports.

```
# ---- Create Clocks ----
create_clock -add -period $clock_period -name VCLK

foreach clock_name $clock_list {
  create_clock -add -period $clock_period [get_ports $clock_name] -name $clock_name
  set_clock_latency $clock_latency [get_clocks $clock_name]
}

set_clock_uncertainty [expr $setup_margin + $clock_jitter] -setup [all_clocks]
set_clock_uncertainty [expr $hold_margin]                  -hold  [all_clocks]

set_driving_cell -lib_cell $clock_driving_cell \
                 -input_transition_rise $max_clock_transition \
                 -input_transition_fall $max_clock_transition \
                 [get_ports $clock_list]

# ---- I/O timing constraints ----
set_input_delay $max_input_constraint -max -clock VCLK \
           [remove_from_collection [all_inputs] $clock_list]
set_input_delay $min_input_constraint -min -clock VCLK \
           [remove_from_collection [all_inputs] $clock_list]

set_output_delay $max_output_constraint -max -clock VCLK [all_outputs]
set_output_delay $min_output_constraint -min -clock VCLK [all_outputs]

# ---- Path groups ----
group_path -name reg2reg -from [all_registers] -to [all_registers]

# ---- Timing exceptions ----
set_multicycle_path 2 -setup -end -from [get_ports DFT*]
set_multicycle_path 1 -hold  -end -from [get_ports DFT*]
%
% # ---- Scan mode ----
```

Figure 8.61 An example of an SDC file. TCL commands are used to specify and constrain the STA behaviour

- **Path groups**: Path groups are a convenient way to help focus optimisation and analysis on a subset of paths. Paths can be selected based on their start points, end points or any common point in between. They are assigned a name. Path groups can be given weights to guide optimisation by emphasising the resolution of timing violations. Timing reports can be created for specific path groups.

- **Timing exceptions**: Occasionally, paths in a design do not conform to the ordinary timing constraints. These include multi-cycle paths (Section 4.9.6), false paths and paths with disabled timing arcs. If a designer expects that the logic will take more than one clock period to resolve, a multi-cycle path can be declared to delay the capture clock edge by a multiple of the clock period.

An example of a **false path** is at the interface of asynchronous clock domains. In this case, the interface is accomplished by inserting special synchronising sequential cells that are designed to reduce the probability of metastability. As long as the synchronising cells are in place, any timing paths between the asynchronous clock domains are false.

- **Case analysis**: Most designs have configuration or reset signals that are not expected to change during normal operation. If these signals do change state, then timing is carefully controlled by external means and the design enters into a different operational mode. Case analysis is used to force these signals to logic one or zero so that only the timing paths that are valid during each mode are checked. The most common pair of modes for which a case analysis is used are scan and functional modes, which are controlled by a scan enable signal (Section 4.7.5). It is necessary to validate the timing using STA in both modes.

Timing constraints are an important part of any design. Any mistake can result in silicon that does not function properly. Therefore, it is important to validate the constraints. EDA vendors provide software to check clock and reset domain crossings and other timing constraints.

8.12.7 Multi-mode Multi-corner Analysis

The massive increase in the number of PVT corners requiring verification at advanced technology nodes has been called the **process corner explosion**, resulting in a need for greater CPU resources and design time. When optimising a design, it is not uncommon for the optimisations performed for one mode and corner combination to conflict with the requirements of another combination. Thus, multiple optimisation algorithms are combined into a complete set of timing sign-off analyses called **multi-mode multi-corner (MMMC)** analysis, which can accommodate the requirements of all combinations simultaneously. Modes are defined by the timing constraints in an SDC file. A range of PVT corners are associated with the modes and used to validate timing across the entire range of corners that need to be validated. Table 8.11 lists some of the common MMMC analyses.

Table 8.11 Typical MMMC configurations, with 40 distinct analysis corners

Timing analysis	Mode	Process corner		Voltage	Temperature	Index
		FEOL	BEOL			
Full-yield maximum-voltage frequency						
Maximum	Functional	SS	C_{worst}	0.90 V	−40°C	1
			RC_{worst}			2
			C_{worst}		125°C	3
			RC_{worst}			4
Half-yield maximum-voltage frequency						
Maximum	Functional	TT	Typical	0.90 V	−40°C	5
					125°C	6
Full-yield nominal-voltage frequency						
Maximum	Functional	SS	C_{worst}	0.81 V	−40°C	7
			RC_{worst}			8
			C_{worst}		125°C	9
			RC_{worst}			10

Timing analysis	Mode	Process corner		Voltage	Temperature	Index
		FEOL	BEOL			
Full-yield minimum-voltage frequency						
Maximum	Functional	SS	C_{worst}	0.72 V	−40°C	11
			RC_{worst}			12
			C_{worst}		125°C	13
			RC_{worst}			14
Maximum-voltage functional hold						
Minimum	Functional	FF	C_{best}	1.10 V	−40°C	15
			RC_{best}			16
			C_{worst}			17
			RC_{worst}			18
			C_{best}		125°C	19
			RC_{best}			20
			C_{worst}			21
			RC_{worst}			22
Minimum-voltage functional hold						
Minimum	Functional	SS	C_{worst}	0.72 V	−40°C	23
			RC_{worst}			24
			C_{worst}		125°C	25
			RC_{worst}			26
Scan frequency						
Maximum	Scan	SS	Typical	0.72 V	−40°C	27
			C_{worst}		125°C	28
Maximum-voltage scan hold						
Minimum	Scan	FF	C_{best}	1.10 V	−40°C	29
			RC_{best}			30
			C_{worst}			31
			RC_{worst}			32
			C_{best}		125°C	33
			RC_{best}			34
			C_{worst}			35
			RC_{worst}			36
Minimum-voltage scan hold						
Minimum	Scan	SS	C_{worst}	0.72 V	−40°C	37
			RC_{worst}			38
			C_{worst}		125°C	39
			RC_{worst}			40

8.12.8 Signal Integrity

A **signal integrity (SI)** analysis looks at all the sources of noise on a signal that can modify timing delays and checks the signals against criteria such as noise threshold voltages and transition time limits. These checks help to ensure that the timing results are accurate and that the design will not propagate erroneous logic states.

8.12.9 Coupling Capacitance

When two wires cross over each other or run parallel with each other, they form a parasitic capacitor, which imparts a coupling capacitance. When one of the wires switches, the coupling capacitance transfers charge to the other wire, which can cause the voltage to deviate from a logic one or zero. If the other wire is also switching at about the same time, the two signals affect each other. If both are switching in the same direction, their transition times can decrease, reducing the delay. Conversely, if they are switching in opposite directions, their transition times can increase or become distorted, which increases the delay. Coupling capacitors are included in the SPEF netlist and the STA software algorithms include their effect on delays when an SI analysis is enabled.

8.12.10 Noise Analysis

Both coupling and Miller capacitance (Section 8.4.6) contribute to noise on the signals in a design. The transistors in each gate have threshold voltages. Signal voltages that are coupled above ground or below the power supply voltage by neighbouring nets switching and thus, surpass the transistor threshold voltage may cause unwanted activity or propagate erroneous logic states. Therefore, one part of STA is to analyse the worst voltage noise and report any violations that surpass specified threshold voltages. This is called **noise analysis**.

8.12.11 Transition Time Limits

Cells are characterised over a wide range of input transition times and output loads. However, if STA determines that the transitions or loads are outside the characterised range, the timing accuracy is in doubt. There can be several reasons for this. The first is that extrapolation beyond the characterised timing table is inherently less accurate than interpolation. The second is that long transition times mean that the driving cell is very weak or that the wire resistance is high relative to the load it is driving. Any inaccuracies in RC extraction, SI analysis or the local instantaneous supply voltage can result in large timing errors. Long transition times are likely to result in a poor quality of results from timing optimisation and may to lead to currents that exceed the electromigration current limits (Section 8.4.5). Finally, long transition times mean that both the N-channel and P-channel transistors of the gate receiving the signal are turned on together for an extended time, leading to higher short-circuit energy use (Section 4.6.2).

In summary, some of the reasons to check transition times against a constraint are:

- avoid timing inaccuracies due to extrapolation

- avoid exacerbating timing inaccuracies due to BEOL extraction, SI analysis or power supply noise

- improve the quality of results from timing optimisations

- remain within the electromigration current limits

- lower the power by reducing the crowbar current.

8.12.12 On-chip Variation

Many factors affect timing in real silicon, and they must be accounted for. Many of them are specific to each instance of a design due to non-uniformity of PVT in location and time. They can be hard to quantify since they are stochastic. Variation due to non-uniformity across a chip is called **on-chip variation (OCV)**.

Global OCV encompasses the entire range of manufacturing tolerances for all lots, wafers and die. The mean of the global variation is a typical transistor that meets the target values for all parameters. The extremes of the global variation are the fastest and slowest transistors that still fall within the manufacturing tolerances even though they rarely occur.

Local OCV is limited to the range of transistors that exist on the same die, within an arbitrarily small distance from one another. The mean of the local variation is the mean transistor on the die, which may be skewed to the slow or fast end of the global process distribution. Figure 8.62 illustrates how local process variation is much narrower than global variation. Two example dies can potentially lie at either ends of the global variation.

However, even within one die, especially a large one, it is unlikely that all the devices will be manufactured uniformly across the entire chip. Thus, process gradients add further variation to timing paths that span large distances. This is known as **spatial variation**.

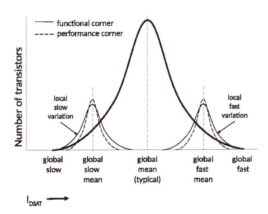

Figure 8.62 Global and localised views of process distributions

For some technologies, foundries may define two types of local process variation. The traditional corner approach assumes that variations in the P-channel and N-channel transistor geometries are unrelated, which means that the transistor performance variations are uncorrelated. The other approach assumes that the P-channel and N-channel transistors are arranged in a configuration with CMOS standard cell gates so that some geometries are shared or in close proximity; therefore, the variations of some parameters are correlated, which leads to less pessimistic timing.

There are a number of ways to estimate the impact of OCV timing. There are two main ways for the cells:

1. **Flat OCV**: The simplest way to account for variation assumes that all cell instances or nets vary in the same proportion and their timing can be scaled by a set of multiplicative derates. A derate is usually expressed as a percentage of the delay. This approach is called flat OCV since it is not specific to each instance of a cell or net but is applied broadly. Flat OCV can be used when more accurate methods are not available.

   An example of flat OCV is shown in Figure 8.63 Here, a process variation of ± 5 per cent was applied to the delay for cells in clock paths, ± 3 per cent was applied to the delay for cells in data paths and -10 per cent was applied to the net delay.

   The reasons for these values are important to understand. Derates for process variation are applied to both the early and late timing paths. That means that the cell-level timing models are characterised at the mean of a global process corner, the global slow corner in this case, and that the percentages represent the potential effect of local process variation on the delay. The percentages applied to clock paths are larger than those applied to data paths. This reflects the desire to be more cautious about clock timing and in the minimum analysis of hold constraints. Because the BEOL extraction corner is RC_{worst}, net delays already represent the maximum timing of late paths. Therefore, a derate is applied to early paths to account for wires that are skewed toward the faster end of the process distribution.

   Timing margins for the spatial variation within a single chip are modelled using LUTs for flat delay derates indexed by distance.

2. **Stage-based OCV**: Flat OCV ignores the differences in variation between different cells and that the delay in paths that have more transistors statistically tends toward the mean. This is addressed by **stage-based OCV (SBOCV)**, which is more commonly known by its commercial name **Advanced OCV**. SBOCV applies a derate to the cell delays from a table that is indexed by the cell type, rising or falling edge, and path depth. Although SBOCV is better than flat OCV, it suffers from several shortcomings. One of these is that only one delay derate table per cell type can be specified, so it is not possible to model the variation for each specific timing arc through the cell, input transition time and output load. Also, transition time variation is ignored.

To address the shortcomings of SBOCV, the LTAB approved the addition to Liberty models of tables with early and late sigmas for every delay arc, transition time and constraint. These new tables are commonly referred to as the **Liberty Variation Format (LVF)**, although EDA vendors tend to use their own proprietary names. The LVF format was later amended to support non-Gaussian distributions with the addition of tables with the first three moments of the distribution, the mean shift, standard deviation and skewness. The mean shift is the difference between the NLDM value and the mean of the distribution. The standard deviation is the sigma of the entire distribution, not just the early or late half. Skewness describes the asymmetry of the distribution. Timing distributions tend to become less Gaussian as the operating voltage decreases relative to the transistor threshold voltage (V_T). With these LVF tables, STA can efficiently and accurately calculate the FEOL timing variation for each path.

LVF gives the user control over their confidence in STA through a **LVF sigma multiplier**. Larger sigma multipliers provide higher confidence in the timing yield but more timing paths need to be optimised. Larger SoC products require higher confidence because they have more timing paths. Figure 8.63 shows the distribution of delay for a timing path due to local variation in relation to the LVF table parameters and the sigma multiplier.

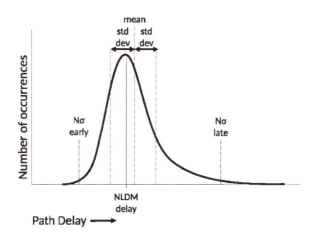

Figure 8.63 LVF path delay distribution and sigma multiplier

A minimum timing analysis requires higher confidence than maximum timing analysis for reasons previously discussed. A maximum timing confidence of 3σ results in a 99.86 per cent probability that all the paths in a slow die will meet the timing. This is acceptable for maximum timing, since there are relatively few critical setup paths and few slow dies. On the other hand, minimum timing confidence needs to be higher because there are usually many near-critical hold paths and these must meet the timing across the entire PVT range. Sigma multipliers of 4.5 or greater may be necessary.

8.12.13 Net Delay Variation

As well as cell OCV, the propagation delay for a net may vary from one die or wafer to another. Variation arises from inconsistencies in the dimensions of the tracks and vias that carry logic signals between cells. These affect the parasitic resistance and capacitance, which, in turn, leads to variations in the net delay. As discussed in Section 4.6.4, the net delay variation did not make up a large proportion of the path delay for older VLSI nodes. However, as transistor and interconnect geometries have reduced, the transistors are proportionally faster and the interconnect is more resistive. This has made the net delay variation increasingly more important.

Since an interconnect often crosses metal layers, a net that uses many layers is manufactured with many independent process steps. Thus, its overall performance will tend towards the mean. However, a net with few layers may be skewed towards one of the BEOL corners, as described earlier. Ideally, the net delay variation is modelled with statistical methods, much like the FEOL variation is modelled with LVF. As of this writing, the statistical modelling of FEOL variation is limited to a few via layers. The most common way to account for net delay variations is to use flat derates.

8.12.14 Voltage Variation

As introduced in Section 8.4.7, supply voltage variations, caused by switching activity, are known as **ground bounce** or **supply droop**, depending on the time scale. These effects are highly correlated with both local and more global behaviour. Local effects whose duration is less than a gate switching time are comparatively easy to integrate into cell characterisation, but the more global voltage droops change in complex ways as instructions and data flow through the SoC.

Supply droops can be very difficult to predict and calculate. Hence, flat delay derates are usually applied to model the timing variation approximately. However, as transistor and interconnect geometries have reduced, the switching currents have become larger, the PDNs have become more resistive and so the timing variations occasionally exceed the assumptions used to develop the derates. This has resulted in first-pass silicon that does not meet the performance expectations due to one or more instances that experience more voltage droop than anticipated. These STA oversights have prompted the EDA industry to invest in software to analyse voltage variation in more detail.

8.12.15 Advanced Topics in STA

STA is constantly evolving as process technologies and market demands require new capabilities. As discussed earlier, modelling the net delay variation and the voltage variation has become more important. Transistor ageing and yield-based analysis are a couple of topics that are also becoming more critical.

Transistor Ageing

The SPICE models for transistors represent fresh transistors early in the lifetime of a product. Two effects are responsible for a gradual decline in transistor performance over time, which together are referred to as transistor ageing.

First, a bias voltage on a transistor gate attracts carriers to charge traps in the interface between the channel and the oxide, causing V_T to shift. Removing the bias can release the charge, thus relaxing the stress and reducing the V_T shift (ΔV_T). Hence, the V_T shift depends on the number of traps in the channel and the length of time the gate is biased. This effect, called *bias temperature instability*, is accelerated by higher temperatures and bias voltages. Figure 8.64 illustrates a statistical V_T shift due to bias temperature instability that is modulated by the length of time the gate is biased.

Second, high switching currents accelerate carriers across the channel. These high-velocity carriers may damage the lattice and become embedded in the gate insulating oxide. This causes a reduction in mobility and a V_T shift. This effect, called **hot carrier injection**, depends on the switching rate.

Foundries can supply SPICE models that reflect some of the effects of transistor ageing. At the time of this writing, they focus on the maximum V_T shift and mobility change. They rarely model relaxation and the statistical V_T shift. Accounting for these effect in STA is becoming more important because the volume of semiconductors in high-reliability applications, like avionics, automobiles and mission-critical data centres, is increasing. This has provided an incentive for the EDA industry to

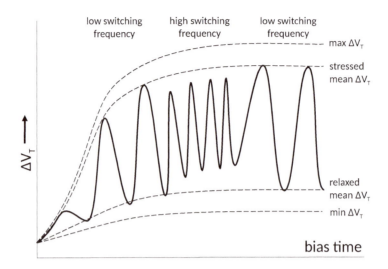

low switching frequency   high switching frequency   low switching frequency

max ΔV_T

stressed mean ΔV_T

relaxed mean ΔV_T

min ΔV_T

ΔV_T ⟶

bias time

Figure 8.64 Statistical V_T shift due to bias temperature instability for various bias times

invest in developing STA solutions. However, modelling is complicated by the many dependencies, the incompleteness of SPICE models and increased characterisation costs.

Yield-based Analysis

So far, the timing distributions that have been discussed reflect the probability of an individual path failing to meet its timing constraint. In reality, the timing yield of a die depends on the combined probability that any one of the many paths will fail to meet its constraint. The probability of one out of many paths failing is less than the probability of an individual path failing. However, paths that share common instances are correlated, which increases their probability of failure.

Yield-based analysis provides an overall timing yield percentage along with static timing results. If the overall timing yield is high enough, then resolving the remaining failing paths adds little value. If the overall timing yield is not high enough, the priority is to resolve the paths that have the highest probability of contributing to failure.

8.12.16 Timing Closure

Commonly, a marketing department will have pre-sold a product with an advertised clock frequency. Making the actual product work at this frequency is known as meeting the **timing closure**. With the design in low-level RTL formal, typical approaches for achieving timing closure include:

▪ replacing standard cells with higher drive-strength variants

▪ using D-type migration to move logic either side of an existing register (Section 4.4.2)

- for bus protocols that are amenable to registering, such as CHI (or AXI with minor additional complexity), adding a further pipeline stage. Not all protocols are suitable for registering (Section 3.1.2)

- with transactional interfaces, adding a one-place FIFO buffer

- altering the floor plan.

The timing sign-off, like all parts of the back-end flow, involves a massive verification effort. Every possible design rule check and cross-check is made. The engineers responsible for timing sign-off always prefer the certainty of a clear pass or fail. Unfortunately, there are many sources of error plus incomplete knowledge, which cloud any such certainty. There are many questions that one must ask to balance models with reality:

- Do the detailed SPICE models of the components and logic cells really reflect the silicon?

- Will the foundry process drift as the manufacturing process matures?

- Do the abstract timing models, BEOL extraction and STA engines conform to the detailed SPICE models?

- Are the timing margins too conservative or too optimistic?

- Is the difficulty of meeting timing negatively impacting the PPA of the product (Section 5.6)?

- Can the timing violations be fixed within the schedule using the resources available?

- Do the STA results really reflect the product timing yield and profitability?

Thus, timing sign-off is as much an art as a science, an art that requires tremendous attention to detail, judicious choices, great management skills and a good bit of luck.

8.13 Summary

This chapter has briefly covered many of the main aspects of the so-called back-end or physical flow. The input is synthesisable RTL, cell libraries, full-custom and specialist cells and silicon process characterisations. The output is a vector graphics file that describes the polygons on each mask. Hence, the back-end flow is also called the RTL-to-GDS flow.

The design flows for an FPGA and ASIC are broadly similar. The choice of which to use in the final product largely depends on the planned production volume. If the final product is envisioned as an ASIC, an FPGA version is useful for a proof of concept of real-time applications (such as modems) and early prototypes in general.

The traditional SoC design flow is divided by the structural RTL level into:

- **Front end**: Specify, explore, design, capture and synthesise ⤳ structural RTL

- **Back end**: Structural RTL ⤳ place, route, mask-making and fabrication.

Today, a handover is more likely to be at the synthesisable RTL level, with the back-end team resynthesising the logic.

The mainstream approach today is to use standard cells in a semi-custom design. A logic synthesiser marries the application-specific design details with a reusable cell library chosen for the target technology node. The principal inputs to a logic synthesiser are synthesisable RTL and the cell library definition, but the design intent files also make a huge difference to the generated design. The output from the synthesiser is a netlist consisting of cell instances from the cell library that embody the behaviour of a portable design.

The back-end steps that follow are placement, routing, tapeout, mask-making, test program generation, fabrication and production testing. In this chapter, we reviewed each of the steps, starting with the synthesis of the RTL. The back-end verification flow is the most time-consuming element. A single error can require a complete chip respin, although this can be sometimes mitigated with a minor change to a few masks or a temporary software workaround (Section 9.3).

In previous decades, it was necessary to iterate many of the steps of an EDA flow to find closure. As an example, if many timing violations remained after the routing step, then a manual adjustment to earlier intent and timing target settings was made before rerunning the routing step. If there were still timing violations, it was necessary to go one step further back in the flow and modify the settings for the synthesis or placement steps and then repeat those steps. Iterating steps is, nowadays, very time-consuming and still does not guarantee that the SoC design will meet the performance targets. Instead, modern EDA tools are physically aware and timing-aware. As an example, logical synthesis considers various physical aspects including an estimate of net length or macrocell area in a coarse placement or Rentian estimate (Section 5.6.6). Also, the placement and routing steps have become timing-aware, since they both automatically iterate (in a trial-and-error approach) until they obtain zero or the minimum number of timing violations.

In this chapter, the reader has been exposed to every step of a traditional flow. Although this flow retains its traditional structure, the challenges of deep submicron geometries, together with market pressure to extract maximum performance from each square millimetre of silicon, mean far greater consideration of the interactions between steps is required. The steps have all become more advanced and complicated. So, in this chapter, we have placed extra emphasis on the new techniques.

8.13.1 Exercises

1. List and describe the main layers of a modern silicon chip.

2. What problems can be found during net routing that would suggest a better placement is needed? How can these be anticipated during placement? Would a constructive placer take these considerations into account?

3. Why is an FPGA larger and slower than the equivalent ASIC?

4. How many FPGA DSP blocks are needed for a 32 × 32 multiplier? What is its latency? What difference does it make if only 32 bits of the result are needed?

5. Design a logic structure that will be very difficult to assess in a production test, but do not include redundant logic. What is the problem? Could such a structure be needed in a real application?

6. What principal data need to be held in a floor plan? Can a good floor plan reduce the number of domain crossing and isolation components needed?

7. Choose one of the reasons listed for limiting the transition times in a design and expand upon the reasoning with examples, simulations or mathematical modelling. Why is the transition time especially important for clock signals?

8. Why does the net delay become a larger proportion of the path delay as process geometries shrink?

9. Why would it be helpful to model the statistical variation of net delays instead of assuming all interconnect segments are at one BEOL corner?

10. Create a list of the sources of timing uncertainty considered during STA. Are there any that were not discussed?

   ▪ Give an example of OCV that is dependent on location and one that is dependent on time. Is there an example that depends on both location and time?

   ▪ What kind of optimisation might be done to fix timing violations with negative slack in maximum timing analysis?

   ▪ What kind of optimisations might be done to lower the power by reclaiming positive slack in a maximum timing analysis?

   ▪ Why can minimum timing violations not be fixed by decreasing the clock frequency?

   ▪ How can reducing the STA positive slack benefit power and area?

- Why is it important that inputs to STA, like Liberty abstract timing models and SPEF netlists, conform to an IEEE standard?

- What kind of optimisations might be done to fix STA minimum timing violations with negative slack?

11. Describe how the yield can be improved if a structure is replicated hundreds of times over a chip? Should the end user be involved in this process? Consult a recent DRAM chip data sheet and discuss the mechanisms likely to be used during a production test and at boot time.

References

[1] V. Gourisetty, H. Mahmoodi, V. Melikyan, E. Babayan, R. Goldman, K. Holcomb, and T. Wood. Low power design flow based on unified power format and Synopsys tool chain. In *3rd Interdisciplinary Engineering Design Education Conference*, pages 28–31, 2013.

[2] C. Mead and L. Conway. *Introduction to VLSI systems*. Addison-Wesley, Reading, Mass, 1980. ISBN 0201043580.

[3] R. H. Dennard, F. H. Gaensslen, L. Kuhn, and H. N. Yu. Design of micron MOS switching devices. In *International Electron Devices Meeting*, pages 168–170, 1972. doi: 10.1109/IEDM.1972.249198.

[4] Mark Horowitz, Elad Alon, Samuel Naffziger, Rajesh Kumar, and Kerry Bernstein. Scaling, power and the future of CMOS. In *Proceedings of the 20th International Conference on VLSI Design held jointly with 6th International Conference: Embedded Systems*, page 23. IEEE Computer Society, 2007.

[5] Jörg Henkel, Heba Khdr, Santiago Pagani, and Muhammad Shafique. New trends in dark silicon. In *Proceedings of the 52nd Annual Design Automation Conference*, DAC '15, New York, NY, USA, 2015. Association for Computing Machinery. ISBN 9781450335201. doi: 10.1145/2744769.2747938. URL https://doi.org/10.1145/2744769.2747938.

[6] H. Esmaeilzadeh, E. Blem, R. S. Amant, K. Sankaralingam, and D. Burger. Dark silicon and the end of multicore scaling. In *38th Annual International Symposium on Computer Architecture (ISCA)*, pages 365–376, 2011.

[7] Texas Instruments. The TTL data book for design engineers, 1976.

[8] ITRS. International technology roadmap for semiconductors 2.0 executive report, 2015.

[9] ITRS. International technology roadmap for semiconductors 2020 update, 2020.

[10] B. Arnold. Shrinking possibilities. *IEEE Spectrum*, 46(4):26–56, 2009. doi: 10.1109/MSPEC.2009.4808761.

[11] John Patrick Hayes. *Digital Logic Design*. Addison Wesley, 1993. ISBN ISBN 0-201-15461-7.

[12] David J. Greaves. *Multi-Access Metropolitan Area Networks*. PhD dissertation, University of Cambridge Computer Laboratory, 1992. URL https://www.cl.cam.ac.uk/users/djg11/pubs/david-j-greaves-phd-dissertation-dec-1992.pdf.

[13] I. Kuon and J. Rose. Measuring the gap between FPGAs and ASICs. *IEEE Transactions on Computer-Aided Design of Integrated Circuits and Systems*, 26(2):203–215, 2007. doi: 10.1109/TCAD.2006.884574.

[14] *IEEE Standard for Universal Verification Methodology Language Reference Manual*. IEEE, 2020. Std 1800.2-2020 (Revision of Std 1800.2-2017).

[15] Europractice IC Service. Price list for general Europractice MPW runs. https://europractice-ic.com, 2021.

Chapter 9

Putting Everything Together

In the early days of SoC design, software engineers, unfortunately, often lacked the motivation to write even a line of code until the physical silicon prototypes had been manufactured and were about to be delivered. This had the bad effect of serialising the work of the hardware and software teams and extended the all-critical time to market. Pre-tapeout virtual models, using ESL or FPGA, changed this. A virtual platform not only allows the software to be developed before the tapeout, but it also gives the software engineers an opportunity to request hardware changes and API improvements. The likelihood of a showstopping post-tapeout bug is, thus, minimised.

Today, nearly all aspects of software development can be completed before the first silicon is fabricated and there are many stories of a whole SoC system running perfectly on the day that the chips arrived. The software effort specifically for a new SoC falls mainly into two classes: bootstrap code and device drivers. Sometimes there is new application code as well, but mostly this can be developed on other computers or on a previous generation of the hardware.

ESL models of devices are likely to be identical to the real hardware, so the device driver (Section 2.7.1) code should be identical and already tested. Exceptions may relate to real-time performance that has not been accurately reported. A high-level model will not be **cycle-accurate**, especially if it has a loosely timed TLM (Section 5.4.4), but also if an FPGA prototype used a different time/space fold (Section 8.5.3).

The boot procedure for the real hardware may be quite different from what was normally used for the ESL model, but the real procedure should also have been tested on the virtual platform. For instance, the ESL model may have simply initialised RAM contents from the file system via backdoor interfaces, whereas for the real system there may be complex interdependencies in boot order for the various cores and subsystems. Power management control needs at least to turn a subsystem on before it can boot, but the complete power structure may not have been reflected in the ESL model. It may be infeasible to use an RTL model for the complete system boot, but Verilog-to-C techniques mitigate this (Section 5.1.1). A secure boot adds complexity (Section 9.1.1).

9.1 Firmware

Software installed in ROM (Section 2.6.2) is called **firmware**. Early embedded systems and microcomputers, such as the Acorn personal computer, put the complete operating system in ROM, but today most systems have only a minimal **bootloader** in ROM. The ROM is put in the memory map at a location that encompasses the reset vector of the **boot core** (Section 1.1.3), which is the first CPU to start operating after a reset. All the others are triggered by it. The job of the bootloader is to load the operating system or embedded application for the SoC.

Multiple levels of bootloader are quite commonly used, with each one loading the next and then transferring execution to it. Each level provides a different level of system configuration and can select which of several alternative next levels to load. For instance, a dual-boot PC must select between Windows or Linux, or different versions of the same operating system, at the appropriate point in the boot chain. One reason for having multiple levels is to simplify software distribution. A particular operating system kernel can be loaded onto a variety of hardware platforms if a prior level of booting has provided sufficient custom initialisation such that the platforms look homogeneous.

Early-stage bootloaders set up the DRAM and important peripherals. DRAM requires timing and voltage selection (Section 4.5) before it can be used and the code that performs this must be small and run entirely from an on-SoC scratchpad (Section 2.3). If the main operating system is to be fetched from disk, USB stick or over a network, the bootloader must contain a rudimentary device driver for the relevant I/O device. For an Ethernet device, it may need to install the MAC in a register, whereas for a file system, it will need sufficient code to traverse a directory structure, in read-only mode, looking for the relevant named file.

As described in Section 3.1.7, an operating system can typically explore the hardware structure to find out how much memory is installed and to see which I/O devices are present. The presence of I/O devices depends on what SoC the code is booted on and on what additional components have been installed on the PCB or plugged in. For ease of software version management, it is now common for a booted image to contain device drivers for devices that are not physically present. Similarly, the booted code may be able to locate additional device drivers on secondary storage or from the cloud. Beyond the critical device drivers, the choice of which devices drivers to hard-include and which to load dynamically is a trade-off of code size and convenience. There is also a security issue. For instance, on a PC, the PS2 port driver may be hard-coded and on a mobile phone, the driver for the button will be hard-coded. This is to prevent operating system spoofing attacks in which a user thinks they are interacting with the device, but instead, they are using an application that is pretending to be the whole device.

Bootstrap code does not typically need to be high performance, so can be put in a slow device, like a serial ROM with 1 bit per word and a transfer rate of just a few Mbps. Moreover, it is common for the bootstrap ROM to be disengaged from the memory map after boot time. A PIO operation (Section 2.7) to a ROM control register will disable it until the next reset. Disengaging the boot ROM frees up memory space (an issue in A32 systems) and provides a degree of protection for secrets and IP embodied in a secure boot.

9.1.1 Secure Bootstrapping

A secure boot is an increasingly common requirement. A **secure bootloader** guarantees that the operating system has been loaded correctly without tampering. It can also provide a number of related operations, such as checking that the appropriate licences have not expired or ensuring the boot operation is logged in a tamper-proof journal that is secure enough to be used as evidence in legal proceedings. A secure bootloader must be installed so that it cannot be bypassed and it must be able to check the authenticity of the software it loads. Typically, it then passes control to the loaded software after sealing a certificate of authenticity in a **secure enclave** (Section 4.9.1), which cannot be modified by any software subsequently run on the SoC and which cannot easily be modified by electronic or mechanical probing. A first-level secure enclave may allow only write access when the boot ROM is engaged. A serial ROM external to the SoC is easy to bypass without specialist tools.

Thus, a common way to prevent a secure bootloader from being bypassed is to put it in mask ROM on the main SoC.

The code in a secure operating system has a digital signature. Digital signatures use **secure hash** functions, such as **SHA-1.2**, which return a 20-byte number or similar for a block of data. The source code for such functions is not secret, but there are no known ways of editing a block of data to give a desired hash. Hence, it is impossible to generate an operating system image that will give the same signature as a known good image. The operating system must have a digital certificate of its hash. Certificates normally use **public key infrastructure (PKI)**. PKI uses pairs of keys. One is kept private and the other made public. These are called, respectively, the **private key** and the **public key**. These are easy to create as pairs, but the private key cannot be generated from the public one. A small amount of data, such as the hash digest and the name of an operating system image, are digitally signed by the issuer by encoding the data with the organisation's private key. The bootloader knows the organisation's public key and hence, can validate the certificate. It will proceed with a boot only if the hash of the image agrees with the one that has been signed. Either the public key is stored in the boot ROM or, if trust is delegated, the public key of a certificate provider is stored. In the latter case, the boot ROM contacts the certificate provider over a network. A secure operating system periodically checks the digital signature of its code, in case malware or a fault has corrupted it. Moreover, it checks the digital signatures of all additionally loaded device drivers and possibly, application code too.

9.2 Powering up

Nearly all SoCs have a UART device (Section 2.7.1). The first program run on most new SoCs prints 'Hello World' to the UART using polled I/O. This program may already be in the on-chip boot ROM or else that ROM contains a low-level **machine-code monitor** that allows memory locations to be viewed and changed and for control to be transferred. The major alternative to a UART is a JTAG debug interface (Section 4.7.3), which, typically, supports the same monitoring primitives. If there is on-chip flash memory, the monitor allows this to be programmed. Since these low-level ports expose an attack surface for malware and jailbreaks, a cryptographic exchange may be needed, as for a secure boot. A **jailbreak** is the installation of an unsigned operating system or application on a platform that should run only approved code.

With a UVM (Section 8.8.1) design flow or otherwise, each IP block is likely to have a software test program that was used during design verification pre-tapeout. These can, typically, be run on **bare metal**, i.e. without operating system support, on the real silicon prior to the operating system boot. However, it is likely the team will try to boot the main software stack at the earliest opportunity. Because of the prior testing on virtual platforms, it should work first time.

9.2.1 Engineering Sample Testing

The first devices received back from a foundry are called **engineering samples**. One or two wafers are produced, yielding up to a hundred devices. These are carefully allocated to various evaluation teams or to special-relationship customers. Fewer are available from a **multi-project wafer (MPW)** run (Section 8.9.1), since the wafer has a mix of well-studied calibration devices and early designs from various companies. Devices are installed on a custom **evaluation board**, which often holds the SoC in a **zero-insertion-force socket** that enables one chip to be swapped with another. Even though a SoC may, typically, be used with only a subset of its peripheral capabilities deployed, an evaluation board supports every option. It also instruments the power supplies and may provide a bread-boarding area onto which additional application-specific hardware can be soldered. Prototypes of the flagship target product, such as a new model of a cell phone, could also be ready for the SoC to be installed. These are termed **alpha prototypes**. They may be conservatively engineered but still require modification before the system works. Modifications may need to be made to the power-supply distribution, DRAM wiring, resistor values or any other respect. These modifications are folded into the next mini-production run, which produces **beta prototypes**. A beta prototype should be very close in design to the final product. These units can be photographed for advertising and loaned to trade journals for pre-release reviews.

A SoC is tested on an evaluation board at various temperatures, power supply voltages and clock frequencies. Energy use and margins are measured at each operating point for voltage and temperature. Multiple samples are checked to assess process variation, the first component of PVT (Section 8.4.4), although if all the samples came from just one or two wafers, the process variation will not be as wide as in general production. Nonetheless, the measurements can be correlated against wafer process parameters measured at the foundry. Not all these data are necessarily released to the customer however.

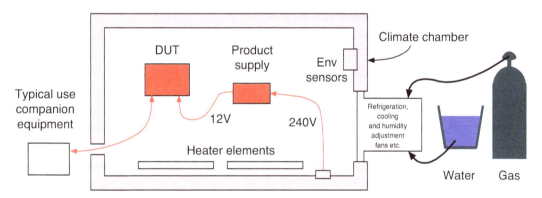

Figure 9.1 Environmental testing under various temperature and humidity conditions in a climate-controlled chamber.

Environmental testing is carried out in a climatic test chamber. Devices often use external mains power supplies. These must be tested with the device under test (DUT). Figure 9.1 shows a typical setup. It is assumed that the companion equipment of a typical use case is tested separately, and so does not have to go inside the chamber. Either the evaluation board or the prototype product are tested. A test chamber contains heater elements and is also connected to a cylinder of liquefied gas (e.g. CO_2), so that the temperature is adjustable (e.g. from $-40°$ C to $+100°$ C). A water supply allows the humidity to be tested up to close to 95 per cent, simulating rainforest conditions. Note that suddenly opening the chamber when it contains very cold air can cause a short shower in the surrounding laboratory!

There may be various on-SoC analogue front ends (AFEs) (Section 2.7.6), such as audio inputs and network transceivers. Their performance is characterised through detailed testing of the sensitivity of the interfaces at different supply voltages and operating temperatures. The DUT may have phase-locked loops (PLLs) (Section 4.9.5) that must correctly acquire incoming frequencies over a specified range. Many such components have a hybrid digital/analogue implementation, requiring coefficients to be loaded that can be correctly determined only on real silicon.

A prototype must be tested for **electromagnetic compatibility (EMC)** and electrical safety and meet various certification standards before it can be marketed. In Europe, the vendor can self-certify their product and then add the **CE mark**. EMC testing involves **electrostatic discharge (ESD)** testing and also measuring its **electromagnetic emissions** and susceptibility to radio waves.

A standard **human body model** consists of a 100-pF capacitor charged to 6000 V in series with a 1.5 kΩ resistor. Such voltages can easily be generated by walking over a dry nylon carpet when wearing certain types of shoes. A device must not be permanently damaged by such discharges and preferably, it should continue to work without interruption. Thus, ESD testing (Section 4.8.1) involves discharging the capacitor into the equipment at places where it is likely to be touched in real use. These include metal parts of the casing and connector pins. This is done with a precharged cable that is disconnected at the other end.

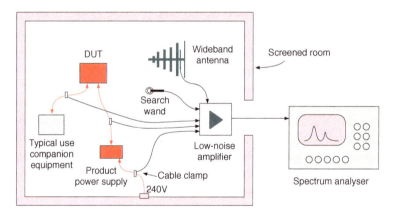

Figure 9.2 EMC testing of radio-frequency interference.

The emissions and susceptibility of a DUT are assessed in an electrically screened chamber or room. Figure 9.2 illustrates the typical setup for emissions testing. Most equipment is designed and tested against the American **Federal Communications Commission (FCC) class B** standard. Companion equipment for typical use cases must be present and included in the test and hence, inside the chamber. For instance, if a device is typically plugged into a laptop using USB, the laptop must be present. **Radiated emissions** are picked up by a wideband directional antenna, which must be pointed at the equipment from a prescribed distance. **Conducted emissions** that pass down the equipment and supply cables are measured with transformers (just a few turns of wire) that are wrapped around the cables. Emission hot spots can be located with a handheld search coil. The signals are amplified and fed to a spectrum analyser. All peaks must be below the standard test levels.

Passing the FCC standard can be a challenge for SoC-based equipment. A clock frequency of 1 GHz means that internal nets are able to generate any frequency within most of the standard radio bands, including HF, VHF and UHF. Harmonics can also easily be generated, spanning down to microwave frequencies. Much of the mitigation is by changing the PCB layout, such as the structure of the ground planes and the position of the connectors. However, within the SoC, various techniques can help reduce electromagnetic emissions, such as using a spread spectrum, which applies frequency modulation to the clocks. An idle system refreshing DRAM also tends to produce pronounced emissions. Again, these can be lightly randomised with a small **pseudorandom binary sequence (PRBS)** generator (Section 3.8), which applies small variations to the refresh interval. These techniques do not actually reduce the emissions, but spread the energy out so that the level at each frequency does not exceed the threshold in the relevant standard. Another solution is to use a metal case or screening boxes on the PCB. These can also isolate delicate receiving AFEs from locally generated noise.

9.3 Success or Failure?

If a SoC does not work, generally, just one subsystem or function is not right. Hopefully, the fault is not in a key component and does not prevent everything from working, as that would be a fault fatal. Prototypes can be shipped with the troublesome feature disabled. Alternatively, a software workaround can be implemented, which may compromise something else, such as battery life or the simultaneous use of two features. At best, the feature can be removed from the product specification and held over to the next version. At worst, a **respin** is needed. As discussed in Section 8.10, a complete respin can sometimes be mitigated by an **engineering change order (ECO)** for a small modification, so that a new batch of engineering samples can be received within a month.

Many SoCs are first fabricated using a **multi-design shuttle**. Ten or so wafers, each containing designs for several different chips, are fabricated together. Every process step may not have been optimised for the devices, but the resulting variation may be characterised well and can be accounted for when the test results are analysed. Such shuttles can be run, say, once a week in a foundry, both to provide early engineering samples to customers and for internal experiments and quality control by the foundry owners.

Chip designers are normally reticent in owning up to design errors that have cost their company thousands or sometimes millions of pounds, especially if a workaround has hidden the error from the customer. Problems can arise from both design mistakes at the front end of the flow and from design process failures in the back end. Here are a few cases from the authors' personal experiences:

- **Signal polarity:** On one device, an output pad was used for two purposes, depending on which of two data serialisers was enabled. The output from the two serialisers was combined with a simple

OR gate at the top level of the module hierarchy and used to drive the pad. This would have worked fine, except that one of the serialisers produced a logic one when idle. This meant that the output from the other serialiser, when in use, was masked by the ORing with a constant true logic value. A software workaround was devised. The one-producing serialiser was enabled at all times, but made to transmit a constant zero when not needed. This involved setting it to a very slow baud rate. Moreover, a periodic timer-triggered daemon stored a few PIO registers every 100 ms, so that the serial data output never changed from zero. The workaround increased the CPU load on one of the cores by a negligible percentage. Less than a milliwatt of electricity was wasted due to a small subsystem being turned on instead of being in sleep mode.

- **Excessive glitch energy**: An AES encryption accelerator (Section 6.4.3) contained, as would be expected, a large number of high-speed XOR gates. The dynamic power modelling was based on a toggle rate (Section 4.6.2) measured from an unannotated simulation in which every path had the same delay. In the real silicon, the net delays varied considerably from each other, due to net length variations. This resulted in a large ratio of glitches to genuine transitions. Because of the high-performance gates, the resulting dynamic energy use was several times greater than modelled and resulted in excessive localised heating. Fortunately, the AES unit had another design error: the data inputs to the XOR gate networks were always active, whereas this input needed to change only while the AES computations were being made. A minor change to the clock gating for the subsystem enabled the input data to be held stable when not in use. This was fixed with an A1 ECO (Section 8.10).

- **Faulty coprocessor or instruction**: Sometimes a single instruction in a custom ISA extension (Section 6.4.1) does not work. In these cases, the instruction can be avoided and replaced with slower code from the core instruction set. This may not hit the design target for energy or performance (or both), but it is possible that something else can be sacrificed, such as the data compression ratio or battery life.

- **AFE sensitivity**: Analogue electronics has its own set of challenges, including tolerance to noise and sensitivity. On one networking project, an **AFE** (Section 2.7.6) for a cable transmission system had to compensate for the skin effect in copper cables (Section 3.8), in which higher frequencies are attenuated far more than lower frequencies. If longer cables are detected, a common solution is to increase the high-frequency gain at the receiver. On one device, the integrated AFE overused this additional gain for shorter cables, resulting in data transmission errors. The solution was made at the PCB level. It would have been possible to add an external AFE chip to the circuit board for each input channel, but it was sufficient to add a passive RC network to build out all cables, with the effect that shorter cables behaved more like long ones but without severely sacrificing performance for genuine longer cable runs. The cost of this was a few pence worth of additional PCB area and passive components.

- **ROM table error**: Intel famously made quite a grave error by shipping chips with a blank mask-programmed ROM that should have contained digits beyond the fifth significant figure in the result of certain floating-point divide operations. Like many complex chips, the silicon contained a revision identifier register, allowing the software to determine readily whether it was running on a faulty chip. It was also easy to run a test division and check what answer was returned. Hence, a software workaround was potentially feasible for all users who were concerned about the error and could recompile their code. This was a costly processor chip, so nearly all devices were socketed and could be replaced with an alternative version of the device that did not have the bug. However, typically, this chip may have been more expensive than all the other components on the PCB put together. Intel offered a free replacement service for any customer who asked for it. Overall, it was a very costly mistake for the company, especially reputationally.

When the device is demonstrably working, scheduled orders for chips will be placed with a foundry. Product manufacturing is often done in a country where the cost of the combined import and export duties is the lowest. This tends to be in the Far East. Of course, many other things, such as cardboard shipping boxes, user manuals, distributors, field repair agents, advertising and so on have to be available too.

Glossary of Abbreviations

A16D8
Address Bus 16 Bits and Data Bus 8 Bits Wide
Address and data specifications for a computer architecture

ABD
Assertion-based Design
A design methodology in which formal statements are included at all steps of the design process

ACE
AXI Coherency Extensions
Protocol additions for cache management and consistency

ACL2
Applicative Common LISP
A formal proof tool

ACM
Association of Computer Machinery
An American trade body

ADC
Analogue-to-digital Convertor
A digitising device that generates a PCM stream from a time-varying voltage

ADSL
Asymmetric Digital Subscriber Line
A form of broadband access using POTS telephone cables

AES
Advanced Encryption Standard
A method of combining blocks of data with a key to get a similar-sized encrypted block

AFE
Analogue Front End
The part of a communications terminal or interface that is not digital and which connects to the physical media

AHB
AMBA High-performance Bus
A SoC interconnect standard from Arm, widely used in the 1990's

ALU
Arithmetic and Logic Unit
A combinational circuit that can perform addition, subtraction and various bitwise logical operations such as AND, OR and XOR

AMBA
Advanced Micro-controller Bus Architecture
A family of SoC interconnect protocols from Arm

| AMS | Analogue and Mixed Signal |
| | Extensions to a digital logic simulator for handling voltage, current and similar analogue quantities |

| AOI | AND-OR-INVERT |
| | A logic function that is efficiently implemented in CMOS and hence, commonly used |

| APB | AMBA Peripheral Bus |
| | A simple and low-performance interconnect standard in the AMBA family |

| API | Application Program Interface |
| | A protocol or standard, typically between a loaded program and the resident operating system, for service access |

| ARQ | Automatic Repeat Request |
| | A message sent in a transport protocol to request that data be sent again |

| ASCII | American Standard Code for Information Interchange |
| | The predominant character encoding used in computers post 1965 |

| ASIC | Application-specific Integrated Circuit |
| | A chip made for a specific application |

| ASSP | Application-specific Standard Part |
| | An ASIC that is widely sold to other equipment manufacturers |

| ATAPI | ATA Packet Interface |
| | A protocol, defined over the original low-level Western Digital register interface for hard disk drives, that conveys a generic, packet-based protocol |

| AVI | Audio Video Interleave |
| | A file format used in early digital cameras that includes JPEG frames and audio |

| AWS | Amazon Web Services |
| | A major cloud computing provider |

| AXI | Advanced eXtensible Interface |
| | An interconnect protocol from Arm |

| BBC | British Broadcasting Corporation |
| | The world's oldest radio and television broadcaster |

| BDD | Binary Decision Diagram |
| | A compact representation of a truth table |

BEOL	Back End-of-Line Variation	
	Changes in the upper layer chip fabrication steps that mostly effect wiring capacitance	
BFM	Bus Functional Model	
	A high-level model of a subsystem with sufficient detail for embedded software to run unaffected	
BIOS	Basic Input/Output System	
	A set of low-level device drivers and bootstrapping code stored in ROM	
BIST	Built-in Self-test	
	Additional hardware for running a test sequence	
BoM	Bill of Materials	
	List of parts needed to assemble a product	
BRAM	Block RAM	
	Blocks of memory found in most FPGA fabrics	
BSI	Battery State Indication	
	A set of sense functions on a battery pack	
BSP	Bulk Synchronous Processing	
	A reference paradigm for parallel computing	
BSV	Bluspec Verilog	
	An HDL with automatic handshaking and scheduling	
BVCI	Basic Virtual Component Interface	
	A split-port protocol from the Open Core Connect (OCP) family	
BWT	Burrows–Wheeler Transform	
	An invertible transformation of a block of text that makes it readily compressible with run-length encoding	
CACTI	Cache Access Tool	
	A delay and energy performance predictor tool for memory and caches	
CAD	Computer-aided Design	
	The generic name for the computerised design tools or processes	
CAE	Computer-aided Engineering	
	See CAD	

| **CAN** | Car-area Network |
| | The predominant control bus used in automotive applications |

| **CAP** | Capability-based Computer |
| | A famous implementation of a hardware protection architecture |

| **CAS** | Column Address Strobe |
| | The input to a DRAM that indicates that the column part of the address is on the multiplexed address bus |

| **CAT5** | Category 5 Twisted-pair Cable |
| | A high-quality in-building wiring standard, using four twisted pairs with 8-pole RJ45 connectors |

| **CBFC** | Credit-based Flow Control |
| | Matching sending and receiving data rates when a source is granted tokens to send FLITs |

| **CBRI** | Clock Domain-crossing Bridge |
| | A bus bridge where each side uses a different clock |

| **CCI** | Coherent Crossbar Interconnect |
| | A wiring generator tool made by Arm |

| **CCIX** | Cache-coherent Interconnect for Accelerators |
| | An interconnect standard for hardware acceleration |

| **CCS** | Concurrent Current Source |
| | A technique for net delay modelling that includes crosstalk effects |

| **CDN** | Clock Delivery Network |
| | The wiring structure used to deliver the clock signal with low skew within a clock domain. |

| **CFR** | Cambridge Fast Ring |

| **CHI** | Coherent Hub Interface |
| | An AMBA protocol for NoC links and ports |

| **CISC** | Complex Instruction Set Computer/Computing |
| | A processor ISA that contains a large number of (variable length) instructions, such as Intel X86 |

| **CLB** | Configurable Logic Block |
| | Components in an FPGA fabric that implement everyday digital logic |

CMN   Coherent Mesh Generator
          An interconnect synthesis tool from Arm

CMO   Cache Management Operation
          A command issued on the interconnect to manage caches, such as the eviction
          of a specified line or a full flush

CMOS   Complementary Oxide of Silicon
          The predominant form of digital logic used in integrated circuits

CMP   Chip Multiprocessor
          A single chip containing multiple processors and associated caches

CNF   Conjunctive Normal Form
          A rearrangement of a Boolean expression into a product of clauses; it is the
          opposite of the sum-of-products form

CNN   Convolutional Neural Network
          A form of AI inference engine used in deep learning, based on multiplication of
          a data vector with static coefficients determined in training

COI   Cone of Influence
          The pattern of cause and effect in which the behaviour of a single point fans
          out to influence several others, which in turn, fan out further

CPI   Clock Cycles per Instruction
          The reciprocal of IPC

CPLD   Complex Programmable Logic Device
          A fast field-programmable chip with low pin-to-pin delay

CPU   Central Processing Unit
          A computer without memory or peripherals, also known as a processor

CRC   Cyclic Redundancy Check
          A sequence of check digits computed using polynomial arithmetic in Galois
          field 2, which can be simply implemented using shift registers and XOR gates

CRV   Constrained Random Verification
          Component testing in which a random stimulus is applied, but sequences
          outside specified constraints are not used

CSMA   Carrier-sense Multiple Access
          A form of media access control (MAC) to a shared resource, such as early
          Ethernet implementations, that reduces the frequency of conflicts between
          simultaneous transmitters

CSP	Communicating Sequential Processes A well-known model of computation from Tony Hoare [1]
CTI	Cross-trigger Interface A test/debug component that helps correlate event sources from different parts of a SoC
CTOR	Constructor A common abbreviation in OO programming for the method that initialises the fields of a new object
CTOV	C-to-Verilog A compiler tool that converts a C program into RTL
CUDA	Compute Unified Device Architecture A reference model and API for synchronising application accelerators
CXL	Compute Express Link An interconnect standard for hardware acceleration
DAC	Digital-to-Analogue Convertor A component that accepts a binary number and produces a voltage in proportion to its value
DAP	Debug Access Port The principal point of attachment between a SoC and an external debugger
DBMS	Database Management System The software that looks after a database, maintaining consistency and indices
DCT	Discrete Cosine Transform A variant of the Fourier transform for a fixed-length sequence or tile of real-valued data
DDC	Display Data Channel A side channel for flat-screen displays that enables a controller to interrogate their resolution and other capabilities
DDR	Double Data-rate A technique used for the data connections to a DRAM chip where data is transferred on both clock edges
DEF	Design Exchange Format The complete physical view of a cell used in the tapeout
DFF	D-type Flip-flop

A synchronous logic element that is edge triggered and stores 1 bit of data

DFFR	A DFF with a reset input
DfT	Design for Testability Adding extra components to a system to make testing easier
DHCP	Dynamic Host Configuration Protocol A means for an Internet-connected device to obtain a suitable IP address
DIL	Dual-in-Line An IC packaging technology with two parallel rows of pins
DIMM	Dual-in-Line Memory Module A number of DRAM chips arranged on a small board to obtain sufficient data bus width and using a double-sided edge connector (two sides have different functions)
DMA	Direct Memory Access A data transfer technique where data moves to/from a peripheral with the host processor not directly involved
DMC	Dynamic Memory Controller The device that sequences operations on a DRAM channel
DMI	Direct Memory Interface A fast path connection between a modelled CPU and its memory model in an ESL platform
DPA	Differential Power Analysis A technique for reverse engineering a device based on measuring minute differences in the supply current as different sequences are run
DRAM	Dynamic Random-access Memory The predominant form of primary storage in modern computer devices; the data are held in minute capacitors that require periodic refreshing to prevent information from leaking away
DRC	Design Rule Check A validation step in which a feature is compared against the rules prescribing that feature, such as the maximum fanout for a gate

DSE	Design Space Exploration
	The process of testing various alternative designs, all of which work, but some of which are better than others under various metrics (cost, energy, performance etc.)
DSL	Domain-specific Language
	In general use, a sub-language or set of constructs inside a general programming language
DSP	Digital Signal Processing
	Processing of analogue signals in the digital domain, or, in FPGAs, a multiply-accumulate block
DUT	Device Under Test
	The part of a design that is being tested
DVD	Digital Versatile Disc
	A plastic disc with embedded metallic layer containing digital information, read by laser beam
DVFS	Dynamic Voltage and Frequency Scaling
	A power control technique that involves changing the power supply voltage and the clock frequency together
DVI	Digital Visual Interface
	A digital interconnect standard between a tuner, DVD player or computer and a display screen
EA-ROM	Electrically Alterable Read-only Memory
	A ROM device whose content can be changed using electricity
ECAD	Electronic Computer Aided Design
	See EDA
ECC	Error-correcting Code
	Check digits that are added to a block of data that enable a small number of transmission errors to be corrected
ECL	Emitter-coupled Logic
	A structure for logic circuits made from bipolar transistors that is non-saturating and so fast, but which uses more power than other circuits
ECO	Engineering Change Order
	An approved request for a change to a design, typically to correct a bug or add a feature

ECSM Effective Current Source Model
A detailed characterisation technique for standard cells

EDA Electronic Design Automation
CAD tools for designing electronic systems such as integrated circuits and printed circuit boards

EDS Event-driven Simulation
Also known as discrete-event simulation. A simulation technique in which time advances only when something changes, as opposed to advancing by a prescribed time step

EEPROM Electrically Erasable Read-only Memory
A form of non-volatile memory, such as flash; both setting bits and clearing blocks are possible using electricity

EIS An End in Itself
A term denoting that an operation must be performed, even if it has no visible use

ELN Electrical Linear Networks
SystemC library with a set of standard electrical components

EMC Electromagnetic Compatibility
A broad term for the interference suffered by a device due to surrounding devices

EMU Event-monitoring Unit

EPROM Erasable Programmable, Read-only Memory
A form of non-volatile memory where bits may be set electronically, but erasure requires another mechanism

ESD Electrostatic Discharge
A harmful impulse current applied to a device, normally arising from lightning or from static electricity producing by shoes rubbing on a carpet

ESL Electronic System Level
A high-level modelling technique capable of faithfully executing embedded software

ETA Estimated Time of Arrival

FAW Frame-alignment Word
A synchronisation pattern in a serial bit stream to delimit word or packet boundaries

FCC	Federal Communications Commission
	An American government agency that regulates radio transmissions
FDTD	Finite-difference, Time Domain Simulation
	A simulation technique where the differences predicted in state variables are added to the state variables to generate the next state
FEC	Forward Error Correction
	An approach to error resilience that relies on always adding ECC digits at the source
FEOL	Front End-of-Line Variation
	Changes in the lower layer chip fabrication steps that mostly effect transistor performance
FET	Field-effect Transistor
	A transistor that uses electrostatic effects (no current flows in the control electrode, the gate)
FFT	Fast Fourier Transform
	An efficient implementation of the discrete Fourier transform
FIB	Focused Ion Beam
	A vacuum device, similar to an electron microscope; metallic atoms in an electron beam are deposited as conductors or else used to cut existing tracks on a chip
FIFO	First-in, First out
	A queue from which items are removed in the order they were inserted
FinFET	Fin Field-effect Transistor
	A FET with a fin
FIQ	Fast Interrupt
	An Arm-specific term where interrupts are serviced using a dedicated (partial) register file
FLIT	Flow-control Element
	A unit of transfer over the interconnect that is subject to flow control
FLOPS	Floating Point Operations per Second
	A measure of computing performance
FO4	Fanout of Four
	A circuit structure commonly used for characterising a silicon process node

FPGA	Field-programmable Gate Array A large piece of silicon that can be electronically programmed to take on the functions of a smaller piece of silicon
FPU	Floating-point Unit A coprocessor optimised for numeric processing, generally using the IEEE floating-point standard
FSM	Finite-state Machine A standard automaton abstraction in which precisely one of several possible states is active at any one time
FU	Functional Unit A generic term for a circuit that performs a prescribed function, such as an adder
GBA	Graph-based Analysis A simple form of static timing analysis where the latest arrival at any node is all that is considered
GDS-II	Graphical Database System A vector graphics format used as the input to mask-making
GIC	Generic Interrupt Controller A device for aggregating and distributing interrupts from multiple sources to multiple CPUs
GND	Ground Rail The zero-volt reference supply rail in a digital logic system
GNU	GNU not Unix A large body of free software that includes Linux
GOPS	Giga-operations per Second A processing rate with multiplier 10^9
GPIO	General-purpose Input/Output A non-dedicated input or output pin on a SoC or microcontroller
GPS	Global Positioning System An array of orbiting satellites and associated radio signals that allow a terminal to find its geolocation, altitude and the current time of day
GPU	Graphical Processing Unit Originally a coprocessor optimised for video operations, such as 3-D rendering and textured shading, but now used as a general-purpose processing unit

GSM	Global System for Mobile Communications A European standard for cell phones, now adopted in much of the world
GUI	Graphical User Interface Unlike a command-line interface, a GUI uses a mouse and windows
HAL	Hardware Abstraction Layer A body of low-level software that gives a uniform higher-level interface over many variants of a hardware platform
HBM	High Bandwidth Memory A die-stacked DRAM memory system, similar to HMC
HCL	Hardware Construction Language A hardware design language used to generate circuit structures using various iterating constructs
HDL	Hardware Description Language A language used to describe a circuit diagram at some level of abstraction
HDMI	High-definition Multimedia Interface A variation of DVI; both carry digital video to a display device
HKMG	High-K Metal Gate A fabrication node where the gate is made of metal and the insulating layer material had increased dielectric constant
HLL	High-level Language A programming language that is portable over various machine architectures and commonly block structured, such as C++ or Java
HLS	High-level Synthesis An approach to generating hardware from software, generally where the assignment of data to RAMs and work to clock cycles is automated and optimised
HMC	Hybrid Memory Cube A die-stacked DRAM memory system, similar to HBM
HoL	Head of Line In the USA, a queue is a called a line. The head-of-line problem arises when a customer who is not at the front of a shared-resource queue wants to use a resource that is free, but cannot get to it since the customer at the front of the queue is waiting for a different resource that is currently busy

HTML	Hypertext Markup Language The script used to describe web pages
H/W	Hardware
IBM	International Business Machines A pioneering computer company
IC	Integrated Circuit
ICI	inter-core/CPU Interrupt An interrupt generated by one CPU to notify another that something is ready to be inspected
IDCT	Inverse Discrete Cosine Transform The inverse of DCT
IDE	Integrated Drive Electronics An interface between a computer and a disk drive; the disk controller is on the far side of the interface (i.e. integrated with the drive)
IDM	Integrated Device Manufacturer A company that both designs and fabs chips, rather than using an outsourced foundry
IEEE	Institute of Electrical and Electronic Engineers An American association that defines standards and sponsors conferences and many other professional activities
II	Initiation Interval The minimum number of clock cycles between an FU accepting one argument and the next
ILP	Instruction-level Parallelism Executing two or more instructions simultaneously since none depends on the result of any other
IOB	Input/output Block A programmable pad for making external connection to an FPGA
IOMMU	Input/Output Memory Management Unit A virtual to physical address translator that provides memory protection and enables DMA devices to use virtual addresses
IoT	Internet of Things

IP block	intellectual Property Block The design for a component to be placed on a SoC, typically licensed from another company
IPC	instructions per Clock Cycle For a super-scalar processor, the average number of instructions executed per clock cycle
IrDA	Infrared Data Association An industry body that develops standards for data exchange using infrared light between adjacent portable computing objects
IRQ	interrupt Request A signal from an external device to a CPU requesting an interrupt
ISA	Instruction Set Architecture The name for the set of instructions executed by a particular processor family
ISCA	International Symposium on Computer Architecture An annual conference at which new developments in computer architecture are presented
ISO	International Standards Office A standards publisher
ISR	Interrupt Service Routine The body of code executed by a CPU in response to an interrupt, also known as an interrupt handler
ISS	Instruction Set Simulator An interpreter for machine code, also known as as an emulator
ISTO	Industry Standards and Technology Organisation A division of the IEEE
ITRS	International Technology Roadmap for Semiconductors A trade body that defines expectations of VLSI progress
JEDEC	Joint Electron Device Engineering Council A trade body that defines standards for memory chips, device packages, etc.
JIT	Just in Time A compilation technique in which code is converted to machine code only if it is used a lot

JPEG   Joint Photographic Experts Group
A trade body that defined the predominant compressed file format for still images

JTAG   Joint Test Action Group
A standard serial data port for debug access and PROM programming

LAN   Local-area Network
A shared-medium computer network covering a building or floor of a large building

LBIST   Logic Built-in Self-test
A self-test mechanism for miscellaneous logic circuits (as opposed to standard functions such as ALUs and RAMs)

LCD   Liquid-crystal Display
A low-energy display technology where regions of a glass panel change in opacity owing to electrostatic effects arising from (AC) voltages applied to transparent conductors

LCRDV   Link Credit Valid
The net in the reverse direction of a credit-controlled link that returns credit to the originator

LEC   Logical Equivalence Checking
The process of checking whether two combinational circuits implement the same logic function

LED   Light-emitting Diode
An efficient and commonly used semiconductor device that converts electricity to light of a pure colour

LEF   Library Exchange Format
The standard description language for standard semi-custom cells

LIFO   Last-in, First-out
A queuing discipline that is the same as a push-down stack

LINQ   Language Integrated Query
A Microsoft standard for connecting the .net runtime to a database query manager

LISP   List Processing Language
An old functional programming language with very simple syntax

LPF Low-pass Filter
A filter that allows DC and all frequencies below a certain cutoff frequency to pass without attenuation

LRU Least-recently Used
A replacement policy for caches that selects the entry that has not been used for the longest amount of time

LSF Linear Signal Flow
A library of AMS modelling components

LSI Large-scale Integration
A term to describe silicon chips containing more than a few hundred components

LTAB Liberty Technical Advisory Board
A committee responsible for new editions of the Liberty cell definition language

LUT Lookup Table
A ROM or RAM containing fixed data and, for an FPGA, implementing an arbitrary logic function with five or six inputs

LVDS Low-voltage Differential Signalling
A way to send digital data that avoids common-mode noise pick-up by using the voltage difference between two wires

LVF Liberty Variation Format
Interpolation coefficients for a detailed model of delay

MAC Media Access Control/Controller
A protocol that controls when data are transmitted on a shared channel

MBIST Memory Built-in Self-test
Additional logic that performs automatic tests on an SRAM macro

MCM Multi-chip Module
A package containing more than one piece of silicon, interconnected with an interposer or through-silicon vias

MESI Modified/Exclusive/Shared/Invalid
A four-state cache-consistency protocol

MIPS (1) Million Instructions per Second
A unit used to measure the processing rate of a CPU

MIPS (2)	A chip manufacturer
MMIO	Memory-mapped Input and Output A style of peripheral operation in which device registers are mapped into the main memory map so they may be accessed with everyday load and store instructions
MMMC	Multi-mode Multi-corner Analysis A verification procedure that explores a predefined list of combinations of variations
MMU	Memory Management Unit A device that converts a virtual address to a physical address for virtual memory system
MOESI	Modified/Owned/Exclusive/Shared/Invalid An enhanced MESI cache-consistency protocol
MOS	Metal Oxide of Silicon A field-effect transistor with an insulated gate (instead of a junction FET that uses a reverse-biased diode)
MOSFET	Metal Oxide of Silicon Field-effect Transistor A transistor that uses an insulator between the gate and the channel; the predominant form of transistor used in SoCs
MP3	Motion Picture Experts Group Audio Layer Level 3 A commonly used, psycho-acoustic audio compression technology and file format
MPEG	Motion Picture Experts Group A family of video compression standards that exploit inter-frame motion and redundancy
MPSoC	Multiprocessor System-on-Chip
MPU (1)	Memory Protection Unit
MPU (2)	Microprocessor
MPW	Multi-project Wafer A prototyping approach in which a wafer carries more than one chip design

MSI	Message-signalled Interrupts Interrupts sent as transactions over the interconnect rather than being conveyed using a dedicated net
NDP	Near-data Processing Processing data near where the data are stored instead of moving them to a central processor
NFET	N-channel Field-effect Transistor A semiconductor device that conducts when there is a positive potential between the gate and substrate
NIC	Network Interface Card A communication port, with associated MAC, buffers and DMA, typically used to connect a device to a LAN
NLDM	Non-linear Delay Model
NMOS	N-channel Metal-oxide Semiconductor A pre-CMOS technology that used only N-channel FETs with the pull-up effected by a weakly conducting transistor
NoC	Metwork-on-Chip
NOP	No-operation An instruction that does not do anything; it just fills space
NRE	Non-recurring Expenses The tooling expenses related to chip development
NRZI	Non-return to Zero, Invert on Ones A simple binary modulation scheme were a one is coded as a change of state
NSF	Next-state Function For a finite-state machine, the function that determines the new state based on the current state and external inputs
NUMA	Non-uniform Memory Access A computer system where different regions of memory have different access times
NVP	Number of Violating Paths The number of paths in a verification procedure that are unsatisfactory (not meeting timing or not routed etc.)

OCIP	Open Core Interconnect Protocol An open-source interconnect standard
OCP	Open Core Connect An open-source SoC bus standard
OCV	On-chip Variation The variation of parameters from one chip to another or across a large chip
OEM	Other/Original Equipment Manufacturer A company elsewhere in the supply chain, typically the provider of parts to be included or re-badged
O/S	Operating System
OSCI	Open SystemC Initiative A trade body, prior to Accellera, that promoted SystemC
OVM	Open Verification Methodology A standard for coding test programs
PAL	Programmable Array Logic A fast, field-programmable logic device containing up to 20 flip-flops
PASTA	Poisson Arrivals See Time Averages A fact/theorem about exponentially arriving traffic, which essentially samples a system at random intervals
PBA	Path-based Analysis A detailed approach to static timing analysis that consides every possible path from end to end
PC (1)	Personal Computer
PC (2)	Program Counter
PC (3)	Protocol Checker
PCB	Printed-circuit Board A multi-layer fibreglass board containing layers of copper wiring with components soldered to the top and bottom
PCDC	Power and/or Clock Domain Convertor A bus bridge that accommodates differences in clocking or power on each side

PCIe   Peripheral Component Interconnect Express
A standard for a board-level interconnect with serial channels

PCM   Pulse Code Modulation
A sampled analogue signal represented as a stream of digital binary numbers

PDN   Power Delivery Network
On-chip regulators, power gates and supply wiring that deliver electricity to the active components

PE   Processing Element

PFET   P-channel Field-effect Transistor
A semiconductor device that conducts when the gate is at a lower potential than the substrate (or N-well)

PHY   Physical Layer
The wire, fibre or antenna used to convey signals in a computer network and the associated amplifiers and transformers

PIO   Programmed Input/Output
A form of input or output in which a processor changes the value of wires (typically GPIO) by storing values to registers or reads back their values with a load instruction

PKI   Public-key Infrastructure
A form of digital signature or cryptographic authentication. Data can be generated only with a privately held secret number, but can be checked using a widely available public key that is known to belong to the signatory

PL   Programmable Logic

PLD   Programmable Logic Device
A field-programmable device that can take on an application-specific function (CPLD, PAL or FPGA)

PLI   Programming Language Interface
A means for plugging arbitrary C/C++ code into an RTL simulator and a library of standard functions for printing, file operations and so on

PLL   Phase-locked Loop
A common structure used for generating a stable clock from a clock of a different frequency or that is jittered

PMIO   Port-mapped Input and Output
The opposite of PIO; mostly found on early computers that had limited addressable space for primary storage

PMU
Performance Management Unit
A subsystem containing counters for various events, such as instruction fetches and cache misses

POD
Plain Old Data
Simple built-in data types in the C and C++ languages, and structs of them, which can be copied with `memcopy` and so on

PoDP
Point of Deep Persistence
The place to which a write must be made before it can be guaranteed to survive a power failure or reboot

POTS
Plain Old Telephone Service
The subscriber connection standard for telephones used throughout the 20th century

PPA
Power, Performance and Area
The three main metrics for the quality of a design in silicon

PRAM
Parallel Random-access Machine
A reference model (or set of similar models) for parallel computing

PRBS
Pseudorandom Binary Sequence
A series of random-looking bits generated by a deterministic shift register and XOR gate structure

PRD
Product Requirements Document
A plain English description of targets and desirable features for a new design

PROM
Programmable Read-only Memory
A form of non-volatile memory in which bits can be set electronically, but with no mechanism to clear them

PS2
A keyboard/mouse port found on many personal computers

PSL
Property Specification Language
An assertion language based on temporal logic for formally specifying hardware

PSU
Power Supply Unit
A circuit that converts mains or battery voltages to stable regulated voltages needed by silicon circuitry

PUF   Physically Unclonable Function
A hardware circuit designed with random behaviour that cannot be
reproduced on any other chip of the same design

PV   Programmer's View

PVT   Process, Voltage and Temperature
The three main sources of performance variation between chip instances for a
nominally identical design

PWL   Piecewise Linear Source
A waveform generator whose output comprises a series of straight lines

PWM   Pulse-width Modulation
A bit stream where the density of ones, and hence the average voltage, is
constrained by an input parameter that varies slowly

QoS   Quality of Service
A set of parameters for mean and peak delay and throughput for traffic in a
packet-switched system

QPI   Quick Path Interconnect
A coherent interface protocol for caches and accelerator interconnection

RAM   Random-access Memory
Memory with the same access delay to every location

RAPL   Running Average Power Limit
An Intel technology that monitors temperature and energy use in various
subsystems and reduces the clock frequency if overheating is detected

RAS   Row Address Strobe
The input to a DRAM that indicates that the row part of the address is on the
multiplexed address bus

RaW   Read After Write

RF   Radio Frequency

RFI   Radio-frequency Interference
Radio waves emitted by a device arising from inadequate shielding or
conductor routing

RGB   Red, Green and Blue
The three primary colours used in most colour display devices

RISC   Reduced Instruction Set Computer/Computing
              An ISA with only commonly used instructions, all of which are one word long

rms   Root-mean Squared

ROM   Read-only Memory
              A non-volatile memory whose content is immutable or seldom changed

RSA   Rivest, Shamir and Adleman
              A public-key authentication system developed by these three gentlemen

RS   Reset-set

RTC   Real-time Clock
              A subsystem, typically permanently powered up using a small battery,
              containing an oscillator and counters; it keeps track of the time and date

RTL   Register Transfer Language
              In general, a way to express the new value of a register on the next clock cycle,
              but mainly used to refer to Verilog and VHLD, which have additional language
              constructs

RTT   Round-trip Time
              The minimum interval between sending a message and receiving a response
              due to channel delays

SAIF   Switching Activity Interchange Format

SAT   Boolean Satisfiability Problem
              A canonical search problem for which there are many effective solver tools;
              these find values for Boolean variables that make an expression hold

SATA   Serial ATAPI
              A serial implementation of the IDE/ATA interface with 23 or so parallel wires,
              including a 16-bit data bus

SCSI   Small Computer System Interface
              A protocol between a computer and disk drive controller, and also the physical
              interface for conveying the protocol

SCU   Snoop Control Unit
              A block that monitors updates to a collection of caches

SDC   Synopsys Design Constraint
              A file format used for timing annotations and directives for static timing
              analysis

SDK	Software Development Kit A set of library files, example designs and compilation scripts to seed software builds for a new platform
SEC	Sequential Equivalence Checking A verification step that checks whether two implementations of an FSM have the same (observable) behaviour
SERDES	Serialiser/Deserialiser A component that sends and receives parallel data words over a serial data channel
SERES	Sugar Extended Regular Expressions A format for describing patterns in a sequence of events
SEU	Single-event Upset A one-off data error in a digital circuit that occurs randomly and is most unlikely to happen again
SEV	Signal Event An Arm instruction for low-level communication
SHA	Secure Hash An algorithm that processes a block of data and yields a compact numeric result with the property that it is infeasible to find a block of data that gives that hash using an exhaustive search or any other method
SIMD	Single-Instruction Multiple-data Words A design point in Flynn's taxonomy [2]
SIMM	Single-in-Line Memory Module A number of DRAM chips arranged on a small board to obtain sufficient data bus width and with a single-sided edge connector (both sides have the same signal)
SMP	Symmetric Multiprocessing A parallel computer design with identical cores
SMT	Satisfiability Modulo Theories A class of automated proof tools that convert a task to a SAT problem using various libraries of standard theories
SMV	Symbolic Model Verifier One of the most famous model checkers

SoC	System-on-Chip	

SOP	Start of Packet
	A signal that indicates the first word of a frame conveyed on a channel

SPD	Serial Presence Detect
	A small ROM containing an electronic data sheet for a SIMM or DIMM

SPEF	Standard Parasitic Exchange Format
	A file format describing capacative loading and other circuit-affecting artefacts arising from a layout

SPICE	Simulation Program with Integrated Circuit Emphasis
	A widely implemented algorithm for simulating analogue circuitry and an associate file format for describing circuits and component models

SQL	Structured Query Language
	The normal language used for updating and interrogating relational databases

SRAM	Static Random-access Memory
	An electronic data store in which each bit is held in a bistable (pair of cross-coupled invertors)

SSD	Solid-state Drive
	A number of flash memory chips packaged in a SATA module as a replacement for a spinning hard disk

SSE2	Streaming SIMD Extension Set 2
	An extension to the Intel x86 architecture for vector processing

SSRAM	Synchronous Static Random-access Memory
	A common form of static RAM where the data is read out the clock cycle after the address was supplied

STA	Static Timing Analysis
	An EDA method that reports the maximum clock frequency and hold-time risks for a synchronous logic circuit

SVA	System Verilog Assertions
	The sub-language for formal proofs embodied in System Verilog

SVGA	Super Video Graphics Adaptor
	A video cable standard used in IBM compatible computers

S/W	Software

TCK	Test Clock One of the five JTAG port terminals
TCL	Tool Command Language A commonly used imperative language that is frequently extended for EDA use with application-specific commands
TCM	Tightly Coupled Memory A region of fast SRAM or scratchpad close to a CPU where a compiler can place frequently used data
TCP	Transmission Control Protocol The predominant transport protocol used in IP networks
TDF	Timed Data Flow A form of AMS modelling where values are exchanged at a predetermined rate
TDI	Test Data Input One of the five JTAG port terminals
TDM (1)	Test Data Mode One of the five JTAG port terminals
TDM (2)	Time-division Multiplexing
TDO	Test Data Output One of the five JTAG port terminals
TGI	Tightly Coupled Generator Interface A channel inside an IP-XACT-based system integrator tool where a child tool is invoked, such as a RAM, wiring or data sheet generator
TLATCH	Transparent Latch A simple flip-flop that, instead of being edge-triggered, allows the value on the output to track the input value for one state of the clock input, which is then called the enable input
TLB	Translation Lookaside Buffer A cache that provides most of the functionality within a memory management unit
TLM	Transaction-level Model/Modelling A style of high-level SoC modelling where IP blocks invoke methods on their peers corresponding to a bus transaction

TMR	Triple Modular Redundancy	
	A form of design resilience in which three instances of a component are provided with the same input values and a majority vote is taken on their output	

TMS	Test Mode Select
	One of the five JTAG port terminals

TPM	Trusted Platform Module
	A physically secure device or part of a chip from which information cannot be read out using side channel attacks, such as DPA

TTL	Transistor-transistor Logic
	A mainstream logic family of the 1970's that exceeded the performance of CMOS at that time

TTM	Time to Market
	The period between product inception and first customer shipment

UART	Universal Asynchronous Receiver and Transmitter
	An historic serial interface that is compatible with electromechanical Teletype model 33 terminals manufactured in 1936 but still commonly used as a simple-to-debug interface

UHF	Ultra-high Frequency
	A radio frequency band ranging from 300 MHz to about 3 GHz

UML	Unified Modelling Language
	A standard language and series of diagrams for capturing various use cases and operating procedures for a product or process

UPF	Universal Power Format
	A standard file format for representing power domains across a SoC

URB	USB Request Block
	A block of data conveyed over a USB port

URL	Uniform Resource Locator
	A string containing a protocol name, followed by a colon and an address, as used for WWW links

USB	Universal Serial Bus
	A low-cost desk-area bus consisting of hubs and end points with a single master being able to discover the topology and send data to and from the end points

UVM   Universal Verification Methodology
A set of standard method names and document structures that facilitate easy integration of third-party IP blocks into an overarching test program

VC   Virtual Circuit or Channel

VCC   Voltage Supply for the Collectors
The name for the +ve supply rail in logic families like 74-series TTL composed mainly of NPN bipolar transistors

VCD   Verilog Change Dump
A standard file format for storing waveforms generated by a digital logic simulator, ready for analysis or visualisation

VCO   Voltage-controlled Oscillator
A pulse or sine wave generator where the frequency is proportional to an external input voltage

VDD   Voltage Supply for the Drains
The positive supply rail in CMOS, which feeds the drains of the N-channel FETs in an NMOS logic family

VGAA   Vertical Gate All Around
Describing a transistor where the source, gate and drain are in a vertical stack

VHDL   Very High-speed Integrated-circuit Hardware Description Language
One of the two mainstream RTLs, the other being Verilog

VHF   Very High Frequency
A radio frequency band ranging from 30 MHz to 300 MHz

VIP   Verification Intellectual Property
An IP block from an EDA vendor that contains assertions or other formal models

VLAN   Virtual Local-area Network
A logical division of a LAN in which traffic is isolated from other divisions for security and management reasons

VLIW   Very Long Instruction Word
A form of computer in which the microarchitecture details are planned at code compile time and explicit in the instructions

VLSI   Very Large-scale Integration
A perhaps meaningless term these days, but originally referring to chips with many thousands of logic gates or more

VM (1)	Virtual Machine
VM (2)	Virtual Memory
VMM	Virtual Machine Monitor A miniature and highly secure operating system that supports some number of fully fledged operating systems on a platform with isolation and perhaps usage charging
VSS	Voltage Supply for the Sources and Substrates Another name for ground or the 0 V rail in CMOS logic families in which the N-channel FETs have their source and substrates connected to ground
VTOC	Verilog to C Compiler A tool that converts from RTL to C++ to generate fast and portable models of a subsystem or entire SoC
WaR	Write After Read
WaW	Write After Write
WDT	Watchdog Timer A device that, like a dead-man's handle, detects when activity has stopped and causes a reset or high-priority interrupt
WFE	Wait for Event An Arm instruction for low-level communication
XML	Extensible Markup Language A human-readable generic file format for exchanging tree-structured data
YUV	Luminance Plus Dual Chrominance A colour matrixing system where the brightness dimension (Y) is factored out for higher-fidelity processing
ZBT	Zero Bus Turnaround A protocol for a tri-state bus that minimises slack time as the bus changes direction between reading and writing

References

[1] Stephen Brookes, C. Hoare, and A. Roscoe. A theory of communicating sequential processes. J. ACM, 31:560–599, 1984. doi: 10.1145/828.833.

[2] M. J. Flynn. Some computer organizations and their effectiveness. IEEE Transactions on Comput- ers, C-21(9):948–960, 1972. doi: 10.1109/TC.1972.5009071.

Index

The Arm Education Media Story

Did you know that Arm processor design is at the heart of technology that touches 70% of the world's population - from sensors to smartphones to super computers.

Given the vast reach of Arm's computer chip and software designs, our aim at Arm Education Media is to play a leading role in addressing the electronics and computing skills gap; i.e., the disconnect between what engineering students are taught and the skills they need in today's job market.

Launched in October 2016, Arm Education Media is the culmination of several years of collaboration with thousands of educational institutions, industrial partners, students, recruiters and managers worldwide. We complement other initiatives and programs at Arm, including the Arm University Program, which provides university academics worldwide with free teaching materials and technologies.

Via our subscription-based digital content hub, we offer interactive online courses and textbooks that enable academics and students to keep up with the latest Arm technologies.

We strive to serve academia and the developer community at large with low-cost, engaging educational materials, tools and platforms.

We are Arm Education Media:
Unleashing Potential

Arm Education Media Online Courses

Our online courses have been developed to help students learn about state of the art technologies from the Arm partner ecosystem. Each online course contains 10-14 modules, and each module comprises lecture slides with notes, interactive quizzes, hands-on labs and lab solutions.

The courses will give your students an understanding of Arm architecture and the principles of software and hardware system design on Arm-based platforms, skills essential for today's computer engineering workplace.

For more information, visit www.arm.com/education

Available Now:

- Professional Certificate in Embedded Systems Essentials with Arm (on the edX platform)

- Efficient Embedded Systems Design and Programming

- Rapid Embedded Systems Design and Programming

- Internet of Things

- Graphics and Mobile Gaming

- Real-Time Operating Systems Design and Programming

- Introduction to System-on-Chip Design

- Advanced System-on-Chip Design

- Embedded Linux

- Mechatronics and Robotics

Arm Education Media Books

The Arm Education books program aims to take learners from foundational knowledge and skills covered by its textbooks to expert-level mastery of Arm-based technologies through its reference books. Textbooks are suitable for classroom adoption in Electrical Engineering, Computer Engineering and related areas. Reference books are suitable for graduate students, researchers, aspiring and practising engineers.

For more information, visit www.arm.com/education

Available now, in print and ePub formats:

Embedded Systems Fundamentals with Arm
Cortex-M based Microcontrollers:
A Practical Approach, FRDM-KL25Z EDITION
by Dr Alexander G. Dean
ISBN 978-1-911531-03-6

Embedded Systems Fundamentals with Arm
Cortex-M based Microcontrollers:
A Practical Approach, NUCLEO-F09IRC EDITION
by Dr Alexander G. Dean
ISBN 978-1-911531-26-5

Digital Signal Processing using Arm Cortex-M
based Microcontrollers: Theory and Practice
by Cem Ünsalan, M. Erkin Yücel and H. Deniz Gürhan
ISBN 978-1911531-16-6

Operating Systems Foundations with Linux
on the Raspberry Pi
by Wim Vanderbauwhede and Jeremy Singer
ISBN 978-1-911531-20-3

Fundamentals of System-on-Chip Design on Arm
Cortex-M Microcontrollers
by René Beuchat, Florian Depraz, Sahand Kashani
and Andrea Guerrieri
ISBN 978-1-911531-33-3

System-on-Chip with Arm Cortex-M Processors
by Joseph Yiu, Distinguished Engineer at Arm
ISBN 978-1-911531-19-7

Arm Helium Technology
M-Profile Vector Extension (MVE) for Arm
Cortex-M Processors
by Jon Marsh
ISBN: 978-1-911531-23-4

www.ingramcontent.com/pod-product-compliance
Lightning Source LLC
LaVergne TN
LVHW080109070326
832902LV00015B/2491